The
Stra
Case

9th Edition

R. I
Texa

Rol
Rice

Mi
Texas A&M University

SOUTH-WESTERN
CENGAGE Learning

Australia • Brazil • Japan • Korea • Mexico • Singapore • Spain • United Kingdom • United States

D1344689

SOUTH-WESTERN
CENGAGE Learning™

The Management of Strategy: Cases, Ninth Edition

R. Duane Ireland, Robert E. Hoskisson, and Michael A. Hitt

VP/Editorial Director:
Jack W. Calhoun

Editor-in-Chief:
Melissa Acuna

Senior Acquisitions Editor:
Michele Rhoades

Director of Development:
John Abner

Senior Editorial Assistant:
Ruth Belanger

Marketing Manager:
Nathan Anderson

Senior Marketing Communications Manager:
Jim Overly

Marketing Coordinator:
Suellen Ruttkay

Content Project Manager:
Jacquelyn K Featherly

Media Editor:
Rob Ellington

Senior Manufacturing Coordinator:
Sandee Milewski

Production House/Compositor:
Cadmus Communications

Senior Art Director:
Tippy McIntosh

B/W Image:
iStockphoto.com/JoLin

Color Image:
Shutterstock Images / Evok20

For product information and technology assistance, contact us at
Cengage Learning Customer & Sales Support, 1-800-354-9706

For permission to use material from this text or product,
submit all requests online at **www.cengage.com/permissions**
Further permissions questions can be emailed to
permissionrequest@cengage.com

ExamView® and ExamView Pro® are registered trademarks of FSCreations, Inc. Windows is a registered trademark of the Microsoft Corporation used herein under license. Macintosh and Power Macintosh are registered trademarks of Apple Computer, Inc. used herein under license.

International Student Edition Cases ISBN-13: 978-0-538-75320-3
International Student Edition Cases ISBN-10: 0-538-75320-X

Cengage Learning International Offices

Asia
cengageasia.com
tel: (65) 6410 1200

Australia/New Zealand
cengage.com.au
tel: (61) 3 9685 4111

Brazil
cengage.com.br
tel: (011) 3665 9900

India
cengage.co.in
tel: (91) 11 30484837/38

Latin America
cengage.com.mx
tel: +52 (55) 1500 6000

UK/Europe/Middle East/Africa
cengage.co.uk
tel: (44) 207 067 2500

Represented in Canada by Nelson Education, Ltd.
nelson.com
tel: (416) 752 9100 / (800) 668 0671

For product information: **www.cengage.com/international**
Visit your local office: **www.cengage.com/global**
Visit our corporate website: **www.cengage.com**

Printed in Canada
1 2 3 4 5 6 7 13 12 11 10

Availability of resources may differ by region. Check with your local Cengage Learning representative for details.

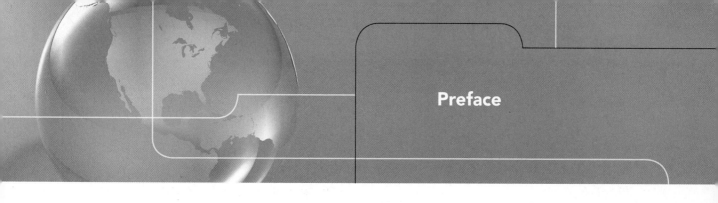

Our goal in writing each edition of this book is to present a new, up-to-date standard for explaining the strategic management process. To reach this goal with the 9th edition of our market-leading text, we again present you with an intellectually rich yet thoroughly practical analysis of strategic management.

With each new edition, we are challenged and invigorated by the goal of establishing a new standard for presenting strategic management knowledge in a readable style. To prepare for each new edition, we carefully study the most recent academic research to ensure that the strategic management content we present to you is highly current and relevant for use in organizations. In addition, we continuously read articles appearing in many different business publications (e.g., *Wall Street Journal, BusinessWeek, Fortune, Financial Times,* and *Forbes,* to name a few); we do this to identify valuable examples of how companies are actually using the strategic management process. Though many of the hundreds of companies we discuss in the book will be quite familiar to you, some companies will likely be new to you as well. One reason for this is that we use examples of companies from around the world to demonstrate how globalized business has become. To maximize your opportunities to learn as you read and think about how actual companies use strategic management tools, techniques, and concepts (based on the most current research), we emphasize a lively and user-friendly writing style.

Supplements

Instructors

New Expanded Instructor Case Notes – To better reflect the varying approaches to teaching and learning via cases, the 9th edition offers a rich selection of case note options:

Basic Case Notes – Each of the 30 cases in the 9th edition is accompanied by a succinct case note designed for ease of use while also providing the necessary background and financial data for classroom discussion.

Presentation Case Notes – For a selection of 13 cases from the 9th edition, a full set of PowerPoint slides has been developed for instructors to effectively use in class, containing key illustrations and other case data.

Rich Assessment Case Notes – Introduced in the 8th edition, these expanded case notes provide details about 13 additional cases from prior editions that are available on the textbook website. These expanded case notes include directed assignments, financial analysis, thorough discussion and exposition of issues in the case, and an assessment rubric tied to AACSB International assurance of learning standards that can be used for grading each case.

Availability of resources may differ by region. Check with your local Cengage Learning representative for details.

Instructor's Resource Manual The Instructor's Resource Manual, organized around each chapter's knowledge objectives, includes teaching ideas for each chapter and how to reinforce essential principles with extra examples. This support product includes lecture outlines, detailed answers to end-of-chapter review questions, instructions for using each chapter's experiential exercises and video cases, and additional assignments. Available on the Product Support Website.

Certified Test Bank Thoroughly revised and enhanced, test bank questions are linked to each chapter's knowledge objectives and are ranked by difficulty and question type. We provide an ample number of application questions throughout, and we have also retained scenario-based questions as a means of adding in-depth problem-solving questions. With this edition, we introduce the concept of certification, whereby another qualified academic has proofread and verified the accuracy of the test bank questions and answers. The test bank material is also available in computerized ExamView™ format for creating custom tests in both Windows and Macintosh formats. Available on the Product Support Website.

ExamView™ Computerized testing software contains all of the questions in the certified printed test bank. This program is an easy-to-use test-creation software compatible with Microsoft Windows. Instructors can add or edit questions, instructions, and answers, and select questions by previewing them on the screen, selecting them randomly, or selecting them by number. Instructors can also create and administer quizzes online, whether over the Internet, a local area network (LAN), or a wide area network (WAN).

Video Case Program. A collection of 13 new videos from Fifty Lessons have been selected for the 9th edition, and directly connected Video Case exercises have been included in the end-of-chapter material of each chapter. These new videos are a comprehensive and compelling resource of management and leadership lessons from some of the world's most successful business leaders. In the form of short and powerful videos, these videos capture leaders' most important learning experiences. They share their real-world business acumen and outline the guiding principles behind their most important business decisions and their career progression.

PowerPoint® An all-new PowerPoint presentation, created for the 9th edition, provides support for lectures, emphasizing key concepts, key terms, and instructive graphics. Slides can also be used by students as an aid to note-taking. Available on the Product Support Website.

Product Support Website (www.cengage.com/international) Our Product Support Website contains all ancillary products for instructors as well as the financial analysis exercises for both students and instructors.

The Business & Company Resource Center (BCRC) Put a complete business library at your students' fingertips! This premier online business research tool allows you and your students to search thousands of periodicals, journals, references, financial data, industry reports, and more. This powerful research tool saves time for students—whether they are preparing for a presentation or writing a reaction paper. You can use the BCRC to quickly and easily assign readings or research projects. Visit http://www.cengage.com/bcrc to learn more about this indispensable tool. For this text in particular, BCRC will be especially useful in further researching the companies featured in the text's 24 cases. We've also included BCRC links for the Strategy Right Now feature on our website as well as in the Cengage NOW product.

Student Premium Companion Site The new optional student premium website features text-specific resources that enhance student learning by bringing concepts to life. Dynamic interactive learning tools include online quizzes, flashcards, PowerPoint slides,

Availability of resources may differ by region. Check with your local Cengage Learning representative for details.

learning games, and more, helping to ensure your students come to class prepared! Ask your Cengage Learning sales representative for more details.

Students

Financial analyses of some of the cases are provided on our Product Support Website for both students and instructors. Researching financial data, company data, and industry data is made easy through the use of our proprietary database, the Business & Company Resource Center. Students are sent to this database to be able to quickly gather data needed for financial analysis.

Make It Yours – Custom Case Selection

Cengage Learning is dedicated to making the educational experience unique for all learners by creating custom materials that best suit your course needs. With our Make It Yours program, you can easily select a unique set of cases for your course from providers such as Harvard Business School Publishing, Darden, and Ivey. See http://www.custom.cengage.com/makeityours/hitt9e for more details.

Acknowledgments

We express our appreciation for the excellent support received from our editorial and production team at South-Western. We especially wish to thank Michele Rhoades, our Senior Acquisitions Editor; John Abner, our Development Editor; Nate Anderson, our Marketing Manager; and Jaci Featherly, our Content Project Manager. We are grateful for their dedication, commitment, and outstanding contributions to the development and publication of this book and its package of support materials.

We are highly indebted to the reviewers of the 8th edition in preparation for this current edition:

Erich Brockmann
University of New Orleans

Scott Elston
Iowa State University

Carol Jacobson
Purdue University

Consuelo M. Ramirez
University of Texas at San Antonio

Deepak Sethi
Old Dominion University

Len J. Trevino
Washington State University

Marta Szabo White
Georgia State University

Diana J. Wong-MingJi
Eastern Michigan University

Bruce H. Charnov
Hofstra University

Susan Hansen
University of Wisconsin-Platteville

Frank Novakowski
Davenport University

Manjula S. Salimath
University of North Texas

Manisha Singal
Virginia Tech

Edward Ward
Saint Cloud State University

Michael L Williams
Michigan State University

Wilson Zehr
Concordia University

Finally, we are very appreciative of the following people for the time and care that went into preparing of the supplements to accompany this edition:

Charles Byles
Virginia Commonwealth University

Paul Friga
University of North Carolina

Availability of resources may differ by region. Check with your local Cengage Learning representative for details.

Richard H. Lester
Texas A&M University

Paul Mallette
Colorado State University

Kristi L. Marshall

R. Duane Ireland
Robert E. Hoskisson
Michael A. Hitt

Availability of resources may differ by region. Check with your local Cengage Learning representative for details.

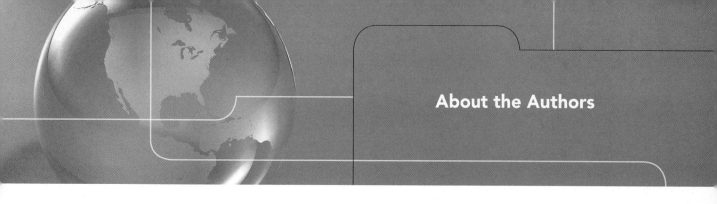
R. Duane Ireland

R. Duane Ireland is a Distinguished Professor and holds the Foreman R. and Ruby S. Bennett Chair in Business from the Mays Business School, Texas A&M University where he previously served as head of the management department. He teaches strategic management courses at all levels (undergraduate, masters, doctoral, and executive). He has over 175 publications including more than a dozen books. His research, which focuses on diversification, innovation, corporate entrepreneurship, and strategic entrepreneurship, has been published in a number of journals, including *Academy of Management Journal, Academy of Management Review, Academy of Management Executive, Administrative Science Quarterly, Strategic Management Journal, Journal of Management, Strategic Entrepreneurship Journal, Human Relations, Entrepreneurship Theory and Practice, Strategic Entrepreneurship Journal, Journal of Business Venturing,* and *Journal of Management Studies,* among others. His recently published books include *Understanding Business Strategy,* 2nd edition (South-Western Cengage Learning, 2009), *Entrepreneurship: Successfully Launching New Ventures,* 3rd edition (Prentice-Hall, 2010), and *Competing for Advantage,* 2nd edition (South-Western, 2008). He is serving or has served as a member of the editorial review boards for a number of journals, including *Academy of Management Journal, Academy of Management Review, Academy of Management Executive, Journal of Management, Strategic Enterprenurship Journal, Journal of Business Venturing, Entrepreneurship Theory and Practice, Journal of Business Strategy,* and *European Management Journal.* He is the current editor of the *Academy of Management Journal.* He has completed terms as an associate editor for *Academy of Management Journal,* as an associate editor for *Academy of Management Executive,* and as a consulting editor for *Entrepreneurship Theory and Practice.* He has co-edited special issues of *Academy of Management Review, Academy of Management Executive, Journal of Business Venturing, Strategic Management Journal, Journal of High Technology and Engineering Management,* and *Organizational Research Methods* (forthcoming). He received awards for the best article published in *Academy of Management Executive* (1999) and *Academy of Management Journal* (2000). In 2001, his co-authored article published in *Academy of Management Executive* won the Best Journal Article in Corporate Entrepreneurship Award from the U.S. Association for Small Business & Entrepreneurship (USASBE).

He is a Fellow of the Academy of Management and is a 21st Century Entrepreneurship Research Scholar. He served a three-year term as a Representative-at-Large member of the Academy of Management's Board of Governors. He received the 1999 Award for Outstanding Intellectual Contributions to Competitiveness Research from the American Society for Competitiveness and the USASBE Scholar in Corporate Entrepreneurship Award (2004).

Robert E. Hoskisson

Robert E. Hoskisson is the George R. Brown Chair of Strategic Management at the Jesse H. Jones Graduate School of Business, Rice University. He received his Ph.D. from the University of California-Irvine. Professor Hoskisson's research topics focus on corporate governance, acquisitions and divestitures, corporate and international diversification, corporate entrepreneurship, privatization, and cooperative strategy. He teaches courses in corporate and international strategic management, cooperative strategy, and strategy consulting, among others. Professor Hoskisson's research has appeared in over 120 publications, including articles in the *Academy of Management Journal, Academy of Management Review, Strategic Management Journal, Organization Science, Journal of Management, Journal of International Business Studies, Journal of Management Studies, Academy of Management Perspectives, Academy of Management Executive, California Management Review,* and 26 co-authored books. He is currently an associate editor of the *Strategic Management Journal* and a consulting editor for the *Journal of International Business Studies,* as well as serving on the Editorial Review board of the *Academy of Management Journal.* Professor Hoskisson has served on several editorial boards for such publications as the *Academy of Management Journal* (including consulting editor and guest editor of a special issue), *Journal of Management* (including associate editor), *Organization Science, Journal of International Business Studies* (consulting editor), *Journal of Management Studies* (guest editor of a special issue) and *Entrepreneurship Theory and Practice.* He has co-authored several books including *Understanding Business Strategy,* 2nd Edition (South-Western Cengage Learning, 2009), *Competing for Advantage,* 2nd edition (South-Western, 2008), and *Downscoping: How to Tame the Diversified Firm* (Oxford University Press, 1994).

He has an appointment as a Special Professor at the University of Nottingham and as an Honorary Professor at Xi'an Jiao Tong University. He is a Fellow of the Academy of Management and a charter member of the Academy of Management Journals Hall of Fame. He is also a Fellow of the Strategic Management Society. In 1998, he received an award for Outstanding Academic Contributions to Competitiveness, American Society for Competitiveness. He also received the William G. Dyer Distinguished Alumni Award given at the Marriott School of Management, Brigham Young University. He completed three years of service as a representative at large on the Board of Governors of the Academy of Management and currently is on the Board of Directors of the Strategic Management Society.

Michael A. Hitt

Michael A. Hitt is a Distinguished Professor and holds the Joe B. Foster Chair in Business Leadership at Texas A&M University. He received his Ph.D. from the University of Colorado. He has more than 260 publications including 26 co-authored or co-edited books and was cited as one of the 10 most-cited scholars in management over a 25-year period in an article published in the 2008 volume of the *Journal of Management.*

Some of his books are *Downscoping: How to Tame the Diversified Firm* (Oxford University Press, 1994); *Mergers and Acquisitions: A Guide to Creating Value for Stakeholders* (Oxford University Press, 2001); *Competing for Advantage,* 2nd edition (South-Western, 2008); and *Understanding Business Strategy,* 2nd edition (South-Western Cengage Learning, 2009). He is co-editor of several books including the following: *Managing Strategically in an Interconnected World* (1998); *New Managerial Mindsets: Organizational Transformation and Strategy Implementation* (1998); *Dynamic Strategic Resources: Development, Diffusion, and Integration* (1999); *Winning Strategies in a Deconstructing World* (John Wiley & Sons, 2000); *Handbook of Strategic Management* (2001); *Strategic Entrepreneurship: Creating a New Integrated Mindset* (2002); *Creating Value: Winners in the New Business Environment* (Blackwell Publishers, 2002); *Managing*

Knowledge for Sustained Competitive Advantage (Jossey-Bass, 2003); *Great Minds in Management: The Process of Theory Development* (Oxford University Press, 2005), and *The Global Mindset* (Elsevier, 2007). He has served on the editorial review boards of multiple journals, including the *Academy of Management Journal, Academy of Management Executive, Journal of Applied Psychology, Journal of Management, Journal of World Business,* and *Journal of Applied Behavioral Sciences.* Furthermore, he has served as consulting editor and editor of the *Academy of Management Journal.* He is currently a co-editor of the *Strategic Entrepreneurship Journal.* He is the current past president of the Strategic Management Society and is a past president of the Academy of Management.

He is a Fellow in the Academy of Management and in the Strategic Management Society. He received an honorary doctorate from the Universidad Carlos III de Madrid and is an Honorary Professor and Honorary Dean at Xi'an Jiao Tong University. He has been acknowledged with several awards for his scholarly research and he received the Irwin Outstanding Educator Award and the Distinguished Service Award from the Academy of Management. He has received best paper awards for articles published in the *Academy of Management Journal, Academy of Management Executive,* and *Journal of Management.*

To my entire family
I love each of you dearly and remain so grateful for your incredibly strong support and encouragement over the years. Your words and deeds have indeed showed me how to "keep my good eye to the sun and my blind eye to the dark."
—R. DUANE IRELAND

To my wonderful grandchildren (Mara, Seth, Roselyn, Ian, Abby, Madeline, Joseph, and Nadine), who are absolutely amazing and light up my life.
—ROBERT E. HOSKISSON

To Ashlyn and Aubrey
Your smiles are like sunshine—they brighten my day.
—MICHAEL A. HITT

Case Title	Manu-facturing	Service	Consumer Goods	Food/Retail	High Tech-nology	Internet	Transportation/Communication	International Perspective	Social/Ethical Issues	Industry Perspective
Biovail			●		●			●	●	
Wal-Mart Stores				●				●	●	
Room and Board				●					●	
Alibaba		●				●		●		
eBay, Inc.		●			●	●		●		●
Boeing	●							●		●
Motorola, Inc.	●		●					●		●
Southwest Airlines		●					●			●
Apple Computer, Inc.	●	●			●	●	●			●
Blockbuster			●	●		●				●
South Beauty Group		●		●				●		
Cinemaplex		●		●						●
JetBlue		●					●	●		●
Dell	●		●		●	●		●		●
Home Depot		●		●				●		
Henkel	●		●					●		
Citibank		●			●	●		●		
Nucor	●						●	●		●
Baidu		●				●		●		
TNK-BP	●							●		
The New York Times Company		●				●	●			●
Tesco versus Sainsbury's			●	●				●		
Under Armour		●						●		●
Barclays		●						●		
United Airlines		●					●	●		●
Netflix		●		●						
Oasis Hong Kong Airlines		●					●	●		
Nintendo			●		●	●		●		●
Pro Clean		●		●						

Case Title	Chapter												
	1	2	3	4	5	6	7	8	9	10	11	12	13
Biovail								●		●	●	●	
Wal-Mart Stores	●	●	●	●									
Room and Board			●	●					●			●	●
Alibaba				●		●		●			●		
eBay, Inc.	●				●	●			●				●
Boeing				●	●			●	●				
Motorola, Inc.		●		●		●	●					●	●
Southwest Airlines		●	●	●	●							●	●
Apple Computer, Inc.			●	●	●				●				●
Blockbuster			●		●	●	●						
South Beauty Group	●	●		●								●	●
Cinemaplex		●	●	●	●				●				
JetBlue		●		●	●								
Dell		●		●	●						●	●	
Home Depot				●	●							●	
Henkel			●	●			●	●			●		
Citibank		●	●	●				●	●		●		
Nucor		●	●	●	●						●	●	
Baidu		●			●			●					
TNK-BP		●				●	●	●		●			
The New York Times Company	●	●		●					●			●	
Tesco versus Sainsbury's					●	●	●	●					
Under Armour	●		●	●				●				●	●
Barclays	●	●	●			●						●	
United Airlines		●		●				●	●				
Netflix		●	●		●							●	
Oasis Hong Kong Airlines		●	●	●				●					
Nintendo		●	●	●				●			●		
Pro Clean		●	●	●								●	●

Case Studies

CASE 1
Accounting at Biovali 1

CASE 2
Wal-Mart Stores,Inc.
(WMT) 17

CASE 3
Room & Board 44

CASE 4
Alibaba.com 49

CASE 5
eBay Inc.: Bidding
for the Future 63

CASE 6
Boeing: Redefining
Strategies to Manage
the Competitive
Market 76

CASE 7
Motorola Inc. 491

CASE 8
Southwest Airlines 104

CASE 9
Apple Computer,
Inc.: Maintaining the
Music Business while
Introducing iPhone
and Apple TV 115

CASE 10
Blockbuster Acquires
Movielink: A Growth
Strategy 134

CASE 11
South Beauty Group: In
Quest of a "Beautiful"
Growth Stroy 147

CASE 12
The Horror Show at the
Cinemaplex? 168

CASE 13
JetBlue Airways:
Challenges Ahead 175

CASE 14
Dell Pursues Growth
in a Challenging
Enivornment 192

CASE 15
The Home Depot 211

CASE 16
Blue Ocean Strategy
at Henkel 222

CASE 17
Citibank's E Business
Strategy for
Global Corporate
Banking 230

CASE 18
Nucor in 2009 243

CASE 19
Baidu: Beating Google
at Its Own Game 265

CASE 20
TNK-BP (Russia)
2008 299

CASE 21
The New York Times
Company 314

CASE 22
Tesco versus Sainsbury's:
Growth Strategies
and Corporate
Competitiveness 332

CASE 23
Under Armor: Working
to Stay on Top of
Its Game 349

CASE 24
Barclays: Matt Barrott's
Journey—Winning
Hearts and Minds 359

CASE 25
United Airlines 365

CASE 26
Netflix 386

CASE 27
Oasis Hong Kong
Airlines: The First
Long Haul, Low Cost
Airliner in Asia 399

CASE 28
Nintendo's Distributive
Strategy: Implications
for the Video Game
Industry 416

CASE 29
Pro Clean,
Tennessee 431

What to Expect From In-Class Case Discussions

As you will learn, classroom discussions of cases differ significantly from lectures. The case method calls for your instructor to guide the discussion and to solicit alternative views as a way of encouraging your active participation when analyzing a case. When alternative views are not forthcoming, your instructor might take a position just to challenge you and your peers to respond thoughtfully as a way of generating still additional alternatives. Often, instructors will evaluate your work in terms of both the quantity and the quality of your contributions to in-class case discussions. The in-class discussions are important in that you can derive significant benefit by having your ideas and recommendations examined against those of your peers and by responding to thoughtful challenges by other class members and/or the instructor.

During case discussions, your instructor will likely listen, question, and probe to extend the analysis of case issues. In the course of these actions, your peers and/or your instructor may challenge an individual's views and the validity of alternative perspectives that have been expressed. These challenges are offered in a constructive manner; their intent is to help all parties involved with analyzing a case develop their analytical and communication skills. Developing these skills is important in that they will serve you well when working for all types of organizations. Commonly, instructors will encourage you and your peers to be innovative and original when developing and presenting ideas. Over the course of an individual discussion, you are likely to form a more complex view of the case as a result of listening to and thinking about the diverse inputs offered by your peers and instructor. Among other benefits, experience with multiple case discussions will increase your knowledge of the advantages and disadvantages of group decision-making processes.

Both your peers and instructor will value comments that contribute to identifying problems as well as solutions to them. To offer relevant contributions, you are encouraged to think independently and, through discussions with your peers outside of class, to refine your thinking. We also encourage you to avoid using "I think," "I believe," and "I feel" to discuss your inputs to a case analysis process. Instead, consider using a less emotion laden phrase, such as "My analysis shows . . . ." This highlights the logical nature of the approach you have taken to analyze a case. When preparing for an in-class case discussion, you should plan to use the case data to explain your assessment of the situation. Assume that your peers and instructor are familiar with the basic facts included in the case. In addition, it is good practice to prepare notes regarding your analysis of case facts before class discussions and use them when explaining your perspectives. Effective notes signal to classmates and the instructor that you are prepared to engage in a thorough discussion of a case. Moreover, comprehensive and detailed notes eliminate the need for you to memorize the facts and figures needed to successfully discuss a case.

The case analysis process described above will help prepare you effectively to discuss a case during class meetings. Using this process results in consideration of the issues required to identify a focal firm's problems and to propose strategic actions through which the firm can increase the probability it will outperform its rivals. In some instances, your instructor may ask you to prepare either an oral or a written analysis of a particular case. Typically, such an assignment demands even more thorough study and analysis of the case contents. At your instructor's discretion, oral and written analyses may be completed by individuals or by groups of three or more people. The information and insights gained by completing the six steps shown in Table 1 often are of value when developing an oral or a written analysis. However, when preparing an oral or written presentation, you must consider the overall framework in which your information and inputs will be presented. Such a framework is the focus of the next section.

Preparing an Oral/Written Case Presentation

Experience shows that two types of thinking (analysis and synthesis) are necessary to develop an effective oral or written presentation (see Exhibit 1). In the analysis stage, you should first analyze the general external environmental issues affecting the firm. Next, your environmental analysis should focus on the particular industry (or industries, in the case of a diversified company) in which a firm operates. Finally, you should examine companies against which the focal firm competes. By studying the three levels of the external environment (general, industry, and competitor), you will be able to identify a firm's opportunities and threats. Following the external environmental analysis is the analysis of the firm's internal organization. This analysis provides the insights needed to identify the firm's strengths and weaknesses.

As noted in Exhibit 1, you must then change the focus from analysis to synthesis. Specifically, you must synthesize information gained from your analysis of the firm's external environment and internal organization. Synthesizing information allows you to generate alternatives that can resolve the significant problems or challenges facing the focal firm. Once you identify a best alternative, from an evaluation based on predetermined criteria and goals, you must explore implementation actions.

In Table 2, we outline the sections that should be included in either an oral or a written presentation: strategic profile and case analysis purpose, situation analysis, statements of strengths/weaknesses and opportunities/threats, strategy formulation, and strategy implementation. These sections are described in the following discussion. Familiarity with the contents of your book's thirteen chapters is helpful because the general outline for an oral or a written presentation shown in Table 2 is based on an understanding of the strategic management process detailed in those chapters. We follow the discussions of the parts of Table 2 with a few comments about the "process" to use to present the results of your case analysis in either a written or oral format.

Table 1 An Effective Case Analysis Process

Step 1: Gaining Familiarity	a. In general—determine who, what, how, where, and when (the critical facts of the case). b. In detail—identify the places, persons, activities, and contexts of the situation. c. Recognize the degree of certainty/uncertainty of acquired information.
Step 2: Recognizing Symptoms	a. List all indicators (including stated "problems") that something is not as expected or as desired. b. Ensure that symptoms are not assumed to be the problem (symptoms should lead to identification of the problem).
Step 3: Identifying Goals	a. Identify critical statements by major parties (for example, people, groups, the work unit, and so on). b. List all goals of the major parties that exist or can be reasonably inferred.
Step 4: Conducting the Analysis	a. Decide which ideas, models, and theories seem useful. b. Apply these conceptual tools to the situation. c. As new information is revealed, cycle back to substeps a and b.
Step 5: Making the Diagnosis	a. Identify predicaments (goal inconsistencies). b. Identify problems (discrepancies between goals and performance). c. Prioritize predicaments/problems regarding timing, importance, and so on.
Step 6: Doing the Action Planning	a. Specify and prioritize the criteria used to choose action alternatives. b. Discover or invent feasible action alternatives. c. Examine the probable consequences of action alternatives. d. Select a course of action. e. Design an implementation plan/schedule. f. Create a plan for assessing the action to be implemented.

Source: C. C. Lundberg and C. Enz, 1993, A framework for student case preparation, Case Research Journal, 13 (Summer): 144. Reprinted by permission of NACRA, North American Case Research Association.

Exhibit 1 Types of Thinking in Case Preparation: Analysis and Synthesis

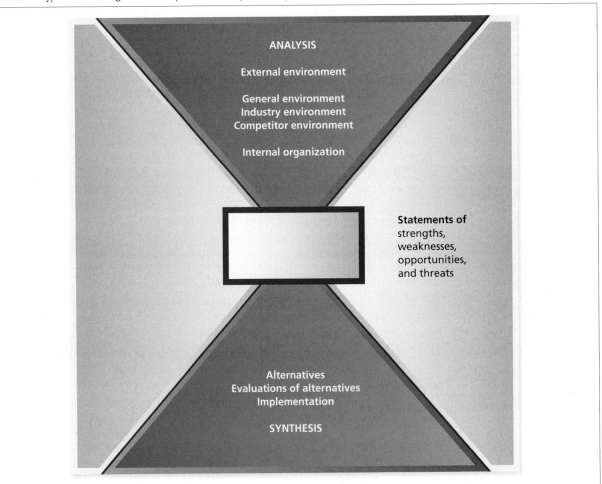

Strategic Profile and Case Analysis Purpose

You will use the strategic profile to briefly present the critical facts from the case that have affected the focal firm's historical strategic direction and performance. The case facts should not be restated in the profile; rather, these comments should show how the critical facts lead to a particular focus for your analysis. This primary focus should be emphasized in this section's conclusion. In addition, this section should state important assumptions about case facts on which your analyses are based.

Situation Analysis

As shown in Table 2, a general starting place for completing a situation analysis is the general environment.

General Environmental Analysis. Your analysis of the general environment should focus on trends in the six segments of the general environment (see Table 3). Many of the segment issues shown in Table 3 for the six segments are explained more fully in Chapter 2 of your book. The objective you should have in evaluating these trends is to be able to *predict* the segments that you expect

Table 2 General Outline for an Oral or Written Presentation

I. Strategic Profile and Case Analysis Purpose

II. Situation Analysis
   A. General environmental analysis
   B. Industry analysis
   C. Competitor analysis
   D. Internal analysis

III. Identification of Environmental Opportunities and Threats and Firm Strengths and Weaknesses (SWOT Analysis)

IV. Strategy Formulation
   A. Strategic alternatives
   B. Alternative evaluation
   C. Alternative choice

V. Strategic Alternative Implementation
   A. Action items
   B. Action plan

to have the most significant influence on your focal firm over the next several years (say three to five years) and to explain your reasoning for your predictions.

Industry Analysis. Porter's five force model is a useful tool for analyzing the industry (or industries) in which

Table 3 Sample General Environmental Categories

Technological Trends
- Information technology continues to become cheaper with more practical applications
- Database technology enables organization of complex data and distribution of information
- Telecommunications technology and networks increasingly provide fast transmission of all sources of data, including voice, written communications, and video information
- Computerized design and manufacturing technologies continue to facilitate quality and flexibility

Demographic Trends
- Regional changes in population due to migration
- Changing ethnic composition of the population
- Aging of the population
- Aging of the "baby boom" generation

Economic Trends
- Interest rates
- Inflation rates
- Savings rates
- Exchange rates
- Trade deficits
- Budget deficits

Political/Legal Trends
- Antitrust enforcement
- Tax policy changes
- Environmental protection laws
- Extent of regulation/deregulation
- Privatizing state monopolies
- State-owned industries

Sociocultural Trends
- Women in the workforce
- Awareness of health and fitness issues
- Concern for the environment
- Concern for customers

Global Trends
- Currency exchange rates
- Free-trade agreements
- Trade deficits

your firm competes. We explain how to use this tool in Chapter 2. In this part of your analysis, you want to determine the attractiveness of an industry (or a segment of an industry) in which your firm is competing. As attractiveness increases, so does the possibility your firm will be able to earn profits by using its chosen strategies. After evaluating the power of the five forces relative to your firm, you should make a judgment as to *how* attractive the industry is in which your firm is competing.

Competitor Analysis. Firms also need to analyze each of their primary competitors. This analysis should identify competitors' current strategies, strategic intent, strategic mission, capabilities, core competencies, and a competitive response profile (see Chapter 2). This information is useful to the focal firm in formulating an appropriate strategy and in predicting competitors' probable responses. Sources that can be used to gather information about an industry and companies with whom the focal firm competes are listed in Appendix I. Included in this list is a wide range of

publications, such as periodicals, newspapers, bibliographies, directories of companies, industry ratios, forecasts, rankings/ratings, and other valuable statistics.

Internal Analysis. Assessing a firm's strengths and weaknesses through a value chain analysis facilitates moving from the external environment to the internal organization. Analysis of the primary and support activities of the value chain provides opportunities to understand how external environmental trends affect the specific activities of a firm. Such analysis helps highlight strengths and weaknesses (see Chapter 3 for an explanation and use of the value chain).

For purposes of preparing an oral or a written presentation, it is important to note that strengths are internal resources and capabilities that have the potential to be core competencies. Weaknesses, on the other hand, are internal resources and capabilities that have the potential to place a firm at a competitive disadvantage relative to its rivals. Thus, some of a firm's resources and capabilities are strengths; others are weaknesses.

When evaluating the internal characteristics of the firm, your analysis of the functional activities emphasized is critical. For instance, if the strategy of the firm is primarily technology driven, it is important to evaluate the firm's R&D activities. If the strategy is market driven, marketing functional activities are of paramount importance. If a firm has financial difficulties, critical financial ratios would require careful evaluation. In fact, because of the importance of financial health, most cases require financial analyses. Appendix II lists and operationally defines several common financial ratios. Included are tables describing profitability, liquidity, leverage, activity, and shareholders' return ratios. Leadership, organizational culture, structure, and control systems are other characteristics of firms you should examine to fully understand the "internal" part of your firm.

Identification of Environmental Opportunities and Threats and Firm Strengths and Weaknesses (SWOT Analysis).

The outcome of the situation analysis is the identification of a firm's strengths and weaknesses and its environmental threats and opportunities. The next step requires that you analyze the strengths and weaknesses and the opportunities and threats for configurations that benefit or do not benefit your firm's efforts to perform well. Case analysts and organizational strategists as well seek to match a firm's strengths with its opportunities. In addition, strengths are chosen to prevent any serious environmental threat from negatively affecting the firm's performance. The key objective of conducting a SWOT analysis is to determine how to position the firm so it can take advantage of opportunities, while simultaneously avoiding or minimizing environmental threats. Results from a SWOT analysis yield valuable insights into the selection of a firm's strategies. The analysis of a case should not be overemphasized relative to the synthesis of results gained from your analytical efforts. There may be a temptation to spend most of your oral or written case analysis on results from the analysis. It is important, however, that you make an equal effort to develop and evaluate alternatives and to design implementation of the chosen strategy.

Strategy Formulation—Strategic Alternatives, Alternative Evaluation, and Alternative Choice.

Developing alternatives is often one of the most difficult steps in preparing an oral or a written presentation. Developing three to four alternative strategies is common (see Chapter 4 for business-level strategy alternatives and Chapter 6 for corporate-level strategy alternatives). Each alternative should be feasible (i.e., it should match the firm's strengths, capabilities, and especially core competencies), and feasibility should be demonstrated. In addition, you should show how each alternative takes advantage of the environmental opportunity or avoids/buffers against environmental threats.

Developing carefully thought out alternatives requires synthesis of your analyses' results and creates greater credibility in oral and written case presentations.

Once you develop strong alternatives, you must evaluate the set to choose the best one. Your choice should be defensible and provide benefits over the other alternatives. Thus, it is important that both alternative development and evaluation of alternatives be thorough. The choice of the best alternative should be explained and defended.

Strategic Alternative Implementation–Action Items and Action Plan.

After selecting the most appropriate strategy (that is, the strategy with the highest probability of helping your firm in its efforts to earn profits), implementation issues require attention. Effective synthesis is important to ensure that you have considered and evaluated all critical implementation issues. Issues you might consider include the structural changes necessary to implement the new strategy. In addition, leadership changes and new controls or incentives may be necessary to implement strategic actions. The implementation actions you recommend should be explicit and thoroughly explained. Occasionally, careful evaluation of implementation actions may show the strategy to be less favorable than you thought originally. A strategy is only as good as the firm's ability to implement it.

Process Issues.

You should ensure that your presentation (either oral or written) has logical consistency throughout. For example, if your presentation identifies one purpose, but your analysis focuses on issues that differ from the stated purpose, the logical inconsistency will be apparent. Likewise, your alternatives should flow from the configuration of strengths, weaknesses, opportunities, and threats you identified by analyzing your firm's external environment and internal organization.

Thoroughness and clarity also are critical to an effective presentation. Thoroughness is represented by the comprehensiveness of the analysis and alternative generation. Furthermore, clarity in the results of the analyses, selection of the best alternative strategy, and design of implementation actions are important. For example, your statement of the strengths and weaknesses should flow clearly and logically from your analysis of your firm's internal organization.

Presentations (oral or written) that show logical consistency, thoroughness, and clarity of purpose, effective analyses, and feasible recommendations (strategy and implementation) are more effective and are likely to be more positively received by your instructor and peers. Furthermore, developing the skills necessary to make such presentations will enhance your future job performance and career success.

Abstracts and Indexes	
Periodicals	*ABI/Inform* *Business Periodicals Index* *InfoTrac* Custom Journals *InfoTrac* Custom Newspapers *InfoTrac* OneFile EBSCO Business Source Premiere Lexis/Nexis Academic *Public Affairs Information Service Bulletin* (PAIS) *Reader's Guide to Periodical Literature*
Newspapers	*NewsBank—Foreign Broadcast Information* *NewsBank-Global NewsBank* *New York Times Index* *Wall Street Journal Index* *Wall Street Journal/Barron's Index* *Washington Post Index*
Bibliographies	*Encyclopedia of Business Information Sources*
Directories	
Companies—General	*America's Corporate Families and International Affiliates* *Hoover's Online: The Business Network* www.hoovers.com/free D&B *Million Dollar Directory* (databases: http://www.dnbmdd.com) *Standard & Poor's Corporation Records* *Standard & Poor's Register of Corporations, Directors, and Executives* (http://www.netadvantage.standardandpoors.com for all of *Standard & Poor's*) *Ward's Business Directory of Largest U.S. Companies*
Companies—International	*America's Corporate Families and International Affiliates* *Business Asia* *Business China* *Business Eastern Europe* *Business Europe* *Business International* *Business International Money Report* *Business Latin America* *Directory of American Firms Operating in Foreign Countries* *Directory of Foreign Firms Operating in the United States* *Hoover's Handbook of World Business* *International Directory of Company Histories* *Mergent's International Manual* Mergent Online (http://www.fisonline.com—for "Business and Financial Information Connection to the World") *Who Owns Whom*
Companies—Manufacturers	*Thomas Register of American Manufacturers* U.S. Office of Management and Budget, Executive Office of the President, *Standard Industrial Classification Manual* *U.S. Manufacturer's Directory, Manufacturing & Distribution, USA*
Companies—Private	D&B *Million Dollar Directory* *Ward's Business Directory of Largest U.S. Companies*

Appendix I Sources for Industry and Competitor Analyses (*Continued*)

Companies—Public	Annual Reports and 10-K Reports *Disclosure* (corporate reports) Q-File Security and Exchange Commision Filings & Forms (EDGAR) http://www.sec.gov/edgar.shtml *Mergent's Manuals:* • *Mergent's Bank and Finance Manual* • *Mergent's Industrial Manual* • *Mergent's International Manual* • *Mergent's Municipal and Government Manual* • *Mergent's OTC Industrial Manual* • *Mergent's OTC Unlisted Manual* • *Mergent's Public Utility Manual* • *Mergent's Transportation Manual* Standard & Poor's Corporation, *Standard Corporation Descriptions:* http://www.netadvantage.standardandpoors.com • *Standard & Poor's Analyst Handbook* • *Standard & Poor's Industry Surveys* • *Standard & Poor's Statistical Service*
Companies—Subsidiaries and Affiliates	*America's Corporate Families and International Affiliates* *Ward's Directory* *Who Owns Whom* *Mergent's Industry Review* *Standard & Poor's Analyst's Handbook* *Standard & Poor's Industry Surveys* (2 volumes) U.S. Department of Commerce, *U.S. Industrial Outlook*
Industry Ratios	Dun & Bradstreet, *Industry Norms and Key Business Ratios* *RMA's Annual Statement Studies* *Troy Almanac of Business and Industrial Financial Ratios*
Industry Forecasts	International Trade Administration, *U.S. Industry & Trade Outlook*
Rankings & Ratings	Annual Report on American Industry in *Forbes* *Business Rankings Annual* *Mergent's Industry Review* http://www.worldcatlibraries.org *Standard & Poor's Industry Report Service* http://www.netadvantage.standardandpoors.com *Value Line Investment Survey* *Ward's Business Directory of Largest U.S. Companies*
Statistics	*American Statistics Index (ASI)* Bureau of the Census, U.S. Department of Commerce, *Economic Census Publications* Bureau of the Census, U.S. Department of Commerce, *Statistical Abstract of the United States* Bureau of Economic Analysis, U.S. Department of Commerce, *Survey of Current Business* Internal Revenue Service, U.S. Treasury Department, *Statistics of Income: Corporation Income Tax Returns* *Statistical Reference Index (SRI)*

Appendix II Financial Analysis in Case Studies

Table A-1 Profitability Ratios

Ratio	Formula	What It Shows
1. Return on total assets	$$\frac{\text{Profits after taxes}}{\text{Total assets}}$$ or $$\frac{\text{Profits after taxes} + \text{Interest}}{\text{Total assets}}$$	The net return on total investments of the firm or The return on both creditors' and shareholders' investments
2. Return on stockholder's equity (or return on net worth)	$$\frac{\text{Profits after taxes}}{\text{Total stockholder's equity}}$$	How profitably the company is utilizing shareholders' funds
3. Return on common equity	$$\frac{\text{Profits after taxes} - \text{Preferred stock dividends}}{\text{Total stockholder's equity} - \text{Par value of preferred stock}}$$	The net return to common stockholders
4. Operating profit margin (or return on sales)	$$\frac{\text{Profits before taxes and before interest}}{\text{Sales}}$$	The firm's profitability from regular operations
5. Net profit margin (or net return on sales)	$$\frac{\text{Profits after taxes}}{\text{Sales}}$$	The firm's net profit as a percentage of total sales

Table A-2 Liquidity Ratios

Ratio	Formula	What It Shows
1. Current ratio	$$\frac{\text{Current assets}}{\text{Current liabilities}}$$	The firm's ability to meet its current financial liabilities
2. Quick ratio (or acid-test ratio)	$$\frac{\text{Current assets} - \text{Inventory}}{\text{Current liabilities}}$$	The firm's ability to pay off short-term obligations without relying on sales of inventory
3. Inventory to net working capital	$$\frac{\text{Inventory}}{\text{Current assets} - \text{Current liabilities}}$$	The extent to which the firm's working capital is tied up in inventory

Table A-3 Leverage Ratios

Ratio	Formula	What It Shows
1. Debt-to-assets	$$\frac{\text{Total debt}}{\text{Total assets}}$$	Total borrowed funds as a percentage of total assets
2. Debt-to-equity	$$\frac{\text{Total debt}}{\text{Total shareholders' equity}}$$	Borrowed funds versus the funds provided by shareholders
3. Long-term debt-to-equity	$$\frac{\text{Long-term debt}}{\text{Total shareholders' equity}}$$	Leverage used by the firm
4. Times-interest-earned (or coverage ratio)	$$\frac{\text{Profits before interest and taxes}}{\text{Total interest charges}}$$	The firm's ability to meet all interest payments
5. Fixed charge coverage	$$\frac{\text{Profits before taxes and interest} + \text{Lease obligations}}{\text{Total interest charges} + \text{Lease obligations}}$$	The firm's ability to meet all fixed-charge obligations including lease payments

Table A-4 Activity Ratios

Ratio	Formula	What It Shows
1. Inventory turnover	$\dfrac{\text{Sales}}{\text{Inventory of finished goods}}$	The effectiveness of the firm in employing inventory
2. Fixed-assets turnover	$\dfrac{\text{Sales}}{\text{Fixed assets}}$	The effectiveness of the firm in utilizing plant and equipment
3. Total assets turnover	$\dfrac{\text{Sales}}{\text{Total assets}}$	The effectiveness of the firm in utilizing total assets
4. Accounts receivable turnover	$\dfrac{\text{Annual credit sales}}{\text{Accounts receivable}}$	How many times the total receivables have been collected during the accounting period
5. Average collecting period	$\dfrac{\text{Accounts receivable}}{\text{Average daily sales}}$	The average length of time the firm waits to collect payment after sales

Table A-5 Shareholders' Return Ratios

Ratio	Formula	What It Shows
1. Dividend yield on common stock	$\dfrac{\text{Annual dividend per share}}{\text{Current market price per share}}$	A measure of return to common stockholders in the form of dividends
2. Price-earnings ratio	$\dfrac{\text{Current market price per share}}{\text{After-tax earnings per share}}$	An indication of market perception of the firm; usually, the faster-growing or less risky firms tend to have higher PE ratios than the slower-growing or more risky firms
3. Dividend payout ratio	$\dfrac{\text{Annual dividends per share}}{\text{After-tax earnings per share}}$	An indication of dividends paid out as a percentage of profits
4. Cash flow per share	$\dfrac{\text{After-tax profits + Depression}}{\text{Number of common shares outstanding}}$	A measure of total cash per share available for use by the firm

Mary-Jane Mastrandrea, Jessica Frisch

Ivey Management Services

Richard Ivey School of Business
The University of Western Ontario

John G. McIntyre leaned back from his computer and considered the just-released "Statements of Allegations of the Staff of the Ontario Securities Commission and the U.S. Securities and Exchange Commission against Biovail Corporation" and four of its current and former executives. His firm, McIntyre and Associates, was a boutique accounting firm that specialized in providing analysis and recommendations to legal firms representing various classes of shareholders in class action lawsuits. McIntyre had the pending Biovail allegations on his radar since late 2003, when Bank of America issued a "sell rating" on Biovail stock, citing the company's aggressive accounting practices. In light of these new charges, McIntyre was convinced that his firm would be engaged by a law firm to provide forensic accounting analysis in this case. McIntyre needed to review the significant amount of information accumulated in the Biovail files and determine which of the many issues should be investigated more fully to support any case.

The Pharmaceutical Industry

The pharmaceutical industry was one of the largest and fastest-growing manufacturing industries in Canada, contributing approximately $6 billion to Canadian GDP in 2005 and boasting an annual industry growth rate of 7.7 percent.[2] The industry was highly competitive and included brand-name corporations, generic drug manufacturers, smaller biopharmaceutical companies, and well-known research and clinical trial organizations. Exhibit 1 provides summary information from some of the largest, multinational players in the industry.

Most large pharmaceutical companies in Canada were clustered in metropolitan areas such as Montreal and Toronto. The pharmaceutical industry was research and development (R&D) intensive. In 2007, the pharmaceutical industry was responsible for $1.96 billion, or 19 percent, of total Canadian R&D spending.[3] The highly skilled Canadian workforce and the Canadian government's commitment to funding pharmaceutical research, either directly or via research and development tax credits, made Canada an attractive investment location for multinational pharmaceutical companies.[4] Furthermore, the North American Free Trade Agreement provided these multinational companies with tariff-free access to the large North American market, enhancing this industry's competitiveness.

Each new drug required a great deal of R&D before it could be approved. The approval process started with preclinical testing. This stage consisted of laboratory tests to show the efficacy and safety of the drug. Following successful preclinical testing, a company filed an Investigational New Drug (IND) application with the Food and Drug Administration (FDA) before it could begin to test the drug on humans. After approval was granted, three phases of clinical trials were conducted. These experimental phases studied the dosage, efficacy, and side effects associated with the drug. The clinical trials included up to 3,000 human volunteers. Lastly, a company had to file a New Drug Application (NDA) with the FDA. In the United States, only five in 5,000 compounds that entered preclinical testing made it to human testing. Moreover, only one of those five tested on people was approved.[5] A company's bottom line could suffer drastically if the FDA did not grant approval.

Mary-Jane Mastrandrea updated this case from a previous version prepared by Jessica Frisch under the supervision of Professor Mary Heisz solely to provide material for class discussion. The authors do not intend to illustrate either effective or ineffective handling of a managerial situation. The authors may have disguised certain names and other identifying information to protect confidentiality.

Exhibit 1 Forbes 2000 Largest Companies, Drug & Biotechnology Industry (in US$ billions)

Global Rank	Company	Country	Sales	Profits	Assets
57	Pfizer	United States	48.42	8.14	115.27
58	Johnson & Johnson	United States	61.10	10.58	80.95
67	Sanofi-aventis	France	40.95	7.68	104.98
72	Novartis	Switzerland	40.22	12.62	71.89
74	Roche Holding	Switzerland	40.65	8.60	67.72
79	GlaxoSmithKline	United Kingdom	45.07	10.35	57.16
148	AstraZeneca	United Kingdom	29.21	5.53	46.91
162	Merck & Co.	United States	24.20	3.28	48.35
167	Abbott Laboratories	United States	25.91	3.61	39.71
171	Wyeth	United States	22.40	4.62	42.72
228	Amgen	United States	14.77	3.17	34.64
229	Eli Lilly & Co.	United States	18.63	2.95	26.79
257	Bristol-Myers Squibb	United States	19.35	2.17	26.17

Source: http://www.forbes.com/lists, accessed September 27, 2008.

Biovail Company Background

Eugene Melnyk started his first company in 1982 when he was just 23 years old. As the son of a Toronto doctor, he recognized the need for physicians to have a more time-efficient way to read the lengthy medical literature available to them. To capitalize on this idea, Melnyk founded a publishing company called Trimel, which focused on creating crib notes for physicians.

In October 1990, Melnyk sold Trimel for Cdn$ 6.5 million and shifted focus toward the drug technologies of the pharmaceutical field. With a particular interest in the area of controlled-release drug delivery,[6] Melnyk acquired the proprietary technology. Melnyk then purchased a half-interest in Biovail SA, a financially troubled but well-respected Swiss pharmaceutical company.[7] The new company's operations were consolidated under the name Biovail.

Initially, Biovail licensed its products early in the development cycle to pharmaceutical companies that conducted clinical trials, regulatory processes, and the manufacturing and sale of their products. However, by the mid-1990s, Biovail had become an international, full-service pharmaceutical company based in Mississauga, Ontario.

In December 2001, Melnyk assumed the position of chief executive officer (CEO) of Biovail. The period during Melnyk's tenure as CEO was the focus of numerous civil, criminal, and regulatory investigations that severely increased expenses and legal fees and distracted the Biovail board and management. Melnyk stepped down from his role of CEO in October 2004.

Melnyk was also chairman of the board of directors during his tenure as CEO, and he remained as chairman until his resignation from the board in June 2007. Melnyk told shareholders at the company's annual meeting that he was resigning because he "can point to a dozen successful business deals in the last dozen years, but [he has] a hard time remembering a dozen quality days at home in the last six months."[8]

As of 2008, Biovail invested over 12 percent of its product sales back into research and development of drug technologies. The company's current commercial portfolio included Zovirax® Cream, Zovirax® Ointment, Wellbutrin XL®, Ultram® ER, Cardizem® LA, and a variety of generic[9] medications for therapeutic categories, including cardiology, depression, and the central nervous system.[10]

In 2007, Melnyk, who was by this time a 48-year-old multi-millionaire and owner of the National Hockey League's Ottawa Senators, was named the seventieth wealthiest person in Canada with a net worth of $759 million.[11] In that year, Biovail reported revenues of US$ 801 million and net income of US$ 195.5 million.[12] Exhibit 2 a, b, and c includes condensed financial statements for the years 2006 and 2007.

Exhibit 2a Biovail Corporation, Consolidated Statements of Income (in accordance with GAAP, all dollar amounts in US$ thousands)

	2007	2006
REVENUE		
Product sales	$801,046	$1,021,278
Research and development	23,828	21,593
Royalty and other	17,944	24,851
	842,818	1,067,722
EXPENSES		
Cost of goods sold	223,680	211,152
Research and development	118,117	95,479
Selling, general and administrative	161,001	238,441
Amortization	48,049	56,457
Legal settlements, net of insurance recoveries	95,114	14,400
Asset impairments, net of gain on disposal	9,910	143,000
Restructuring costs	668	15,126
Contract costs (recovery)	(1,735)	54,800
	654,804	828,855
Operating income	188,014	238,867
Interest income	24,563	29,199
Interest expense	(9,745)	(35,203)
Foreign exchange gain	5,491	(2,360)
Equity loss	(2,528)	(529)
Other income (expense)	2,944	—
Income from continuing operations before provision for income taxes	208,739	229,974
Provision for income taxes	13,200	14,500
Income from continuing operations	195,539	215,474
Loss from discontinued operation	0	–3,848
Net income	$ 195,539	$ 211,626

Sources: http://www.biovail.com.

Exhibit 2b Biovail Corporation, Consolidated Balance Sheets (in accordance with GAAP, dollar amounts in US$ thousands)

	2007	2006
ASSETS		
Current	2007	2006
Cash and cash equivalents	$ 433,641	$ 834,540
Marketable securities	3,895	—

(Continued)

Exhibit 2b Biovail Corporation, Consolidated Balance Sheets (in accordance with GAAP, dollar amounts in US$ thousands) (*Continued*)

	2007	2006
Accounts receivable	111,114	129,247
Insurance recoveries receivable	62,942	—
Inventories	80,745	78,871
Prepaid expenses and other current assets	14,680	15,056
	707,017	1,057,624
Marketable securities	24,417	5,677
Long-term investments	24,834	56,442
Property, plant and equipment, net	238,457	211,979
Intangible assets, net	630,514	697,645
Good will	100,294	100,294
Deferred tax assets, net of valuation allowance	20,700	—
Other long-term assets, net	35,882	62,781
	$ 1,782,115	$ 2,192,442
LIABILITIES		
Current		
Accounts payable	50,415	44,988
Dividends payable	—	80,222
Accrued liabilities	74,363	101,219
Accrued legal settlements	148,000	14,400
Accrued contract costs	45,065	54,800
Income taxes payable	647	41,596
Deferrend revenue	49,088	61,916
Current portion of long-term liabilities	—	11,146
	$ 367,578	$ 410,287
Deferred revenue	55,653	73,621
Income taxes payable	54,100	—
Long-term obligations	—	399,379
Other long-term liabilities	6,965	6,898
	484,296	890,185
SHAREHOLDER'S EQUITY		
Common shares, no par value, unlimited shares authorized,161,023,729, and 160,444,070 issues and outstanding at December 31, 2007 and 2006, respectively	1,489,807	1,476,930

(*Continued*)

Exhibit 2b Biovail Corporation, Consolidated Balance Sheets (in accordance with GAAP, dollar amounts in US$ thousands) (*Continued*)

	2007	2006
Additional paid in capital	23,925	14,952
Deficit	(278,495)	(232,733)
Accumulated other comprehensive income	62,582	43,108
	$ 1,782,115	$ 2,192,442

Sources: http://www.biovail.com.

Exhibit 2c Biovail Corporation, Consolidated Statements of Cash Flows (in accordance with GAAP, dollar amounts in US$ thousands)

	2007	2006
CASH FLOWS FROM OPERATING ACTIVITIES		
Net income	$195,539	$211,626
Adjustments to reconcile net income to net cash provided by continuing operating activities		
Depreciation and amortization	94,985	92,150
Amortization and write-down of deferred financing costs	4,821	2,300
Amortization and write-down of discounts on long-term obligations	962	1,291
Accrued legal settlements, net of insurance recoveries	78,652	14,400
Gains on disposal of investments and intangible assets	24,356	4,000
Impairment charges and asset write-offs	21,268	151,140
Stock-based compensation	10,633	14,794
Accrued contract costs	9,735	54,800
Premium paid on early extinguishment of debt	7,854	—
Equity loss	2,528	529
Loss from discontinued operations	—	3,848
Other	5,578	2,083
Changes in operating assets and liabilities		
Accounts receivable	18,052	4,688
Insurance recoveries receivable	7,994	—
Inventories	3,023	10,906
Prepaid expenses and other current assets	376	311
Accounts payable	3,273	12,999
Accrued liabilities	26,496	13,694
Income taxes payable	7,514	3,897
Deferred revenue	30,796	42,319

(*Continued*)

Exhibit 2c Biovail Corporation, Consolidated Statements of Cash Flows (in accordance with GAAP, dollar amounts in US$ thousands) (*Continued*)

	2007	2006
Net cash provided by continuing operating activities	340,853	522,517
CASH FLOWS FROM INVESTING ACTIVITIES		
Proceeds on disposals of investments, net of costs	52,669	—
Additions to property, plant, and equipment, net	35,086	44,802
Additions to marketable securities	34,534	3,196
Proceeds from sales and maturities of marketable securities	3,282	4,854
Additions to long-term investments	1,376	1,303
Proceeds on disposals of intangible assets	—	4,000
Acquisitions of intangible assets	—	—
Net cash provided by (used in) continuing investing activities	15,045	40,447
CASH FLOWS FROM FINANCING ACTIVITIES		
Redemption of Senior Subordinated Notes	406,756	1,098
Dividends paid	321,523	80,062
Repayments of other long-term obligations	11,250	25,280
Issuance of common shares	11,217	15,634
Repayment of deferred compensation obligation, net	338	175
Financing costs paid	—	1,275
Payment on termination of interest rate swap	—	—
Net cash used in continuing financing activities	728,650	92,256
CASH FLOWS FROM DISCONTINUED OPERATION		
Net cash used in operating activities	—	558
Net cash used in investing activities	—	—
Net cash used in discontinued operation	—	558
Effect of exchange rate changes on cash and cash equivalents	1,943	5
Net increase (decrease) in cash and cash equivalents	400,899	389,251
Cash and cash equivalents, beginning of year	834,540	445,289
Cash and cash equivalents, end of year	$ 433,641	$ 834,540

Sources: http://www.biovail.com.

The Truck Accident

On October 1, 2003, a fatal traffic accident occurred involving one of Biovail's delivery trucks. Before long, Biovail would blame this accident for its weak third-quarter revenues. Eight people were killed and 16 people were injured when an 18-wheeler truck crashed into a tour bus. The tour bus, in turn, crashed into Biovail's contract carrier. Though no one in the Biovail vehicle was hurt, the vehicle was loaded with finished goods that management claimed were severely damaged and, therefore, not salable. Shortly after the accident, Biovail issued a press release[13] warning that the company's revenues for the third quarter of 2003 would be lower than previously expected. According to management, Biovail's ill-fated shipment contained $15 million to $20 million of one of the company's main revenue drivers, Wellbutrin XL®, an anti-depression medication.

Skeptical analysts questioned the timing of the truck accident as well as the quantity of inventory involved. One analyst said, "It is a curious thing when a company's financials are so dependent on one truckload of products that it just happens to be shipping on the last day of the quarter."[14]

Even before these events, by 2003, Biovail had earned a questionable reputation. With a number of class action lawsuits outstanding and a chief executive officer whose conduct was constantly challenged by analysts, Biovail received widespread scrutiny from the media. Furthermore, Biovail's accounting methods were being questioned, leading investors to wonder whether the company had actually achieved the level of success that was previously reported in their statements.

Bank of America's Research Report

On October 8, 2003, seven days after the accident, Biovail's stock dropped 33 percent on the TSX to $25.20 per share. The plummet in stock value was assumed to be due to the aftermath of the inability for Biovail to meet its earnings forecast and to the October 2003 Bank of America research report that labelled Biovail's stock with a "sell rating." A TSX stock chart and historical prices for Biovail are presented in Exhibit 3.

The Bank of America report sought out the opinions of three forensic accounting experts who studied Biovail's press releases, transcripts, and most recent public filings. In

Exhibit 3 Biovail Stock Price History

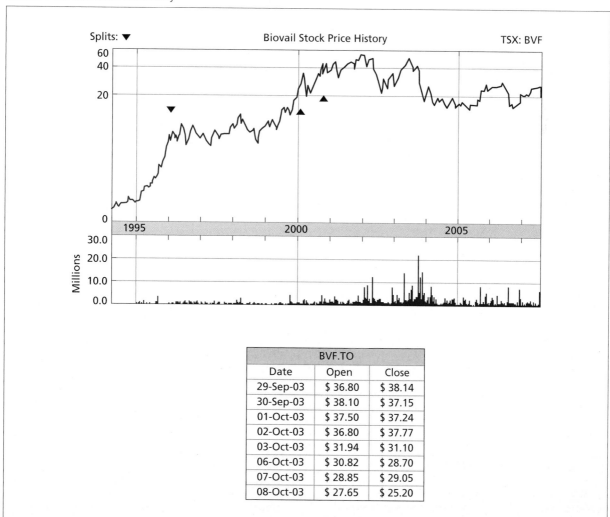

BVF.TO		
Date	Open	Close
29-Sep-03	$ 36.80	$ 38.14
30-Sep-03	$ 38.10	$ 37.15
01-Oct-03	$ 37.50	$ 37.24
02-Oct-03	$ 36.80	$ 37.77
03-Oct-03	$ 31.94	$ 31.10
06-Oct-03	$ 30.82	$ 28.70
07-Oct-03	$ 28.85	$ 29.05
08-Oct-03	$ 27.65	$ 25.20

Source: http://ca.finance.yahoo.com/q/bc?s. Copyright 2008 Yahoo! Inc., http://finance.yahoo.com.

the final report, one expert noted that Biovail's practices may be "aggressive but legal"; another noted that while Biovail's practices did not show that there was any widespread accounting impropriety, there was "perhaps aggressiveness beyond what we have observed at peer companies."[15]

The forensic accountants went on to criticize the company in many areas. The experts questioned the truck accident, noting that after they undertook further investigation, the situation seemed even more surprising. Having studied the photographs and video of the accident scene, they noted that, contrary to Biovail's high damage estimates, one-third to one-half of the truck interior appeared to be empty.

In addition to the peculiar traffic accident, the Bank of America report referenced many other reasons for the sell rating. For example, the experts noted that Biovail's product sales growth had become negative in 2003. Product sales growth, normally the company's primary growth driver, had significantly slowed for Biovail. In the company's statements, overall sales appeared solid but had been helped by royalties and licensing revenue gains. The experts questioned the sustainability of these two types of revenue streams.

Other areas of criticism included Biovail's declining R&D spending, its highly leveraged balance sheet, and the company's low tax rate. Biovail's research and development spending had dropped substantially. In addition, the report noted that in 2003, each of Biovail's top 10 selling products was purchased rather than developed in-house. The company's balance sheet contained an extremely high level of debt relative to its peer companies. In addition, Biovail's tax rate was 6.9 percent, as compared to the next lowest tax rate in its peer group at 19.8 percent, and the report questioned whether or not this lower rate was sustainable.[16]

Finally, Biovail's quality for earnings troubled the forensic accountants—specifically, the company's long history of reporting operating earnings results that differed substantially from its earnings as measured by generally accepted accounting principles (GAAP). The accounting team was particularly concerned with the company's reliance on pro forma earnings.[17] While regulatory filings, including quarterly and annual reports, are prepared using GAAP, press releases and conference calls provide management with other opportunities to communicate with investors about a company's performance using information that was generally not audited prior to its release.

As noted by Biovail management:

Management utilizes a measure of net income and earnings per share on a basis that excludes certain charges to better assess operating performance. Each of the items excluded is considered to be of a non-operational nature in the applicable period. Management has consistently applied this measure when discussing earnings or earnings guidance and will continue to do so going forward. Management believes that most of the Company's shareholders prefer to analyze the Company's results based on this measure, as it is consistent with industry practice. Earnings excluding charges are also disclosed to give investors the ability to further analyze the Company's results.[18]

Bank of America contended that the gap between Biovail's pro forma earnings and its GAAP earnings was among the largest in its peer group. Skepticism surrounded the non-GAAP earnings, which portrayed a company that was growing faster than its underlying organic growth.[19] Exhibit 4 provides actual and pro forma financial statements for Biovail for the years 2001 and 2002 and the second quarter of 2003. Exhibit 5 provides select information from the Bank of America

Exhibit 4 Biovail Corporation Earnings Release Income Statement (US$ millions)

	2001	2002	2003 2Q cum
Revenue			
Product sales	$521.2	$646.0	$284.6
Research and development	14.6	28.4	6.3
Co-promotion, royalty and licensing	47.5	113.6	117.8
	583.3	788.0	408.7
Expenses			
Cost of goods sold	126.0	164.7	48.7
Research and development	51.0	52.2	39.8
Seling, general and administrative	110.1	165.7	103.1
Amortization	44.5	71.5	86.4

(Continued)

Exhibit 4 Biovail Corporation Earnings Release Income Statement (US$ millions) (*Continued*)

	2001	2002	2003 2Q cum
Write-down of assets	80.5	31.9	—
Acquired research and development	—	167.7	84.2
Settlements	—	—	(34.1)
	412.1	653.7	328.1
Operating income (loss)	171.2	134.3	80.6
Interest income	2.7	3.6	4.7
Interest expense	(36.2)	(32.0)	(19.5)
Other income	—	3.4	6.7
Debt conversion premiums	(34.9)	—	—
Income (loss) before provision for income taxes	102.8	109.3	72.5
Provision for income taxes	15.3	21.5	10.4
Net income (loss)	$87.5	$87.8	$62.1
Diluted earning per share	$0.58	$0.55	$0.39
Net income (loss)	$ 87.5	$87.8	$62.1
Add (deduct) certain items			
Write-down of assets	80.5	31.9	—
Acquired research and development	—	167.7	84.2
Other income	—	(3.4)	—
Debt conversion premiums	34.9	—	—
Net income excluding certain items	$202.9	$284.0	$146.3
Diluted earnings per share excluding certain items	$1.35	$1.77	$0.91

Source: www.sedar.com, Biovail press release.

research report for Biovail and two of its competitors, Abbott Laboratories and Cephalon, Inc. Exhibits 6 and 7 provide earnings releases for the same two competitors.

Pointing Fingers

As it has been throughout his career, Melnyk's entrepreneurial drive could be inspiring and effective in his organization. It could also be annoying and frustrating even to his own shareholders because Melnyk would not let even the slightest criticism from regulators and analysts pass.[20]

In March 2006, while he was executive chairman of the Biovail board of directors, Melnyk brought action against 22 defendants, alleging a market manipulation scheme was the reason for the drastic decline in Biovail's stock market price in recent years.[21] Specific allegations were released against Bank of America Securities in response to their October 2003 report. Melnyk accused reporters of influencing independent analysts to broadcast materially false and misleading information about Biovail.[22]

Exhibit 5 Excerpts from Bank of America Research Report, Earnings Quality Analysis

Aggregate ProForma Earnings versus Aggregate GAAP Earnings from 1998 to 2002				
Company	**ProForma EPS**	**GAAP EPS**	**Absolute Difference**	**Relative Earnings Ratio***
Median**	$4.07	$3.05	$0.53	12%
Abbott Labs	$8.90	$7.63	$1.27	14%
Cephalon	$(3.83)	$(5.60)	$1.77	46%
Biovail	$4.75	$(0.59)	$5.34	112%

*Calculated as (ProForma earnings – GAAP earnings)/ProForma Earnings.
**Median represents the median return on invested capital for 16 companies in Biovail's peer group.

Return on Invested Capital*—GAAP Earnings versus ProForma Earnings				
ROIC – GAAP Earnings				
Company	**2000**	**2001**	**2002**	**2003 2Q**
Median**	13.20%	11.40%	14.10%	14.40%
Abbott	29.70%	13.50%	19.90%	15.70%
Cephalon	N/A	−2.80%	13.80%	9.20%
Biovail	−18.90%	10.40%	8.00%	4.20%
ROIC – ProForma Earnings				
Company	**2000**	**2001**	**2002**	**2003 2Q**
Median**	14.90%	13.70%	16.30%	17.90%
Abbott	29.70%	24.10%	22.90%	20.90%
Cephalon	N/A	2.40%	7.40%	4.40%
Biovail	14.80%	20.90%	21.40%	17.70%

*Return on Invested Capital is calculated using the formula: (Net Income – Dividends)/Total Capital.
**Median represents the median return on invested capital for 16 companies in Biovail's peer group.

Source: Bank of America Research Report, October 10, 2003.

Exhibit 6 Abbott Laboratories Income Statement (US$ millions)

	2001	2002
Net sales	$16,285.2	$17,684.7
Cost of products sold	7,748.4	8,506.3
Research & development (R&D)	1,577.5	1,561.8
Acquired in-process R&D	1,330.4	107.7
Selling, general & administrative	3,734.9	3,978.8
Total operating cost and expenses	14,391.2	14,154.6
Operating earnings	1,894.0	3,530.1
Net interest expense	234.8	205.2
Net foreign exchange loss	31.4	74.6

(Continued)

Exhibit 6 Abbott Laboratories Income Statement (US$ millions) (*Continued*)

	2001	2002
(Income) from TAP Pharm. Products Inc. joint venture	(333.8)	(666.8)
Other (income)/expense, net	78.5	243.7
Earnings before taxes	1,883.1	3,673.4
Taxes on earnings	332.8	879.7
Net earnings	$1,550.3	$2,793.7
Net earnings excluding acquired in-process R&D and other one-time charges	$2,942.8	$3,242.5
(Note 1)		
Diluted earnings per common share (US GAAP)	$0.99	$1.78
Diluted earnings per common share excluding acquired in-process R&D and other one-time charges	$1.88	$2.06
Average no. of common shares outstanding plus dilutive common stock options	$1,566.0	$1,573.3

Note 1: Year 2002 excludes a non-cash charge of $0.05 for acquired in-process research and development related to the acquisition of Biocompatibles' stent business and the Medtronic alliance, $0.06 for one-time charges related to the consent decree with the FDA, a $0.09 non-cash charge related to the decline in the value of certain equity investments, and $0.08 related to previously announced restructuring expenses. Year 2001 excludes a non-cash charge of $0.56 for acquired in-process research and development, $0.17 for a one-time adjustment to income from TAP joint venture, and $0.16 for other one-time charges related to the acquisition of the pharmaceutical business of BASF.

Source: http://www.abbott.com.

Exhibit 7 Cephalon Inc. Income Statement (US$ millions)

	2001	2002
Revenues		
Product sales	$226.1	$465.9
Other revenues	35.9	41.0
	262.0	506.9
Cost and Expenses		
Cost of product sales	44.9	74.2
Research and development	83.0	128.3
Selling, general and administrative	96.2	172.8
Merger and integration costs	0.1	—
Acquired in-process research and development	20.0	—
	244.2	375.3
EBITDA (a)	17.9	131.6
Depreciation and amortization	(14.4)	(35.5)
Debt exchange expense	(52.4)	—
Gain (charge) on early extinguishment of debt	3.0	(7.1)
Other income (expense), net	(9.4)	(26.6)

(*Continued*)

Exhibit 7 Cephalon Inc. Income Statement (US$ millions) (*Continued*)

	2001	2002
Income (loss) before income taxes	(55.4)	62.4
Income tax benefit (expense), net	—	112.6
Income before cumulative effect of changing inventory costing method	(55.4)	175.0
Cumulative effect of changing inventory costing method from FIFO to LIFO	—	(3.5)
Net income (loss)	(55.4)	171.5
Dividends on convertible exchangeable preferred stock	(5.7)	—
Income (loss) applicable to common shares	$(61.1)	$ 171.5
Basic income (loss) per common share		
Income (loss) per common share excluding cumulative effect of changing inventory method	$(1.27)	$3.17
Cumulative effect of changing inventory costing method	$ —	$(0.06)
	$ (1.27)	$ 3.11
Diluted income (loss) per common share		
Income (loss) per common share excluding the effect of changing the inventory method	$ (1.27)	$ 3.07
Cumulative effect of changing inventory costing method	$ —	$ (0.06)
	$ (1.27)	$ 3.01
Weighted average number of common shares outstanding	48.3	55.1
Weighted average number of common shares outstanding - assuming dilution	48.3	57.0
Reconciliation of Income (loss) applicable to common shares to adjusted net income:		
Income (loss) applicable to common shares	$ (61.1)	$ 171.5
Certain charges:		
Deferred tax valuation adjustment	—	(116.7)
CNS joint venture (b)	—	6.5
Short-term bridge financing and other merger related expenses	1.6	—
Acquired in-process research and development	20.0	—
Debt exchange expense	52.4	—
(Gain) charge on early extinguishment of debt	(3.0)	7.1
Cumulative effect of changing inventory costing method	—	3.5
Adjusted net income	$ 9.9	$ 71.9
Basic adjusted net income per common share	$ 0.20	$ 1.31
Diluted adjusted net income per common share	$ 0.19	$ 1.26

(a) Earnings (loss) before net interest, depreciation, amortization, debt exchange expense, foreign currency exchange, dividends on convertible exchangeable preferred stock and cumulative effect of changing inventory costing method.
(b) Includes $3,508,000 from selling, general and administrative expense and $2,973,000 from other expense.

Source: Cephalon, Inc.

In April 2006, weeks after Melnyk's market manipulation allegations, Melnyk found himself at the center of media attention as the OSC and SEC acknowledged probable suspicious trading activity.[23] Melnyk was accused of failing to file insider trading reports and acting contrary to public interest by failing to disclose his holdings to the public and understating his ownership stake in the company. The investigation encompassed a large number of trades in Cayman Island trust accounts where Melnyk was believed to be a beneficiary.[24] These trades occurred throughout Melnyk's tenure as chief executive officer from December 2001 to October 2004.

On May 14, 2007, Eugene Melnyk and other Biovail executives received Wells Notices[25] from the U.S. Securities and Exchange Commission. The Wells Notices encompassed alleged violations of federal securities laws in accounting and disclosure practices.[26] Specific enforcement action against Melnyk was expected regarding his trading and reporting ownership positions of Biovail securities.

On May 18, Melnyk settled allegations from the Ontario Securities Commission concerning his failure to disclose US$ 1.3 billion in trades of Biovail shares. To settle this dispute, Melnyk paid the OSC Cdn$ 1

million and agreed to step down as executive chairman of the board of Biovail Corporation and from all other director and officer roles relating to Biovail subsidiaries.[27]

On June 30, Melnyk retired from the board of Biovail Corporation. Since then, the role of executive chairman was assumed by Douglas Squires.[28] Squires had served Biovail as a director since 2005 and as lead director since 2007. Other new appointments included William Wells as the chief executive officer. Appointments were decided and announced by the Compensation, Nominating, and Corporate Governance Committee of the board of directors.[29] This committee was designed to insure independence and strategic appointments for Biovail leadership.

On February 25, 2008, Melnyk resigned as director and officer of BLS, another Biovail subsidiary. As of this date, Melnyk was no longer employed by or a director of Biovail Corporation or any of its subsidiaries.

OSC and SEC Bring Charges

On March 24, 2008, not unexpectedly, both the Ontario Securities Commission and the U.S. Securities and Exchange Commission released a Statement of

Exhibit 8 Summary of Key Allegations in the OSC and SEC Reports

Biovail Corporation engaged in chronic fraudulent conduct, including financial reporting fraud and other intentional public misrepresentations. Obsessed with meeting quarterly and annual earnings guidance, Biovail executives repeatedly overstated earnings and hid losses in order to deceive investors and create the appearance of achieving that goal. When it became impossible to conceal the company's poor performance, Biovail actively misled investors to create the appearance of meeting their goals.

The financial reporting fraud involves three accounting schemes that affected reporting periods from 2001 to 2003. They are:

1. A transaction through which Biovail, over a period of several reporting periods in 2001 and 2002, improperly moved off its financial statements to the statements of a special purpose entity known as Parmatech. Revenent transactions included the movement of expenses incurred in the R&D of Biovail products that totaled $47 million through September 30, 2002, and liabilities that exceeded $51 million through that date.
2. A fictitious bill and hold transaction that Biovail created to record approximately $8 million in revenue in the second quarter.
3. An intentional misstatement of foreign exchange losses that caused Biovail's second-quarter 2003 loss to be understated by about $3.9 million.

In October 2003, Biovail intentionally and falsely attributed nearly half of its failure to meet its third-quarter 2003 earnings guidance to a truck accident involving a shipment of Wellbutrin XL®. Biovail intentionally misstated in press releases and public statements both the effect of the accident on Biovail's third quarter earnings as well as grossly overstating the value of the product involved in the truck accident. The accident, in fact, had no effect on third-quarter earnings.

Each of the fraudulent accounting schemes had a material effect on Biovail's financial statements from the relevant quarter and years and was engineered by Biovail's senior management in order to manage Biovail's earnings. With these schemes, Biovail management also intentionally deceived its auditors as to the true nature of the transactions. The truck accident misstatements were intended to and did mislead analysts and the investing public concerning the significance of Biovail's failure to meet its own guidance.

Biovail's then-chairman and chief executive, Eugene Melnyk, also violated share ownership disclosure provisions by failing to identify his beneficial ownership held by several trusts in which he continued to exercise both investment and trading authority.

Source: Statement of Allegations of Staff of the Ontario Securities Commission in the Matter of Biovail Corporation, Eugene N. Melnyk, Brian H. Crombie, John R. Miszuk, and Kenneth G. Howling, March 24, 2008; Securities and Exchange Commission against Biovail Corporation, Eugene N. Melnyk, Brian Crombie, John Miszuk, and Kenneth G. Howling, March 24, 2008.

Allegations targeting Biovail Corporation and four former and current executives[30] and the company's financial reports for 2001, 2002, and Q1 and Q2 of 2003 (see Exhibit 8 for a summary of the key allegations).

The SEC's statement was particularly scathing, accusing the company and its management team of chronic fraudulent conduct, including financial reporting fraud and other intentional public misrepresentations, as a result of their obsession with meeting quarterly and annual earnings targets. The SEC continued by alleging that when it "ultimately became impossible to continue to conceal the company's poor performance, Biovail actively misled investors and analysts as to its cause"[31] referring to the October 1, 2003, truck accident.

The alleged financial reporting fraud involved three accounting schemes that affected reporting periods from 2001 to 2003, including the improper use of a special purpose entity, revenue manipulation, and an intentional misstatement of foreign exchange losses.

Biovail created a special purpose entity, Pharmaceutical Technologies Corp. (Pharmatech), a development-stage company, to undertake an estimated $125 million[32] in research and development activities on behalf of Biovail in return for royalties in mid-2001. Pharmatech's sole shareholder, a past consultant for Biovail, invested US$1 million, of which $350,000 was immediately refunded as a fee. The remainder was fully secured by Biovail.[33] As well, the company entered into a share option agreement with the sole shareholder of Pharmatech permitting Biovail to purchase all of the stockholder's Pharmatech shares at any time until December 31, 2006, in exchange for a fixed purchase price. On December 27, 2002, as a result of Pharmatech's banker's refusal to extend financing directly to Pharmatech, Biovail exercised its purchase option and repaid the bank (which also happened to be the company's principal bank) in full. As a result of these transactions, the SEC concluded that Biovail's financial reports were materially false and misleading, causing net income to be overstated by approximately 50 percent in the third quarter of 2001, 32 percent in the 2001 annual financial statements, 15 percent in the first quarter 2002, 18 percent in the second quarter 2002, and 16 percent in the third quarter 2002, and understated by approximately 17 percent in the 2002 annual financial statements.[34]

In October 2001, Biovail entered into an agreement with a distributor whereby Biovail would produce Wellbutrin XL (WXL), which had not yet received FDA approval, and then sell it to the distributor. Biovail was to produce sample products (sold at cost), which the distributor could distribute to physicians as a promotional tool, as well as trade products (sold at normal markups) packaged and labeled for commercial sale. By June 2003, the FDA had indicated that WXL was "approvable" subject to some labeling changes. Final approval was not received until August 29, 2003. On June 19, 2003, Biovail contacted its distributor and requested that, prior to June 30, 2003, the distributor place an order for trade WXL. Biovail committed to segregating the specific inventory related to the purchase order in a separate location in its Manitoba warehouse.[35] Biovail further indicated that if the distributor failed to place such an order, the company would not fully commit its manufacturing facilities to producing WXL tablets in advance of the product launch. The distributor sent Biovail a purchase order, and Biovail invoiced the distributor for approximately US$ 8 million, resulting in an increased second quarter operating income of US$ 4.4 million.[36] Subsequent to the receipt of the purchase order, management became concerned about the expiration date on the segregated inventory. The segregated inventory was then used to fill orders from the distributor for sample products (at sample- or cost-based prices).

In December 2002, Biovail acquired the rights to certain drugs and assumed a liability denominated in Canadian dollars. Since Biovail reported its results in U.S. dollars, it was required to account for this liability in its financial statements in U.S. dollars by converting the liability at the current rate at each balance sheet date. On March 31, 2003, the Canadian dollar had strengthened against the U.S. dollar compared to its December 31, 2002, rate. Though the company correctly accounted for the liability on its 2002 year-end balance sheet, it continued to use the exchange rate from December 2002 on its March 31, 2003, and June 30, 2003, balance sheets. As a result, the quarterly financial statements for first two quarters of 2003 did not reflect the resultant exchange loss or an accurate statement of the liability. Biovail overstated its net income by approximately US$ 5 million and US$ 4 million in the first and second quarters of 2003, respectively. According to the OSC and the SEC, the chief financial officer (CFO) at the time became aware of the error in early July 2003, but took no steps to correct the error or to disclose the error until the company's March 3, 2004, press release.

As McIntyre pondered the two Statements of Allegations in front of him, he found it particularly interesting that Biovail's claim that the truck accident had caused the company to miss its third quarter earnings target appeared to have precipitated the OSC and SEC's investigation. Much of both documents focused on the allegations that the statements made in the company's October 3, 2003, press release were materially misleading or untrue.

Class Action Lawsuit

McIntyre and Associates had significant experience in providing forensic accounting analysis to law firms involved in class action lawsuits against corporations accused of breaching securities laws by making false and misleading statements about the state of their business. A class action lawsuit organized the claims of numerous people, in this case shareholders, with a common interest to engage corporate entities in legal action to rectify any immoral actions committed by these entities.[37]

The typical process for a class action lawsuit involved the hiring of legal representation and soliciting the court for "class action" case certification. The certification of "class action" was contingent on the number of shareholders involved in the suit, the extent of commonality in damages experienced by these shareholders, and whether the legal representation was aligned with and representative of the shareholder interests.[38] A time period was established for the start and end of the claims period, and only holders of shares during that period were eligible to participate in the class action lawsuit. Once class-action certification was granted, all eligible shareholders were informed and prompted to contribute input. Eligible shareholders then became entitled to a prorated portion of any awards received, net of legal expenses.

Class action claims could be settled through negotiation agreements with the corporation, or they could be brought to trial where a judge would render a decision. In order to gain negotiating leverage, the plaintiff had to prove that management intentionally misled shareholders through their actions or through the information that they distributed and that those actions lead to a destruction of shareholder value.[39]

McIntyre's Task

As he sifted through the Biovail files, McIntyre knew there were several issues to consider when preparing the supporting arguments for a law firm to take the lead in a possible class action suit on behalf of Biovail shareholders. Much of what he had read about the actions of Biovail executives might be construed as just poor management judgment; on the other hand, as noted by the OSC and SEC, perhaps this was a case of fraudulent conduct. McIntyre would also have to identify a period of time in which the issues would have impacted shareholders and new purchasers of Biovail shares. The chosen time period would determine the eligible members of the class action suit and the market value destruction that had occurred to their investments in Biovail. McIntyre took a sip of his cappuccino and began to investigate the issues that he believed warranted further examination.

NOTES

1. This case has been written on the basis of published sources only. Consequently, the interpretation and perspectives presented in this case are not necessarily those of Biovail Corporation or of any of its employees.
2. http://www.ic.gc.ca/epic/site/lsi-isv.nsf/en/li00256e.html, accessed October 20, 2008.
3. http://www.newswire.ca/en/releases/archive/October2008/23/c8768.html, accessed November 17, 2008.
4. Ibid.
5. http://www.allp.com/drug_dev.htm, accessed June 23, 2003.
6. Rather than an individual taking several doses of the same pill in one day, controlled-release technology allows people to take only one dosage of medication, and the technology releases the drug at a controlled pace.
7. Report on business, The Globe and Mail, October 2008.
8. http://www.cbc.ca/money/story/2007/05/16/biovailmelynk.html, accessed October 2, 2008.
9. A generic drug is the proven bioequivalent to its branded counterpart. Generic drugs are offered at a lower price.
10. http://www.biovail.com, accessed October 23, 2008.
11. http://www.canadianbusiness.com/after_hours/article.jsp?content=20071128_210746_3160&page=2, October 23, 2008.
12. Triangle Business Journal, April 21, 2003.
13. Known as the "October 3, 2003" press release.
14. Ibid.
15. Bank of America report, October 10, 2003.
16. Ibid.
17. Pro forma reporting had long been used by companies to paint a "what if" picture, where pro forma numbers were used to show the comparability of financial information in a year when a company acquired or divested of another company to how the financial statements would have looked had the merger taken place at an earlier time or not at all. In recent years companies, including Biovail, have been using unregulated pro forma earnings as a means of showing shareholders a more sustainable view of company profits. Pro forma earnings were often higher than GAAP earnings since companies often excluded a number of expenses they considered to be non-recurring, such as asset write-downs, litigation settlements, merger/acquisition-related expenses, restructuring charges, amortization expenses, research and development charges, and stock-related compensation expenses.
18. Biovail press release, March 4, 2003.
19. Ibid.
20. Report on Business, The Globe and Mail, October 2008.
21. http://www.sedar.com, Notice of Annual Meeting of Shareholders & Management Proxy Circular, June 25, 2008.
22. http://www.globeandmail.com, March 28, 2006.
23. http://www.globeandmail.com, April 4, 2006.
24. http://www.globeandmail.com, July 31, 2006.
25. A Wells Notice is a letter that the U.S. Securities and Exchange Commission sends to people or firms when it is planning to bring an enforcement action against them.

26. http://www.reportonbusiness.com, May 14, 2007.

27. http://www.globeandmail.com, March 24, 2008.

28. http://www.sedar.com, Management discussion and analysis, November 2007.

29. http://www.sedar.com, Biovail press release, June 28, 2007.

30. Executives included Eugene Melnyk, Brian Crombie (former CFO), John Miszuk (VP, Controller and Assistant Secretary), and Kenneth Howling (Senior VP and CFO).

31. Securities and Exchange Commission, Statement of Allegations, March 24, 2008.

32. Ontario Securities Commission, Statement of Allegations, March 24, 2008.

33. Ibid.

34. Securities and Exchange Commission, Statement of Allegations, March 24, 2008.

35. Hence the designation of this transaction as a "bill and hold" transaction.

36. Ontario Securities Commission, Statement of Allegations, March 24, 2008.

37. http://www.classaction.ca, accessed November 17, 2008.

38. http://classactiondefense.jmbm.com/2006/05/defending_against_class_action_4.html, accessed November 17, 2008.

39. http://www.web-access.net/~aclark/frames45.htm, accessed November 17, 2008.

CASE 2
Wal-Mart Stores, Inc. (WMT)

Francine Barley, David Bragg, Misty Dawson, Hammad Shah, Brian Sillanpaa, Nathan Sleeper
Dominik Steinkuler, Prof. Lutz Kaufmann, Daniel Schmidt

Arizona State University

Lee Scott ignored his fear of public speaking as he prepared to step in front of 20,000 people at the Bud Walton Arena in Fayetteville, Arkansas, on June 1, 2007.[1] For his seventh year as Wal-Mart CEO, Scott addressed his company's shareholders at its annual meeting.

Outside the building, the local "Against the Wal" protesters were back for the fourth year in a row, clutching a list of seven demands: "living wage," "affordable health care," "end discrimination," "zero tolerance on child labor," "respect communities," "respect the environment," and "stop union busting."[2]

Inside the arena, shareholders had their own concerns, with declining share prices and 11 shareholder proposals—all opposed by the company.[3] Since Scott became CEO in 2000, Wal-Mart's stock price has dipped about 27 percent, from $64.50 to the $47 range.[4]

In the same timeframe, competitor Costco's stock price has appreciated roughly 20 percent, and Target's has climbed more than 70 percent[5] (see Exhibit 1). Analysts are saying Wal-Mart's "glory days are over" and its stock is "dead money."[6] Some observers are speculating that Scott's days as CEO may be numbered if he is unable to get the company back on track soon.

It is a big company to change. From its humble origins 45 years ago as a single shop in the Ozarks, Wal-Mart has grown to 1.8 million employees supporting more than 6,700 stores in 14 countries, serving 175 million customers per week and pulling in an average of $6.6 billion in weekly sales.[7] Over the past decade, Wal-Mart doubled its store count, tripled its revenue, and nearly quadrupled its net income[8] (see Exhibits 2 and 3). Wal-Mart earned more in its first quarter of fiscal 2007

Exhibit 1 Changes in Stock Price: Wal-Mart, Target, and Costco, January 3, 2000, through May 14, 2007

Source: 2007, Yahoo! Finance, http://finance.yahoo.com/charts#chart6:symbol=wmt;range=20000103,20070518;compare=cost+tgt;indicator=volume;charttype=line;crosshair=on;logscale=on;source=undefined, May 17.

© Don Hammond/Design Pics/Corbis

Exhibit 2 Wal-Mart Retail Units and Sales, 1997–2007

	2007	2006	2005	2004	2003	2002	2001	2000	1999	1998	1997
Number of retail units											
Wal-Mart Stores	1,074	1,209	1,353	1,478	1,568	1,647	1,736	1,801	1,869	1,921	1,960
Supercenters	2,257	1,980	1,713	1,471	1,258	1,066	888	721	564	441	344
Neighborhood Markets	112	100	85	64	49	31	19	7	4	0	0
SAM'S Clubs	579	567	551	538	525	500	475	463	451	443	436
US Stores Total	4,022	3,856	3,702	3,551	3,400	3,244	3,118	2,992	2,888	2,805	2,740
International Stores	2,760	2,181	1,480	1,248	1,163	1,050	955	892	605	568	314
Total Stores	**6,782**	**6,037**	**5,182**	**4,799**	**4,563**	**4,294**	**4,073**	**3,884**	**3,493**	**3,373**	**3,054**
Percentage of total retail units											
Wal-Mart Stores	26.7%	31.4%	36.5%	41.6%	46.1%	50.8%	55.7%	60.2%	64.7%	68.5%	71.5%
Supercenters	56.1%	51.3%	46.3%	41.4%	37.0%	32.9%	28.5%	24.1%	19.5%	15.7%	12.6%
Neighborhood Markets	2.8%	2.6%	2.3%	1.8%	1.4%	1.0%	0.6%	0.2%	0.1%	0.0%	0.0%
SAM'S Clubs	14.4%	14.7%	14.9%	15.2%	15.4%	15.4%	15.2%	15.5%	15.6%	15.8%	15.9%
International	40.7%	36.1%	28.6%	26.0%	25.5%	24.5%	23.4%	23.0%	17.3%	16.8%	10.3%
Sales by segment											
Wal-Mart	$226,294	$209,910	$191,826	$174,220	$157,120	$139,131	$121,889	$108,721	$95,395	$83,820	$74,840
SAM'S Clubs	$41,582	$39,798	$37,119	$34,537	$31,702	$29,395	$26,798	$24,801	$22,881	$20,668	$19,785
International	$77,116	$59,237	$52,543	$47,572	$40,794	$35,485	$32,100	$22,728	$12,247	$7,517	$5,002
Total	**$344,992**	**$308,945**	**$281,488**	**$256,329**	**$229,616**	**$204,011**	**$180,787**	**$156,250**	**$130,523**	**$112,005**	**$99,627**
Percentage of sales by segment											
Wal-Mart	65.6%	67.9%	68.1%	68.0%	68.4%	68.2%	67.4%	69.6%	73.1%	74.8%	75.1%
SAM'S Clubs	12.1%	12.9%	13.2%	13.5%	13.8%	14.4%	14.8%	15.9%	17.5%	18.5%	19.9%
International	22.4%	19.2%	18.7%	18.6%	17.8%	17.4%	17.8%	14.5%	9.4%	6.7%	5.0%
Percentage of sales											
Domestic	77.6%	80.8%	81.3%	81.4%	82.2%	82.6%	82.2%	85.5%	90.6%	93.3%	95.0%
International	22.4%	19.2%	18.7%	18.6%	17.8%	17.4%	17.8%	14.5%	9.4%	6.7%	5.0%
Percentage change in sales											
Domestic	7.3%	9.1%	9.7%	10.6%	12.0%	13.3%	11.4%	12.9%	13.2%	10.4%	2.0%
International	30.2%	12.7%	10.4%	16.6%	15.0%	10.5%	41.2%	85.6%	62.9%	50.3%	25.9%
Percentage sales change											
Domestic	50.4%	75.6%	80.2%	74.6%	79.3%	85.4%	61.8%	59.3%	74.5%	79.7%	
International	49.6%	24.4%	19.8%	25.4%	20.7%	14.6%	38.2%	40.7%	25.5%	20.3%	

Source: 2007, 2002, Wal-Mart Annual Reports.

Exhibit 3 Wal-Mart Income, 1997–2007

Income Statement
(figures in $ millions; fiscal year ends 1/31)

	2007	2006	2005	2004	2003	2002	2001	2000	1999	1998	1997
Total Operating Revenue	$348,650	$312,101	$284,310	$252,791	$226,479	$201,166	$178,028	$153,345	$129,161	$112,005	$99,627
Cost of Sales	$264,152	$237,649	$216,832	$195,922	$175,769	$156,807	$138,438	$119,526	$101,456	$88,163	$78,897
Gross Operating Profit	**$ 84,498**	**$ 74,452**	**$ 67,478**	**$ 56,869**	**$ 50,710**	**$ 44,359**	**$ 39,590**	**$ 33,819**	**$ 27,705**	**$ 23,842**	**$20,730**
Gross Margins	24.2%	23.9%	23.7%	22.5%	22.4%	22.1%	22.2%	22.1%	21.4%	21.3%	20.8%
Operating, Selling, G&A Exp.	$ 64,001	$ 55,739	$ 50,178	$ 43,877	$ 39,178	$ 34,275	$ 29,942	$ 25,182	$ 21,469	$ 18,831	$ 16,437
Operating Income	**$ 20,497**	**$ 18,713**	**$ 17,300**	**$ 12,992**	**$ 11,532**	**$ 10,084**	**$ 9,648**	**$ 8,637**	**$ 6,236**	**$ 5,011**	**$ 4,293**
Net Interest Expense	$ 1,529	$ 1,178	$ 980	$ 825	$ 930	$ 1,183	$ 1,194	$ 837	$ 595	$ 716	$ 807
Income Before Taxes	$ 18,968	$ 17,535	$ 16,320	$ 12,167	$ 10,602	$ 8,901	$ 8,454	$ 7,800	$ 5,641	$ 4,295	$ 3,486
Taxes	$ 6,365	$ 5,803	$ 5,589	$ 3,071	$ 2,662	$ 2,183	$ 2,008	$ 2,218	$ 1,432	$ 871	$ 508
Effective Tax Rate	33.6%	33.1%	34.2%	25.2%	25.1%	24.5%	23.8%	28.4%	25.4%	20.3%	14.6%
Net Income from Operations	$ 12,603	$ 11,732	$ 10,731	$ 9,096	$ 7,940	$ 6,718	$ 6,446	$ 5,582	$ 4,209	$ 3,424	$ 2,978
Other Items	$ (894)	$ (177)	$ (215)	$ (42)	$ 15	$ (126)	$ (211)	$ (258)	$ 188	$ 80	$ 64
Net Income	$ 11,709	$ 11,555	$ 10,516	$ 9,054	$ 7,955	$ 6,592	$ 6,235	$ 5,324	$ 4,397	$ 3,504	$ 3,042
Shareholder Income											
EPS (diluted) ($dollars)	$ 2.71	$ 2.68	$ 2.41	$ 2.07	$ 1.79	$ 1.50	$ 1.44	$ 1.25	$ 0.94	$ 0.76	$ 0.65
Dividend ($dollars)	$ 0.67	$ 0.60	$ 0.52	$ 0.36	$ 0.30	$ 0.28	$ 0.24	$ 0.20	$ 0.16	$ 0.14	$ 0.11

Source: 2007, 2002, Wal-Mart Annual Reports.

($78.8 billion) than Target made all year ($59.5 billion).[9] Wal-Mart's revenue gave it the No. 1 spot on *Fortune's* April 2007 list of America's largest corporations.[10] By contrast, its profit as a percentage of revenue came in at 3.2 percent, and its total return to investors was 0.1 percent, earning Wal-Mart sub-par ranks by those measures (no. 354 and no. 355, respectively).[11]

Over the past several years, Wal-Mart has stumbled upon a variety of compounding difficulties. Opposition has been mounting against not only Wal-Mart's practices, but also its very presence, due to multiple relationship issues with employees, communities, and governments.[12] It is increasingly challenging for the company to expand at its current rate, both in the United States and abroad. Meanwhile, key competitors have been "growing two to five times faster than Wal-Mart" in same-store sales.[13]

As a result, the company has gradually been losing some of its luster, even in the eyes of its former admirers. In 2004, Wal-Mart had been number one on *Fortune* magazine's list of "America's Most Admired Companies" for the second year running, notwithstanding "a year of bad press and lagging stock price."[14] In 2007, by contrast, Wal-Mart was tied for number 19, behind Costco (no. 18) and Target (no. 13).[15]

What had worked in the past was no longer sustainable in the current competitive environment. Scott wondered whether the change efforts he had started over the past few years would begin to have a positive effect or whether he should somehow adjust Wal-Mart's course.

Company History

Origins

Before founding Wal-Mart, Sam Walton accumulated experience in variety store retailing as a JCPenney management trainee and a franchisee of Ben Franklin stores.[16] Anticipating discount market growth, Walton opened his first Wal-Mart store in Rogers, Arkansas, in 1962, the same year Kmart and Target were founded.[17] Wal-Mart opened 24 more stores by 1967.[18] This start was slow compared with Kmart, which had already opened 162 stores by 1966.[19] Wal-Mart went public in 1970, giving it access to the financial resources needed to begin a decades-long expansion campaign that led to the opening of 3,800 stores by 2005.[20] Wal-Mart opened its first Sam's Club warehouse in 1983 and its first international store in 1991, and the company's national and international multiplatform expansion continues[21] (see Exhibit 4).

Recent History

Wal-Mart's growth soared in recent years, with the company adding nearly one new store every day (since 2006).[22] The company's rapid expansion brought its total retail store presence to 6,782 units worldwide as of February 8, 2007.[23] Wal-Mart spread with a missionary zeal, to "save people money so they can live better."[24] As Wal-Mart's presence continued to grow, so did its sales, to a record $345 billion in the fiscal year ended January 31, 2007 (hereafter referred to as 2007).

The company's massive growth brought with it massive controversies, however. Wal-Mart faced multiple accusations, charges, and lawsuits, many resulting in fines, including environmental violations, child labor law violations, use of illegal immigrants by subcontractors, and allegedly poor working conditions for associates.[25] Side effects of these issues include communities rejecting expansion of Wal-Mart stores into their neighborhoods.[26] Anti-Wal-Mart press is also on the rise, with books such as *How Wal-Mart Is Destroying America and the World: And What You Can Do About It* by Bill Quinn, and Robert Greenwald's film, *Wal-Mart: The High Cost of Low Price*. By one estimate, Wal-Mart's reputation issues have cost it $16 billion in market capitalization and an unknown amount of lost business in each store category or business segment.[27]

Business Segments

Wal-Mart's three business segments are Wal-Mart Stores, Sam's Club, and Wal-Mart International.[28] The Wal-Mart Stores segment includes walmart.com and three retail store formats in all 50 of the United States, including 2,257 Supercenters, 1,074 Discount Stores, and 112 Neighborhood Markets.[29] The Neighborhood Markets have the smallest format, with an average size of 42,000 square feet, and a primary focus on grocery products.[30] Wal-Mart's Discount Stores "offer a wide assortment of general merchandise and a limited variety of food products" within 107,000 square feet of selling space.[31] Supercenters average 187,000 square feet and add a full line of food products to Discount Stores' typical selection.[32] Wal-Mart converted 147 Discount Stores into Supercenters in 2007.[33] Overall, Wal-Mart Stores opened 303 new units in 2007 (276 Supercenters, 15 Discount Stores, and 12 Neighborhood Markets).[34]

Membership-based Sam's Club operates in a retail warehouse format, as well as online at samsclub.com. The segment's 579 clubs average 132,000 square feet, and provide "exceptional value on brand-name merchandise at 'members only' prices for both business and personal use."[35] Sam's Club opened 15 new units in 2007.[36]

Wal-Mart International added 576 (net) new stores in 2006—on its way to doubling its total retail unit count over the past few years.[37] Wal-Mart now operates 2,760 stores outside the United States in various formats, under diverse brand names, in 13 foreign countries and territories.[38] Wal-Mart International includes "wholly owned operations in Argentina, Brazil, Canada, Puerto Rico,

Exhibit 4 Wal-Mart Key Events, 1962–2004

1960s

1962:   Company founded with opening of first Wal-Mart in Rogers, Arkansas.
1967:   Wal-Mart's 24 stores total $12.6 million in sales.
1968:   Wal-Mart moves outside Arkansas with stores in Missouri and Oklahoma.
1969:   Company incorporated as Wal-Mart Stores, Inc., on October 31.

1970s

1970:   Wal-Mart opens first distribution center and home office in Bentonville, Arkansas. Wal-Mart stock first traded over the counter as a publicly held company. 38 stores now in operation with sales at $44.2 million. Total number of associates is 1,500.
1971:   Wal-Mart is now in five states: Arkansas, Kansas, Louisiana, Missouri, and Oklahoma.
1972:   Wal-Mart approved and listed on the New York Stock Exchange.
1973:   Wal-Mart enters Tennessee.
1974:   Wal-Mart stores now in Kentucky and Mississippi.
1975:   125 stores in operation with sales of $340.3 million and 7,500 associates. Wal-Mart enters ninth state: Texas.
1977:   Wal-Mart enters its 10th state: Illinois.
1979:   Wal-Mart is the first company to reach $1 billion in sales in such a short period of time: $1.248 billion. Wal-Mart now has 276 stores, 21,000 associates and is in its 11th state: Alabama.

1980s

1981:   Wal-Mart enters Georgia and South Carolina.
1982:   Wal-Mart enters Florida and Nebraska.
1983:   First Sam's Club opened in April in Midwest City, Oklahoma. Wal-Mart enters Indiana, Iowa, New Mexico, and North Carolina. For eighth year straight Forbes magazine ranks Wal-Mart No. 1 among general retailers.
1984:   Wal-Mart enters Virginia.
1985:   Wal-Mart has 882 stores with sales of $8.4 billion and 104,000 associates. Company adds stores in Wisconsin and Colorado.
1986:   Wal-Mart enters Minnesota.
1987:   Wal-Mart's 25th anniversary: 1,198 stores with sales of $15.9 billion and 200,000 associates.
1988:   First Supercenter opened in Washington, Missouri.
1989:   Wal-Mart is now in 26 states with the addition of Michigan, West Virginia, and Wyoming.

1990s

1990:   Wal-Mart enters California, Nevada, North Dakota, Pennsylvania, South Dakota, and Utah.
1991:   Wal-Mart enters Connecticut, Delaware, Maine, Maryland, Massachusetts, New Hampshire, New Jersey, and New York. International market entered for first time with the opening of two units in Mexico City. Wal-Mart has entered 45 states with the addition of Idaho, Montana, and Oregon. Wal-Mart enters Puerto Rico.
1993:   Wal-Mart enters Alaska, Hawaii, Rhode Island, and Washington.
1994:   Three value clubs open in Hong Kong. Canada has 123 stores and Mexico has 96.
1995:   Wal-Mart Stores, Inc., has 1,995 Wal-Mart stores, 239 Supercenters, 433 Sam's Clubs, and 276 International stores with sales at $93.6 billion and 675,000 associates. Wal-Mart enters its 50th state, Vermont, and builds three units in Argentina and five in Brazil.
1996:   Wal-Mart enters China through a joint-venture agreement.
1997:   Wal-Mart replaces Woolworth on the Dow Jones Industrial Average.
1998:   Wal-Mart enters Korea through a joint venture agreement.
1999:   Wal-Mart has 1,140,000 associates, making the company the largest private employer in the world.

2000s

2000:   Wal-Mart ranked 5th by Fortune magazine in its Global Most Admired All-Stars list.
2001:   Wal-Mart named by Fortune magazine as the third most admired company in America.
2002:   Wal-Mart ranked #1 on the Fortune 500 listing.
2002:   Wal-Mart has the biggest single day sales in history: $1.43 billion on the day after Thanksgiving.
2003:   Wal-Mart named by Fortune magazine as the most admired company in America.
2004:   Fortune magazine placed Wal-Mart in the top spot on its "Most Admired Companies" list for the second year in a row.

Source: 2007, The Wal-Mart Timeline, Wal-Mart Facts, http://www.walmartfacts.com/content/default.aspx?id=3, April 1.

and the United Kingdom; the operation of joint ventures in China; and the operations of majority-owned subsidiaries in Central America, Japan, and Mexico."[39] In 2006, Wal-Mart divested its operations in Germany and Korea.[40] Mike Duke, vice chairperson of Wal-Mart Stores and head of the International Division, commented that it had "'become increasingly clear that in Germany's [and South Korea's] business environment it would be difficult to obtain the scale and results we desire.' Wal-Mart seeks markets where it feels that there is potential for it to become a top three retailer, an opportunity that did not exist for it in Germany [or South Korea]."[41] Wal-Mart International's U.K.-based Asda subsidiary brings in the largest share of the company's international revenue, at

Exhibit 5 International Wal-Mart Retail Units and Banners, 2007

2,760 total units

Country	Retail Units	Date of Entry
Mexico	889	November 1991
Puerto Rico	54	August 1992
Canada	289	November 1994
Argentina	13	November 1995
Brazil	302	May 1995
China	73	August 1996
United Kingdom	335	July 1999
Japan	392	March 2002
Costa Rica	137	September 2005
El Salvador	63	September 2005
Guatemala	132	September 2005
Honduras	41	September 2005
Nicaragua	40	September 2005

Wal-Mart Stores, Inc.
These are our banners worldwide. We are united in saving our customers money so they can live better.

Sources: 2007, International Data Sheet, Wal-Mart Stores, http://walmartstores.com/Files/Intl_operations.pdf, February 8; 2007, Wal-Mart Annual Report, 24.

37.4 percent.[42] Wal-Mart de Mexico provides the next largest share, at 23.6 percent of Wal-Mart International sales[43] (see Exhibit 5).

One of the challenges for each of Wal-Mart's segments is determining the appropriate product offerings for each location.

Product/Service Diversification

Wal-Mart continues to build on the discount general-store concept that reflects founder Sam Walton's ideals: "a wide assortment of good quality merchandise; the lowest possible prices; guaranteed satisfaction with what you buy; friendly, knowledgeable service; convenient hours; free parking; [and] a pleasant shopping experience."[44] The company's Neighborhood Market locations provide an average of 29,000 items per store; its Discount Stores offer 120,000 items in each store; and its Supercenters stock more than 142,000 different items. Walmart.com offers customers 1 million SKUs (stock keeping units or items in stock), multiple times the number offered in Wal-Mart's retail stores.[45] Sam's Club features appliances, electronics, furniture, jewelry, and office products, plus healthcare, business, personal and financial services.[46] Interestingly, Wal-Mart "caters heavily to customers with little or no access to banking services, often described as the 'unbanked.'"[47] This category fits 20 percent of Wal-Mart's customer base and, as such, Wal-Mart provides substantial financial services for this customer segment by providing services such as check cashing. It has 170 money centers in its approximately 4,000 U.S. stores.

Product and service offerings are just one of the many complex decisions that Wal-Mart's strategic leaders have to make.

Strategic Leaders

Ultimate leadership control has remained in the Walton family, with chairmanship changing hands only once, from father to son. Successors to the highest executive positions at Wal-Mart have always come from within the company. After eight years as CFO and executive vice president, David Glass succeeded Sam Walton as president and later as CEO.[48] H. Lee Scott joined Wal-Mart in 1979 and was named CEO by David Glass in 2000[49] (see Exhibit 6).

Decision Makers

Twenty-five senior Wal-Mart officers meet via weekly videoconferences "to review the Company's ongoing performance, focus on initiatives to drive sales and customer service, and address broader issues"[50] (see Exhibit 7). Eight of these senior officers currently have the most critical roles.

The most powerful among them is S. Robson (Rob) Walton, first son of Sam Walton and chair of the board of directors since 1992.[51] Rob Walton was initiated into the fledgling family business one night in the early 1960s after he earned his driver's license when Sam recruited him to truck goods from a garage in Bentonville to a Wal-Mart store.[52] Rob officially joined the company in

1969, shortly after graduating from law school, worked his way up to the vice chair position, and became board chair in 1992 after his father died.[53] "We lead when we embrace my dad's vision," according to Rob, "to improve the lives of everyday people by making everyday things more affordable."[54] Rob now lives in Colorado, where he races bicycles and sports cars in his spare time, and flies the company jet to his Bentonville office.[55] He continues to serve as the primary conduit for Walton family input related to company proceedings.[56]

CEO Lee Scott "rose through the ranks by excelling at the mechanical aspects of retailing, playing an indispensable part in Wal-Mart's technology-induced rebound in the latter half of the 1990s."[57] The son of a gas station owner and a music teacher in small-town Kansas, Scott worked factory night shifts to pay for college, while he, his wife, and their baby lived in a mobile home.[58] He put his business degree to use in logistics, first as a dispatcher for Yellow Freight, then as a "headstrong," "aggressive, even abrasive" Wal-Mart transportation manager.[59] His skill in reducing costs helped him ascend to senior logistics jobs, then into the top merchandising post, where he cut billions in excess inventory in the late 1990s.[60] Next Scott ran the 2,300-unit Wal-Mart Stores Division for a year before becoming Wal-Mart's chief operating officer and vice chairperson in 1999.[61] He became CEO in January 2000.[62]

Mike Duke, an industrial engineer who had 23 years of experience with Federated and May Department Stores, followed Scott's path, climbing the distribution and logistics ladder to the leadership of Wal-Mart Stores Division.[63] Now he oversees international operations as vice chairperson.[64]

John Menzer, who joined Wal-Mart in 1995 after 10 years with Ben Franklin Retail Stores, served as Wal-Mart's chief financial officer before becoming CEO of Wal-Mart International in 1999.[65] He led the acquisitions of Seiyu (a majority-owned subsidiary in Japan) and Asda.[66] Now as vice chairperson, Menzer is responsible for Wal-Mart Stores and various corporate functions, including strategic planning.[67]

A native of Ecuador, Eduardo Castro-Wright leads the Wal-Mart Stores Division in the United States after leading Wal-Mart de Mexico from 2001 to 2005, following a distinguished career with Nabisco in the Latin America and Asia-Pacific regions.[68]

Doug McMillon became president and CEO of Sam's Club after a 15-year career with Wal-Mart, first as a buyer, then as a merchandising manager and leader.[69]

Nineteen-year Target veteran John Fleming ascended through Walmart.com in the early 2000s to become Wal-Mart Stores' chief marketing officer, prior to his January 2007 induction as chief merchandising officer for Wal-Mart Stores.[70]

Exhibit 6 History of Leadership Succession at Wal-Mart

History of Leadership Succession at Wal-Mart			
Year	President	CEO	Chairman
1962	Sam Walton	Sam Walton	Sam Walton
1984	David Glass	Sam Walton	Sam Walton
1988	David Glass	David Glass	Sam Walton
1992	David Glass	David Glass	Rob Walton
2000	H. Lee Scott	H. Lee Scott	Rob Walton

Sources: 2007, The Wal-Mart Timeline, Wal-Mart Facts, http://www
.walmartfacts.com/content/default.aspx?id=3, April 1; D. Longo, 1998,
Wal-Mart hands CEO crown to David Glass, *Discount Store News*, February 15.

Exhibit 7 Wal-Mart Senior Officers, May 2007

Eduardo Castro-Wright
Executive Vice President and President and Chief Executive Officer, Wal-Mart Stores Division

M. Susan Chambers
Executive Vice President of People Division

Patricia A. Curran
Executive Vice President, Store Operations, Wal-Mart Stores Division

Leslie A. Dach
Executive Vice President, Corporate Affairs and Government Relations

Linda M. Dillman
Executive Vice President, Risk Management and Benefits Administration

Michael T. Duke
Vice Chairman, Responsible for International

Johnnie C. Dobbs
Executive Vice President, Logistics and Supply Chain

John E. Fleming
Executive Vice President and Chief Merchandising Officer, Wal-Mart Stores Division

Rollin L. Ford
Executive Vice President, Chief Information Officer

Craig R. Herkert
Executive Vice President and President and Chief Executive Officer, The Americas, International

Charles M. Holley, Jr.
Executive Vice President, Finance and Treasurer

Thomas D. Hyde
Executive Vice President and Corporate Secretary

Gregory L. Johnston
Executive Vice President, Club Operations, SAM'S CLUB

Thomas A. Mars
Executive Vice President and General Counsel

C. Douglas McMillon
Executive Vice President and President and Chief Executive Officer, SAM'S CLUB

John B. Menzer
Vice Chairman, Responsible for U.S.

Stephen Quinn
Executive Vice President and Chief Marketing Officer, Wal-Mart Stores, Inc.

Thomas M. Schoewe
Executive Vice President and Chief Financial Officer

H. Lee Scott, Jr.
President and Chief Executive Officer

William S. Simon
Executive Vice President and Chief Operating Officer, Professional Services and New Business Development

Gregory E. Spragg
Executive Vice President, Merchandising and Replenishment, SAM'S CLUB

S. Robson Walton
Chairman of the Board of Directors of Wal-Mart Stores, Inc.

Claire A. Watts
Executive Vice President, Merchandising, Wal-Mart Stores Division-US

Steven P. Whaley
Senior Vice President, Controller, Wal-Mart Stores Inc.

Eric S. Zorn
Executive Vice President and President, Wal-Mart Realty

Source: 2007, Senior Officers, WalMartStores.com, http://walmartstores.com/GlobalWMStoresWeb/navigate.do?catg=540, May 25.

After 13 years in marketing roles with PepsiCo, Stephen Quinn joined Wal-Mart as senior vice president of marketing in 2005, and then in January 2007 took over Fleming's former position as chief marketing officer for Wal-Mart Stores.[71]

These eight leaders are supported and monitored by the board of directors.

Board of Directors

Wal-Mart has an active, high-caliber, 14-member board of directors that may soon get even more powerful. "The Board has been instrumental in encouraging the company to more quickly address critical issues, and I am extremely pleased that they are not reticent about sharing their opinions," Rob Walton recently wrote, adding: "Today's Board is the furthest thing from a rubber stamp."[72] Two out of three board members have held

CEO positions and/or chaired the boards of various companies. Retail turnaround guru Allen Questrom, who overhauled JCPenney, joined the board in June 2007.[73] Questrom recently told *Women's Wear Daily*: "[Wal-Mart is] never going to be a leader in fashion apparel. That's not their calling. But can they improve on that, sure they can."[74] The most famous former board member is New York Senator and Democratic presidential candidate Hillary Rodham Clinton, who served on the Wal-Mart board from 1986 to 1992 as a "loyalist reformer"[75] (see Exhibit 8).

Several board members are among the largest shareholders in the company.

Shareholders

Of the 4.1 billion Wal-Mart shares outstanding, insiders and beneficial owners hold 42 percent, while institutional investors and mutual funds hold 37 percent.[76]

Exhibit 8 Wal-Mart Board of Directors, May 2007

Aida M. Alvarez, 57
Former Administrator of the U.S. Small Business Administration; joined board in 2006

James W. Breyer, 45
Managing Partner of Accel Partners; joined board in 2001

M. Michele Burns, 49
Chairman and CEO of Mercer Human Resources Consulting; joined board in 2003

James Cash, Jr., Ph.D., 59
Retired Professor of Business Administration at Harvard Business School; joined board in 2006

Roger C. Corbett, 64
Retired CEO and Group Managing Director of Woolworths Limited; joined board in 2006

Douglas N. Daft, 64
Retired Chairman of the Board and CEO of The Coca-Cola Company; joined board in 2005

David D. Glass, 71
Former President and CEO of Wal-Mart Stores, Inc.; joined board in 1977

Roland A. Hernandez, 49
Retired Chairman and CEO of Telemundo Group, Inc.; joined board in 1998

Allen I. Questrom, 67
Former Chairman and CEO of JCPenney Company; Barneys New York, Inc.; The Neiman Marcus Group, Inc.; and Federated Department Stores, Inc.; standing for election in June 2007

H. Lee Scott, Jr., 58
President and Chief Executive Officer of Wal-Mart Stores, Inc.; joined board in 1999

Jack C. Shewmaker, 69
Retired Vice Chairman of Wal-Mart Stores, Inc.; joined board in 1977

Jim C. Walton, 58
Chairman of the Board and CEO of Arvest Bank Group, Inc.; joined board in 2005

S. Robson Walton, 62
Chairman of the Board of Directors of Wal-Mart Stores, Inc.; joined board in 1978

Christopher J. Williams, 49
Chairman and CEO of The Williams Capital Group, L.P.; joined board in 2004

Linda S. Wolf, 59
Former Chairman of the Board and CEO of Leo Burnett Worldwide, Inc.; joined board in 2005

Sources: 2007, Board of Directors, WalMartStores.com, http://walmartstores.com/GlobalWMStoresWeb/navigate.do?catg=502, May 25; 2007, Wal-Mart Stores, Inc., Form DEF 14A, Proxy Statement, Notice of 2007 Annual Shareholders' Meeting, U.S. SEC, April 19.

The Walton family owns almost 1.7 billion shares through its holding company, Walton Enterprises, LLC, whose directors were five of America's ten wealthiest individuals in 2005: Sam's three sons, Rob Walton, director Jim C. Walton, and John T. Walton (d. 2005); daughter Alice L. Walton; and widow Helen R. Walton (d. 2007).[77]

Top non-Walton inside shareholders include CEO Lee Scott (1.2 million shares), director David D. Glass (1.2 million shares), director Jack C. Shewmaker (557,674 shares), Mike Duke (413,213 shares), and John Menzer (401,883 shares).[78]

Some 1,127 institutions own Wal-Mart stock.[79] Nearly 536 million Wal-Mart shares are owned by 785 mutual funds.[80]

In total, as many as 312,423 shareholders held common stock in Wal-Mart on March 16, 2007, when the company finalized its annual report for fiscal 2007.[81]

Financial Results

Fiscal 2007 and Recent Years[82]
Over the past 10 years, Wal-Mart's net income has nearly quadrupled, from $3 billion in 1997 to $11.7 billion in 2007. Revenues have more than tripled, from $100 billion to $345 billion. Meanwhile, operating, selling, and general administration expenses have quadrupled, outstripping the increase in revenue and net income, averaging 14.6 percent of sales. Despite the increase in expenses, steadily higher gross margins have boosted operating income (refer to Exhibit 3).

Wal-Mart had assets totaling $151 billion in 2007, up from $39 billion in 1997. Concurrent with the increase in assets, liabilities have grown 319 percent over the same period, from $21.4 billion to $89.6 billion. Shareholder return on equity measured 22 percent in 2007, close to its 10-year average. Total shareholder equity rose from $17.2 billion in 1997 to $61.8 billion in 2007 (see Exhibit 9).

Wal-Mart has improved its profitability over the last several years. Compared with an average operating profit margin of 5.1 percent in the prior three-year period, Wal-Mart has averaged 6.0 percent in the past three years. In 1997, Wal-Mart's operating profit margin was 4.3 percent. From a debt perspective, Wal-Mart has fluctuated up and down, with a debt ratio between 55.1 percent and 61.5 percent over the last 10 years. As of 2007, it measured 59.3 percent, 150 basis points over its 10-year median (see Exhibit 10).

Comparative Revenue[83]
Sales by Region. Of nearly $345 billion in total sales in 2007 (not including Sam's Club fees), domestic U.S. revenues totaled nearly $268 billion, or 77.6 percent of sales, while international revenues were $77 billion, or 22.4 percent of sales. International operations are becoming increasingly important to the company. Driving

Exhibit 9 Wal-Mart Balance Sheet, 1997–2007

Balance Sheet
(all figures in $millions; fiscal year ends 1/31)

	2007	2006	2005	2004	2003	2002	2001	2000	1999	1998	1997
Assets											
Inventories	33,685	$ 31,910	29,419	26,263	24,098	21,793	20,710	18,961	16,058	16,005	15,556
Other Current Assets	$ 12,903	$ 11,915	$ 8,494	$ 7,285	$ 4,769	$ 4,122	$ 4,086	$ 4,021	$ 3,445	$ 2,584	$ 1,829
Total Current Assets	$ 46,588	$ 43,825	$ 37,913	$ 33,548	$28,867	$25,915	$24,796	$22,982	$19,503	$18,589	$17,385
Net Property, Equipment & Leases	$ 88,440	$ 77,865	$ 66,549	$ 57,591	$50,053	$44,172	$39,439	$34,570	$24,824	$23,237	$19,935
Goodwill & Other Long-term Assets	$ 16,165	$ 13,934	$ 12,677	$ 11,316	$11,309	$ 9,214	$10,082	$ 9,738	$ 2,739	$ 2,395	$ 1,251
Total Assets	$151,193	$135,624	$117,139	$102,455	$90,229	$79,301	$74,317	$67,290	$47,066	$44,221	$38,571
Return on Assets	8.8%	9.3%	9.8%	9.7%	9.6%	9.0%	9.3%	10.1%	9.6%	8.5%	8.0%
Liabilities & Shareholder Equity											
Current Liabilities	$ 51,754	$ 48,348	$ 42,609	$ 37,308	$31,752	$26,309	$28,096	$25,058	$15,848	$13,930	$10,432
Long-Term Debt	$ 27,222	$ 26,429	$ 20,087	$ 17,088	$16,545	$15,632	$12,453	$13,650	$ 6,875	$ 7,169	$ 7,685
Long-Term Leases	$ 3,513	$ 3,667	$ 3,073	$ 2,888	$ 2,903	$ 2,956	$ 3,054	$ 2,852	$ 2,697	$ 2,480	$ 2,304
Other Liabilities	$ 7,131	$ 4,009	$ 1,974	$ 1,548	$ (432)	$ (788)	$ (693)	$ (148)	$ 505	$ 2,123	$ 999
(minority interest, discontinued ops, deferred taxes)											
Total Liabilities	$ 89,620	$ 82,453	$ 67,743	$ 58,832	$50,768	$44,109	$42,910	$41,412	$25,925	$25,702	$21,420
Shareholder Equity	$ 61,573	$ 53,171	$ 49,396	$ 43,623	$39,461	$35,192	$31,407	$25,878	$21,141	$18,519	$17,151
Return on Equity	22.0%	22.9%	23.1%	22.4%	21.8%	20.7%	23.0%	24.5%	22.0%	19.6%	18.8%

Source: 2007, 2002, Wal-Mart Annual Reports.

Exhibit 10 Wal-Mart Financial Ratios, 1997–2007

	2007	2006	2005	2004	2003	2002	2001	2000	1999	1998	1997
Stability											
Debt Ratio	59.3%	60.8%	57.8%	57.4%	56.3%	55.6%	57.7%	61.5%	55.1%	58.1%	55.5%
Stockholders Equity to Assets	40.7%	39.2%	42.2%	42.6%	43.7%	44.4%	42.3%	38.5%	44.9%	41.9%	44.5%
Leverage	2.50	2.46	2.36	2.32	2.27	2.31	2.47	2.43	2.30	2.32	n/a
Debt to Equity Ratio	1.46	1.55	1.37	1.35	1.29	1.25	1.37	1.60	1.23	1.39	1.25
Debt to Capitization Ratio	0.38	0.39	0.34	0.33	0.33	0.34	0.32	0.39	0.32	0.39	0.39
Liquidity											
Current Ratio	0.90	0.91	0.89	0.90	0.91	0.99	0.88	0.92	1.23	1.33	1.67
Quick Ratio	0.25	0.25	0.20	0.20	0.15	0.16	0.15	0.16	0.22	0.19	0.18
Profitability											
Operating Profit Margin	5.9%	6.0%	6.1%	5.1%	5.1%	5.0%	5.4%	5.6%	4.8%	4.5%	4.3%
Operating Ratio	18.4%	17.9%	17.6%	17.4%	17.3%	17.0%	16.8%	16.4%	16.6%	16.8%	16.5%
Net Profit Margin	3.3%	3.6%	3.6%	3.6%	3.5%	3.3%	3.5%	3.5%	3.4%	3.1%	3.1%
Total Asset Turnover	2.4	2.5	2.6	2.6	2.7	2.6	2.5	2.7	2.8	2.7	n/a

Source: 2007, 2002, Wal-Mart Annual Reports.

Wal-Mart's overall growth, international sales growth has averaged 33.6 percent over the past 10 years, whereas domestic sales have grown an average of only 11.0 percent in the same period. In the last three years, domestic sales growth has averaged 8.7 percent versus average international growth of 17.8 percent (refer to Exhibit 2).

Wal-Mart has experienced varying rates of growth in international markets. Nonetheless, international revenue has been a constant source of sales growth for Wal-Mart, outpacing the revenue contribution from the Sam's Club segment since 2001.

Sales by Segment. Wal-Mart Stores brought in 65.6 percent of all sales in 2007, down from 75.1 percent of sales in 1997. Wal-Mart International was responsible for 22.4 percent of sales, up from 5.0 percent a decade earlier, while Sam's Club accounted for 12.1 percent of sales in 2007, down from 19.9 percent in 1997 (refer to Exhibit 2).

Sam's Club has suffered against rival Costco for years, losing the battle for comparable-store sales in "64 of the past 73 months," according to one researcher, as well as the battle for membership renewals.[84] Average annual sales per warehouse were $73 million for Sam's Club versus $135 million for Costco in fiscal 2006.[85]

Wal-Mart's online business has not been a significant source of revenue, bringing in an estimated $135 million in sales in 2002, the same year JCPenney.com had sales of $324 million and Amazon.com reached sales greater than $3 billion.[86]

Wal-Mart Supercenters drove 56.1 percent of the company's sales, reflecting the company's competitive strength in traditional nonmembership discount formats.

Results Relative to Competitors

Market Leadership. Wal-Mart is the number one retailer in 77 of the 100 largest general merchandise markets in America, squaring up against Target or Costco in all but 11 of these markets.[87] Either Wal-Mart, Costco, or Target holds the top position in 91 of the top 100 largest general merchandise markets in the United States.[88] Geographically, Wal-Mart is the dominant retailer in the South and throughout midsized and small-town markets, while Costco is the leader in California and Washington.[89] According to ACNielsen, (the world's leading marketing information company), in the United States, Wal-Mart "controls 20 percent of dry grocery, 29 percent of non-food grocery, 30 percent of health and beauty aids, and 45 percent of general merchandise sales."[90] It also controls 45 percent of the retail toy segment.[91] However, Target, Kroger, and Family Dollar Stores are all growing revenue faster than Wal-Mart, threatening its dominance (see Exhibit 11).

Financial Ratios. From a competitive profitability perspective, Wal-Mart's 5.87 percent operating margin and 3.23 percent net margin put it in the middle of the pack relative to its key competitors (refer to Exhibit 11). Target enjoys higher margins, closer to those of JCPenney, while Costco has lower margins, closer to those of Dollar General and Kroger. Wal-Mart's

Exhibit 11 Comparison of Financial Ratios

| | Financial Ratios of Select Retailers (sorted by revenue growth, as of May 26, 2007) | | | | | |
| | Quarterly Growth (yoy) | | Profitability (ttm) | | Management Effectiveness (ttm) | |
	Revenue Growth	Earnings Growth	Net Profit Margin	Operating Margin	Return on Assets	Return on Equity
Amazon.com, Inc.	32.30%	117.60%	2.18%	3.74%	10.37%	73.86%
Target Corporation	16.30%	19.20%	4.69%	8.52%	8.93%	18.68%
Kroger Co.	14.50%	36.50%	1.69%	3.47%	7.10%	23.95%
Family Dollar Stores, Inc.	12.20%	66.00%	3.49%	5.70%	9.44%	17.68%
Wal-Mart Stores, Inc.	9.60%	8.10%	3.23%	5.87%	8.81%	21.80%
Costco Wholesale Corp.	7.50%	−15.80%	1.73%	2.55%	6.25%	12.07%
J.C. Penney Corporation	3.10%	13.30%	5.90%	9.73%	9.57%	26.43%
Dollar General Corp.	3.00%	−65.50%	1.50%	2.67%	5.24%	7.96%
Sears Holdings Corporation	1.30%	26.50%	2.81%	4.59%	5.06%	12.25%

Sources: 2007, Key Statistics, Capital IQ, A Division of Standard & Poor's, Yahoo! Finance, http://finance.yahoo.com/q/ks?s=WMT, http://finance.yahoo.com/q/ks?s=TGT, http://finance.yahoo.com/q/ks?s=COST, http://finance.yahoo.com/q/ks?s=KR, http://finance.yahoo.com/q/ks?s=DG, http://finance.yahoo.com/q/ks?s=FDO, http://finance.yahoo.com/q/ks?s=SHLD, http://finance.yahoo.com/q/ks?s=JCP, http://finance.yahoo.com/q/ks?s=AMZN, May 26.

margins are nearest those of Family Dollar Stores and Sears Holdings (Kmart and Sears). Wal-Mart's profit margin may be held down somewhat by its presence in the lower margin grocery business, especially in its Neighborhood Markets format.[92] In Supercenters, groceries serve a larger role of driving store traffic and drawing customers toward higher margin products. From a management effectiveness standpoint, Wal-Mart is creating a return on equity that is higher than Target's and much higher than Costco's and a return on assets that is nearly identical to Target's and higher than Costco's.

First Quarter, Fiscal 2008 (Quarter Ending April 30, 2007)

Wal-Mart had a difficult first quarter. Revenue and earnings "were not where we would have expected [them] to be, nor where we believe they should be," according to CEO Scott.[93] "Quite honestly, we're not satisfied with our overall performance."[94] Wal-Mart increased company sales (not including Sam's Club fees) by 8.3 percent in the first quarter to $85.3 billion.[95] Overall operating income increased 7.9 percent year-over-year, with nearly 53.1 percent of the change coming from Wal-Mart's international operations[96] (see Exhibit 12).

Closing out the first quarter on a down note, Wal-Mart's April same-store sales decrease was the worst ever recorded in 28 years of tracking: an overall U.S. comparable-store sales slide of 3.5 percent for the month, with a 4.6 percent drop at Wal-Mart Stores offset by a 2.5 percent increase at Sam's Clubs.[97] Much of the April decline was blamed on the apparel

business, which constitutes 10 percent of Wal-Mart's sales.[98] Recent failed forays into fashion appear to have dragged down overall same-stores sales.[99] Wal-Mart wasn't the only retailer to have a bad April. The International Council of Shopping Centers reported an average 2.3 percent drop in same-store sales across 51 chains.[100] Against the trend, Costco posted a 6 percent same-store sales gain in April (see Exhibit 13).

The financial situation might be better considered with an understanding of the competitive situation in Wal-Mart's industry.

Competitive Situation

We face strong sales competition from other discount, department, drug, variety and specialty stores and supermarkets, many of which are national, regional or international chains, as well as internet-based retailers and catalog businesses. Additionally, we compete with a number of companies for prime retail site locations, as well as in attracting and retaining quality employees ("associates"). We, along with other retail companies, are influenced by a number of factors . . . cost of goods, consumer debt levels and buying patterns, economic conditions, interest rates, customer preferences, unemployment, labor costs, inflation, currency exchange fluctuations, fuel prices, weather patterns, catastrophic events, competitive pressures and insurance costs. Our Sam's Club segment faces strong sales competition from other wholesale club operators, catalogs businesses, internet-based and other retailers."

—*2007 WAL-MART ANNUAL REPORT, 28–29*

Exhibit 12 Wal-Mart Fiscal 2008 First Quarter Results versus Target

Wall-Mart Stores, Inc. Fiscal 2008 First Quarter Results Quarters Ending 4/30, all figures in $millions			
Income	Q1 2008	Q1 2007	YoY% Chng
Total Operating Revenue	$86,410	$79,676	8.5%
Cost of Sales	$65,311	$60,237	8.4%
Gross Operating Profit	**$21,099**	**$19,439**	8.5%
Gross Margins	24.4%	24.4%	
Operating, Selling, G&A Exp.	$16,249	$14,944	8.7%
Operating Income	**$ 4,850**	**$ 4,495**	7.9%
Net Interest Expense	$ 392	$ 368	6.5%
Income Before Taxes	$ 4,458	$ 4,127	8.0%
Provision for Taxes	$ 1,532	$ 1,388	10.4%
Effective Tax Rate	34.4%	33.6%	2.2%
Net Income from Operations	$ 2,926	$ 2,739	6.8%
Other Items	$ (100)	$ (124)	
Net Income	**$ 2,826**	**$ 2,615**	8.1%
Shareholder Income ($dollars)			
EPS (diluted)	$ 0.68	$ 0.63	7.9%
Dividend	$ 0.67	$ 0.60	
Comparable-Store Sales Growth	**0.6%**	**3.8%**	
Wal-Mart Stores	–0.1%	3.8%	
Sam's Club (excl. fuel)	4.7%	4.3%	
Segment Breakdown			
Revenue by Segment			
Wal-Mart Stores	$55,437	$52,499	5.6%
Sam's Club	$10,323	$ 9,775	5.6%
International	$19,627	$16,561	18.5%
Total (excludes other income)	$85,387	$78,835	8.3%
Operating Income by Segment			
Wal-Mart Stores	$ 3,927	$ 3,858	1.8%
Sam's Club	$ 363	$ 303	19.8%
International	$ 903	$ 757	19.3%
Total (excludes other income)	$ 5,193	$ 4,918	5.6%
Operating Margins by Segment			
Wal-Mart Stores	7.1%	7.3%	–3.6%
Sam's Club	3.5%	3.1%	13.4%
International	4.6%	4.6%	0.7%
Total (excludes other income)	6.1%	6.2%	–2.5%
Cash Flows			
Net Income	$ 2,826	$ 2,615	
Change in Inventories	$ (1,280)	$ 259	
Accounts Payable	$ (1,115)	$ (442)	
Accounts Receivable	$ 62	$ 219	
Cash Flows from Operating Activities	**$ 493**	**$ 2,651**	

Target Corporation Fiscal 2008 First Quarter Results Quarters Ending 5/5/07 and 4/29/06, all figures in $millions			
Income	Q1 2008	Q1 2007	YoY%Chng
Total Operating Revenue*	$14,041	$12,863	9.2%
Cost of Sales	$ 9,186	$ 8,473	8.4%
Gross Operating Profit	**$ 4,855**	**$ 4,390**	10.6%
Gross Margins	34.6%	34.1%	
Operating, Selling, G&A Exp.**	$ 3,655	$ 3,373	8.4%
Operating Income	**$ 1,200**	**$ 1,017**	18.0%
Net Interest Expense	$ 136	$ 131	3.6%
Income Before Taxes	$ 1,064	$ 886	20.2%
Provision for Taxes	$ 413	$ 332	24.5%
Effective Tax Rate	38.8%	37.5%	3.6%
Net Income from Operations	$ 651	$ 554	17.6%
Other Items	$ –	$ –	
Net Income	**$ 651**	**$ 554**	17.5%
Shareholder Income ($dollars)			
EPS (diluted)	$ 0.75	$ 0.63	19.6%

*includes sales and net credit card revenues
**includes SG&A, credit card expenses, depreciation and amortization

Comparable-Store Sales Growth	4.3%	5.1%	

Sources: 2007, Wal-Mart Stores, Inc., Form 8-K, U.S. SEC, May 15; and 2007, Target Corporation, Form 8-K, U.S. SEC, May 23.

Exhibit 13 April 2007 Same-Store Sales Growth

April 2007 Same-Store Sales Growth

Discounters

Wal-Mart	−3.5%
Costco	+6.0%
Target	−6.1%
Dollar General	−2.4%

Department Stores

Federated	−2.2%
JCPenney	−4.7%
Nordstrom	+3.1%
Dillard's	−14.0%
Neiman Marcus	+1.0%
Saks	+11.7%

Apparel

TJX	−1.0%
Kohl's	−10.5%
Gap	−16.0%
Limited	−1.0%
AnnTaylor	−12.8%

Teen Apparel

Abercrombie & Fitch	−15.0%
American Eagle Outfitters	−10.0%

Source: J. Covert, 2007, Retail-sales slide fuels concern: Decline of 2.3% in April among worst on record; even Wal-Mart slipped, *Wall Street Journal*, May 11, A3.

Competitors

Target. Target Corporation operates 1,318 general merchandise stores and 182 SuperTarget stores in 47 states, in addition to its online business, target.com.[101] Target describes itself as "an upscale discounter that provides high-quality, on-trend merchandise at attractive prices in clean, spacious and guest-friendly stores."[102] Target has grown revenue from $33 billion in 2001 to more than $59 billion in 2006, a compound annual growth rate of 12.5 percent.[103] Profits have risen as well, as earnings from continuing operations averaged an annual growth rate of 20.4 percent over the same period[104] (see Exhibit 14).

Costco. Costco Wholesale Corporation runs 510 warehouses, averaging 140,000 square feet, in 38 states, six foreign countries (Canada, Mexico, the United Kingdom, Taiwan, Korea, and Japan), and Puerto Rico.[105] Costco offers three kinds of membership and roughly 4,000 products, 10 to 15 times fewer than many competitors, according to the company.[106] Costco benefits from a limited number of products sold in high volumes, high inventory turnover, low costs via purchasing discounts and a no-frills approach, and favorable real estate locations. Gross margins have averaged about 10.6 percent over the past five years, and operating income has increased an average of 10.5 percent over the same period[107] (see Exhibit 15).

Kroger. The Kroger Co. is "one of the nation's largest retailers, operating 2,468 supermarket and multi-department stores under two dozen banners including Kroger, Ralphs, Fred Meyer, Food 4 Less, King Soopers, Smith's, Fry's, Fry's Marketplace, Dillons, QFC, and City Market."[108] Kroger's operating income fell 13.1 percent between 2002 and 2006, from $2.8 billion to $2.2 billion, despite an increase in revenue of 27.7 percent.[109] Operating margins have averaged 24.8 percent over the last three years, up from 15.7 percent in the three years prior[110] (see Exhibit 16).

Other General Discount Competitors. Sears Holdings (Kmart and Sears) offer some additional U.S. competition in general merchandise, while Tesco of Britain and Carrefour of France compete with Wal-Mart internationally. Carrefour is the second-largest retailer in the world

Exhibit 14 Target Performance, 2001–2006

Target	2001	2002	2003	2004	2005	2006
Revenue	$33,021	$ 37,410	$42,025	$46,839	$52,620	$59,940
COGS	$23,030	$25,948	$28,389	$31,445	$34,927	$39,399
Gross Margin	$ 9,991	$11,462	$13,636	$15,394	$ 17,693	$20,541
Gross Margin %	30.3%	30.6%	32.4%	32.9%	33.6%	34.3%
Operating Income/EBIT	$ 2,246	2,811	3,159	3,601	4,323	5,069
		25.2%	12.4%	14.0%	20.0%	17.3%
Net Income	$ 1,101	$ 1,376	$ 1,619	$ 1,885	$ 2,408	$ 2,787
Net Income % chg		25.0%	17.7%	16.4%	27.7%	15.7%

Note: $ in millions

Source: 2006, Target Corporation Annual Report.

Exhibit 15 Costco Performance, 2001–2006

Costco	2001	2002	2003	2004	2005	2006
Revenue	$ 34,137,021	$ 37,994,608	$ 41,694,561	$ 47,148,627	$ 51,879,070	$ 58,963,180
COGS	$ 30,598,140	$ 33,983,121	$ 37,235,383	$ 42,092,016	$ 46,346,961	$ 52,745,497
Gross Margin	$ 3,538,881	$ 4,011,487	$ 4,459,178	$ 5,056,611	$ 5,532,109	$ 6,217,683
Gross Margin %	10.4%	10.6%	10.7%	10.7%	10.7%	10.5%
Operating Income/ EBIT	$ 992,267	1,131,535	1,156,628	1,385,648	1,474,303	1,625,632
		14.0%	2.2%	19.8%	6.4%	10.3%
Net Income	$ 602,089	$ 699,983	$ 721,000	$ 882,393	$ 1,063,092	$ 1,103,215
Net Income % chg		16.3%	3.0%	22.4%	20.5%	3.8%

Note: $ in thousands

Source: 2006, Costco Wholesale Corp. Annual Report.

Exhibit 16 Kroger Performance, 2001–2006

Kroger	2001	2002	2003	2004	2005	2006
Revenue	$49,000	$51,760	$53,791	$56,434	$60,553	$ 66,111
COGS	$36,398	$ 37,810	$39,637	$42,140	$45,565	$ 50,115
Gross Margin	$12,602	$13,950	$14,154	$14,294	$14,988	$ 15,996
Gross Margin %	25.7%	10.6%	10.7%	25.3%	24.8%	24.2%
Operating Income/ EBIT	$ 2,359	$ 2,573	$ 1,374	$ 843	$ 2,035	$ 2,236
		9.1%	−46.6%	−38.6%	141.4%	9.9%
Net Income	$ 877	$ 1,202	$ 285	$ (104)	$ 958	$ 1,115
Net Income % chg		37.1%	−76.3%	−136.5%	$ 1021.2%	$ 16.4%

Note: $ in millions

Source: 2006 The Kroger Co. Annual Report.

(after Wal-Mart) and is probably its closest international competitor from a strategy perspective, as it focuses on hypermarkets (similar to Supercenters), in addition to a variety of other formats.[111] Tesco emphasizes convenience and competes primarily in groceries, but also in general merchandise against Wal-Mart's U.K. subsidiary Asda.[112] Tesco is looking to expand to the West Coast of the United States in 2007.[113] Amazon.com adds another level of global competition for Wal-Mart due to its high number of SKUs and its convenience.

Niche Competitors. Other retailers compete with Wal-Mart at the department level, including Safeway, Best Buy, Circuit City, Home Depot, Ace Hardware, Lowe's, Kohl's, Mervyn's California, Barnes & Noble, and Borders, among others. In order to provide lower prices than its competitors, Wal-Mart has developed a unique relationship with its suppliers.

Suppliers

Wal-Mart's 1,600-member Global Procurement Services team, based in 23 countries, buys merchandise from suppliers in more than 70 countries, including 61,000 suppliers in the United States.[114] Leveraging its size, "Wal-Mart not only dictates delivery schedules and inventory levels but also heavily influences product specifications. In the end, many suppliers have to choose between designing goods their way or the Wal-Mart way."[115] In return, companies with a streamlined product and supply chain can benefit greatly. "If you are good with data, are sophisticated, and have scale, Wal-Mart should be one of your most profitable customers," says a retired consumer-products executive.[116] "Wal-Mart controls a large and rapidly increasing share of the business done by most every major U.S. consumer products company," about 28 percent of the total sales of Dial and almost a quarter of the sales of Del Monte Foods, Clorox, and Revlon.[117]

Customers

Wal-Mart attracts 175 million people to its stores each week.[118] According to ACNielsen (the world's leading marketing information company), the typical Wal-Mart shopper has an annual household income of $10,000 to $50,000.[119] These shoppers account for 54 percent of Wal-Mart's sales.[120] Wal-Mart also attracts an affluent segment (with household incomes of at least $75,000) that accounts for 26 percent of its customer base.[121] The affluent segment cross-shops the most with Costco (27 percent) and Target (28 percent).[122] These upscale shoppers likely have lower price elasticity, a relatively lower switching cost, but a higher sensitivity to brand reputation.

Even though Wal-Mart recently hired some well-known public relations experts and ended its relationship with its Ad Agency of 32 years in hopes of creating a more positive image, according to a 2004 study, "2 to 8 percent of Wal-Mart consumers surveyed have ceased shopping at the chain because of 'negative press.'"[123] Shoppers interviewed by the authors of this case have strong opinions about Wal-Mart (see Exhibits 17 and 18).

Wal-Mart's recent struggles with bad press and lawsuits have created urgency to find a way to protect its market share from potential entrants or substitutes.

Other Sources of Competition

Customers have many alternatives for each of the products and services that Wal-Mart provides, but few alternatives exist for the large-scale discount superstore or warehouse shopping experience. The same products can be purchased at different types of retailers, but it is difficult to replicate the convenience, price, and diversity of merchandise found at a Wal-Mart. Also, new potential market entrants with similar scale would have difficulty competing in any substantial volume on price across a wide array of merchandise. Other large incumbents such as Target and Costco have also built economies of scale that would be difficult for a start-up to replicate. Supply chains must be extensive and very efficient. Product differentiation is usually minor in discount store merchandise. However, switching retailers would be easy for customers in well-served areas.

Beyond these retail industry forces, more general external trends also influence Wal-Mart's competitive situation.

External Trends

Government. Wal-Mart has become a "poster company" on political issues related to trade, health care, the environment, discrimination, worker pay, and general anticorporate sentiment. Many activists even contend that Wal-Mart is breaking antitrust laws by using its "power to micromanage the market, carefully coordinating the actions of thousands of firms from a position above the market."[124] Concerns about Wal-Mart's handling of hazardous waste have prompted local, state, and federal officials in the southwestern United States to initiate official actions. In addition to activists and union groups, U.S. political figures are lashing out against Wal-Mart. Democratic presidential candidates are "denouncing Wal-Mart for what they say are substandard wages and health care benefits."[125] Wal-Mart's political action committee's contributions to candidates (even to a former board member) are being returned as a sign of protest.[126] This sentiment is not only surfacing nationally, but locally as well. Governments in Inglewood, California, Cedar Mill, Oregon, and Vancouver, Canada, have rejected Wal-Mart expansion plans.[127]

Exhibit 17 Wal-Mart Shopper Profile

Income	% of sales
<$50,000	54%
$50-$75000	20%
$75,000 +	26%

Education	% of sales
Less than a High School Diploma	20%
High School Diploma (incl. some college)	57%
Bachelor Degree and above	23%

Leisure Pursuits—Typical Customer	% of customers
Tend Their Garden	43%
Listen to Country Music	30%
Like Auto Racing	17%
Go Fishing	17%
Go Camping	19%

Leisure Pursuits—Affluent Customer	% of customers
Listen to Talk Radio	34%
Go to a Theme Park	32%
Listen to Contemporary Music	25%
Go to the Museum	21%
Go to the Zoo	18%

Source: S. Kapinus, 2006, Rollback sushi and discount organics: What Wal-Mart's push to upscale consumers means to you, *ACNielsen Consumer Insight Magazine*, http://us.acnielsen.com/pubs/2006_q2_ci_rollback.shtml, Q2.

Exhibit 18 Interviewee Perspectives on Wal-Mart, 2007

The environment steps are baby steps at the moment. We hope they will take substantive and [significant] action around the critical issues of the environment. Sadly, in the past, much of their efforts have been about publicity and positive spin, not about substance. We will wait to see what level of real commitment they will make around the environment.

 —ROBERT GREENWALD, PRODUCER/DIRECTOR,

 WAL-MART: THE HIGH COST OF LOW PRICE (2007, E-MAIL INTERVIEW, MAY 22)

[Wal-Mart has] a problem with blight. They leave behind in some cases blight by opening a new Supercenter and leaving their old stores empty. They need to have a plan for communities and not leave those huge buildings empty. In Hood River, the community didn't want Wal-Mart to open a Supercenter because they would leave the old store vacant, and Wal-Mart listened. They didn't open the Supercenter.

 —FRED G.,

 55, SUBURBAN WAL-MART SHOPPER (2007, PERSONAL INTERVIEW, MAY 21)

[B]eing the low-cost provider loses some of the service, the pleasure of going shopping. Target has wider aisles, and less product on the shelf. In contrast, Wal-Mart bombards you with tons of products.

 —OLIVER DAVIS,

 TARGET SHOPPER (2007, PERSONAL INTERVIEW, MAY 21)

There was a long time I didn't shop at Wal-Mart, and that had to do with the store's image of ruthlessness when it came to destroying the competition. To be honest, I feel a certain amount of shame at shopping there. As a mother, though, I'm afraid budget and convenience rule. In other words, I've sold out.

 —LILI N.,

 34, AFFLUENT SHOPPER (2007, E-MAIL INTERVIEW, MAY 19)

I shop at Wal-Mart for convenience-type items, but if the item I need is over $100 or is something that I need of quality, I will shop elsewhere. . . . I do not believe that Wal-Mart is capable of becoming related to quality items in the near future like Target and I do not believe that they will be successful at both discount and high quality.

 —ANDRE S.,

 26, BUDGET-CONSCIOUS SHOPPER (2007, PERSONAL INTERVIEW, MAY 20)

The [Wal-Mart] store itself is a little overwhelming—too many people, parking is usually tight, and the lines at the check-out are long. Also, there are so many [unfamiliar] employees working in a single Wal-Mart, that my shopping experience has no personal touch. I enjoy going to my neighborhood HEB [grocery store] because I see familiar faces—both at the check-out and in the aisles. If Wal-Mart would be willing to downsize a bit and have more of a neighborhood feel to it, I might consider stopping in more often.

 —ANGIE R.,

 29, AFFLUENT SHOPPER (2007, E-MAIL INTERVIEW, MAY 20)

Wal-Mart . . . lets you stay in their parking lot overnight. Friends stay at the "Wally-World" when we go windsurfing in Hood River. You can use their facilities and treat the parking lot like a campground. I like to shop there because of that corporate policy.

 —FRED G.,

 55, SUBURBAN WAL-MART SHOPPER (2007, PERSONAL INTERVIEW, MAY 21)

I shop at Wal-Mart very infrequently because I find it hard to find things, [and the store is] often not very clean. There doesn't seem to be well-laid-out aisles like Target; it is more of a jumbled maze. However, one plus is the live fish they have. Kids love to go by and see them! And they usually have better prices. If I am looking for a particular item, like a kids' outdoor toy/sandbox, that is what usually gets me there, because you can find it cheaper.

 —CRYSTAL B.,

 35, AFFLUENT SHOPPER (2007, E-MAIL INTERVIEW, MAY 21)

Wal-Mart neighborhood grocery is OK if you just need staples—it'll be cheap. I won't go into the 24-hour Supercenter down here. I think that was the store that had a stabbing over a Black Thursday laptop deal or something like that. SuperTarget is almost as bad during midday Sunday, but at least the store is cleaner and the meat looks a little better.

 —MICHAEL C.,

 35, WAL-MART SHOPPER (2007, E-MAIL INTERVIEW, MAY 21)

(continued)

Exhibit 18 Interviewee Perspectives on Wal-Mart, 2007 *(Continued)*

When I was an Operations Manager for a Fortune 500 company, we were having a yearly employee appreciation picnic . . . [so] my secretary and I hopped into a company van, shot down to Sam's Club, loaded up four shopping carts of hamburgers, hotdogs, beverages, and all the fixings, got to the checkout, pulled out my Visa, and then found out that Sam's club didn't accept Visa. After a few minutes of arguing with an unhelpful and unsympathetic manager, I left all four carts at the checkout and have never been back since.

> —Brian S.,
> former Sam's Club member (2007, discussion-board posting, May 22)

Wal-Mart has been such a negative experience that it would be hard for me to go back. I have been hesitant to go to a neighborhood Wal-Mart because of my poor shopping experiences around the country at different big-box Wal-Marts. The Wal-Mart I am closer to is a lower socioeconomic neighborhood, and I drive past it to go to Target because I perceive it as being safer and I feel that I am getting a higher quality product.

> —Oliver Davis,
> Target shopper (2007, personal interview, May 21)

[Wal-Mart] will continue to grow, and will make many changes in that time. Some are for the better and some are not. Unfortunately, sometimes plans that are not well [thought-out] are implemented and mandated, which only causes frustration/irritation. Other times workers are stuck in [their] ways and don't want to change.

> —Anonymous
> Wal-Mart manager (2007, e-mail interview, May 21)

[Wal-Mart needs better] price marking, more UPC scanners in the store. I see something and the price is ambiguous. They don't mark the prices. They can also make checkout faster. Why is it so slow? I don't go to Kmart anymore because a lot of times the UPC of something doesn't ring up at the cash register. It isn't in their system. If it is on the shelf, the UPC should be in the computer. Wal-Mart is also getting worse at this.

> —Fred G.,
> 55, suburban Wal-Mart shopper (2007, personal interview, May 21)

[Wal-Mart] does offer a big variety [of benefits for associates], some much better than other companies and some not so good in my opinion. Some examples of good discounts are 10% discount on most items (excludes grocery, clearance, and a few other items—biggest complaint on this is that tax in most areas eats up most of the discount), vacation (depends on variety of factors, but generally 2 weeks for full time and 1 week for [part-time] 1st year, and increases thereafter), personnel days (day off with pay—earned up to a certain # each year (average 2)), sick days, holiday pay, etc. On the other side of the coin, [I] think much more needs to be done to provide better health care for its workers, and a goal should be done to improve this every year. Many co-workers I know have dropped [their] coverage or rely on state assistance programs. Wal-Mart also did away with some of its [benefits], such as Christmas bonuses, unless you are grandfathered in (must have been hired before the change was made).

> —Anonymous
> Wal-Mart manager (2007, e-mail interview, May 21)

We have an Associates Fund that everyone chips into in case someone is in critical need. For example, if a cashier were to, heaven forbid, have their house burn down, the fund would immediately come to help out by supplying a place to stay, warm clothes, and food, pretty much everything that the associate would need to get back on her feet, up to and including a replacement house, if that's what it takes. . . . A happy associate is more productive.

> Sergio Jimenez,
> Wal-Mart store co-manager (2007, personal interview, May 20)

Wal-Mart takes care of their people in dire situations. When my friend's wife died, they brought them groceries and really took care of them.

> —Wendy S.,
> 46, friend of Wal-Mart associate (2007, personal interview, May 20)

One thing the company does . . . every year is [to] hold [grassroots] meetings for associates to come and vent about things they don't like, in the hope that something will change. Sadly, most associates (workers) feel that they are allowed to vent, but not without [retaliation] any more, or at best [their] input will not change anything. I think the

(continued)

company should not just write down the input they are being given, but act on it when possible. If they would do so it would boost morale, and more effort would be given, [causing] customer satisfaction to go up and sales to boost as well.

—ANONYMOUS

WAL-MART MANAGER (2007, E-MAIL INTERVIEW, MAY 21)

If I [were] to change Wal-Mart, I would reduce product on the shelves and change the lighting, and widen the aisles. [T]he bouncing ball for Wal-Mart gives it a cartoon-ish edge, whereas Target does an ad that goes coast to coast, with a heavy CGI aspect that it isn't cartoon-y. It has a big-city feel whereas Wal-Mart has a small-town middle America feel. I am partial to bigger cities. . . . Smaller towns that have limited options [make] me feel constrained, which is one of the reasons I like Target, which has hip trends, whereas Wal-Mart just has the bouncy smiley face. [T]he smiley face reduces [Wal-Mart's] seriousness. I would go to more subtle references to being the low-cost provider, and pitch one-stop shopping, but push the option to have your own personal brand, and reduce the number of SKUs on the walls so you don't feel overwhelmed by the experience there.

—OLIVER DAVIS,

TARGET SHOPPER (2007, PERSONAL INTERVIEW, MAY 21)

I would LOVE a coupon for a certain amount off any item the store. Sort of what Michael's has (40% off any item) or Bed Bath and Beyond has (20% off). I also find Target's returns the most convenient I've ever experienced: they can locate the item you purchased by sliding your credit card through the reader so you don't have to go searching for your receipt. I appreciate that kind of convenience.

—LILI N.,

34, AFFLUENT SHOPPER (2007, E-MAIL INTERVIEW, MAY 19)

Legal. Class-action lawsuits against Wal-Mart have become commonplace. In *Savaglio v. Wal-Mart Stores, Inc.,* the "plaintiffs allege that they were not provided meal and rest breaks in accordance with California law, and seek monetary damages and injunctive relief."[128] A jury ruled in favor of those plaintiffs and awarded them a total of $198 million.[129] In *Dukes v. Wal-Mart Stores, Inc.,* currently pending on behalf of all present and past female employees in all of Wal-Mart's retail stores and warehouse clubs, Wal-Mart is alleged to have "engaged in a pattern and practice of discriminating against women in promotions, pay, training, and job assignments."[130] These lawsuits are providing ample fodder for Wal-Mart opponents to inflict ongoing reputation damage.

Global. The globalization trend that began in the 1990s persists. As trade barriers continue to come down around the world and as technology enables greater access to information, the world is becoming one mega-market of labor, capital, goods, and services. Bilateral and multilateral free trade agreements are continuing to shape markets.

Technology. The development of radio frequency identification (RFID) is expected to play a major part in the next evolution of supply chain management in the retail industry. This technology may better enable retailers to track inventory locations, store shelving status, packages en-route to and from suppliers, warehouses, shelves, and even shoplifting.[131] Recent developments in the technology include a movement toward "common standards and practices that could make RFID as ubiquitous as bar codes," and a push to lower the cost per RFID tag from the current 10-cent mark to the Wal-Mart target of 5-cents.[132] RFID chips are increasingly "able to hold much more information and fit into different shapes and sizes—woven inside clothing, slipped into a paper-thin tag or molded inside a key chain."[133]

Another technology development impacting the retail industry is the unabated growth of electronic commerce, and the increasing pervasiveness of broadband Internet access in most developed countries. As consumers at various socioeconomic levels come to rely more on the Web for information, entertainment, and shopping, retailers are discovering the need to use their online presence not just to spur online sales, but to drive traditional-format sales as well.

Demographics. Americans, like those in many developed nations, are getting older. The Census Bureau estimates the number of those aged 65 and up will rise from approximately 35 million in 2000 to 86.7 million by 2050. The age 65 and up cohort made up 12.4 percent of the total U.S. population in 2000; by 2050, it will make up 20.7 percent of a projected population of nearly 420 million.[134]

The country is also becoming more diverse.[135] Ethnic and gender diversity in the U.S. workforce is on the rise. In 1995, whites/non-Hispanics made up 76 percent of the workforce, but this is projected to decrease to 68 percent in 2020. According to the U.S. Department of Labor, women comprised 46 percent of the labor force in 2006.[136] The percentage of women over the age of 16 in the labor force has risen 23 percent in 44 years to 59 percent in 2004.[137]

The distance in America between the "haves" and the "have-nots" is growing. Increasing returns to education have created a bifurcation in income distribution.[138] The bottom quintile has seen its mean income increase 34.5 percent in real terms from 1967 to 2005, whereas the top income quintile had an increase in mean income of 80.8 percent over the same time period.[139] Average income growth for the bottom three quintiles was only 30.4 percent. The typical Wal-Mart customer is in the middle-income quintiles.

As Wal-Mart's competitive landscape continues to evolve, the company is taking its strategic cues from Sam Walton's words of wisdom: "Everything around you is always changing. To succeed, stay out in front of that change."[140]

Current Strategies

To manage its competitive environment, Wal-Mart is currently deploying a variety of strategies, most of which stem from its relentless core generic strategy of cost leadership, but some of which represent beyond-cost approaches. "Our everyday low price position is the basis for our business," wrote Rob Walton in Wal-Mart's 2006 annual report.[141] He added, "While this core principle is critical to our growth and business strategy, by itself it is not enough anymore."[142] According to Scott in this year's shareholder letter, Wal-Mart is confronting "a period of perhaps the most rapid and profound change in our Company's history. With our transformation plan, we are committed to staying 'Out in Front' of the changes around us."[143] The corporate plan, encompassing previous change initiatives as well as newer ones, rests on "five pillars": "broadening our appeal to our customers, making Wal-Mart an even better place to work, improving operations and efficiencies, driving global growth, and contributing to our communities.[144]

Strategies to Deal with External and Reputational Challenges. Wal-Mart is pursuing two key strategies that will help them overcome external issues affecting the company, including environmental and community-impact issues, among others. These strategies include sustainability efforts and localized charitable giving to help portray it as being a responsible corporate citizen and a good neighbor. Wal-Mart launched its global environmental sustainability initiative in 2004 and has since taken action toward several sustainability goals: sell 100 million compact fluorescent bulbs by 2008; reduce packaging by five percent by 2013; buy fish from certified fisheries; sell "more organic and environmentally friendly products"; and make company facilities and trucks more energy-efficient.[145] The Wal-Mart Foundation in 2006 gave "more than $415 million in cash and in-kind merchandise to 100,000 organizations worldwide," making it the "largest corporate cash contributor in America."[146] The Foundation "gave most of the money at the local level where [it] can have the greatest impact."[147]

Wal-Mart has beefed up pro-community, prosustainability, pro-health care information on its Web site, on its television ads, and in its annual report. The company recently launched *In Front with Wal-Mart*, a 30-minute television show airing on the Lifetime and USA networks that "gives [Wal-Mart] a chance to showcase [its] incredible associates and the variety of ways they give back to their communities, bettering the lives of America's working families" and "sheds light . . . on some of [Wal-Mart's] eco-friendly practices."[148] Wal-Mart created an interactive Web site on sustainability, dedicated a page of its 2007 annual report to sustainability, and will soon publish a separate Sustainability Report.[149]

In its public outreach, Wal-Mart also stresses its benefits to suppliers and communities, as well as its commitment to providing affordable health care and competitive wages for its associates.[150] These efforts tie into its supply-chain innovation and people strategies.

Supply-Chain Innovation and People Strategies

As previously mentioned, Wal-Mart creates value for customers with a highly efficient and innovative supplychain management operation. This operation combines tough, low-cost procurement tactics, leading-edge information systems and "rocket-science" logistics.[151]

There's not much negotiation at all. The manufacturer walks into the room. I've been in these little cubicles, I've seen it happen. The buyer says, "Look, we want you to sell it to us for 5 percent on a dollar—at cost—lower this year than you did last year." They know every fact and figure that these manufacturers have. They know their books. They know their costs. They know their business practices—everything, you know? So what's a manufacturer left to do? They sit naked in front of Wal-Mart. You know, Wal-Mart calls the shots. "If you want to do business with us, if you want to stay in business, then you're going to do it our way." And it's all about driving down the cost of goods.

—**FORMER WAL-MART STORE MANAGER JON LEHMAN ON FRONTLINE IN 2004**[152]

All Wal-Mart suppliers must participate in Retail Link, a computerized system in which they "plan, execute, and analyze their businesses."[153] Along with electronic data interchange, suppliers receive purchase order information and supply invoices electronically, thereby lowering expenses and increasing productivity. Suppliers must meet Wal-Mart's strict lead-time and shipping requirements by using the technology and complying with operating procedures. The Wal-Mart logistics team uses an Internet-based Transportation Link system that complements a Backhaul Betty telephone voice-response system to help them move goods. In one year, Wal-Mart estimated nearly 1 million loads of general merchandise moved to Distribution Centers throughout the country.[154] Store-bound shipments travel by the company's 7,000 trucks, one of the largest fleets in the world.[155] The company relentlessly strives to develop its supply-chain process. For example, "[t]o ensure greater supply chain visibility, satellite-based tracking technology is being installed in the Company's entire fleet of over-the-road trailers. The data generated . . . increases productivity, reduces costs and enhances security."[156]

In the stores, Wal-Mart's legendary inventory management capability is driven by its advanced Texlon barcode system. In addition to tracking the sales price, inventory levels of each product, and a history of quantities sold, Texlon can record trends and predict future needs. Quantities sold can be traced to specific weeks, days, or even hours of each day. Seasonal projections can be documented, and shopping habits are noted. Information is sent daily at midnight to the warehouses, so depleted products are restocked the following night. Reliance on this kind of technology to drive the supply chain enables Wal-Mart's suppliers to use "pull production" instead of "push production." The barcode system will eventually be replaced by an RFID-based system, technology Wal-Mart is driving.

Wal-Mart's technological supply-chain sophistication is intended to provide "value for customers, associates, and shareholders."[157] The system depends on Wal-Mart's 1.8 million associates to provide the final link in the value chain to customers. Wal-Mart's people strategy involves "[g]iving our associates the tools and opportunities they need to be as productive as possible," which has enabled "workforce productivity gains in every quarter of the last two years."[158] Associates who feel overworked may create a weak link in the value chain.

I would say that some customers are happy, but most are not. . . . [M]any workers feel they are being overworked due to mainly understaffing issues, which causes workers to treat the customers worse, then causing customers to become upset. Many customers have at one time been [Wal-Mart] associates and understand how things are handled at each store level and can relate. Personally, [I] believe that overall morale a few years ago was much higher with workers, and that attitude was passed along to the customers. Today many customers feel that [Wal-Mart] only wants them for [their] money, and does not care about them."

—**ANONYMOUS WAL-MART MANAGER (2007, E-MAIL INTERVIEW, MAY 21)**

Reassuring its "valued long-term associates" that the company "is listening to them," Wal-Mart "again increased [its] average full-time hourly wage in the United States."[159] The company is against unionization of its associates.

Wal-Mart's operational effectiveness goals of improving return on investment, comparable-store sales, and working capital productivity are setting the agenda for its business-segment strategies.[160]

Wal-Mart Stores Segment Strategies

The Wal-Mart Stores segment is in its second year of a three-year strategic plan to improve ROI, people development, and customer relevancy.[161] Customers have become the prime focus since January 2007, when Wal-Mart Stores elevated its new marketing and merchandising chiefs and completed its management reshuffle.

In 2006, Wal-Mart Stores rolled out a $4 generic prescription program, a clear opening-price-point approach. Merchandising has been characterized by the product-focused "opening price point" strategy, which relied on attractive low prices on entry-level items in every category to set the stage for higher-margin prices on more desirable items.[162] This single strategy has served to focus each of the two dozen departments at a typical Wal-Mart Supercenter (see Exhibit 19). Wal-Mart stores often offer retail space to other vendors that provide services, such as nail salons, hair salons, coffee shops, food and beverage vendors (e.g., McDonald's and Subway), full-service banks, and even employment agencies in some locations.

Recently, Wal-Mart Stores "realigned [its] merchandising . . . around five key power categories—entertainment, grocery, health and wellness, apparel, and home."[163] Global Procurement meanwhile is "establishing groups of technical experts—specialists that focus on the many important dynamics of a particular category purchase."[164]

Exhibit 19 List of Departments in Wal-Mart

Wal-Mart Departments	
Grocery	Pharmacy
Bakery	Health & Beauty
Produce	Vision Center
Deli	Jewelry
Frozen Foods	Lawn & Garden
Apparel	Portrait Studio
Housewares	Photo Lab
Entertainment	Hardware
Electronics	Furniture
Tire & Lube Express	Sporting Goods
Automotive	Toys & Games
School Supplies	Office Products & School Supplies

Source: http://www.walmart.com.

The Wal-Mart Stores customer segmentation and merchandising strategies have been in flux over the past few years, with three different strategies in play to move Wal-Mart Stores toward a more customer-focused position.

The first customer-focused strategy—mimicking Target's upscale, fashion-forward appeal—flopped. "In working to broaden our appeal to our customers, we moved too quickly in the rollout of some of our fashion-forward apparel in the United States," according to Scott.[165] Wal-Mart Stores has at least partially retreated from this strategy.

The second customer-focused strategy—localizing selections based on store-neighborhood demographics—continues to drive various store changes, though it may be waning. In 2006, Wal-Mart "launched six different types of customized stores to attract different demographics, from inner-city residents, to affluent suburbanites, to rural shoppers."[166] With these stores, Wal-Mart attempted to target African-Americans, Hispanics, empty-nesters, suburbanites, rural residents, and the affluent. Wal-Mart expanded and empowered regional marketing teams, moving many executives away from headquarters into regions to better understand Wal-Mart's wide customer base.[167] These changes were inspired by localized merchandizing selection in Wal-Mart de Mexico stores aimed at different mixes of inventory for different income levels.[168] For example, the localization strategy expanded the mix of hip-hop, gospel, and R&B music in a store outside Chicago and led to plans for larger pharmacy sections and fewer children's clothes at a store geared toward empty-nesters.[169] In his March letter to shareholders, Scott wrote, "We continue to strive to make sure every Wal-Mart store is a 'Store of the Community'—one that reflects the individual needs of each neighborhood we serve."[170]

The third customer-focused strategy—appealing to the three universal types of low-price-seeking customers who currently shop at Wal-Mart—now guides merchandising and marketing decisions. According to Fleming and Quinn, the three types are "'brand aspirationals' (people with low incomes who are obsessed with names like Kitchen Aid), 'price-sensitive affluents' (wealthier shoppers who love deals), and 'value-price shoppers' (who like low prices and cannot afford much more)."[171] For these types, the Wal-Mart Stores segment is concentrating on developing unique, innovative products and providing distinguished brands (such as the recently added Dell desktop computers) to better appeal to its core customers as the low-price leader on well-known brands.[172]

This is a much better strategy for Wal-Mart than the store segmentation strategy path . . . they were going down before . . . because it aligns with their basic brand proposition (EDLP) and basic consumer rather than trying to attract a new consumer by adding high-end fashion and complicated assortments. For the same reason, it aligns better with Wal-Mart's supply chain strength. It's far easier to roll out a national brand in stores nationally than it is to ship different assortments to different stores within a region without disrupting the cost efficient supply chain that is Wal-Mart's core competitive advantage. I'm not sure what took them so long but it looks like Wal-Mart is back to a strategy that is sustainable and executable for them.

—*Forrester Research senior analyst Lisa Bradner*[173]

Sam's Club Segment Strategies

Sam's Club, meanwhile, is focused on three areas: "reinvigorating the brand" by broadening products and services; improving inventory management and other performance measures; and optimizing the "in-club experience."[174] Sam's Club stores offer members products such as frozen and dry food goods in bulk, electronics, computer equipment, clothing, books, electronic entertainment, and general merchandise. Sam's Club recently restructured its management layers to give stores additional flexibility and to boost service.[175] Rumors have circulated that Sam's Club may spin off from Wal-Mart, in part to set its own direction in attracting and retaining members and associates, two key groups who are generally less loyal to Sam's Club than to its rival Costco.[176]

Wal-Mart International Segment Strategies

Wal-Mart International's strategy is to prioritize "where the greatest growth and greatest returns exist," what the segment calls "majoring in the majors."[177] The majors appear to include the Americas primarily, followed by the United Kingdom and Japan, as well as China and India over the long term.[178] Wal-Mart International is labeling this strategy "focused portfolio execution."[179] Its second strategy is global leverage, or "taking full advantage of our worldwide assets, including formats, information systems, purchasing organizations, category expertise, and shared best practices."[180] In the past year, it has concentrated on turning around Asda in the United Kingdom through "improved execution in all phases of customer service, differentiation with competitors, and development of new channels and formats."[181] To better compete against U.K. leader Tesco, second-largest Asda reportedly may be considering acquiring the third-largest U.K. retailer, the J. Sainsbury chain of grocery and convenience stores.[182] Wal-Mart's international stores are varied in their mix of products and services, and they stick to the motto of "offering working families the things they need at the prices they can afford."[183]

Just as the business segments are looking to focus on the right challenges for their short- and long-term success in the marketplace, the company must ensure it is applying its greatest resources against its greatest strategic challenges across the enterprise.

Strategic Challenges

The challenges Wal-Mart faces today are actually not much different from what they have been for the past several years. These following quotes come from an article in April 2003: "Even though it is the nation's largest apparel retailer with more than 12 percent of the market, Wal-Mart could be doing better in this category"; "It would like to be a fashion retailer and take on Target with good quality at a low price-point, but it hasn't convinced the American consumer it should be a destination for casual fashion"; "Wal-Mart is . . . looking abroad for future sales growth"; "Wal-Mart will need to struggle against the urge to centralize operations and eliminate decision making from the frontlines where managers have face-to-face contact with customers"; and "The only area in which Wal-Mart has not been able to pummel its competition is against Costco."[184] One of the company's challenges may be to stop proliferating nearly identical sets of challenges

each year. Like the stock price, the challenges appear to be stuck in a holding pattern.

One key new challenge is the sluggishness of same-store sales relative to Wal-Mart's competitors. According to *BusinessWeek,* Wal-Mart faces "the diciest conundrum in retailing today . . . can it seduce . . . middle-income shoppers into stepping up their purchases in a major way without alienating its low-income legions in the process?"[185]

Another growing challenge is the difficulty of expanding in the domestic market, whether because of community opposition or geographic saturation (see Exhibits 20 and 21).

These and other strategic challenges are weighing on the minds of Wal-Mart's shareholders, especially on the two with the most responsibility for the company's fate.

Questions Wal-Mart Leaders Must Address
CEO Lee Scott and Chairman Rob Walton are grappling with some vexing questions as they head into the 2007 Wal-Mart Annual Shareholders' Meeting:

- How can Wal-Mart Stores and Sam's Club increase same-store sales?
- How should the company capture share of middle- and upper-income wallets?
- Should Wal-Mart Stores fully retreat from fashion-forward merchandising and marketing? Will its neighborhood-store-localization strategy increase sales enough to offset the associated costs? What should it do to make its new three-types-of-customers segmentation strategy work?
- Should the company spin off Sam's Club? If not, what should it do to compete more effectively against Costco?
- Is Wal-Mart expanding the right kind of new stores at the right pace and in the right places? How and where should the company continue to grow internationally? Should Asda buy J. Sainsbury?
- What will it take to restore the company's reputation in America?
- Should Lee Scott change Wal-Mart's course? If so, how?
- Should Rob Walton replace Lee Scott? If so, when and with whom?

Exhibit 20 Spread of Wal-Mart Stores, 1970–1995

Source: E. Basker, 2004, Job creation or destruction? Labor-market effects of Wal-Mart expansion, University of Missouri, January, Figure 1, 28.

Exhibit 21 Number of Counties Having a Wal-Mart Store, 1963–2006

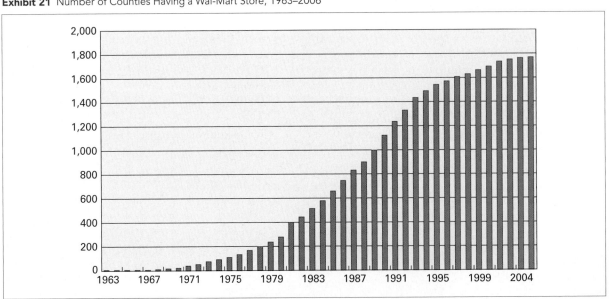

Source: 2005, The economic impact of Wal-Mart, Global Insight, Business Planning Solutions, Global Insight Advisory Services, November 2, Figure 4, 33.

NOTES

1. A. Bianco, 2006, The Bully of Bentonville: The High Cost of Wal-Mart's Everyday Low Prices, New York: Doubleday Publishing, 1.

2. 2007, 7 demands for change, Against * The * Wal, http://www.againstthewal.net/7demands.html, May 18.

3. 2007, Notice of 2007 Annual Shareholders' Meeting, DEF 14A, Proxy Statement, Wal-Mart Stores, Inc., U.S. SEC, April 19, 52–68.

4. A. Bianco, 2006, The Bully of Bentonville: The High Cost of Wal-Mart's Everyday Low Prices, 267; 2007, Yahoo! Finance, http://finance.yahoo.com/charts#chart6:symbol=wmt;range=20000103,20070518;compare=cost+tgt;indicator=volume;charttype=line;crosshair=on;logscale=on;source=undefined, May 17.

5. 2007, Yahoo! Finance, http://finance.yahoo.com/charts#chart6:symbol=wmt;range=20000103,20070518;compare=cost+tgt;indicator=volume;charttype=line;crosshair=on;logscale=on;source=undefined, May 17.

6. A. Bianco, 2007, Wal-Mart's midlife crisis, BusinessWeek, April 30, 46–52.

7. 2007, Wal-Mart Data Sheet, http://walmartstores.com/Files/US_operations.pdf, February 8.

8. 2007, Wal-Mart Annual Report.

9. 2007, Wal-Mart Stores, Inc., Form 8-K, U.S. SEC, May 15; and 2007, Company Overview, Target.com, http://investors.target.com/phoenix.zhtml?c=65828&p=irol-homeProfile, May 25.

10. L. Michael Cacace & K. Tucksmith, 2007, Fortune 500 largest U.S. corporations, Fortune, April 30, F2.

11. Ibid.

12. A. Bianco, 2007, Wal-Mart's midlife crisis, 49–52.

13. A. Bianco, 2007, Wal-Mart's midlife crisis, 46.

14. 2004, Wal-Mart Tops Fortune's List of America's Most Admired Companies, Fortune, http://www.timeinc.net/fortune/information/presscenter/fortune/press_releases/02232004AMAC.html, February 23.

15. 2007, America's Most Admired Companies 2007, Fortune, CNNMoney.com, http://money.cnn.com/magazines/fortune/mostadmired/2007/top20/, May 18.

16. W. Zellner, 2004, Sam Walton: King of the discounters, BusinessWeek, August 9.

17. Ibid.

18. Ibid.

19. A. A. Thompson & A. J. Strickland, Strategic Management, Concepts & Cases, 10th ed., New York: Irwin/McGraw-Hill.

20. 2007, The Wal-Mart Timeline, Wal-Mart Facts, http://www.walmartfacts.com/content/default.aspx?id=3, April 1; D. Longo, 1998, Wal-Mart hands CEO crown to David Glass, Discount Store News, February 15, 1988.

21. 2007, Wal-Mart Annual Report, 19; 2007, The Wal-Mart Timeline, Wal-Mart Facts, http://www.walmartfacts.com/content/default.aspx?id=3, April 1.

22. A. Bianco, 2007, Wal-Mart's midlife crisis, 46–54.

23. 2007, Data Sheet, Wal-Mart Stores, http://walmartstores.com/Files/US_operations.pdf, February 8, May 25; and 2007, International Data Sheet, Wal-Mart Stores, http://walmartstores.com/Files/Intl_operations.pdf, February 8, May 25.

24. 2007, Wal-Mart Annual Report, 1.

25. A. Biesada, 2007, Wal-Mart Company Overview, Hoovers Online, http://premium.hoovers.com, May.

26. Ibid.

27. P. Engardio, 2007, Beyond the green corporation, imagine a world in which eco-friendly and socially responsible practices actually help a company's bottom line. It's closer than you think, BusinessWeek Online, January 29.

28. 2007, Wal-Mart Annual Report, 18-19.

29. 2007, Wal-Mart Annual Report, 31.

30. 2007, Wal-Mart Annual Report , 28.

31. Ibid.

32. Ibid.

33. 2007, Wal-Mart Annual Report, 31.

34. Ibid.

35. 2007, Wal-Mart Annual Report, 28.

36. 2007, Wal-Mart Annual Report, 36.

37. 2007, Wal-Mart Annual Report, 32.

38. 2007, International Data Sheet, Wal-Mart Stores, http://walmartstores.com/Files/Intl_operations.pdf, February 8.

39. 2007, Wal-Mart Annual Report, 32.

40. 2007, Wal-Mart Annual Report, 51-52.

41. 2006, IGD looks at Wal-Mart's decision to pull out of Germany, http://www.igd.com/CIR, March 8.

42. 2007, Wal-Mart Annual Report, 32.

43. 2007, Informe Anual 2006, Wal-Mart de Mexico, http://library.corporate-ir.net/library/19/194/194702/items/231792/AR06.pdf, May 21; and 2007, CIA World Fact Book, Mexico, https://www.cia.gov/library/publications/the-world-factbook/geos/mx.html#Econ, May 21.

44. 2007, Wal-Mart Facts: The Wal-Mart Story, http://www.walmartfacts.com/content/default.aspx?id=1, April 1.

45. 2006, CNBC Interview with Carter Cast, http://www.hoovers.com/global/co/interviews/player.xhtml, November 7.

46. 2007, About Sam's Club, Samsclub.com, http://pressroom.samsclub.com/content/?id=3&atg=524, March 1.

47. K. Hundson, 2007, Wal-Mart Pushes Financial-Services Menu, Wall Street Journal, June 6, A3.

48. 2007, The Wal-Mart Timeline, Wal-Mart Facts, http://www.walmartfacts.com/content/default.aspx?id=3, April 1; D. Longo, 1998, Wal-Mart hands CEO crown to David Glass, Discount Store News, February 15.

49. 2007, The Wal-Mart Timeline, Wal-Mart Facts, http://www.walmartfacts.com/content/default.aspx?id=3, April 1.

50. 2007, Wal-Mart Annual Report, 14; 2007, Senior Officers, Wal-Mart Stores, http://walmartstores.com/GlobalWMStoresWeb/navigate.do?catg=540, May 6.

51. 2007, S. Robson Walton, Wal-Mart Stores, http://walmartstores.com/GlobalWMStoresWeb/navigate.do?catg=540&contId=15, May 6; 2005. Forbes: America's richest 400, MSN Money, http://moneycentral.msn.com/content/invest/forbes/P129955.asp, September 23.

52. A. Bianco, 2006, The Bully of Bentonville: The High Cost of Wal-Mart's Everyday Low Prices, 61.

53. 2007, S. Robson Walton, Wal-Mart Stores.

54. 2007, Wal-Mart Annual Report, 13.

55. A. Bianco, The Bully of Bentonville: The High Cost of Wal-Mart's Everyday Low Prices, 104.

56. Ibid.

57. A. Bianco, The Bully of Bentonville: The High Cost of Wal-Mart's Everyday Low Prices, 79.

58. Ibid.

59. A. Bianco, The Bully of Bentonville: The High Cost of Wal-Mart's Everyday Low Prices, 80.

60. A. Bianco, The Bully of Bentonville: The High Cost of Wal-Mart's Everyday Low Prices, 81.

61. 2007, H. Lee Scott, Jr., Senior Officers, WalMartStores.com, http://walmartstores.com/GlobalWMStoresWeb/navigate.do?catg=540&contId=17, May 25.

62. Ibid.

63. 2007, Michael T. Duke, Senior Officers, WalMartStores.com, http://walmartstores.com/GlobalWMStoresWeb/navigate.do?catg=540&contId=22, May 25.

64. Ibid.

65. 2007, John B. Menzer, Senior Officers, WalMartStores.com, http://walmartstores.com/GlobalWMStoresWeb/navigate.do?catg=540&contId=19, May 25.

66. Ibid.

67. Ibid.

68. 2007, Eduardo Castro-Wright, Senior Officers, WalMartStores.com, http://walmartstores.com/GlobalWMStoresWeb/navigate .do?catg=540&contId=41, May 25.

69. 2007, C. Douglas McMillon, Senior Officers, WalMartStores.com, http://walmartstores.com/GlobalWMStoresWeb/navigate .do?catg=540&contId=33, May 25.

70. 2007, John E. Fleming, Senior Officers, WalMartStores.com, http://walmartstores.com/GlobalWMStoresWeb/navigate .do?catg=540&contId=42, May 25.

71. 2007, Stephen Quinn, Senior Officers, WalMartStores.com, http://walmartstores.com/GlobalWMStoresWeb/navigate .do?catg=540&contId=6396, May 25.

72. 2007, Wal-Mart Board of Directors, Walmart.com, June 28.

73. M. Halkias, 2007, Questrom nominated to Wal-Mart board, *Dallas Morning News*, http://www.dallasnews.com/sharedcontent/dws/bus/ industries/retail/stories/042507dnbusquestrom.36b21ad.html, April 24.

74. Ibid.

75. S. Braun, 2007, At Wal-Mart, Clinton didn't upset any carts, *Los Angeles Times*, http://www.latimes.com/news/nationworld/nation/ la-na-hillary19may19,0,5168474.story?coll=la-home-center, May 19.

76. 2007, Morningstar, Wal-Mart Stores (WMT), http://quicktake .morningstar.com/StockNet/powerbrokers.aspx?Country=USA& Symbol=WMT&stocktab=owner, May 6; 2007, Wal-Mart Stores Inc. (WMT), Major Holders, Yahoo! Finance, http://finance.yahoo. com/q/mh?s=WMT, May 6.

77. 2007, Wal-Mart Stores Inc. (WMT), Major Holders, Yahoo! Finance, http://finance.yahoo.com/q/mh?s=WMT; May 6; and 2005, Forbes: America's richest 400, MSN Money, http://moneycentral.msn.com/ content/invest/forbes/P129955.asp, September 23; 2002, Proxy, Wal-Mart Stores, http://www.walmartstores.com/Files/proxy_2002/ proxy_pg05.htm; M. Weil and M. Barbaro, 2005, John T. Walton, 58; Heir to Wal-Mart Fortune, *The Washington Post*, http:// www.washingtonpost.com/wp-dyn/content/article/2005/06/27/ AR2005062701471.html, June 28; 2007, Associated Press, *Washington Post*, Helen R. Walton; Philanthropic wife of Wal-Mart chief, http://www.washingtonpost.com/wp-dyn/content/ article/2007/04/20/AR2007042002060.html, April 21.

78. 2007, Wal-Mart Stores Inc. (WMT), Insider Roster, Yahoo! Finance, http://finance.yahoo.com/q/ir?s=WMT, May 6.

79. 2007, Wal-Mart Stores Inc. (WMT), Major Holders, Yahoo! Finance, http://finance.yahoo.com/q/mh?s=WMT, May 6.

80. 2007, Morningstar, Wal-Mart Stores (WMT), http://quicktake .morningstar.com/StockNet/powerbrokers.aspx?Country=USA&Sym bol=WMT&stocktab=owner, May 6.

81. 2007, Wal-Mart Annual Report, 64.

82. 2007, 2002 Wal-Mart Annual Reports.

83. Ibid.

84. 2007, Sam's Club vs. Costco: Battle of the brands, *BloggingStocks*, AOL Money & Finance, http://www.bloggingstocks. com/2007/04/12/sams-club-vs-costco-battle-of-the-brands/, April 12.

85. T. Otte, 2007, Spinoff in Bentonville revisited, Value Investing, MotleyFool.com, http://www.fool.com/investing/value/2007/05/07/ spinoff-in-bentonville-revisited.aspx, May 7.

86. M. Wagner, 2003, Where's Wal-Mart: Wal-Mart's web revenue hardly registers on its ledger, *Internet Retailer*, http://www.internetretailer .com/internet/marketing-conference/70624-wheres-wal-mart.html, April.

87. D. Pinto, 2005, Mass market retailers, http://www .massmarketretailers.com/articles/Every_winner.html, May 16.

88. Ibid.

89. Ibid.

90. A. Bianco, 2007, Wal-Mart's, midlife crisis, 48.

91. D. Pinto, Mass market retailers.

92. M. Holz-Clause & M. Geisler, 2006, Grocery Industry, Grocery Retailing Profile, AgMRC, http://www.agmrc.org/agmrc/markets/ Food/groceryindustry.htm, September.

93. 2007, Wal-Mart F1Q08 (Qtr End 4/30/07) Earnings Call Transcript, SeekingAlpha.com, http://retail.seekingalpha.com/article/35633, May 15.

94. Ibid.

95. 2007, Wal-Mart 1st Quarter 2008 Earnings Release, May 10.

96. Ibid.

97. 2007, Wal-Mart April Sales News Release, May 10.

98. R. Dodes & G. McWilliams, 2007, Fashion faux pas hurts Wal-Mart, *Wall Street Journal*, May 21, A8.

99. G. McWilliams, 2007, Wal-Mart net rises as weakness persists, *Wall Street Journal*, May 16, C6.

100. J. Covert, 2007, Retail-sales slide fuels concern: Decline of 2.3% in April among worst on record; even Wal-Mart slipped, Wall Street Journal, May 11, A3.

101. 2007, Target Corporation, Form 8-K, U.S. SEC, May 23; 2007, Company Overview, Target.com, http://investors.target.com/ phoenix.zhtml?c=65828&p=irol-homeProfile, May 25.

102. Ibid.

103. 2006, Target Annual Report, 2.

104. Ibid.

105. 2007, Company Profile, Costco Wholesale Investor Relations, http://phx.corporate-ir.net/phoenix.zhtml?c=83830&p=irol-homeprofile, May 5.

106. 2006, Costco Annual Report, 9.

107. 2006, 2002 Costco Annual Report.

108. 2007, The Kroger Co., Form 10-K, U.S. SEC, April 4.

109. Ibid.

110. Ibid.

111. 2007, Carrefour profile, Hoovers, Lexis/Nexis Academic, May 8.

112. 2007, Tesco profile, Hoovers, Lexis/Nexis Academic, May 8.

113. Ibid.

114. 2007, Global Procurement, WalMartStores.com, http:// walmartstores.com/GlobalWMStoresWeb/navigate.do?catg=337, May 26.

115. A. Bianco & W. Zellner, 2003, Is Wal-Mart too powerful? *BusinessWeek*, http://www.businessweek.com/magazine/ content/03_40/b3852001_mz001.htm, October 6.

116. Ibid.

117. Ibid.

118. 2007, Wal-Mart Facts, http://www.walmartfacts.com/ FactSheets/3142007_Corporate_Facts.pdf, March 14.

119. S. Kapinus, 2006, Rollback sushi and discount organics, *ACNielsen Consumer Insight*, http://us.acnielsen.com/pubs/2006_q2_ci_ rollback.shtml, Q2.

120. Ibid.

121. Ibid.

122. Ibid.

123. Barney Gimbel, 2006, Attack of the Wal-Martyrs, http://money.cnn .com/magazines/fortune/fortune_archive/2006/12/11/8395445/ index.htm, November 28.

124. B. C. Lynn, 2006, It's time to enforce antitrust law and break up Wal-Mart, *Harper's Magazine*, July.

125. A. Nagourney & M. Barbaro, 2006, Eye on election, Democrats run as Wal-Mart foe, *New York Times*, August 17.

126. Ibid.

127. 2006, Beaverton council rejects Cedar Mill Wal-Mart plan, *Beaverton Valley Times*, August 8; 2005, No Wal-Mart for Vancouver, *CBC News*, June 29; 2004, Inglewood Wal-Mart proposal defeated, http://www.laane.org/pressroom/stories/ walmart/040407CityNewsService .html, April 6.

128. 2007, Wal-Mart Annual Report, 56.

129. Ibid.

130. Ibid.

131. C. Harrison, 2003, Commitment from Wal-Mart may boost tracking technology, *Dallas Morning News*, July 15.

132. Ibid.

133. Ibid.

134. 2004, U.S. Census Bureau, Interim Projections Consistent with 2000 Census, http://www.census.gov/population/www/projections/ popproj.html, March.

135. Ibid.

136. 2007, U.S. Department of Labor, Women's Bureau: Statistics & Data, http://www.dol.gov/wb/stats/main.htm, May 14.

137. E. L. Chao & K. P. Utgoff, Women in the labor force: A databook, U.S. Bureau of Labor Statistics, May 2005, 1.

138. G. Becker & K. Murphy, 2007, The upside of income inequality, *The American*, May/June, 24–28.

139. 2007, U.S. Census Bureau, Historical Income Inequality Tables, http://www.census.gov/hhes/www/income/histinc/ineqtoc.html, May 21.

140. 2007, Wal-Mart "Out in Front," Fact Sheets, WalMartFacts.com, http://www.walmartfacts.com/FactSheets/4112007_Wal-Mart__Out_in_Front_.pdf, April 11.

141. R. Walton, 2006, Wal-Mart Annual Report, inside cover.

142. Ibid.

143. H. L. Scott, 2007, Wal-Mart Annual Report, 10.

144. 2007, Wal-Mart "Out in Front."

145. 2007 Wal-Mart Annual Report, 5, 12; and Wal-Mart Stores Overview, http://walmartstores.com/GlobalWMStoresWeb/navigate.do?catg=345, May 25.

146. 2007 Wal-Mart Annual Report, 8, 12.

147. Ibid.

148. 2007, In Front with Wal-Mart, Wal-Mart Stores, Inc., http://www.infrontwithwalmart.com/about.aspx, May 20.

149. 2007, Wal-Mart Annual Report, 5.

150. 2007, Wal-Mart Annual Report, 11.

151. 2003, Knowledge@Wharton, The Wal-Mart Empire: A Simple Formula and Unstoppable Growth, Research at Penn, http://www.upenn.edu/researchatpenn/article.php?631&bus, April 9.

152. 2004, FRONTLINE co-production with Hedrick Smith Productions, Inc., WGBH Educational Foundation, http://www.pbs.org/wgbh/pages/frontline/shows/walmart/etc/script.html.

153. 2007, Wal-Mart supplier requirements and processes, http://walmartstores.com/GlobalWMStoresWeb/navigate .do?catg=331, May 19.

154. Ibid.

155. 2007, Wal-Mart Sustainability, http://walmartstores.com/microsite/walmart_sustainability.html, May 19.

156. 2007, Wal-Mart Annual Report, 16.

157. Ibid.

158. 2007, Wal-Mart Annual Report, 11.

159. Ibid.

160. 2007, Wal-Mart Annual Report, 21.

161. 2007, Wal-Mart Annual Report, 18.

162. S. Hornblower, 2004, Always low prices: Is Wal-Mart good for America? *Frontline*, http://www.pbs.org/wgbh/pages/frontline/shows/walmart/secrets/pricing.html, November 23.

163. 2007, Wal-Mart Annual Report, 18.

164. 2007, Wal-Mart Annual Report, 17.

165. H. L. Scott, 2007, Wal-Mart Annual Report, 11.

166. B. Helm & D. Kiley, 2006, Wal-Mart leaves draft out in the cold, *BusinessWeek*, http://www.businessweek.com/bwdaily/dnflash/content/dec2006/db20061207_540888.htm?campaign_id=rss_innovate, December 7.

167. A. Zimmerman, 2006, To boost sales, Wal-Mart drops one-size-fits-all approach, *Wall Street Journal*, http://online.wsj.com/article/SB115758956826955863.html?mod=hps_us_pageone, September 7.

168. Ibid.

169. Ibid.

170. H. L. Scott, 2007, Wal-Mart Annual Report, 11.

171. M. Barbaro, 2007, It's not only about price at Wal-Mart, *New York Times*, http://www.nytimes.com/2007/03/02/business/02walmart.html?ex=1330491600&en=5a72ddc69030ce62&ei=5088&partner=rssnyt&emc=rss&pagewanted=print, March 2

172. 2007 Wal-Mart Annual Report, 17; P. Svensson, 2007, Dell to sell computers at Wal-Mart, Associated Press, Yahoo! Finance, http://biz.yahoo.com/ap/070524/dell_wal_mart.html?.v=11, May 24.

173. T. Ryan, 2007, From RetailWire: Wal-Mart classifies customers for growth, *Supply Chain Digest*, http://www.scdigest.com/assets/newsViews/07-03-27-2.php?cid=977, March 27.

174. 2007, Wal-Mart Annual Report, 19.

175. 2007, Wal-Mart cutting managers at Sam's Club, Reuters, http://www.reuters.com/article/businessNews/idUSN2628417520070426?feedType=RSS, April 26.

176. T. Otte, 2007, Spinoff in Bentonville revisited, value investing, MotleyFool.com, http://www.fool.com/investing/value/2007/05/07/spinoff-in-bentonville-revisited.aspx, May 7.

177. 2007, Wal-Mart Annual Report, 19.

178. Ibid.

179. Ibid.

180. Ibid.

181. 2007, Wal-Mart F1Q08 (Qtr End 4/30/07) Earnings call transcript, retail stocks, *SeekingAlpha*, http://retail.seekingalpha.com/article/35633, May 15.

182. 2007, Wal-Mart evaluating options in possible bid for the UK's J. Sainsbury chain, *Supply Chain Digest*, http://www.scdigest.com/assets/newsViews/07-03-27-3.php?cid=978, March 27.

183. 2007, Wal-Mart Retail Divisions, http://www.walmartfacts.com/articles/2502.aspx, April 4.

184. 2003, The Wal-Mart Empire: A simple formula and unstoppable growth, *Knowledge@Wharton*, http://www.upenn.edu/researchatpenn/article.php?631&bus, April 9.

185. A. Bianco, 2007, Wal-Mart's midlife crisis, 56.

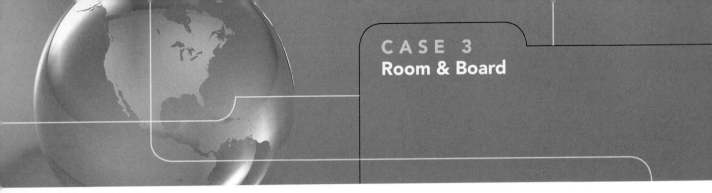

Edward D. Hess

University of Virginia, Darden School Foundation

Room & Board was a privately owned home-furnishings retailer, offering products that combined classic, simple design with exceptional quality. Approximately $50 million of revenue a year was generated through Room & Board's fully integrated, multichannel sales approach, consisting of its eight national retail stores, an annual catalog, and a Web site. Based in Minneapolis, Minnesota, Room & Board's story is one of contrarian success as a company that had abandoned the standard retail-industry business model, disavowed debt and equity-growth financing, and embraced a unique multiple-stakeholder model that valued quality and relationships ahead of the bottom line while producing stellar financial results. That the company had achieved consistency and harmony between its values and actions also added to its uniqueness. Its culture supported an energized, positive growth environment for its employees that fostered high employee engagement and in turn, high customer engagement.

Room & Board was wholly owned by John Gabbert, who had created it more than 25 years earlier. Having reached the age of 60, Gabbert was now confronting his biggest challenge: how to institutionalize the unusual business model, culture, and employee environment he had built. His primary objective was to preserve and protect his "relationship" business model, which was the heart and soul of Room & Board's success.

History

Gabbert grew up working in a family retail business that sold traditional home furnishings; at the age of 24, he succeeded his father as the CEO. Family dynamics proved challenging, so when he was 33, he left the family furniture business to start his own furniture company initially based on IKEA's business model. He also diversified

into other businesses. By the late 1980s however, feeling overextended and unfulfilled, he decided to focus all his energy on building a business with people he liked and on a model that represented quality. All this drew him into the design aspect of the furniture business.

To Gabbert, quality relationships were just as important as quality home furnishings. This belief helped shape Room & Board into a business focused on creating long-lasting relationships with customers, vendors, and employees, who were all fully integrated into the model of selling quality furnishings. At Room & Board, quality was also about providing value. That value was inherent in the firm's products, which lasted and whose style and design were timeless—furniture that customers could count on enjoying for many years. But Room & Board went further by believing that a customer's home should be a place where he or she can create a meaningful environment. This was made possible by offering customers a multitude of special-order products, ranging from fabric choices on throw pillows to customer-designed solid-wood storage pieces.

Supply Chain

The retail-furniture industry was generally controlled by large manufacturers that dictated style, product availability, and price, and that made many products overseas with cheaper labor than could be found in the United States. Room & Board decided early on that it did not want to compete by the traditional rules associated with the retail-furniture industry. In contrast, the firm created its own supply chain of approximately 40 different vendors, nearly all privately owned family businesses, many having grown alongside Room & Board over the years. Soon, more than 85 percent of the

This case was prepared by Edward D. Hess, Professor of Business Administration and Batten Executive-in-Residence. It was written as a basis for class discussion rather than to illustrate effective or ineffective handling of an administrative situation.

company's products were made in the United States—in places like Newton, North Carolina; Martinsville, Virginia; Minneapolis, Minnesota; Grand Forks, North Dakota; Shell Lake, Wisconsin; and Albany, Oregon—by craftsmen and artisans using high-quality hardwoods, granite, and steel. Most of these products were made exclusively for Room & Board, and more than 50 percent of the products were manufactured by 12 key vendors. Room & Board met with its vendors frequently to plan growth, discuss needs, and share financial data and results to ensure that everyone was making a fair living while creating high-quality, well-designed products.

These vendor relationships evolved over the years into true partnerships, which allowed Room & Board to set an annual goal of having 85 percent of its products in stock at all times, contributing to quick deliveries. Special-order products were programmed ahead of normal production with the aim of delivering the product as quickly as possible to the customer.

Under this model, Room & Board was more in control of its destiny; it had control over product quality, inventory availability, and the risk of supply-chain disruptions. This unique model carried its own risks however, as almost all of Room & Board's suppliers were private, family-owned businesses that shared the company's challenge of growing at a rate that sustained their economic health.

Culture

Room & Board had rejected common attributes of private-company culture: hierarchy, command and control from the top, information on a need-to-know basis, and, in the retail industry, high turnover resulting in customer-service challenges. Its culture was based on the principles of trust, respect, relationships, transparency, entrepreneurial ownership of one's job and career, and the importance of a balanced life. Room & Board eschewed rules, lengthy policy manuals, and elitism. Rather, it believed that individuals thrive in an environment where they are empowered to make decisions and everyone's view is heard and respected. These core beliefs were outlined in its *Guiding Principles,* partially based on the following expectation:

At Room & Board we hope you find meaning in your work. There is both tremendous productivity for the company and personal fulfillment for each staff member when someone finds their life's work. It's a wonderful circle of success.

Room & Board tried to achieve this "circle of success" by creating an environment of collaboration and engagement. This engagement was evidenced by deep relationships with customers, fellow employees, and suppliers. Respect for different views, openness to

feedback, and responsibility for one's actions all drove the staff's behavior.

What worked for Room & Board as it tried to achieve balance was defined by Gandhi: Harmony exists when what you feel, what you think, and what you do are consistent. Many businesses talked a good game, but Room & Board actually tried to "walk the talk." In this company environment, there was a heightened sensitivity regarding the impact of actions across functions and an awareness of the real message being communicated.

Room & Board believed that success was rooted in shared accountability; therefore, there were no rules for personal leave or sick pay. All 670 employees were shown the company's annual strategy priorities and a complete detailed financial package every month so that they could understand the goals of the business. All financial and operating numbers were transparent to encourage responsibility for owning and, in turn, affecting Room & Board's success. In discussing the company's normal eight-hour day, Gabbert stated:

I learned a long time ago that most people only have so many productive hours a day—it is the number of productive hours that count, not the number of hours at work. We strive to have an environment which results in energy and productivity. That is why we have a full physical-fitness facility with classes going on during the workday, a masseuse, as well as a great kitchen for employees to prepare healthy lunches.

Room & Board also operated on the principle that people who have a balanced life, with a life outside work, were happier and dealt well with customers and with each other. Gabbert, who recognized that what set his company apart was its engaged employees who tried to make every customer experience special, said, "I never wanted to be the biggest. I never thought about size. I just wanted to be the best and to spend my time at work with good people doing something more meaningful than just making money or keeping score."

Employees

The retail industry is known for high employee turnover, with companies using many part-time employees to keep expenditures on employee benefits low and commission-based compensation to lower fixed costs. But Room & Board was proof that a very profitable, high-quality business could be built by not following any of those common retail practices.

Instead, Room & Board had very low employee turnover, mostly full-time employees, provided full benefits for part-time employees, and pay based on salary rather than on individual sales. The rejection of a commission-based structure, together with its integrated and multichannel purchasing options, allowed Room & Board customers to shop and purchase in the manner that made the most sense to them. "We want customers to rely on us for the best advice and to trust that we have their best interests in mind—sales commissions run against that type of trust," said Gabbert. The breakdown of Room & Board's employees by staff divisions is shown in Exhibit 1.

Room & Board stores more than five years old had average employee tenure of more than five years, which was very high for the retail industry. Delivery and warehouse personnel in delivery centers open for more than four years had an average tenure of five years. Employee tenure was 5.7 years for the central office, and total employee tenure for the company averaged nearly five years.

Room & Board also took a different approach to measuring employee satisfaction: The company tracked how many employees referred family and friends for jobs and how many employees participated in the company's 401(k) program. Room & Board believed that these measures truly contributed to long-term employee engagement. Following the philosophy that employees needed good physical, mental, and financial health, Room & Board offered an extensive physical-fitness facility, a healthy-lunch program, and personal financial-planning services and 401(k) investment advice from an outside financial consulting firm at no cost. In addition, all employees could buy Room & Board products at a substantial discount.

Leadership Team

Room & Board was led by a six-member advisory board made up of John Gabbert and the members (see Exhibit 2). The leadership team received generous bonuses if key company objectives were met.

Key Expectations for Employees and Leaders

Room & Board's *Guiding Principles* was the foundation for the company's expectations and also served as a tool to help employees understand their connection to the business. The document, which spoke primarily to

Exhibit 1 Room & Board Staff Divisions

Type	Number
Store personnel	237
Delivery personnel	220
Store and delivery leadership team	62
Central office staff	100

Exhibit 2 Leadership Team

Member	Title	Tenure
Bruce Champeau	Vice President of Distribution Delivery/Technology	16 years
Kimberly Ruthenbeck	Vice President of Retail Customer Experience & Vendor Managements	15 years
Mark Miller	Chief Financial Officer	11 years
Betsey Kershaw	Director of Brand Experience	5 years
Nancy McGough	Director of Human Resources	16 years

respect individual accountability and engaging the business, included the following statements:

- Respect is foundational to our work environment. Everyone is expected to build relationships based upon mutual respect and collaboration.
- Use good judgment when making decisions and apply principle, not rules, to each situation.
- The more you seek to understand how your role is related to our business objectives and tied to the broader success of the company, the more rewarding, enjoyable, and challenging the effort.

Just as all employees were expected to understand and embrace the core beliefs outlined in *Guiding Principles,* leaders were expected to adhere to their own additional roadmap. Room & Board set forth a number of leadership objectives for its central office, store, and delivery/distribution leadership team, including the following:

- You take ownership for your business—you're independent and therefore do not wait to be told what to do.
- You lead less with rules and rely more on principles.
- You value building relationships; collaboration is much more important to you than competition.
- You appreciate and desire longevity within your role. You do not seek to move from location to location or from department to department to get ahead; your growth occurs from richer experiences within your current role.

Financial Results

The Skokie, Illinois, store opened in 1986; the Edina, Minnesota, store in April 1989; the Denver store in 1991; and the Chicago store in 1993 (see Exhibits 3 and 4).

Exhibit 3 Room & Board Financial Results

Year	Sales (in millions [$])	New-Store Openings
1995	$33	
1996	$45	
1997	$53	Oakbrook, IL
1998	$67	
1999	$82	
2000	$98	
2001	$92	
2002	$95	South Coast, CA
2003	$110	
2004	$132	New York, NY; downtown Chicago store moves to Rush & Ohio location
2005	$173	San Francisco, CA
2006	$208	
2007	$229	

Source: Room & Board.

Delivery Centers

Another point of differentiation from other retailers was Room & Board's philosophy regarding deliveries. Many furniture chains outsourced their deliveries. Room & Board did not, operating its own delivery centers staffed by full-time Room & Board professionals. These teams delivered all the local products. For national deliveries, Room & Board had an exclusive relationship with a Minneapolis company. To ensure ongoing collaboration, a few employees from the national shipping company's office worked out of Room & Board's central location.

In addition, the company had dedicated delivery teams for just Room & Board products. It was not unusual for customers to assume that these delivery professionals were Room & Board employees, not just because of their Room & Board uniforms, but also because they adhered to the same principles that all Room & Board employees followed: namely, that the customer experience during

Exhibit 4 Room & Board Financial Results

Key Metrics	Goals
Sales growth	10% annual
Net profit	8% pretax
Customer satisfaction	>96%
Product in warehouse at time of sale	>85%
Vendor lead time	<7 weeks
Channels of Distribution	**Approximate-Breakdown**
Store sales	70%
Phone sales	2%
Web sales	18%
Markets	**($ in millions)**
Colorado	$18
Minneapolis	$24
Chicago	$44
San Francisco	$33
Southern California	$23
New York City	$46
National sales	$42
Main Product Lines	
Sofas and chairs	36%
Bedroom	17%
Dining room	12%

Source: Room & Board.

every step of the process was hassle-free and treated as an opportunity to create long-lasting relationships. The individuals who had the last interaction with customers about purchases were viewed as brand ambassadors and acted as such.

Room & Board's goal of providing a great customer experience at every step of the buying-and-receiving process required delivery personnel to deliver and set up the product and leave the customer happy. Delivery times were scheduled to allow time for customer interaction, discussions, and the proper placement of the new purchases. If there was a problem, delivery personnel were empowered to solve it on the spot because they were trained to "leave the customer in a good place." The focus on interaction with the customer, from the beginning of the experience to the end, drove customer satisfaction, in terms of loyalty and referrals, to a rate of more than 95 percent.

Real Estate

To avoid the high rent typical in retail malls, Room & Board owned most of its locations and searched out freestanding sites with ample parking and easy access for customers. The company often chose to renovate an existing location, blending its store in with a particular environment rather than building a new one. This practice served as inspiration to customers who dealt with similar challenges when designing and furnishing their own spaces. Moreover, it prevented Room & Board from adopting a "cookie cutter" image for its stores and fostered the company's philosophy of unique design. The central-office facility was furnished with Room & Board products, so even employees who were not in customer-facing roles understood what the company sold, its quality, and its lasting design.

Pricing Model

Room & Board's pricing model was simple: no sales, no volume discounts, and no discounts for interior designers. Everyone paid the same price. As John Gabbert put it, "Nothing makes me madder than to buy something and then see it go on sale. I feel taken advantage of. That is why we have no sales, and we guarantee all prices for a year after purchase for each calendar year. If we sell a product within a year of your purchase for less than you paid, we will refund the difference."

Competition

Direct comparison with other retailers was impossible because Room & Board's exclusive designs, corporate structure, and long-lasting heirloom-quality products were not offered by any other company. Ultimately, Room & Board was competing for any of the dollars that customers spent on their homes no matter what the other retailer sold. Design Within Reach and Crate and Barrel were two companies that carried similar modern home furnishings and mid-century products.

Design Within Reach was a public company. In fiscal 2006, it had $110 million in sales through its 63 stores, which ranged in size from 1,100 square feet to 11,000 square feet. Although Room & Board stores were fewer in number, they were much bigger, at 30,000 square feet. Crate and Barrel had grown from a small family business, started in 1962, to a chain of over 160 mall-based stores owned by the private German company Otto, which also owned Spiegel and Eddie Bauer. More than 50 percent of Crate and Barrel products were imported from Europe.

Conclusion

Room & Board achieved the enviable market position of managing its growth and avoiding the capital-market pressures produced by debt financing and equity partners or by being a public company. It built a loyal and highly engaged workforce dedicated to its way of doing things, and managed to be a model of productivity and engagement without sacrificing quality. The company did not strive for the lowest operational costs, but instead embraced a vertically integrated business model and earned good net margins.

The beauty of the Room & Board success story was how it had created a consistent, seamless, self-reinforcing system that cut across culture, structure, execution philosophy, employee hiring, and benefits. The result was a company with a high-performance environment that manufactured 85 percent of its products in the United States, paid its people well, sold high-quality products, and made good profits.

Room & Board adhered to a multiple-stakeholder philosophy of capitalism, much like the European model and less like the sole-stakeholder model more common in the United States. It believed it would do well if its customers, employees, and suppliers did well. To create shareholder value had not been Room & Board's sole purpose. But now the company was looking at expanding—into Los Angeles, Seattle, Atlanta, Miami, and Washington, D.C.—but at its own pace and on its own terms. Room & Board's task was figuring out how to institutionalize its way of doing business beyond the life of its founder and how to strengthen its culture and high employee and customer engagement, while growing at a rate that sustained its economic health.

Ali Farhoomand

University of Hong Kong

China is a place where miracles are made.

JACK MA, FOUNDER AND CHAIRMAN OF ALIBABA GROUP[1]

On November 6, 2007, Alibaba.com debuted on the Hong Kong Stock Exchange, raising US$1.5 billion to become the world's biggest Internet stock offering since Google's initial public offering (IPO) in 2004. On the first trading day, frenzied purchases of the stock pushed prices up by 193 percent, the fourth-largest first-day gain in Hong Kong's stock exchange in three years. The closing price of US$5.09[2] per share gave Alibaba.com a value of about US$25.6 billion, making it the fifth-most-valuable Internet company and the largest in Asia outside Japan. It also made the company's stock among the most expensive on the Hong Kong exchange,[3] trading at 306 times its projected 2007 earnings of US$83.6 million.[4] In contrast, Yahoo!, a globally recognized "dot-com" brand that held a 39 percent stake in pre-IPO Alibaba.com, and Japan's SoftBank, which owned 29.3 percent of Alibaba.com prior to the IPO, traded at only around 60 times their projected earnings. In other words, shareholders had displayed extreme optimism about Alibaba.com's prospective earnings by paying a significant premium to own the company's shares.

Barely a week after the IPO, Alibaba.com was already reported to be in talks with SoftBank to set up a joint venture in early 2008 in Japan. Although the Japanese telecom giant disclosed no details regarding the proposed venture, it was likely that Alibaba.com would expand its service to mobile users in Japan, a market that had been impenetrable to the Chinese e-commerce company.[5] On its home turf, parent company Alibaba Group had already proven its mettle by topping EachNet, an older rival backed by global leader eBay.[6] Founder and Chairman

Jack Ma had made it his aim to make the Alibaba Group one of three largest Internet companies in the world and a Fortune 500 company.[7] Could the IPO be the first step to Alibaba.com's global market dominance, or would it be overtaken just as quickly as it rose to regional pre-eminence?

Internet and E-Commerce in China

The world's most populous nation had 162 million Internet users as of June 2007.[8] Although the Chinese Internet-using population was second only to that of the United States,[9] China's Internet penetration rate of 12.3 percent significantly trailed those of the United States, Japan, and South Korea, whose penetration rates were all more than 65 percent.[10] Nevertheless, with the penetration rate growing at around three percentage points annually (see Exhibit 1), China was expected to experience even more rapid growth in the scale of penetration, having crossed the critical threshold of 10 percent and heading into the steep phase of the S-curve.[11]

Similarly, e-commerce was still in its infancy in China. Official figures estimated that only 25.5 percent of Internet users in China had engaged in online shopping, whereas the figure was 71 percent in the United States. The utilization rate of online sales and marketing was also very low—a mere 4.3 percent compared to 15 percent in the United States. The only exception to the trend was the rate of online stock transactions, which was 14.1 percent, narrowly beating the U.S. rate of 13 percent. The official explanation was the frenzy over the financial markets in China that started around 2006.[12]

Ricky Lai prepared this case under the supervision of Professor Ali Farhoom and for class discussion. This case is not intended to show effective or ineffective handling of decision or business processes.

Exhibit 1 China's Internet Penetration Rate

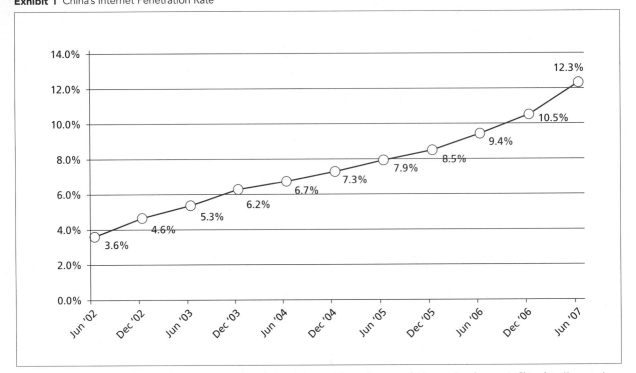

Source: China Internet Network Information Center, 2007, The 20th CNNIC Statistical Survey Report on the Internet Development in China, http://www.cnnic. net.cn/download/2007/20thCNNICreport-en.pdf (accessed November 19, 2007).

Chinese Internet media market researcher, iResearch Consulting Group, valued the Chinese online shopping market at US$1.5 billion in the first quarter of 2007. The online shopping market comprised the customer-to-customer and business-to-customer segments, with the former accounting for US$1.3 billion, or 89.7 percent of the market in China. Overall, the Chinese online shopping market recorded a 14.8 percent rise in the first quarter of 2007 compared to the preceding quarter and a massive 64.1 percent jump over the previous year (see Exhibit 2).[13] By comparison, the online business-to-business (B2B) market was much bigger, valued at US$65.7 billion in the second quarter of 2007, increasing 10.4 percent quarter-on-quarter and a staggering 69.8 percent year-on-year (see Exhibit 3).[14]

SMEs in China

Small and medium-sized enterprises (SMEs) have been a key driving force in the booming Chinese economy. In 2004, SMEs contributed 68.8 percent to the nation's gross industrial output (in current prices).[15] iResearch estimated that the number of SMEs in China would rise from 31.5 million in 2006 to 50 million in 2012 (see Exhibit 4).[16] Out of these 31.5 million Chinese SMEs, a mere 8.8 million, or 28 percent, utilized

third-party B2B e-commerce platforms. With the Chinese government's "11th Five-Year Planning for the Development of E-Commerce" encouraging SMEs to use third-party e-commerce platforms, however, the numbers were expected to rise to 41 million and 82 percent, respectively, in 2012 (see Exhibit 5).[17] The implication was that e-commerce had plenty of room for growth in China, at least among SMEs, where the market was expected to almost quadruple between 2007 and 2012.

The rising popularity of e-commerce among SMEs in China was fueled by several challenges in the traditional trade environment, including:

- Limited geographic presence restricting SMEs' ability to develop customer and supplier relationships beyond their immediate vicinity
- Fragmentation of suppliers and buyers, which made it difficult to find and communicate with suitable trading partners
- Limited communication channels and information sources through which to market and promote products and services or to find new markets and suppliers
- A relatively small scale of operation, limiting SMEs' resources for sales and marketing
- Absence of efficient mechanisms for evaluating the trustworthiness of trading partners[18]

Exhibit 2 Growth of the Chinese Online Shopping Market

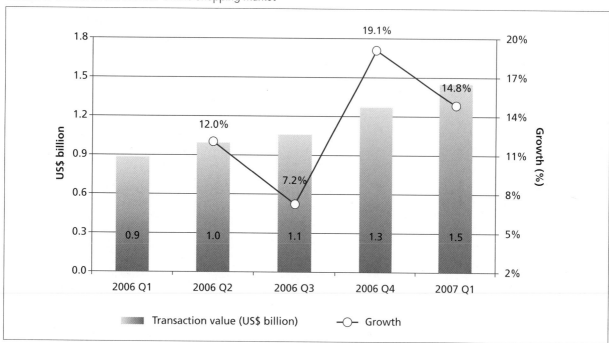

Source: iResearch Inc., 2007, China's online shopping market worth RMB 10.8 billion in Q1 of 2007, http://www.iresearchgroup.com.cn/html/Consulting/Online_Shopping/DetailNews_id_65929.html, June 18 (accessed November 20, 2007).

Exhibit 3 Growth of the Chinese B2B E-Commerce Market

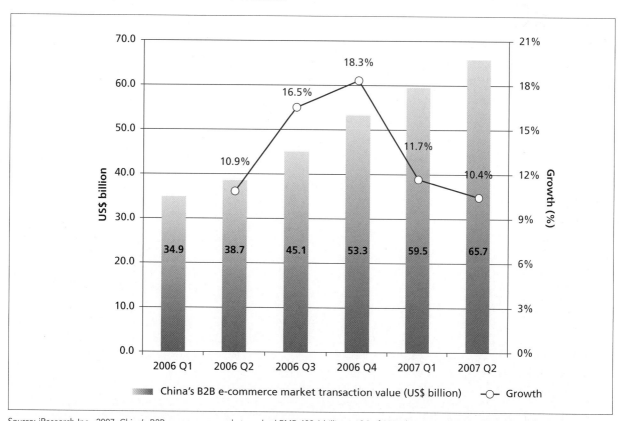

Source: iResearch Inc., 2007, China's B2B e-commerce market reached RMB 489.1 billion in Q2 of 2007, http://www.iresearchgroup.com.cn/html/consulting/B2B/DetailNews_id_72299.html, November 5 (accessed November 20, 2007).

Exhibit 4 Growth of Chinese SMEs

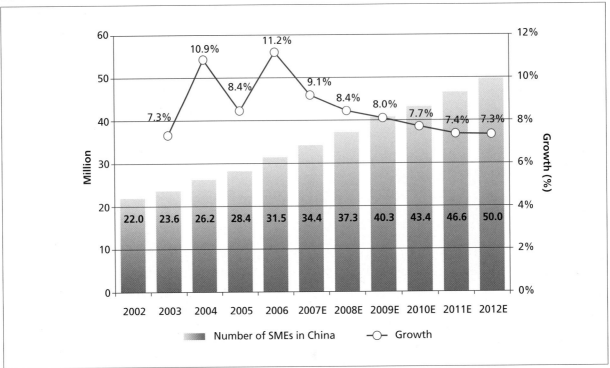

Source: iResearch Inc., 2007, China SME number to reach 50 million in 2012, http://www.iresearchgroup.com.cn/Consulting/others/DetailNews.asp?id=65361, June 6 (accessed November 22, 2007).

Exhibit 5 Usage of Third-Party E-Commerce among Chinese SMEs

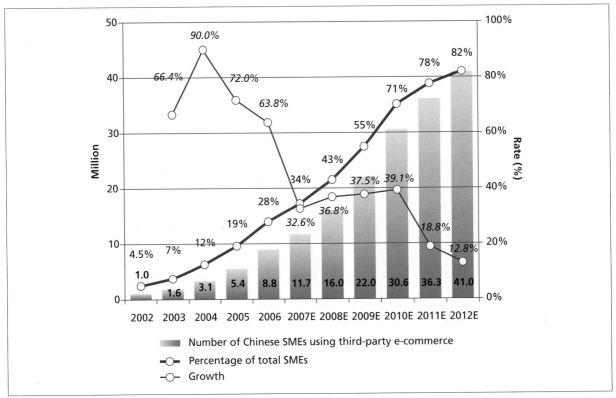

Source: iResearch Inc., 2007, B2B e-commerce should start with interest of SMEs, http://www.iresearchgroup.com.cn/html/Consulting/B2B/DetailNews_id_67225.html, July 12 (accessed November 22, 2007).

Alibaba.com

History

Alibaba's first online marketplace was launched as Alibaba Online in December 1998. Originally, the China-based Web site operated as a bulletin board service for businesses to post, buy, and sell trade leads. In June 1999, Jack Ma and 18 other founders formed the parent company, Alibaba Group, inaugurating its Web site in simplified Chinese to serve the Chinese mainland market. Three months later, a major operating subsidiary in China, Alibaba China, was established to carry out the business of operating B2B marketplaces. Within months, three more sites were launched: an English site for international users, a Korean site for Korean users, and a traditional Chinese site for Chinese users outside of China. In October 2000, Alibaba launched the Gold Supplier membership service for Chinese exporters, followed in August 2001 by the launch of International TrustPass, a membership service catering to exporters outside of China. China TrustPass was launched in March 2002 to serve SMEs engaged in domestic trade.

In September 2006, to facilitate the IPO of its B2B business, Alibaba underwent a restructuring of its B2B arm, Alibaba.com (see Exhibit 6). The principal company emerging from the restructuring, Alibaba.com Limited, became 17 percent–owned by public shareholders, with the remaining shares of the company held by the parent company, employees, and consultants.

Jack Ma

Lead founder and chairman of Alibaba Group, Jack Ma is a native of Hangzhou, located about 100 miles southwest of Shanghai, where the company's headquarters are located.

Exhibit 6 Corporate Structure of Alibaba.com Before and After Restructuring

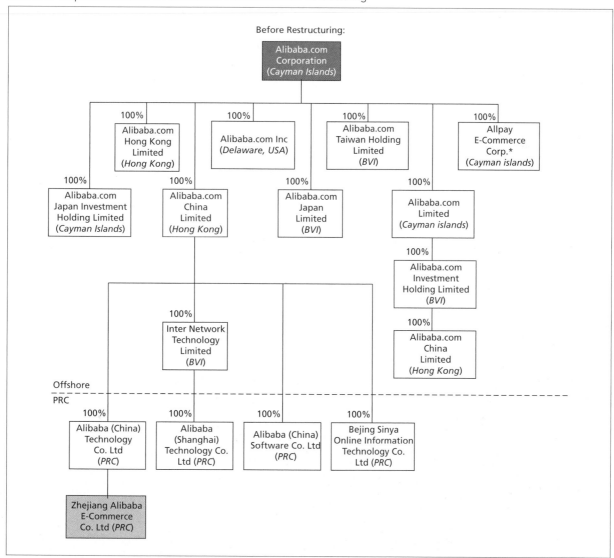

(Continued)

Exhibit 6 Corporate Structure of Alibaba.com Before and After Restructuring (*Continued*)

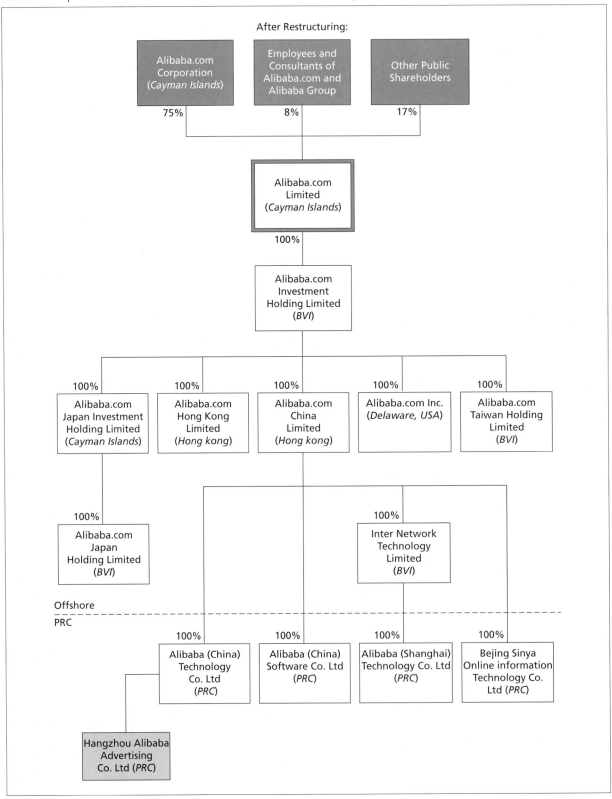

Notes:

_____ Denotes equity ownership

_ _ _ _ _ Denotes contractual relationship

* Formerly known as Alibaba.com E-Commerce Corp.

Source: Alibaba.com, 2007, Global Offering Prospectus, 63–64.

Growing up during China's Cultural Revolution, Ma became interested in learning English. Starting at age 12, and for the next 8 years, he rode his bicycle 40 minutes every morning to a hotel near the West Lake and worked on his English by giving free tours to foreigners. In spite of this effort, he failed his university entrance examinations twice before being accepted to a teachers' university.[19] The low-paying teaching job he was offered after graduation did not interest Ma, and in 1995 he found himself employed by the Chinese government to settle a dispute between a Chinese firm and its U.S. partner. Purportedly, Ma was held captive by the U.S. partner at gunpoint for two days before he regained his freedom by agreeing to become a partner in an Internet startup in China, even though he had no concept of the Internet at all.[20]

Although he never carried out his end of the deal, Ma came into his first contact with a computer and the Internet in Seattle, Washington, and was surprised to find nothing when he searched for "beer" and "China." He then returned to China, borrowed US$2,000, and started a company and Web site called China Pages. The Web site shared a strikingly similar ideology with Alibaba.com: to list Chinese companies on the Internet and help foreigners find their Web sites. Eventually, China Telecom would buy out Ma's stake and he would end up returning to civil service to promote e-commerce. Always looking for a chance to fulfill his dream of setting up his own e-commerce company, Ma stepped out of the civil service again in 1998 and resumed work on his vision to connect Chinese companies to the world through the Internet. This vision was realized in December of that year with the launch of Alibaba Online.

Business Model

By the second quarter of 2007, Alibaba.com was the largest online B2B e-commerce company in China, based on the number of registered users and market share by revenue.[21] The international marketplace was served by their English-language Web site, Alibaba.com, which focused on global importers and exporters. The Chinese marketplace was served by their Chinese-language interface, Alibaba.com.cn, which focused on suppliers and buyers trading domestically in China.

The two B2B marketplaces provided a platform to facilitate e-commerce between business sellers, whom Alibaba.com referred to as "suppliers," and wholesale buyers (see Exhibit 7 for Alibaba. com's value proposition). Suppliers and buyers used the marketplaces to establish their presence online, identify potential trading partners, and conduct business with each other. Suppliers and some buyers used the marketplaces to host their company profiles and catalogues in standardized formats known as "storefronts" and post "listings" such as products, services, and trade leads. Users could view storefronts and listings in over 30 industry categories and nearly 5,000 product categories by either searching for keywords or browsing through the online industry directory (see Exhibit 8 for a typical trading process). For many suppliers, their storefront or listing was their only presence on the Internet. As of June 30, 2007, there were more than 2.4 million storefronts. In the first half of 2007, users posted a monthly average of 2.9 million new listings on the marketplaces.

Through active listings, inquiry exchanges, instant messaging, discussion forums, and other user-friendly community features, suppliers and buyers formed large, interactive online communities on Alibaba.com's marketplaces. In June 2007, Alibaba.com registered more than 540,000 peak simultaneous online users of TradeManager, an instant messaging tool for trade communications. The two marketplaces collectively hosted more than 200 online forums and more than 4.2 million registered users.

To enhance the breadth and depth of the marketplaces, Alibaba.com offered basic features and services to all registered users free of charge. Revenue was generated from suppliers who purchased services, primarily membership packages that provided priority placement

Exhibit 7 Alibaba.com's Value Proposition

Suppliers		Buyers
• Access to active global buyer community		• Access to active global supplier community
• Targeted marketing to reach buyers	Alibaba.com	• Broad selection of listings
• Customer service and training		• Access to high-quality, organized information • Easy-to-use interface
• Always online		• Convenient, real-time medium
• Budget certainty through a fixed subscription fee model		• Authentication and trust profiles of suppliers

Source: Alibaba.com, 2007, Global Offering Prospectus, 78.

Exhibit 8 Typical Trading Process in the Alibaba.com Marketplace

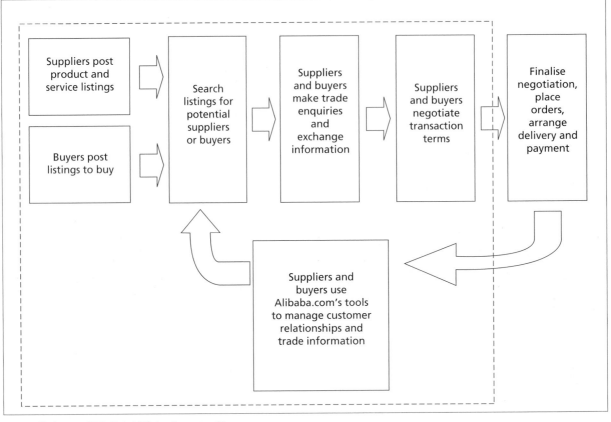

Source: Alibaba.com, 2007, Global Offering Prospectus, 83.

of storefronts and listings in the industry directory and search results. These paying members generated additional revenue by subscribing to value-added services, including purchases of additional keywords to improve their rankings in search results and premium placement on Alibaba.com's Web pages for enhanced exposure and visibility.

Results

Alibaba.com experienced significant growth in the number of registered users (Table 1) and in the number of paying members (Table 2) from 2004 to mid-2007.[22]

For the international marketplace, as of the end of June 2007, about 17.7 percent of users were based in the United States, followed by 8.7 percent from the European Union (excluding the United Kingdom), 8.2 percent from India, 6.2 percent from the United Kingdom, and 2.7 percent from Canada.

For the Chinese marketplace, as of the end of June 2007, Guangdong led in the regional breakdown of registered users with a 21.5 percent share, followed by Zhejiang with 8.5 percent, Jiangsu with 6.6 percent, Shandong with 5.3 percent, and Shanghai with 4.6 percent.

Revenue increased at a staggering cumulative annual growth rate of 94.8 percent from US$48.3 million at the end of 2004 to US$183.2 million at the end of 2006. According to Alibaba.com's detailed financial data (see Exhibit 9), the international marketplace had been

Table 1 Growth in the Number of Alibaba.com's Registered Users

	End of 2004	End of 2005	Year-on-Year	End of 2006	Year-on-Year
Total registered users	6.0 million	11.0 million	+82.6%	19.8 million	+80.2%
International marketplace	1.2 million	1.9 million	+67.2%	3.1 million	+59.8%
Chinese marketplace	4.8 million	9.0 million	+86.3%	16.6 million	+84.6%

Table 2 Growth in the Number of Alibaba.com's Paying Members

	End of 2004	End of 2005	Year-on-Year	End of 2006	Year-on-Year
Total paying members	77,922	141,614	+81.7%	219,098	+54.7%
International marketplace	11,450	19,983	+74.5%	29,525	+47.8%
Chinese marketplace	66,472	121,631	+83.0%	189,573	+55.9%

Exhibit 9 Alibaba.com Financial Data, 2004–2007

	Year ending 31 December						Six months ending 30 June			
	2004		2005		2006		2006		2007	
	Amount	% of revenue	Amount	% of revenue	Amount	% of revenue	Amount	% of revenue	Amount	% of revenue
							(unaudited)			
				(in thousands of Rmb, except percentages)						
Revenue										
International marketplace	254,765	70.9	527,227	71.4	991,869	72.7	431,481	72.7	695,398	72.6
Chinese marketplace	104,670	29.1	211,070	28.6	371,993	27.3	162,156	27.3	260,965	27.3
Others	—	—	—	—	—	—	—	—	1,353	0.1
Total	359,435	100.0	738,297	100.0	1,363,862	100.0	593,637	100.0	957,716	100.0
Cost of revenue[1]	(62,569)	(17.4)	(126,509)	(17.1)	(237,625)	(17.4)	(109,131)	(18.4)	(122,717)	(12.8)
Gross profit	296,866	82.6	611,788	82.9	1,126,237	82.6	484,506	81.6	834,999	87.2
Sales & marketing expenses[1][2]	(194,773)	(54.2)	(393,950)	(53.4)	(610,198)	(44.8)	(299,034)	(50.3)	(307,428)	(32.1)
Product development expenses[1][2]	(19,151)	(5.4)	(35,678)	(4.8)	(105,486)	(7.7)	(47,256)	(8.0)	(58,278)	(6.1)
General and administrative expenses[1][2]	(57,639)	(16.0)	(101,082)	(13.7)	(159,969)	(11.7)	(59,820)	(10.1)	(88,432)	(9.2)
Other operating (loss) income, net	(426)	(0.1)	14,465	1.9	17,645	1.3	800	0.1	1,190	0.1
Profit from operation	24,877	6.9	95,543	12.9	268,229	19.7	79,196	13.3	382,051	39.9
Interest income	3,591	1.0	7,876	1.1	23,159	1.7	10,340	1.7	17,699	1.8
Profit before income taxes	28,468	7.9	103,419	14.0	291,388	21.4	89,596	15.1	399,705	41.7
Income tax credits (charges)	45,393	12.6	(32,965)	(4.5)	(71,450)	(5.3)	(28,253)	(4.8)	(104,543)	(10.9)
Profit for the year/ period attributable to equity owners	73,861	20.5	70,454	9.5	219,938	16.1	61,283	10.3	295,207	30.8

Notes:

(1) Includes share-based compensation expenses, which are allocated as follows:

(Continued)

Exhibit 9 Alibaba.com Financial Data, 2004,2007 *(Continued)*

	Year ending 31 December						Six months ending 30 June			
	2004		2005		2006		2006		2007	
	Amount	% of revenue	Amount	% of revenue	Amount	% of revenue	Amount	% of revenue	Amount	% of revenue
							(unaudited)			
			(in thousands of Rmb, except percentages)							
Cost of revenue	1,936	0.5	8,766	1.2	23,335	1.7	13,258	2.2	6,207	0.7
Sales & marketing expenses	5,259	1.5	26,920	3.6	50,068	3.7	21,975	3.7	21,517	2.2
Product development expenses	1,382	0.4	5,126	0.7	16,344	1.2	7,727	1.3	6,582	0.7
General and administrative expenses	2,838	0.8	8,079	1.1	24,157	1.8	10,442	1.8	20,183	2.1
Total share-based compensation expenses	11,415	3.2	48,891	6.6	113,904	8.4	53,402	9.0	54,489	5.7

(2) Includes expenses of Alibaba Group not related to the B2B business as follows:

	Year ending 31 December						Six months ending 30 June			
	2004		2005		2006		2006		2007	
	Amount	% of revenue	Amount	% of revenue	Amount	% of revenue	Amount	% of revenue	Amount	% of revenue
							(unaudited)			
			(in thousands of Rmb, except percentages)							
Sales & marketing expenses	—	—	35,959	4.9	83,186	6.1	58,661	9.9	—	—
Product development expenses	—	—	1,414	0.2	6,748	0.5	3,705	0.6	—	—
General and administrative expenses	9,594	2.7	29,972	4.0	47,573	3.5	18,818	3.2	—	—
Total	9,594	2.7	67,345	9.1	137,507	10.1	81,184	13.7	—	—

Source: Alibaba. Com, 2007, Globl Offering Prospectus, 102–103.

steadily contributing slightly more than 70 percent of revenue, while the Chinese marketplace brought in just short of 30 percent. Specifically, Alibaba.com derived around 71 percent of its revenue from Gold Supplier members of the international marketplace, who paid at least US$5,373.60 per year for a standard package and US$8,060.40 for a premium package. Alibaba.com indicated that it would merge the two tiers of membership beginning November 2007, with the new rate starting at US$6,717.00 per year.[23]

Strengths

Alibaba.com believed that it had certain competitive strengths to merit such moves as the membership merger, which would effectively produce more revenue.

First, Alibaba.com had built a premier brand in the e-commerce domain, boasting the highest traffic among all online B2B marketplaces. According to Internet statistics compiler Alexa.com, Alibaba.com was the most visited site in the e-commerce and international business and trade categories,[24] in addition to being the largest online B2B company in China. Alibaba.com attracted suppliers on the strength of the large number of potential buyers that used the marketplaces, which in turn attracted more buyers to sign up with Alibaba.com. Alibaba.com's breadth and depth in its marketplaces were difficult to replicate, thus creating an effective barrier to new entrants and a virtually insurmountable lead over competitors.

Second, Alibaba.com focused exclusively on the highly lucrative SME sector. Providing tools and solutions tailored to SMEs, Alibaba.com was confident in the value proposition of its service offerings. For example, Alibaba.com provided trust ratings for suppliers and buyers, thus facilitating the process of selecting potential trading partners. The fixed subscription fee model also gave budget certainty to SMEs, which were often budget-sensitive and averse to ad-hoc expenditures. Users and subscribers had responded positively, leading to the formation of interactive communities at the online marketplaces. Alibaba.com had also installed staff dedicated to enhancing the community experience of users to build up loyalty to and trust in the brand.

Third, Alibaba.com was confident about its sales force and customer service support in attracting and retaining users, especially those who paid for subscriptions. As of mid-2007, Alibaba.com maintained more than 1,900 full-time field salespeople in 30 cities across China, more than 800 telephone salespeople, and more than 400 full-time customer-service employees, all of whom were grouped into teams in direct, daily contact with current and prospective customers. The customer service arm provided customer feedback to the sales force which, in turn, made use of the findings and worked with the product development team to deliver services that more closely met customers' needs. For example, a number of services available to Alibaba.com users, such as e-mail and instant messaging, had initially been proposed by customers and later developed by Alibaba.com.

Strategy

Alibaba.com's mission was to make it easy to do business anywhere.[25] To accomplish this mission, Alibaba.com set forth a multi-pronged strategy to make its online marketplaces more effective for SMEs around the world.

First, Alibaba.com tried to increase the size of its marketplaces through the expansion of its user base and active listings. The company believed that the breadth and quality of users and listings were critical to the success of the marketplaces. To that end, Alibaba.com continued to leverage the networking aspect of its online marketplaces, its leading market position, and the "Alibaba" brand name to increase its user base worldwide. It also planned to conduct targeted marketing to potential users in specific industries and geographic locations.

Second, Alibaba.com planned to enhance community experiences to further improve user loyalty and activity through continued development and introduction of new features and tools. Specifically, it planned to invest further in the existing instant messaging service, online forums, and other communication services. Alibaba.com also planned to continue organizing regular meetings, training, and offline events for registered users and paying members to further build the sense of community.

Third, Alibaba.com was keen to monetize its user base after providing years of free service to the majority of its members. The company would strive not only to convert more users into paying members, but also to generate more revenue from existing paying members through sales of value-added services, such as additional keyword listing and premium listing placement.

Fourth, Alibaba.com planned to selectively expand its sales and customer service capabilities into international markets, either directly or through third-party agents, to acquire more paying members and sell premium services outside China. The company had already taken the first step by offering Gold Supplier membership packages to Hong Kong suppliers in 2007. Alibaba.com was already in talks with Japanese telecommunications giant SoftBank about a joint venture to tap the Japanese market, for which significant upgrades to Alibaba.com's Japanese language Web site were already in the pipeline.

Fifth, Alibaba.com believed that its online marketplace platform could be extended beyond pure trade marketing to address users' daily business processes, such as customer relationship management and internal operations. It aimed to enhance the loyalty of its users by providing business applications through the marketplace platform and becoming an integral part of users' business operations. For example, it launched an Internet-based business management application called Alisoft Export Edition, developed by sister company Alisoft, for users based in China.

Finally, Alibaba.com was set to expand its business through acquisitions, investments, licensing arrangements, and partnerships. The underlying objectives would be to expand its user and revenue base, widen geographic coverage, enhance content and service offerings, advance its technology, and strengthen its talent pool. Alibaba.com also considered leveraging its relationship with parent company Alibaba Group to seek cross-selling, cross-marketing, and licensing arrangements and other opportunities.

Competition from Global Sources

Despite Alibaba.com's dominance in the online B2B market in China, the company was not immune to competition from both domestic and international competitors (see Exhibit 10). Chief among Alibaba.com's competitors in the international marketplace was international B2B giant Global Sources, whose online

directory was bolstered by the many other B2B services it offered, such as print business directories and exhibitions.

Founded in Hong Kong in 1971 as a monthly trade magazine for consumer products made in Asia for export to Western markets, Global Sources claimed to have a community of over 647,000 buyers and 160,000 suppliers as of the end of September 2007.[26] Global Sources also boasted the following:

- It enabled suppliers to sell to hard-to-reach buyers in over 230 countries.
- It delivered information on 2 million products annually.
- It operated 14 online marketplaces that delivered more than 23 million sales leads annually.
- It published 13 monthly magazines and over 100 sourcing research reports per year.
- It organized 9 trade-specific exhibitions that ran 22 times a year across seven cities.

In mainland China, Global Sources had over 2,000 staff members in 44 locations and a community of over one million registered online users and magazine readers of its Chinese-language media.

Global Sources clearly posed a threat to Alibaba.com because it was earning more and more of its revenue online, as evidenced by its 2006 annual report demonstrating that its online businesses generated more than 40 percent of its total revenue (Table 3).

Exhibit 10 Market Share of China's Online E-Commerce Market, by Revenue

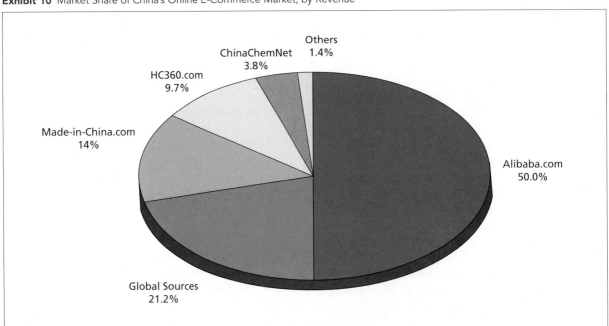

Source: iResearch Inc., 2007, China's B2B e-commerce market reached RMB 489.1 Billion in Q2 of 2007, http://www.iresearchgroup.com.cn/html/consulting/ B2B/DetailNews it 72299 html, November 5 (accessed November 20, 2007).

Table 3 Contributors to Global Sources's 2006 Revenue[27]

	Revenue (US$ million)	% of total
Online	64.4	41.2
Print	48.7	31.1
Exhibitions	42.1	26.9
Miscellaneous	1.3	0.8
Total	156.5	

The growth strategy of Global Sources was built around four key foundations:[28]

- Market penetration through increasing revenue from exhibitions by selling more booths and increasing the average revenue per booth; cross-selling to clients not using online, print, or shows, particularly the large number of new clients patronizing only exhibitions; and expanding the online customer base by offering new services and pricing packages for the new Global Sources Online 2.0.
- New product development: Global Sources actively increased its online marketplaces, magazines, and exhibitions. In 2007, it added 11 new online marketplaces, monthly publications, and trade shows and announced eight new exhibitions to be launched in 2008 and 2009.
- Expansion into China's domestic B2B market: domestic trade in China was an attractive growth market and was synergistic with Global Sources's existing media serving China's export and import sectors. Global Sources launched new exhibitions in China in the hopes of attracting volume buyers as attendees. To complement these exhibitions and other vertical, industry-focused markets, the company launched China Global Sources Online to enable international suppliers to sell to China's domestic B2B market.
- Acquisitions and alliances: Global Sources, like Alibaba.com, was on the lookout for complementary businesses, technologies, and products that would help it to achieve and maintain leading positions in the markets it served. In 2007, in support of its plans to expand online business within China, Global Sources acquired the business and Web site assets of a Beijing-based online media company, Blue Bamboo China Ventures.

Given the similarities between the current positioning and growth strategies of Alibaba.com and Global Sources, competition between the two companies for the vast and growing Chinese market is bound to intensify.

Other Competition and Constraints

Competitors in Alibaba.com's Chinese marketplace include domestic B2B e-commerce platforms such as HC360.com, the Web site operated by HC International. As a generalized e-commerce platform, Alibaba.com also had to contend with specialized platforms that focused on vertical coverage of specific industries, such as ChinaChemNet, which catered to the chemical industry in China. Because Alibaba.com founded its success on the breadth of its horizontal coverage of industries, it would be tremendously difficult for it to pursue vertical coverage of a specific industry without upsetting its basic business model. In addition, there was indirect competition from other marketing service providers, such as Internet search engines and traditional trading channels, including exhibitions, trade magazines, classified advertisements, and outdoor advertising.

As Alibaba.com served mostly Chinese SMEs, it was also captive to the same problems that impeded offline commerce, ranging from China's credit and foreign exchange controls to the deficient national distribution network. Many procedures involved in a successful business deal, such as financing and shipping, were simply beyond Alibaba.com's scope. Alibaba.com also faced other issues with online commerce, such as fears about fraud, privacy, and trust that discouraged businesses from adopting the Internet as a medium of commerce.

Internally, Alibaba.com's executives regarded their charismatic and visionary founder and chairman Jack Ma as the company's cornerstone. However, Ma has indicated that his plan is to eventually exit to make room for the next generation of leadership. Despite the fact that many senior executives and potential future leaders of Alibaba.com were handpicked by Ma, questions remained over the issue of succession, especially with Ma's departure looming on the horizon.

At the end of 2007, Alibaba.com experienced a reshuffling of its senior management, with several executives going on study sabbaticals outside of China. Some industry watchers believed the move was a precursor to taking the company global by equipping its Chinese executives with international experience. Such speculation was heightened by reports that Alibaba.com had encountered difficulties in recruiting international business talent.[29]

The Way Forward

Four months into a record-breaking IPO that significantly raised both the capital and profile of the company, Alibaba.com's share price had slipped to around half of the launch value. Could investor optimism about

Alibaba.com be slipping? How could Alibaba.com best utilize the proceeds from the IPO to scale new heights in the B2B e-commerce industry and beyond?[30] Would it be able to emerge from the shadows of its totemic founder and mature into an international conglomerate? Would Alibaba.com thrive under a rising Chinese economy, or would its success only last for "One Thousand and One Nights"?

NOTES

1. R. Kwong & T. Mitchell, 2007, Alibaba shares soar on first day of trading, *Financial Times* (Asia Edition), November 7.
2. US$1 = HK$7.76425 on November 6, 2007.
3. R. Kwong & T. Mitchell, 2007, Alibaba shares soar on first day of trading, *Financial Times* (Asia Edition), November 7.
4. US$1 = RMB 7.4638 on November 6, 2007.
5. R. Kwong, 2007, SoftBank and Alibaba in Talks, *Financial Times* (Asia Edition), November 14.
6. B. Liu, 2007, US Giant eBay Loses Ground to Taobao, *China Daily*, April 17.
7. J. Macartney, 2007, Workaholic's road to fortune "like riding on a blind tiger," *The Times, London*, November 7.
8. China Internet Network Information Center, 2007, The latest statistics, http://www.cnnic.net.cn/en/index/0O/index.htm (accessed November 19, 2007).
9. CIA, 2007, *The World Fact Book*, https://www.cia.gov/library/publications/the-world-factbook/rankorder/2153rank.html (accessed November 19, 2007).
10. China Internet Network Information Center, 2007, The 20th CNNIC statistical survey report on the Internet development in China, http://www.cnnic.net.cn/download/2007/20thCNNICreport-en.pdf (accessed November 19, 2007).
11. China Internet Network Information Center, 2007, The 20th CNNIC statistical survey report on the Internet development in China, http://www.cnnic.net.cn/download/2007/20thCNNICreport-en.pdf (accessed November 19, 2007).
12. China Internet Network Information Center, 2007, The 20th CNNIC statistical survey report on the Internet development in China, http://www.cnnic.net.cn/download/2007/20thCNNICreport-en.pdf (accessed November 19, 2007).
13. iResearch Inc., 18 June 2007, China's Online Shopping Market Worth Rmb 10.8 Billion in Q1 of 2007, http://www.iresearchgroup.com.cn/html/Consulting/Online_Shopping/DetailNews_id_65929.html (accessed 20 November 2007).
14. iResearch Inc., 2007, China's B2B e-commerce market reached RMB 489.1 billion in Q2 of 2007, http://www.iresearchgroup.com.cn/html/consulting/B2B/DetailNews_id_72299.html, November 5 (accessed November 20, 2007).
15. National Statistics Bureau of China, 2006, *China Statistical Yearbook*, Chapter 14–1.
16. iResearch Inc., 2007, China SME number to reach 50 million in 2012, http://www.iresearchgroup.com.cn/Consulting/others/DetailNews.asp?id=65361, June 6 (accessed November 22, 2007).
17. iResearch Inc., 2007, B2B e-commerce should start with interest of SMEs, http://www.iresearchgroup.com.cn/html/Consulting/B2B/DetailNews_id_67225.html, July 12 (accessed November 22, 2007).
18. Alibaba.com, 2007 Global Offering Prospectus, 74–75.
19. R. Fannin, 2008, How I did it—Jack Ma, Alibaba.com, *Inc.*, 30(1): 105.
20. C. Chandler, 2007, China's Web king, *Fortune*, December 10, 172.
21. iResearch Inc., 2007, Alibaba IPO Financial Research Report, http://www.iresearchgroup.com.cn/html/Consulting/B2B/Free_classi_id_1076.html, November 5 (accessed December 11, 2007).
22. Alibaba.com, 2007, Global Offering Prospectus, 102.
23. Alibaba.com, 2007, Global Offering Prospectus, 24.
24. Alexa.com, 2008, Browse: E-Commerce, http://www.alexa.com/browse?&CategoryID=298214; Alexa.com, 2008, Browse: International business and trade, http://www.alexa.com/browse?&CategoryID=42647 (accessed January 2, 2008).
25. Alibaba. com, 2007, Global Offering Prospectus, 80.
26. Global Sources, 2007, Investor Relations Factsheet, http://www.corporate.globalsources.com/IRS/IRFACT.HTM (accessed January 22, 2008).
27. Global Sources, 2006, Annual Report, 24–25.
28. Global Sources, 2007, Investor Relations Factsheet, http://www.corporate.globalsources.Com/IRS/IRFACT.HTM (accessed January 22, 2008).
29. S. So, 2008, Alibaba reshuffle a precursor to global expansion, *South China Morning Post*, January 29.
30. Alibaba.com stated its intention to allocate the net proceeds from the IPO as follows: 60 percent for strategic acquisitions and business development initiatives, 20 percent to increase the existing businesses both in China and internationally, 10 percent to purchase computer equipment and development of new technologies, and 10 percent to fund working capital and for general corporate purposes. Source: Alibaba.com, 2007, Global Offering Prospectus, 130.

Kazi Ahmed, Phillip Feller, Tara Ferrin, Jeffrey Fletcher,
Fidel Rodriguez, Juliet Taylor, Robin Chapman

Arizona State University

"Our purpose is to pioneer new communities around the world built on commerce, sustained by trust and inspired by opportunity."[1]

Introduction

John Donahoe took over as president and CEO of eBay Inc. in March 2008, during an unfavorable time for the company.[2] Since its inception in 1995, eBay has experienced revenue and earnings growth year after year, but the growth rate has slowed since 2006. For the first time, eBay's revenues fell from the previous year, down by 7 percent in the fourth quarter of 2008.[3] Although eBay is still the industry leader for online retailing with 17 percent market share, it has lost market share to innovative key competitors such as Amazon, Yahoo!, and Google. The expensive acquisition of Skype (a communications software company) did not have the outcome former CEO, Meg Whitman, expected. The company's venture into China failed, and changes in seller fees have not provided the results that eBay executives had anticipated. In addition, there have been lawsuits related to counterfeit products. In March 2008, Meg Whitman stepped down as CEO and was succeeded by John Donahoe, who has to confront the current situation. In a fast-cycle market such as online retailing, how can Donahoe discover new competitive advantages and regain eBay's market share and growth rate while confronting a more complex international and legal environment? In particular, Donahoe now faces a global economic downturn, a struggling e-commerce industry, and company shares trading between $10 and $11 below their prior year price of $40.

Company Leaders and Overview

In 1995, shortly after conducting a successful online auction for a broken laser pointer costing $14.83, Pierre Omidyar realized that the Internet enabled market efficiency by allowing millions of buyers and sellers to view products and conduct transactions. This inspired him to launch AuctionWeb, an online marketplace for buyers and sellers.[4] AuctionWeb officially became eBay in 1997 and hosted more auctions per month in that year than it did in all of 1996. Within four years and with the help of Meg Whitman, eBay grew from a programmer's experiment into a major publicly traded company, trading on NASDAQ with the symbol EBAY[5] (see Exhibit 1 for more details on eBay's history).

Meg Whitman was recruited as eBay's second president and CEO in 1998 and helped bring eBay public in September of that year. At the time eBay's registered users had grown six-fold, to over 2 million, from the prior year. Under Whitman's leadership the company grew to over 200 million users globally and over $7 billion in revenue. During her tenure, Whitman helped eBay enter China, integrated globally recognized brands like PayPal and Skype into the eBay portfolio, and most notably, successfully steered the company through the dot-com bust by staying focused on its core users and core competency—online auctions. She continues to serve on eBay's board of directors.

After a 20-year career at Bain & Company, Donahoe joined eBay in February 2005 as president of eBay marketplaces, where he served for three years. Donahoe's prior executive experience made him an ideal candidate to help expand marketplaces, eBay's core business. Under his leadership eBay acquired Shopping.com, StubHub, Gumtree, and LoQUo, giving it a strategic

The authors would like to thank Professor Robert E. Hoskisson for his support and guidance during the development of this case. This case is not intended to illustrate either effective or ineffective handling of managerial situations. The case is solely intended for class discussion.

Exhibit 1 eBay History

1995: Pierre Omidyar successfully conducted an online auction for a broken laser pointer which cost $14.83. Omidyar realized the Internet enabled market efficiency by allowing millions of buyers and sellers to view products and interact. It was this experiment that led Omidyar to found AuctionWeb, an online marketplace for buyers and sellers.

1996: AuctionWeb expanded greatly, with revenue topping which cost $10,000. In June Omidyar hired Jeff Skoll as president.

1997: AuctionWeb officially became eBay and hosted more auctions per month than it did in all of 1996.

1998: Meg Whitman joined as president and CEO and in September; eBay went public listing on NASDAQ under the symbol EBAY.

1999: eBay started its international expansion with marketplaces in the United Kingdom, Germany, and Australia.

2000: eBay became the number one e-commerce Web site, acquired Half.com to enter into the fixed price market, and continued international expansion with marketplaces in Austria, Canada, France, and Taiwan.

2001: eBay dramatically accelerated its international expansion through marketplaces in Ireland, Italy, Korea, New Zealand, Singapore, and Switzerland.

2002: eBay boosted revenues by acquiring Paypal.com, the primary payment method used on eBay.

2003: eBay expanded into Hong Kong; integrated PayPal Buyer Protection Services, protecting buyers and sellers in the eBay marketplace.

2004: eBay expanded into Malaysia and the Philippines, started strategic alliance in China, and acquired Rent.com. eBay purchased 28 percent ownership in online marketplace rival Craigslist.com for a reported $15 million.

2005: eBay diversified by acquiring Shopping.com, Skype, and foreign classified Web sites LoQUo and Gumtree while launching U.S. classified Web site Kijiji.com.

2006: Launched eBay express adding brand new fixed-price items to its marketplace, thereby further enhancing eBay as a primary shopping location.

2007: eBay acquired online ticket Web site Stubhub.com and Stumbleupon.com, which enhanced its Web presence while strategically partnering to enter India. eBay also partnered with Wal-Mart and Myspace.com to market Skype, and Northwest and Southwest Airlines to make PayPal a payment option. Major League Baseball named StubHub as its official provider of secondary tickets. In June, eBay cancelled its advertising on Google as a result of Google's push for Google Checkout as an eBay payment option.

2008: eBay announced that large-volume sellers with the highest feedback ratings will have preferential search locations and lower fees. eBay removed the option for buyers to receive negative feedback. On March 31, Meg Whitman stepped down as CEO and John Donahoe took over as president and CEO. On October 6, eBay announced a massive stream-lining process which entailed laying off 10 percent of its workforce and restructuring charges of $70 to 80 million. It acquired Bill Me Later and two Danish classified ad Web sites. In mid-2008 eBay signed a deal with Buy.com allowing some sellers to directly negotiate their seller fees, dramatically increasing its items listed, but angering many of its smaller "powersellers." On July 15, a U.S. District Court judge ruled that eBay did not bear legal responsibility for sales of counterfeit goods in its marketplace. On September 16, eBay lowered fees on fixed-cost auctions by more than 70 percent in an effort to better compete with Amazon.com while also eliminating the use of checks and money orders as payments, and shifted to PayPal as the sole payment option for most auctions.

Sources: 2008, eBay history, http://www.ebay.com, November 3; J. Swartz, 2008, eBay to lay off 1,600 employees, cites economy, *USA Today*, October 7, 2B; 2008, eBay 2007 Form 10-K, http://www.ebay.com, November 25, 51; 2008, eBay major direct shareholders, http://finance.yahoo.com, November 26; B. Stone, 2008, Buy.com deal with eBay angers sellers, *New York Times*, July 14, 1; C. Wolf, 2008, eBay cuts fixed-price sales fees by 70%, *Washington Post*, August 21, D03; J. Schofield, 2008, Technology, *The Guardian*, February 21, 3; J. Swartz, 2008, Listings down 13% in boycott of eBay, *USA Today*, February 28, 3B; D. Rushe, 2008, Silicon Valley culture clash as eBay sues Craigslist, *The Times (London)*, April 27, B9; 2008, Judge rules for eBay over fake Tiffany jewelry sales, *International Herald Tribune*, July 15, F12; 2008, Google cancels 'Freedom' party to appease eBay, http://www.techweb.com, June 14; 2008, eBay Fact Sheet, http://www.ebay.com, November 28; 2008, eCommerce marketsize and trends, www.goecart.com/ecommerce_solutions_facts.asp, November 30; 2008, World's most valuable general retailers, http://galenet.galegroup.com. November 30.

presence in the growing online comparison shopping industry, ticket sales, and classifieds. At the time of his transition to CEO, eBay's market share was declining and it had failed to gain in its number of unique visitors. In an attempt to reinvigorate growth, Donahoe shifted eBay's emphasis closer to other competitors by moving from auctions to fixed price listing, which has been the profit engine for Wal-Mart.com, Amazon.com, and Yahoo.com. He also streamlined the organization with a 10 percent workforce reduction and the acquisition of Bill Me Later, a transaction-based credit business with a total payment volume of over $1 billion, as a complementary payment method to PayPal.

Consisting of over 88 million active users in 39 global markets (see Exhibit 2 for eBay marketplace locations), eBay offers anyone the opportunity to be an entrepreneur.[6] The company's marketplace segment operates online auctions, classified ad sites, and other sites where people can conduct commercial transactions. Unlike other e-commerce companies, eBay does not operate the online equivalent of a store; it is more like an online mall or flea market. Its payment segment provides ways for individuals to transfer money to complete an e-commerce transaction. Its third segment, communications, offers technology that enables voice and video communications between computers, and from a computer to an ordinary telephone.[7]

The e-commerce industry is attractive because it is relatively simple to enter. Most of the major players in the industry, including Yahoo!, Google, and eBay, began as small entrepreneurial ventures with little more than an Internet connection and lines of code. Despite relatively low entry barriers, growth is difficult due to strong industry rivalry.

Competitors

Amazon.com Inc.

Amazon.com Inc. (Amazon) was founded in 1994 as an online bookstore. Over the years it expanded to include items ranging from books and CDs to clothing and electronics. This expansion occurred through partnerships with companies including Toys "R" Us, AOL, and Hoover's.[8] Amazon sells other companies' products on its Web site and uses its distribution network to ensure prompt and accurate delivery. After a relatively unsuccessful attempt to add an auction component, Amazon created the Amazon marketplace, which allows sellers to place used items on the site, featuring them alongside identical new items sold by Amazon.[9]

Amazon aims to be the low-cost leader in the e-commerce industry. In order to continue attracting new customers, Amazon continues to add innovative

Exhibit 2 Locations of eBay Marketplaces

Argentina	Malaysia
Australia	Mexico
Austria	Netherlands
Belgium	New Zealand
Brazil	Panama
Canada	Peru
Chile	Philippines
China	Poland
Colombia	Switzerland
Costa Rica	Singapore
Dominican Republic	Sweden
Ecuador	Taiwan
France	Thailand
Germany	Turkey
Hong Kong	United Kingdom
India	United States
Ireland	Uruguay
Italy	Venezuela
Korea	Vietnam

Source: 2008, eBay Web site, http://www.ebay.com.

value-added services such as "frustration-free packaging"—which eliminates difficult-to-open product containers—and the ability for customers to pay with installment payment plans.[10] Amazon is also attempting to vertically integrate as a supplier of kitchenware through its new division, Pinzon.

In 2008, even though third-quarter profit was up 48 percent, Amazon reduced fourth-quarter projections, citing expectations, along with the rest of the retail sector, for a bleak holiday season.[11]

Yahoo! Inc.

Originally known primarily as a search engine, Yahoo! Inc. ventured into the e-commerce industry in 1998 with the purchase of Viaweb. In addition to e-commerce services, Yahoo! products include advertising, e-mail, news and information, photo sharing, and Internet browser toolbars and add-ons.[12] Yahoo! has a presence in more than 20 countries. It appeals to advertisers by creating a Web site that users go to for all of their needs, thereby creating the most exposure for its ads.[13]

While the company currently operates a Yahoo! Shopping site, it discontinued its auction site in the United States and Canada in June 2007. However, Yahoo! still runs auction Web sites in Hong Kong, Singapore, and Taiwan.[14]

In recent years, Yahoo! was involved in a takeover bid by Microsoft. The software giant saw Yahoo! as a way to compete with Google for advertising dollars. After a friendly acquisition was rejected, Microsoft attempted and failed at an unsolicited takeover. Investors have criticized Yahoo!'s board for not dealing more effectively with Microsoft and for not acting in their interest.[15] Although Microsoft is reportedly no longer interested in a full takeover, it may still try to purchase the Yahoo! search engine segment.[16]

Google, Inc.

Google Inc. (Google) is a search engine site that was founded in 1998. It uses proprietary software to "understand exactly what you mean and give back exactly what you want" when searching on the Internet.[17] While Google continually adds applications, such as e-mail and file sharing, 70 percent of its resources are directed toward improving its search engine capabilities. This builds on Google's dominance in this industry, which is derived from its popularity as a search engine. Google also has a strong international presence, with its site available in 116 languages.[18]

From an e-commerce perspective, Google Product Search is an application that will search for items available for purchase on the Internet and display a side-by-side comparison. Google does not have an auction site available, although sellers do have the option of setting a negotiable price for their products. In order to compete with eBay's financial service segment, PayPal, Google launched Google Checkout in 2006 and began charging for its use in February of 2008.[19]

Craigslist

A successful new entrant in the e-commerce industry is Craigslist. A private company, Craigslist began in San Francisco as a way for local residents to list events and classified ads. Craigslist differentiates itself by not charging to list or sell products on its Web site.

All revenue comes from fees for job postings and brokered apartment listings in selected cities such as New York. Craigslist keeps its overhead low in many ways, such as by continuing to operate out of a house instead of an office building and by having a staff of only 25 employees.[20] While confirmed financials are not available, some experts estimate the value of Craigslist to be near $5 billion.[21] As part of eBay's growth and acquisition strategy it has *acquired* a portion, roughly 28 percent, of Craigslist (see Exhibit 3 and Exhibit 4 for competitors' financial data).

Acquisitions

eBay's revenue growth has come largely through acquisitions. The acquisitions have also allowed it to increase its geographic reach, move into related businesses such as online payments, and obtain technology that will strengthen its product differentiation.[22] eBay has completed many acquisitions, and some of the more noteworthy ones are discussed here.

Half.com was one of eBay's first acquisitions and allowed eBay to enter the fixed price marketplace. It was acquired in 2000 for $312.8 million. Half.com allows eBay users to sell used books, games, CDs, and DVDs at fixed prices. Sellers are paid directly by Half.com and eBay operates the Half.com Web site separately from eBay.com but allows eBay.com user profiles to be shared between the Web sites.

In 2002 eBay purchased PayPal for $1.5 billion, thereby enabling sellers of any size to receive online payments from a buyer's credit card or checking account. This greatly reduced the payment and shipment times and provided another source of revenue for eBay. PayPal's transaction fee for transactions less than $3,000 is 2.9 percent of the amount transferred.[23] Revenues for PayPal in 2008 were $2.4 billion, making up 28 percent of eBay's total revenue.[24] In September 2008, eBay announced that PayPal was the sole payment option for a majority of its marketplace listings.[25]

In 2004 eBay acquired Shopping.com, Rent.com, and 28 percent ownership of Craigslist. It purchased Shopping.com for $620 million. Shopping.com allows people to search for products and compare prices (similar to Google's product search formerly known as Froogle). This acquisition gave eBay a new channel for buyers and sellers to interact and a new medium for ad revenue.[26]

eBay acquired Rent.com for $415 million. Rent.com joins landlords with tenants online, charging property owners for each lease produced.[27] The acquisition of Rent.com gave eBay entry into the online classifieds market, while increasing revenue streams and online exposure.

Exhibit 3 Key Competitor Financials

	eBay	Google	Amazon	Yahoo!	Overstock	Craigslist
Annual Sales (in Billions)	8.69	20.92	18.14	7.32	0.873	N/A
Employees	15,500	16,805	17,000	14,300	844	25
Market Value (in Billions)	6.57	86.99	17.84	13.87	0.166	N/A
Total Cash (in Billions)	3.64	14.41	2.32	3.21	0.07	N/A
Beta	1.54	1.57	1.84	1.2	2.54	N/A
Gross Profit Margin (in Billions)	5.91	9.94	3.35	4.13	0.124	N/A
EBITDA (in Billions)	2.93	7.62	1.06	1.29	0.001	N/A
Net Income (in Billions)	1.94	5.05	0.627	0.933	−0.02	N/A
Return on Equity	18.0%	20.8%	38.1%	8.94%	−148%	N/A
Return on Assets	9.7%	14.4%	8.8%	2.51%	−9.03%	N/A
Total Debt/Equity	N/A	N/A	0.172	0.005	N/A	N/A
Market Capitalization (in Billions)	16.34	80.99	18.23	14.16	0.16	N/A

Sources: 2008, Yahoo! Finance, http://finance.yahoo.com, November 24; 2008, Craigslist Fact Sheet, http://www.craigslist.org/about/factsheet, November 24

eBay acquired its partial ownership of Craigslist for an undisclosed amount. eBay's relationship with Craigslist has always been somewhat icy. eBay purchased its shares from an owner that went against the other stockholders' wishes to not sell to a public company. Craigslist alleges that eBay placed a variety of excessive demands on it, such as giving eBay blocking rights on all forms of corporate transactions. In 2008 eBay accused Craigslist of diluting eBay's ownership interest by more than 10 percent; Craigslist countersued a month later accusing eBay of unlawful competition and copyright infringement because it launched the international classified-ad site Kijiji.[28] These lawsuits are yet to be resolved.

eBay acquired Skype in 2005 for $2.6 billion. Skype is an Internet phone provider, allowing users to make calls to almost every country with their computers using Voice Over Internet Protocol (VOIP).[29] eBay's plan for Skype was to integrate it to allow buyers and sellers to communicate prior to transactions.[30] Skype is a free service if both parties are using Skype, but it charges non-Skype users for in-and-out calls.[31] The number of Skype users has increased from 57 million in 2005 to 400 million in 2008.[32] In 2007, eBay declared a $1.4 billion asset impairment for Skype, meaning that either eBay overpaid for Skype or that the strategic integration of Skype was not going as planned. Thus, to maximize Skype's potential, eBay has announced that it plans to make Skype a stand-alone business and will conduct an initial public offering in the first half of 2010.[33]

eBay acquired Stubhub.com in 2007 for $310 million. Stubhub.com is a secondary ticket marketplace that integrates guaranteed fulfillment and shipment using FedEx.[34] Stubhub partners with American Express for concert tickets and over 60 teams for sporting events.[35] In 2007 Stubhub was named the official secondary market for tickets by Major League Baseball.[36] Stubhub features a season-ticketholder option, encouraging customer loyalty, and an easy method for season ticketholders to re-sell tickets.[37] eBay operates Stubhub.com independently from eBay.com.

eBay's purchase of Fraud Sciences Ltd. for $169 million in 2008 adds to its technology portfolio. eBay has long operated on the notion that trust is the key to its success, and it has announced plans to improve the level of trust that it provides. Fraud Sciences has developed ways to detect fraudulent purchases and provides eBay with the technology that it needs but lacks the capability to develop.

Exhibit 4 Historical Financial Overview of eBay and its Competitors

eBay.com	2003	2004	2005	2006	2007	2008 Q1	2008 Q2	2008 Q3
Net Revenues	$2,165,096	$3,271,309	$4,552,401	$5,969,741	$7,672,329	$2,192,223	$2,195,661	$2,117,531
Cost of Net Revenues	416,058	614,415	818,104	1,256,792	1,762,972	525,412	562,103	560,963
Net Income (Loss)	441,771	778,223	1,082,043	1,125,639	348,251	459,718	460,345	492,219
Google.com	**2003**	**2004**	**2005**	**2006**	**2007**	**2008 Q1**	**2008 Q2**	**2008 Q3**
Net Revenues	$1,465,934	$3,189,223	$6,138,560	$10,604,917	$16,593,986	$5,186,043	$5,367,212	$5,541,391
Cost of Net Revenues	1,123,470	2,549,031	4,121,282	7,054,921	11,509,586	3,639,808	3,789,247	2,173,390
Net Income (Loss)	105,648	399,119	1,465,397	3,077,446	4,203,720	1,307,086	1,247,391	1,289,939
Amazon.com	**2003**	**2004**	**2005**	**2006**	**2007**	**2008 Q1**	**2008 Q2**	**2008 Q3**
Net Revenues	$5,264,000	$6,921,000	$8,490,000	$10,711,000	$14,835,000	$4,135,000	$4,063,000	$4,265,000
Cost of Net Revenues	4,007,000	5,319,000	6,451,000	8,255,000	11,482,000	3,179,000	3,096,000	3,266,000
Net Income (Loss)	35,000	588,000	359,000	190,000	476,000	143,000	158,000	119,000
Yahoo.com	**2003**	**2004**	**2005**	**2006**	**2007**	**2008 Q1**	**2008 Q2**	**2008 Q3**
Net Revenues	$1,625,097	$5,257,668	$6,425,679	$6,969,274	$6,969,274	$1,817,602	$1,798,085	$1,786,426
Cost of Net Revenues	358,103	2,096,201	2,675,723	2,675,723	2,838,758	755,083	765,911	772,227
Net Income (Loss)	237,879	1,896,230	751,391	660,000	660,000	542,163	131,215	54,348
Overstock.com	**2003**	**2004**	**2005**	**2006**	**2007**	**2008 Q1**	**2008 Q2**	**2008 Q3**
Net Revenues	$234,603	$490,621	$794,975	$780,137	$765,902	$202,814	$188,836	$186,855
Cost of Net Revenues	209,320	424,183	678,502	690,333	641,352	168,843	155,627	154,736
Net Income (Loss)	(11,981)	(4,414)	(25,212)	(106,762)	(48,036)	(4,724)	(7,359)	(1,589)

Sources: 2008, http://www.ebay.com; http://www.google.com; http://www.yahoo.com; http://finance.yahoo.com; http://www.overstock.com; http://www.amazon.com

Also, eBay has expanded into Europe and Asia through acquisitions. It increased its auction reach with Alando in Germany, iBazar in France, Tradera in Sweden, Internet Auction in South Korea, and Baazee in India. eBay incorporated international classified ad Web sites into its portfolio with purchases of Loquo in Spain, Gumtree in the United Kingdom, Marktplaats in the Netherlands, and Den Bla Avis in Denmark. Each international acquisition allows eBay to expand and diversify its revenue base by purchasing established Web sites that the local culture understands.[38] This is an extremely important element when developing any sort of presence in a foreign country as eBay learned through its experience in China (discussed in the Customer Demographics and International Experience subsection).

Alliances

In addition to acquisitions, eBay uses alliances with small entrepreneurs and large companies to increase revenues and enhance the number of items available in the marketplace.

In 2004, eBay established a certified provider program consisting of exams, references, and an annual fee.[39] Partners provide services and products that sellers might need and eBay itself does not wish to offer, such as inventory management software, outbound logistics, or a full consignment business.[40] This helps eBay to attract sellers that might not otherwise use its services, or who wish to conduct a high number of transactions but lack expertise in certain areas. Having these services and products available helps sellers move more product than they would otherwise.[41] Activia is one of the best-known certified companies, providing marketplace listing tools to sellers of multiple items.[42] This alliance allows entrepreneurs to use the eBay name to grow their business while providing eBay fee revenue.

In 2006, eBay aligned with Yahoo! in a marketing alliance to promote revenue growth for both companies. Under the alliance Yahoo! became the exclusive advertising provider on eBay, the companies have a co-branded toolbar, and PayPal became Yahoo!'s preferred payment provider.[43] eBay also aligned with Google in 2006, making Google the primary advertiser on eBay's Web sites outside of the United States.[44] Google has sought to integrate Skype into the alliance as a method to further sales from Web advertising.

In 2007, eBay aligned with Northwest and Southwest Airlines to enable PayPal as a payment option, and with Wal-Mart and Myspace.com to promote the growth of Skype.[45] The alliance with Wal-Mart will allow eBay to sell Skype phone equipment in 1,800 retail locations.[46] These alliances help expand the brand name of both PayPal and Skype while also increasing revenue for eBay.

Although initially many smaller sellers were angered by eBay's 2008 alliance with Buy.com because Buy.com does not pay listing fees and its volume, free shipping, and ability to take returns hurt smaller sellers, this alliance is one of the largest potential revenue generators for eBay. Buy.com is a middle-of-the-market tool that links retailers with buyers, and it immediately added five million fixed-price listings to the eBay marketplace.[47] eBay executives have responded to the objections about its alliance with Buy.com by stating, "eBay is aggressively using price as a lever to improve the value and selection on eBay.com. Consistent with our goals, we have entered into a partnership with Buy.com to bring their new-in-season merchandise onto eBay.com. We expect to learn a great deal from this partnership and we will build upon the results."[48]

It appears that eBay will continue to use partnerships as a large part of its growth strategy. Alliances with online competitors such as Yahoo! have allowed online exposure growth, and certified provider programs have given eBay the opportunity to fill the gaps that they are unable or unwilling to fill.

eBay also seeks growth through internal innovation. Product development accounts for almost 18 percent of the company's operating expenses.

Internal Innovation

eBay's early innovations include My eBay, the feedback forum, and final value fees.[49] My eBay is a personal account on eBay that allows users to track their buying and selling activity, send and receive e-mail, update personal information, and view feedback reports. The feedback forum is intended to form trust between buyers and sellers. Each eBay member has a feedback profile that consists of three main elements: the feedback score, the feedback percentage, and the feedback reports. The feedback score is a rating of a member's trade history—the number of good reports about a member minus the number of bad reports. The feedback percentage is the percentage of users that have reported a positive feedback experience with a seller in a given year. The feedback report displays both positive and negative reports from buyers and sellers who have traded with a member and includes information about each transaction. The final value fees are the portion that eBay takes when an item sells (or ends with a winning bid). For items less than $25, the final value fee is 8.75 percent; for items between $25 and $1,000, the final value fee is 8.75 percent of the initial $25 plus 3.5 percent of the remaining value; for items over $1,000, the final value fee is 8.75 percent of the initial $25 plus 3.5 percent of the initial $25 to $1,000 plus 1.5 percent of the remaining value.

In 2005, eBay unveiled Kijiji.com, an online classified Web site resembling Craigslist. By 2008, Kijiji attracted five million unique monthly visitors and was available in over 1,000 cities across the globe.[50] In 2006, eBay launched eBay Express in the United States, the United Kingdom, and Germany, providing buyers with the ability to buy multiple items, much like Amazon .com. However, due to feedback from both buyers and sellers, eBay closed eBay Express in all three markets in 2008 to focus more on its main eBay site.[51] David Hsu, a management professor at Wharton describes eBay's internal innovation as, "a poor job of identifying synergistic opportunities . . . eBay's research group has not been able to drive much growth by internal innovation. … [eBay] has to get that spark the company had in the early days."[52]

Economic Downturn

When it makes its acquisition, alliance, and innovation decisions, eBay first considers the environmental factors that may influence its success. The increasing unemployment rate and the mortgage crisis have also contributed to a decline in disposable income. This may increase the number of sellers on eBay as those who are unemployed seek ways to make extra money, but fewer people are buying, and those who are demand low prices.[53] Thus, in September 2008 eBay lowered fees on fixed-cost sales by more than 70 percent in an effort to better compete with Amazon.com;[54] and starting in June 2009 infrequent sellers will be able to offer up to five items every 30 days without paying a listing fee.[55]

Customer Demographics and International Experience

An aging population poses potential challenges. Currently, 50 percent of eBay buyers are over the age of 45, 53 percent are male, and 72 percent earn more than $50,000 per year; but as baby boomers age, the number of consumers in this age group will decline.[56]

Additionally, significant shifts in ethnic composition are occurring in the United States. For example, the Hispanic population is growing and is expected to triple over the next 40 years. This will likely alter the type of products desired for purchase on eBay.[57] Furthermore, as eBay continues to pursue international expansion, the products in demand will change and it will need to broaden its understanding of business practices and levels of service that are required to attract consumers in specific countries.

eBay did not succeed in its first attempt to establish a presence in China, most likely because it lacked insight into the Chinese culture. eBay entered China in 2002 by purchasing a third of China's principal online auction site, Eachnet.com. In 2003, eBay purchased and became the sole owner of Eachnet.com, but by 2005 it had lost significant market share to Taobao, the consumer auction segment of China's largest ecommerce company.[58] eBay failed to understand that its popularity in the United States would not automatically make it successful in China. Some of the complaints were that eBay did not provide phone service or allow bartering, and it did not react quickly enough when Taobao entered the market without charging user fees.[59] Despite its failure with Eachnet.com, eBay is in China for the long haul, as Whitman said, "market leadership in China will be a defining characteristic of leadership globally," and failure to establish itself there would be an "astronomical" setback for the company as a whole.[60] Therefore in 2007 it established a partnership with a Beijing-based Internet company, Tom Online Inc., taking a 49 percent stake in the company and possessing administration rights. This allows eBay to have strong local management that understands the culture and consumer desires. Tom eBay has done much to win the trust of Chinese consumers such as using an escrow service to hold payments until the buyer confirms satisfaction with the product. Whitman stated, "Whatever we do elsewhere to assure trust and safety, in China we have to do more."[61] eBay has had some success in China with Skype; Skype has grown faster in China than anywhere else.[62]

Technology and Competitive Challenges

Various technological trends may pose challenges for eBay. Staying aware of the trends and responding quickly is essential—as eBay learned from its misfortune in Japan. eBay lost significant market share to Yahoo! and pulled out of Japan in 2002 mostly due to failing to be up to date with the technology that Japanese users expected to be available on an auction site.[63] Another possible issue is that Skype's technology may threaten eBay's profitability by giving buyers and sellers an opportunity to conduct the transaction without using eBay and thereby circumventing eBay's fees.

Another aspect of technology that poses a challenge is that retailers have put great effort into improving their Web sites to make online shopping easier for consumers. Stores such as Best Buy, Nordstrom, Target, and Wal-Mart carry items in four out of five of eBay's top volume categories (electronics, computers, clothing/accessories, and home/garden). Consumers may prefer these retailers over eBay because they have greater confidence in their ability to return items and to have some sort of recourse if a purchased item is never received or is broken upon receipt. However, eBay was founded on its judicious use of technology and it has recently developed some technology to help it limit the number of legal proceedings related to counterfeit products.

Legal Issues

Fashion fakes constitute a $600 billion industry worldwide[64] and despite eBay's efforts to crack down on counterfeit merchandise, some eBay users continue to sell it. This has led to lawsuits against eBay from companies such as Rolex, Tiffany & Co., Hermès, Louis Vuitton, and L'Oreal. Lawsuit results have been mixed. Rolex first instigated a trial against eBay in 2001. The original ruling was overturned by a German court in 2007 because the judge believed that eBay could not be held liable for damages, but it should monitor its site to prevent fakes from being sold. Again in early 2009 Rolex brought a case against eBay, but the judge ruled in favor of eBay.[65] In the case against Tiffany & Co. in July 2008, a U.S. District Court judge ruled that eBay did not bear legal responsibility for sales of counterfeit goods in its marketplace and that "it is the trademark owner's burden to police its mark."[66] However eBay was not as fortunate in the French courts in the cases against Hermès and Louis Vuitton. It was ordered to pay Hermès $30,000 in damages because "by failing to act within [its] powers to prevent reprehensible use of the site, both the seller and eBay committed acts of counterfeiting;"[67] eBay was also instructed to compensate Louis Vuitton $63 million for "culpable negligence," and an additional $20 million in damages for unauthorized sales of its perfume.[68] Most recently, though, courts in Paris have ruled in favor of eBay in a case against L'Oreal, stating that "preventing the sale of counterfeit goods on the eBay platform encounters major difficulties when it comes to perfumes and cosmetics."[69]

eBay is dedicated to thwarting the sale of counterfeit products on its site. It has developed a filter program that detects offerings that blatantly violate trademark rights, established a team that works closely with law enforcement agencies, and even launched an anti-counterfeit campaign that aimed to educate buyers on how to avoid counterfeit products.

Tax law also may present challenges for eBay. Currently, if a consumer orders merchandise from a company that does not operate in his or her state of residence, no sales tax is paid on the item.[70] However, there is a possibility that legislation will pass requiring Internet purchases to be taxed. The IRS has also proposed that certain types of Internet companies, including eBay, should be required to collect and report individuals' earnings, allowing the IRS to ensure income taxes are being paid.[71] If this legislation passes, eBay users may move their business to sites that are not required to adhere to this policy.

To this point, eBay has been able to successfully navigate the company through environmental obstacles; it will need to continue to do so in order to remain profitable.

Financial Results

eBay derives most of its income from transaction costs associated with online sales. The product category that brings in the most revenue for eBay is vehicles (see Exhibit 5). Revenues from its businesses outside of the main eBay auction marketplaces have grown to 44 percent of total revenue. In 2008, of its $8.5 billion total net revenues, PayPal made up $2.3 billion (27 percent), Skype made up $551 million (6 percent), and marketplace transactions made up $5.6 billion (66 percent); 46 percent came from the United States, and 54 percent came from international sources.[72] In recent years, more and more of eBay's revenue is generated from international operations (see Exhibit 6).

In 2008 eBay was ranked second among the world's most valuable retail Web sites, only trailing Amazon in unique visitors and year-over-year growth.[73] In annual sales, eBay trails Google ($20.92 billion) and Amazon ($18.14 billion), beating Yahoo! ($7.32 billion) and Overstock ($.873 billion) (see Exhibits 3 and 4). Craigslist is not a public company and thus its sales data is not public information.

Marketplace revenue depends on gross merchandise volume (GMV). eBay breaks down GMV into the number of listings multiplied by the conversion rate (the percentage of items that sold) multiplied by the average sale price.[74] New-listing and GMV growth in 2008 came primarily from the international marketplace (see Exhibit 6). In 2008 eBay marketplaces had 86.3 million active users and 140 million listings at any given time.[75] Vehicles, parts, and accessories made up 31.5 percent of the top 16 GMV categories for the years 2006–2008, while consumer electronics and computers composed 16.4 percent, clothing and accessories was 8.5 percent, and home and garden was 6.8 percent (see Exhibit 5). eBay's expansion into fixed-price sales is positive, as this area increased to 45 percent of total GMV in 2008.[76] Regardless of the positive financial results that eBay

Exhibit 5 eBay Categories and Trends

	$1 billion categories trend data (in millions)								
	30-Sep-06	31-Dec-06	31-Mar-07	30-Jun-07	30-Sep-07	31-Dec-07	31-Mar-08	30-Jun-08	30-Sep-08
Vehicles	12,376	11,552	11,832	13,536	13,328	12,424	12,672	13,532	11,688
Parts and Accessories	3,764	4,172	4,680	5,016	4,596	4,768	5,348	5,392	4,620
Consumer Electronics	3,876	5,872	4,880	4,608	4,620	6,788	5,796	5,200	4,992
Computers	3,600	3,996	4,052	3,688	3,688	4,132	4,248	3,656	3,500
Clothing and Accessories	3,704	4,744	4,540	4,496	4,340	5,564	5,348	5,288	4,652
Home and Garden	3,036	3,496	3,584	3,640	3,700	4,120	4,244	4,184	3,840
Collectibles	2,208	2,804	2,684	2,388	2,380	2,948	2,772	2,468	2,232
Books/Movies/Music	2,780	3,032	3,124	2,720	3,000	3,288	3,456	2,952	2,864
Sports	2,496	2,668	2,584	2,892	2,836	2,884	2,940	3,232	2,992
Business & Industrial	1,752	2,012	2,232	2,220	2,140	2,300	2,584	2,452	2,212
Toys	1,700	2,564	2,136	1,940	1,940	2,748	2,396	2,144	1,952
Jewelry & Watches	1,644	2,184	1,972	1,960	1,924	2,508	2,332	2,216	1,988
Cameras & Photo	1,404	1,636	1,524	1,548	1,504	1,752	1,672	1,672	1,508
Antiques & Art	1,012	1,304	1,352	1,248	1,164	1,484	1,508	1,364	1,096
Coins & Stamps	900	1,044	1,320	1,068	1,028	1,192	1,428	1,188	1,032
Tickets & Travel	972	916	1,088	1,336	1,772	1,980	1,496	2,012	2,260
Total	47,224	53,996	53,584	54,304	53,960	60,880	60,240	58,952	53,428
Percentage Growth	14%	14%	-1%	1%	-1%	13%	-1%	-2%	-9%

Source: 2008, eBay Annual Report, http://www.ebay.com

Exhibit 6 eBay Growth: U.S. vs. International

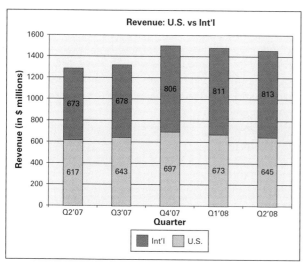

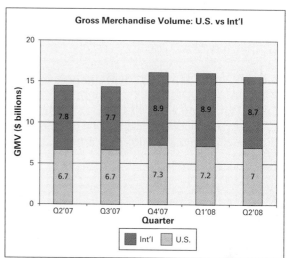

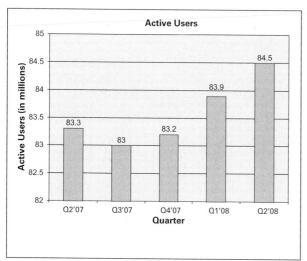

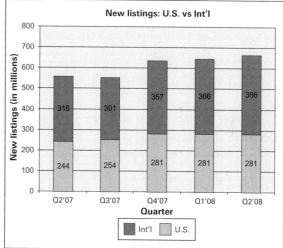

Source: 2008, Investor Relations, eBay company website, http:// www.ebay.com.

posted in 2008, there are some significant challenges for which the new CEO and other leaders must determine solutions.

Overview of Challenges

eBay is currently in a fast-cycle market, causing it to experience extreme external competitive pressure. This competitive pressure is from both dominant Internet companies such as Amazon, Yahoo!, and Google as well as small private companies such as Craigslist. eBay faces the challenge of differentiating itself from these competitors, while at the same time striving to attract

buyers and increasing revenues on each transaction. In an effort to attract more listings and higher revenues, eBay's alliance with Buy.com has sparked boycotts and a loss of some its core customers. eBay needs to find a balance between satisfying buyers and creating economically beneficial cost structures for large strategic alliance partners.

Given the current budget deficits of many states, they may push to overturn the 1992 Supreme Court ruling that liberated mail-order merchants from having to collect sales tax from a consumer in a state in which they do not have a physical presence. This would result in eBay having to ensure that sales tax is collected on each transaction, leading to increased costs and more book-keeping for eBay.[77]

Counterfeit merchandise affects eBay's image as a trustworthy auction site and poses the threat of more time and money spent in lawsuits. Current competition is fierce in the fast-cycle VOIP marketplace and potential government regulations of the VOIP industry could further affect the Skype brand. Additionally, Skype's technology is licensed from third parties and although there are contracts in place, future license renewals could increase costs or make it illogical for eBay to use this third-party software.[78]

eBay is currently at a unique period in company growth as its acquisition strategy has created a large conglomerate of companies that intertwine within the online marketplace arena, while looking for new avenues to gain market share and revenue. The e-commerce industry as a whole is in a growth-stage and competitors are gaining market share as they innovate at a faster pace than eBay. With Meg Whitman's retirement and the company's recent shift toward focusing on the fixed-price marketplace, eBay has entered a defining phase of its business.

NOTES

1. 2008, eBay: The world's online marketplace, http://pages.ebay.com/aboutebay/thecompany/companyoverview.html, December 4.
2. A. Schmidt, 2008, eBay CEO Meg Whitman to retire, MSNBC, http://www.msnbc.com, January 23.
3. R. Waters, 2008, eBay revenue to decline for first time, Financial Times, October 16; F. Ross, 2009, eBay's 4th quarter earnings—The recession? All Business, http://www.allbusiness.com, February 14.
4. 2008, eBay History, http://www.ebay.com, November 3.
5. Ibid.
6. 2008, eBay Form 10-K, http://www.ebay.com.
7. 2008, eBay Form 10-K, http://www.ebay.com.
8. 2008, Hoover's Company Records: Amazon.com Inc., November 1.
9. T. Wolverton, 2000, Amazon, Sotheby's closing jointly operated auction site, Cnet News, http://news.cnet.com, October 10.
10. 2008, Amazon announces beginning of multi-year frustration-free packaging initiative, Forbes, http://www.forbes.com, November 3.
11. B. Stone, 2008, Profit is up at Amazon, but outlook is reduced, New York Times, October 23, B3.
12. 2008, Hoover's Company Records: Yahoo! Inc., November 25.
13. 2008, 2007 Yahoo! Inc. Form 10K, http://www.yahoo.com, February 27.
14. 2007, Yahoo! to close North American auction site, MSNBC, http://www.msnbc.msn.com, May 9.
15. A. Sorkin & S. Lohr, 2008, Pursuing Yahoo! again, Microsoft shows need for a Web franchise, New York Times, May 19, A1.
16. B. Stone, 2008, Now comes the hard part as Yahoo! wrestles with a question of direction, New York Times, November 18, B1.
17. 2008, Corporate information: Our philosophy, http://www.google.com, November 28.
18. Ibid.
19. 2007, Google Inc., Form 10-K, http://www.google.com.
20. 2008, craigslist fact sheet, http://www.craigslist.org, November 16.
21. J. Fine, 2008, Can Craigslist stay oddball? BusinessWeek, May 19, 75.
22. 2008, The Portfolio Story, http://ebayinkblog.com/wp-content/uploads/ThePortfolioStory_24Oct08.pdf, October.
23. 2008, Transaction fees domestic transactions, PayPal company Web site, http://www.paypal.com, December 3.
24. 2008, eBay 2007 Form 10-K, 51.
25. C. Wolf, 2008, eBay cuts fixed-price sales fees by 70%.
26. 2008, eBay to buy Shopping.com for $620 million, http://news.cnet.com, December 3.
27. 2008, eBay to buy Rent.com for $415 million, http://news.cnet.com, December 3.
28. 2008, eBay files corporate governance suit to protect its investment in Craigslist, eBay News, http://www.news.ebay.com, April 22; 2008, Craigslist-eBay suit details icy relationship, PC Magazine, www.pcmag.com, May 13; 2008, eBay goes public with Craigslist complaint, USA Today, http://www.usatoday.com, May 1.
29. 2008, About Skype, Skype company Web site, http://www.skype.com, December 3.
30. 2008, eBay to buy Skype in $2.6bn deal, http://news.bbc.co.uk, December 3.
31. 2008, About Skype.
32. 2009, Skype available on Apple App store, About Skype, http://www.skype.com, March 31; 2008, What to do with Skype, http://news.cnet.com, December 3.
33. 2009, eBay Inc. announces plan for 2010 initial public offering of Skype, About Skype, http://www.skype.com, April 14.
34. 2008, Is Stubhub the ticket for eBay, BusinessWeek, http://www.businessweek.com, December 3.
35. 2008, About Stubhub, Stubhub company Web site, http://www.stubhub.com/, December 3.
36. 2008, eBay 2007 Form 10-K.
37. 2008, About Stubhub.
38. 2008, The portfolio story.
39. Ibid.
40. 2008, eBay certified provider program, http://www.ebay.com, November 16.
41. 2008, Inside eBay's innovation machine—case studies, CIO Insight, http://www.cioinsight.com, November 16.
42. 2008, Certified providers program.
43. 2008, Yahoo!, eBay in Web advertising pact, MSNBC, http://www.msnbc.msn.com, December 3.
44. 2008, Google and eBay form an alliance to tailor adds to every customer, http://www.guardian.co.uk, December 3.
45. 2008, eBay 2007 Form 10-K, http://www.ebay.com, November 25, 51.
46. 2008, Wal-Mart to sell Skype phone gear, MSNBC, http://www.msnbc.msn.com, December 3.
47. B. Stone, 2008, Buy.com deal with eBay angers sellers, New York Times, July 14, 1.
48. R. Smythe, 2008, eBay partners with Buy.com, http://www.ebayinkblog.com, May 3.
49. A. Hsiao, 2009, Understanding the eBay feedback system, About.com, www.ebay.about.com, May 20; 2009, Final value fees, http://www.ebay,com, May 20; 2009, Using My eBay, http://www.ebay.com, May 20.
50. 2008, About Kijiji, http://bayarea.kijiji.com, December 3.
51. 2008, About eBay express, http://www.ebay.com, December 3.
52. 2008, eBay, After Meg, Forbes, http://www.forbes.com, December 3.
53. R. Waters, 2008, Add eBay to the cart, Financial Times, http://www.ft.com, October.
54. C. Wolf, 2008, eBay cuts fixed-price sales fees by 70%, Washington Post, August 21, D03.
55. R. Metz, 2009, eBay cuts auction listing fees for casual sellers, The Boston Globe, http://www.boston.com, May 12.

56. 2008, eBay Seller Central, http://www.ebay.com, November; 2008, The changing nature of retail: Planting the seeds for sustainable growth, *Deloitte Consulting*, http://www.deloitte.com, November 18.

57. 2005, Changing demographics result in shifting consumer habits, http://www.retailforward.com, November 4.

58. K. Hafner & B. Stone, 2006, eBay is expected to close its auction site in China, *New York Times*, http://www.nytimes.com, December 19.

59. Ibid., R. Hof, 2006, eBay's China challenge, *BusinessWeek*, http://www.businessweek.com, December 19.

60. K. Hafner & B. Stone, eBay is expected to close its auction site in China; B. Powell & J. Ressner, 2005, Why eBay must win in China, *Time*, http://www.time.com, August 22.

61. V. Shannon, 2007, eBay is planning to re-enter the China auction business, *New York Times*, http://www.nytimes.com, June 22.

62. Ibid.

63. B. Powell & J. Ressner, Why eBay must win in China; 2001, How Yahoo! Japan beat eBay at its own game, *BusinessWeek*, http://www.businessweek.com, June 4.

64. A. Szustek, 2009, eBay victorious over Rolex in latest counterfeiting lawsuit, *Finding Dulcinea*, http://www.findingdulcinea.com, February 27.

65. D. Woollard, 2009, Rolex loses eBay lawsuit, http://www.luxist.com, February 26.

66. 2008, Judge rules for eBay over fake Tiffany jewelry sales, *International Herald Tribune*, July 15, F12.

67. C. Matlack, 2008, Hermes beats eBay in counterfeit case, *BusinessWeek*, http://www.businessweek.com, June 6.

68. R. Waters, 2008, eBay wins court battle with Tiffany, *Financial Times*, http://www.ft.com, July 14; R.Waters, 2008, Moment of truth for eBay on luxury goods, *Financial Times*, http://www.ft.com, June 30.

69. I. Steiner, 2009, eBay fends off L'Oreal's counterfeiting lawsuit, *Auction Bytes*, http://www.auctionbytes.com, May 13.

70. A. Broache, 2008, Tax-free Internet shopping days could be numbered, *CNET News*, http://www.cnetnews.com, April 15.

71. 2008, Internet broker tax reporting, eBay Government Relations, http://www.ebay.com, November 20.

72. 2008, eBay 2007 Form 10-K, http://investor.ebay.com/annuals.cfm, 51, November 25.

73. 2009, eBay narrows the gap, but Amazon tops in traffic again, Nielsen says, *Internet Retailer*, http://www.internetretailer.com, February 27.

74. 2008, Q3 20008 Earnings Slides, eBay company Web site, http://www.ebay.com, November 16.

75. 2008, eBay 2007 Form 10-K, http://www.ebay.com, 51.

76. 2008, eBay Fact Sheet, http://www.ebay.com, November 28.

77. 2008, Sales tax on the Internet, http://www.nolo.com, December 4.

78. 2008, eBay 2007 Form 10-K, 29.

Ryan Gust, Brandon Barth, Joey O'Donnell, Drew Forsberg, Robin Chapman

Arizona State University

Introduction

In 1992 Boeing and Airbus parent, EADS, agreed to conduct a joint study on the prospects for a superjumbo airplane. With a forecasted 5 percent annual growth in air travel, both companies saw the need for a new aircraft large enough to support this growth. However, the world will not be permitted to see what the brain trust of the two aerospace industry giants could have produced. Airbus and Boeing reached different conclusions concerning market trends, and the joint effort was called off.

The average size of aircraft grew until the late 1990s; however, this trend began to change as carriers shifted their primary focus to profits as opposed to market share. Strong competition among airlines prompted ticket prices to fall in recent years. As a result, carriers dramatically reduced costs and aggressively expanded their networks. The assumption reached by many carriers was that in order to become more flexible, a smaller aircraft must be used to reach many regional airports rather than larger aircraft that can only access hub airports in major cities.[1]

As both companies considered which options to pursue in order to satisfy the growing market, Airbus speculated that the hub-and-spoke system would prove to be the future for airlines and decided to launch the A-380 project in December 2000. Boeing's aircraft, dubbed the 787, was launched in 2005. This aircraft represents a fundamentally different vision, one anchored in the belief that the point-to-point system is the most sensible growth platform.

What is at stake for Boeing and Airbus? Boeing invested more than $8 billion in development for the 787, while Airbus went over budget, investing more than $14 billion and experienced a two-year delay in delivery to its customers. Boeing received solid orders for the midsized 787 and is determined to deliver the 787 in May 2008 as promised to avoid the problems that have plagued its competitor. Some manufacturing problems threatened to delay delivery, however, and are minimizing Boeing's margin for error.[2]

This case discusses the history of Boeing and the salient industry forces affecting the company, leading to the critical decisions faced by both competitors. The key strategic issues driving Boeing's competitive strategies are also outlined along with a discussion of strategies used to manage the competitive environment by both Boeing and Airbus, and the challenges facing both companies.

Boeing's History

William E. Boeing originally worked in the timber industry, and his knowledge of wooden structures led him to design and build an airplane, the B&W Seaplane. When the B&W was ready to fly, the test pilot was late and Mr. Boeing grew impatient, which prompted him to pilot the aircraft himself.[3] This example illustrates Mr. Boeing's level of determination, a key quality of his character, which was incorporated into his airplane manufacturing company.

Established on July 15, 1916, the company was originally called Pacific Aero Products Company. A year later Mr. Boeing changed the name to what is now the Boeing Airplane Company. Edgar Gott, William Boeing's first cousin, became president of the company in 1922.[4] Gott helped Boeing Co. obtain business contracts with the military; succeeding presidents, Philip G. Johnson and Clairmont L. Egtvedt, maintained this relationship with the government throughout WWII. Boeing became a powerhouse in large part due to its war effort, essentially because the military ordered numerous B-17 Bombers.

After the war many of the Bomber orders were canceled, so Boeing's management team tried to recover by

The authors would like to thank Professor Robert E. Hoskisson for his support and under whose direction the case was developed. The case solely provides material for class discussion. The authors do not intend to illustrate either effective or ineffective handling of a managerial situation. This case was developed with contributions from Hal Hardy and Emily Little.

diversifying its product offerings. Boeing began selling a luxurious four-engine commercial aircraft known as the Stratocruiser.[5] However, this aircraft was not the commercial success Boeing had hoped for and as a result, Boeing once again found itself at the drawing board.

William M. Allen took control of Boeing in 1945 and oversaw the building of the United States' first commercial jet airliner, the 707. The 707 had capacity for 156 passengers and helped the United States become a leader in commercial jet manufacturing. The 720 jet plane, which was faster, soon followed, but it had a shorter flying range. A demand for planes capable of flying long routes led Boeing to develop the 727.[6] This aircraft utilized one less engine than previous models and was thought to be significantly more comfortable and reliable than competitors' products.[7] Because most models are eventually discontinued to allocate resources to "new and improved models," the 727 was discontinued in 1984; however, by the beginning of 2000 almost 1,300 of these planes were still in service. Boeing achieved additional commercial success in 1967 and 1968 with the production of the 737 and 747. The 737 would become the best-selling commercial jet aircraft in history while the 747 would hold the passenger seating capacity record for 35 years. The 747 utilizes a double-decker configuration, allowing for a maximum of 524 passengers on board.[8]

In 1994, under the leadership of Frank Shrontz, Boeing developed the 777. This aircraft would actually be the first aircraft designed entirely by computer. "Throughout the design process, the airplane was 'pre-assembled' on the computer, eliminating the need for a costly, full-scale mock-up."[9] This aircraft became the longest range twin-engine aircraft in the world.

Thornton "T" Wilson became president of Boeing in 1968 and continued as CEO until 1986. Malcolm T. Stamper became president in 1972 and, in collaboration with Mr. Wilson, he led Boeing's development of the single-aisle 757 and the larger twin-aisle 767 in the wake of a new European competitor, Airbus. During these years Boeing also participated in space programs and military projects, such as the International Space Station and the development of new sophisticated missiles. Today, "Boeing is organized into two business units: Boeing Commercial Airplanes and Boeing Integrated Defense Systems," with the latter making Boeing the world's second-largest defense company.[10]

Philip M. Condit took over in 1996 but was quickly relieved of his position in 1997 because he underestimated Airbus's ability to compete with Boeing. Harry Stonecipher succeeded Condit and faced even more intense rivalry with Airbus. By 2003, Airbus had become the market leader, sending Boeing scrambling frantically to pursue new projects, such as the Sonic Cruiser. The Sonic Cruiser aimed to please customers with a faster, more comfortable ride for long-distance travel. The Cruiser would cut an hour off traditional travel time by flying at a higher elevation and a Mach speed of .98 (most aircraft fly at Mach .80).[11] When Lew Platt became board chair in December of 2003, Boeing abandoned the Sonic Cruiser project in order to focus its efforts on the 787 Dreamliner. Airlines were favoring planes that boasted fuel efficiency over those that offered faster speed. The Dreamliner, slated to fly in May 2008, is popular in the industry because of its potential fuel economy, one-piece composite fuselage sections, and eco-friendliness. It will cost slightly more than half of Airbus's complementary product, and currently has more than twice as much order-book value.[12]

Although each of Boeing's leaders sought to improve the organization during his tenure (for additional biographical information on Boeing's previous leadership, please refer to Exhibit 1), the rivalry with Boeing's key competitor is still intense.

Airbus: Boeing's Key Competitor

The industry for large commercial aircraft (LCA) is a duopoly composed of Boeing Co. and Airbus Industries. These two manufacturing giants have emerged in an unsteady industry whose fortune is based upon strategic timing and luck. Market share is overwhelmingly the most important consideration for each company when making strategic decisions. Essentially, market share determines success. Airbus, once considered a small player, swiftly emerged as an industry giant by focusing on the needs of the market, a standard product line, efficient production methods, and successful marketing ploys. Other players such as Douglas Aircraft Corporation and Lockheed Martin, who were successful and competitive corporations, fell from their positions due to failure in their demand forecast strategies and they merged with other competitors; especially significant was the merger between McDonnell Douglas and Boeing.[13]

Airplanes are grouped into families based on size, range, and technology. At the low end of the market are two single-aisle airplanes; the Boeing 737 and the Airbus A-320, which both seat about 190 people. These planes have each been extremely successful in generating sales, but fall short as revenue earners for both companies. The most profitable market segment has been the middle market, filled with the medium-sized aircraft, which seat from 200 to 300 passengers. Boeing's 757 and Airbus's A330-200 are the most popular planes in this segment. High-end jumbo airplanes fill the remaining segment of the market and are characterized by long-range flight capability, 300+ seats, and maximum use of technology. Each company attempts to develop its products to match the forecasted market demands by producing

Exhibit 1 Biographical Information on Boeing's Previous Leadership

Walter James McNerney Jr.
President, Chief Executive Officer, and Chairman of the Board of Directors of The Boeing Company, 2005–Present

McNerney received a BA from Yale University in 1971 and an MBA from Harvard in 1975. While receiving his education, Mc-Nerney played varsity baseball and hockey. McNerney started his executive career at General Electric in 1982. Over the next 19 years he held many positions including president and CEO of GE Aircraft Engines, GE Lighting, and GE Electrical Distribution and Control. He also spent time as president of GE Asia-Pacific and GE Information Services, and executive vice president of GE Capital. In 2001 McNerney joined 3M as CEO. After turning down two offers in two years, 3M CEO McNerney finally accepted the position as CEO and chairman of The Boeing Company in June of 2005. McNerney had already been a member of the board of directors at Boeing since 2001. He is the chair of the U.S.-China Business Council and serves on the World Business Council for Sustainable Development.

James A. Bell
Interim Chief Executive Officer of the Boeing Company, March 2005–June 2005; Chief Financial Officer, 2004–Present

James A. Bell received a BA in accounting from California State University. Mr. Bell started his career as an accountant at The Rockwell Company. He advanced through management at Rockwell, holding positions as senior internal auditor, accounting manager, and manager of general and cost accounting. When Rockwell's aerospace division was acquired by Boeing in 1996, Bell moved with it. At Boeing, Bell held positions as the vice president of contracts and pricing for the company's space and communications division, as well as senior vice president of finance and corporate controller. In 2004, following the firing of Michel M. Sears (due to a government contract scandal), Bell accepted the position as the chief financial officer of The Boeing Company. Bell also served as an interim CEO for a few months in 2005 between the time that Harry Stonecipher was forced to resign and James McNerney Jr. accepted the position.

Harry C. Stonecipher
President; 1997–2005; Chief Executive Officer of The Boeing Company, 2003–2005

Harry C. Stonecipher received a BS in physics from Tennessee Technological University in 1960. He began his career as a lab technician at General Motors. He then moved to GE's large engine division and worked his way up to become a vice president and then a division head. He left GE to go to Sundstrand where he became president and CEO after two years. After that he served as president and CEO of McDonnell Douglas until the merger with Boeing in 1997. At Boeing he served as the president and COO until 2003 when he filled the shoes of Philip M. Condit as CEO. In 2005, however, Stonecipher resigned at the request of the board after news of a "consensual relationship" with a female board member surfaced (violating Boeing's Code of Conduct).

Philip Murray Condit
Chief Executive Officer, 1996–2003; Chairman of the Board, 1997–2003 of The Boeing Company

Condit earned a Bachelor's degree in mechanical engineering from the University of California, Berkley; a master's degree in Aeronautical Engineering from Princeton; an MBA from the MIT Sloan School of Management; and a PhD in engineering from Science University of Tokyo. Condit started at Boeing in 1965 as an aerodynamics engineer, he then advanced to a lead engineer and soon after became a marketing manager. After a short break to earn his MBA he returned to Boeing, working through a myriad of leadership positions until he ascended to CEO in 1996 and board chair in 1997. His time as CEO and chairperson was characterized by a number of mergers and acquisitions as well as a struggle with increasing competition with Airbus. Condit was forced to resign in 2003 amidst corruption charges involving his freezing of a contract with the U.S. Air Force in 1997.

Thornton "T" A. Wilson
President, 1968–1972; Chief Executive Officer, 1969–1986; Chairman of the Board, 1972–1987; Chairman Emeritus of The Boeing Company, 1987–1993

Wilson received an aeronautical engineering degree from Iowa State University in 1943 and a master's degree in aeronautical engineering from the California Institute of Technology in 1948. Wilson begins his career with Boeing in 1943 and advanced rapidly. His first assignment of note was as project engineer on the B-52 and then was general manager of the proposal team for the Minuteman intercontinental ballistic missile program. Wilson became a vice president in 1963 and was put in charge of planning the Boeing corporate headquarters in 1964. He was named executive vice president in 1966 and president in 1968. Wilson became the CEO in 1969 and board chair in 1972.

Louis Gallois
Chief Executive Officer of Airbus, 2006–Present

Gallois graduated from both the Ecole Des Hautes Etudes Commerciales (where he received an education in economic science) and the Ecole Nationale de l'Administration. In 1972 Gallois started with the Treasury Department of the French government. During1982–1987, Gallois worked his way up at the Cabinet Office of the Ministry of Research. His appointment as the Head of Civil and Military Cabinet Office of the French Ministry of Defense took place in 1988. It was in 1989 that Gallois shifted his career from government to the private sector when be became board chair and CEO of SNECMA, an airplane engine manufacturer. He then moved to Aerospatiale, another aerospace manufacture, as board chair and CEO. Gallois was chair of the French National Railways from 1996 to 2006. In October 2006, Gallois became CEO of Airbus.

Source: Executive Biographies, Wikipedia, http://en.wikipedia.org; http://www.boeing.com.

an airplane that offers the appropriate size, range, fuel efficiency, and technology. These forecasts are based on huge uncertainties, such as what size of airplane will airlines need in order to carry an unknown amount of people to and from large hub airports or smaller regional airports. These variables make accurate short-term projections and assumptions key to long-term success in an industry that is constantly changing.[14]

Airbus became a competitive global manufacturer of LCAs with the help of "launch aid," a form of government subsidies implemented to help a company, such as Airbus, compete and survive in industries where competitive giants such as Boeing have established distribution networks and economies of scale. Airbus was able to establish a significant market share and a brand name by making airplanes that addressed the needs of the market. Airlines had been "crying" for midsized cost efficient airplanes, and Airbus answered by building the A-320. The "commonality" that the A-320 had with other Airbus airplanes was attractive to airlines because of its potential to reduce pilot and attendant training costs as well as improve airplane turnaround time.[15]

Despite Airbus's strategy, Boeing had not embraced commonality among its products because of the changes and high costs that would be incurred at its current stage. As a result, the manufacturing giant fell from its number one position. In order for Boeing to survive its newfound misfortune, it needed to make serious changes in its strategy and business processes. The first aspect considered for business-process change would be its relationships with suppliers.

Suppliers

The importance of suppliers to aircraft manufacturers has shifted with advancements in technology. Chuck Agne, a former director of supplier management for Boeing's Integrated Defense Systems, said in 2004 that Boeing's strategy was to "move up the value chain," meaning that Boeing was going to focus less on the many details and more on their core competence, integration, and assembly. As part of this strategy, Boeing consolidated its supplier list and managed relationships only with those that provide quality products with the best value. Agne said, "What we have found is, the suppliers we're sticking with are the ones who are able to move up that value chain with us."[16]

Traditionally, most manufacturers similar to Boeing completed all research and production in-house. Technological research and development is seen as a competitive advantage that must be closely guarded within the airplane production industry. Boeing's key technical expertise—such as wing technology and new lightweight materials such as composites—are considered its core competencies. Boeing traditionally believed that outsourcing these components to suppliers would give the suppliers control over manufacturing and ultimately place the supplier in control when determining its share of revenue. However, it is no longer a sensible option for Boeing to keep an entire production line in-house. Thus, a new trend emerged in the production of new aircraft, such as the 787 Dreamliner. For the first time Boeing announced it would "offload" (Boeing's term for *outsourcing*)[17] the design of it wings and parts of its fuselage to Japan, and also outsource its fuselage panel work to an Italian company. It is estimated that now 70 percent of the components of a given airplane are outsourced. As such, Boeing is responsible for plane assembly, assuming the title of "Systems Integrator."[18]

Boeing also sought strategic partnerships globally in an effort to reduce costs and perhaps generate sales. By outsourcing to countries such as China and India, Boeing entered what is called an "offset agreement," such that they obtain aircraft sales in return for manufacturing work. This arrangement allowed Boeing to gain more substantial entry into two of the largest and fastest growing airplane markets (China and India).[19]

One of the main attractions for establishing strategic partnerships is the ability to distribute some of the risk associated with the large investment required to build an airplane. By outsourcing, LCA manufacturers are able to share risks and focus their efforts on marketing and supplier relationships. By developing components of the 787 Dreamliner in Japan, Boeing also acquires support from Asian Airlines through the purchase of planes, aided by Japanese government incentives. Another indirect financial benefit to Boeing is the fact that the Japanese and Italian companies are all subsidized by their governments. If successful, the projects present multiple opportunities for Boeing to develop and market their product in an entirely new way.[20] However, risk sharing also equates to profit sharing.

In addition to diminished profits, other implications related to outsourcing are worth noting. First of all, many Boeing employees, including the engineers, are against the outsourcing for obvious reasons; they feel that their jobs are at stake and believe that Boeing has lost sight of its larger interests.[21] Former CEO Harry Stonecipher countered outsourcing concerns by stating, "We have to understand that the go-it-alone approach doesn't work in today's world. Companies will increasingly focus on their core competencies. As they do, they will outsource (a) where the markets are, and (b) where the best people to do the job are."[22] Eventually union leaders and employees were able to acknowledge that outsourcing is about more than just cutting jobs, it is about competing efficiently in a global industry.[23]

Additional controversy centers on whether Boeing is transferring knowledge vital to U.S. military security and commercial competitiveness. The United States has given Boeing's aerospace and defense divisions many subsidies to develop technology. Some of this technology has presumably been transferred to Boeing's aircraft manufacturing division. Japanese suppliers may use the technology shared by Boeing to eventually design their own airplanes. Over the past three years, "The Japanese government and its heavy industrial firms have openly sought to establish Japan as an aerospace power for generations."[24] A Japanese aerospace giant would pose a huge threat to both Boeing and Airbus because it would be able to capitalize on political and trade ties with the flourishing Asia-Pacific markets.[25]

Comparatively, Airbus has kept tighter control over the knowledge it shares with suppliers. In fact, in late 2005 Airbus tightened control over tier one suppliers, directing them to outsource only minimal amounts of work to Asian countries.[26] As such, most of their suppliers are associated with European Union countries, most of which have some ownership in Airbus's parent, EADS. Airbus models its relationship with suppliers after Wal-Mart and utilizes JIT, just-in-time delivery. To further develop efficiencies it follows the approach of the auto industry and requests that its suppliers deliver all components in prepackaged trays that can be loaded onto carts similar to a chest of drawers. Assembly line workers are able to get everything they need without having to leave their stations. As a result, some of Airbus's assembly lines have nearly doubled their efficiency in the past two years.[27]

Clearly, Airbus and Boeing are utilizing relatively different strategies concerning value chain logistics. Consequently, the question remains: Which strategic approach to value chain management will provide better efficiency and long-run strategic advantage? Boeing must continuously monitor and evaluate over time these key concerns in order to maintain positive relations with its stakeholders, specifically its customers and employees.

Customers

Boeing's mission statement signifies that one of its core competencies lays in "detailed customer knowledge and focus."[28] Customers have the choice of buying new or used planes and to license them or purchase them entirely. The customers for Boeing's commercial division are the airlines of the world, and governments are the customers for the defense division. For the commercial division, carriers in China and India are becoming valuable overseas customers, as income rises in these countries along with a forecasted air traffic growth of 8.8 percent in China through the year 2024, and 25 percent growth yearly in India.[29] Half of the orders for the Boeing 787 Dreamliner are from Asia-Pacific clients. Although it is early in the process, the Airbus A-380 currently has

not been purchased by any American carriers, which may suggest that Boeing will dominate the superjumbo aircraft market within the United States.[30] Australia's carrier, Qantas, has indicated it will purchase 115 of its 787 Dreamliners valued at more than $14 billion.[31]

United Airlines has traditionally been Boeing's largest domestic customer,[32] and low-cost airlines have also been key clients for Boeing. However, successful sales campaigns by Airbus resulted in some lost sales for Boeing with the low-cost airlines. JetBlue, when it first emerged in the low-cost industry, announced its decision to purchase Airbus's A-320 over Boeing's 737.[33] JetBlue liked the wider seats, more leg room, and more overhead storage that the A-320 could offer its passengers.

Through early 2004, a major problem seemed to lay in the fact that Boeing had a weak sales force and Airbus was consistently pricing its products below Boeing's prices.[34] These factors, coupled with superior technology in the A-320, won Airbus a considerable amount of Boeing's previous contracts. Boeing's list of lost deals was getting longer and longer, with notable losses to Airbus from United Airlines, AirBerlin, Air Asia, and Southwest. The situation became extremely alarming to Boeing, and in the latter half of 2004 and the beginning of 2005, numerous changes were made in Boeing's sales force. Senior executives and board members were sent into the field to garner sales, decision making was sped up, and the salespeople were empowered to take more risks in pricing.[35]

Frustration with the two-year delay in delivery of the Airbus A-380 (as discussed later in the case) allowed Boeing to acquire some valuable customers from Airbus, including FedEx. FedEx is experiencing growing demand for international freight shipments and needs more planes in its fleet sooner than Airbus can deliver, which resulted in a $2.3 billion loss for Airbus and a $3.6 billion gain for Boeing in new orders.[36] Virgin, also frustrated with the Airbus delays, canceled its order for the A-380 and partnered with Boeing, ordering 15 of its 787s.[37]

In addition to the battle for sales, Boeing and Airbus have been engaged in an ongoing dispute concerning the role that governments play in the success of the two companies.

Government Issues

Boeing attributes much of Airbus's success to its extensive financial support through subsidies called "launch aid" from Spain, France, Germany, and Great Britain, the four member countries that have ownership interests in EADS, the parent of Airbus. During the 1980s Airbus was able to create its multitude of products because of the financial support it relied on from these countries. Airbus still receives a debatable amount, thought to be $1.7 billion for the year 2005.[38]

Boeing was able to further its case against "launch aid" when Airbus released plans to develop the A-350 in response to Boeing's 787, which suspiciously will be developed despite the huge financial losses Airbus accumulated due the problems associated with its A-380 superjumbo jet.[39] Boeing sought protection from the World Trade Organization from these subsidies because they threaten its competitiveness in the global economy. Conversely, Airbus fired back, claiming that Boeing also receives subsidies from the U.S. government. This financial aid comes in the form of "federal research and development contracts from NASA and the Pentagon and, more recently, tax breaks from Washington State."[40] Those in support of Boeing counter with the argument that these contracts are business deals associated with its defense business (not its commercial airlines business) and for which other companies can compete and therefore are not defined as subsidies.[41] Nonetheless, Airbus argues that the government funded technology assists in commercial plane development because such technology is transferable.

For example, about half of the 787 will consist of composites of which knowledge can be directly drawn from Boeing's experience with the B-2 stealth bomber program. However, Airbus also has the ability to draw on military technology from its parent company EADS, so the true validity within this argument is uncertain. Both companies decided to file complaints with the WTO in 2004. The acceptance of government subsidies by global corporations, known as "extraterritorial income," is deemed illegal by the WTO. In reality both companies receive almost equal support from their governments, and tracking or even ending these funds is difficult. The WTO has little judicial power and really only provides leverage to settle disputes.

It is understood that WTO cases are fraught with risk and have uncertain outcomes and often last for years. Also, the European Union and the United States, the two sides in this dispute, are the strongest members in the WTO. The outcome is yet to be determined, but the ultimate conclusion is likely to have an impact on the finances of both firms.[42]

Financials

Boeing's revenue increased nearly 15 percent from 2005 to 2006 ($53,621 million to $61,530 million). In part, this extraordinary growth can be attributed to the record-breaking number of orders and a one-third increase in production capacity. Boeing's net profit on this revenue more than doubled from $464 million in 2005 to $980 million in 2006. This jump equates to net change of 111.2 percent. For investors it is great news. It allowed Boeing to increase its earnings per share (EPS) from $0.59 in 2005 to $1.28 in 2006 (see Exhibits 2, 3, and 4).

Boeing's financial margins indicate how well the organization is utilizing sales dollars. Boeing's gross margin increased at the end of 2006 to 17.6 percent from 14.6 percent in 2005. Gross margin provides insight into the profit available from the sales dollars. Generally, the higher the percentage of gross margin, the more flexible the organization can be in its operating decisions. The gross margin for the industry average is 13.8 percent for 2006 (see Exhibits 2, 3, and 4). Due to its increased flexibility Boeing increased its spending for R&D by nearly $1 billion.

Operating margin (or operating profit margin) increased 2.7 percentage points in 2006 from 2005, moving from 3.9 percent to 6.6 percent. This ratio is useful in determining the earnings before taxes (EBIT) on each dollar. The stronger the ratio, the better, and when coupled with growth year over year, this ratio equates to a favorable analysis. Net margin also increased from 2005 (3.3%) to 2006 (5.6%) for a net change of 2.3 percentage points, indicating that Boeing is doing a better job at controlling its costs and converting its revenue dollars into profit (see Exhibits 2, 3, and 4). Cash flow grew to be 12 percent of revenues, up $.5 billion from $7 billion in 2005 (see Exhibit 7).

Boeing is heavily leveraged compared to its industry; its debt-to-equity ratio is 2.01, compared to the industry average of 0.96. However, when building products with budgets discussed in terms of billions of U.S. dollars, leveraging perhaps allows for better use of assets. This rationale can be seen in Boeing's 2006 credit rating of A3, as provided by Moody's Investors Service.[43] Despite the positive credit rating it is especially important for Boeing to contain its debt levels and use its financial resources wisely in order to come out on top with its strategy versus Airbus's strategy. (For a broader picture of Boeing's financial condition and a comparison of Airbus's financials please refer to Exhibits 5, 6, 7, and 8.)

Opposing Strategies

In comparing the strategies of Boeing and Airbus, one analyst concluded the following: "In today's marketplace, distinct differences in the way competitive products work have become increasingly rare. But functional product differentiation is exactly what the rivalry between the Airbus A-380 and the Boeing 787 Dreamliner is all about: Two companies with fundamentally different products, based on diametrically opposite visions of the future."[44] Boeing maintains that increased fragmentation in the form of point-to-point travel will not only solve the problem of airport congestion, but also appeal to travelers. Airbus on the other hand believes that hub-to-hub travel, especially between major cities will continue to grow—with an emphasis on the Asian markets.

Case 6: Boeing: Redefining Strategies to Manage the Competitive Market

Exhibit 2 Boeing Financial Ratios with Contrast

Growth Rates %	Company	Industry	S&P 500
Sales (Qtr vs year ago qtr)	26.20	16.40	13.60
Net Income (YTD vs YTD)	−14.00	28.10	24.40
Net Income (Qtr vs year ago qtr)	111.20	57.40	80.80
Sales (5-Year Annual Avg.)	1.12	8.39	13.12
Net Income (5-Year Annual Avg.)	−4.83	58.28	22.42
Dividends (5-Year Annual Avg.)	12.03	11.41	9.95

Price Ratios	Company	Industry	S&P 500
Current P/E Ratio	33.1	22.2	21.9
P/E Ratio 5-Year High	65.3	88.0	61.3
P/E Ratio 5-Year Low	9.0	20.9	14.8
Price/Sales Ratio	1.20	1.28	2.77
Price/Book Value	15.63	7.46	4.06
Price/Cash Flow Ratio	19.80	16.10	14.80

Profit Margins %	Company	Industry	S&P 500
Gross Margin	18.0	13.8	36.8
Pre-Tax Margin	5.2	5.1	19.1
Net Profit Margin	3.6	2.7	13.4
5Yr Gross Margin (5-Year Avg.)	15.3	14.5	35.6
5Yr PreTax Margin (5-Year Avg.)	4.3	5.5	17.2
5Yr Net Profit Margin (5-Year Avg.)	3.5	4.0	11.8

Financial Condition	Company	Industry	S&P 500
Debt/Equity Ratio	2.01	0.96	1.32
Current Ratio	0.8	1.2	1.2
Quick Ratio	0.5	0.8	1.0
Interest Coverage	12.5	11.1	24.7
Leverage Ratio	10.9	5.5	4.6
Book Value/Share	6.01	18.51	19.14

Investment Returns %	Company	Industry	S&P 500
Return On Equity	27.9	24.5	21.6
Return On Assets	3.9	5.5	8.0
Return On Capital	8.2	9.8	10.5
Return On Equity (5-Year Avg.)	20.8	16.5	20.2
Return On Assets (5-Year Avg.)	3.5	4.0	6.6
Return On Capital (5-Year Avg.)	6.1	6.5	8.7

Management Efficiency	Company	Industry	S&P 500
Income/Employee	14,325	18,312	104,736
Revenue/Employee	399,546	315,545	856,844
Receivable Turnover	11.7	19.5	17.5
Inventory Turnover	6.3	9.6	8.9
Asset Turnover	1.1	1.1	0.8

Source: Boeing Company Financial Ratios, *Reuters*, http://stocks.us.reuters.com/stocks/ratios.asp?symbol=BA&WT.

Exhibit 3 Boeing Performance Summary, 10 years

	Avg P/E	Price/Sales	Price/Book	Net Profit Margin (%)
12/06	28.20	1.14	14.79	3.6
12/05	19.50	1.05	5.08	4.8
12/04	21.30	0.82	3.82	3.5
12/03	39.50	0.68	4.36	1.4
12/02	13.90	0.50	3.43	4.3
12/01	15.10	0.55	2.86	4.9
12/00	19.90	1.12	5.01	4.1
12/99	16.50	0.66	3.15	4.0
12/98	37.70	0.57	2.48	2.0
12/97	−286.40	1.04	3.68	−0.4

	Book Value/Share	Debt/Equity	Return on Equity (%)	Return on Assets (%)	Interest Coverage
12/06	$6.01	2.01	46.5	4.3	12.0
12/05	$13.82	0.97	23.2	4.3	9.3
12/04	$13.56	1.08	16.1	3.2	5.7
12/03	$9.67	1.77	8.4	1.3	NA
12/02	$9.62	1.87	29.8	4.4	10.9
12/01	$13.57	1.13	26.1	5.8	10.7
12/00	$13.18	0.80	19.3	5.0	6.7
12/99	$13.16	0.59	20.1	6.4	7.3
12/98	$13.13	0.57	9.1	3.0	3.6
12/97	$13.31	0.53	−1.4	−0.5	−0.4

Source: Boeing Company Financial Ratios, *Reuters,* http://stocks.us.reuters.com/stocks/ratios.asp?symbol=BA.

The solution for Boeing is the 787 Dreamliner, a midsized twin-engine airplane with long-haul capabilities, longer than any of Boeing's previous models. Boeing has championed the 787 as "revolutionary," encompassing major changes in all aspects of the airplane including design, production, and finance. Based on a decade of focus groups and scientific studies, the objective for the 787 has been to offer the passenger the most comfortable point-to-point travel experience with as few intermediate stops as possible. The 787 will have more standing room, larger windows and bathrooms, ambient light settings in the cabin to adjust to the time of day, and the cabin will also be set at a higher humidity level. For the airlines it is an attractive product because it is fuel efficient (burning 27 percent less fuel per passenger than the A-380[45]), made from lightweight composite materials, and simple to operate.[46]

Airbus's offering is dubbed the A-380, or commonly referred to as the "superjumbo." The A-380 will be the largest aircraft in the world, 35 percent larger than the current largest, the Boeing 747-400. The A-380 is 239 feet long and stands over 80 feet tall.[47] It can be configured with bars and specialty boutiques. With a wing span of almost 300 feet, the A-380 can transport 550 passengers in a typical three-class layout.[48] Airbus claims the A-380 will allow 10 million additional passengers per year to fly between airports with no increase in flights.[49] Despite a size that provides boasting rights, it also creates challenges because the A-380 will only be able to utilize the largest airports—most facilities are unable to accommodate this aircraft. Airports are having to spend millions of dollars to accommodate this new superjumbo plane. For example, London's Heathrow airport has already spent $909 million for upgrades to prepare for the A-380.[50] Thus, Boeing has the opportunity to exploit smaller airports. The success of Boeing's strategy will depend largely upon its marketing approach. (See Exhibits 9 and 10 to view the differences in features and success between the 787 and A-380.)

Marketing Approach

As a result of the billions of dollars already spent, and the future of the firm at stake, Boeing has marketed the 787 extensively. Boeing recognized that as its products became more sophisticated, it needed to revamp its marketing approach. Rob Pollack, vice president of branding at Boeing, said, "We realized that if you have the most

Exhibit 4 Financial Highlights

Financial Highlights			
Sales	61.53Bil	Revenue/Share	78.68
Income	2.21Bil	Earnings/Share	2.85
Net Profit Margin	3.59%	Book Value/Share	6.01
Return on Equity	27.93%	Dividend Rate	1.40
Debt/Equity Ratio	2.01	Payout Ratio	43.00%

Revenue–Quarterly Results (in Millions)			
	FY (12/06)	FY (12/05)	FY (12/04)
1st Qtr	14,264.0	12,681.0	12,903.0
2nd Qtr	14,986.0	14,684.0	13,088.0
3rd Qtr	14,739.0	12,355.0	13,152.0
4th Qtr	17,541.0	13,901.0	13,314.0
Total	61,530.0	53,621.0	52,457.0

Earnings Per Share–Quarterly Results			
	FY (12/06)	FY (12/05)	FY (12/04)
1st Qtr	$0.91	$0.68	$0.77
2nd Qtr	–$0.21	$0.71	$0.75
3rd Qtr	$0.90	$1.28	$0.56
4th Qtr	$1.30	$0.62	$0.24
Total	$2.90	$3.29	$2.32

Qtr. over Qtr. EPS Growth Rate			
	FY (12/06)	FY (12/05)	FY (12/04)
1st Qtr	47%	183%	—
2nd Qtr	NA	4%	–3%
3rd Qtr	NA	80%	–25%
4th Qtr	44%	–52%	–57%

Yr. over Yr. EPS Growth Rate		
	FY (12/06)	FY (12/05)
1st Qtr	34%	–12%
2nd Qtr	NA	–5%
3rd Qtr	–30%	129%
4th Qtr	110%	158%

Source: Boeing Company Financial Highlights, *Reuters*, http://stocks.us.reuters.com/stocks/financialHighlights.asp?symbol=BA.

state-of-the-art products in the world, how you represent yourself has to be done with state-of-the-art marketing techniques." The new strategy presents Boeing as not just a manufacturer, but a "life cycle partner," providing its customers with business solutions through the full lifespan of its products.[51] "Trade shows are now more about creating an immersion than a spectacle. Media is designed to bring the brand to life. Press events strive to stamp an indelible message."[52] Prospective clients are now invited to Boeing's Customer Experience Center, a 30,000-square-foot facility that allows an interactive experience in which Boeing's sales force can address the needs, concerns, and challenges of its customers. "The studio is facilitating discussions that might never have taken place between Boeing and its clients."[53]

The effort taken to improve its marketing and sales approach will hopefully prove to benefit Boeing as it strives to overcome the challenges that lay ahead.

The Challenges Ahead

As previously mentioned, Airbus has experienced significant delays and other problems surrounding the A-380 project. Not only has Airbus run 50 percent over budget, but they also face hundreds of millions of dollars in penalties for delays. EADS's earnings will decrease by $6 billion over the next four years, and the share price has declined 21 percent in the past year (2006). Additionally, Christian Streiff was forced to quit after only three months in his position as CEO.[54] The problems started when mechanics spent weeks routing 348 miles of bundled electrical wiring in each plane, but came up short when attempting to connect one section to another. The cause was determined to be the fact that engineers in Hamburg were drawing on two-dimensional computer programs whereas engineers in Toulouse were using three-dimensional programs.[55]

Multiple redesigns of the proposed A-350 model intended to compete with Boeing's 787 Dreamliner have been delayed as well, resulting in more bad press for Airbus. Six years ago, Airbus executives said the company would need to sell 250 A-380s to break even on the investment. This number has now risen to more than 400 due to delays and cancelations. The company has ramped up production of its A-320 model, the single-aisle aircraft purchased by many low-cost carriers, in an effort to earn badly needed cash. This tactic could prove disastrous if suppliers are not able to keep up with

Exhibit 5 Boeing Income Statement

Boeing	2006	2005	2004	2003	2002
Period End Date	12/31/2006	12/31/2005	12/31/2004	12/31/2003	12/31/2002
Period Length	12 Months	12 Months	12 Months	12 Months	12 Months
Stmt Source	10-K	10-K	10-K	10-K	10-K
Stmt Source Date	2/16/2007	2/16/2007	2/16/2007	2/28/2005	2/28/2005
Stmt Update Type	Updated	Reclassified	Reclassified	Restated	Restated
Revenue	61,530.00	53,621.00	51,400.00	50,256.00	53,831.00
Total Revenue	**61,530.00**	**53,621.00**	**51,400.00**	**50,256.00**	**53,831.00**
Cost of Revenue, Total	50,437.00	44,984.00	43,968.00	44,150.00	45,804.00
Gross Profit	**11,093.00**	**8,637.00**	**7,432.00**	**6,106.00**	**8,027.00**
Selling/General/Administrative Expenses, Total	4,171.00	4,228.00	3,657.00	3,200.00	2,959.00
Research & Development	3,257.00	2,205.00	1,879.00	1,651.00	1,639.00
Depreciation/Amortization	0	0	3	0	0
Interest Expense (Income), Net Operating	−146	−88	−91	−28	49
Unusual Expense (Income)	571	0	0	892	−2
Other Operating Expenses, Total	226	−520	−23	−7	−44
Operating Income	**3,014.00**	**2,812.00**	**2,007.00**	**398**	**3,426.00**
Interest Income (Expense), Net Non-Operating	−240	−294	−335	−358	−320
Gain (Loss) on Sale of Assets	0	0	0	0	0
Other, Net	420	301	288	460	37
Income Before Tax	**3,194.00**	**2,819.00**	**1,960.00**	**500**	**3,143.00**
Income Tax, Total	988	257	140	−185	847
Income After Tax	**2,206.00**	**2,562.00**	**1,820.00**	**685**	**2,296.00**
Minority Interest	0	0	0	0	0
Equity In Affiliates	0	0	0	0	0
U.S. GAAP Adjustment	0	0	0	0	0
Net Income Before Extra Items	**2,206.00**	**2,562.00**	**1,820.00**	**685**	**2,296.00**
Total Extraordinary Items	9	10	52	33	−1,804.00
Accounting Change	0	17	0	0	−1,827.00
Discontinued Operations	9	−7	52	33	23
Net Income	**2,215.00**	**2,572.00**	**1,872.00**	**718**	**492**
Total Adjustments to Net Income	0	0	0	0	0

Source: Boeing Company Financial Statements, *Reuters*, http://stocks.us.reuters.com/stocks/incomeStatement.asp.

Exhibit 6 Boeing Balance Sheet

Boeing	2006	2005	2004	2003	2002
Period End Date	12/31/2006	12/31/2005	12/31/2004	12/31/2003	12/31/2002
Stmt Source	10-K	10-K	10-K	10-K	10-K
Stmt Source Date	2/16/2007	2/16/2007	2/28/2006	2/28/2005	2/27/2003
Stmt Update Type	Updated	Restated	Restated	Restated	Updated
Assets					
Cash and Short-Term Investments	6,386.00	5,966.00	3,523.00	4,633.00	2,333.00
Cash & Equivalents	6,118.00	5,412.00	3,204.00	4,633.00	2,333.00
Short-Term Investments	268	554	319	0	0
Total Receivables, Net	5,655.00	5,613.00	5,269.00	5,522.00	6,296.00
Accounts Receivable—Trade, Net	5,285.00	5,246.00	4,653.00	4,466.00	5,007.00
Accounts Receivable—Trade, Gross	5,368.00	5,336.00	0	0	0
Provision for Doubtful Accounts	−83	−90	0	0	0
Notes Receivable—Short-Term	370	367	616	857	1,289.00
Receivables—Other	0	0	0	199	0
Total Inventory	8,105.00	7,878.00	6,508.00	5,338.00	6,184.00
Prepaid Expenses	0	0	0	0	0
Other Current Assets, Total	2,837.00	2,449.00	2,061.00	3,798.00	2,042.00
Total Current Assets	**22,983.00**	**21,906.00**	**17,361.00**	**19,291.00**	**16,855.00**
Property/Plant/Equipment, Total—Net	7,675.00	8,420.00	8,443.00	8,597.00	8,765.00
Goodwill, Net	3,047.00	1,924.00	1,948.00	1,913.00	2,760.00
Intangibles, Net	1,426.00	671	955	1,035.00	1,128.00
Long-Term Investments	4,085.00	2,852.00	3,050.00	646	0
Note Receivable—Long-Term	8,520.00	9,639.00	10,385.00	10,057.00	10,922.00
Other Long-Term Assets, Total	4,058.00	14,584.00	14,082.00	11,447.00	11,912.00
Other Assets, Total	0	0	0	0	0
Total Assets	**51,794.00**	**59,996.00**	**56,224.00**	**52,986.00**	**52,342.00**
Liabilities and Shareholders' Equity					
Accounts Payable	16,201.00	16,513.00	14,869.00	13,514.00	13,739.00
Payable/Accrued	0	0	0	0	0
Accrued Expenses	0	0	0	0	0
Notes Payable/Short-Term Debt	0	0	0	0	0
Current Port. of LT Debt/Capital Leases	1,381.00	1,189.00	1,321.00	1,144.00	1,814.00
Other Current Liabilities, Total	12,119.00	10,424.00	6,906.00	3,741.00	4,257.00
Total Current Liabilities	**29,701.00**	**28,126.00**	**23,096.00**	**18,399.00**	**19,810.00**
Total Long-Term Debt	8,157.00	9,538.00	10,879.00	13,299.00	12,589.00
Long-Term Debt	8,157.00	9,538.00	10,879.00	13,299.00	12,589.00
Deferred Income Tax	0	2,067.00	1,090.00	0	0

Exhibit 6 Boeing Balance Sheet *(Continued)*

Boeing	2006	2005	2004	2003	2002
Minority Interest	0	0	0	0	0
Other Liabilities, Total	9,197.00	9,206.00	9,873.00	13,149.00	12,247.00
Total Liabilities	**47,055.00**	**48,937.00**	**44,938.00**	**44,847.00**	**44,646.00**
Redeemable Preferred Stock	0	0	0	0	0
Preferred Stock—Non Redeemable, Net	0	0	0	0	0
Common Stock	5,061.00	5,061.00	5,059.00	5,059.00	5,059.00
Additional Paid-In Capital	4,655.00	4,371.00	3,420.00	2,880.00	2,141.00
Retained Earnings (Accumulated Deficit)	18,453.00	17,276.00	15,565.00	14,407.00	14,262.00
Treasury Stock—Common	−12,459.00	−11,075.00	−8,810.00	−8,322.00	−8,397.00
ESOP Debt Guarantee	−2,754.00	−2,796.00	−2,023.00	−1,740.00	−1,324.00
Other Equity, Total	−8,217.00	−1,778.00	−1,925.00	−4,145.00	−4,045.00
Total Equity	**4,739.00**	**11,059.00**	**11,286.00**	**8,139.00**	**7,696.00**
Total Liabilities & Shareholders' Equity	**51,794.00**	**59,996.00**	**56,224.00**	**52,986.00**	**52,342.00**
Total Common Shares Outstanding	788.74	800.17	832.18	841.48	799.66
Total Preferred Shares Outstanding	0	0	0	0	0

Source: Boeing Company Financial Statements, *Reuters,* http://stocks.us.reuters.com/stocks/balanceSheet.asp.

Airbus's schedule. However, Airbus executives insist that losses will be recouped by 2010.[56]

Boeing also invested heavily in its 787 project and faced criticism over weight issues and composite construction materials. Although both firms experienced setbacks, Airbus has taken the brunt of these setbacks, as already noted. Boeing's challenges have more to do with potential production delays and meeting its massive order-backlog on time. In 2007, Boeing had already announced some delays. Boeing officials noted that "it is possible to overcome a nearly four-month delay in the 787 Dreamliner program and deliver the first jet on time in May [2008]."[57] However, "Industry observers and a number of the plane's suppliers say it would be the aerospace equivalent of hitting a hole in one on a golf course." The complexity of producing an aircraft is significant, but when you have to simultaneously bring together a large array of suppliers and the various parts that they produce to meet a deadline, the possibilities for error increase geometrically.

In the long term, Boeing must wonder whether it is going to create a new competitor in Japan and eventually in China, given its outsourcing strategy. Also,

Airbus countered Boeing's 787 product strategy with the A-350 in addition to the A-380 (Boeing does not have a comparable product, unless they can effectively update the 747). Thus, both Boeing and Airbus face significant strategic challenges.

Conclusion

Both Boeing and Airbus spent billions of dollars in developing their unique strategies. Airbus bet that the way to cope with increased customer demand is to offer a platform, namely the A-380, capable of moving mass amounts of people using the hub system. Alternatively, Boeing focused on the 787 to offer consumers long-range capabilities while at the same time using direct connections. Initial trends indicate support for Boeing strategies based on accumulated orders for the 787, numbering nearly 500, whereas Airbus's A-380 has not received the amount of orders originally forecasted. Airbus also experienced major setbacks with the two-year delivery delay while running nearly 50 percent over budget[58] and losing orders from frustrated customers. Thus, Boeing currently

Exhibit 7 Boeing Statement of Cash Flows

Boeing	2006	2005	2004	2003	2002
Period End Date	12/31/2006	12/31/2005	12/31/2004	12/31/2003	12/31/2002
Net Income/Starting Line	2,215.00	2,572.00	1,872.00	718	492
Depreciation/Depletion	1,445.00	1,412.00	1,412.00	1,306.00	1,362.00
Amortization	100	91	97	94	88
Non-Cash Items	1,552.00	1,807.00	1,538.00	1,737.00	2,907.00
Discontinued Operations	−14	12	−51	63	76
Unusual Items	344	−437	102	1,068.00	2,723.00
Other Non-Cash Items	1,222.00	2,232.00	1,487.00	606	108
Changes in Working Capital	2,187.00	1,118.00	−1,415.00	−1,079.00	−2,513.00
Accounts Receivable	−244	−592	−241	357	−155
Inventories	444	−1,965.00	535	191	1,507.00
Prepaid Expenses	−522	−1,862.00	−4,355.00	−1,728.00	−340
Other Assets	718	600	−425	−1,321.00	−2,038.00
Accounts Payable	−744	1,147.00	1,321.00	−132	−441
Accrued Expenses	114	30	214	311	67
Taxes Payable	933	628	1,086.00	320	322
Other Liabilities	1,677.00	3,086.00	705	876	−978
Other Operating Cash Flow	−189	46	−255	47	−457
Cash from Operating Activities	**7,499.00**	**7,000.00**	**3,504.00**	**2,776.00**	**2,336.00**
Capital Expenditures	−1,681.00	−1,547.00	−1,246.00	−836	−1,001.00
Purchase of Fixed Assets	−1,681.00	−1,547.00	−1,246.00	−836	−1,001.00
Other Investing Cash Flow Items, Total	−1,505.00	1,449.00	−200	896	−381
Acquisition of Business	−1,854.00	−172	−34	289	−22
Sale of Business	123	1,709.00	194	186	157
Sale of Fixed Assets	225	51	2,285.00	95	0
Sale/Maturity of Investment	2,850.00	2,725.00	1,323.00	203	140
Purchase of Investments	−2,815.00	−2,866.00	−4,142.00	−102	−505
Other Investing Cash Flow	−34	2	174	225	−151
Cash from Investing Activities	**−3,186.00**	**−98**	**−1,446.00**	**60**	**−1,382.00**
Financing Cash Flow Items	395	70	23	0	0
Other Financing Cash Flow	395	70	23	0	0
Total Cash Dividends Paid	−956	−820	−648	−572	−571
Issuance (Retirement) of Stock, Net	−1,404.00	−2,529.00	−654	18	67
Issuance (Retirement) of Debt, Net	−1,680.00	−1,378.00	−2,208.00	18	1,250.00
Cash from Financing Activities	**−3,645.00**	**−4,657.00**	**−3,487.00**	**−536**	**746**
Foreign Exchange Effects	38	−37	0	0	0
Net Change in Cash	**706**	**2,208.00**	**−1,429.00**	**2,300.00**	**1,700.00**
Net Cash, Beginning Balance	5,412.00	3,204.00	4,633.00	2,333.00	633
Net Cash, Ending Balance	6,118.00	5,412.00	3,204.00	4,633.00	2,333.00

Source: Boeing Financial Statements, *Reuters,* http://stocks.us.reuters.com/stocks/cashFlowStatement.

Exhibit 8 Airbus Select Financials

(Euro, million)	2006	2005	2004	2003
EBIT	(572)	2307	1919	1353
Total Revenue	25190	22179	20224	19048
Assets	33958	33226	35044	29290
Goodwill	6374	6987	6883	6342
Liabilities	24096	20553	17019	17501
Provisions	6272	4205	0	0
Capital Expenditures	1750	1864	2778	2027
Depreciation, Amortization	1140	1131	1088	1628
R&D	2035	1659	1734	1819
Exchange Rate	0.757855	0.844589	0.738788	0.793869

(U.S., million)	2006	2005	2004	2003
EBIT	(433)	1948	1418	1074
Total Revenue	19090	18732	14941	15122
Assets	25735	28062	25890	23252
Goodwill	4831	5901	5085	5035
Liabilities	18261	17359	12573	13894
Provisions	4753	3551	0	0
Capital Expenditures	1326	1574	2052	1609
Depreciation, Amortization	864	955	804	1292
R&D	1542	1401	1281	1444

Source: 2006, 2005, 2004, *EADS Annual Reports*, www.eads.com/1024/en/investor/Reports/Archive/Archives.html.

Exhibit 9 Dreamliner (787) vs. Superjumbo (A-380)

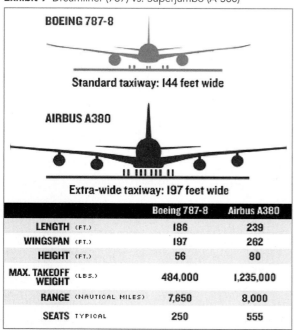

	Boeing 787-8	Airbus A380
LENGTH (FT.)	186	239
WINGSPAN (FT.)	197	262
HEIGHT (FT.)	56	80
MAX. TAKEOFF WEIGHT (LBS.)	484,000	1,235,000
RANGE (NAUTICAL MILES)	7,650	8,000
SEATS TYPICAL	250	555

Source: 2007, Dissecting the A-380's troubles, *Fortune*, http://www.fortune.com, March 5.

Exhibit 10 Boeing vs. Airbus Orders

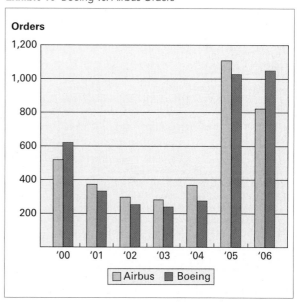

Source: 2007, Dissecting the A-380's troubles, *Fortune*, http://www.fortune.com, March 5.

holds the lead in the aerospace industry. However, the Asian markets are growing, and demand for large aircraft to meet air traffic increases is also likely to grow. Boeing may be confident in its strategy, but recent minor delays serve as a reminder that Boeing cannot get too comfortable. The first A-380 is slated to be delivered to Singapore Airlines on October 15, 2007.[59] Will this aircraft become a sensation? Will Airbus be able to recoup its costs by 2010 and flourish in the industry? Will Boeing realize continued strategic success, given Airbus's A-350 program, which was established to compete with the 787?

NOTES

1. 2001, Aviation competition: Regional jet service yet to reach many small communities, United States General Accounting Office, http://www.gao.gov, February, 5–10; D. Schlossberg, 2007, FAA fights proliferation of small planes, http://www.consumeraffairs.com, August 23.

2. J. L. Lunsford, 2007, Boeing's 787 faces less room for error: Dreamliner flight tests pushed by months; sticking to delivery date, Wall Street Journal, September 6, A13.

3. 2007, Boeing, Wikipedia, http://en.wikipedia.org/wiki/Boeing.

4. 2007, Boeing History, http://www.boeing.com/history/chronology.

5. 2007, Boeing History, http://www.boeing.com/history.

6. 2007, Boeing History: Beginnings—Building a company, Aviation History, http://www.wingsoverkansas.com/history/article.asp?id=404.

7. R. J. Gordon, 1983, Energy efficiency, user cost change, and the measurement of durable goods prices, The U.S. national income and product accounts: Selected topics, Chicago: University of Chicago Press, 235.

8. 2007, Boeing, Wikipedia, http://en.wikipedia.org/wiki/Boeing_747-8.

9. 2007, Boeing history, http://www.boeing.com/history/boeing/777.

10. 2007, Boeing, http://www.careerbuilder.com.

11. 2001, Boeing's Sonic Cruiser skirts the edge of the sound barrier, Popular Mechanics, http://www.popularmechanics.com, October.

2. L. Laurent, 2007, Boeing's Dreamliner, Airbus's nightmare, Forbes, http://www.forbes.com, July 9.

13. J. Newhouse, 2007, Boeing Versus Airbus, Toronto, Canada: Alfred A. Knopf.

14. Ibid.

15. Ibid.

16. J. Destefani, 2004, A look at Boeing's outsourcing strategy, Manufacturing Engineering, March.

17. Ibid.

18. Ibid.

19. 2006, Boeing's global strategy takes off: The aerospace titan is taking a measured approach to outsourcing, with help from local teams, BusinessWeek, http://www.businessweek.com, January 30.

20. Ibid.

21. Ibid.

22. Harry C. Stonecipher, 2004, Outsourcing, the real issue, Orange County Business Council Annual Meeting and Dinner, http://www.boeing.com/news/speeches, June 2.

23. 2006, Boeing's global strategy takes off.

24. E. F. Vencat, 2006, A Boeing of Asia? It could happen, now that Airbus and Boeing build planes in global factories, Newsweek International, http://www.msnbc.msn.com, May 15.

25. Ibid.

26. J. Newhouse, Boeing versus Airbus.

27. C. Matlack & S. Holmes, 2007, Airbus revs up the engines; to generate badly needed cash, it's boosting output of its popular A-320 to record levels, BusinessWeek, March 5, 4024: 41.

28. 2004, There where they're needed, Boeing Frontiers, http://www.boeing.com, December.

29. V. Kwong & A. Rothman, 2006, Boeing vs. Airbus: The next bout, International Herald Tribune, http://www.iht.com, February 16.

30. L. Wayne, 2007, Airbus superjumbo takes a lap around America, New York Times, http://www.nytimes.com, March 20.

31. A. Burgos, 2005, Qantas sets $14 billion order for Boeing planes, Forbes, http://www.forbes.com, December 14.

32. J. Newhouse, Boeing versus Airbus.

33. 1999, JetBlue chooses the Airbus A-320, Press Releases, http://www.jetblue.com, July 14.

34. L. Timmerman, 2004, Boeing sales to get new leadership, The Seattle Times, http://www.seattletimes.com, December 4.

35. D. Drezner, 2005, Competition has been good for Boeing, http://www.danieldrezner.com, April 13.

36. M. Schlangenstein, 2007, FedEx dumps Airbus for Boeing, The News Tribune (Tacoma, WA), http://www.thenewstribune.com, September 25.

37. P. Olson, 2007, Branson turns his back on Airbus, Forbes, http://www.forbes.com, April 25.

38. D. Ackman, 2005, Boeing, Airbus showdown at 40,000 feet, Forbes, http://www.forbes.com, May 31.

39. M. Adams, 2006, Airbus announces new jet to rival Boeing Dreamliner, USA Today, http://www.usatoday.com, July 18.

40. D. Ackman, Boeing, Airbus showdown at 40,000 feet.

41. Ibid.

42. J. Audley & K. Saleh, 2004, Boeing vs. Airbus: Trade fight could prove costly for everyone, The Seattle Times, http://www.seattletimes.com, December 6.

43. 2006, Moody's boosts Boeing's credit rating, International Business Times, http://in.ibtimes.com, March 15.

44. M. E. Babej & T. Pollak, 2006, Boeing versus Airbus, Forbes, http://www.forbes.com, May 24.

45. P. Olson, Branson turns his back on Airbus.

46. M. E. Babej & T. Pollak, Boeing versus Airbus.

47. 2007, Anatomy of an A-380, Fortune, March 5, 101–106.

48. J. Newhouse, Boeing versus Airbus.

49. Ibid.

50. R. Stone, 2007, Airbus A-380 promises less for big airports, Wall Street Journal, September 5, D7.

51. 2007, Ground Control, Event Marketer, http://www.eventmarketer.com, February 11.

52. Ibid.

53. Ibid.

54. N. D. Schwartz, 2007, Big plane, big problems, Fortune, March 5, 95–98.

55. 2007, Anatomy of an A-380.

56. G. Parkinson, 2006, Crisis at Airbus as chief quits after only 100 days, The (London) Independent, http://www.findarticles.com, October 10.

57. J. L. Lunsford, 2007, Boeing's tall order: On-time 787; suppliers say Dreamliner delivery could hit may target—if all goes right, Wall Street Journal, September 17, A8.

58. D. Michaels, 2007, More super, less jumbo for this carrier, Wall Street Journal, September 25, B8.

59. Ibid.

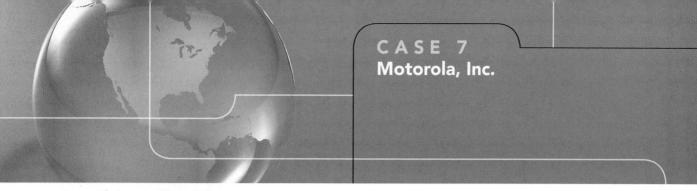

Aaron Christensen, Victor Delagarza,
Aric Griggs, Lubka Robertson,
Tamara Stuart, Michael Valverde

Arizona State University

In November 2008, Motorola announced the postponement of its highly publicized spinoff of the Mobile Device segment, a struggling business segment that is pulling down the results of the entire firm. In light of the challenging economy, Motorola faces the decision of if and when to spin off this division and which new market opportunities to explore in order to return to the profitable company it was for so many years.

Company History

In 1928, Paul and Joseph Galvin incorporated Galvin Manufacturing[1] after acquiring "battery eliminator operations"[2] from the bankrupt Stewart Storage Battery Company.[3] A battery eliminator is a device that allows "battery-powered radios [to] run on a standard household electric current"[4] instead of batteries. Galvin Manufacturing used the technology as the groundwork for its first car radio named Motorola.[5] The name Motorola is a combination of "'motor' (for motor car) and 'ola' (which implied sound)."[6] Galvin Manufacturing introduced its first Motorola car radio in 1930, the Motorola Police Cruiser radio in 1936,[7] and home radios in 1937.[8] By the end of 1937, B. F. Goodrich had partnered with Galvin Manufacturing to become the first national Motorola dealer.[9]

Starting in 1940, Galvin Manufacturing expanded its product line to include two-way communication devices.[10] The first product was the Handie-Talkie SCR536 AM Radio, which was used extensively by the military during World War II.[11] The success of the Handie-Talkie and a strong belief in the sustainable demand for its communication products led Galvin Manufacturing to create a separate product division and establish a sales subsidiary, Motorola Communications and Electronics, Inc.[12] Leveraging its experience with military radios, Galvin Manufacturing introduced its first commercial line of Motorola FM vehicular two-way radio systems and equipment in 1941.[13] By the end of 1943, Galvin Manufacturing successfully completed its first initial public offering with its stock selling for $8.50 per share.[14] Building upon earlier success, Galvin Manufacturing produced the world's first portable backpack FM radio (SCR300), more commonly known as a "walkie-talkie."[15] In 1946, Galvin Manufacturing partnered with Bell Telephone Company to enable car radio-telephone service via Motorola communication equipment for the Chicago area.[16]

Galvin Manufacturing officially changed its name to Motorola, Inc. in 1947.[17] As part of a diversification strategy, Motorola acquired the car radio manufacturer Detrola, a supplier to Ford Motor Company, and entered the television market with the Golden View VT71.[18] Motorola sold more than 100,000 Golden View television units within the first year and became the fourth-largest U.S. television manufacturer.[19] Motorola illustrated its commitment to product development and innovation through the establishment of its R&D operations in Phoenix, Arizona, in 1949.[20] This R&D effort led to advances in semiconductor and transistor technology, including the germanium transistor technology Motorola used in its 1955 car radios.[21] The germanium transistor "was the world's first commercial high-power transistor . . . [and] Motorola's first mass-produced semiconductor."[22]

By 1954, Motorola had outgrown its existing organizational structure, causing Paul Galvin to decide to reorganize the company[23] into product-line divisions.[24] The following year, Galvin's son, Robert, became Motorola's president.[25] Robert Galvin continued to

Note: This case was written to be used as a basis for class discussion rather than to illustrate either effective or ineffective handling of an administrative situation. We would like to thank Robert E. Hoskisson and Robert E. White for useful feedback in writing this case. Data was collected from publically available sources.

lead the company by following its communication and television expertise but "shifted the company's strategy toward selling directly to government and business."[26] In 1958, Motorola introduced the Motrac vehicular radio that "enabled the radio to transmit without running the vehicle's engine."[27] Motorola also introduced a three-amp power transistor,[28] a small radio receiver used extensively in hospitals (more commonly known as a pager[29]) and color television sets[30] during the 1950s and 1960s. In 1969, Motorola's radio transponder on *Apollo 11* "relayed the first words from the Earth to the Moon . . . [and] transmitted telemetry, tracking, voice communications, and television signals from the Earth to the Moon."[31]

By 1968, frustrations over limitations concerning car-based communication technology led the Federal Communications Commission (FCC) to propose allocating bandwidth to new technologies that would address this problem.[32] Thus, Motorola pioneered the cellular phone industry by creating the first commercial cellular phone, the Motorola DynaTAC phone.[33]

Motorola continued its pioneering efforts in the world of manufacturing. In 1968, Motorola developed the Six Sigma quality improvement process.[34] Six Sigma is an analytical, statistical approach that is used to improve the quality of manufacturing processes and to eliminate defects.[35] Since its introduction, Six Sigma has become a global standard.[36]

During the 1990s Motorola extended its traditional product offerings into the digital arena. Motorola acquired General Instrument Corporation, the company that developed the all-digital high-definition television (HDTV) technical standard.[37] In 1991, Motorola developed the first digital cellular phone prototype[38] and by 1994 Motorola produced its Integrated Digital Enhanced Network (iDEN) digital radio, which combined paging data, cellular communications, and voice dispatch in a single radio network and handset.[39] Motorola continued to enhance product features and produce phones with more integrated features through the end of the 1990s.[40]

In 2000, Motorola partnered with Cisco Systems, Inc. to expand operations into the United Kingdom with BT Cellnet by supplying the "world's first commercial General Packet Radio Service (GPRS) cellular network."[41] Motorola then introduced the wireless cable modem which allowed computer networking, a 700-MHz high-speed data system for public safety, a cellular PDA handset that combined Linux and Java technology, and demonstration of the first WiMAX mobile hand-offs.[42]

In 2004, Motorola's introduction of the RAZR (see Exhibit 1) was a huge success as indicated by the facts that the firm sold more than 750,000 units in the first 90 days and held a 16 percent share of the cell phone

Exhibit 1 Motorola RAZR Phone

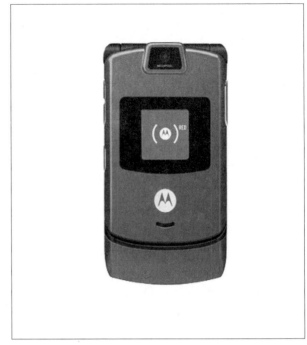

Source: 2009, http://www.motorola.com.

market until 2007.[43] Motorola tried to extend the RAZR's success by introducing the Q in 2005, but it ultimately failed to invoke the same response as its predecessor.[44] In 2006, Motorola expanded its international product offerings again by introducing the MING touch screen smartphone with advanced handwriting software and the Chinese alphabet targeted for the Asian market.[45] Despite continued efforts in the mobile device market segment, Motorola's market share decreased from 22.2 percent in 2006 to 12 percent in 2007.[46]

Edward Zander, the first non-Galvin CEO, was hired by the board of directors in January 2004 to replace Chris Galvin when he retired.[47] Zander steered the company toward products that focused on combining Internet technologies with wireless phone technologies.[48] In 2007, Motorola merged with Symbol Technologies in order to expand its product offerings in mobile computing, advanced data capture, and radio frequency identification (RFID).[49] Motorola also acquired Good Technology in 2007 to expand access to enterprise applications, intranets, and corporate applications for mobile employees.[50] Disappointing returns in 2007 led Motorola's second largest shareholder, Carl Icahn, to demand changes in the organization and the board of directors.[51] Greg Brown replaced Zander in January 2008.[52] Prior to being appointed as CEO, Brown held the president and COO positions. Brown possessed almost 25 years of high-tech experience and had been with Motorola since 2003.[53] However, his appointment did not help ease shareholder frustrations over Motorola's struggling mobile device business, and during his tenure there has been significant turnover in upper management positions, ultimately affecting the company.[54] Therefore, Motorola leaders have thoughtfully considered the direction the company should take, specifically which products it should offer, in order to resume successful operations.

Product Offerings

In 2007 when Motorola restructured the organization, it aligned its business into three operating segments: Home and Networks Mobility, Enterprise Mobility Solutions, and Mobile Devices.[55] The firm's product portfolio consists of wireless handsets, accessories, and access systems as well as digital entertainment devices, voice and data communications systems, and enterprise mobility products.[56]

The Home and Networks Mobility segment competes in the cable set-top box, broadband cable modem, cellular infrastructure, and wireless broadband systems industries.[57] In the third quarter of 2008, this division contributed 32 percent of Motorola's net sales.[58]

The Enterprise Mobility Solutions segment competes in areas such as two-way radio, wireless broadband systems, and private networks for both enterprise and government use.[59] Furthermore, Motorola provides broadcast interactive networks, third-party switching for broadband networks to include: Code Division Multiple Access (CDMA),[60] Global System for Mobile Communication (GSM), and Universal Mobile Telecommunications System[61] (UMTS), all of which are technologies used for mobile communication networking.[62] This division contributed 27 percent of Motorola's net sales in the third quarter of 2008.[63]

The Mobile Devices segment competes in the wireless handset industry. This segment manufactures and sells analog and digital two-way radios, voice and data communication products for private networks, and intellectual property in the form of licenses and patents.[64] This segment comprised 42 percent of Motorola's net sales in third quarter 2008.[65] In the same quarter Motorola held approximately 8.4 percent market share (25.4 million units) in the global handset market. There are several competitors that have taken market share from Motorola.

Competitors

In the wireless handset industry, Motorola's top competitors are Nokia, Samsung, and Sony Ericsson Mobile Communications. LG Electronics, Apple Inc., Research in Motion and HELIO are also competitors but do not pose as large a threat.

Nokia[66]

In 1998 Nokia became and has since been the leading cell phone manufacturer. In 2008 it had net sales of $70.5 billion from 468 million units shipped. This was a seven percent increase over 2007. In 2008 Nokia controlled 39 percent of the mobile communication device market. In 2008 alone Nokia introduced 26 different phones that were focused in five different categories. Smartphone sales made up 13 percent of total cell phones shipped, totaling 61 million units. Nokia is especially dominant in the European and Asian Pacific markets.

Nokia started a joint venture with Siemens in 2007 to provide industry leading consumer Internet service. Nokia has been actively acquiring other businesses to expand its dominance in the mobile phone industry. Since 2006, Nokia has acquired nine businesses in the consumer software field that range from file sharing and music services to advertising and security. Nokia has been affected by the global crisis that started toward the end of 2007; however, the firm has been able to reduce the negative effects of the crisis through its effective use of strategic acquisitions, partnerships, and industry-leading research and development.

Samsung Electronics[67]

Samsung produces and sells products ranging from televisions to home appliances to mobile devices. It is also a major supplier for both LCD screens and memory-based semiconductor chips. Samsung's Telecommunication Networks division, which manufactures and sells the firm's wireless handsets, generates approximately 23 percent of Samsung's sales revenue. With strong brand awareness, consumer-driven design, and aggressive expansion into developing markets, Samsung increased its net profit by 42 percent from 2006 to 2007.

Samsung has been able to launch premium products and rapidly penetrate emerging markets with its mid-range products. As such, it is currently the world's second-largest mobile phone maker, with a 14.3 percent market share. Its premium products, such as the Ultra Edition smartphone, have captured the attention of consumers with features such as a touchscreen, high megapixel cameras, and music capabilities. Samsung was voted "best brand" six years in a row in the United States and captured the number one market spot in France and Russia.

Sony Ericsson Mobile Communications[68]

With the joint venture between Sony and Ericsson in 2001, Sony Ericsson Mobile Communications was able to offer a variety of mobile handsets and other mobile devices that supported multimedia applications and other personal communication services. This is in line with the firm's vision to "be the prime driver in an all-communicating world … in which all people can use voice, text, images and video to share ideas and information whenever and wherever they want."

China, the United States, and India are Sony Ericsson's top three markets. However, by increasing the sales of lower-priced handsets in emerging markets such as Latin America, Sony Ericsson sold over 100 million handsets in 2007—an increase of 18 percent from the previous year. Sony Ericsson believes it is in a prime position to build on its recent strong performance and continues to develop its mid- to low-range products while establishing brand awareness with its high-end products.

LG Electronics[69]

The Mobile Communications division of LG Electronics (LG) is a global leader in the worldwide mobile market.[70] By strategically reallocating its resources, LG plans on becoming a member of the "Global Top 3." LG aims to anticipate customer needs and surpass them with products using the latest technology and presenting consumers with stylish product designs. This strategy seems to be effective as illustrated by a 13 percent increase in mobile handset sales worldwide and a 10 percent increase in global revenue in 2007.

Apple Inc.[71]

Most commonly known for designing and producing software, computers, computer peripherals, and portable music players, Apple Inc. entered the mobile communications devices market with the introduction of the iPhone through a partnership with AT&T Mobility LLC. The iPhone combines cellular communications, a portable music player, and Internet access using Wi-Fi into a single product, all through the control of a touchscreen. Many well-established companies have tried to imitate the capabilities of the iPhone in their respective smartphones.

For fiscal 2008, Apple generated annual revenue of $32 billion versus 2007 annual revenue of $24 billion. Profit margins increased from 14.6 percent in 2007 to 14.9 percent in 2008. Also, Apple's handset division revenue jumped up from approximately $250 million to $1.8 billion in 2008.

Research in Motion[72]

Founded in 1984, Research in Motion (RIM) is a leading designer and manufacturer of innovative wireless solutions.[73] RIM is best known for its telecommunication handheld device, the BlackBerry. It supports mobile telephony, text messaging, e-mail, and Web browsing.

By the end of fiscal year 2008, Blackberrys were available in more than 135 countries. Hardware generates 79 percent of RIM's revenue, which amounted to $6 billion in fiscal 2008, nearly double the revenue of 2007. Profit margins for 2008 were 21 percent versus 27 percent for 2007. The company plans on expanding its selection of mobile devices with several new smartphones as well as enhancing software and services to gain new market share.

HELIO, Inc.[74]

In January 2005, HELIO, Inc. was formed via a joint venture between EarthLink, Inc. and SK Telecom Co., Inc. with the purpose of developing wireless telecommunications services, including but not limited to handsets. Services that are included are integrated Imaging, an Ultimate Inbox, and other popular applications such as MySpace and YouTube.[75] A 282 percent increase in equipment sales and other revenue from 2006 to 2007 indicates that HELIO has successfully established itself in the U.S. market.

In addition to the main competitors in the handset market, Motorola is constantly faced with competition from emerging technologies such as Mobile Internet Devices (MIDs).

Mobile Internet Devices (MIDs)[76]

MIDs are devices that allow consumers to "communicate with others, enjoy [their] favorite entertainment, and access information on-the-go" by connecting to wireless hotspots around town. This new technology provides all of the Internet capabilities consumers want as well as the ability to have a conversation using Voice over Internet Protocol (VoIP). Industry-leading companies, such as Intel, are forming a Mobile Internet Device Innovation Alliance.[77] The MID Alliance is comprised of industry-leading original manufacturers as Asus, BenQ, Compal, Elektrobit, HTC, Inventec, and Quanta.[78] The members of the alliance are working together to solve engineering challenges with respect to power management, wireless communications, and software integration.[79]

Each of these firms is vying for business from the customers Motorola seeks to serve as it operates in its three business segments.

Motorola's Customers

Motorola's Mobile Device Segment has several large customers including Sprint Nextel, Verizon, China Mobile, AT&T, and America Movil. Motorola has stated that "the loss of one or more of [these companies] could have a material adverse effect on the Company."[80] Sales to these five companies accounted for 42 percent of total revenue in the Mobile Devices segment.[81]

Customers of the Home and Networks Mobility segment include Comcast, Verizon, KDDI, China Mobile, and Sprint Nextel. Sales to these five customers account for 43 percent of total net sales for this division. Similar to the Mobile Devices segment, the loss of any one customer could be detrimental.[82]

Enterprise Mobility Solutions segment customers include the U.S. government, Scansource, IBM, Ingram Micro, and Wal-Mart.[83] Sales to these customers generate 19 percent of the division's net sales. Other customers include resellers and distributors, who then sell to the commercial enterprise market.

Because of the late 2008 financial crisis and the tightening of credit, Motorola is concerned that customers will defer purchases, be unable to obtain financing, and submit more requests for vendor financing by Motorola.[84]

Motorola's Suppliers

Motorola's suppliers include Freescale, Qualcomm, ATI, Spansion, Texas Instruments, and STMicroelectronics. One drawback is that some of the inputs required to manufacture Motorola's products are only available from a single supplier. In 2003 and 2004, Motorola suffered from product delays due to supply shortages caused by a lack of a sufficient number of suppliers.[85] Also, with the current financial crisis, Motorola is concerned that its suppliers may become capacity constrained because of credit issues and thus cause possible product delays.[86]

However, Motorola actively works with suppliers to assist them in reducing lead times and improving efficiency. David Buck, the director of procurement, states "We look for opportunities for our suppliers to be more successful."[87] Motorola works with suppliers early in the design phase of a product, enabling a fast ramp-up of production. At times, "purchasers involved in design are co-located with designers."[88] These activities contribute directly to Motorola's bottom line since parts can be ramped up and delivered faster, with increased quality and lower cost.

Financial Performance

Motorola reported financial losses and a decline in annual sales in 2007 (see Exhibit 2). Net sales in 2007 totaled almost $36.7 billion, down 15 percent compared to net sales of $42.8 billion in 2006.[89] The Mobile Devices segment's net sales in 2007 were $19 billion, representing 52 percent of the Company's consolidated net sales, but experiencing a 33 percent decrease from the previous year. The Home and Networks Mobility segment's net sales in 2007 were $10 billion, representing 27 percent of the Company's consolidated net sales, a 9 percent increase from the previous year. The Enterprise Mobility Solutions segment's net sales in 2007 were $7.7 billion, representing 21 percent of the Company's consolidated net sales, a 43 percent increase in net sales from the previous year.[90]

Additionally, Motorola reported operating losses of $553 million (see Exhibit 2). In the previous year, the firm reported operating earnings of $4.1 billion.[91] Operating margins were 1.5 percent of net sales in 2007 compared to 9.6 percent in 2006—another substantial decline.[92]

Exhibit 2 Motorola, Inc. and Subsidiaries

Income Statement			
	Years Ended December 31		
(In millions, except per share amounts)	2007	2006	2005
Net sales	$ 36,622	$ 42,847	$ 35,310
Costs of sales	26,670	30,120	23,881
Gross margin	9,952	12,727	11,429
Selling, general and administrative expenses	5,092	4,504	3,628
Research and development expenditures	4,429	4,106	3,600
Other charges (income)	984	25	(404)
Operating earnings (loss)	(553)	4,092	4,605

Exhibit 2 Motorola, Inc. and Subsidiaries (*Continued*)

Income Statement			
	Years Ended December 31		
(In millions, except per share amounts)	**2007**	**2006**	**2005**
Other income (expense)			
Interest income, net	91	326	71
Gains on sales of investments and businesses, net	50	41	1,845
Other	22	151	(109)
Total other income (expense)	163	518	1,807
Earnings (loss) from continuing operations before income taxes	(390)	4,610	6,412
Income tax expense (benefit)	(285)	1,349	1,893
Earnings (loss) from continuing operations	(105)	3,261	4,519
Earnings from discontinued operations, net of tax	56	400	59
Net earnings (loss)	$ (49)	$ 3,661	$ 4,578
Earnings (loss) per common share			
Basic			
Continuing operations	$ (0.05)	$ 1.33	$ 1.83
Discontinued operations	0.03	0.17	0.02
	$ (0.02)	$ 1.50	$ 1.85
Diluted			
Continuing operations	$ (0.05)	$ 1.30	$ 1.79
Discontinued operations	0.03	0.16	0.02
	$ (0.02)	$ 1.46	$ 1.81
Weighted average common shares outstanding			
Basic	2,312.7	2,446.3	2,471.3
Diluted	2,312.7	2,504.2	2,527.0
Dividends paid per share	$ 0.20	$ 0.18	$ 0.16

Source: Motorola 2007 Annual Report, http://www.motorola.com.

The firm incurred a loss from continuing operations of $105 million which resulted in $0.05 per diluted common share.[93] This was down from the stated $1.30 per diluted common share in 2006 with continuing operations of $3.3 billion, as shown in Exhibits 2 and 3.

Another significant decrease from previous years occurred in the stated operating cash flow of $785 million in 2007 (see Exhibit 4). Generated operating cash flows from 2005 through 2007 are $4.3 billion, $3.5 billion, and $785 million, respectively, showing a continuation of a decreasing trend.[94]

The less-than-stellar financial situation has led management to consider different strategies that would best solve this predicament.

Exhibit 3 Motorola, Inc. and Subsidiaries

Balance Sheet		
	December 31	
(In millions, except per share amounts)	2007	2006
Assets		
Cash and cash equivalents	$ 2,752	$ 2,816
Sigma Fund	5,242	12,204
Short-term investments	612	620
Accounts receivable, net	5,324	7,509
Inventories, net	2,836	3,162
Deferred income taxes	1,891	1,731
Other current assets	3,565	2,933
Total current assets	22,222	30,975
Property, plant and equipment, net	2,480	2,267
Investments	837	895
Deferred income taxes	2,454	1,325
Goodwill	4,499	1,706
Other assets	2,320	1,425
Total assets	$34,812	$38,593
Liabilities and stockholders' equity		
Notes payable and current portion of long-term debt	$ 332	$ 1,693

Balance Sheet		
	December 31	
(In millions, except per share amounts)	2007	2006
Accounts payable	4,167	5,056
Accrued liabilities	8,001	8,676
Total current liabilities	12,500	15,425
Long-term debt	3,991	2,704
Other liabilities	2,874	3,322
Stockholders' equity		
Preferred stock, $100 par value	—	—
Common stock, $3 par value	6,792	7,197
Issued shares:	2,264	2,399
Outstanding shares:	2,236	2,397
Additional paid-in capital	782	2,509
Retained earnings	8,579	9,086
Non-owner changes to equity	(706)	(1,650)
Total stockholders' equity	15,447	17,142
Total liabilities and stockholders' equity	$34,812	$38,593

Source: Motorola 2007 Annual Report, http://www.motorola.com.

Exhibit 4 Motorola, Inc. and Subsidiaries

Statement of Cash Flows			
	Years Ended December 31		
(In millions)	2007	2006	2005
Operating			
Net earnings (loss)	$ (49)	$ 3,661	$ 4,578
Less: Earnings from discontinued operations	56	400	59
Earnings (loss) from continuing operations	(105)	3,261	4,519
Adjustments to reconcile earnings (loss) from continuing operations to net cash provided by operating activities:			
Depreciation and amortization	903	558	540
Non-cash other charges	213	49	106
Share-based compensation expense	315	276	14
Gains on sales of investments and businesses, net	(50)	(41)	(1,845)
Deferred income taxes	(747)	838	1,000
Change in assets and liabilities, net of effects of acquisitions and dispositions			
Accounts receivable	2,538	(1,775)	(1,303)
Inventories	556	(718)	(19)
Other current assets	(705)	(388)	(721)
Accounts payable and accrued liabilities	(2,303)	1,654	2,405
Other assets and liabilities	170	(215)	(388)
Net cash provided by operating activities from continuing operations	785	3,499	4,308
Investing			
Acquisitions and investments, net	(4,568)	(1,068)	(312)
Proceeds from sale of investments and businesses	411	2,001	1,538
Capital expenditures	(527)	(649)	(548)

Exhibit 4 Motorola, Inc. and Subsidiaries (*Continued*)

	Statement of Cash Flows		
	Years Ended December 31		
(In millions)	**2007**	**2006**	**2005**
Proceeds from sale of property, plant and equipment	166	85	103
Proceeds from sales (purchases) of Sigma Fund investments, net	6,889	(1,337)	(3,157)
Proceeds from sales (purchases) of short-term investments	8	(476)	8
Net cash provided by (used for) investing activities from continuing operations	2,379	(1,444)	(2,368)
Financing			
Net proceeds from (repayment of) commercial paper and short-term borrowings	(242)	66	11
Repayment of debt	(1,386)	(18)	(1,132)
Net proceeds from issuance of debt	1,415	—	—
Issuance of common stock	440	918	1,199
Purchase of common stock	(3,035)	(3,826)	(874)
Excess tax benefits from share-based compensation	50	165	—
Payment of dividends	(468)	(443)	(394)
Distribution from (to) discontinued operations	(75)	(23)	283
Net cash used for financing activities from continuing operations	(3,301)	(3,161)	(907)
Effect of exchange rate changes on cash and cash equivalents from continuing operations	73	148	(105)
Discontinued Operations			
Net cash provided by (used for) operating activities from discontinued operations	(75)	(16)	297
Net cash used for investing activities from discontinued operations	—	(13)	(16)
Net cash provided by (used for) financing activities from discontinued operations	75	23	(283)
Effect of exchange rate changes on cash and cash equivalents from discontinued operations	—	6	2
Net cash provided by (used for) discontinued operations	—	—	—

Exhibit 4 Motorola, Inc. and Subsidiaries (*Continued*)

Statement of Cash Flows			
	Years Ended December 31		
(In millions)	**2007**	**2006**	**2005**
Net increase (decrease) in cash and cash equivalents	(64)	(958)	928
Cash and cash equivalents, beginning of year	2,816	3,774	2,846
Cash and cash equivalents, end of year	$ 2,752	$ 2,816	$ 3,774
Cash Flow Information			
Cash paid during the year for:			
Interest, net	$ 312	$ 322	$ 318
Income taxes, net of refunds	440	463	703

Source: Motorola 2007 Annual Report, http://www.motorola.com.

Motorola's Strategies

Motorola's current strategies are framed around efforts to return the firm to profitability. In the past couple of years there has been much discussion about spinning off the Mobile Devices segment as an independent company, similar to what Motorola had previously done with Free Scale. In a press release, Greg Brown stated the following: "Creating two industry-leading companies will provide improved flexibility, more tailored capital structures, and increased management focus—as well as more targeted investment opportunities for our shareholders."[95] However, as a result of the 2008 economic downturn, Motorola postponed the spin-off until the third quarter of 2009.[96]

Motorola is going to direct its efforts to better understand consumer demand.[97] In addition, it plans to pursue a product upgrade cycle and initiate operational changes to cut costs and make the company leaner.[98] This entails cutting approximately 3,000 jobs—2,000 of which will be from the handset division.[99] In addition, Motorola is considering reducing its emphasis on the European market.[100]

Motorola also invested heavily in the newly developed WiMax technology.[101] There are high expectations for WiMax as the next-generation wireless technology because it supports high-speed data transmission.[102] WiMax is capable of transmitting data at speeds from 1 to 5 megabits per second.[103] Furthermore, it works on

a radius of over 20 miles.[104] Motorola believes competing in this technological and product domain is crucial for its mobility strategy.[105] In November 2008, Motorola announced the deployment of its first trial network in Vietnam.[106] Dr. Ray Owen, head of Technology for Asia and general director of Motorola Vietnam, said: "Launching the trial network for Vietnam Datacommunications Company is another milestone in Motorola's long history of leading WiMAX development in the industry."[107]

Historically, Motorola has not limited the number of operating systems it supports in the Mobile Devices segment. However, recently the firm reduced the number of operating systems it supports to only P2K (Motorola's legacy platform for low-end devices),[108] Windows Mobile, and Android.[109] Motorola has been a featured partner with Google since the inception of the Android platform alliance.[110] Android will feature social networking applications such as Facebook and MySpace.[111] Moreover, analysts believe that social networking phones are expected to be a hit with the 16- to 34-year-old age segment, expected to comprise 23 percent of cell phone users by the end of 2012.[112]

Motorola's cost-reduction actions may expose the firm to additional risks.[113] Similar to most firms in this very competitive market, Motorola is confronted with an uncertain future.

Exhibit 5 Competitor Financials*

Key Numbers	Sony Ericsson Mobile	Nokia	Nokia (Mobile Phones)	Samsung	Samsung (Telecom)	RIM (2008)	RIM (Devices) (2008)	Apple (2008)	Apple (Headsets) (2008)	LG (Headsets)	Industry	Market
Competitor Financials												
Annual Sales ($ mil.)	47.50	75,203.30	32,309.00	105,018	16,114	6,009.40	4,914	32,479	1,800	3,136		
Net Income ($ mil.)			5,434.00	8,446	2,407	1,294.00	370	4,834				
Employees		100,534	3,614			8,387		35,100				
Market Cap ($ mil.)				48,700								
Profitability											Industry	Market
Gross Profit Margin		33.90%									33.40%	52.70%
Pre-Tax Profit Margin		16.20%									0.50%	4.70%
Net Profit Margin	7.40%	14.10%	7.45%	8.04%	11.60%	21.53%	7.53%	14.88%		6%	-0.30%	2.70%

* Aside from Motorola, Nokia is the only publicly traded company on the U.S. exchanges; therefore, those companies traded on non-U.S. exchanges are not required by the Securities and Exchange Commission to report all necessary financials.

Source: 2008, http://hoovers.com; 2008, http://www.samsung.com; 2008, http://www.apple.com; 2008, http://www.lge.com; 2008, http://www.rim.net.

The Future for Motorola

Motorola has struggled to maintain pace with the change in technology that consumers desire. Indeed, the firm has struggled to have a top-performing product within the Mobile Devices segment since its introduction of the RAZR. Will a spinoff of this division help the rest of Motorola's business improve its financial performance? Can the new CEO and top-management team establish a positive reputation and limit the turnover that has taken place in upper management since he took over? These and other questions are at the forefront of the minds of the board of directors and stockholders alike.

NOTES

1. 2008, Motorola Inc Timeline, *Motorola Inc,* http://www.motorola.com.
2. 2008, Motorola – Early History, *Free Encyclopedia of Ecommerce,* http://ecommerce.hostip.info/pages/751/Motorola-Inc-EARLY-HISTORY.html.
3. Ibid.
4. 2008, Motorola Inc. Timeline.
5. 2008, Motorola Inc.—Early History.
6. 2008, Motorola Inc. Timeline.
7. Ibid.
8. 2008, Motorola Inc.—Early History.
9. Ibid.
10. 2008, Motorola Inc. Timeline.
11. Ibid.
12. 2008, Motorola Inc.—Early History.
13. 2008, Motorola Inc. Timeline.
14. Ibid.
15. Ibid.
16. Ibid.
17. Ibid.
18. 2008, Motorola Inc.—Early History.
19. Ibid.
20. Ibid.
21. 2008, Motorola Inc. Timeline.
22. Ibid.
23. 1990, Paul Galvin: Motorola, *American National Business Hall of Fame,* http://www.anbhf.org/laureates/pgalvin.html.
24. 2006, Illinois Hall of Fame; Paul Galvin, *Illinois Review,* http://illinoisreview.typepad.com/illinoisreview/2006/11/illinois_hall_o_2.html.
25. 2008, Motorola Inc. Timeline.
26. 2008, Motorola Inc., *Encyclopedia Britannica,* http://www.britannica.com, November 30.
27. 2008, Motorola Inc. Timeline.
28. 2008, Motorola Inc.—Early History.
29. Ibid.
30. 2008, Motorola Inc. Timeline.
31. Ibid.
32. 2008, Motorola DynaTAC—35th Anniversary, Motorola Inc., http://www.motorola.com.
33. 2008, Motorola Inc. Timeline, Motorola Inc., http://www.motorola.com/content.jsp?globalObjectId=7632.
34. 2008, Motorola Inc. Timeline, Motorola Inc., http://www.motorola.com/content.jsp?globalObjectId=7632.
35. 2008, Six Sigma: Motorola does it right, Motorola Inc., http://www.motorola.com.
36. 2008, Motorola Inc. Timeline.
37. Ibid.
38. Ibid.
39. Ibid.
40. Ibid.
41. Ibid.
42. Ibid.
43. 2008, 20 Moments in Motorola History, *ChannelWeb,* http://www.crn.com/networking/206906014;jsessionid=F0MYJEPAOMV5UQSNDLPCKH0CJUNN2JVN?pgno=3.
44. Ibid.
45. 2008, Motorola Inc. Timeline.
46. 2008, CCID Consulting reviews Motorola performance in the mobile phone market, *Reuters,* http://www.reuters.com, June 11.
47. 2008, 20 moments in Motorola history.
48. Ibid.
49. 2008, Motorola Inc. Timeline.
50. 2008, 20 moments in Motorola History.
51. Ibid.
52. Ibid.
53. 2007, Motorola names Greg Brown CEO, *BusinessWeek,* http://www.businessweek.com, November 30.
54. A. Dannin, 2008, Motorola Inc., http://library.morningstar.com.ezproxy1.lib.asu.edu/stocknet/MorningstarAnalysis.aspx?Country=USA&Symbol=MOT.
55. 2008, Motorola Inc. company description, *BusinessWeek,* http://investing.businessweek.com.
56. 2008, Motorola 2007 Annual Report, http://www.motorola.com.
57. 2008, Form 10-Q: Motorola, Inc., United States Securities and Exchange Commission, http://sec.gov/Archives/edgar/data/68505/000095015208008426/c47113e10vq.htm.
58. Ibid.
59. Ibid.
60. 2008, CDMA – Code Division Multiple Access, Birds-Eye.net, http://www.birds-eye.net/definition/c/cdma-code_division_multiple_access.shtml.
61. 2008, UMTS – Universal Mobile Telecommunications System, Birds-Eye.net, http://www.birds-eye.net/definition/u/umts-universal_mobile_telecommunications_system.shtml.
62. 2008, Motorola Inc. company description, *BusinessWeek.*
63. 2008, Form 10-Q: Motorola, Inc.
64. 2008, Motorola Inc. company description.
65. 2008, Form 10-Q: Motorola, Inc.
66. 2008, Nokia Annual Report, http://www.nokia.com; 2007, Nokia in 2007, *Nokia,* http://media.corporate-ir.net/media_files/irol/10/107224/reports/ann_acc_2007.pdf_.
67. Samsung Electronics 2007 Annual Report, http://www.samsung.com.
68. Ericsson Annual Report 2007, http://www.ericsson.com.
69. LG Annual Report 2007, http://www.lg.net.
70. 2008, About LG: Mobile communications, http://www.lge.com.
71. 2007, Apple Form 10-K, Securities and Exchange Commission, http://www.sec.gov, December 31.
72. Research in Motion 2008 Annual Report, http://www.rim.net.
73. 2008, RIM: Company, Research in Motion, http://www.rim.com.
74. 2008, Helio, Inc, and Helio LLC Exhbit 99.1, Helio, http://documents.scribd.com/docs/qk9y5wyxvrrcweuad2d.pdf
75. 2008, Don't call us a phone company, Helio, http://www.helio.com.
76. 2008, Mobile internet devices, Intel Corporation, http://www.intel.com.
77. Ibid.
78. Ibid.
79. Ibid.
80. 2008, SEC Form 10-Q: Motorola, Inc, *AOL Money and Finance,* http://finance.aol.com.
81. Ibid.

82. Ibid.
83. Ibid.
84. 2008, Motorola Form 10-Q.
85. T. Krazit, 2004, After delays, Motorola brings V400 to North America, *InfoWorld*, http://www.infoworld.com, January 16.
86. 2007, Motorola Form 10-Q.
87. P. Teague, 2007, The ABCs of spend analysis: Change the way you source, *Purchasing*, http://www.purchasing.com, May 3.
88. J. Carbone, 2007, Time-to-Market is key, *Purchasing*, http://www.purchasing.com, March 15.
89. 2008, Motorola 2007 Annual Report.
90. Ibid.
91. Ibid.
92. Ibid.
93. Ibid.
94. Ibid.
95. Ibid.
96. A. Dannin, Motorola Inc.
97. J. Zounis, 2008, Motorola Inc., http://library.morningstar.com.ezproxy1.lib.asu.edu/stocknet/AnalysisArchive.aspx?docId=234200&Year=2008&Country=USA&Symbol=MOT.
98. Ibid.
99. O. Kharif, 2008, Motorola's turnaround plans meet with skepticism, *BusinessWeek*, http://www.businessweek.com, October 31.
100. Ibid.
101. A. Dannin, Motorola Inc.
102. M. Reardon, 2005, Motorola, Intel team on mobile WiMax, CNET News, http://news.cnet.com, October 27.
103. Ibid.
104. Ibid.
105. Ibid.
106. Motorola Media Center, 2008, Motorola deploys its First WiMAX 802.16e trial network in Vietnam, http://www.motorola.com, November 27.
107. Ibid.
108. http://www.funambol.com/blog/capo/2008/10/motorola-focusing-on-android-why-it-is.html.
109. A. Dannin, Motorola Inc.
110. D. Gardner, 2008, Motorola reportedly trimming operating systems in favor of android, *Information Week*, http://www.informationweek.com, October 29.
111. O.Kharif, 2008, Motorola readies its own android social smartphone, *BusinessWeek*, http://www.businessweek.com, October 17.
112. Ibid.
113. Ibid.

James Francart, Harry Fry, Denis Grigorov,
Leonard Muhammad, Regina Pelkman,
Kyle Schlabach, Robin Chapman

Arizona State University

The worst sort of business is one that grows rapidly, requires significant capital to engender the growth, and then earns little or no money. Think airlines. Here a durable competitive advantage has proven elusive ever since the days of the Wright Brothers. Indeed, if a farsighted capitalist had been present at Kitty Hawk, he would have done his successors a huge favor by shooting Orville down.[1]

—*WARREN BUFFETT IN A 2008 LETTER TO BERKSHIRE HATHAWAY SHAREHOLDERS*

Some of the best minds in business have entered the commercial airline industry and failed. Included in this group is Warren Buffett, who invested in U.S. Air during the 1990s and was unsuccessful in saving the airline.[2] Since the inception of commercial flight, more than 200 airlines have tried and failed in the commercial airline industry.[3] These companies are a reminder that this business is tumultuous, complex, and in many cases, futile. Herb Kelleher, one of Southwest Airlines's founders, illustrates his awareness of how difficult it is to achieve any modicum of profitability in this industry with his comment, "If the Wright brothers were alive today Wilbur would have to fire Orville to reduce costs."[4]

Financial distress in the airline industry can be tied to the high costs incurred by the airlines to offer their services and low costs demanded by customers to travel. In an already extremely challenging industry, Southwest also faces dilemmas associated with its growth strategy, costs incurred to meet safety regulations on its aircraft, and a dispute with a labor union.[5]

These issues make the current and future decisions of the company more critical than ever. Fortunately for Southwest, the current president and CEO has a vast amount of experience within the company.

Key Leader

Gary C. Kelly replaced Herb Kelleher, one of the founders and chairman of the board, as president when he resigned in May 2008.[6] Kelly began his 22-year career with Southwest in the finance department as controller.[7] In that time, he has risen to the top of Southwest Airlines, holding positions such as vice president of finance, executive vice president, chief financial officer, and vice chairman.[8] Kelly, with such initiatives as fuel hedging, has been instrumental in Southwest's recent success.[9]

History of Southwest

Southwest Airlines, originally known as Air Southwest, was founded by Rollin King and Herb Kelleher. Southwest took its first flight in June 1971, serving three major cities: Dallas, Houston, and San Antonio.[10] Within the first two years Southwest suffered operating losses and was forced to make a difficult decision: lay off employees or sell one of its four aircraft. As an early indication of Southwest's loyalty to its employees, it chose to sell the aircraft.[11] This established the company's "no layoff policy" that is still in force.[12]

Southwest was able to sustain a four-aircraft schedule using only three aircraft by utilizing the "ten-minute turn."[13] Southwest turned its first annual profit in 1973. Southwest's expansion strategy flourished after 1973. By 1977 Southwest operated six airplanes and had transported five million customers.[14] New flight destinations were added such as Rio Grande Valley, Austin, Corpus Christi, El Paso, Lubbock, and Midland/Odessa.[15] Between 1979 and 1980, Southwest established its first interstate service to New Orleans and Albuquerque, followed by Oklahoma City and Tulsa.[16] Southwest expanded west in 1982, when it added service to Phoenix, Las Vegas, and San Diego.[17] In late 1984 the first 737-300 was added to its fleet and was used to service flights to Chicago Midway and St. Louis.[18]

In 1986, Southwest opened a new multi-million dollar training center for flight crews.[19] Since customer satisfaction was Southwest's main focus, it began a frequent flyer program, "The Company Club," in 1987. In 1988,

Southwest won its first monthly Triple Crown award for having the best on-time record, best baggage handling, and fewest customer complaints. All of its achievements allowed it to reach the billion-dollar revenue mark and become a major airline by 1989.[20] In 1990, Southwest created its corporate culture committee to take the lead in preserving the airline's unique culture.[21]

Southwest began to offer service to many new cities such as Nashville, Sacramento, Cleveland, and Columbus, and finally entered the east coast market in 1993 when it offered service to Baltimore/Washington International Airport.[22] With the acquisition and integration of Morris Air in 1994, the company was able to add service to seven new cities, including Seattle, Spokane, Portland, Salt Lake City, and Boise. That same year Southwest became the first airline to introduce Ticketless Travel in four cities, which eventually expanded system-wide in January of 1995.[23] Later in 1995, Southwest became one of the first airlines to have its own Web site, and the following year the Ticketless Travel system debuted online.[24]

After 25 years of service, Southwest owned a fleet of 243 aircraft and it saw an opportunity to introduce a fuel cost management program. The Asian market plummeted in 1998, causing jet fuel costs to drop to 35 cents per gallon. Southwest took advantage of this opportunity and hedged its fuel costs. Within two years fuel costs had increased as crude oil increased from $11 to $34 per barrel.

Further expansion, tangible asset improvements, and technology upgrades continued between 1999 and 2006. Southwest expanded to serve locations such as Long Island and Raleigh-Durham. It teamed up with IBM to introduce approximately 250 self-service check-in kiosks.[25] This project was "part of a nationwide effort to reduce the amount of time Southwest customers spend in line and to improve the airport experience."[26] By 2004, Southwest was offering online boarding passes via its Web site, allowing passengers to go directly to the departure gates without having to stop at the ticket counter.[27] Customer convenience increased even more in 2005, when Southwest "extended online check-in to 24 hours prior to departure."[28] By 2006, Southwest was ranked number one among airlines in customer satisfaction.[29]

Southwest updated its boarding procedure in 2007. Passengers are now assigned a boarding letter and a number that assigns them a specific place in line.[30] Select fare increases aligned with continuous cost-cutting policies resulted in the year-end revenue of $9.8 billion and $645 million in profits.[31]

In November 2008, Southwest purchased one of its main competitors, ATA Airlines, which allowed it to obtain boarding slots at New York's LaGuardia Airport.[32]

Acquiring ATA has the potential to provide Southwest with means to connect to foreign destinations. Southwest also partnered with WestJet Airlines, a low-cost carrier, to synch flights between Canada and the United States.

Southwest followed other carriers in early 2009 by increasing fare prices $10 per leg in the domestic market and up to $40 per leg for international routes.[33]

Southwest's technological innovations, procedure changes, price increases, and recent acquisitions are attempts to overcome the looming challenges in the airline industry.

Industry Challenges

Factors such as increased fuel costs and other high operating expenses, a decrease in business travelers due to budget cuts, and increased regulation have placed strains on airline companies. Many airlines have subsequently been forced out of business or acquired by competitors. This is illustrated by the fact that the large group of airlines that made up the industry 30 years ago has narrowed to six major firms that control a majority of the market (see Exhibit 1). These six carriers constitute five traditional airline companies (American, Continental, Delta, United, and US Airways) and Southwest, the low-cost leader.

Additionally, many airlines have been forced to file for bankruptcy. From 2005 to 2007, US Airways, UAL Corporation (United Airlines), ATA Airlines, Northwest Airlines, and Delta Air Lines all emerged from bankruptcy proceedings.[34] In 2008, Frontier Airlines, Skybus Airlines, Inc., Aloha Airlines, and ATA Airlines (for the second time) filed for bankruptcy.[35] All of these

Exhibit 1 Airline Domestic Market Share (March 2009)

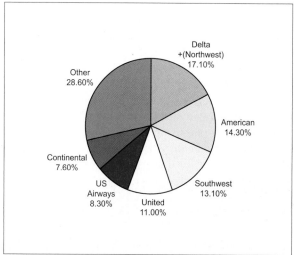

Source: 2008, Research and Innovative Technology Administration, http://www.transtats.bts.gov.

bankruptcies demonstrate the difficult and competitive nature of the industry.

Competitive Environment

Southwest considers any airline offering a flight on the same route it does a competitor, regardless of the overall size of that competitor's operation. Since Southwest now operates in many geographic markets throughout the United States, essentially every airline that offers service to domestic cities is viewed as a competitor.[36]

New companies still occasionally try to replace Southwest as the low-cost leader. Many of these new airlines have disappeared as fast and unspectacularly as they flashed into existence. For example, Skybus, founded by an ex-Southwest employee, copied Southwest's operating model and began its operations in May 2007. Within one year it discontinued operations, citing the weakened state of the economy and increasing fuel costs as the reasons for its ruin.[37]

Although it was able to sustain operations for a longer period of time, the final days of Frontier were no less tragic. When Frontier filed for bankruptcy in April 2008, six days after Skybus,[38] it was the fourth airline to close its doors that week.[39]

JetBlue, also founded by an ex-Southwest employee, emerged in 1999 and is one of the few new entrants to successfully become a principle competitor to Southwest both in terms of route coverage and low-cost, low-fare strategies.[40] It is currently the seventh-largest airline in the United States and holds 4 percent market share compared to Southwest's 13 percent. It operates mostly with point-to-point routes and reaches 52 destinations in 19 states as well as South and Central America and the Caribbean. It just opened its own terminal at JFK airport in New York and claims it has started a new airline category, the "value airline" based on service, cost, and style.[41]

Traditional carriers have recently also adopted cost-cutting practices to more effectively compete with their low-cost counterparts.[42] More than 200 aircraft were grounded in 2008, Continental cut 3,000 jobs, and airlines offered fewer flights.[43] Although the major carriers are still offering higher fares overall, their business models are beginning to mirror those of low-cost rivals. Thus, Southwest has to increasingly improve its marketing efforts to differentiate itself.

Marketing Strategy

Due to the industry-wide move to promote value, Southwest aims to differentiate itself from its competitors by utilizing quirky, humor-driven advertising.[44] One of its first ads, featuring the slogan, "How do we love you? Let us count the ways" illustrated that by offering many flights throughout the day to its first three destinations, Southwest loved its customers (see Exhibit 2).

Another example relates to the recent checked bags fees charged by most other airlines. In response, Southwest began promoting a "no fees" policy in its advertisements such as with its "The Other Side" ad, illustrating a desk clerk with two faces: one face offering only the competitor's airfare; the other face demanding additional fees.

To further develop its unconventional niche in the airline industry and achieve success as a low-cost provider, Southwest distinguishes itself using both quantitative and qualitative characteristics.

Low Costs

An efficiency technique that has consistently saved Southwest both time and expense is the standardization of its airline fleet. It was the first company to put into practice the "one-model-fleet" tactic,[45] meaning that it has focused on purchasing only one aircraft model. It started in 1971 with a fleet of Boeing 737-200s, and it has used the Boeing 737 model ever since, being one of the launch customers for the Boeing 737-700, 737-500, and 737-300 series.[46] This model has been deemed "the workhorse of the aviation industry" and has gained a reputation of being excellent in the areas of cost, reliability and flexibility.[47] "Having a single airplane model in a fleet also lowers inventory, record keeping and maintenance costs, and it minimizes the number of technical manuals, tools and spare parts. Also, fleet management is greatly simplified [and] maintenance crews do not have to modify their routines to service different models."[48]

Another tactic that Southwest employs to maintain its low costs is fuel hedging. Southwest began this practice in the late 1990s and it has played a major role in its 36 years of profitability.[49] Although Southwest is renowned for using this methodology, the idea of oil futures contracts is nothing new in the airline industry (see Exhibit 3). "All the major airlines have hedged fuel prices since the 1980s, but as the major carriers have run into financial difficulties in recent years, they have no longer had the cash—or the creditworthiness—to play the oil-futures market."[50] Nonetheless, Southwest has successfully hedged "at least 70 percent" of its fuel consumption, saving the company $727 million in 2007.[51] Fuel costs fluctuated significantly during 2008, starting out at $91, hitting $151 during the summer, and closing the year at $51. The significant change in oil prices did not provide Southwest with cost savings like those in 2007, but it

Exhibit 2 Southwest Advertisement

How do we love you? Let us count the ways.

Dallas/Ft. Worth to Houston		Houston to Dallas/Ft. Worth	
Depart	Arrive	Depart	Arrive
7:30 a*	8:18 a	7:30 a*	8:18 a
8:45 a*	9:33 a	8:45 a	9:33 a
10:00 a	10:48 a	10:00 a*	10:48 a
11:15 a*	12:03 p	11:15 a	12:03 p
12:30 p	1:18 p	12:30 p*	1:18 p
1:45 p**	2:33 p	1:45 p	2:33 p
3:00 p	3:48 p	3:00 p**	3:48 p
4:15 p**	5:03 p	4:15 p	5:03 p
5:30 p	6:18 p	5:30 p**	6:18 p
6:45 p**	7:33 p	6:45 p	7:33 p
8:00 p	8:48 p	8:00 p**	8:48 p
9:15 p**	10:03 p	9:15 p**	10:03 p

Dallas/Ft. Worth to San Antonio		San Antonio to Dallas/Ft. Worth	
Depart	Arrive	Depart	Arrive
7:00 a*	7:50 a	8:15 a*	9:05 a
9:30 a	10:20 a	10:45 a	11:35 a
12:00 n	12:50 p	1:15 p	2:05 p
2:30 p	3:20 p	3:45 p	4:35 p
5:00 p	5:50 p	6:15 p	7:05 p
7:30 p**	8:20 p	8:45 p**	9:35 p

*Except Sunday.
**Except Saturday.

SOUTHWEST AIRLINES
The somebody else up there who loves you.

Source: 2008, Southwest Airlines Historical Advertising Gallery, http://www.southwest.com.

did allow it to secure a good hedging contract through 2013 based on the fourth quarter fuel prices ($51). This is expected to save $600 million in fuel costs annually compared to 2008.[52]

Southwest exercised other cost-saving measures concerning fuel consumption, such as the implementation of blended winglets on all of its 737-700s.[53] These blended winglets would "improve performance by extending the airplane's range, saving fuel, lowering engine maintenance costs and reducing takeoff noise."[54] (See Exhibit 4 for estimates on fuel savings.) Testing on the blended winglets demonstrated "gross fuel mileage improvement … in the range of 4 to 5 percent."[55] In 2003, Southwest announced that performance-enhancing "blended winglets" would be installed on all existing and future aircrafts, though this action was not carried out until 2007.[56]

In 2008, Southwest initiated a contract with Pratt & Whitney to use its EcoPower® engine wash services. EcoPower uses atomized water to wash aircraft engines and prevent potential contaminant runoff. This system is more efficient and effective than traditional engine washing processes and extends on-wing time for Pratt & Whitney, International Aero Engines, General Electric, Rolls-Royce, and CFMI engines. By using this engine wash, Southwest anticipates saving "more than $20 million in fuel costs [at 2008 prices]."[57]

The following measures not only help Southwest save on costs, but also to retain its reputation for being reliable and punctual.

Exhibit 3 Southwest Advertisement

Southwest's Profitable Bet

Percentage of each airline's fuel needs that are hedged against higher fuel prices and have been disclosed, with the price caps of their hedges.

	2007 4th quarter		**2008** full years		**2009**		**2010**	
	HEDGED	PRICE CAP	HEDGED	PRICE CAP	HEDGED	PRICE CAP	HEDGED	PRICE CAP
Alaska[1]	50%	$62	32%	$64	5%	$68	0	
American[1]	40	69	14	n.d.†	0		0	
Continental[2]	30	93	10*	93	0		0	
Delta[2]	20	99	0		0		0	
JetBlue[2]	47	83	0		0		0	
Northwest[1]	50	73	10*	84	0		0	
Southwest[1]	90	51	70	51	55	51	25%	$63
United[2]	18	93	0		0		0	
US Airways[1]	56	73	15	73	0		0	

[1]Price based on crude oil.

[2]Price based on heating oil, which is more expensive.

*First quarter only. †Price not disclosed.

Source: 2008, Southwest Airlines manages risk through oil price hedges. http://www.artdiamondblog.com/archives/energyenvironment/, March 18.

Exhibit 4 Improvements from Winglets

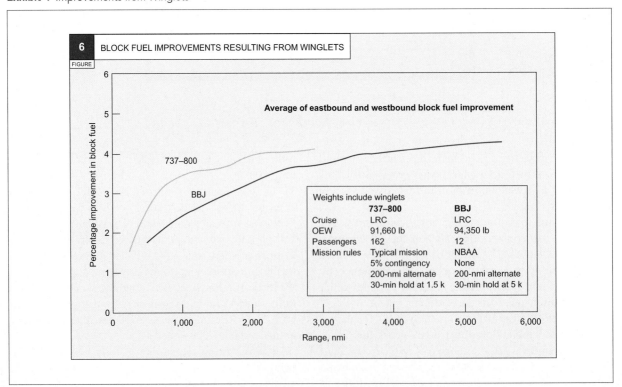

Source: Aero 17 – Blended Winglets, fig. 6, http://www.boeing.com/commercial/aeromagazine/aero_17/winglet_story.

Punctuality

Timeliness has been a defining characteristic for Southwest since its beginning. In the 1970s, the company had a 10-minute turnaround time for aircraft while the industry average was four to six times longer.[58] Southwest's "turnarounds now average 23 minutes, but that's still . . . half the time it takes other airlines."[59] It is able to maintain this quick turnaround rate because it uses point-to-point service (curtailing connection times and luggage transfers) and secondary airports for the bulk of its flights (reducing potential congestion).[60] Instead of point-to-point service most legacy carriers use a hub-and-spoke system where small feeder airlines from smaller cities feed into larger international airports such as Delta's hub in Atlanta.

The boarding process with unassigned seating is another of Southwest's differentiating qualities, but one for which it has received mixed reviews from customers.[61] Although this tactic aids in quicker gate turnaround,[62] it is flawed from a customer service standpoint and has a reputation as "cattle call" check-in. It favors customers who are able to arrive at the gate early, no matter when the ticket was purchased (even with an "A" boarding pass—see Exhibit 5). In response to customer complaints Southwest initiated a new check-in process in 2007. Kelleher believes, "Customers are like a force of nature: You can't fool them, and you ignore them at your own peril."[63] The new method gives passengers a group letter (A, B, C) and a number (1 to 60) based on order of check-in, thus it reserves more of a semblance of a place in line than the previous process.[64] Even though this distinction creates perceived value for the customer in terms of time savings, there is still controversy about this method among Southwest customers. Recently, adjustments were made to accommodate families with small children, who did not receive priority seating when the change was first made.[65]

Exceptional Customer Service Begins at Home

A unique aspect of Southwest's customer service perspective is that the end-user is not the primary focus, the employees are; "If [Southwest] can effectively make employees feel good about what they're doing on a daily basis, satisfied employees will deliver [a] . . . sense of friendliness and care to Southwest passengers."[66]

In 2008, Southwest was the highest-rated airline in *Fortune's* list of "America's Most Admired Companies."[67] It ranked first in the categories "people management" and "quality of management." Southwest's reputation for being a great employer is further illustrated by the fact that in 2007, Southwest received 329,200 resumes from job seekers.[68] In 1973, the airline adopted the first profit-sharing plan in the U.S. airline industry, and employees now own at least 8 percent of the company stock.[69] It would be safe to assume that these factors are key contributors to the low employee turnover rate that Southwest enjoys.[70] However, there have been some recent issues related to union activities and contract negotiations that could possibly tarnish Southwest's reputation as an employer (see the Additional Challenges section).

Exhibit 5 Southwest's Boarding Process

How it worked before:

- Each passenger's boarding pass was assigned to Group A, B, or C, based on check-in.
- A and B groups had 45 passengers, with everyone else in Group C.
- Families with young children boarded before the groups were called.
- In the gate area, passengers in each of the groups lined up, often 30 to 45 minutes before boarding, in either the A, B, or C line.
- Passengers boarded by group letter.
- Seats were unassigned.

The new boarding drill:

- Passenger boarding passes will have a group letter (A, B, or C) and a number (1 to 60), based on order of check-in.
- In combination, the letter and number reserves passengers' places in line, leaving them free to relax or get something to eat.
- Groups A and B contain 60 passengers each; those remaining are in Group C.
- Families with young children must now wait until the A group has boarded, unless they hold A passes.
- At the gate, six stainless steel columns divide passengers into groups of five on each side. For example, the first column has passengers holding 1–5 passes on one side and those with 31–35 on the other. The second column has spaces for those holding 6–10 and 36–40.
- Electronic monitors indicate which group is boarding. Those with A passes standing on the first side of the column will board, followed by those on the other side. As the second half boards, Group B will assemble.
- Seats are still unassigned.

Source: S. Marta, 2007, Southwest launches streamlined boarding, *The Dallas Morning News*, http://www.dallasnews.com, October 15.

Reward Programs

Nearly every major airline has attempted to increase customer loyalty through reward programs. These programs offer repeat customers perks such as an accelerated check-in process, upgrades, and even free flights and hotel stays. However, it is debatable how effective these programs are. Leisure travelers may not travel enough to allow these programs to influence their purchasing decisions; and business and other frequent travelers, who are much more concerned about convenience and scheduling, are often members of many, if not all, frequent flyer programs from each airline. The end result is that Rewards programs have not had a major impact on Southwest's bottom line.

Financial Results

Southwest Airlines reported an operating profit of $449 million for the year 2008, despite rising operating expenses marking 71 consecutive quarters of profitability. Total operating expenses for the year increased 16 percent compared to 2007 and were driven primarily by higher fuel costs (44 percent), as well as ongoing maintenance costs (see Exhibit 6). However, Southwest did make 2008 its thirty-sixth consecutive year with annual operating profits.[71]

In 2008, Southwest boasted an operating profit margin (4 percent) much higher than its competitors such as Delta (−36 percent), JetBlue (3.2 percent),

Exhibit 6 Southwest Airlines—Consolidated Statement of Income

	Years Ended December 31		
	2007	2006	2005
	(In millions, except per share amounts)		
Operating Revenues:			
Passenger	$9,457	$8,750	$7,279
Freight	130	134	133
Other	274	202	172
Total operating revenues	9,861	9,086	7,584
Operating Expenses:			
Salaries, wages, and benefits	3,213	3,052	2,782
Fuel and oil	2,536	2,138	1,341
Maintenance materials and repairs	616	468	446
Aircraft rentals	156	158	163
Landing fees and other rentals	560	495	454
Depreciation and amortization	555	515	469
Other operating expenses	1,434	1,326	1,204
Total operating expenses	9,070	8,152	6,859
Operating Income	791	934	725
Other Expenses (Income):			
Interest expense	119	128	122
Capitalized interest	(50)	(51)	(39)
Interest income	(44)	(84)	(47)

Exhibit 6 Southwest Airlines—Consolidated Statement of Income (*Continued*)

	Years Ended December 31		
	2007	**2006**	**2005**
	(In millions, except per share amounts)		
Other (gains) losses, net	(292)	151	(90)
Total other expenses (income)	(267)	144	(54)
Income before income taxes	1,058	790	779
Provision for income taxes	413	291	295
Net income	$645	$499	$484
Net income per share, basic	$.85	$.63	$.61
Net income per share, diluted	$.84	$.61	$.60

Source: 2008, Southwest Airlines 2007 Annual Report, http://www.southwest.com.

United (−21.9 percent), and American (−7.9 percent).[72] This is an indication of Southwest's ability to control costs in an industry that has historically struggled in this area. Continued emphasis on cost cutting has allowed Southwest to avoid filing for bankruptcy, unlike many of its competitors (see Exhibit 7).

In the airline industry, a high ROA indicates a company's ability to generate high income proportionate to its held assets, which are primarily composed of aircraft and other flight equipment, property (including airport operating slots), and fuel hedge contracts. In 2008, Southwest operated with an ROA of 1.2 percent, double that of the next-closest competitor, JetBlue (−1.3 percent). This demonstrates Southwest's outstanding ability to avoid excess capacity and service outages.

Many airlines rely heavily on debt financing, since many investors avoid sinking cash into this industry. Southwest has been able to maintain low levels of debt and position itself with the lowest D/E ratio (77.6) among major airlines (the industry average D/E is 330). Southwest has been able to generate income, have positive profit margins, and maintain low debt levels because it puts great effort into wisely carrying out its strategies.

Part of Southwest's efforts to maintain positive operating margins and low debt levels is to expand its service to greater destinations.

Expansion Plans

Kelly has expressed a desire to expand Southwest beyond the 64 cities it currently serves, calling the airline "an adolescent" in the airline industry.[73] Although the airline is cutting certain less profitable routes, the net result of the additional flights will increase the company's overall flights by nine.[74]

In March 2009, flights between Chicago and Minneapolis were added. "The people of Minnesota have been asking for Southwest Airlines' service for many years, and we can't wait to introduce them to our legendary customer service, as well as our low fares, on-time flights, and no hidden fees."[75] Even though its strategy is primarily limited to domestic expansion with a push into Denver, Southwest is exploring ways to launch services to the Caribbean and England.[76] It recently announced the addition of flights to Mexico through code-sharing with Volaris. "Volaris has a stellar reputation for being a highly efficient airline with a dedication to customer service, which makes it a natural fit for Southwest Airlines."[77] Growth initiatives also include possible acquisitions of flights once belonging to now defunct airlines such as Ted (United Airlines attempt at a lower cost approach).[78]

Additional Challenges

Technology

The airline companies' widespread integration of the Internet into the booking process acts as a double-edged sword. Customers value the ease provided by online booking, which in turn draws in customers. Southwest obtained first-mover advantage using this technology when it became the first airline to offer the service. However, now that this has become the industry

Exhibit 7 Financial Analysis of Southwest Airlines and Selected Key Competitors

	Southwest Airlines[1]	JetBlue Airways[2]	American Airlines[3]	Delta Air Lines[4]	United Airlines[5]
Period	*2007*	*2007*	*2007*	*2007*	*2007*
Annual Revenue					
Passenger	9,457	2,636	20,705	11,803	18,317
Freight and other	404	206	2,230	1,555	1,826
Total	*9,861*	*2,842*	*22,935*	*13,358*	*20,143*
Employees (FTE)	34,378	10,219	85,500	55,044	44,861
Operating Profit Margin	8.0%	5.9%	4.2%	6.0%	5.1%
Pre-Tax Profit Margin	10.7%	1.4%	2.2%	3.9%	3.5%
Net Profit Margin	6.5%	0.6%	2.2%	2.4%	2.0%
Return on Equity	9.6%	1.8%	49.1%	−18.0%	17.7%
Return on Assets	4.3%	0.3%	1.7%	1.2%	1.6%
Total Debt/Equity	1.42	4.40	9.75	2.21	9.02
12-month Revenue Growth	8.5%	20.3%	1.6%	nm	nm

[1] 2008, Southwest Airlines 2007 Annual Report, http://www.southwest.com.
[2] 2008, JetBlue Airways Corporation 2007 Annual Report, http://www.jetblue.com.
[3] 2008, AMR Corporation 2007 Annual Report, http://www.aa.com.
[4] 2008, Delta Air Lines, Inc. 2007 Annual Report, http://www.delta.com.
[5] 2008, UAL Corporation 2007 Annual Report, http://www.united.com.

standard, it has significantly increased consumer ability to apply some pressure on ticket prices. Travel search engine sites such as Expedia.com, Travelocity.com, Orbitz.com, Kayak.com, and others have further exasperated this issue for the airlines. Southwest has long refused to submit pricing information or allow the purchase of its tickets from these sites. Since there are many airlines and negligible switching costs, this is truly an industry that has long lacked customer loyalty.

Violations of Safety Requirements. Early in 2008, it was revealed that Southwest had flown at least 117 aircraft that were in violation of mandatory safety checks.[79] As a result, the airline had to temporarily ground 47 of its aircrafts for re-inspection, and the Federal Aviation Administration charged the airline with $10.2 million in fines.[80] Southwest claims, "[it] discovered the missed inspection area, disclosed it to the FAA, and promptly

reinspected all potentially affected aircraft in March 2007. The FAA approved our actions and considered the matter closed as of April 2007." FAA inspectors contest that Southwest continued to use the planes in question before inspections were complete, thus the airline did not take immediate corrective action.[81] Gary Kelly states, "Our interpretation of the guidance that we got from the FAA at the time was that we were in compliance with all laws and regulations … the important point is that at no time were we operating in an unsafe manner, and I think our history proves it."[82]

Union Walkout

The company that once enjoyed superior employee relations compared to its competitors ran into problems in 2008. Complaints of unequal pay for members of ground crew and no raises since 2005 prompted a walkout by the labor union on November 20, 2008.[83] In March

2009 an agreement was reached. The union president admitted that the negotiations were conducted with a spirit of cooperation that is part of Southwest's culture: "Southwest Airlines flight attendants have always been an integral part of the airline's success and it is great news that together they have negotiated a contract that recognizes their contribution."[84] Flight attendants will gain wage increases and a boost in 401k contributions, but only to the degree that such increases will allow Southwest to keep its low-cost advantage.

Questions to Address

As the airline industry as a whole suffers, due to threats from fuel price increases, ever-escalating operational costs, potential security threats, and the current global economic crisis, can Southwest maintain its 36-year streak of profitability? With fluctuating oil prices, can Southwest continue to depend on fuel hedging as an important source of cost control? As it expands its domestic flight operations, will "point-to-point" methodology still prove to be useful? As the major traditional airlines become more like their low-cost counterparts, will they ultimately become more of a competitive threat to Southwest? Using its current strategy, will Southwest be able to expand internationally? Can it maintain its positive relations with employees and avoid future union walkouts and negotiations? If the current economic crisis persists, how will the present expansion plans by Southwest fare? As environmental uncertainties mount, what overall strategies and as well as competitive tactics should Southwest consider to maintain it low cost position and perception of customer loyalty?

NOTES

1. Sykes, 2008, Buffett letter offers great lessons for investors, http://www.bloggingstocks.com, March 3.
2. 2008, Warren Buffett, airlines hasn't always been a successful marriage, *Local Tech Wire*, http://localtechwire.com, January.
3. 2008, Defunct airlines of the United States, http://en.wikipedia.org.
4. H. Kelleher, 1994, *USA Today*, June 8.
5. M. McSherry & M. Lewis, 2008, Southwest Airlines union pickets over wages, *Reuters*, http://www.reuters.com, November.
6. T. Maxon, 2008, Kelleher to preside over his last Southwest meeting Wednesday, *The Dallas Morning News*, http://www.dallasnews.com, May 20; 2008, Southwest officer biographies, http://www.southwest.com.
7. G. C. Kelly, 2008, *Forbes*, http://people.forbes.com/profile/gary-c-kelly/73447.
8. 2008, Southwest officer biographies, http://www.southwest.com.
9. S. Taylor, 2005, To provide the best customer service, put customers second, says Southwest President Colleen Barrett, *McCombs School of Business*, http://www.mccombs.utexas.edu, April 18.
10. 2008, Southwest Airlines, Wikipedia, http://en.wikipedia.org.
11. D. Koenig, 2008, Southwest leader Kelleher steps down, *USA Today*, http://www.usatoday.com, May 21.
12. 2003, What makes Southwest Airlines fly, *Knowledge@Wharton*, http://knowledge.wharton.upenn.edu, April 23.
13. 2008, About Southwest Airlines, http://www.southwest.com.
14. Ibid.
15. Ibid.
16. Ibid.
17. Ibid.
18. Ibid.
19. Ibid.
20. Ibid.
21. Ibid.
22. Ibid.
23. Ibid.
24. Ibid.
25. Ibid.
26. Ibid.
27. Ibid.
28. Ibid.
29. Ibid.
30. Southwest Airlines, Wikipedia.
31. About Southwest Airlines.
32. Ibid.
33. M. Schlangenstein, 2009, Delta, Southwest airlines raise most U.S. tickets $20, http://www.Bloomberg.com, June 17.
34. 2008, Southwest Airlines 2007 Annual Report, http://www.southwest.com..
35. J. Bunch & K. Yamanouchi, 2008, Frontier Airlines files Chapter 11, *The Denver Post*, http://www.denverpost.com, April 11; 2008, Southwest Airlines bids on 14 LaGuardia slots, *Queens Chronicle*, http://www.zwire.com, November; 2008, Skybus becomes third airline to close this week, CNN, http://www.cnn.com, April 4.
36. 2008, Southwest Airlines 2007 Annual Report.
37. Ibid.
38. J. Bunch & K. Yamanouchi, Frontier Airlines files Chapter 11.
39. Skybus becomes third airline to close this week.
40. 2008, America's most admired companies, *Fortune*, http://money.cnn.com, March 17.
41. 2009, JetBlue 2008 Annual Report, http://www.jetblue.com, June 17.
42. M. Maynard, 2008, As costs rise, airlines cut services and raise fares, *The New York Times*, http://www.nytimes.com, June 6.
43. Ibid.
44. 2008, Southwest Airlines historical advertising gallery, http://www.southwest.com.
45. 2002, The secret behind high profits at low-fare airlines, Boeing News Release, http://www.boeing.com, June 14.
46. 2008, Southwest Airlines Fact Sheet, http://www.southwest.com.
47. The secret behind high profits at low-fare airlines.
48. Ibid.
49. D. Reed, 2008, Can fuel hedges keep Southwest in the money? *USA Today*, http://www.usatoday.com, July 23.
50. E. Roston, 2005, Hedging their costs, *Time*, June 20.
51. Southwest Airlines 2007 Annual Report.
52. 2009, Southwest Airlines 2008 Annual Report, http://www.southwest.com, June 11, 9.
53. 2003, Southwest Airlines Boeing 737-700 fleet takes wing with sleek new look, Boeing News Release, http://www.boeing.com, June 17.
54. Ibid.
55. Ibid.

56. Ibid.

57. G. Brostowicz & J. Whitlow, 2008, Southwest Airlines to save millions in fuel costs and significantly reduce carbon dioxide emissions with Pratt & Whitney EcoPower® Engine wash services, *Pratt & Whitney*, http://www.pw.utc.com, June 11.

58. 2007, Something special about Southwest Airlines, CBS News, http://www.cbsnews.com,_September 2.

59. Ibid.

60. 2008, Southwest Airlines Company (LUV), Wikinvest, http://www.wikinvest.com.

61. D. Grossman, 2007, New Southwest boarding policy pits business travelers against families, *USA Today*, http://www.usatoday.com, October 28.

62. W. Haas, 2007, How Southwest Airlines plans for success, *Associated Content*, http://www.associatedcontent.com, February 2.

63. B. McConnell & J. Huba, 2001, The wild turkey, *Creative Customer Evangelists*, http://www.creatingcustomerevangelists.com, September 1.

64. S. Marta, 2007, Southwest launches streamlined boarding, *The Dallas Morning News*, http://www.dallasnews.com, October 15.

65. Ibid.

66. To provide the best customer service, put customers second.

67. America's most admired companies, *Fortune*.

68. Southwest Airlines Fact Sheet.

69. Ibid.

70. T. Tripp, Best practices case study: Best perks, Southwest Airlines, *Vault*, http://www.vault.com/nr/newsmain.jsp?nr_page=3&ch_id=402&article_id=19258&cat_id=1123.

71. Southwest 2008 Annual Report; 2008, Southwest Airlines reports third quarter financial results, http://www.southwest.com, October 16; 2008, Southwest Airlines reports fourth quarter earnings and 35th consecutive year of profitability, http://www.southwest.com, January 23.

72. 2009, Delta, Southwest, AMR, UAL, and JetBlue, *Reuters*, http://www.reuters.com, June 11.

73. J. Bottiglieri, 2008, Gary C. Kelly: Aspire to something greater; Southwest Airlines' CEO talks about sustaining profitability and mitigating risk, *Bnet Business Network*, March; R. Velotta, 2008, Southwest Airlines announces code share with Mexican airline, *Las Vegas Sun*http://www.lasvegassun.com, November 10.

74. 2008, Southwest Airlines cuts 31 flights, adds 40 flights, *DWS Aviation*, http://www.dancewithshadows.com, June.

75. 2008, Southwest Airlines announces schedule, fares for its new Minneapolis-Chicago service, *DWS Aviation*, http://www.dancewithshadows.com/aviation, November.

76. Ibid.

77. 2008, Southwest to partner with Volaris on international flights, *Austin Business Journal*, http://www.bizjournals.com, November.

78. 2008, Southwest Airlines bids on 14 LaGuardia slots, *Queens Chronicle*, http://www.zwire.com, November.

79. D. Griffin & S. Bronstein, 2008, Records: Southwest Airlines flew "unsafe" planes, *CNN*, http://www.cnn.com, March 6.

80. Ibid.

81. Ibid.

82. D. Griffin & S. Bronstein, 2008, Southwest Airlines CEO calls FAA's threats of fine "unfair", *CNN*, http://www.cnn.com, March 7.

83. Southwest Airlines union pickets over wages.

84. J. Horwitz, 2009, Arriving today, a tentative agreement for Southwest flight attendants that protects employees and the LUV airline's future, TWU News Room, http://www.twu.org, March 26.

Apple Computer, Inc.: Maintaining the Music Business While Introducing iPhone and Apple TV*

Robin Chapman, Robert E. Hoskisson

Arizona State University

"This will go down in history as a turning point for the music industry," said Apple Computer CEO Steve Jobs. "This is landmark stuff. I can't overestimate it!"[1] Jobs was referring to the April 2003 debut of Apple's iTunes Online Music Store, the first legal online music service to have agreements with all five major record labels. Although initially available only for Macintosh users, iTunes sold more than 1 million songs by the end of its first week in operation. Not only did iTunes change the nature of the music industry, it also added greatly to Apple's revenues by way of promoting the purchase of the iPod—a portable digital music device that can store downloaded iTunes songs. In 2007, Apple controlled more than 70 percent of the digital music market,[2] and its net income was $3.5 billion (see Exhibits 1 and 2). Jobs hopes further that the success of iTunes will flourish with the launch of Apple TV and iPhone in 2007. In May 2007, Apple was named by *BusinessWeek* as the most innovative company for the third year in a row. Apple's focus on innovation has helped it maintain a competitive advantage and marketing prowess over other industry players that have historically been much stronger than Apple.[3] However, Apple must beat the competition on a number of levels. iTunes faces stiff competition from new and existing online music and video download services both legal and illegal. The iPod, Apple TV, and iPhone all face the threat of lower-priced rivals and possible substitutes. Apple's innovative ability and the quality of its marketing strategy will likely determine the outcome of the company's foray into the music, mobile phone, and video-on-demand businesses.

Early Company History

On April 1, 1976, Steve Jobs and Stephen Wozniak began the partnership that would eventually become Apple Computer. Both electronics gurus, Jobs and Wozniak had known each other since high school and had worked together previously on other projects.[4] In early 1976, Wozniak had been working on combining video monitors with computers. His idea was to invent a user-friendly computer that ordinary consumers could buy. Wozniak, who worked for Hewlett-Packard (HP) at the time, decided to approach his employer with his idea. HP, however, did not see a future for personal computers (PCs) and soundly rebuffed him. At that point, Steve Jobs told his friend Wozniak that they should go into business together and sell computers themselves.[5]

Their first computer, the *Apple I*, was built in the garage of Jobs's parents (see Exhibit 3). Known as a "kit computer," the original Apple consisted merely of a circuit board and did not even have an exterior casing. It was intended to be sold to hobbyists only. Jobs called the computer an "Apple" in honor of his days working at an orchard while seeking enlightenment—and because neither he nor Wozniak could come up with a better name.[6] The *Apple I* received mixed responses from hobbyists, and the duo decided it was time to expand the market for personal computers by building a more attractive and useful machine, the *Apple II*.[7]

Growth

After taking on new partners to fund expansion plans, the company officially became Apple Computer, Inc., in early

* This case is intended to be used as the basis for class discussion rather than to illustrate effective or ineffective handling of an administrative or strategic situation. We appreciate the previous input on an earlier case focused only on the music industry by Jeff Berrong, Marilyn Klopp, Max Mishkin, Jimmy Pittman, and Adrian Ray under the direction of Professor Robert E. Hoskisson.

Apple Computer, Inc., by Robin Chapman and Robert E. Hoskisson. Reprinted by permission of the authors.

1977.[8] Within months, the recapitalized company introduced the *Apple II*, the first computer to come with a sleek plastic casing and color graphics.[9] Annual sales increased dramatically to $10 million, and the company began to grow quickly in size, adding thousands of employees.[10] On December 12, 1980, Apple became a public company. On the first day of trading, its share price increased from an initial $22 offering to $29.[11] By the end of the year, Apple reached $100 million in annual sales.[12] The fledgling company, however, soon faced some experienced competition.

In 1981, IBM released its first personal computer. IBM's sheer size ensured its domination of the young PC market. Steve Jobs realized that Apple would have to move fast in order to remain a viable company. Over the next few years, the company released several new computer models, most notably the *Apple III* and the *Lisa*. Neither of these models sold particularly well.

In 1983, Jobs recruited Pepsi-Cola CEO John Sculley as Apple's president and CEO. Jobs hoped that this change would bring more structure and

Exhibit 1 Consolidated Statements of Cash Flows

(In millions)	Three Fiscal Years Ended September 29		
	2007	2006	2005
Cash and cash equivalents, beginning of the year	$ 6,392	$ 3,491	$ 2,969
Operating Activities: Net income	3,496	1,989	1,328
Adjustments to reconcile net income to cash generated by operating activities:			
Depreciation, amortization, and accretion	317	225	179
Stock-based compensation expense	242	163	49
Provision for deferred income taxes	78	53	50
Excess tax benefits from stock options	—	—	428
Gain on sale of Power School net assets	—	(4)	—
Loss on disposition of property, plant, and equipment	12	15	9
Changes in operating assets and liabilities:			
Accounts receivable, net	(385)	(357)	(121)
Inventories	(76)	(105)	(64)
Other current assets	(1,540)	(1,626)	(150)
Other assets	81	(1,040)	(35)
Accounts payable	1,494	1,611	328
Other liabilities	1,751	1,296	534
Cash generated by operating activities	5,470	2,220	2,535

Source: Apple's 2007 Fiscal Year 10K, www.apple.com/investor.

organization to the young company.[13] Apple's biggest computer achievement, the Macintosh (Mac), was released. After initially opposing it, Jobs had personally taken on the task of developing the Mac, which became the first PC featuring a graphical interface and a mouse for navigation. Apple first presented the now-famous Macintosh computer with a riveting January 1984 Super Bowl commercial. The memorable commercial featured an Orwellian *1984* world filled with stoic human zombies, all watching a large-screen image of "Big Brother." A young woman rushes into the room and dramatically destroys the screen. Apple used this *1984* imagery to depict IBM's computer dominance being destroyed by the new Macintosh.[14] With features that made the Mac easy to use for publishing and a marketing strategy that concentrated on universities, the new computer sold very well, pushing Apple's fiscal 1984 sales to an unprecedented $1.5 billion.[15]

Shake-Up

By 1985, however, Jobs and Sculley began to disagree over the direction they wanted the company to take. After Jobs's attempt to remove Sculley failed, Jobs left Apple in May to start his own new business, NeXT Computers. Meanwhile, Microsoft benefited from Apple's poor negotiation of a contract that cleared the way for successive versions of the Windows operating system to use graphical user interface (GUI) technology similar to that of the Mac. With this agreement, "Apple had effectively lost exclusive rights to its interface design."[16]

In 1990, Microsoft released Windows 3.0, the first universal software that could run on nearly every PC regardless of the manufacturer. Although Apple's worldwide sales had reached $7 billion by 1992, Apple soon found itself fighting an uphill battle against the movement toward standardized software. More and more businesses and consumers wanted compatible operating

Exhibit 2 Apple Computer, Fourth-Quarter Fiscal 2007 10Q Report

Net Sales (net sales in millions and unit sales in thousands)	Three Months Ended		
	12/29/07	12/30/06	Change
Net Sales by Operating Segment:			
Americas net sales	$ 4,298	$ 3,521	22%
Europe net sales	2,471	1,712	44%
Japan net sales	400	285	40%
Retail net sales	1,701	1,115	53%
Other segments net sales (a)	738	482	53%
Total net sales	$ 9,608	$ 7,115	35%
Unit Sales by Operating Segment:			
Americas Macintosh unit sales	841	625	35%
Europe Macintosh unit sales	705	491	44%
Japan Macintosh unit sales	91	70	30%
Retail Macintosh unit sales	504	308	64%
Other segments Macintosh unit sales (b)	178	112	59%
Total Macintosh unit sales	2,319	1,606	44%

(Continued)

Exhibit 2 Apple Computer, Fourth-Quarter Fiscal 2007 10Q Report (*Continued*)

Net Sales (net sales in millions and unit sales in thousands)	Three Months Ended		
	12/29/07	12/30/06	Change
Net Sales by Product:			
Desktops (c)	$ 1,515	$ 955	59%
Portables (d)	2,037	1,455	40%
Total Macintosh net sales	3,552	2,410	47%
iPod	3,997	3,427	17%
Other music-related products and services (e)	808	634	27%
iPhone and related products and services (f)	241	—	NM
Peripherals and other hardware (g)	382	297	29%
Software, service, and other sales (h)	628	347	81%
Total net sales	$ 9,608	$ 7,115	35%
Unit Sales by Product:			
Desktops (c)	977	637	53%
Portables (d)	1,342	969	38%
Total Macintosh unit sales	2,319	1,606	44%
Net sales per Macintosh unit sold (i)	$ 1,532	$ 1,501	2%
iPod unit sales	22,121	21,066	5%
Net sales per iPod unit sold (j)	$ 181	$ 163	11%
iPhone unit sales	2,315	—	NM

(a) During the third quarter of 2007, the Company revised the way it measures the Retail Segment's operating results to a manner that is generally consistent with the Company's other operating segments. Prior period results have been reclassified to reflect this change to the Retail Segment's operating results along with the corresponding offsets to the other operating segments. Further information regarding the Company's operating segments may be found in Notes to Condensed Consolidated Financial Statements at Note 7, "Segment Information and Geographic Data."
(b) Other Segments include Asia Pacific and FileMaker.
(c) Includes iMac, eMac, Mac mini, Mac Pro, Power Mac, and Xserve product lines.
(d) Includes MacBook, iBook, MacBook Pro, and PowerBook product lines.
(e) Consists of iTunes Store sales, iPod services, and Apple-branded and third-party iPod accessories.
(f) Derived from handset sales, carrier agreements, and Apple-branded and third-party iPhone accessories.
(g) Includes sales of Apple-branded and third-party displays, wireless connectivity and networking solutions, and other hardware accessories.
(h) Includes sales of Apple-branded operating system, application software, third-party software, AppleCare, and Internet services.
(i) Derived by dividing total Mac net sales by total Mac unit sales.
(j) Derived by dividing total iPod net sales by total iPod unit sales.

Source: Apple Company, 2007 4Q Form 10Q, hwww.apple.com/investor, 22.

Exhibit 3 Select Apple Product Releases

1976	Apple I
1977	Apple II
1980	Apple III
1983	Lisa
1984	Macintosh Graphical user interface (GUI)
1986	Macintosh Plus
1987	Macintosh II
1991	Macintosh Quadra PowerBook 100
1994	PowerMac 6100
1997	PowerBook G3
1998	iMac
1999	iBook
2001	iTunes iDVD iPod
2003	iLife suite iTunes 4 (online music store w/200,000 downloadable songs)
2004	iPod Mini eMac iPod (Click Wheel) iPod (U2 Special Edition) iPod Photo
2005	iPod Shuffle iPod nano iPod color iPod with video
2006	MacBook Mac mini
2007	Apple TV iPhone

Source: www.apple-history.com.

systems, but the Macintosh still ran exclusively on Mac OS, a system not available to other computers. By 1993, Apple's board of directors replaced Sculley as CEO. Apple moved through two CEOs over the next five years.

During this time, Apple partnered with IBM and Motorola to produce the PowerPC chip, which would run the company's new line of PowerMacs, allowing it to outperform computers powered by Intel microprocessors.[17] Despite this and Apple's attempts to reorganize, losses mounted in 1996 and 1997. In December 1996, Apple acquired NeXT, with the plan of using its technology as the basis for a new operating system. After being gone for more than a decade, Jobs returned to the company he had originally cofounded with Wozniak.

Jobs's Return

One of the first problems Steve Jobs moved to fix was the ongoing dispute between Apple and Microsoft over the Windows graphical user interface (GUI). Microsoft not only paid an undisclosed amount to Apple, but also made its Office 98 suite compatible with Macintoshes.[18] Jobs then proceeded to change the company's sales strategy in 1997 to encompass direct sales—both online and by phone. In a flurry of product releases, Apple introduced the new generation of PowerMacs, PowerBooks, and the highly anticipated iMac and iBook, which were less expensive computers aimed at the low-end computer market. After an entire year without showing a profit, the first quarter of 1998 began three years of profitable quarters for Apple.[19]

Jobs stated that he wanted to transform the company by making the Mac "the hub of [the consumers'] digital lifestyle." To do this, Apple introduced iLife in 2002, a software suite including applications such as iPhoto, iMovie, iTunes, and eventually the iPod. With the advent of Napster and peer-to-peer music sharing, Apple saw a way to capitalize on the emerging trend of cheap music downloads by creating a legal online music distribution network. iTunes would be the key to exploiting this market. Once downloaded by way of iTunes, music could then be transferred only to an iPod (due to encryption). With iTunes, Apple has quite possibly revolutionized the distribution of music and hopes to do the same with the distribution of movies on demand. Similar changes may be expected with the iPhone in the mobile or smartphone industry segments and with Apple TV in the mobile media and set-top box industry segments.

iTunes: Apple's Online Music Store

Apple ventured into the market of legal downloads with the introduction of its iTunes Music Store.[20] iTunes offers downloads at a specified price without requiring a subscription or monthly fees. Originally offered exclusively on Apple's own Mac, iTunes can now be installed on PCs as well. The idea behind iTunes was to provide a solution to the illegal pirating of music and software from rival sources such as Kazaa.

iTunes offers its users a selection of more than 6 million songs, with new songs continually added.[21] Titles are from just about every genre of music. Users can perform a search by type of music, artist name, or title of track or album. Each song available can be previewed without making a purchase. Purchasers have the option of purchasing an entire album or single songs. Each song is $0.99, and a complete album starts at $9.99. Downloads can be made not only to a Mac or PC, but also directly to an iPod. All new song additions are encoded in AAC format, which many say is superior to MP3, although iTunes does still carry the MP3 format on some of its older selections.

Once songs are downloaded, they are stored as a digital music library. As this collection grows, this list of songs can be arranged in many different ways. Songs can be arranged by personal rating, artist, or genre. This feature allows for a customizable playlist for playback or burning to a CD.

In addition iTunes offers a collection of more than 10,000 audiobooks ranging in price from $2.95 to $15.95, including many different language lessons. Also available are downloadable versions of public radio shows. Gift certificates are also available in different denominations and can be sent electronically through e-mail.

As previously mentioned, in its first week of existence, the number of downloads from iTunes surpassed the 1 million mark. This feat is amazing considering that at the time of iTunes' introduction, the download service was available only for the Mac. In addition, at that time, Mac users comprised less than 5 percent of U.S. computer users.[22] When iTunes became available for use on the PC, sales increased even more rapidly. iTunes PC downloads reached the 1 million mark in three days, less than half the time it took for the Mac version. But the success of iTunes is not measured in number of downloads sold per day or week, since after paying royalties, Apple makes only approximately 10 cents per song. iTunes is simply used as a means to boost the sale of iPods, iPhones, and Apple TVs, which generate a substantial profit per sale. For example, the iPod has been labeled "the profit machine" for Apple, as it tends to produce a 50 percent profit margin, per unit, before marketing and distribution costs.[23]

iTunes, iPod, iPhone, and Apple TV

iPod

For music lovers, the iPod is the greatest invention since the Walkman. With up to 160 GB of storage, it allows users to carry up to 40,000 songs or 200 hours of video wherever they go.[24] There are currently four different iPod styles: the iPod shuffle, iPod classic, iPod nano, and iPod touch. iPod owners can purchase accessories such as the armband, the radio remote, and the universal dock and remote to make using the iPod even more enjoyable. In 2007, with more than 100 million products sold, the closest competitor to Apple's iPod had only 8 percent of the market share, leaving Apple with the vast majority. While others are seeking to simply duplicate the complementary and innovative relationships between iPod and iTunes, Apple continues to innovate with new products such as the iPhone and Apple TV.[25] (See Exhibit 4 for more details about the iPod products.)

iPhone

In first-quarter 2007, Apple launched its "revolutionary" product, the iPhone. The iPhone combines three concepts popular with consumers: a mobile phone, a widescreen iPod, and an Internet communication device. The iPhone brags "an entirely new user interface based on a large multi-touch display and pioneering software," which users can control with just their fingers.[26] The iPhone's default Internet browser will be Apple's own Safari,** but it is open to other software as well.[27] The iPhone allows for 8 hours of talk time, 24 hours of audio playback time, and 10 days of standby time.[28] Apple sold 1 million iPhones less than three months after this product was available to consumers. Apple expects this trend to continue during 2008 and to reach sales of 10 million iPhones, stealing 1 percent of the mobile phone market share.[29]

Apple TV

In addition to the iPhone, Apple also introduced the Apple TV in 2007. With this product, Apple intends to revolutionize the Internet video industry, as it did with the music download industry. Users can download movies and TV shows via the iTunes online service or via YouTube as well as view digital photos and home videos.[30] Some negative hype claims that the Apple TV will be a flop just like the Apple III and the Power Mac

---

** Safari is Apple's Internet browser that was introduced in 2003. It is part of Apple's strategy to gain more market share by having both hardware and software products. Apple suggests that Safari is the fastest browser available. It blocks pop-up advertising and has a built-in text reader that reads the site pages aloud. In addition to being the default browser for the iPhone, it is the default browser for the iPod Touch and the Mac computer. Safari's user share was estimated to be 6 percent in early 2008. (P. Festa, 2003, Welcome to the browser jungle, Safari, CNET News, www.news.com, January 7; 2008, Wikipedia, http://en.wikipedia.org.)

Cube. Some of the features that made the first edition unpopular include the following:

- Users are not able to download a movie from iTunes directly to their TV; they have to download it to their PC first.
- It requires an HDTV, but the movies that can be downloaded are of such low resolution that the picture looks fuzzy and old-fashioned.
- It has no DVD drive.

Steve Jobs announced at the Macworld Conference & Expo in January 2008 that the upgraded version of Apple TV will allow owners to order movies directly from the TV rather than having to download to the PC.[31] Also, critics do compliment the fact that the Apple TV plays a slideshow of digital photos.[32]

The price to rent a movie using Apple TV is $2.99 for library titles, $3.99 for new releases, and $1 extra to view the movie in high definition.[33]

One key component that must be in place to have good media content for the three products mentioned is the relationship that Apple has with each of its media and phone service suppliers.

Service Suppliers: iTunes, Apple TV, and iPhone

iTunes

iTunes has agreements with all five major record labels (BMG, EMI, Sony Music Entertainment, Universal, and Warner Bros.) as well as more than 200 independent labels. These agreements allow iTunes to sell the music owned by these labels and pay the record label each time a song is downloaded. This deal is considered a reseller agreement, meaning that Apple is not licensing content from these labels, but rather buying it wholesale and reselling it to consumers.[34] Apple gets to keep its share, while the portion the label receives must be divided among many parties including artists, producers, and publishers. Labels earn approximately 70 cents per song sold on iTunes. This figure may seem small, but it is still greater than losing money to the millions of illegal downloads that nearly crippled the music industry.

The revenues for record label companies have been dropping in the past year due to tough market conditions, and Apple has introduced a strategy that may help increase revenues by at least a small percentage. It has already contracted with EMI to make its entire catalog available to iTunes' users in two formats, the traditional download option, which includes the Fairplay digital rights management (DRM) software and DRM-free versions. The DRM software limits the number of times a song can be copied, which decreases the quality of the song. The DRM-free versions would deliver greater quality music but would require a higher price tag. iTunes will start the DRM-free songs at $1.29 per song versus the traditional $0.99 per song. Other record labels may enter into the same agreement with Apple depending on how successful this strategy is with EMI.[35]

NBC recently cancelled its agreement with Apple to provide its TV shows on iTunes due to pricing disputes. Walt Disney Studios previously offered its new releases, and Paramount, Metro-Goldwyn-Mayer (MGM), and Lionsgate allowed older library titles to be purchased on iTunes, but the supplier agreements have changed with the launch of Apple TV.[36]

Apple TV

Apple did not have an easy time finalizing with movie studios contracts that will allow Apple to sell movies on iTunes for use on the iPod and Apple TV. Not only were the studios concerned about losing significant revenues from the sales of DVDs and Blu-ray discs, but some studios urged Apple to require a watermark on digital video for it to play on its devices. Their concern is heightened given the pirating experienced in the music download business. One movie-studio executive said, "Our position is, if you want our content, you have to protect our business." Apple, however, responded that it trusts its consumers not to play pirated movies.[37]

The limited number of movie downloads available on iTunes would significantly diminish the success of Apple TV. Thus, Apple's CEO was persistent in his negotiations with the movie studios. Jobs announced at the Macworld Expo in 2008 that Apple had reached agreement with each of the following major studios: Twentieth Century Fox, The Walt Disney Studios, Warner Bros., Paramount, Sony Pictures Entertainment, MGM, Lionsgate, and New Line Cinema.[38] Despite NBC's issues with Apple concerning TV shows, Universal Pictures (owned by NBC and General Electric) has agreed to allow Apple to rent its movies via iTunes.

The supplier agreement between Apple and the movie studios is that new movies will not be available for rent until 30 days after the DVD is distributed. Within a 24-hour period, customers will be able to watch a film as many times as they like once the movie is started. Movies that are downloaded but not started will not be available for viewing after 30 days.[39]

iPhone

Cingular was selected as the exclusive wireless carrier for the iPhone in the United States because, according to Steve Jobs, Cingular is the best and most popular carrier in the United States.[40] Together these companies

Exhibit 4 iPod Product Descriptions

	iPod shuffle		iPod nano		iPod classic		iPod touch	
Capacity[1]	1GB	Up to 240 songs	4GB	Up to 1,000 songs, up to 3,500 photos, up to 4 hours of video, or some of each	80GB	Up to 20,000 songs, up to 25,000 photos, up to 100 hours of video, or some of each	8GB	Up to 1,750 songs, up to 10,000 photos, up to 10 hours of video, or some of each
	2GB	Up to 500 songs	8GB	Up to 2,000 songs, up to 7,000 photos, up to 8 hours of video, or some of each	160GB	Up to 40,000 songs, up to 25,000 photos, up to 200 hours of video, or some of each	16GB	Up to 3,500 songs, up to 20,000 photos, up to 20 hours of video, or some of each
							32GB	Up to 7,000 songs, up to 25,000 photos, up to 40 hours of video, or some of each
Price	1GB	$49	4GB	$149	80GB	$249	8GB	$299
	2GB	$69	8GB	$199	160GB	$349	16GB	$399
							32GB	$499
Color display			2-inch		2.5-inch		3.5-inch Multi-Touch	
Wireless data[2]							Wi-Fi (802.11b/g)	
Battery life[3]	Up to 2 hours of audio		Up to 24 hours of audio / Up to 5 hours of video		Up to 40 hours of audio / Up to 7 hours of video		Up to 22 hours of audio / Up to 5 hours of video	

1. 1 GB = 1 billion bytes; actual formatted capacity is less. Music capacity is based on 4 minutes per song and 128-Kpbs AAC encoding; photo capacity is based on iPod-viewable photos transferred from iTunes; video capacity is based on H.264 1.5-Mbps video at 640-by-480 resolution combined with 128-Kbps audio; actual capacity varies by content.

2. Internet access is required; broadband is recommended; fees may apply.

3. Testing was conducted by Apple in August 2007 using preproduction hardware and software. For audio playback, the playlist contained 358 unique audio tracks consisting of content imported from CDs using iTunes (128-Kbps AAC) and content purchased from the iTunes Store (128-Kbps AAC); all settings were default except that Ask to Join Networks was turned off for iPod touch. For video playback, video content was purchased from the iTunes Store; all settings were default except that Ask to Join Networks and Auto-Brightness were turned off for iPod touch. Battery tests are conducted with specific iPod units; actual results may vary. Rechargeable batteries have a limited number of charge cycles and may eventually need to be replaced (see www.apple.com/support/ipod/service/battery). Battery life and number of charge cycles vary by use and settings. See www.apple.com/batteries for more information.

Source: www.apple.com/ipod/whichipod.

developed the Visual Voicemail feature that allows users to listen to the voicemails they prefer rather than having to listen to all messages in succession. Since the agreement was made between Cingular and Apple, Cingular was acquired by AT&T. iPhone owners are required to sign a two-year service agreement with AT&T. AT&T offers four different plans, with monthly fees ranging from $59.99 to $119.99. All plans include the visual voicemail, unlimited access to the Internet, and roll-over minutes.[41]

Hardware

Concerning its hardware suppliers, Apple is usually not forthcoming with this information. However, a disassembled iPhone reveals that the microprocessor chip is supplied by Samsung; Philips, Texas Instruments, and Linear Technology all play a role in providing the batteries, and many other companies provide chips that are central to the camera, display, and motion sensor.[42]

Many companies have expressed frustration in working with Apple because Steve Jobs is very clear on his vision for his products and can tend to be controlling. Maintaining good supplier relationships and keeping enough control to provide the quality of products expected of Apple is a balance that Apple will have to find in order to stay ahead of its competitors.

Competitors

iTunes

Since the October 2003 launch of iTunes.com for Windows, Apple has faced a multitude of competitors. During the late 1990s, the emergence of music sharing came about with Napster, a freeware program offering free downloads using peer-to-peer transfers. Peer-to-peer transfers allow users to connect directly with other users without the need for a central point of management.[43] However, in recent years due to legal proceedings, Napster and all other competitors have become a subscription service similar to iTunes.

Napster. In May 1999, 19-year-old Shawn Fanning created Napster while studying at Northeastern University. The name Napster came from the Internet "handle" he had used as a programmer. He created a type of software that allowed music fans anywhere to "share" MP3s in one forum. During the first year of service, Napster was obtaining more than 250,000 new users a week while maintaining a free service.[44] This software creation led to the ever-growing controversy of the availability of MP3s on the Internet. Music sharing exploded in the late 1990s, and Napster's servers were overloaded with millions of requests a day for media downloads. Music artists considered this new "sharing" forum to be a continuous copyright violation. Fanning soon became the target of their animosity and became one of the most disliked people in the music industry.

During 2000, Napster was in and out of court and was finally slated to shut down on July 26, 2000. The decision was reversed two days later on July 28, 2000.[45] In 2001, Konrad Hilbers, a 38-year-old German, became CEO of the rapidly declining music file-sharing site. In June 2001, Napster had more than 26 million users, but growth was declining fast, going from 6.3 billion to 2.2 billion minutes used a day. On March 7, 2002, Napster closed its servers while opting to implement a fee-based service to comply with the federal judge's decision. On June 3, 2002, Napster filed for Chapter 11 bankruptcy in an effort to secure court-ordered protection from creditors. This move was part of the overall financial restructuring strategy of Bertelsmann AG, which was proceeding with its takeover of the once popular file-sharing system. By July 2003, Roxio, Inc., had acquired Napster and was planning a Napster 2.0 launch for December 2003. Napster 2.0 is a successful, legal fee-based service.[46]

Through restructuring and quality legal representation, Napster finally has a legal base that is expected to stand. Currently, Napster 4.0 is online with content agreements from five major record labels and hundreds of independent labels; therefore, its library is made up of more than 5 million songs. Members have unlimited access to the library for $12.95 per month. Napster 4.0 now accommodates the use of its software for Mac and Linux users.

Kazaa. Sharman Networks Limited was founded in January 2002 as a private limited company. Sharman Networks develops and markets world-class Internet applications. Kazaa Media Desktop and Kazaa Plus are products of Sharman Networks. Sharman Networks earns revenue by soliciting companies to advertise on its software. Users that prefer ad-free use of the software can purchase an upgrade, Kazaa Plus for $29.95. This upgrade will also allow for greater search capabilities and more download sources.[47]

Being Australian-based, the company avoided legal intervention in allowing the file sharing, but in 2005, the Federal Court of Australia ruled that Kazaa had knowingly allowed users to illegally download copyrighted songs. The company was charged to change its software to prohibit copyrighted music or videos from being shared.[48] Kazaa owners agreed to pay the four major record labels (Universal Music, Sony BMG, EMI, and Warner Music) $100 million.[49]

Kazaa Media Desktop is a program rumored to be littered with spyware and ad-based programs that "infect" consumer systems; thus many users have become wary of accessing Kazaa's site.[50]

RealNetworks, Inc. RealNetworks, through its RealPlayer Music Store, sought a price war with Apple by dropping the price to $0.49 per song and $4.99 per album compared to Apple's price of $0.99 and $9.99, respectively. Analysts indicated that RealNetworks was pricing below the cost of purchasing the music from the record companies, and eventually it did increase its price to $0.99 per song; however, it still offers, select songs for $0.49 a track. As part of its battle to reduce Apple's market share, RealNetworks launched technology called Harmony, which allows RealNetworks users to translate songs purchased from RealPlayer Music Store into a format that can be played on an iPod. It also allows RealNetworks music to be played on Microsoft formats.[51] RealPlayer is a RealNetworks medium through which it competes in the video-on-demand market. Video can be downloaded from the Web to an iPod, PC, CD, and DVD. RealPlayer customers can subscribe to its SuperPass membership, which combines the benefits of RealPlayer and the RealPlayer Music Store. The $14.99 monthly fee provides subscribers with $10.00 worth of music downloads and full-length movies per month.

Sony. Sony started a music download service called Connect in the spring of 2004. Despite its efforts to compete in the music downloading market, it did not realize significant success; thus, Connect closed at the end of March 2008.[52] Instead, Sony is focusing its attention on gaining market share in the video download segment.[53]

Virgin Media. Virgin offers more than 15,000 record labels in addition to computer games and videos and Blockbuster movies. Similar to iTunes, customers can listen to a 30-second sample before purchase and download exclusive tracks through Virgin's V2 music label before the tracks are released to the general public.[54]

Wal-Mart. Wal-Mart launched its own online music store. It is currently the number-one music retailer in the nation, followed by iTunes.[55] Initially Wal-Mart offered music in MP3 format for $0.88 per song, $0.11 cheaper than Apple, but currently it offers songs for $0.94 and albums starting at $7.88.[56]

Yahoo! Music Unlimited. Subscribers to Yahoo! Music Jukebox have access to more than 2 million songs. Users can listen to 150 LAUNCHcast radio stations or download songs to any PC. After paying a monthly $6.00 fee, subscribers pay only $0.79 per song. Nonsubscribers can also download songs for $0.99 each.[57] At this time, Yahoo! offers only music on its site; video and TV shows are not available.

Apple TV

Amazon Unbox. The Amazon Unbox was introduced in 2006. Users download films or TV shows to the Amazon Unbox Player or on Windows Media Player. In addition, Amazon established a partnership with

TiVo in 2007 that allows consumers to purchase movies or TV shows through Amazon's Unbox and send it to the TiVo machine to view. Amazon's service is similar to its competitors in that once a movie or show is downloaded, it must be viewed within 30 days and once it is started, it must be viewed within 24 hours. Amazon also has agreements with most of the major movie studios such as Paramount Pictures, Universal Studios, Warner Bros., CBS, and Fox.[58] NBC contracted with Amazon to offer its TV shows for download after NBC cancelled its agreement with Apple for the iTunes service.[59]

CinemaNow. This company seemed to have been ahead of the game, entering the video download market in 1999. It was the first to offer pay-per-view movies from the major Hollywood studios, the first to offer Download-to-Own services, and the first distributor of Burn-to-DVD movies. It is headquartered in Marina Del Rey, California, and its library consists of more than 10,000 movie titles, television programs, music concerts, and shorts. It has enabled users to download movies to the Microsoft Xbox 360 video game console as part of its strategy of providing multiple platforms on which to download movies. It has recently been creating joint ventures to differentiate itself in the industry. It originated as a distributor of videos via the Internet and has progressed most recently to wireless Internet "infotainment," a new feature available in select new car models. Its agreement with USTelematics, Inc. will allow it to offer a package of features and functions, including the creation of a mobile Wi-Fi Internet hotspot to enable online computer usage in the car, as well as DVD, movies, TV, Xbox, and other computer games.[60]

Disney. Disney, through an agreement made with Microsoft in 2007, offers movie download service for use on the Xbox 360. This service is one of the few that offers movies in high-definition format. Consumers have access to the Walt Disney Studios library, including titles from Walt Disney Pictures, Touchstone Pictures, Hollywood Pictures, and Miramax Films.[61]

HP. HP announced at the beginning of 2008 that it had reached an agreement with Sony Pictures Home Entertainment (SPHE) to deliver movies on demand. HP's manufactured-on-demand service will produce a DVD of any movie, TV show, or other content offered through SPHE. HP believes this service will aid movie studios in trying to match supply and demand for movies it sells on DVD. The current list of items available for order are classic TV shows never released on DVD, foreign movies, specialty cable programming, independent movies, specialty genres such as religion and education, and recently broadcast TV shows.[62]

Movielink. Recently acquired by Blockbuster, Movielink began in 2002 and was owned by five of the top movie studios: Universal Studios, Paramount Pictures, Sony Pictures, MGM, and Warner Bros. It operates as a subsidiary of Blockbuster and offers 3,300 movie titles.[63] Consumers who purchase a movie from Movielink must view it using a computer, a TV connected to a computer, or an Xbox 360 game console or via a set-top box company.

Netflix. Like many of its competitors, Netflix has teamed up with a technology company, LG, to become a stronger player in the video-on-demand market. In January 2008, Netflix announced that through LG's set-top box, customers can stream movies directly on their TVs. The device is expected to be available in the second half of 2008.[64] In the meantime, Netflix subscribers can stream to their PC an unlimited number of movies per month, unconstrained by hourly limits, for a monthly fee with plans starting at $8.99 per month. The on-demand library offers viewers the option of 6,000 titles of movies and TV shows.[65]

Sony. In the United Kingdom and Ireland, Sony offers video-on-demand service through its PlayStation Portable device. It has partnered with British Sky Broadcasting to provide the movies.[66] It also offers this service in Japan, but it is currently not available in the United States.

Vudu. Vudu, headquartered in Santa Clara, California, entered the video-on-demand market in April 2007.[67] Vudu's black box connects to the TV and Internet, and the built-in hard drive gives users the option of viewing 5,000 movie titles instantly. The box costs $400. The service has no monthly service charge, but a rental costs $2.00 to $4.00 per movie. As such, Vudu claims to be the cure-all for the movie rental business; it saves customers from running back and forth from the video store or waiting for the movie to come in the mail from Netflix or Blockbuster; it offers more movie titles than video-on-demand providers; and it is more functional than Internet download services because it does not require a PC. Similar to Vudu's competitors, once a movie is downloaded, it must be viewed within 24 hours.

Vudu offers movies from all major Hollywood studios. But since it is subject to the distribution windows, the time frame in which select movies are available may not match consumer demand. Only some movies have previews, and some are available only for purchase and not for rent.[68]

Wal-Mart. In December 2006, Wal-Mart entered the movie download segment of the entertainment industry, but only a year later it exited the business because it had not caught on with consumers. Raul Vasquez, Wal-Mart's CEO for walmart.com, stated that the download service was an experiment. "We want to understand what the customers want. And I think what we learned is that the initial experience of buying and downloading content needs to be better. We thought it was going to be easier for the customer to understand."

iPhone

Motorola. Motorola has been a long-time leader in mobile phone sales in the United States. However, since Apple's iPhone and Research In Motion's (RIM) Blackberry have been gaining ground, the leader is falling hard and fast. Motorola's RAZR phone has lost its popularity, and its smartphone made in partnership with Microsoft, the Motorola Q, has not performed as expected. Motorola announced in January 2008 that it is seeking alternatives for its handset business, most likely a divestiture.[69]

Palm. Despite the fact that Palm sold 689,000 Treos in the first quarter of 2007, a 21 percent increase from the previous year, Palm is struggling to remain a major player in the smartphone market amid the success of the Blackberry and the iPhone. The competition with the iPhone is especially fierce since AT&T is the phone service provider for both products. Palm introduced its Centro in October 2007 as a low-cost strategy to increase market share. Although the Centro sells for $99, it does not have all of the features of the iPhone. But cost-conscious consumers may choose it over the iPhone given the iPhone's $399 price tag.[70]

Research In Motion. The Blackberry created by Research In Motion (RIM) has been a popular product among corporate consumers who mainly needed e-mail service and a calendar. To stay in the competitive game, however, RIM has been adding features to make its product more appealing to users who want the fun features in addition to the features that aid in their work. Blackberrys now have cameras and can play music. There is a rumor that RIM is going to introduce a Blackberry 9000, which will have a touch-sensitive screen, making it similar to the iPhone.[71] Conversely, Apple has recently released tools that make its iPhone more corporate-user friendly, and it will now be compatible with Microsoft's Exchange platform.[72]

Exhibit 5 illustrates a comparison of the product features for the iPhone relative to its key competitors.

Exhibit 5 iPhone properties and its competitors

	Apple iPhone - $499 to $599	Moto Q - $499	BlackBerry Pearl - $299	Palm Treo 750 - $649
	N/A	FM Radio with Software Sold Separately	No	FM Radio with Software Sold Separately
	Bluetooth Wireless Technology v2.0 + EDR	Bluetooth Wireless Technology v1.2	**Bluetooth Wireless Technology v2.0**	Bluetooth Wireless Technology v1.2
	N/A but most likely	Video Capture/Camcorder QCIF-quality	N/A	Video Capture/Camcorder QCIF
	Full QWERTY Soft Keyboard	QWERTY Keyboard Backlit with thumbwheel	QWERTY Keyboard	QWERTY Keyboard Backlit
	N/A	**Infrared Port**	No	**Infrared Port**
	N/A	**Use Phone as Modem via USB Cable, Bluetooth, or IR**	**Use This Phone as a Modem**	**Use Phone as Modem via USB Cable, Bluetooth, or IR**
	iSynch via Bluetooth or Wi-Fi Mac or PC	PC Synch via Cable: Infrared or Bluetooth: Active Sync	PC Synchronization	PC Synch via Cable: Infrared or Bluetooth: Active Sync
	Full Color Display 3.5" 320 x 480 Pixels at 160 ppi	Color Display 320 x 240 Pixels, 65K Colors, QVGATFT	Color Display 240 x 260 Pixels, 65K Colors	Color Display 320 x 320 Pixels, 65K Colors, TFT
	Multi Touch Screen	No		**Touch Screen**
	Speakerphone	**Speakerphone**	**Speakerphone**	**Speakerphone**
	Widgets	To-Do List, Alarm, Calculator, Calendar, etc.	To-Do List, Alarm, Calculator, Calendar, etc.	To-Do List, Alarm, Calculator, Calendar, etc.
	N/A	**Voice Memo**	N/A	**Voice Memo**
	N/A	Vibrate	Vibrate	Vibrate
	N/A	**Voice recognition**	**Voice-activated Dialing**	No
	Predictive Text Entry with corrector	N/A	**Predictive Text Entry**	No
	Advanced Sensors for Rotation Detection	No	No	No
Messaging & Internet Features				
	Safari Full Rich HTML Browser	Pocket Internet Explorer HTML	**Full HTML Web Browser**	Blazer Browser Supports
	N/A	MMS	MMS	MMS
	SMS	**SMS**	**SMS**	**SMS**
	POP3/IMAP Push Email services	Pocket Outlook Supports POP, IMAP, APOP, ESMTP	**Push Email POP3, IMAP, SMTP**	Pocket Outlook Supports POP, IMAR, APOP, ESMTP
	Google Maps Built in	No	No	No
	Widgets	No	No	No
	Visual Voice Mail	No	No	No
	N/A	IM	IM	IM
Technical Specifications				
	OSX	Windows Mobile 5.0 + BREW	BlackBerry OS with Intel XScale Processor + Java	Palm OS 5.4 with Intel 312 Mhz XScale Processor
	Data Download Speed - EDGE + WiFi (802.11 b/g)	Data Download Speed - EV-DO and 1xRTT	Data Download Speed - EDGE	Data Download Speed - EV-DO and 1xRTT
	GSM Quad Band 850, 900, 1800, 1900	**GSM Quad Band 850, 900, 1800, 1900**	**GSM Quad Band 850, 900, 1800, 1900**	**GSM Quad Band 850, 900, 1800, 1900**
	Built-in Memory - 4GB or 8GB Available	Built-in Memory - 64 MB Available	Built-in Memory - 64 MB Plus Online Photo	Built-in Memory - 123 MB Available
	None	**SecureDigital (SD) Card Format Compatible Slot**	**MicroSD Card Format Compatible Slot**	**SecureDigital (SD) Card Format Compatible Slot**
	Dimension - 115 x 61 x 11.6mm	Dimension - 116 x 63 x 11.5mm	**Dimension - 107 x 50 x 14.5mm**	Dimension - 111.8 x 58.4 x 20.3mm
	Weight - 4.8 oz	Weight - 6.40 oz	**Weight - 3.2 oz**	Weight - 6.40 oz
Battery Life				
	Up to 300 Minutes Talk/Video/Browsing	Talk Time - Up to 240 Minutes	Talk Time - Up to 210 Minutes	Talk Time - Up to 282 Minutes
	N/A	Standby Time - Up to 192 Hours	Standby Time - Up to 360 Hours	Standby Time - Up to 300 Hours
	Up to 16H Audio Playback	N/A	N/A	N/A
	No	**Removable**	**Removable**	**Removable**

iPod

Some of the iPod's major competitors include Rio Karma, Dell Digital Jukebox DJ, Samsung Napster YP-910GS, and the Gateway Jukebox Player DMP-X20 (see Exhibit 6).[73] Some of the differences from the iPod include a longer battery life, such as a 16-hour battery life for the Dell MP3 player. The weight also varies from one competitor to the next, ranging from 7.7 ounces to 5.5 ounces. (For a detailed list of the major competitors' specifications, see Exhibit 7.)

The Microsoft Zune premiered in the fall of 2006. Due to its lack of tremendous success, in the fall of 2007, Microsoft exerted great energy in combating the success of the iPod with its improved Zune. The Zune offers options of 4, 8, or 80 gigabytes of storage with prices ranging from $150 to $300. The newest edition of the Zune is smaller, has a better viewing screen, and allows users to wirelessly synchronize the gadget with the music on their computers. It also includes a touch-sensitive pad that allows users to navigate through songs with more precise control than the iPod, according to Microsoft executives.[74] But critics suggest that the Zune does not pose a significant threat to the iPod because it does not offer any significant technological breakthroughs.[75] Only 1.2 million Zunes sold during 2007 while Apple sold more than 41 million iPods. Apple's success can likely be attributed to its marketing competency.

Marketing

Up until this point, Apple's marketing endeavors have earned it awards, product sales, and a devoted base of customers, both new and old. In 2003, Apple was awarded *Advertising Age's* Marketer of the Year for its upbeat, original, and (most importantly) memorable advertisements for both its iPod and iTunes.[76] Apple has been hailed as one of the best marketers by many different sources and has had a reputation over the years of being a brand that can gain customers through its well-thought-out and carefully executed marketing strategies.

Marketing has been one of Apple's strengths; however, staying on top of the game will become more difficult as Apple develops a broader range of products and markets them to the mainstream customer rather than just the "tech-savvy fanatics" in fields such as education and design.[77] "The customer base is now more diverse, including students and mainstream consumers, and it's harder to satisfy as a whole," says Lopo L. Rego, a marketing professor at the University of Iowa.[78] Business leaders today have a daunting job in balancing shareholder demands and running a successful company. Businesses want to market new products aggressively to try and ensure their products' success. Apple

heavily promoted the iPhone when it was introduced in July 2007. Customer and investor expectations, due to Apple's reputation, boosted the stock price. But when customers don't believe that the marketing promises have been delivered, stock price, brand equity, and investor confidence are significantly affected.[79] Apple's success lies in a carefully thought-out plan.

Marketing Plan

A marketing plan begins with design of the product.[80] In an industry of low profit margins and cost cutting, Apple takes a different approach to the design of its products. While competitors are doing everything they can to keep costs down, Apple does what it can to make its product different. In 2007, for the third year in a row, Apple was named as the Most Innovative Company by *Business-Week*.[81] Its CEO, Steve Jobs is "a legend for his design sense."[82] Even employees of one of Apple's biggest competitors, Microsoft, have recognized Apple's dominance in the design of eye-catching products. The employees created a mock promotion for the iPod had it been created by Microsoft and circulated it on YouTube.[83]

Steve Jobs is essential to the public relations and promotional aspect of Apple, especially with the iPod.[84] He maintains relationships with the media and has been called the "public face and champion of the brand."[85] He is an expert when it comes to talking with the press, maintaining relationships with magazine editors, and continually creating new relationships.[86] Because of his dynamic, high-energy personality, he usually holds a new idea that he is energetic about and is always ready and willing to share the idea to gain exposure.

Jobs also takes action in response to customer feedback to show that he is listening and concerned. For example, three months after the iPhone was available in stores, Apple cut the price of this product by one-third. This was a strategic move to increase demand and meet sales goals; it was not the result of a faulty product. Consumers who had purchased the iPhone in the first three months for the higher price expressed great dissatisfaction. Jobs responded by promising these consumers a $100 Apple store credit.[87]

A more recent advantage in Apple's marketing strategy is its retail stores. Apple has opened more than 200 retail stores located worldwide. At the time that Apple opened its first retail store in 2001, analysts predicted that Apple would report huge losses and shut the store within two years. At the time, no computer manufacturer had proved profitable in running its own branded store.[88] However, Apple's retail stores contributed an estimated $200 million, 15 to 16 percent of its profits during the past two years (see Exhibit 8).[89] Apple's philosophy behind the stores is brand exposure. Apple believes that the more people can touch an Apple product

Exhibit 6 Products of Competitors to iPod

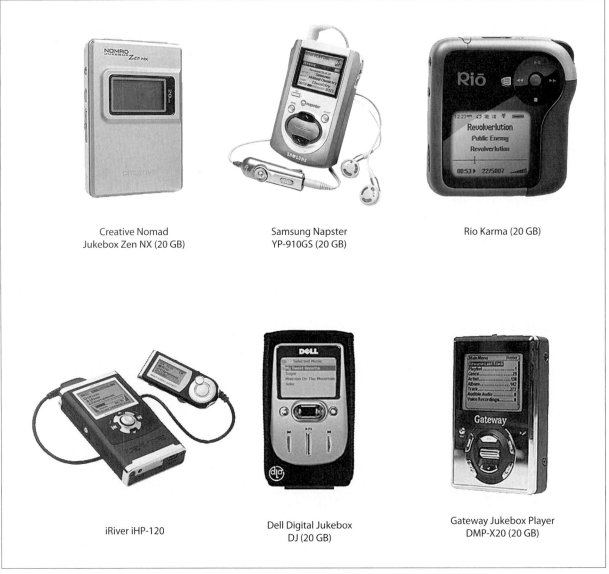

Creative Nomad
Jukebox Zen NX (20 GB)

Samsung Napster
YP-910GS (20 GB)

Rio Karma (20 GB)

iRiver iHP-120

Dell Digital Jukebox
DJ (20 GB)

Gateway Jukebox Player
DMP-X20 (20 GB)

Source: http://reviews.cnet.com/4520-6497-5093864.html.

and see what it can do with their own eyes, the greater the potential market share.[90] In addition, the stores provide free group workshops, personal training, and personal assistance for Apple customers.[91]

Apple offers a One-to-One program for an annual fee of $99; subscribers can attend a tutorial session with an Apple expert for an hour once a week for one year. Apple customers can also consult with the staff at the "Genius Bar" by appointment. The Genius Bar is where Apple product users meet face-to-face with Apple's "geniuses" for answers to technical questions and for problem troubleshooting. In addition, customers wanting to purchase a new computer or other equipment can schedule an appointment with a shopping assistant, who helps ensure that the customer selects the right equipment for his or her needs. Apple has apparently struck a chord with customers because its staff conducts more than 50,000 training sessions per week.[92] "Apple has become the new gathering place," said Steven Addis, chief executive of Addis Creson, a brand strategy and design firm in Berkeley. "You can't help but get caught up with it when you first walk in."[93]

As so eloquently stated in a *USA Today* article, "Apple's arsenal of attention-getting tools holds lessons for any company: design cool, innovative products. Have

Exhibit 7 Details of Products of Competitors to iPod

Basic Specs	Creative Nomad Jukebox Zen NX (20 GB)	Samsung Napster YP-910GS (20 GB)	Rio Karma (20 GB)	iRiver iHP-120	Dell Digital Jukebox DJ (20 GB)	Gateway Jukebox Player Product DMP-X20 (20 GB)
Product type	Digital player	Digital player / recorder / radio	Digital player	Digital player / voice recorder / radio	Digital player / voice recorder	Digital player / voice recorder / radio
PC interface(s) supported	Hi-Speed USB	Hi-Speed USB	Hi-Speed USB	Hi-Speed USB	Hi-Speed USB	Hi-Speed USB
Flash memory installed	8 MB	Info unavailable	Info unavailable	Info unavailable	Info unavailable	Info unavailable
Storage capacity	20 GB	20 GB	20 GB	20 GB	20 GB	20 GB
Digital formats supported	MP3	MP3	MP3	MP3	MP3	MP3
Weight	7.2 oz	6 oz	5.5 oz	5.6 oz	7.6 oz	7.7 oz
Resolution	132 × 64	Info unavailable	160 × 128	Info unavailable	160 × 104	160 × 128
Battery technology	Lithium ion	Lithium polymer	Lithium ion	Lithium polymer	Lithium ion	Lithium ion
Mfr estimated battery life	14 hour(s)	10 hour(s)	15 hour(s)	16 hour(s)	16 hour(s)	10 hour(s)
Software included	Creative MediaSource	Drivers & Utilities	Drivers & Utilities	Drivers & Utilities	Drivers & Utilities	Drivers & Utilities

Source: http://reviews.cnet.com/4520-6497-5093864.html.

a streamlined product line. Invest in memorable ads. Work your customer base to make customers feel special and create word-of-mouth agents. Most important: keep the world and media surprised, to generate gobs of attention."[94]

Finally, Apple has garnered major success for iPod and iTunes by way of strategic partnerships with other well-known brands. Apple has created marketing agreements with Volkswagen of America, Burton Snowboards, Nike, and Starbucks. By affiliating itself with different brands, Apple gains consumer confidence as well as exposure through marketing partner advertisements.

Strategic Agreements

All of the strategic agreements that are currently known by the public are agreements related to the iPod. It remains to be seen what alliances or joint ventures Apple enters in order to create awareness for the iPhone and Apple TV.

Volkswagen. In early 2003, Volkswagen of America (VW) offered a free iPod to customers who purchased a 2003 hardtop Beetle 10. The ad campaign was aptly named "Pods Unite."[95] The deal brought iPod enthusiasts (and people who just wanted to learn more about the iPod) into the Volkswagen stores, and both products benefited from the advertisement. For three months, iPods were shown in Volkswagen showrooms.[96] Also, the Volkswagen sold iPod connectivity wiring and a cradle for the iPod to be used in the new VW Beetle.[97] Because both brands are known for unique design, it is likely that the promotion brought in consumers who highly value the design aspect of a product, whether it is a car or a digital music player.

Exhibit 8 Retail Sales as a Contribution to Overall Apple Revenue

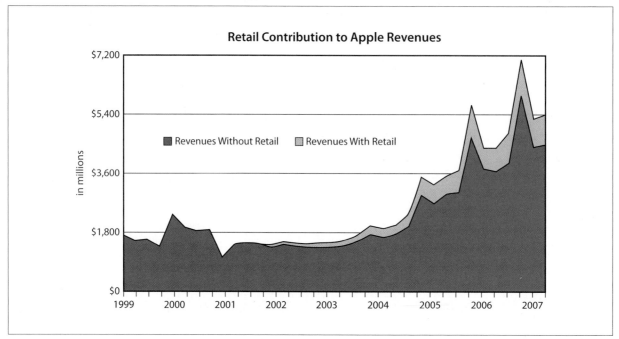

Source: 2007, Retail Stores' Importance Highlighted, http://ifoapplestore.com, August 17.

In the fall of 2007, rumors came out that Apple and VW were in discussions about furthering their relationship to create an iCar. This car would feature products that Steve Jobs fashioned. No details have been specified by either company's leaders.[98]

Burton Snowboards. In January 2004, Burton released a snowboarding/snow-skiing jacket made especially for use with the iPod (Exhibit 9). The jacket has a built-in iPod control electronic system on the sleeve of the jacket so that the wearer can operate the iPod without removing gloves, digging in pockets, or fumbling with zippers.[99] The iPod rests in a protected chest pocket in the inner lining of the jacket. With this jacket, Apple places a product into the hands of those who use iPods and creates exposure for the iPod by way of young snowboarders and skiers showing off and wearing the special jacket.

Nike. Nike and Apple have teamed up to create a smart running shoe. When runners combine a pair of Nike athletic shoes, an iPod nano, and the iPod Sport Kit, they are able to track their run in real time, with time, distance, pace, and calories burned displayed on the iPod. The iPod Sport Kit became available in 2006. Users' playlists can be selected based on the desired workout. If runners need a sudden burst of energy, they can press the Power Song button. An additional feature is the voice feedback that tells runners when they reach a personal best, whether it is in regard to pace, distance, time, or calories burned.[100] The personal data can be uploaded to Nike's Web site, and runners can compete virtually against one another.[101] The most recent partnership between Nike and Apple will shift to the gym. Teaming up with gym equipment makers and 24-Hour Fitness and Virgin Athletic Clubs, Apple and Nike will allow club members to plug their iPod nanos into the cardio equipment to track workouts, upload the information to Nike's Web site, and set goals based on personal history or to compete with others tracked on the Web site.[102]

Starbucks. In September 2007, Starbucks and Apple announced a joint venture that allows Starbucks customers to access (at no cost) the iTunes Wi-Fi Music store at more than 600 participating Starbucks locations. Customers can browse, search, and preview all songs available on the iTunes store, including the "Now Playing" service, which displays the name of the song playing at that moment in Starbucks. "Getting free access to the iTunes Wi-Fi Music Store and the 'Now Playing' service at Starbucks is a great way for customers to discover new music," said Steve Jobs.[103] If customers have to leave the Starbucks store before the download of a song is complete, their personal computer will complete the download automatically at a later time. Every song purchased in a Starbucks participating location syncs back to the users' computer the next time they connect.

In addition to these agreements with domestic companies, Apple is seeking opportunities to create demand for its products in the global market.

Exhibit 9 Complementary Product Advertised with iPods

Source: www.burton.com/Burton/gear/products.asp?productID=728.

Going Global

To stay on top of its game, Apple is pursuing opportunities to sell the iPhone globally. Apple has a goal of capturing 1 percent of the global cell phone business by the end of 2008. It already has partnership agreements with cell phone carriers in France, Germany, and Great Britain. It has also entered the Middle East and Africa regions, ranking fifth next to Nokia, Research In Motion, HTC, and Motorola.[104] Considering that Japan is one of the world's largest and most demanding mobile phone markets with almost 100 million mobile phone users, Steve Jobs has been meeting with officials in Japan in hopes of making a partnership agreement with some of the major telecommunications companies in Japan. This market will be difficult to penetrate, as many other foreign companies have tried unsuccessfully to compete with the 10 domestic handset makers in Japan. Some analysts wonder whether Apple will be able to develop a relationship with the Japanese carriers due to Apple's tight control over the design of the phone, but others believe Apple will succeed. Apple already has a positive brand image in Japan related to the Macintosh computer and the iPod and has seven Apple retail stores already in place.[105]

Stephen Kobrin, a Wharton Multinational management professor explained in a recent interview that companies that are high-tech and driven by technology that demands that they expand into many countries simultaneously are "born global." He clarifies by further stating, "Companies that are born global 'tend to have high-tech products that immediately find acceptance in many different cultures and societies.'"[106] Thus, it is likely that the iPhone will experience success in many different markets, as will the Apple TV and other new products that Apple may launch when they become part of its global strategy.

Future Opportunities and Challenges

As Apple tries to expand its product line to include media and software in addition to hardware and as it tries to reach many different consumers rather than its traditional niche of "cult followers," the tech-savvy consumers who work in fields such as education and design, the company will find it more difficult to keep a positive brand image among all consumers. The technology and entertainment industries are constantly and rapidly changing. Will Apple be able to keep its reputation related to innovative design and continually launch products that will be the "latest hit"? Competition has become extremely fierce in the technology sector, and Apple needs to be concerned not only about major competitors, but also about start-up companies. For example, in relation to the iPhone, GotVoice is a Web-based company that allows subscribers to record voicemail messages in MP3 format and send those messages to their e-mail account to view the subject line and the message length. This capability rivals Apple's Visual Voicemail on the iPhone, and the service is free unless users prefer to pay $10 to avoid ad pop-ups.[107]

Interestingly, GotVoice has an advantage over Apple's Visual Voicemail in that it works not only with cell phones, but also with home and work phones.[108] It will be a challenge for Apple to maintain its competitive advantage in new product hardware and to create strong relationships with powerful suppliers of media and other services as well as fend off startups such as GotVoice in software and other areas.

NOTES

1. D. Leonard, 2003, Songs in the key of Steve, *Fortune*, April 28.
2. D. Chmielewski & M. Quinn, 2007, Technology; Movie studios fear the sequel to iPod; They see risk that new Apple TV signals effort to control distribution, *Los Angeles Times*, June 11, C1.
3. R. E. Hoskisson, 2007, Strategic Focus: Apple: Using innovation to create technology trends and maintain competitive advantage, Hitt, Ireland, & Hoskisson, *Strategic Management: Competitiveness and Globalization*, 8th Edition.
4. Ibid.
5. Apple history, www.apple-history.com/frames.
6. Ibid.
7. L. Kimmel, 1998, Apple Computer, Inc.: A History, www.geocities.com/Athens/3682/applehistory.html.
8. Ibid.
9. http://apple-history.com.
10. Apple Computer History Weblog, http://apple.computerhistory.org.
11. L. Kimmel, 1998, Apple Computer, Inc.: A history.
12. Apple Computer History Weblog.
13. http://apple-history.com.
14. Ibid.
15. Apple Computer History Weblog.
16. http://apple-history.com.
17. Ibid.
18. Ibid.
19. Ibid.
20. http://www.apple.com/itunes.
21. 2008, iTunes store, www.apple.com/itunes/store/, January 8.
22. P. Hardy, 2003, Apple launches Windows-based iTunes, *Music & Copyright Magazine*, October 29.
23. A. Hesseldahl, 2005, Unpeeling Apple's Nano, *BusinessWeek*, www.businessweek.com, September 22.
24. 2007, www.apple.com.
25. R. E. Hoskisson, Strategic Focus: Apple.
26. 2007, Apple reinvents the phone with iPhone, Apple Inc. press release, www.apple.com/pr/library/2007/01/09iphone.html, January 9.
27. K. Allison, 2007, Apple encroaches on Window's turf, *The Financial Times*, www.ft.com, June 11.
28. 2007, iPhone delivers up to eight hours of talk time, Apple Inc. press release, www.apple.com/pr/library/2007/06/18iphone.html, June 18.
29. 2007, In three months, iPhone sales top a million, *New York Times*, www.nytimes.com, September 11.
30. Ibid.
31. M. Quinn & D. C. Chmielewski, 2008, Studios join Apple's movie-rental service, *Los Angeles Times*, www.latimes.com, January 16.
32. B. Schlender, 2007, The trouble with Apple TV, *Fortune*, June 11,155(11): 56.
33. 2008, www.apple.com/appletv/rentals.
34. W. Cohen, www.rollingstone/news/newsarticle.asp?nid =18075.
35. K. Regan, 2007, EMI revenue falls but DRM-free iTunes sales promising, *Ecommerce Times*, www.ecommercetimes.com, August 6.
36. M. Garrahan & K. Allison, 2007, Apple signs film deal with Fox studio, *Financial Times*, www.ft.com, December 27.
37. D. C. Chmielewski & M. Quinn, 2007, Technology; Movie studios fear the sequel to iPod; They see risk that new Apple TV signals effort to control distribution, *Los Angeles Times*, June 11, C1.
38. 2008, Apple premieres iTunes movie rentals with all major film studios, Apple press release, www.apple.com/pr/library, January 15.
39. M. Quinn & D. C. Chmielewski, Studios join Apple's movie-rental service.
40. 2007, Apple chooses Cingular as exclusive U.S. carrier for its revolutionary iPhone, Apple Inc. press release, www.apple.com/pr/library/2007/01/09cingular.html, January 9.
41. 2008, www.apple.com/iphone.
42. A. Hesseldahl, 2007, Take the iPhone apart, *BusinessWeek*, www.businessweek.com, July 2.
43. 2001, Napster's History, http://w3.uwyo.edu/~pz/nap2.htm.
44. 2001, The history of the Napster struggle, www.theneworleanschannel.com/news/457209/detail.html.
45. 2003, Napster 2.0 to launch by Christmas, www.roxio.com/en/company/news/archive/prelease030728.jhtml.
46. Ibid.
47. J. Ketola, 2003, Kazaa Plus service launched, www.afterdawn.com, August.
48. 2008, Wikipedia, http://en.wikipedia.org/wiki/kazaa.
49. 2006, Kazaa settlement, *BBC News*, http://news.bbc.co.uk., July 27.
50. 2003, Kazaa Usage Map, http://tools.waglo.com/kazaa.
51. N. Wingfield, 2004, Price war in online music, *Wall Street Journal*, www.wsj.com, August 17.
52. 2008, http://musicstore.connect.com.
53. Y. I. Kane, 2007, Sony to challenge Apple in TV, movie downloads, *Wall Street Journal*, www.online.wsj.com, September 4.
54. 2008, www.virgin.com/VirginProducts/Shopping/Musicdownloads.aspx.
55. 2008, iTunes now the number two music retailer in the United States, Apple press release, www.apple.com/pr/library.
56. 2008, http://musicdownloads.walmart.com.
57. 2008, http://music.yahoo.com.
58. B. Stone, 2007, Amazon and TiVo in venture to put downloaded movies on TV, *New York Times*, www.nytimes.com, February 7.
59. G. Sandoval, 2007, NBC says goodbye to Apple, hello to Amazon, www.news.com, September 4.
60. 2008, CinemaNow Inc., *BusinessWeek*, http://investing.businessweek.com, March 14; 2008, www.cinemanow.com; 2008, Wikipedia, http://en.wikipedia.org; A. Gonsalves, 2007, *Information Week*, www.informationweek.com, July 18.
61. 2007, The Walt Disney Studios to offer movie rentals on demand through Xbox Live starting now, *MicrosoftNews*, www.microsoft.com/presspass, July 10.
62. 2008, HP and Sony Pictures Home Entertainment announce manufactured-on-demand content licensing agreement, *HP News Release*, www.hp.com/hpinfo/newsroom, January 24.
63. 2007, Blockbuster acquires Movielink, *New York Times*, www.nytimes.com, August 9.
64. 2008, Netflix and LG unveil video-on-demand service, *Appliance Magazine*, www.appliancemagazine.com, January 7.
65. 2008, Netflix now offers subscribers unlimited streaming of movies and TV shows on their PCs for the same monthly fee, Netflix press release, www.netflix.mediaroom.com, January 14.
66. Leipzig, 2007, PSP (PlayStation Portable) video download service, Sony Computer Entertainment Europe press release, www.scei.co.jp/corporate/release, August.
67. 2008, Wikipedia, http://en.wikipedia.org.

68. D. Pogue, 2007, High-speed video store in the living room, *New York Times*, www.nytimes.com, September 6.

69. J. Goldman, 2008, Motorola hangs up on handsets, www.cnbc.com, January 31; A. Hasseldahl, 2008, Blackberry vs. iPhone: Who wins? *BusinessWeek*, www.articles.moneycentral.msn.com, January 3.

70. E. M. Rusli, 2007, Palm wilts, *Forbes*, www.forbes.com, October 2.

71. A. Hesseldahl, 2008, Blackberry vs. iPhone: Who wins?

72. J. Goldman, 2008, iPhone vs. Blackberry: Apple launches new software, www.cnbc.com, March 6.

73. www.reviews.cnet.com/html.

74. N. Wingfield, 2007, Microsoft tunes its Zunes to catch up with iPod, *Wall Street Journal Online*, www.wsj.com, October 3, D8.

75. Ibid.

76. A. Cuneo, 2003, Apple transcends as lifestyle brand, *Advertising Age*, December 15.

77. 2007, A bruise or two on Apple's reputation, *BusinessWeek*, www.businessweek.com, October 22.

78. Ibid.

79. J. Quelch, 2007, How marketing hype hurt Boeing and Apple, *Harvard Business*, http://discussionleader.hbsp.com, November 2.

80. Ibid.

81. J. Smykil, 2007, *BusinessWeek* names Apple most innovative, http://arstechnica.com, May 6.

82. L. Gomes, 2006, Above all else, rivals of Apple mostly need some design mojo, *Wall Street Journal*, May 24, B1.

83. Ibid.

84. Cuneo, Apple transcends as lifestyle brand.

85. Ibid.

86. Ibid.

87. 2007, In 3 months, iPhone sales top a million.

88. R. Stross, 2007, Apple's lesson for Sony's stores: Just connect, *New York Times*, www.nytimes.com, May 27.

89. Ibid.; 2007, Retail stores' importance highlighted, http://ifoapplestore.com, August 17.

90. Cuneo, Apple transcends as lifestyle brand.

91. www.apple.com/findouthow/retail/.

92. J. Boudreau, 2008, Apple tutorial classes help create bond with customers, *The Mercury News*, www.mercurynews.com, March 3.

93. Ibid.

94. J. Graham, 2007, Apple buffs marketing savvy to a high shine, *USA Today*, www.usatoday.com, March 3.

95. Wong.

96. Ibid.

97. Ibid.

98. C. Campellone, 2007, Apple and Volkswagen team up for possible iCar, http://media.www.theloquitur.com, September 20.

99. Ibid.

100. www.apple.com/ipod/nike/run.html.

101. E.C. Baig, 2006, Apple, Nike exercise iPods to track workouts, *USA Today*, www.usatoday.com, May 23.

102. 2008, Nike, Apple plug iPods into gym equipment, *USA Today*, www.usatoday.com, March 4.

103. 2007, Apple and Starbucks announce music partnership, Apple press release, www.apple.com/pr/library, September 5; http://www.apple.com/itunes/starbucks.

104. N. Gohring, 2008, Apple beats Microsoft and Motorola in 4Q phone sales, IDG News Service, February 6.

105. Y. I. Kane & N. Wingfield, 2007, For Apple iPhone, Japan could be the next big test, *Wall Street Journal Online*, www.wsj.com, December 19, B1.

106. 2007, What makes a global leader? *India Knowledge at Wharton*, http://knowledge.wharton.upenn.edu/india, October 4.

107. M. S. Lasky, 2007, iPhone versus your phone: Tips to avoid iPhone envy, *PC World*, www.pcworld.com, June 27.

108. 2008, www.gotvoice.com.

Florence Nightingale,
Vara Vasanthi

ICFAI Business School

*Blockbuster is committed to keeping pace with the changing
needs of customers by offering them an expanding array of
convenient ways to access entertainment content."*[1]

> — JAMES W. KEYES, CHAIRMAN AND CEO OF
> BLOCKBUSTER

Blockbuster Inc. is a leading global provider of in-home
movie and game entertainment, with approximately
8,000 stores located throughout America, Europe, Asia,
and Australia. The video rental market has undergone
many changes and continues to constantly change with
new product offerings from companies. The biggest
change in the video rental market is the transition from
store-based video rental to online video rental. To tackle
the changes taking place in the industry, Blockbuster
wanted to identify and implement initiatives designed
to regenerate the company's activities and enhance its
organizational structure to improve profitability. As part
of these initiatives, in August 2007 Blockbuster acquired
Movielink, a movie download service provider. This
acquisition enabled Blockbuster to offer video downloading services to its customers. Blockbuster acknowledged that this acquisition was its next logical step in
the planned transformation of the company.[2] It, however,
remains to be seen if the acquisition will generate the
expected synergies.

The Video Rental Market

In-home filmed entertainment includes video rentals
and purchases of various video products such as DVDs
with rentals being the most significant portion of this
market. A key driver of this market is the affordability
and improvement of high-quality DVD technology.
Consumer spending on video rentals is nearly three
times greater than the theatrical box office.[3] The home
video market was the largest segment of consumer movie
spending in 2007, generating just over $24 billion in rev-
enue.[4] The breakdown for the revenue in the home video
market was approximately $15.9 billion in sales and $8.2
billion in rentals.[5] Customer preferences are changing daily, making an exclusively bricks-and-mortar[6]
approach to video sales and rentals unprofitable.[7]

In-home filmed entertainment is offered through various distribution channels such as the retail home video
industry, the online video industry, movie downloads,
the cable industry, and the satellite industry. Of these
distribution channels, the retail home video industry
includes the sale and rental of movies on DVD (including in the Blue-Ray format) and VHS by traditional video
store retailers such as Blockbuster and other businesses.
Online video retailers include Blockbuster Online, Movie
Gallery, Netflix, Amazon.com, CinemaNow, and other
retailers (Exhibit 1).

As home-viewing technology improves and becomes
cheaper, downloading movies over the Internet and
watching on wide-screen televisions at home is an
emerging trend. By using a computer and a broadband
link, movies can be downloaded from online video retailers for as low as $2 to $5 and watched by customers on
their computers.[8] Online DVD rental services are convenient and allow customers to find, rent, and watch movies whenever they wish. Online video retailers such as
Movielink and CinemaNow provide various methods of

This case was written by Florence Nightingale, ICFAI Business School, Chennai and Vara Vasanthi, ICFAI Business School Case Development Centre, under the
direction of Doris Rajakumari John, ICFAI Business School, Chennai. It is intended to be used as the basis for class discussion rather than to illustrate either
effective or ineffective handling of a management situation. The case was compiled from published sources.

Exhibit 1 Online Video Rental Companies

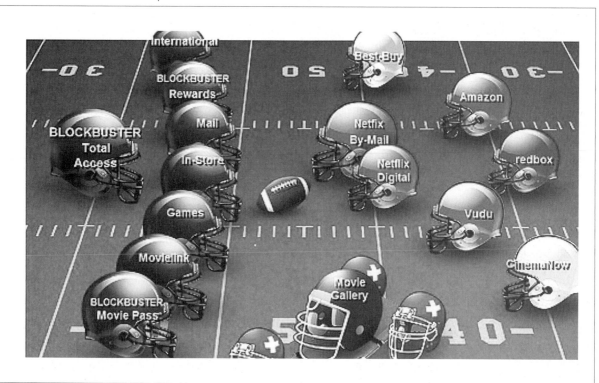

Source: Blockbuster's new paradigm and its impact on competitors, http://finance.paidcontent.org/paidcontent?Page=QUOTE&Ticket=Bbl, November 15, 2007.

access to customers for watching movies. Movielink, for example, offers two options to either buy or rent a movie. It provides a license to watch a movie and also allows for unlimited viewing. The movie can be stored on a hard disc.[9] The price to purchase a movie ranges between $8.99 and $19.99, and a movie rental from $0.99 to $4.99. As technology advances, it is likely to be easier to send a movie from a computer to a television. The major players in movie downloads are Sony, Universal, and Warner Bros., which embarked on a major endeavor to have movies transferred into digital designs. These companies also provide access to movies, similar to online video retailers. CinemaNow.com also provides free movie downloads and allows users to choose from a wide array of movies, ranging from major studio blockbusters to hard-to-find classics.

Despite the emergence of new technologies such as movie downloads and online movie purchases, the online rental business remains popular. The United States (the world's largest market for video rentals) and Europe generated more than $1 billion in consumer spending in this area in 2005.[10] By the end of 2005, there were about 6.3 million online DVD rental subscribers in the United States and Europe.[11] The United Kingdom dominates the European market, followed by Germany and thriving markets in France and Scandinavia. The online sector already accounts for more than 1 in 10 video rentals

in the United Kingdom.[12] According to recent research, 70 percent of Americans prefer watching movies at home, and Americans rented about 10 million movies in September 2007.[13] It is expected that by the end of 2009, more than half of the United Kingdom's rental transactions and rental spending will be online.[14]

The growth in the sector is further aided by customer-friendly strategies adopted by retailers. The retailers no longer insist on return dates or charge late fees for DVD rentals, thereby giving customers more freedom to keep the DVDs as long as they desire. The online rental companies allow customers to pay a monthly fee for access to unlimited rentals, which arrive and are returned by mail. In this fast-growing video rental market, Blockbuster Inc. was one of the early players and was the largest video rental chain in the United States.

The Blockbuster Business Model

Headquartered in Dallas, Texas, Blockbuster Inc. was founded by David Cook in 1982. In October 1985, Cook opened the first Blockbuster Video outlet in Dallas, with 8,000 tapes covering 6,500 titles. At the start of 1987, Blockbuster owned 15 stores and franchised 20 other stores. By the end of 1987, Blockbuster was operating 133 stores and had become the fifth-largest video chain in terms of revenue in the United States.[15] The company's basic revenues were from their stores and from late fees charged for rentals. In August 2004, Blockbuster introduced an online DVD rental service to compete with the established market leader, Netflix. Blockbuster offers services primarily through traditional retail outlets, online retailers, and cable and satellite providers. The company owns various trademarks such as Blockbuster, Blockbuster Video, "torn ticket" Logos, Blockbuster.com, Blockbuster Online, Blockbuster Night, Blockbuster GiftCards, Blockbuster Game Pass, Blockbuster Movie Pass word marks and logos, Blockbuster Rewards, related Blockbuster Family of Marks, Game Rush word mark and logo, and Life After Late Fees.[16]

Blockbuster's business model features a state-of-the-art distribution network and 41 distribution centers in the United States, which can reach most customers with one-day delivery, and an online recommendation system that lets customers select from 65,000 video titles. Blockbuster introduced a package that could travel as first-class mail, making it easy for customers to return DVDs at no charge to them. Blockbuster later launched a new online movie rental program to provide customers both Internet convenience and in-store benefits (see Exhibit 2). Blockbuster projects itself as a home entertainment enterprise with a diversified set of products and services, which includes an expanded games selection, DVD sales, online rentals, game trading, and various other businesses.

Later, the company introduced Blockbuster Total Access, a movie rental program that gives online customers the option of exchanging their DVDs through the mail or returning them to a nearby Blockbuster store in exchange for free in-store movie rentals, which was different from the existing model (Appendix I). In addition, most of Blockbuster's online subscribers had the option of exchanging their online movies for discounted in-store game rentals as well as free in-store movie rentals at more than 5,000 Blockbuster stores. Blockbuster reported, "We want to give consumers the most convenient access to media entertainment, whether that's through our stores or by mail, and are dedicated to doing that with flexible plans and pricing."[17] With more than 65,000 titles to choose from online, Blockbuster delivers DVDs to the subscribers' mailboxes in prepaid postage return envelopes. To increase its business, Blockbuster launched advertising campaigns and also undertook joint promotions with fast food outlets such as Domino's Pizza and McDonald's.

Blockbuster designed marketing and advertising campaigns to maximize opportunities in the marketplace, working closely with customers to connect and drive business. Blockbuster customized its stores' merchandise selection, quantity, and formats to meet the needs and preferences of local customers. As the new business was gaining ground, Blockbuster underwent several changes in its business-level strategy, focusing mainly on cost-cutting programs and selling products such as DVDs. This strategy made an impact, and the sales of DVDs increased as compared to DVD rentals. The popularity of online video rentals, however, was increasing with

Exhibit 2 Blockbuster Online Movie Rental Plan

video-on-demand (VoD) services gaining prominence. VoD services, in which video is streamed over the Internet, deviated from the firm's existing business model, which depended heavily on store ownership and increasing sales per store. Both VoD and online video-rental services diverted focus from the sale of DVDs.[18] Blockbuster developed a good understanding of how the online rental channel worked and what online customers were doing in their stores.

In 2005, as part of a comprehensive business trans-formation initiative, Blockbuster engaged Accenture, a global management consulting and technology services company, to develop the systems and processes and to launch the online business.[19] Both companies jointly built a network of distribution centers fully dedicated to service online customers. Blockbuster wanted to offer a "one-day" delivery to as many customers as possible. Working with Accenture, Blockbuster also identified sites for distribution centers that enhanced its cus-tomer service. The company's online rental program was unique and encouraged former customers to return to Blockbuster's stores.

Blockbuster reported worldwide revenues of more than $5.5 billion and a profit of $54.7 million in 2006.[20] In the same year, Blockbuster Online had about 1.4 million online subscribers.[21] To concentrate more on its online subscriber business, Blockbuster closed nearly 300 stores in the United States in 2006. Blockbuster continued to invest in its Total Access program and added more than 700,000 online subscribers[22] and more than 4 million total subscribers[23] in 2006. This action facilitated Blockbuster's efforts to compete with Netflix. Blockbuster reported, "We have invested heavily in Total Access during the first half of 2007 to capture market share in the overall video rental market and to set the stage for the expected future profitability of our online rental business."[24] Blockbuster's Total Access had a positive impact on its online movie rental revenue. In the first quarter of 2007, revenues reached about $108.9 million.[25] Total Access also helped Blockbuster generate more cross-channel sales and traffic. The average store had about 4,800 shoppers and 45,000 rentals per month. Blockbuster reported, "Growing the revenue of Total Access had helped to offset the in-store revenue decline."[26]

Michael Pachter, an analyst at Wedbush Morgan Securities,[27] said, "Under Keyes, Blockbuster will likely be looking for ways to maximize its customer base and leverage its chain of stores—the main differentiator with Netflix—all while also preparing for the fact that physical DVD rentals may not be its core business in just a few years."[28] Blockbuster focused on protecting its core rental business, developing new retail opportu-nities, and becoming the preferred provider of digital entertainment.[29] In 2007, Blockbuster had 27 percent of the U.S. video rental market and served more than 87 million customers in the United States, its territories, and 25 other nations.[30]

While Blockbuster tried to make its mark in the online movie rental business, the firm encountered stiff competitions from Apple, Amazon.com, and Wal-Mart, as well as market leader Netflix. In 2007, Netflix was already an established player with 75 percent[31] of the market. Netflix's success was attributed to the firm's business model. Netflix's innovative subscription service, for example, allowed customers to keep videos as long as they wished. There are no due dates or late fees nor does the customer incur any shipping charges. Netflix's success inspired a number of other DVD rental companies both in the United States and abroad (see Exhibit 3).

Both Blockbuster and Netflix offer three movie rent-als for a monthly fee of $17.99 (the price of this service changes in response to competitive challenges) and allow customers to return their rentals by mail. However, as part of the Total Access program, Blockbuster accepts returns at its stores and rewards subscribers with a free rental for each store return. Consumers were willing to pay a premium for convenience, and Blockbuster capital-ized on that. As a result, Blockbuster gained subscribers from Netflix, which had no bricks-and-mortar presence and could not match with Blockbuster's Total Access plan.

Netflix, for its part, still posted a 36 percent increase in revenue to $305.3 million for the year 2007. Netflix was also investing more than $40 million in new digi-tal download technology.[32] Blockbuster responded to these competitive actions by aggressively trying to take customers away from Netflix.[33] Reducing its prices and enhancing the layouts of its retail stores are examples of the competitive actions Blockbuster decided to initi-ate while competing against Netflix. Blockbuster also provides printable e-coupons for two free in-store movie or game rentals, and other special offers. Both companies were organized to focus on the key consider-ations such as selection, price, and customer satisfaction (see Exhibit 4).

Pachter said, "Netflix has tried to grab the lead in the digital distribution channel, but Blockbuster is signaling it's not going to give that up easily."[34] Blockbuster and Netflix offer similar plans and have repeatedly lowered prices or modified services in an effort to win customers. Blockbuster, in addition to the entertainment content provided through its stores and by mail, had taken an important step towards making movie downloading available to computers, portable devices, and directly to televisions in homes.

In 2007, Blockbuster introduced a wider range of subscription plans, including Blockbuster Total Access

Exhibit 3 Netflix—How it Works

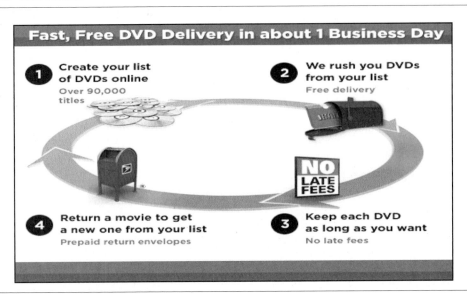

Source: Netflix—How it works, http://www.netflix.com/HowItWorks.

Exhibit 4 Comparison of Blockbuster Online DVD Rentals and NetFlix.com

	BLOCKBUSTER Online Blockbuster Online DVD Rental	NETFLIX. Netflix
No Late Fees	Keep the DVDs as long as you want **No Late Fees**	Keep the DVDs as long as you want **No Late Fees**
Selections	Over 40,000 titles	Over 40,000 titles
Turn-around Time	1 Day	1 Day
Unlimited DVD Rentals	YES	YES
Delivered to Your Mailbox	YES	YES
Free Shipping & Postage	**Free** first-class postage both ways	**Free** first-class postage both ways
No Return Dates	YES	YES
Distribution Centers	23 across the United States Will start using their **4,500** stores in coming year	35 across the United States.
Free In-Store Coupons	**YES** – Two e-coupons for **FREE** in-store movie or game rentals. Print coupons yourself.	**NO**
Gift Subscriptions	YES	YES
Special Offers	**$9.99 for First Month**	2-week free trial
$$ Cost $$	**$17.99 – 3 titles out** $29.99 – 5 titles out $37.49 – 8 titles out	$11.99, 4 DVDs a month, 2 titles out **$17.99 – 3 titles out** $29.99 – 5 titles out $47.99 – 8 titles out *Eight subscription plans offered*

Source: DVD Rental Services Comparison, http://www.acmetech.com/shopping/movies/dvd_rental.php.

Premium™, Blockbuster Total Access™, and Blockbuster® by Mail. The new subscription plans were available to all current and new subscribers to Blockbuster's online rental service with pricing as low as $4.99 a month[35] (see Appendix 2). Blockbuster's online movie rentals increased by 121.3 percent from $174.2 million in 2006 to $385.5 million in 2007.[36] Despite the increase in the online movie rentals, Blockbuster reported losses in 2007 (see Appendix 3).

According to the projected figures for 2008 in the Online DVD rental report published by *Online DVD Rental Reviews 2008*, Netflix ranked first, with Blockbuster second (see Appendix 4). To survive in the market, Blockbuster needed to increase its market share and establish its reputation in the online download business. According to PricewaterhouseCoopers, by 2010, annual revenue for the online video download business is expected to increase by $3.7 billion and DVD rentals and sales are expected to increase to about $29.5 billion.[37] For these reasons, Blockbuster decided to acquire Movielink.

Movielink Acquisition: The Strategic Rationale

When Blockbuster released its financial results for the year 2007, the firm's shareholders questioned the long-term sustainability of the company's current business model. In response to these concerns, company officials said, "Our goal is to continue to increase our membership base by providing even more ways for customers to get the entertainment they want through our stores, through the mail, and through new technologies."[38] As part of this goal, in August 2007, Blockbuster acquired Movielink, a leading movie downloading service.

Movielink offers movies for download through its video-on-demand Internet distribution service. Movielink was founded as a joint venture among five studios—Paramount Pictures, Sony Pictures Entertainment, MGM, Universal Studios, and Warner Bros.—who were responding to consumers' adoption of high-speed Internet access.[39] Movielink offers about 400 movies, which take 30 to 90 minutes to download, but the customers have the option of watching the movie after 10 minutes of downloading.[40] The Movielink Web site has two stores, a purchase store and a rental store, with a common home page. At the rental store, customers can browse the site and view trailers of movies without any charge. The customer can register with Movielink and pay for the rental by credit card.

Bruce Anderson, Movielink's vice president of engineering and operations, said, "As Movielink's business continues to grow, it is vital that our content delivery infrastructure continues to provide the quality of service our customers have come to expect."[41] Movielink has distribution agreements with the five studios that founded it, as well as Lionsgate and 20th Century FOX. Blockbuster's chief executive, James W. Keyes, said, "The acquisition immediately puts us in the digital download business. Clearly, our customers have responded favorably to having other convenient ways to access movies and entertainment."[42] The acquisition provided Blockbuster with a way to send movies straight to televisions and computers, complementing its store and movie-by-mail operations. Pachter stated, "The acquisition is a defensive move by Blockbuster to keep up with Netflix."[43]

Movielink CEO Jim Ramo said, "The studios' goal with the Movielink service has always been to make digital entertainment content more conveniently, more widely, and more securely available to consumers. This acquisition should further that goal."[44] He added, "With Blockbuster's ability to leverage its store network, online assets, and marketing expertise, Blockbuster should be able to grow the market for digitally-delivered entertainment content, and we believe that's good news for consumers and content providers alike."[45]

Blockbuster believed that the 1,400 movie titles in the Movielink catalog gave it a strong presence among firms offering movies for digital download via online capabilities. Customers are allowed to rent movies for $0.99, and they can store the movie for 30 days on their computers. Movielink announced that it was working on a plan that would allow customers to copy films to DVD.

Movielink's services, however, failed to catch on because the only way to watch films from Movielink on a television was to buy a set-top box. The company offered a network between a PC and television. Analysts felt the issue was that Movielink downloads could not be burned to discs.[46] Movielink did not provide a download-and-burn[47] service because of a misunderstanding between Movielink and the five studios.[48] In contrast, Blockbuster's competitor Netflix's movie download service was favorably received by customers. Movielink ended up failing to reach a wide audience and posted a net loss of $10.16 million in 2007.

Blockbuster's acquisition of Movielink failed to immediately expand the firm's business beyond the store-based movie-rental market. Competition from cable providers offering video-on-demand and DVD-rental services such as Netflix also posed problems for Blockbuster. Whether Blockbuster can use the Movielink acquisition to increase its market share and profitability in the video rental market and whether this acquisition offers Blockbuster an increased online presence remains to be seen.

NOTES

1. C. Metz, 2007, Blockbuster reels in MovieLink, http://www .theregister.co.uk/2007/08/09/blockbuster_buys_netflix, August 9.

2. K. Regan, 2007, Blockbuster chases online box office with movielink buy, http://www.ecommercetimes.com/story/58751.html, August 9.

3. EMA's 2007 Annual Report is now available, http://www.entmerch .org/annual_reports.html.

4. Ibid.

5. The Entertainment Merchant Association, http://www.entmerch.org/ annual_reports.html.

6. Companies that have a physical presence can offer face-to-face consumer experiences.

7. G. Millman, 2005, Blockbuster's bricks and clicks, http:// www.accenture.com/Global/Research_and_Insights/Outlook/ BlockbustersClicks.htm, June.

8. Blockbuster's bricks and clicks, op.cit.

9. D. Gynn, 2006, Download movies with Movielink/Optaros and reduce risk, http://opensource.syscon. com/read/256611.htm, August 8.

10. A. Wood & H. J. Davis, 2005, The outlook for online DVD rental: A strategic analysis of the U.S. and European markets, http://www .screendigest.com/reports/05onlinedvdrental/readmore/view.html, November.

11. Ibid.

12. The outlook for online DVD rental: A strategic analysis of the U.S. and European markets, op.cit.

13. 2007, Frost & Sullivan Commends DVDPlays Innovative Services in the Automated DVD Rental Machine Market, http://www.frost.com/ prod/servlet/press-release.pag?docid=110114449, October 23.

14. Ibid.

15. Blockbuster Inc., http://www.fundinguniverse.com/company- histories/Blockbuster-Inc-Company-History.html.

16. Blockbuster Inc., 2007, http://custom.marketwatch.com/custom/ nyt-com/htmlcompanyprofile. asp?MW=http://marketwatch. nytimes.com/custom/nyt-com/htmlcompanyprofile. asp&symb=BBI &sid=153477#compinfo, August 11.

17. 2007, Blockbuster announces expanded online subscription offerings, http://goliath.ecnext.com/coms2/summary_0199- 6786323_ITM, July 26.

18. Diversity, http://www.blockbuster.com/corporate/diversity

19. Blockbuster's bricks and clicks, op.cit.

20. 2006, Blockbuster profit, 1.4 million online subscribers, http://www .hackingnetflix.com/2006/07/blockbuster_pro.html, July 27.

21. Ibid.

22. C. Spielvogel, 2007, Blockbuster Q4 income down, revenue up, http://www.videobusiness.com/article/CA6419949.html, February 27.

23. 2007, Blockbuster emphasizes its online program over stores, http://www.internetretailer.com/dailyNews.asp?id=22946, June 29.

24. Blockbuster profit, 1.4 million online subscribers, op.cit.

25. Ibid.

26. 2007, Blockbuster Q1 2007 Earnings Call Transcript, http://www .seekingalpha.com/article/34304-blockbuster-q1-2007-earnings- call-transcript, May 2.

27. It is recognized among securities professionals as a leading investment banking and brokerage firm.

28. Blockbuster chases online box office with movielink buy, op.cit.

29. 2007, Blockbuster reports third quarter 2007 results, new strategic initiatives and decisive actions taken to improve near-term profitability, http://www.b2i.us/profiles/investor/ ResLibraryView.asp?BzID=553&ResLibraryID=22067&Category=1 027, November 1.

30. Blockbuster Inc., op.cit.

31. J. M. Spool, 2006, Innovation is the new black, http://www.uie.com/ articles/innovation_from_experience_design/, June 1.

32. Blockbuster emphasizes its online program over stores, op.cit.

33. J. Love, 2006. E-retailing's brightest stars at IRCE 2007, http: //www.internetretailer.com/internet/marketing-conference/89902- e-retailings-brightest-stars-at-irce-2007.html, December.

34. Blockbuster chases online box office with movielink buy, op.cit.

35. Blockbuster announces expanded online subscription offerings, op.cit.

36. 2007, Blockbuster turns in a weaker third quarter performance, http://www.internetretailer.com/dailyNews.asp?id=24278, November 1.

37. Video download service, http://videodownloadservice.net.

38. A. Chowdhry, 2007, Blockbuster revenue drops 5.7 percent; focusing on membership gain, http://pulse2.com/category/ blockbuster, November 3.

39. Movielink, LLC Company Profile, http://biz.yahoo.com/ ic/106/106424.html.

40. Movielink, http://dvd-rental-review.toptenreviews.com/movielink-details .html

41. 2005, Equinix to provide connectivity infrastructure for Movielink video-on-demand service, http://findarticles.com/p/articles/mi_ m0EIN/is_2005_Jan_17/ai_n8694997, January 17.

42. 2007, Blockbuster acquires Movielink, http://www.nytimes. com/2007/08/09/business/09movie.html?_r=1&n= Toppercent2f Newspercent2f Businesspercent 2fCompanies percent2fBlockbu ste rpercent20Incpercent2e&oref=slogin, August 9.

43. Ibid.

44. Blockbuster reels in Movielink, op.cit.

45. Ibid.

46. G. Sandoval, 2007, Blockbuster acquires Movielink, http://www .news.com/2100-1026_3-6201609.html, August 8.

47. The service allows the consumers to purchase, download, and burn a complete DVD for instant gratification.

48. E. Bangeman, 2007, Is action better than inaction? Blockbuster buys Movielink for a song, http://arstechnica.com/news.ars/ post/20070809-is-action-better-than-inaction-blockbuster- buys-movielink-for-asong.html?rel, August 9.

Appendix 1 Blockbuster Business

SELECT MOVIES
Make your list online from over 75,000 titles.

RECEIVE BY MAIL
Free shipping. Keep your online movies as long as you want.

MAIL BACK

OR

EXCHANGE IN-STORE
Return by mail OR exchange in-store (up to monthly plan limits on exchanges) at a participating store*.

NEXT DVDS ON THE WAY

Rent Online – Return by Mail Or In-Store with Blockbuster Total Access™

Only Blockbuster Total Access™ gives the convenience of renting movies online and the choice of how to return them: by mail or bringing them to participating Blockbuster store, where customers can exchange them for new movies or discounted game rentals on the spot (up to monthly plan limits on exchanges).*

In-Store Exchanges

For only $17.99 a month (plus taxes) customers can receive up to 3 DVDs at a time with up to 5 in-store exchanges for free movie rentals or discounted game rentals. When customers finish watching a DVD, they can send it back in the provided postage-paid envelope or return it to a participating Blockbuster store.

Special In-Store Monthly Offers

As a Blockbuster Online member, customers are eligible for exclusive deals and discounts each month at participating Blockbuster stores.

More than 75,000 Titles, Including New Releases

Online DVD library has more than 75,000 titles, and it is growing every week. Customers can find classic cinema, modern favorites, television shows, children's programming, health and fitness workouts, and of course, the hottest new releases from Blockbuster.

Delivered Right to the Mailbox

Renting DVDs is as easy as picking up the mail. DVDs usually arrive within 1–2 business days**. Return the DVD by placing the DVD in the provided postage paid envelope and send it back through the mail or return it to a participating store. Then, the next DVD will be on its way.

Free Shipping and Postage

Shipping is always free. Both ways. There are no postage charges.

No Return Dates on Online Rentals

Blockbuster online rental members can keep online rentals out as long as they want. There are never any due dates*. Watch the DVD when it is convenient for you, and send it back only when you are ready for a new selection.

No Extended Viewing Fees or Late Fees on Online Rentals

As a Blockbuster Online rental member, customers pay a flat monthly rate. There are no extended viewing fees or late fees on DVDs rented online.

* Separate, complimentary in-store membership required for in-store rentals. In-store movie rentals are subject to store rental terms and conditions, including due dates and charges which may apply to rentals not returned by the due date. See store for complete in-store rental terms and conditions. Free in-store rentals must be returned to the store where they were originally rented.

** One business day delivery for Blockbuster based on more than 90 percent of our subscribers being within one-day postal delivery zone. Certain subscribers may experience longer delivery times.

Source: Blockbuster Movies, https://www.blockbuster.com/signup/rp/howItWorks.

Appendix 2 Blockbuster Membership Plans

Blockbuster Online offers the following membership plans:

- $4.99 per month—offers 2 DVD rentals per month and allows 1 movie rental at a time.
- $8.99 per month—offers unlimited DVD rentals per month and allows 1 movie rental at a time.
- $13.99 per month—offers unlimited DVD rentals per month and allows for 2 movie rentals at a time.
- $16.99 per month—offers unlimited DVD rentals per month and allows for 3 movie rentals at a time.

Blockbuster Total Access offers the following membership plans:

- $7.99 per month—2 DVD rentals per month, allowing 1 movie rental at a time or 2 in-store exchanges 1 movie at a time.
- $9.99 per month—offers unlimited DVD rentals per month, allows 1 movie rental at a time and up to 2 in-store exchanges per month.
- $14.99 per month—offers unlimited DVD rentals per month, allows 2 movie rentals at a time and up to 3 in-store exchanges per month.
- $17.99 per month—offers unlimited DVD rentals per month, allows 3 movie rentals at a time and up to 5 in-store exchanges per month.

Blockbuster Total Access Premium plans include:

- $16.99 per month—offers unlimited DVD rentals per month, unlimited in-store exchanges, 1 movie at a time.
- $21.99 per month—offers unlimited DVD rentals per month, unlimited in-store exchanges, 2 movies at a time.
- $24.99 per month—offers unlimited DVD rentals per month, unlimited in-store exchanges, 3 movies at a time.

Source: Blockbuster Online, http://dvd-rental-review.toptenreviews.com/blockbuster-online-review.html.

Appendix 3 Blockbuster Income Statement – 2007

All amounts in millions except per-share amounts	Q3–2007 09/2007	Q2–2007 06/2007	Q1–2007 03/2007	Q4–2006 12/2006
Operating Revenue	1,238.20	1,263.20	1,473.00	1,463.10
Total Revenue	1,238.20	1,263.20	1,473.00	1,463.10
Adjustment to Revenue	0.00	0.00	0.00	0.00
Cost of Sales	396.30	441.00	531.60	536.90
Cost of Sales with Depreciation	570.40	627.70	711.00	699.90
Gross Margin	667.80	635.50	762.00	763.20
Gross Operating Profit	841.90	822.20	941.40	926.20
R&D	0.00	0.00	0.00	0.00
SG&A	603.20	624.30	654.50	610.70
Advertising	27.50	54.80	76.60	47.50
Operating Profit	−5.60	−13.70	−18.40	50.10
Operating Profit before Depreciation (EBITDA)	211.20	143.10	210.30	268.00
Depreciation	217.00	234.50	228.70	212.80
Depreciation Unreconciled	42.90	47.80	49.30	49.80
Amortization	0.00	0.00	0.00	0.00
Amortization of Intangibles	0.00	0.00	0.00	0.00
Operating Income After Depreciation	−5.80	−91.40	−18.40	55.20

Appendix 3 Blockbuster Income Statement – 2007 (*Continued*)

All amounts in millions except per-share amounts	Q3–2007 09/2007	Q2–2007 06/2007	Q1–2007 03/2007	Q4–2006 12/2006
Interest Income	1.30	1.90	1.90	2.60
Earnings from Equity Interest	0.00	0.00	0.00	0.00
Other Income, Net	−1.10	1.70	−0.40	1.60
Income Acquired in Process R&D	0.00	0.00	0.00	0.00
Interest Restructuring and M&A	0.20	77.70	0.00	0.00
Other Special Charges	0.00	0.00	0.00	−5.10
Total Income Available for Interest Expense (EBIT)	−5.40	−10.10	−16.90	54.30
Interest Expense	20.70	21.10	23.60	24.40
Income Before Tax (EBT)	−26.10	−31.20	−40.50	29.90
Income Taxes	8.70	3.00	8.50	10.30
Minority Interest	0.00	0.00	0.00	0.00
Preferred Securities of Subsidiary Trust	0.00	0.00	0.00	0.00
Net Income from Continuing Operations	−34.80	−34.20	−49.00	19.60
Net Income from Discontinued Operations	−0.20	−1.10	2.60	−6.70
Net Income from Total Operations	−35.00	−35.30	−46.40	12.90
Extraordinary Income/Losses	0.00	0.00	0.00	0.00
Income from Cumulative Effect of Accounting Change	0.00	0.00	0.00	0.00
Income from Tax Loss Carryforward	0.00	0.00	0.00	0.00
Other Gains (Losses)	0.00	0.00	0.00	0.00
Total Net Income	−35.00	−35.30	−46.40	12.90
Normalized Income	−35.00	−111.90	−49.00	24.70
Net Income Available for Common	−37.60	−37.00	−51.80	16.70
Preferred Dividends	2.80	2.80	2.80	2.90
Excise Taxes	0.00	0.00	0.00	0.00
Per-Share Data				

(*Continued*)

Appendix 3 Blockbuster Income Statement – 2007 (*Continued*)

All amounts in millions except per-share amounts	Q3–2007 09/2007	Q2–2007 06/2007	Q1–2007 03/2007	Q4–2006 12/2006
Basic Earnings Per Share (EPS) from Continuing Operations	−0.20	−0.19	−0.27	0.09
Basic EPS from Discontinued Operations	0.00	−0.01	0.01	−0.04
Basic EPS from Total Operations	−0.20	−0.20	−0.26	0.05
Basic EPS from Extraordinary Income	0.00	0.00	0.00	0.00
Basic EPS from Cumulative Effect of Accounting Change	0.00	0.00	0.00	0.00
Basic EPS from Other Gains (Losses)	0.00	0.00	0.00	0.00
Basic EPS Total	−0.20	−0.20	−0.26	0.05
Basic Normalized Net Income/ Share	−0.20	−0.62	−0.27	0.11
Diluted EPS from Continuing Operations	−0.20	−0.19	−0.27	0.09
Diluted EPS from Discontinued Operations	0.00	−0.01	0.01	−0.04
Diluted EPS from Total Operations	−0.20	−0.20	−0.26	0.05
Diluted EPS from Extraordinary Income	0.00	0.00	0.00	0.00
Diluted EPS from Cumulative Effect of Accounting Change	0.00	0.00	0.00	0.00
Diluted EPS from Other Gains (Losses)	0.00	0.00	0.00	0.00
Diluted EPS Total	−0.20	−0.20	−0.26	0.05
Diluted Normalized Net Income/ Share	−0.20	−0.62	−0.27	0.11
Dividends Paid per Share	0.00	0.00	0.00	0.00
Additional Data				
Basic Weighted Shares Outstanding	190.60	190.00	189.40	187.10
Diluted Weighted Shares Outstanding	190.60	190.00	189.40	189.00

Source: Blockbuster Inc. Income Statement, http://finance.google.com/finance?fstype=ii&q=BBI.

Appendix 4 Projected Figures – 2008 Online DVD Rental Report

		Excellent
■■■■□		Very Good
■■■□□		Good
■■□□□		Fair
□□□□□		Poor

	Netflix	Blockbuster Online	DVD Avenue	Gameznflix	CafeDVD.com	eHit.com	Intelliflix	Peerflix	Number Slate	iLetYou
Rank	GOLD	SILVER	BRONZE	4	5	6	7	8	9	10
Reviewer Comments	READ REVIEW	READ REVIEW	READ REVIEW	READ REVIEW	READ REVIEW	READ REVIEW	READ REVIEW	READ REVIEW	READ REVIEW	READ REVIEW
Lowest Price	BUY $4.99	BUY $4.99	BUY $9.99	BUY $8.99	BUY $14.95	BUY $13.99	BUY $24.95	BUY Varies	BUY $9.95	BUY Varies
Overall Rating	■■■■□	■■■■□	■■■□□	■■■■□	■■■□□	■■■□□	■■■□□	■■□□□	■■□□□	■■□□□
Ratings										
Inventory	■■■■	■■■■	■■■□	■■■□	■■■□	■■□□	■■■■	■■□□	■■□□	■■□□
Membership Features	■■■■□	■■■■□	■■■□	■■■□	■■□□	■■■□	■■■■□	■■□□	■■■□	■■□□
Movie Arrival Time	■■■■	■■■■	■■■□	■■■□	■■■□	■■■□	■■□□	■■□□	■■□□	■■□□
Movie Information	■■■■	■■■■	■■■□	■■■□	■■□□	■■□□	■■■□	■■■□	■■■□	■■□□
Search Capabilities	■■■□	■■■□	■■■□	■■■■	■■■□	■■■□	■■■■	■■□□	■□□□	■□□□
Inventory										
DVDs	✓	✓	✓	✓	✓	✓	✓	✓	✓	✓
Games				✓			✓			✓
TV Series	✓	✓			✓		✓	✓		✓
Movie Titles	85,000	75,000	25,000	28,000	13,000	5,000	60,000	unknown	5,000	unknown

Membership Features										
Unlimited DVDs per month	✓	✓	✓	✓	✓	✓	✓		✓	
Monthly Plans	✓	✓	✓	✓		✓	✓		✓	
Pay Per Movie					✓		✓	✓		✓
No Due Date	✓	✓	✓	✓		✓	✓		✓	
No Late Fees	✓	✓	✓	✓		✓	✓		✓	
Free Two-Way Shipping	✓	✓	✓	✓		✓	✓			
Free Trial	✓		✓	✓		✓			✓	
Number of Plans	4	11	4	4	4	4	4	1	1	1
Option to Purchase DVD	✓	✓		✓	✓			✓		
Download Movies	✓									
Average Days to Receive your DVD	1-2	1-2	2-5	2–5	2-4	2-4	1–3	varies	varies	varies
Movie Information										
Title	✓	✓	✓	✓	✓	✓	✓	✓	✓	✓
MPAA Rating	✓	✓	✓	✓	✓	✓	✓		✓	✓
Critic Rating		✓	✓	✓		✓	✓			
Movie Synopsis	✓	✓	✓	✓	✓	✓	✓	✓	✓	✓
Actors	✓	✓	✓	✓	✓	✓	✓	✓	✓	✓
Director	✓	✓	✓	✓	✓	✓	✓	✓	✓	✓
Genre	✓	✓	✓	✓	✓	✓	✓	✓	✓	
Movie Studio	✓	✓	✓	✓						
Awards	✓	✓	✓							
Movie Reviews (Critics)	✓	✓		✓		✓	✓		✓	
Trailers/Previews	✓	✓		✓						

Case 10: Blockbuster Acquires Movielink: A Growth Strategy?

Appendix 4 Projected Figures – 2008 Online DVD Rental Report (*Continued*)

	Netflix	Blockbuster Online	DVD Avenue	GameznFlix	CafeDVD.com	eHit.com	Intelliflix	Peerflix	Number Slate	iLetYou
Search Capabilities										
Title	✓	✓	✓	✓		✓	✓	✓		✓
Actor	✓	✓	✓	✓		✓	✓	✓		✓
Director	✓	✓	✓	✓			✓	✓		✓
Year							✓			
Rating		✓		✓		✓	✓			
Synopsis			✓				✓			
Genre	✓	✓	✓	✓	✓	✓	✓	✓	✓	✓
New Releases	✓	✓		✓	✓	✓		✓	✓	✓
Coming Soon				✓						✓
Production Studio				✓						
Screen Format				✓						
Language			✓	✓		✓	✓			
Subtitles				✓			✓			
Awards		✓					✓			
Support/Documentation										
Phone Support	✓		✓	✓						✓
FAQ	✓	✓	✓	✓	✓	✓	✓	✓	✓	✓
eMail/Online Form		✓	✓		✓	✓	✓	✓	✓	

Source: Top Ten Reviews, http://dvd-rental-review.toptenreviews.com/index.html#anchor, 2007.

X. U. Leiping

China Europe International Business School

It was the morning of October 18, 2007. In Beijing, the autumn air was clear and crisp. Zhang Lan, the founder and chair of the board of the South Beauty Group, sat in her office with her management team to discuss the future plans for her seven-year-old company.

As a successful player in China's catering industry, by September 2007 the South Beauty Group had expanded to a total of 20 plush restaurants in the most commercially valuable locations across Beijing, Shanghai, and Chengdu, with three different brands. South Beauty, the Group's flagship brand with 19 restaurants, targeted the upper-middle-class segment of businesspeople; LAN Club, the new luxury brand with two restaurants (one opened), targeted the upper-class dining segment; SUBU, the company's latest brand slated to shortly open its first restaurant in Beijing, would cater to health-conscious youth. All the restaurants were owned and operated by the group. Occupying more than 40,000 square meters in total, employing around 2,600 people, and registering more than 3.5 million footfalls a year, the South Beauty Group was regarded as an innovative and leading player in the Chinese restaurant market. It won a prestigious contract to become a Food Service Partner of Chinese cuisine for the 2008 Beijing Olympics, which would provide more revenue than the group's estimated revenues in 2007.

However, as Zhang Lan sat with her team that morning, daunting challenges lay ahead for the company as it sought to expand its operations from the existing 20 restaurants in China to a total of 100 worldwide (35 in China and 65 in the international market) over the next three years. To achieve this scale of expansion, the company needed to make critical decisions on a number of issues: the standardization of the process of preparing the dishes to increase efficiency and quality, which was a tough task to achieve with Chinese cuisine; the prioritization of markets to enter (i.e., whether to focus on the local market to realize its full potential before venturing abroad, or to do both at the same time); entry into new businesses, such as airline catering and the supply of semi-processed food to retail outlets such as supermarkets; and the expansion model (i.e., through owned outlets,

This case was prepared by research fellow X. U. Leiping under the guidance of Prof. S. Ramakrishna Velamuri in collaboration with South Beauty Group for the purpose of class discussion, as opposed to illustrating either effective or ineffective handling of an administrative situation. Certain names and other identifying information may have been changed to maintain confidentiality.

Zhang Lan[1]

as had been the case until now, or through franchising). With so many areas to study, Zhang Lan realized that she and her team had their work cut out for them.

Zhang Lan: The Founder of South Beauty

Zhang Lan was born in Beijing. Her father was a professor of civil engineering at Tsinghua University. However, the Cultural Revolution in China shattered her carefree childhood. Her family was exiled to a farm in an impoverished mountainous area of the Hubei province, which was built to "reform" intellectuals through labor. Although moving to such an environment was devastating for a young girl, she secretly dabbled in drawing and music with her parents. Significantly, at the age of nine, she also learned to prepare simple meals for her parents, who returned exhausted after their daily toil on the farm.

At the age of 17, Zhang Lan and her parents returned to Beijing after the collapse of the Cultural Revolution. At that time, there was no opportunity for young people to study in universities. Her first job was as a worker in a factory. It was much later, in 1985, as a 27-year-old mother of a two-year-old boy, that Zhang Lan decided to study business administration at Beijing Business College[2] through an adult education program. When she graduated in 1987, she joined a civil engineering company as an office worker with a salary much higher than the average level at that time. But she was not content with things as they were, because her life was leisurely and carefree and she wanted something different. In early 1989, she obtained a visa to study in Canada with the help of her uncle, a Canadian resident. Once in Canada,

she worked part time in restaurants, hotels, and hair salons to support herself, working as many as four jobs at a time.

Following the Tiananmen Square protests in the summer of 1989, the Canadian government offered green cards to all Chinese students in the country. Zhang Lan was one of the few who rejected this opportunity. She was faced with the dilemma of staying in a prosperous country for the rest of her life or returning to an impoverished China to stay with her family. She finally decided to return to China as soon as her savings reached USD 20,000 (RMB 108,000 at that time).[3] Just four days before Christmas 1990, Zhang Lan's bank account met the target and she returned to China immediately.

When Zhang Lan reached Beijing with her substantial savings, she was brimming with ideas for possible business ventures—a pizza store, a dumpling-wrapping business, a frozen foods store, and even a paper production plant based on high-quality Canadian paper pulp technology—but soon realized that her savings could only support a business that required limited capital. During windy springtime in Beijing, with a gauze kerchief on her head, she rode a bicycle through the streets in search of business opportunities. She found that consumers' needs for dining out were increasing; however, many old and traditional restaurants could not meet this trend. Opening a small restaurant in Beijing seemed to be a relatively safe venture in that the total investment would be relatively low.

In April 1991, an attractive opportunity presented itself to open a small restaurant of only 96 square meters in Dong Si, Beijing's downtown area. Zhang Lan believed the restaurant business would help her realize her dream of doing something in China while enabling her to benefit from her extensive experience in several Canadian restaurants serving Chinese and Western food. She knew how to operate a Chinese restaurant, from the purchase of raw materials to customer reception. Her friends regarded the restaurant business as unsuitable for Zhang Lan; in spite of this, she remained adamant about pursuing her dream.

In the initial phase, Zhang Lan invested considerable time and effort to formulate her business plan. She selected Sichuan food as the restaurant's main cuisine. She believed that among the eight main Chinese cuisines, Sichuan food best expressed the Chinese culture. Sichuan food is known as "Bai Cai Bai Ge, Bai Cai Bai Wei," literally "a hundred dishes, a hundred flavors," which means that it is liked by people across the world.

Further, Zhang Lan wanted to provide a unique and comfortable ambience in her restaurant. In this pursuit, she traveled to Pi Xian, a county in Sichuan, to transport 13-meter-long bamboo shoots to Beijing by train. Three bamboo weavers designed her restaurant as a bamboo house. Zhang Lan named her restaurant

"A Lan," which sounded like her childhood nickname. "Lan" is the Chinese word for orchid or fragrance. Although bamboo was cheaper than other regular materials, by the time the restaurant was ready to open, Zhang Lan's savings were almost fully depleted.

In the early 1990s, China, especially Beijing, was staid and lacking in diversity because of slow economic and social growth. Zhang Lan's small restaurant was thus able to tap a large customer base as its unique style and offerings contrasted with the environment. Zhang Lan initially managed all operational issues (ordering dishes, purchasing, etc.) pertaining to the restaurant by herself. In a short time, A Lan Restaurant became known as a special small restaurant in Beijing.

In 1997, encouraged by the success of A Lan Restaurant, Zhang Lan opened a larger restaurant, Bai Niao Yuan Seafood and Shark's Fin Restaurant[4] in Beijing, which was quite different from the A Lan Restaurant (Exhibit 1). At that time, expensive shark's fin and abalone were popular in many Chinese cities. This popularity was influenced by Guangdong and Hong Kong cuisines. Zhang Lan capitalized on this business opportunity, seeking to exploit the demand for new tastes and accumulate profits from these relatively expensive dishes. At the same time, she was also occupied with other investments, including real estate, stocks, mobile phone retailing, and even a nightclub. In 1999, Zhang Lan sold all her restaurants and other assets and made a profit of RMB 60 million (USD 7.26 million).[5] She explained this surprising action afterwards: "I thought it was hard to earn high profits through cooking the dishes one by one in a traditional way. After selling out all my assets in 1999, I spent half a year to calm my mind and continuously ask myself … what activity should I pursue in the end?"[6]

After six months of hard and careful reflection, Zhang Lan realized that her heart was still in the restaurant business. Possessing a large cash reserve, she went to France to see her son, who was studying fashion design in Paris. While in Paris, she visited a few well-known restaurants and decided to do something different this time—start a restaurant to carry forward Chinese cuisine to the world, as opposed to the idea of opening an unoriginal restaurant in China. Zhang Lan explained the logic behind her decision:

When I was involved with the restaurant business, I felt that I should take up the responsibility of enhancing Chinese cuisine. Although China has a 5,000-year catering culture, Chinese cuisine is regarded as low-end. French cuisine, on the other hand, is regarded as high-end. I did not agree with this. However, I thought that it would take my whole life to do this job (to prove the detractors wrong). Moreover, it would also require several generations' efforts because the restaurant business is a difficult venture, which needs assiduousness, diligence, thriftiness, zealousness, earnestness, and willingness for undertaking hard work.[7]

The Birth of South Beauty

Zhang Lan took the second step in her journey as an entrepreneur. She discovered that there were only a few restaurants offering Guangdong cuisine in plush office buildings in Beijing. These restaurants were too expensive to attract average businesspeople and their potential buying power. These customers looked for a high-quality, stylish, and comfortable environment as well as hygienic and delicious food presented aesthetically at a reasonable cost. Therefore, she decided to build a top-notch Chinese restaurant brand by targeting these businesspeople:[8] "There is a big misunderstanding of Chinese cuisine in the world. A lot of foreigners regard Chinese cuisine as the Mapo Tofu and Sweet and Sour Pork that you find in Chinatown. In fact, there are deep cultural meanings inside Chinese cuisine. More and

Exhibit 1 Pictures of A Lan Restaurant and Bai Niao Yuan Restaurant

Zhang Lan in A Lan Restaurant, 1991   Mockup Pictures of Bai Niao Yuan Restaurant

Source: South Beauty Group provided the picture of A Lan Restaurant; the mockup pictures were selected from http://food.yoolink.com to simulate the environment of Bai Niao Yuan Restaurant at that time.

more foreigners and businesspeople are in Beijing now. But there are few Chinese restaurants with special and elegant atmosphere. I wanted to build a Chinese restaurant for global business people to understand Chinese catering culture in the shortest time."[9]

Zhang Lan selected a prestigious office building for her first new restaurant, located in the proximity of her target customers—white collar office workers—who were still an untapped niche market in China at that time.

In April 2000, she launched an upper-middle-class restaurant, "South Beauty" (in Chinese: Qiao Jiang Nan[10]), at Guomao (China World Trade Center), a high-end office building in Beijing. In those days, Chinese restaurants were acclaimed for their delicious offerings, while Western restaurants were credited for their ambience. But Zhang Lan had her own intuition: "People prefer visual pleasures to those offered to the taste buds. When customers walk into your restaurant, they first observe the ambience and only then decide what to eat. Therefore, the first glance at the restaurant is critical."[11]

Among 10 designers, Zhang Lan selected Jack Tam, a Chinese-American designer who graduated from Harvard University, to design her new restaurant. It was the first time that a Chinese restaurant in China was designed by a foreign artist. Zhang Lan believed that only Tam could understand both Western restaurant-styling practices and the Chinese catering culture. Once completed, Tam's work did not disappoint Zhang Lan. The targeted customers took to the restaurant almost instantly (see Exhibit 2).

Zhang Lan also decided to provide Sichuan food in her new restaurant, just as she had in her earlier

Exhibit 2 Pictures of the First South Beauty Restaurant at Guomao in Beijing

Source: Company internal information.

A Lan Restaurant. Sichuan food was regarded as a kind of low-middle-level cuisine in China due to its popular raw materials. However, South Beauty Restaurant introduced several innovations and improvements with regard to traditional Sichuan food, not only in terms of new raw materials, but also the process of preparing the dishes and the customer experience. For example, South Beauty launched a new Sichuan dish, "Stone-heated Tofu Congee," which was much appreciated by office workers. To prepare this dish, waiters poured cold liquid Tofu into a glass bowl, which contained three Sichuan-origin river stones heated to 200°C, in front of the customers. Then the bowl was covered. After five minutes, the Tofu congee was ready for customers to mix with various flavors. Zhang Lan also devised various creative ways to present Sichuan delicacies. For example, inspired by the countryside experience of washing clothes in the river after work and hanging them up under the setting sun, she created a new way to present a traditional Sichuan dish, "Cold Boiled Pork with Garlic Puree." In a highly innovative and visually impactful way, slices of meat were hung from a bamboo beam. In addition, she renamed this dish as "Hanging Meat." She had utensils of different shapes and colors in her office, allowing her to experiment with food presentation styles (see Exhibit 3).

With its unique positioning as an innovative Sichuan restaurant, providing businesspeople with pleasant ambience and located at prestigious office buildings, South Beauty was a success, although the initial four months were very difficult because of low market awareness. Zhang Lan once explained the difference between A Lan Restaurant and South Beauty Restaurant: "A Lan was just like other normal traditional Chinese restaurants and my purpose with that venture was just to earn money. South Beauty was different. South Beauty is a brand, actually."[12]

Some staff members of the A Lan restaurant moved to South Beauty in the finance and restaurant development divisions. Zhang Lan and her team also surmounted the SARS[13] crisis in 2003. Under a group of experienced managers, the company established a sound reputation and opened more restaurants successfully in other business buildings. Each restaurant was run autonomously and the role of the head office was minimal.

By mid-2007, the South Beauty Group had expanded to 19 restaurants, under the brand name of South Beauty, in three key cities: Beijing, Shanghai, and Chengdu. Zhang Lan also attempted to build new restaurant brands, LAN Club and SUBU. One LAN Club restaurant opened in Beijing in November 2006, a location of more than 5,000 square meters designed by the well-known designer Philip Stark with a total investment of over RMB 100 million. It was profitable from its first month. The Group expected to recover its investment on this first LAN Club in two years. Moreover, one new LAN Club restaurant was to open in Shanghai in April 2008, and one SUBU restaurant was scheduled to open soon in Beijing (see Exhibits 4–7). With estimated revenues of

Exhibit 3 Examples of Innovative Sichuan Dishes from South Beauty

Note: Top row (left to right) Stone-heated tofu congee; hanging meat; shredded chicken with spicy sauce; bottom row (left to right): four seasons; seasonal Williams pear aspic; spare ribs fried deeply with chili and spices; fried mandarin fish with Ziran and spicy sauce.

Source: Company internal information.

Exhibit 4 Coverage of South Beauty in China (2007)

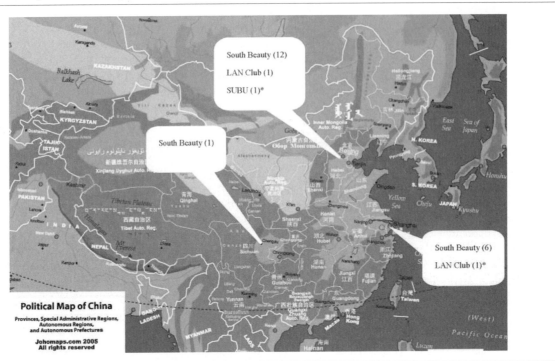

*SUBU and LAN Club's outlets in Beijing and Shanghai, respectively, are currently being furnished and are expected to open shortly.

Source: The map was copied from http://www.xxcha.com/All/449/8224_1.htm and company internal information.

Exhibit 5 Pictures of Various South Beauty Restaurants

Note: Names of these restaurants (top row, left to right): South Beauty at China World Trade Center in Beijing; South Beauty in Chengdu; South Beauty at Super Brand Mall in Shanghai; (bottom row, left to right) South Beauty at Beijing Yinzuo; South Beauty at Shanghai 881; South Beauty at Beida Resource in Beijing.

Source: Company internal information.

Exhibit 6 Pictures of LAN Club

The internal décor of LAN Club in Beijing

Source: Company internal information.

Exhibit 7 Design Effect of SUBU in Beijing

The design effect of SUBU Restaurant in Beijing, opening soon

Source: Company internal information.

RMB 384 million in 2007,[14] and around 10,000 footfalls every day, the Group became one of the benchmarks of the Chinese restaurant market (see Exhibit 8). Because of the highly fragmented nature of China's catering market, the market share of South Beauty in the total industry was less than 0.1 percent; however its market share in the Chinese dinner category[15] was an estimated two percent in 2006. In terms of the niche market of high-end Chinese dinner, South Beauty's share was more than 7 percent.[16] The company was also regarded as an innovative company, with 55 percent annual growth. The Group had also won the bid for providing food services for the 2008 Beijing Olympics. During the Olympic Games, South Beauty prepared food for around 150,000 people every day. It was the first time for Chinese food to be designated as one of the cuisines for the Olympic Games.

South Beauty's Business Model

From 2005 forward, the South Beauty Group slowed down its speed of expansion and started to develop functional management expertise at its head office with a view to coordinating the management of its restaurants, all of which were directly owned and managed by the Group. Under the recently adjusted structure, the Group had two divisions: one for head office functions and another one for restaurant operations (Exhibit 9).

The head office made decisions regarding the overall development of the Group, such as those pertaining to strategy, financial management, human resources, marketing, market expansion, engineering, R&D, and quality control of the food supply.

The three restaurant brands (South Beauty, LAN Club, and SUBU) had different missions. Within South Beauty, each restaurant handled its own daily business operations. A new department was also set up to manage the franchising business in local and overseas markets, mainly for the South Beauty restaurant brand. Luo Yun, who was personal assistant to the board chairman, commented on the change in the management structure in the following manner:

To select the management direction, we spent two years considering how to conduct our business. Before 2005, we formulated operations for individual restaurants, not considering the overall company strategy. Later, we realized that we were not just a single restaurant business; in fact, we felt that we should use the company's central management to achieve greater synergies. Thus, we decided to move from single-restaurant-based operations to company-based management.

During the last two years, we have also been thinking about ways to differentiate ourselves from our competitors to capture greater market share. In China, we need to distinguish ourselves from numerous restaurants. We also set up the "Restaurant Chain Management Company" to try the franchising model to expand our business size.[17]

The size of a normal South Beauty Restaurant was between 2,000 and 3,000 square meters. In each restaurant, there were 100 to 150 workers, of which 30 to 40 percent worked in the kitchen. Usually, each restaurant offered more than 380 dishes, of which 60 to 70 percent belonged to the Sichuan cuisine, while the remaining were Cantonese and other cuisines.

The unique features of South Beauty's business model were related to its brand positioning, menu innovation, location, pricing, interior decoration, IT application, and people management. With these

Exhibit 8 Chronology—South Beauty Group (2000–2007)

Year	Restaurants Number	Employees	Location and Number of Restaurants	Total Revenue (in RMB million)*
2000	2	200	Beijing (2)	10
2001	6	600	Beijing (6)	40
2002	8	800	Beijing (7); Shanghai (1)	60
2003	11	1,300	Beijing (8); Shanghai (3)	110
2004	16	1,900	Beijing (11); Shanghai (4); Chengdu (1)	200
2005	18	2,200	Beijing (12); Shanghai (5); Chengdu (1)	280
2006	20	2,600	Beijing (13); Shanghai (6); Chengdu (1)	350
2007	20	2,600	Beijing (13); Shanghai (6); Chengdu (1)	Est. 384

*Total revenue provided by company.

Source: Company internal information.

Exhibit 9 South Beauty's Organization Structure (2007)

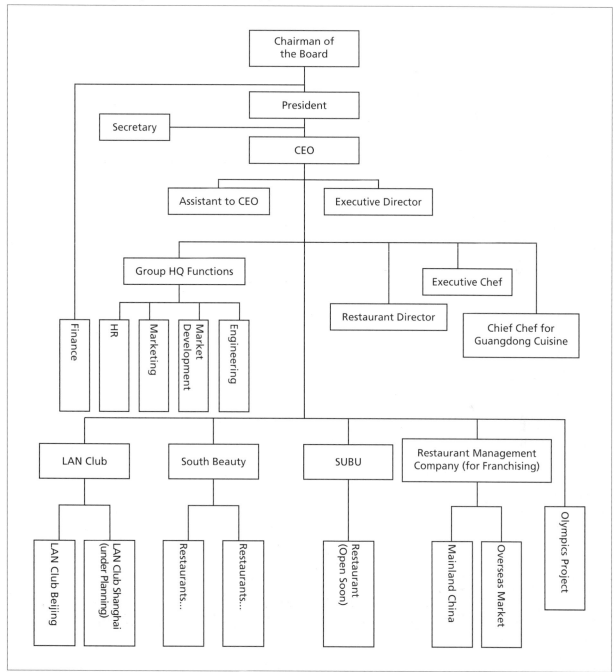

Source: Company internal information.

features, South Beauty could surpass almost all local competitors.

Positioning and Branding

With its positioning as an upmarket restaurant focused on office workers and businesspeople, South Beauty's occupancy rate was quite low during public holidays, such as the Golden Weeks,[18] because its target customers usually went on vacation at this time. In contrast, the business of other popular restaurants or fast food chains, such as McDonald's, fared well during these holidays; this proved the correctness of the brand positioning of South Beauty.

Danny Wang, Zhang Lan's only child and executive director of the Group, was in charge of developing LAN Club and SUBU. He did his high school, university, and MBA education in France and Canada and visited upmarket restaurants all over the world. When he returned to China in 2004, Zhang Lan asked him to consider a multi-brand strategy for the Group. Danny

Wang mentioned the basic consideration of LAN Club brand and SUBU:

At the beginning, the company just wanted to build a flagship restaurant under the South Beauty Brand. But I did not agree with that. As a metropolis, Beijing lacks the attributes of a modern city. I think that Beijing needs a place for leisure with an international standard to provide the 360-degree experience of an exclusive and healthy lifestyle. It is the original positioning of LAN Club. LAN is the name of my mother and also means "orchid," a symbol of Chinese culture.

As the newest brand in the Group, SUBU was to be different from the luxury LAN Club and the business-segment-focused South Beauty. SUBU was to focus on innovative healthy food. Moreover, a special store was to be inside a SUBU restaurant to sell the SUBU-style CDs and tablewares, etc.[19]

In fact, no competitor in the Chinese restaurant market had such brand architecture. Almost all of them just operated their single brands without clear brand positioning, and their brand image was relatively inferior. Luo Yun explained the company's branding strategy thusly: "We focused on brand differentiation to cater to a wide range of customers. Thus, South Beauty targets businesspeople aged 30–45 years. LAN Club targets successful businesspeople aged over 45 years. SUBU targets younger and more fashionable office workers. We hope that our business would be like that of BMW, which rolls out 7-, 5-, and 3-series products at the same time."[20]

In order to promote these three brands systematically, the company built consistent brand identities and launched some outdoor and print advertisement. The company explored cooperation with certain international airlines, including Air France and KLM Royal Dutch Airlines, to provide business travelers flying between China and Europe with South Beauty–branded Chinese dishes (see Exhibit 10). In addition, it wanted to diversify into the business of partially cooked frozen foods—such as dumplings—for retail outlets.

Menu Innovations

The Group developed a range of innovations with regard to Sichuan cuisine. An independent R&D team was placed in charge of creating new dishes, and the executive chef was responsible for food quality. Under a strict assessment system, only 2 percent of all new dishes could be launched. Although many competitors copied the Group's dishes, Zhang Lan reminded her team to focus on continuous innovations to stay ahead of its followers instead of worrying about being copied by them. In addition, to enrich its variety and cater to the tastes of different people, the company also added certain

Cantonese cuisine and other flavors to its menu. As a brochure said:

The South Beauty Group primarily offers Sichuan flavors, but we also offer Cantonese and other dishes. We innovatively combine Chinese and Western cuisine that breaks with tradition and creates original new flavors. It is the first Chinese restaurant to offer Chinese food in a western style, and the first to mix food presentation with artistic elements.... For many years the Group has charged itself with the mission of developing the culture of Chinese cuisine and advocating a stylish and healthy lifestyle. It has always been focused on drawing from China's deep traditional culture while at the same time making bold innovations and improvements.... Some of the factors that make the Group's cuisine different from others are the strict requirements placed on raw ingredients, the innovation on traditional cuisine, the exacting criteria placed on a dish's nutritional value, and the strong emphasis on the visual appeal of each dish.[21]

Location and Pricing

In order to remain close to its targeted customer base, the Group's restaurants were located in top-notch office buildings in key cities. Although the operational costs were higher in comparison with those of other restaurants, meals could be more expensively priced to cover the costs. This combination of high-end location and high pricing was also helpful in developing the upper-middle-class brand image.

Interior Decoration

Each South Beauty restaurant had a different décor, designed by well-known artists in the field. Zhang Lan and her team insisted that people came to the restaurants not only for the food but also for the ambience. South Beauty never hesitated to invest in interior décor, and sought to combine both Chinese and Western designs in the restaurants. On average, the Group invested RMB 8 million (around USD 1 million) on the furniture, interior decoration, and in setting up the kitchen of a new South Beauty restaurant. Moreover, for the luxury LAN Club, the total investment on interior decoration was over RMB 100 million (around USD 13 million), including USD 2 million in design fees. In this way, the Group became unique in the Chinese restaurant market. In contrast, no competitor could invest so heavily in interior decoration.

IT Applications

In the South Beauty Group, advanced IT applications (e.g., portable order placement) were seen as potent tools to enhance the upper-middle-class image of the restaurant and to improve efficiency. Well before other Chinese restaurants constructed CRM systems, the Group built its own CRM system to record customer information

Exhibit 10 Branding Activities of South Beauty

(Left) Restaurant Signage in Shanghai; (Right) Outdoor Advertising in Beijing

Airline Food Cooperation between Air France and South Beauty

The Brand Logos of South Beauty, LAN Club, and SUBU

Source: Company internal information; the pictures of airline food cooperation with Air France were copied from http://www.cnsphoto.com/NewsPhoto/printNews.asp?ID=359106.

and use that information to provide tailor-made services and make promotional communications. An ERP system was established to control the key financial variables and the purchasing process. Meanwhile, the company tested its remote conference system to increase internal communication among various restaurants located at different places. These IT applications were quite innovative for the traditional Chinese catering industry, as most restaurants remain committed to their old ways of operating their businesses.

People Management

Zhang Lan believed that a dedicated workforce could surmount challenges pertaining to financial capital and market potential. In 2003, when the threat of the SARS virus had the population terrified and almost all other restaurants temporarily closed and dismissed their staffs, Zhang Lan resisted this course of action. She paid her more than 1,000 staff members their full salaries and provided them with proper accommodations to limit their risk of catching the disease.

The Group sought to apply performance management techniques with regard to the management team. At the same time, it worked with a consulting firm to design a new people management system to motivate its staff. Danny Wang regarded people management as a key part of the daily operation, stating: "Our industry is a labor-intensive business. Although the top management is critical (for efficient performance), it is the waiters who are the first point of contact with our customers. The process of training and managing these front-line people, who are young and inexperienced, is the most difficult issue. We initiated a large-scale training program for our staff last year."[22]

In 2006, waiters had to undertake a three-month course at a company training center, evaluated on metrics such as setting a table within three minutes. Restaurant managers, meanwhile, had to complete a two-year on-the-job training program. For two weeks each year, they were sent to tour restaurants in Europe, the United States, and Asia in order to compare service levels and bring back ideas. Zhang Lan also recruited Chinese executives who had previously managed the operations of McDonald's and Coca-Cola in China to work for South Beauty.

China's Restaurant Market

The Shandong, Sichuan, Guangdong, Fujian, Jiangsu, Zhejiang, Hunan, and Anhui cuisines, also known as the "Eight Cuisines," are the most popular in China. The essential factors that establish a particular cuisine are complex, and include history, cooking habits, geography, climate, resources, and lifestyles. A typical Chinese restaurant offers one or two cuisines.

Since the 1990s, China's catering industry had been booming with a compound annual growth rate (CAGR) of more than 15 percent. In 2007, the catering market size of RMB 1,200 billion (USD 155 billion) accounted for 4.87 percent of the gross domestic product (GDP) in China. This percentage was only 1.5 percent in 1978. In 2004, Eastern China contributed at least 50 percent of total industry revenue (see Exhibits 11 and 12).

Exhibit 11 Market Development—China's Catering Industry (1995–2007)*

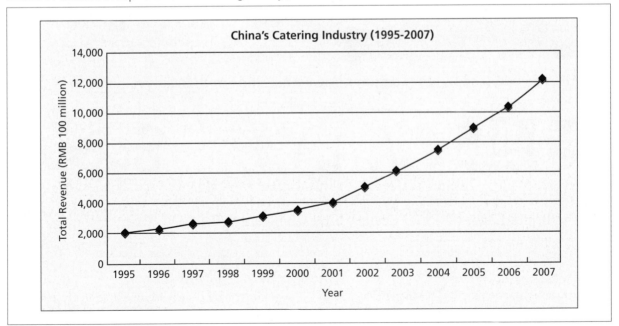

*The data for 2007 were estimated.

Source: Information from industry interviews.

Exhibit 12 Area Difference—China's Catering Industry (2004)

Area	Number of Provinces	Total Revenue of Restaurant Industry (in RMB billion)	% of Total	Annual Growth Rate (in %)
National Total	**31**	**748.6**	**100**	**21.6**
East China	11	418.3	55.7	22.0
Middle China	8	180.0	24.0	20.1
West China	12	152.0	20.3	23.8

Source: 2004, China catering industry analysis, *Economic Daily*, March 16, 2005.

There were three main sections in China's catering industry: breakfast stands, street hawkers, and restaurants. Although there were many breakfast stands and street hawkers, the restaurants section was especially significant (see Exhibit 13). In China, the restaurants section was divided into four subcategories: dinner (mainly Chinese cuisine), hot pot, fast food (Western and Chinese), and teahouses (including coffeehouses). Generally speaking, the growth of the Chinese dinner category was slower than that of the other three categories.

In 2006, the average profitability of the restaurant market was pegged at about 10 percent of total revenues; raw material costs were 43.6 percent of total revenues; labor costs were 11.92 percent; and rental costs were 8.75 percent. The labor costs in China were lower, while the overhead costs were higher, as compared with those in other developed countries.[23]

Beneath the prosperous surface, China's restaurant market faced critical problems. As a result of low entry barriers, thousands upon thousands of new restaurants emerged. However, the service quality, hygiene levels, and managerial capabilities of those in charge were often unsatisfactory.

Growth Dream

China's restaurant market was competitively challenging, not only in terms of the number of players, but also in terms of food varieties. This market was also affected by high rates of turnover (openings and closures) and fragmentation. Since 2001, half of the top 100 restaurant companies in China have been replaced by other emerging companies. In 2006, the sales revenue of the top 50 restaurant companies accounted for just 5 percent of the national restaurant market. In contrast, the sales revenue of the top 50 restaurant companies in the United States represented 20 percent of that market.[24] The global player, Yum! Brands, ranked at the top of China's catering industry, reaching annual revenues of more than RMB 11 billion; however, the revenue of the next biggest player in China was only around five billion, and that of the tenth biggest was less than one billion.[25]

Nevertheless, shocked by the success of Western fast food in China, the leading Chinese players explored how to expand their scale. It was believed that expanding the scale of the leading restaurants in China was critical for the market's healthy development. It was also believed that scaling required standardization. However, for traditional Chinese cuisine, standardization was difficult to implement. As an industry observer commented:

The features of Chinese catering culture are different from those of the Western one. Chinese cuisine has a wider range of raw materials, more varied consumption of dishes per meal, and more flexible ways of preparing dishes. It conflicts with the tenets of standardization, such as few product types, standardized processes and criteria,

Exhibit 13 Structure Difference—China's Catering Industry (2004)

Type	Number (in thousands)	Daily Revenue for Each Outlet (in RMB)	Est. Investment for Each Outlet (in RMB)	Estimated Employee Number
Breakfast Stander	1,900	<100	<500	1
Street Hawkers	1,000	300–400	2,000	2–3
Restaurants (100–400 seats)	600	5,000–10,000	300,000	20–50
Restaurants (400–800 seats)	200	15,000–30,000	2,000,000	150–200
Restaurants (800+ seats)	1	50,000–120,000	5,000,000	300–400

Source: Constraints on Chinese restaurant development: Reason and analysis; *Xinhua Daily*, April 27, 2005, and industry interviews.

etc. Comparatively speaking, it is easier for the sections of hot pot and Chinese fast food to explore standardization and expand scale through chain restaurants. However, for the Chinese dinner section, standardization is not an easy job. That's why the scaling of Chinese dinner restaurants is slower than that of the hot pot and Chinese fast food restaurants.[26]

Expanding Chains

The rapid development of many restaurant chains was notable, both in the hot pot and the Western fast food markets, especially with regard to the trend of franchising (see Exhibits 14 and 15). In 2006, the top 100 restaurants in China had 14,489 outlets, of which about 39 percent were directly owned while 61 percent were franchisees. In addition, the operational indicators of the dinner/hot pot restaurant chains were also distinct from those of fast food chains (see Exhibit 16).

Because expansion required significant investment, in 2006, at least 10 restaurant chains announced their intentions to launch initial public offerings (IPOs). Certain venture capital firms (VCs), which were normally in the business of technology, media, and telecom (TMT) deals, bought stakes in restaurant businesses. They expressed their increasing interest in this evolving traditional industry: "The restaurant business has better

cash flow and lower risk than the TMT businesses. China is at the critical point of the booming consumption economy. There are many opportunities to foster leading companies in a traditional business. The VCs would like to select valuable companies who have the long-term dream to be great players in their industries."[27]

The restaurant chains' expansion was much quicker than the rate of economic growth and raised a great deal of issues. Besides the difficulties inherent in standardizing Chinese cuisine, the lack of human resources and management skills were bottlenecks as well. Although the franchising model became popular for chain expansion, the franchisees sometimes crept out of the control of the principal companies and gradually set up their own similar brands. In addition, a restaurant could quickly and easily copy any new dish created by another restaurant. Because of these issues, few Chinese restaurant chains could build their core competitiveness for the long term.

However, a few far-sighted restaurant chains were planning to avoid the potential risk of unplanned expansion and took actions to improve the quality of their business operations. For example, Little Sheep, which was the biggest hot pot chain and had received USD 25 million from venture capitalists, reduced its outlets from 721 to 326 in the summer of 2007. Even though the

Exhibit 14 Top 100 Restaurants—China's Restaurant Market (2006)

Type	Restaurant Chains	Restaurant Outlets	Total Revenue (in RMB billion)	% of Top 100
Hot Pot	22	6,682	30	36
Fast Food	15	4,375	23	27.8
Chinese Dinner	42	1,690	19.5	23.5
Tea/Coffee House	N/A	N/A	10.6	12.7

Source: The fast development of Chinese key restaurant companies, *China Business Newspaper*, June 15, 2007.

Exhibit 15 Restaurant Chains—China's Restaurant Market (2006)*

Type	Revenue (in RMB billion)			Restaurant Outlets		
	2005	2006	Growth (in %)	2005	2006	Growth (in %)
Western Fast Food	14.7	18.5	25.8	2,330	2,757	18.3
Chinese Fast Food	1.8	2.0	11.6	1,191	1,075	−10.8
Hot Pot	13.1	14.9	14	2,454	2,799	13.6
Chinese Dinner	139.0	151.0	9.5	1,507	1,545	2.25

*Because of various sampling, some data in Exhibit 15 are different from those in Exhibit 14; however, Exhibit 15 reveals the yearly difference between 2005 and 2006.

Source: *China Chain Store Business Year Book* 2007.

Exhibit 16 Dinner/Hot Pot Chains vs. Fast Food Chains in China (2006)

Index	Dinner/Hot Pot Chains		Fast Food Chains	
	2005	2006	2005	2006
Number of Restaurants	4,244	5,066	4,213	4,843
Total Size (10,000 m²)	338.2	426.6	123.6	140.7
Staff (10,000 people)	27.8	32.9	20.6	20.6
Seats (10,000)	191.6	212.6	49.2	55.7
Total Revenue (in RMB billion)	22.8	27.8	20.4	24.9
Purchased Product (in RMB billion)	9.5	11.24	7.35	8.43
By Central Distribution	3.99	4.74	6.74	7.75
By Owned Distribution Center	2.73	3.54	4.94	5.63
By Third-Party Distribution Center	1.26	1.19	1.79	2.10

Source: Adapted from *China Statistical Year Book 2007.*

majority of the closed restaurants were franchisees, only 30 percent of the remaining restaurants were directly controlled; the rest continued to be franchisees.[28]

Innovative Chinese Restaurants

Certain emerging, innovative Chinese restaurants, including South Beauty, sought to revamp the image of Chinese cuisine. For example, the appearance of the hot pot was considered unappealing and, therefore, it was not treated as refined food. However, the Hot Loft Restaurant in Beijing experimented with certain simple innovations in the dish, thereby elevating the image of the traditional hot pot.

Some of the innovative Chinese dinner restaurants also paid more attention to their brand statement, which dealt with the entire process of daily operations from raw material purchases to service delivery. These restaurants selected their menus carefully and limited customers' choices, although they had the capability to prepare a great variety of dishes in their kitchens. The founders of these restaurants realized the importance of innovative business ideas, a unique menu, and an impressive decoration style. They believed that unless such initiatives were undertaken, Chinese cuisine would not be able to catch up with the changing tastes of consumers. Paul Hsu, owner of Night Shanghai, suggested that "People only want to visit restaurants that have an impressive ambience. The food can be extremely simple, and they order a small number of dishes and enjoy them slowly."[29]

The most important innovation among Chinese dinner restaurants was the attempt to standardize raw material purchases, preparation of semi-cooked dishes, logistics, and customer service. For example, Jade Garden, with 11 top-grade Shanghainese Cuisine chain restaurants in Shanghai and Beijing, set up a central kitchen in 2002. At the beginning, its intention was just to manage various suppliers centrally for the quality control of raw materials. After a few years' operation, the central kitchen evolved into a production center for meals to be heated as well as to prepare dim sums and semi-cooked dishes with packs of well-mixed sauces. The chefs at each restaurant could prepare the food easily according to the required process. Li Jun, one of the founders of Jade Garden, shared her experience:

At the beginning, the Chief Chef was against the central kitchen, because he was worried that he had to make his cooking knowledge public. But I told him, with the central kitchen, he would be a Chief Chef supervising 500 chefs, not just 50 chefs at the current time. Then we separated the food preparing process into many steps, with each chef in the central kitchen just handling part of the entire process.

In this way, except the Chief Chef, nobody can grasp the whole process. But we are able to overcome the bottleneck of production and prepare Chinese dishes in a standardized way. Moreover, we also have unexpected results, such as lower stock of raw materials, and fewer chefs in each chain restaurant.

Operating several restaurants under the same brand does not necessarily constitute a real chain. A real chain requires a consistent business model and operation. With the standardized raw material purchases, food preparation and sauce mix, we believe that we are building a real restaurant chain. However, we would not request standardized interior decoration for each restaurant. We are not McDonald's, which makes simple standardized fast food; we are standardizing complex Chinese dishes to keep steady quality.[30]

Fast Food Players

The growth of international fast food brands such as KFC, McDonald's, and Pizza Hut in China have increased the food options available to consumers. For instance, since November 1987, KFC had launched 2,000 restaurants and covered more than 400 cities. The restaurant chain's next objective in China was to rapidly penetrate into smaller cities, with plans of opening one outlet every day. China had become the second-largest market for KFC, after the United States. Its main competitor, McDonald's, had 820 outlets and intended to reach 1,000 restaurants in 2008.

These Western fast food chains showed what standardization and logistics could achieve in the restaurant business. For example, by 2006, Yum! Brands, the parent company of KFC, Pizza Hut, and Taco Bell, established 16 distribution centers in China. Its newest East China distribution center, which was also the group's largest facility in Asia, was 15,500 square meters in area and nine meters high. It could manage more than 3,500 items to cover more than 300 restaurants and deliver at least five million cartons of food over three million kilometers every year. At the same time, in Shanghai, Yum! was testing its new brand, Dong Fang Ji Bai Chain Restaurant, focusing exclusively on Chinese fast food. This new brand had the same standardized operational system as KFC and showed encouraging results.

Local fast food chains, such as Kungfu, Ajisen Noodle, Malan Noodle, and Da Niang Dumpling, borrowed the best practices of these international brands. For example, Kungfu—a fast-growing local player with 200 restaurants—planned to establish three logistics centers in China to carry out the key functions of raw material procurement, food processing, and delivery. Kungfu also announced plans to open 2,000 restaurants by 2012. Most successful local chains had attracted foreign capital and also planned to offer IPOs to gain greater resources for scaling up their operations. However, they lagged far behind the international brands in some areas, especially food and process standardization and central logistics capability.

South Beauty's Competitors

Being positioned in the high-end Chinese dinner segment, South Beauty would not compete directly with fast food, hot pot, and "ordinary" restaurants. Among the top 100 restaurant companies in China in 2007, 10 were in this segment, including Shanghai Jingjiang (ranked No. 4), Beijing Shunfeng (No. 18), Guangzhou Jiujia (No. 28), Shanghai Xiaonanguo (No. 32), Shanghai Renjia (No. 60), Shanghai Jade Garden (No. 88), Shanghai Shenjia Garden (No. 91), and South Beauty itself (No. 72). These competitors focused on various Chinese cuisines; for example, Beijing Shunfeng and Guangzhou Jiujia mainly served Guangdong cuisine, and Jingjiang, Xioananguo, Renjia, Jade Garden, and Shengjia Garden in Shanghai offered Jiangsu and Zhejiang dishes. Thus, South Beauty, which focused on Sichuan cuisine, did not compete with these restaurants directly in terms of cuisine. Normally, people selected the type of cuisine they were in the mood for first and the restaurant later.

The most crucial issue for South Beauty was that of restaurants claiming to be South Beauty franchises. In 2005, South Beauty found there were at least 16 "fake" restaurants in cities South Beauty had not penetrated, such as Nanjing, Xiamen, Tianjing, Qingdao, and Hong Kong. Generally speaking, the imposters used the same Chinese name as South Beauty (i.e., Qiao Jiang Nan), with one or two additional Chinese characters. The counterfeit logos enlarged the size of the "Qiao Jiang Nan" characters and minimized the other elements. In this way, these counterfeit restaurants attracted innocent customers and provided them with poor service and atmosphere. However, the unhappy customers complained to the "real" South Beauty. South Beauty attempted to use legal means to protect its brand, but because of the local protection the copiers enjoyed in some cities, the process was sometimes quite slow, and the results were not very encouraging.

Consumer Trends and Opinions

In recent years, as Chinese urban consumers' disposable incomes have increased, they have spent more on meals in restaurants. The annual expenditure per capita on restaurant meals increased from RMB 534 (USD 65) in 2004 to an estimated RMB 800 (USD 105) in 2007. However, compared with developed markets, there is still great potential for growth—the corresponding figure in the United States was USD 1,600 per capita, and, in France, USD 1,050.[31] Moreover, in more advanced cities, such as Shanghai, Guangzhou, and Beijing, this number was three to five times higher than the national average. In these cities, consumers had more choices of restaurants and made selections based on word of mouth. According to a Web site survey, 63 percent of consumers obtained restaurant information from word-of-mouth publicity, 15 percent from traditional media (newspaper, TV, radio, etc.), 12 percent from the Internet, and 10 percent from outdoor advertising.[32]

Since the 1990s, consumption in restaurants has evolved into various segments, such as office workers having lunches, family members dining out, friends gathering, lovers dating, and business-related meals. Different segments have different needs. The office workers select fast food (Western 30 percent and Chinese 70 percent) as their lunch for its convenience and quickness. This huge segment constituted one fourth of the total catering industry. The main consideration of families dining out is value for their money. The restaurant selection for a gathering of friends depends on the social status of the people; those with higher status select better restaurants. Lovers prefer a romantic restaurant for their dates.

Because of the booming economy in China, the business meals had more potential than the other segments because they could absorb higher prices. Also, businesspeople were not satisfied with simple eating and drinking—they required more in terms of the restaurant's atmosphere, food taste, location, and so on. These businesspeople were the target consumers of the South Beauty Group.

A popular restaurant review Web site stated:

Promoting "Refined or Improved Sichuan Food," South Beauty has elevated Sichuan food from the level of austerity to one fit for the nobility. The dishes have a unique taste, appearance, and preparation style. The ambience is also excellent—an elegant, grand, Western style—quite different from that offered by ordinary Chinese restaurants. The waiters and waitresses wear well-designed uniforms and are hospitable. It is a good place to entertain guests, although the charges are higher in comparison with normal restaurants.[33]

However, in Chengdu, the birthplace of Sichuan food, customers were of the opinion that the Sichuan food offered by South Beauty was not as spicy as the original cuisine. Others did not view South Beauty as a genuine Sichuan food restaurant. Nonetheless, they were pleased that South Beauty offered a range of innovative dishes that were presented elegantly (see Exhibit 17).

2008 Beijing Olympics Opportunity

The 2008 Olympic Games in Beijing were estimated to generate sales of RMB 18 billion for the catering industry in the city. Thirteen million meals would be provided for athletes, support personnel, media reporters, and other guests for three months. This revenue was divided between Western (estimated at 70 percent of meals) and Chinese cuisine (30 percent).

However, the mainstream international media challenged the food security situation in China. The Chinese government tried to ensure food supply safety for the Olympic Games. Following the completion of the bidding process based on strict food standards, six companies were selected as the food suppliers: South Beauty Group, along with three other local companies and two international ones, McDonald's and ARAMARK. Bian Jiang, the chief secretary of the China Restaurant Association, commented to the press: "The 2008 Beijing Olympic Games will facilitate the internationalization of the Beijing restaurant market. The food suppliers for the Olympic Games will suffer a critical technical transition,

Exhibit 17 Customer Ratings of South Beauty Restaurants (October 2007)

	Beijing (Among 420 customers)	Shanghai (Among 1,153 Customers)	Chengdu (Among 187 customers)
Rating (max. 30)			
Taste	18–21	17–18	17
Environment	24–27	21–26	27
Service	20–22	15–20	22
Consumption (RMB/per person)	102–141	149–180	115
Category Perception (%)			
Business Entertainment	34%	27%	41%
Sichuan Food	23%	18%	10%
Gathering of Friends	13%	8%	0%
Innovative Sichuan Food	0%	0%	33%
Dinner for Dating	16%	8%	16%

Source: Information collected from http://www.dianping.com in October 2007 based on customers' comments on a typical restaurant in each city.

especially in terms of the food and process standardization and logistics capacity, which will also lead to a change in the restaurant market. Restaurants that can upgrade their operations in response to the large-scale requirements of the Olympics are likely to fare well in China's catering industry in the future."[34]

Future Plans

Zhang Lan believed that the Chinese entrepreneurs of her generation should take greater responsibility to rejuvenate Chinese culture because they have access to better opportunities than previous generations:

I am thinking about how to develop Chinese cuisine to enter the mainstream restaurant market in Western countries as opposed to opening the kind of Chinese restaurants you find in Chinatown. The South Beauty Group has catered to more than 100,000 foreign guests from all over the world, and they all enjoyed our food. Thus, now is the time to expand. We have met success in China, and now we wish to build an international brand, which will have a presence in New York, Paris, London, Milan, Geneva, Tokyo, and other important international cities of the world.[35]

Undoubtedly, redefining Chinese cuisine and maintaining quality in the midst of rapid domestic and global expansion will not be an easy job. Luo Yun commented on the difficulties:

Having objectives and ambitions are not enough; we have to act to meet these objectives. Top management is thinking about the big picture. We also need to consider how to execute the tasks and foresee difficulties. For example, we should constantly improve the menu through R&D, improve people management practices, etc.; we also should train people to do things in a standardized way. It is difficult to do so, and until now, no one (in the China's dinner category) has been able to do it very successfully.[36]

The Challenges Ahead

The existing business of the South Beauty Group was flourishing, but the management team did not halt their efforts to improve the Group's operational efficiency through standardization, which was also the foundation for scaling up. To expand, the Group had to consider the prioritization of markets to enter (i.e., whether to focus on the local market to realize its full potential before venturing abroad, or to do both at the same time); entry into new businesses, such as airline catering and the supply of semi-processed food to retail outlets; the expansion model (i.e., through owned outlets as had been the case until now or through franchising); and the way to finance the expansion, which posed many challenges.

Seeking Standardization

It was easier for a fast food chain or a Western restaurant to standardize its food and processes—for example, McDonald's offered only 40 to 50 dishes and T.G.I. Friday's around 100. Each South Beauty restaurant carried 380 items on the main menu, excluding soft drinks and wines. Raw materials depended on local suppliers, and the quality of each dish relied on the experience of the chef. Although there was a team with three main chefs at the head office to develop new dishes and control the quality, the process of standardization was still in its nascent phase.

Jacy Yang, who joined the Group in July 2007 as executive director, had 25 years of experience in Western food companies such as McDonald's, T.G.I. Friday's, and Gino's. He was assigned the task of setting up a system to enhance operational efficiency. He described the challenges and the company's reactions:

In fast-food restaurants, such as KFC and Kungfu, it is easier to handle standardization. However, the same can be quite difficult to manage in high-end Chinese dinner restaurants. Before I came on board, the chefs did not define the inputs because these were regarded as their secrets, and some were even offended when asked to write down the recipes. Subsequently, I looked up the recipes, read the local menu, spoke to professional cooks, and studied the terminology to understand the entire process.

I think it is easy for a restaurant to elaborate on its two success factors. The first is service, which can be stipulated manually and standardized easily through training, rules, inspections, and the right incentive systems. The second is the menu. We are working on an idea for a central kitchen to prepare the main dishes and distribute them to each restaurant to ensure the same taste of key dishes at different times across various restaurants.

At present, in each restaurant, we have a kitchen that is 300–400 square meters in area. The function of a central kitchen that is 2,000 square meters in area is to prepare the main dish packets with uncooked raw materials and send them to the various company restaurants for cooking. The central kitchen will be set up in each city of operation. Currently, we are building two, in Beijing and Shanghai. In this way, we can achieve standardization and control the average cost. Our central kitchen will handle dishes prepared from expensive materials and the ones that can be easily standardized. However, the kitchens in individual restaurants will also prepare some dishes with fresh materials, such as vegetables, and other special requests, so they will still be required to make certain raw material purchases.[37]

Jacy Yang's other role was to standardize the Group's cost management. He explained his ideas this way:

Some people in our company say they have cut 30 percent of the cost, but I am not sure about it. They should provide data. I will set the standard, ask the chef, and nail down the recipe and the input cost, factor in the processing cost, and then arrive at a standard cost for each dish. Meanwhile, we will control the use of raw materials with computer software to calculate the number of dishes sold and the raw materials used, and check the stock situation to evaluate materials usage. In this way, we will be able to control the cost of raw materials, which constitutes the largest part of the cost structure.[38]

Venturing into Newer Markets

The South Beauty Group's domestic business was concentrated in Beijing and Shanghai. The city selection was a critical decision (see Exhibit 18). This same issue was raised with regard to international markets. In 2005, Zhang Lan planned to open two restaurants in Hong Kong, but little progress had been made on this front. Zhang Lan also wanted to test the market in the United Arab Emirates. Recently, the Group had communicated its ongoing projects to open restaurants in well-known international cities such as New York, Paris, and Tokyo, although the details of this plan have not been disclosed.

When Zhang Lan stated her scale expansion objectives, she projected the Group to have 30 restaurants in short term and 100 outlets in the next three years, of which 35 restaurants would be located in China and 65 in the international market in cooperation with strategic partners in Tokyo, New York, and other cities. The Group was also trying to expand its scale through entering into new product areas, such as airline catering in the global market and the supply of semi-processed food to retail outlets in the domestic market.

The scaling up of fast food restaurants has been achieved by several brands, both international and Chinese, but the expansion of upper-middle-class dinner restaurants posed a bigger challenge. Therefore, South Beauty Group's targets looked extremely ambitious and certain observers expressed their worries. According to a well-known international media publication, "There is no other successful national restaurant chain in this market segment, and South Beauty has still not covered all the major Chinese cities. Entering a mature (Western) market will involve working in a radically different operating environment."[39]

Expansion Model

The South Beauty Group was trying to develop a franchising system to expand its restaurant chain in China. There were two new restaurants at the stage of signing franchise contracts. The company also announced its plan to seek franchisees on its Web site and was flooded with questions from interested entrepreneurs. Luo Yun expressed his concerns:

It is a huge and extremely difficult transition for the company, because Chinese cuisine has not been standardized well with regard to operations. We studied the central management style, for example, of the McDonald's chain, which has 16 staff members in its financial division for 800 outlets. However, we recruited

Exhibit 18 Top 10 Cities—China's Catering Industry (2006)

Rank by Size	City	Total Revenue of Catering Industry (in RMB billion)	Rank by Growth	City	Annual Growth (in %)
1	Shanghai	45.2	1	Shanghai	29.0
2	Beijing	36.2	2	Jinan	21.8
3	Guangzhou	35.0	3	Qingdao	21.7
4	Tianjing	21.0	4	Chongqing	20.0
5	Chengdu	20.9	5	Zhengzhou	19.3
6	Chongqing	19.4	6	Hefei	19.1
7	Wuhan	17.7	7	Wuhan	17.9
8	Jinan	14.0	8	Hangzhou	17.9
9	Dalian	13.4	9	Tianjing	17.4
10	Zhengzhou	13.0	10	Changsha	17.2

Source: China's catering industry: Top 10 cities in 2006; *China Chain Store Business Year Book 2007*.

more than 80 people in the same department for only 20 restaurants. That is the big difference.[40]

However, in the international market, both owned and franchised restaurants might be risky models for expansion because of the lack of local market knowledge and the difficulties of managing the franchisees. The Group contacted local partners with complementary resources in target cities to seek cooperation. For example, Royal Company, a potential strategic partner for the group in Japan, controlled over 1,000 restaurants and provided airline food in the Japanese market. In addition, the requirements for the restaurant's size, style, and cuisine in the international market would be different from those in the domestic market. The Group had to adjust its plan accordingly.

Financing by IPO

In China, it was difficult for a private restaurant to apply for a bank loan because banks were hesitant to provide capital to restaurants because of the perceived risks involved in this industry. In addition, the government did not consider this industry as a priority area. The South Beauty Group funded its growth plans by reinvesting its profits. The company's cash flow was sufficient to maintain its current operations and to pursue moderate growth. However, the company needed external funding for its expansion plan and other projects related to standardization, new business development, and the Olympic Games contract.

Several private venture capitalists and investment banks, such as Citigroup and Credit Suisse, had expressed their wishes to cooperate with the South Beauty Group. In 2006, the Group announced the launch of a possible IPO in the international or domestic stock market, although a decision regarding the exact date of the IPO was not made. Zhang Lan discussed her company's IPO:

Our IPO is not just for funding. Our main objective is to build an open company with the supervision of the shareholders. I do not like the family company, because it is difficult to be a giant under family members' management. A long-life company could be built through a well-designed management system and a clear arrangement with the shareholders about their equity and responsibility.[41]

Dream Big but Do Small

At the break of the 2007 meeting with her management team, Zhang Lan looked out of her office window. She saw Beijing National Stadium (the "Bird's Nest") being built for the 2008 Olympics—the stadium's main body had already taken shape.[42] Zhang Lan sat back and pondered:

Should the Group scale up its size at a rapid pace? How can the company improve standardization of Chinese cuisine? Where should the targeted domestic and international markets be located? How can the company achieve the right balance between owned and franchised restaurants? What would be the correct time to invite external capital and launch an IPO?

Zhang Lan realized that she had to dream big for the future, but, at the same time, take small steps to keep everything on track. She knew that the road ahead was just like the Bird's Nest Stadium, which had an exciting outer shape and a complex inner structure as well.

NOTES

1. Picture of Zhang Lan from 2006, Zhang Lan: Planning to open South Beauty in New York and Paris, *China Entrepreneur*, December.
2. This school's name was changed to Beijing Technology and Business University in 1999.
3. Exchange rate in 1991: USD 1=RMB 5.4.
4. "Bai Niao Yuan" means a garden with a lot of birds.
5. Exchange rate in 1999: USD 1=RMB 8.27.
6. 2007, Boss town: Dialogue with Zhang Lan, http://www.sina.com.cn, January 19.
7. Ibid.
8. Businesspeople include entrepreneurs, professional managers, and some middle-level office workers.
9. 2008, LAN Club and its hostess, *Lifeweek*, February 4.
10. Qiao Jiang Nan: "Qiao" means beautiful and "Jiang Nan" stands for the area south of Yangtze.
11. 2006, South Beauty: Chinese food in a Western way, winning with details, *Eastern Entrepreneur*, March 2006.
12. Case writer's interview with Zhang Lan, October 16, 2007.
13. SARS is the acronym for Severe Acute Respiratory Syndrome.
14. This number was provided by the company. As a cautious private company that was contacting venture capitalists, South Beauty was sensitive about providing its financial data. However, some media (such as Zhang Lan: A woman behind South Beauty, *Money Talk*, April 17, 2008) estimated that the annual revenue of the South Beauty Group would be over RMB 1 billion in 2007, with 20,000 to 30,000 footfalls every day. According to another source, the company's actual revenue in 2005 was RMB 460 million, with an average annual growth of 55.6 percent in the past three years (*China Entrepreneur*, May 20, 2006).
15. Dinner is the main meal of the day, whether eaten at midday or in the evening. The Chinese dinner category includes Chinese restaurants that provide the main meals of Chinese cuisine, not fast food or hot pot.
16. The market share of the top player, Yum!, was around 1 percent. The market share of South Beauty was estimated by the case authors and industry observers.
17. Case writer's interview with Luo Yun, October 16, 2007.
18. Golden Week is a twice-yearly week-long Chinese holiday.
19. 2007, South Beauty promotes its multibrand strategy and plans the overseas market expansion, *China New Age*, October; case writer's interview with Danny Wang, October 16, 2007.
20. Case writer's interview with Luo Yun on October 16, 2007.
21. The brochure was printed by the South Beauty Group.

22. Case writer's interview with Danny Wang on October 16, 2007.

23. 2007, The out-of-order competition in China's catering industry," *Economic Policy Information*, January 15.

24. 2008, Who is the biggest in China's catering industry? *Lifeweek*, February 4.

25. 2007, China Catering Industry Report, Hu Nan Science and Technology Publishing Company, October.

26. 2008, Who is the biggest in China's catering industry? *Lifeweek*, February 4.

27. 2007, China's catering industry becomes a hotspot, *China Business News*, January 15.

28. 2007, Little Sheep Restaurant Chain: Plan an IPO in Hong Kong for HK$ 2 billion, *Oriental Morning Post*, August 3.

29. The features of Chinese restaurants, http://brand.hr.com.cn/html/40724.html.

30. 2008, Jade Garden: Dialectic of high end Shanghainese cuisine development, *Lifeweek*, February 4.

31. The data of personal consumption came from "China's catering industry is developing fast," *International Business Newspaper*, October 18, 2006, with adjustment based on *China Statistical Year Book 2004*. Exchange rate in October 2007: USD 1 = RMB 7.5; in 2004: USD 1 = RMB 8.27.

32. 2008, Restaurant consumer survey through Internet, *Pin Week*, March 15.

33. Adapted from the Web site: http://www.dianping.com.

34. 2007, Olympics 2008 will create RMB 18 billion business for China's catering industry, *Consumption Daily*, July 30.

35. Information combined from case interview and the media report, 2006, LV (Zhang Lan's South Beauty wants to be LV brand in the restaurant market, http://www.netease.com, January 26; China's 400 richest, http://www.forbes.com/global/2006/1113/098.html.

36. Case Writers' interview with Luo Yun on October 16, 2007.

37. Case Writers' interview with Jacy Yang on October 16, 2007.

38. Ibid.

39. China's 400 richest, http://www.forbes.com/global/2006/1113/098.html.

40. Case Writers' interview with Luo Yun on October 16, 2007.

41. 2008, LAN Club and its hostess, *Lifeweek*, February 4.

42. Please refer to http://en.wikipedia.org/wiki/Beijing_National_Stadium.

Steve Gove

Virginia Tech

Brett P. Matherne

Loyola University of New Orleans

If the motion picture industry's performance in 2007 were a feature presentation, the marquee would read "Massive Box Office: Smashing Records—the Sequel!" At $9.63 billion, box office revenue set another record in 2007, a full 5 percent above the record set in 2006.[1] An astonishing 1.4 billion tickets were sold in 2007. But beyond the headlines, the industry is a study in contradictions:

- The number of theaters is declining, but the number of screens is at an all-time high.
- Revenues are up, but attendance is largely flat—1.4 billion tickets sold is little improved from 1997, when 1.35 billion tickets were sold, and is a fraction of the 4 billion sold in 1946. In 1946, the average person attended 28 films a year. Today, it is 6.[2] (see Exhibits 1 and 2).
- The U.S. population is increasing, but the size of the market in the core demographic group is growing more slowly (see Exhibit 3).

- Americans spend more time than ever on entertainment—3,500 hours annually—but only 12 of those hours are spent at the movies.[3] The average person watches that much television every three days.

Movies remain as popular as ever, but opportunities for viewing outside the theater have greatly increased. While motion picture studios increased revenues through product licensing, DVD sales, and international expansion, the exhibitors—movie theaters—have seen their business decline. Movies are more available than ever, but fewer are venturing to the theater to see them. Many theaters have ceased operation, driven from the market by consolidation and a lack of patrons.

Will the marquee at the local theater soon change to: "A Horror Show at the Cinemaplex?" How has this come to be? What can exhibitors do to respond?

Exhibit 1 Domestic Tickets Sold and Box Office Gross

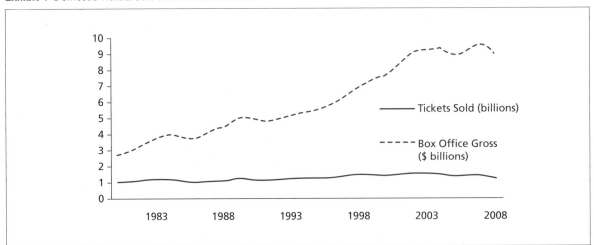

Source: http://boxofficemojo.com & U.S. Census.

Exhibit 2 Average Movie Ticket Price

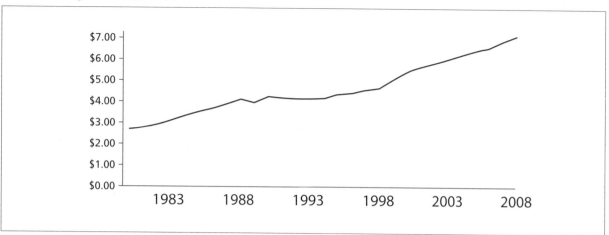

Source: http://boxofficemojo.com.

The Motion Picture Industry Value Chain

The motion picture industry value chain consists of three stages: studio production, distribution, and exhibition. All stages of the value chain are undergoing consolidation.

Studio Production

The studios produce the lifeblood of the industry; they create content. Films from the top 10 studios produce over 90 percent of domestic box office receipts (see Exhibit 4). Studios are increasingly part of larger corporations,

managed as any other profit center. Management is a challenge as investments are large and there is no one formula for success. Because of this, profitability swings wildly. The cost of bringing a typical feature to market is more than $100 million, up 25 percent in the past five years.[4] Typically, marketing expenses are a third of these costs.

Studios know their core audience is 12 to 24 years old. This age group purchases nearly 40 percent of theater tickets. Half are "frequent moviegoers" attending at least one movie per month. Profits are driven by the studios' ability to satisfy this fickle audience. In 2008, films based on two successful comic book characters met

Exhibit 3 Population Trend among 14 to 17 and 18 to 24 Age Groups (Millions)

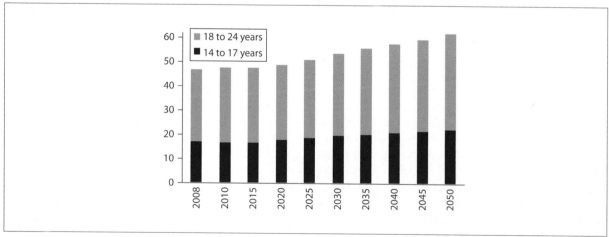

Source: U.S. Census.

Exhibit 4 Market Share of Film Production (2007)

Studio Parent & Label	2007 Combined Share (%)
Time Warner (Warner Brothers & New Line)	19.8
Sony (Sony & MGM)	16.7
Viacom (Viacom & Paramount)	15.5
Disney (Disney, Buena Vista Pictures, & Miramax)	15.4
Universal Studios	11.4
News Corp. (20th Century FOX)	10.5
Lions Gate	3.6
DreamWorks SKG*	0.0
	92.9

Note: *DreamWorks share in 2005 was 5.7%.

Source: Adapted from Mintel Report: Movie Theaters, United States, February 2008.

with wildly different fates.[5] Paramount's successful *Iron Man* was produced for $140 and grossed $318 million at the domestic box office. Warner Brothers's *Speed Racer*, produced for $20 million less and released the following weekend, was a flop, grossing just $44 million.

Demographic trends are unfavorable. The U.S. population will increase 17 percent by 2025, an increase of 54 million people. However, the number of 12- to 24-year-olds is expected to increase only 9 percent—just 4 million more potential viewers. Based on the current number of theaters and screens, this is an increase of less than 700 additional viewers per theater, or roughly 100 per screen.

Distribution

Distributors are the intermediaries between the studios and exhibitors. Distribution entails all steps following a film's artistic completion, including marketing, logistics, and administration. Exhibitors negotiate a percentage of gross from the studio or purchase rights to films and profit from the box office receipts. Distributors select and market film to exhibitors, seeking to maximize potential attendees. Distributors coordinate the manufacture and distribution of the film to exhibitors. They also handle collections, audits of attendees, and

other administrative tasks. There are over 300 active distributors, but much of this work is done by a few major firms, including divisions of studios. Pixar, for example, co-produced *Finding Nemo* with Disney and distribution was handled by Disney's Buena Vista.

Exhibition

Studios have historically sought full vertical integration through theater ownership, allowing greater control over audiences and capturing exhibition profits. A common practice was for the studio to use their ownership to reduce competition by not showing pictures produced by rivals. This practice ended in 1948 with the Supreme Court's ruling against the studios in *United States v. Paramount Pictures.* Theaters were soon divested, leaving them to negotiate with studios for film access and rental.

Theaters are classified according to the number of screens at one location (Exhibit 5). Single-screen theaters were the standard from the introduction of film through the 1980s. They have since rapidly declined in number, replaced by theater complexes. These include miniplexes (2 to 7 screens), multiplexes (8 to 15 screens), and megaplexes (16 or more screens). The number of theaters decreased more than 15 percent between 2000 and 2007, but the number of screens increased because of growth in megaplexes. Nearly 10 percent of theaters are now megaplexes, and the number of screens is at a historical high of 40,077.[6] Many analysts argue the industry has overbuilt and too many theaters and screens exist to make the business profitable.

Movie attendance usually increases as the economy declines. In 2008, there were rapid increases in gas prices, a large stock market decline, and significant layoffs. One summer movie patron commented, "There's not a whole lot you can do for $10 anymore."[7] Movies do remain a

Exhibit 5 Number of Theaters by Complex Size

	2000	2007	% Change
Single Screens	2,368	1,748	−26.18%
Miniplexes (2–7 Screens)	3,170	2,296	−27.57%
Multiplexes (8–15 Screens)	1,478	1,617	9.40%
Megaplexes (16+ Screens)	405	616	52.10%
Total	7,421	6,277	−15.42%

Sources: Developed by author from: Entertainment Industry, 2007 Report, Motion Picture Association of America, and Mintel Report "Movie Theaters, United States, February 2008."

Exhibit 6 Exhibition Market Leaders

Company	Theater Brands	# U.S Theater Locations	# U.S. Screens	Avg. Screens per Theater
Regal	Regal, United Artists, Edwards	526	6,355	12
AMC	AMC, Loews	315	4,585	14
Cinemark	Cinemark, Century	284	3,606	12
Carmike	Carmike	280	2,412	8
	Total for four leading companies	1,405	16,958	
	Industry total	7,421	40,077	

Source: Mintel Report "Movie Theaters, United States, February 2008," SEC filings and author estimates.

bargain in the entertainment business. Four tickets to a movie can cost under $27 (depending on the time of day and location) compared to $141 for an amusement park or $261 for a pro football game.[8] For many, the air-conditioned comfort of a dark theater and the latest Hollywood release offer a break not just from the summer heat, but from reality. "It's escapism, absolutely. It's probably a subconscious thing, and people don't realize it. But there's just so much going on, with people trying to pay their mortgages and get by. It's an escape for a couple of hours."[9]

Declining ticket sales and the increased costs associated with developing megaplexes led to a wave of consolidation among exhibitors. There are now four dominant exhibitors: Regal, AMC, Cinemark, and Carmike. While operating 1,405 theaters in the country (just 19 percent), these companies control 42 percent of screens. This market share provides these exhibitors with negotiating power for access to films, prices for films and concessions, and greater access to revenues from national advertisers.

There is little differentiation in the offerings of the major theater exhibitors—prices within markets differ little, the same movies are shown at the same times, and the food and services are nearly identical. Competition between theaters often comes down to distance from home, convenience of parking, and proximity to restaurants. Innovations by one theater chain are quickly adopted by others. The chains do serve different geographic markets and do so in different ways.[10] Regal focuses on mid-size markets using multiplexes and megaplexes. Regal's average ticket price of $7.43 is the highest among the leaders. AMC concentrates on urban areas with megaplexes and on large population centers, such as those in California, Florida, and Texas. Cinemark

serves smaller markets, operating as the sole theater chain in over 80 percent of its markets. Cinemark's average ticket price last year of $5.11 was the lowest of the majors. Carmike concentrates on small to mid-sized markets, targeting populations of less than 100,000 that have few other entertainment options. Carmike's average ticket price in 2007 was $5.89, but at $3.05, their average concession revenue per patron is the highest among the majors.

The different approaches of the companies are reflected in the cost of fixed assets per screens. These costs result from decisions made on how to serve customers, such as the level of technology and finish of the theater—digital projection and marble floors cost more than traditional projectors and a carpeted lobby.[11] Despite multi- and megaplex facilities, Regal's cost per screen is the highest at $430,000. Carmike, the rural operator, is the lowest at just $206,000. Cinemark is in the middle at $367,000. Data is not available for AMC, but costs are thought to be near or above those of Regal.

The Business of Exhibition

There are three primary sources of revenue for exhibitors: box office receipts, concessions, and advertising. Managers have low discretion; their ability to influence revenues and expenses is limited. Operating margins among exhibitors average a slim 10 percent. This is before significant expenses such as facility and labor costs. The result is marginal or negative net income. Overall, the business of exhibitors is best described as loss leadership on movies: the firms make money selling concessions and showing ads to patrons who are drawn by the movie.

Box Office Revenues

Ticket sales constitute two thirds of exhibition business revenues. The return on these receipts, however, is quite small. A power imbalance results in contracts that return the vast majority of box office receipts to the studios. The record-setting revenues at the box office have been the result of increases in ticket prices and have flowed back to the studios.

Concessions

Moviegoers frequently lament the high prices for concessions. Concessions average 25 to 30 percent of revenues. Direct costs are less than 15 percent of the selling price, making concessions the largest source of exhibitor profit. These are influenced by the three factors: attendance, pricing, and material costs. The most important is attendance: more attendees equal more concession sales. Sales per patron are influenced by prices. The $3.75 price point for a large soda is not by accident, but the result of market research and profit-maximization calculation. Costs are influenced by purchase volume, with larger chains able to negotiate better prices on everything from popcorn and soft drinks to cups and napkins.

Advertising

Exhibitors also generate revenue through pre-show advertising. Though this constitutes just 5 percent of revenues, it is highly profitable. Mintel reports that advertising revenues among exhibitors are expected to increase at a rate of approximately 10 percent over the coming decade.[12] Audiences signal consistent dislike for advertising at the theater. Balancing the revenues from ads with audience tolerance is an ongoing struggle for exhibitors.

Overall, the exhibitor has limited control over both revenues and profits. Box office receipts are the bulk of revenues, but yield few profits. Strong attendance numbers allow for profitable sales of concessions and advertisements, but there are significant caps on the volume of concession sales per person and selling prices seem to have reached their maximum. Advertising remains an attractive avenue for revenues and profits, but audiences loathe it.

The Process of Exhibition

The fundamentals of film exhibition have changed little since the early 1940s. To show a picture, each theater receives a shipment of physical canisters containing a "release print" from the distributor. Making these prints requires $20,000 to $30,000 in up-front costs and $1,000 to $1,500 for each print. Thus, a modern major motion picture opening on 2,500 screens simultaneously requires $2.50 to $3.75 million in print costs. This is borne by the studios, but paid for by movie attendees.

Each release print is actually several reels of 35-mm film, which are manually loaded onto projector reels, sequenced, and queued for display by a projector operator. The film passes through the projector, which shines intense light through the film, projecting the image through a lens that focuses the image on the screen. A typical projection systems costs $50,000, with one needed for each screen.

Digital cinema is becoming economically viable. Digital cinema involves a high resolution (4096 × 2160) digitized image projected onto the screen. Basic digital systems cost $150,000 to $250,000 per screen. Conversion of an existing eight-screen theater to digital thus involves an investment of $1.2 to $2 million. The costs for digital "release prints" are far lower than traditional film, but these costs savings most directly benefit the studio whereas the exhibitors must pay any costs to convert theaters. The number of digital theaters is expanding rapidly. In 2004, there were less than 100, and there are now approximately 4,600, or 12 percent of screens. Because of the cost involved, most theaters use a mixture of technologies, with a minority of screens in any one facility featuring digital projection.

The Theater Experience

For a significant number of moviegoers, the draw of the theater is far more than what film is showing. Moviegoers describe attending the theater as an experience, with the appeal based on:[13]

- the giant theater screen
- the opportunity to be out of the house
- not having to wait to see a particular movie on home video
- the experience of watching the movies with a theatrical sound system
- the theater as a location option for a date

The ability of theaters to provide more than what audiences can experience at home appears to be diminishing. Of the reasons why people go to the movies, only the place aspects—the theater as a place to be out of house and as a place for dating—may be immune from substitution. Few teenagers want to watch a movie and eat popcorn with their date at home with their parents next to them on the sofa.

The overall "experience" currently offered by theaters falls short for many. Marketing research firm Mintel reports the reasons for not attending the theater more frequently are largely the result of the declining experience. Specific factors include the overall cost, at-home viewing options, interruptions such as cell phones in the theater, rude patrons, the overall hassle, and ads prior to the show.[14] A recent *Wall Street Journal* article reported on interruptions ranging from the intrusion of soundtracks in adjacent theaters to cell phones. "The interruptions capped a night of moviegoing already marred by out-of-order ticketing kiosks and a parade of preshow ads so long that, upon seeing the Coca-Cola polar bears on screen, one customer grumbled: 'This is obscene.'"[15] Recounting bad experiences is a lively topic for bloggers. A typical comment: "I say it has gotten worse. I hate paying $9.00 for a ticket and the movie is 90–100 minutes long, people talking on the cell phone, the people who work at the theaters look like they are bored, and when you ask them a question, the answer is very rude. I worked as an usher in the late '60s and we had to wear uniforms and white gloves on Friday and Saturday nights, those days are long gone."[16]

A trip to the local cinemaplex can be eye opening even for industry insiders. In 2005, Toby Emmerich, New Line Cinema's head of production, faced a not-so-common choice: attending "War of the Worlds" in a theater or in a screening room at actor Jim Carrey's house. Said Emmerich in an *LA Times* article, "I love seeing a movie with a big crowd, but I had no idea how many obnoxious ads I'd have to endure—it really drove me crazy. After sitting through about 15 minutes of ads, I turned to my wife and said, 'Maybe we should've gone to Jim Carrey's house after all.'"[17]

The unique value proposition offered by movie theaters—large screens, the long wait for DVD release, and advantages of theatrical sound systems—also appears to be fading. Increasingly larger television sets, DVD content, and the adoption of high-definition technology are all part of this change. One blogger posts, "Whereas the electronics industry has been innovating to create immersive experiences from the comfort of our own home, the US theater industry has been dragging their feet."[18]

Home Viewing Technology

Home television sets are increasingly large, high-definition sets coupled with inexpensive, yet impressive audio systems. In 1997, the screen size of the average television was just 23 inches. Currently, almost half of LCD televisions sold have screens 36 inches or larger.[19] Because set size is measured as the diagonal screen size, increases in viewable area are greater than the measurement suggests. In recent years, the viewing area of sets doubled from 250 inches to 550 inches.

The FCC requirement that all broadcasters convert to digital broadcasts by June 12, 2009, is widely credited with starting a consumer movement to upgrade televisions. Since the 1950s, television transmissions were formatted as 480 interlaced vertical lines (480i) of resolution. The new digital format is high definition (HD), providing up to 1080 vertical lines of resolution (1080p).[20] Three quarters of all televisions sold since 2006 are HD capable.

As LCD technology became the standard for both computer and television screens, manufacturing costs declined. Wholesale prices for televisions fell 65 percent from the late 1990s to 2007.[21] In 2006, the average television retailed for $29 per diagonal inch of set size. This is expected to decrease to $22 within five years.[22] Consumers, however, are actually spending more on every television, consistently electing to purchase larger sets to achieve a better viewing experience. Sharp, a leading manufacturer of televisions predicts that by 2015 the average screen will reach 60 inches.[23]

Large screen televisions, DVD players, and audio and speaker components are commonly packaged as low-cost home theaters. The average DVD player now costs just $72[24] and high-definition DVD players are beginning to penetrate the market. Retail price wars during the 2008 Christmas season led to HD Blu-Ray players dropping below $200. These home theater systems offer a movie experience that rivals many theaters, all for $1,000 to $2,000. Says Mike Gabriel, Sharp's head of marketing and communications: "People can now expect a home cinema experience from their TV. Technology that was once associated with the rich and famous is now accessible to homes across the country."[25]

Content Availability and Timing

Even the best hardware offers little value without content for display. Rental firm Netflix advertises a selection of more than 100,000 titles extending well beyond new and classic films to include television shows, sports, and music performances. HD content is increasingly available to maximize the experience offered by those HD televisions. Satellite and cable television providers have engaged in a game of one-upmanship to provide the greatest percentage of HD content available to subscribers. By the end of 2009, 2,000 movies were available on Blu-Ray DVD.[26]

Movie fans no longer have to wait long for the summer's blockbuster to appear on DVD. The time period between theatrical and DVD release has declined 40 percent since 2000. The top five films in 2000 were released on DVD an average of 37 weeks after their box office opening. In 2007, the lag was just 23 weeks. And, studios are experimenting with simultaneous releases to theaters, pay per view, and DVD.

Overall, the visual and audio experience available in the home is rapidly converging with that available at the movie theater. As a blogger on the movie fan site Big Picture posted:

I used to go to the movies all the time—even my blog is called the Big Picture. Then I started going less—and then less still and now—hardly at all. My screen at home is better, the sound system is better, the picture is in focus, the floors aren't sticky and the movies start on time. My seat is clean. And there's no idiot chattering away 2 rows behind me, and (this is my favorite) THERE'S NO CELL PHONES RINGING. EVER.[27]

Is this a horror show at the cinemaplex?

NOTES

1. Motion Picture Association of America (MPAA), 2007, Entertainment industry market statistics.
2. A. Serwer, 2006, Extreme makeover: With big screens and high-def in more and more living rooms, movie theaters are taking radical new measures to woo filmgoers, *Fortune*, 153: 108–116.
3. Mintel Report, 2008, Movie theaters—U.S., February.
4. MPAA, 2007, Entertainment industry market statistics.
5. All data on these two films from http://www.boxofficemojo.com.
6. Developed by author from: Entertainment Industry, 2007 Report, Motion Picture Association of America.
7. J. Woestendiek & C. Kaltenbach, 2008, $10 is small price for a big escape: Movie box office figures are flourishing despite, or because of, economic worries, *Baltimore Sun*, July 8.
8. MPAA, 2007, Entertainment industry market statistics.
9. J. Woestendiek & C. Kaltenbach, 2008, $10 is small price for a big escape: Movie box office figures are flourishing despite, or because of, economic worries, *Baltimore Sun*, July 8.
10. Data on the firms, screen sizes, location, from Web sites and SEC filings.
11. All data is from SEC filings, based on net property, plant, and equipment reported in 2007 balance sheet and on the number of screens.
12. Mintel Report, 2008, Segment performance: cinema advertising, Movie theaters—U.S., February.
13. Mintel Report, 2008, Reasons to go to the movies over watching a DVD, Movie theaters—U.S., February.
14. Mintel Report, 2008, Reasons why attendance is not higher, Movie theaters—U.S., February.
15. K. Kelly, B. Orwall, & P. Sanders, 2005, The multiplex under siege, *Wall Street Journal*, December 24, P1.
16. Blog comment, Over the past years…, http://cinematreasures.org/polls/22/ (accessed December 11, 2008).
17. Incident reported in Patrick Goldstein, 2005, Now playing: A glut of ads, *Los Angeles Times*, July 12, E-1.
18. Designs of the week: The Movie Theater Experience, 2008, November 23, http://www.sramanamitra.com/2008/11/23/designs-of-the-week-the-movie-theater-experience/.
19. DuBravac, 2007.
20. DuBravac, 2007.
21. DuBravac, 2007.
22. B. Keefe, 2008, Prices on flat-screen TVs expected to keep falling, *Atlanta Journal-Constitution*, March 15.
23. Average TV size up to 60-inch by 2015, says Sharp, TechDigest, http://www.techdigest.tv/2008/01/average_tv_size.html (accessed December 11, 2008).
24. MPAA, 2007, Entertainment industry market statistics.
25. Average TV size up to 60-inch by 2015, says Sharp, TechDigest, http://www.techdigest.tv/2008/01/average_tv_size.html (accessed December 11, 2008).
26. http://www.movieweb.com.
27. The Big Picture, Why is movie theatre attendance declining?, http://bigpicture.typepad.com/comments/2005/07/declining_movie.htm (accessed December 11, 2008).

Theodore Bosley, Christopher Calton, Jeffrey Deakins, Tomoko Nakajima, Sally Orford, Robin Pohl, Robin Chapman

Arizona State University

Introduction

We're going to bring humanity back to air travel.
— **DAVID NEELEMAN**
FOUNDER AND CHAIRPERSON

David Neeleman, JetBlue's founder and chairperson, sought to "bring the humanity back to air travel."[1] Since launching operations in February 2000, JetBlue distinguished itself from its competitors by providing superior customer service at low fares. The JetBlue experience included brand new airplanes, leather seats, and personal satellite TV service. The firm experienced rapid early growth. In a period when most U.S. airlines struggled in the aftermath of the September 11, 2001, terrorist attacks, JetBlue reported 18 consecutive quarterly profits.

Then in 2005, JetBlue announced its first net loss of $20 million. The disappointing results were attributed to spiraling fuel prices, aggressive competition, and increasing operating costs. Global events such as war, political turmoil, and natural disasters contributed to the rise in fuel prices. The average price for a barrel of oil in 2003 was $30, by the summer of 2005 prices had climbed above $60 per barrel. The legacy airlines were becoming more competitive after exiting bankruptcy and streamlining their operations to benefit from economies of scale.[2] Analysts speculated that JetBlue was experiencing growth pains:, their maintenance costs on aging planes were increasing, employees were becoming more senior, and new profitable routes were harder to obtain.[3] The company continued to lose money in 2006. While major competitors, such as AMR, the parent company for American Airlines, and Continental, reported higher than expected returns, JetBlue announced a narrow third-quarter loss of $500,000. Following its third-quarter loss, JetBlue announced plans to slow down growth by delaying deliveries of some aircraft, selling others, and eliminating some cross-country flights.[4] Despite these actions, in a recent interview Neeleman insisted, "We're still a growth airline."[5] It remains to be seen how JetBlue will continue to grow in the face of increasing strategic challenges.

History

Founding History of Jet Blue

David Neeleman founded JetBlue Airways Corporation in 1999, after raising $130 million in investment capital. Building on his past experiences, Neeleman hired talented executives, such as David Barger, previous vice president of the Newark, New Jersey, hub for Continental, and John Owen, previous vice president of Operations Planning and Analysis for Southwest.[6] JetBlue chose John F. Kennedy International Airport in New York as its hub and initially obtained 75 takeoff and landing slots.

Neeleman's vision was to provide "high-end customer service at low-end prices."[7] Although JetBlue imitated competitor Southwest Airlines with a single seat class, it did so with Airbus A-320 narrow-body jets instead of Boeing 737s. The A-320 provided wider cabins and wider seats for JetBlue passengers with more room for carry-on baggage.[8] JetBlue implemented innovative IT programs such as an Internet booking system that allowed customers to make reservations online or with a touch-tone phone, and a paperless cockpit to allow pilots to prepare for flight more quickly, helping planes to stay on schedule.[9] JetBlue also provided complementary, unlimited snacks and beverages, preassigned seating, and a selection of first-run movies available from Fox InFlight on flights longer than two hours. For further differentiation, JetBlue installed 36 channels of free DIRECTV programming.

The authors would like to thank Professor Robert E. Hoskisson for his support under whose direction the case was developed. The authors do not intend to illustrate either effective or ineffective handling of a managerial situation. The case solely provides material for class discussion.

Early in 2000, the first JetBlue flights departed from New York to Fort Lauderdale, with a fleet of two planes. JetBlue gradually increased its destinations during the year to include 12 additional airports in California, Florida, New York, Utah, and Vermont. By December, Neeleman announced the landmark of JetBlue's millionth customer and reported $100 million in revenues.

Rapid Growth in 2000–2004

The September 11, 2001, terrorist attacks on America resulted in a widespread fear of air travel, negatively impacting most of the airline industry. While other airlines announced millions in lost revenue following 9/11, JetBlue made a profit and within eight weeks expanded its network to include six more destinations and resumed IT spending to further improve services offered.[10] In February 2002, JetBlue won the 2002 Air Transport World "Market Development Award" for its successful first two years of service, and also was named "Best Overall Airline" by *Onboard Service* magazine.[11] On April 11, 2002, JetBlue announced its initial public offering (IPO) of 5.86 million shares of common stock at a price of $27 per share.[12] JetBlue grew steadily between 2003 and 2004, with annual operating revenues growing from $998.4 million in 2003, to $1.27 billion in 2004. Exhibits 1 through 3 show JetBlue's financial statements for the years 2001 to 2005.

Slowed Growth in 2005–2007

In November 2005 JetBlue decided to add nine new Embraer E190s to its fleet. JetBlue ordered the aircraft with a 100-seat configuration, bigger television screens than the Airbus A-320, and 100 channels from XM Satellite Radio. Also, in late 2005, JetBlue decided to fund $80 million of an airport expansion project at John F. Kennedy Airport, which had a total budget of $875 million. The expansion would allow for more than double the number of flights at JetBlue's hub airport within three years.[13]

Exhibit 1 Consolidated Statement of Income

JetBlue Airways Corporation (in $ millions, year ended December 31)					
	2006	2005	2004	2003	2002
Operating Revenues					
Passenger	$ 2223	$ 1620	$ 1220	$ 965	$ 615
Other	140	81	45	33	20
Total Operating Revenues	2363	1701	1265	998	635
Operating Expenses					
Salaries, wages, and benefits	553	428	337	267	162
Aircraft fuel	752	488	255	147	76
Landing fees and other rents	158	112	92	70	44
Depreciation and amortization	151	115	77	51	43
Aircraft rent	103	74	70	60	41
Sales and marketing	104	81	63	54	27
Maintenance materials and repairs	87	64	45	23	9
Other operating expenses	328	291	215	159	127
Total Operating Expenses	2236	1653	1154	831	530
Operating Income	$ 127	$ 48	$ 111	$ 167	$ 105
Other Income (Expenses)					
Interest expense	(173)	(107)	(53)	(29)	(21)
Capitalized interest	27	16	9	5	5
Interest income and other	28	19	8	8	5
government compensation				23	
Total other income (expense)	(118)	(72)	(36)	7	(10)
Income (Loss) before income taxes	9	(24)	75	174	95
Income tax expense (benefit)	10	(4)	29	71	40
Net Income (Loss)	$ (1)	$ (20)	$ 46	$ 103	$ 55

Source: JetBlue Airways Corporation 2006 Annual Report.

Exhibit 2 Consolidated Balance Sheet

JetBlue Airways Corporation
(in $ millions, except share data)

Assets	December 31				
	2006	2005	2004	2003	2002
Cash and short-term Investments	$ 699	$ 484	$ 450	$ 607.31	$ 257.85
Total receivables, net	77	94	37	16.72	11.93
Total inventory	27	21	10	8.3	4.84
Prepaid expenses	124	36	17	13.42	5.59
Other current assets, total	0	0	0	0	2.85
Total Current Assets	$ 927	$ 635	$ 514	$ 645.74	$ 283.06
Property/Plant/Equip, total	$ 3438	$ 2978	$ 2130	$ 1421	$ 997
Goodwill, net	0	0	0	0	0
Intangibles, net	32	43	54	62	68
Long-term investments	0	0	0	0	0
Note receivable long-term	0	0	0	0	0
Other long-term assets, total	446	236	99	57	30
Other assets, total	0	0	0	0	0
Total Assets	$ 4843	$ 3892	$ 2797	$ 2186	$ 1379

Liabilities and Shareholders' Equity	December 31				
	2006	2005	2004	2003	2002
Accounts payable	$ 136	$ 99	$ 71	$ 53	$ 46
Payable/Accrued	0	0	0	0	0
Accrued expenses	164	111	94	85	54
Notes payable/Short-term debt	39	64	44	30	22
Current port. of LT debt/capital	175	158	105	67	51
Leases					
Other current liabilities, total	340	243	174	135	98
Total Current Liabilities	$ 854	$ 676	$ 488	$ 370	$ 270
Long-term debt and leases	$ 2626	$ 2103	$ 1396	$ 1012	$ 640
Deferred income tax	136	116	121	99	39
Minority interest	0	0	0	0	0
Other liabilities, total	275	86	38	34	17
Total Liabilities	$ 3891	$ 2981	$ 2043	$ 1515	$ 964
Redeemable preferred stock	$ 0	$ 0	$ 0	$ 0	$ 0
Preferred stock-non	0	0	0	0	0
Common stock	2	2	1	1	1
Additional paid-in capital	813	764	581	552	407
Retained earnings	144	145	165	120	16
Other equity, total	(7)	0	7	(2)	(9)
Total Equity	952	911	754	671	415
Total Liabilities & Shareholders' Equity	$ 4843	$ 3892	$ 2797	$ 2186	$ 1,379

Source: JetBlue Airways Corporation 2006 Annual Report.

Exhibit 3 Consolidated Statement of Cash Flows

JetBlue Airways Corporation
(in $ millions)

	December 31				
	2006	2005	2004	2003	2002
Cash Flows from Operating Activities					
Net Income	$ (1)	$ (20)	$ 46	$ 103	$ 55
Operating Activities					
Deferred income taxes	10	(4)	29	69	40
Depreciation	136	101	67	45	25
Amortization	18	16	11	7	2
Stock-based compensation	21	9	2	2	
Changes in certain operating assets and liabilities					
Increase in receivables	(12)	(28)	(20)	(4)	7
Increase in inventories	(28)	(20)	(6)	(11)	(4)
Increase in air traffic liabilities	97	69	39	37	46
Increase in accounts payable and other accrued liabilities	33	54	21	38	35
Other, Net	0	(7)	10	1	11
Net Cash Provided by Operating Activities	274	170	199	287	216
Cash Flows from Investing Activities					
Capital expenditures	(996)	(941)	(617)	(573)	(544)
Predelivery deposits for flight equipment	(106)	(183)	(180)	(160)	(109)
Purchase of held-to-maturity investment	(23)	(5)	(19)	(26)	(11)
Proceeds from maturities of held-to-maturity investment	15	18	25	9	2
Purchase of available-for-sale securities	(1002)	(79)	76	(235)	(80)
Increase in restricted cash and other assets	(16)	(86)	(5)	(2)	(1)
Net Cash Used in Investing Activities	$ (1307)	$ (1276)	$ (720)	$ (987)	$ (744)
Cash Flows from Financing Activities					
Proceeds from:					
Issuance of common stock	28	178	20	136	174
Issuance of long-term debt	855	872	499	446	416
Aircraft sale and leaseback transactions	406	152		265	0.3
Short-term borrowings	45	68	44	33	150
Repayment of long-term debt	(390)	(117)	(77)	(57)	27
Repayment of short-term debt	(71)	(47)	(30)	(25)	(71)
Other, Net	−15	(13)	(19)	(9)	(34)
Net Cash Provided by Financing Activities	$ 1037	$ 1093	$ 437	$ 789	$ (5)
Increase in Cash and Cash Equivalents	$ 4	$ (13)	$ (84)	$ 89	$ 129
Cash and cash equivalent at beginning of period	$ 6	$ 19	$ 103	$ 14	$ 117
Cash and cash equivalent at end of period	$ 10	$ 6	$ 19	$ 103	$ 247

Source: JetBlue Airways Corporation 2006 Annual Report.

However, JetBlue's quarterly financial report started to show growth saturation. Quarterly growth records of operating revenue in 2005 were 29.5 percent, 34.5 percent, 40.2 percent, and –5.2 percent, respectively. JetBlue announced a fourth quarter net loss of $42.4 million, representing a loss per share of $0.25. It was JetBlue's first quarterly net loss.[14]

In 2006, the firm announced unstable earnings, and reported a loss of $32 million, a profit of $14 million, and a loss of $0.5 million in the first three quarters, respectively.[15] Even though JetBlue served 47 destinations with up to 470 daily flights, it decided to reduce its rate of growth over the next three years by delaying the delivery of additional planes.[16] Data for destination and service commenced

Exhibit 4 JetBlue's Destinations

Destination	Service Commenced
New York, New York	February 2000
Fort Lauderdale, Florida	February 2000
Buffalo, New York	February 2000
Tampa, Florida	March 2000
Orland, Florida	June 2000
Ontario, California	July 2000
Oakland, California	August 2000
Rochester, New York	August 2000
Burlington, Vermont	September 2000
West Palm Beach, Florida	October 2000
Salt Lake City, Utah	November 2000
Fort Myers, Florida	November 2000
Seattle, Washington	May 2001
Syracuse, New York	May 2001
Denver, Colorado	May 2001
New Orleans, Louisiana	July 2001
Long Beach, California	August 2001
Washington, D.C. (Dulles Airport)	November 2001
San Juan, Puerto Rico	May 2002
Las Vegas, Nevada	November 2002
San Diego, California	June 2003
Boston, Massachusetts	January 2004
Sacramento, California	March 2004
Aguadilla, Puerto Rico	May 2004
Santiago, Dominican Republic	June 2004
San Jose, California	June 2004
New York, New York (LGA Airport)	September 2004
Phoenix, Arizona	October 2004
Nassau, The Bahamas	November 2004
Burbank, California	May 2005
Portland, Oregon	May 2005
Ponce, Puerto Rico	June 2005
Newark, New Jersey	October 2005
Austin, Texas	January 2006
Richmond, Virginia	March 2006
Hamilton, Bermuda	May 2006
Sarasota-Bradenton, Florida	September 2006
Cancun, Mexico	November 2006
Island of Aruba	November 2006
Chicago, Illinois	January 2007
White Plains, New York	March 2007
San Francisco, California	May 2007

Source: JetBlue Airways Corporation Form 10-K, Fiscal year ending December 31, 2006.

are listed in Exhibit 4. Effort to slow the growth rate was intended to preserve cash, enabling JetBlue to remain stable among competitors.

The first quarter of 2007 did not get off to a great start for JetBlue. Bad weather in February resulted in many cancelled flights and stranded passengers. The climax of the crisis occurred when nine airplanes full of angry passengers sat on the tarmac for six hours, because JetBlue leaders had expected the weather to clear and did not cancel flights. CEO David Neeleman received bad press for his management of the situation. Neeleman responded by humbly admitting "that his company's management was not strong enough. [It] was the result of a shoestring communications system that left pilots and flight attendants in the dark, and an undersize reservation system."[17] Rapid efforts were made to regain its brand image such that a JetBlue Customer Bill of Rights was created, a customer advisory council was formed, plans were made to cross-train crew members, and new communication strategies were put in place.[18] In addition JetBlue waived change fees and fare differences to assist customers who may be affected by additional storms throughout the winter of 2007. Despite his sincere efforts to bounce back from this predicament, Neeleman eventually had to step down as CEO in order to appease shareholders. David Barger, former COO succeeded Neeleman as CEO and needed to establish a strong position against JetBlue rivals.

Competitive Environment

In 1978, the Airline Deregulation Act eliminated government control over fares and routes, opening up the industry to increased competition. The airline industry is now highly competitive, consisting of 43 mainline carriers and 79 regional airlines. The U.S. Department of Transportation (DOT) classifies airlines into three categories based on annual revenue: major (revenue more than $1 billion), national (revenue between $100 million to $1 billion), and regional/commuter (revenue less than $100 million).[19] With annual revenue of $1.7 billion, JetBlue is one of the smaller major carriers and competes primarily on point-to-point routes. Its major competitors are low-cost carrier Southwest Airlines and traditional carriers, AMR Corp, United Airlines, US Airways, Continental Airlines, and Delta Air.[20]

Southwest is JetBlue's most obvious competitor, but the traditional airlines are becoming more aggressive in the low-fare market. Following recent bankruptcies, legacy airlines are emerging with clean balance sheets and lower cost structures. As the major airlines become more competitive and expand their domestic businesses, the low-cost airlines struggle to find new markets.[21]

Competition also comes from the regional carriers, which typically partner with the major airlines to share routes, risk, and costs. For example, Mesa partners with United Airlines and operates as United Express, with Delta Airlines as Delta Express, and with US Air as US Air Express. In exchange for an agreed proportion of revenue, Mesa operates flights on select local routes, while its partners handle reservations and marketing. In recent years, the regional airlines fared better than most, growing twice as fast as the national carriers.[22] However, as the competitive environment toughens, many of the large airlines are renegotiating the agreements, and in some cases—such as Atlantic Coast, a former partner of United Airlines—regional airlines are deciding to operate independently.[23]

The major airlines also form alliances—with each other and international carriers—to share marketing and scheduling capabilities. American Airlines partners with British Airways, Quantas, and various European airlines to form the One World Alliance, which serves 135 countries and operates a shared frequent flyer program. The Star Alliance, spearheaded by United Airlines, with Lufthansa, Scandinavian Air System, All Nippon Airways, and Air Canada, serves 157 countries.[24] Such alliances increase the market power of their members, and research has shown they increase passenger volume by an average of 9.4 percent.[25] Although the benefit is more significant for global carriers seeking to expand their network abroad, researchers observed an average improvement in number of tickets booked by 7.4 percent on short-haul flights.

Although JetBlue does not currently participate in any alliances, it has had discussions about forming one with international airlines in an effort to leverage its power at the hub in JFK. JetBlue does not want to enter a traditional agreement with other airlines, because many of these agreements include increased overhead costs. JetBlue is hoping to create an agreement that will increase traffic without increasing costs.[26]

Fare pricing is an important competitive factor within the industry. For many years excess capacity posed a significant problem, causing airlines to either leave planes on the ground or fly planes with empty seats. In order to avoid this dilemma, carriers try to increase market share by discounting tickets. Even the legacy airlines slash fares in order to compete on low-cost routes. Although low-cost airlines, like JetBlue, still offer the greatest number of discounted fares, some of the cheapest tickets are now available from traditional airlines, such as American, Delta, and United.[27]

Rumors of consolidation in the industry could change the competitive landscape. US Airways made a hostile bid for bankrupt Delta Airlines in fourth quarter 2006, but withdrew its offer in January 2007 due to the inability to reach financial agreement with Delta creditors.[28] The merger would have created the largest airline in a fragmented industry and would likely have triggered further consolidations.[29] Even though a wave of consolidation may create a more efficient airline industry with fewer major players, consolidations affect ticket prices, usually leading to higher ticket prices, and complicate the flight paths offered by airlines. Therefore, consolidations affect all competitors within the industry.

Key Competitors

Southwest Airlines

Southwest is the leading low-fare, no-frills, U.S. carrier. The company was founded in 1967 as a Texas-based airline to serve Dallas, Houston, and San Antonio. The airline now flies to more than 63 cities across the United States. In 2006, Southwest reported a $499 million profit and net sales of $9.86 billion.[30] Exhibit 5 compares key financial data for the major airlines. In 2005, America West's CEO, Douglas Parker, described Southwest as follows: "They really were at one point the scrawny kid who was lifting weights in his basement. Now they come out and they're bigger than anybody else and stronger than anybody else."[31]

Southwest's strategy emphasizes low costs; the firm was the first to sell tickets online and to introduce unassigned seating. It operates a single aircraft fleet of 481

Exhibit 5 U.S. Major Airlines' Select Financials for Year Ended 2006 (in $millions)

	JetBlue	UAL	SWA	Delta	Continental	US Airways	AMR Corp.
Total revenues	$2,363	$ 19,340	$ 9,086	$ 17,171	$13,128	$11,557	$ 22,563
Cost of revenues	1,653	14,114	6,311	14,430	11,007	9,049	17,659
Gross profit	570	5,226	2,573	1,694	1,453	1,814	4,904
Profit as % of revenue	24%	27%	28%	10%	11%	16%	22%
Operating income (loss)	127	23,381	934	(6,148)	468	558	1,060
Net income (loss)	$ (1)	$ 22,386	$ 499	$ (6,203)	$ 343	$ 304	$ 231
Total assets	$4,843	25,369	$13,460	$ 19,622	$11,308	$ 7,576	$ 29,145
Current assets	927	6,273	2,601	5,385	4,129	3,354	6,902
Total liabilities	$3,891	$ 23,221	$ 7,011	$ 33,215	$10,961	$ 6,606	$ 29,751
Current liabilities	854	7,945	2,887	5,769	3,955	2,712	8,505
Total owner equity	$ 952	$ 2,148	$ 6,449	$ (13,593)	$ 347	$ 970	$ (606)

Source: 2007, MSN Money Central, http://moneycentral.msn.com/investor/research/welcome.asp, July 24.

Exhibit 6 Top 10 U.S. Airlines, Ranked by August 2006 Domestic Scheduled Enplanements

Passenger numbers in millions

August 2006 Rank	Carrier	August 2006 Enplanements	August 2005 Rank	August 2005 Enplanements
1	Southwest	8.7	1	8.1
2	American	6.5	3	6.8
3	Delta	5.4	2	7.0
4	United	5.1	4	5.0
5	Northwest	4.1	5	4.2
6	Continental	3.1	7	2.9
7	US Airways	2.6	6	3.1
8	America West	1.8	8	1.9
9	AirTran	1.8	9	1.5
10	JetBlue	1.7	13	1.3

Note: Percentage changes based on numbers prior to rounding.

Source: Bureau of Transportation Statistics, T-100 Domestic Market.

Boeing 737s. The company is also lauded for its unique and friendly culture and its high level of customer service.[32] However, evidence now indicates a shift in its strategy—from serving underserved routes, to competing in major markets such as Denver and Philadelphia. Southwest is now the largest U.S. airline in terms of number of passengers (Exhibit 6), and in order to continue to grow, Southwest is competing against United in its Denver hub, and US Airways, on routes out of Philadelphia.[33]

AMR Corp.

As the world's largest airline, American Airlines (AMR's main subsidiary) offers flights to 150 destinations throughout North America, Latin America, the Caribbean, Europe, and Asia. It has had its share of success and failures; two of its planes were hijacked during the September 11, 2001, terrorist attacks and the firm barely avoided bankruptcy in 2003.[34] In 2006, AMR Corp. reported net earnings of $231 million, an improvement over its net loss of $861 million in 2005 and other significant losses in preceding years.[35] In order to return to profitability, the firm streamlined costs and expanded its routes in Asia.

United Airlines

United also lost two planes on September 11, 2001, and after several years of financial difficulties, UAL eventually filed for Chapter 11 bankruptcy in 2002.[36] UAL emerged from bankruptcy as a more competitive firm. In February 2004, United launched its own low-cost off-shoot, Ted. The firm is now looking for new ways to expand and improve profitability. Global expansion is central to UAL's strategy; in July 2006, the firm announced plans to expand its Asia/Pacific routes.[37] Recent rumors report that UAL hired Goldman Sachs to assess possible merger options.[38]

US Airways

US Airways Group is the product of a merger between US Airways and America West. CEO Parker believes this acquisition strategy is successful; when comparing the firm's post-bankruptcy performance to United, he stated, "The big difference is we were able to generate synergies that United was not able to."[39] Shareholders experienced a 45 percent increase in stock price during the first full year after the merger.[40]

Delta Air

With an 11.8% domestic market share, Delta places third among traditional airline icons.[41] Delta is strongly focused on international expansion, adding 50 new international routes in 2005–2006. Delta now serves over 450 destinations in 95 countries. Delta filed for bankruptcy and was a target acquisition by US Airways just before it emerged from bankruptcy in April 2007.

Continental Airlines

Continental targets the business traveler by serving diverse U.S. and international routes.[42] Continental has a strong balance sheet, having recently retired $100 million in debt.[43] In the third quarter of 2006, Continental followed in the path of the other legacy airlines by reporting stronger than expected results. The positive results were attributed to greatly increased number of passengers, especially on Continental's regional and Latin American routes.[44]

As well as domestic competitors, the international airline market conditions are a factor that JetBlue must consider.

International Market Conditions

The demand for international travel has increased significantly over the past decade (see Exhibit 7). The international travel growth rate is more than double the domestic travel growth rate in the United States.[45] Travel to Southeast Asia and China increases every year by about 7.3 percent and 8.0 percent. Looking forward, the number of transatlantic plane tickets purchased is expected to grow by 4.6 percent annually. Global business transactions have contributed, as well as more discretionary income for consumers, and lower airfare resulting from greater efficiencies in international travel.

The international market is attractive to many airlines because they can include fuel surcharges in the ticket price and recover some of the costs associated with higher-priced fuel.

However, the airline industry is monitored more scrupulously by the government than any other industry conducting business internationally. The government has many regulations on when, where, and how airlines can fly, how much they can charge, and how they can market international travel.[46] Many lobbyist firms and politicians in the United States have been fighting for deregulation and less restrictions on international air travel so that the United States might be more of a force in the international market. The European airline industry, more specifically AirFrance/KLM, has taken the lead in revenues for international aviation.[47]

Not only is it important for JetBlue to consider its competitive environment, but it is also important to understand the companies/industries that supply the provisions necessary to remain competitive.

Key Suppliers

Fuel

Fuel is usually the second-highest expense for an airline next to labor.[48] Therefore, fuel price increases are a major contributor to rising operating costs in the airline industry. A Merrill Lynch analyst indicated that for every $1

Exhibit 7 U.S. Commercial Air Carriers Total U.S. Passenger Traffic

Fiscal Year	Revenue Passenger Enplanements (millions)			Revenue Passenger Miles (billions)		
	Domestic	International	System	Domestic	International	System
Historical*						
2000	641.2	56.4	697.6	512.8	181.8	694.6
2001	626.8	56.7	683.4	508.1	183.3	691.4
2002	574.5	51.2	625.8	473.0	158.2	631.3
2003	587.8	54.2	642.0	492.7	155.9	648.6
2004	628.5	61.4	689.9	540.2	177.4	717.7
2005	661	86.2	747.2	573.7	221.5	795.1
Forecast						
2006	660.9	89.7	750.6	577.6	232.5	810.1
2007	693.3	75.8	769.1	603.3	221.5	824.7
2008	713.8	79.8	793.6	624.6	234.5	859.0
2009	735.7	84.0	819.7	647.7	247.9	895.6
2010	758.9	88.3	847.2	671.9	262.1	934.1
2011	782.6	92.9	875.5	697.6	276.9	974.5
2012	807.7	97.6	905.2	724.5	291.9	1,016.4
2013	833.4	102.3	935.7	752.6	307.4	1,059.9
2014	860.5	107.2	967.7	782.2	323.5	1,105.7
2015	888.4	112.3	1,000.7	813.3	340.2	1,153.5
2016	917.7	117.6	1,035.3	846.1	357.5	1,203.6
2017	848.4	123.1	1,071.6	880.6	375.2	1,255.8
Average Annual Growth 2005–2017	2.9%	5.0%	3.1%	3.6%	5.5%	4.1%

Source: Forms 41 and 298-C, U.S. Department of Transportation.

increase in price for a barrel of fuel, the airline industry experiences a $450 million loss in pretax profits.[49] According to the FAA, jet fuel costs rose by 20.1 percent in 2004, 40.5 percent in 2005, and 30.4 percent in 2006.[50] In 2006, fuel costs became JetBlue's largest operating expense at 33.65 percent.[51] The FAA forecasts fuel costs will remain high for the next several years. Neeleman seriously considers fuel costs and is investigating alternative sources of energy, such as liquid coal. Because the United States has an abundant supply of coal, Neeleman is urging his customers to support a new bill to fund additional coal-to-liquid plants.[52]

Airlines engage in fuel hedging in order to manage unpredictable costs. However, the jet fuel commodities market is illiquid, and it is especially difficult for the large airlines to hedge sufficient quantities of fuel.[53] JetBlue is increasing its efforts to systematically hedge against future fuel needs. JetBlue also seeks more efficient fuel usage through the planes purchased and improved flight planning.[54]

Aircraft Manufacturers

The aircraft industry is dominated by two companies, Airbus and Boeing. Due to the weak economy following September 11, 2001, their orders for new commercial planes fell sharply. However, as commercial business improved, the large manufacturers profited from the buoyant space and defense markets. Embraer, the number four aircraft manufacturer, has seen lackluster commercial sales, but is benefiting from increased sales in the military sector.

Typically, the low-cost airlines operate few aircraft types, reducing their maintenance, scheduling, and training costs. JetBlue currently owns two airplane models, and its growth plans include the addition of 96 Airbus A-320s and 92 Embraer E190s.[55] Cost efficiencies would be lost if JetBlue switched suppliers, exposing the firm to any problems related to either of its aircraft suppliers. But currently more pressing for JetBlue are the challenges associated with the airline industry.

General Environment

A number of new trends are emerging in air travel. After September 11, 2001, the industry saw a drop in the number of corporate travelers, but five years later this trend appeared to be reversing. According to a survey by the National Business Travel Association, 65 percent of businesses expect employees to take more flights in 2007, and 75 percent predict an increase in the amount of business travel.[56]

Another factor in the environment of air travel is the characteristics of the airport and FAA density regulations. JetBlue experiences general performance setbacks by operating in high traffic areas such as the northeastern United States, and the airport congestion hampers performance statistics.[57] The FAA regulates airport slot (a slot is a time frame allotted for takeoff and landing)[58] allocations with the intent to ease congestion problems and enhance airport capacity. For example, recent measures at New York La Guardia airport include growth limitations, regulations encouraging use of larger aircraft, and a proposal for 10-year slot reallocation.[59]

Natural disasters and annual weather patterns also affect the performance statistics for air travel. Florida is quite popular during the winter months and the western states during summer months. Air travel is also affected by winter weather in the Northeast and tropical storms along the Atlantic and Gulf coasts.[60]

In the airline industry, more than 60 percent of employees are unionized.[61] Although JetBlue is non-unionized, it can be affected by the industry environment. In June 2006, the International Association of Machinists and Aerospace Workers campaigned to represent JetBlue's ramp service workers. The bid was unsuccessful; however JetBlue's management commented, "We can expect ongoing attempts by unions to organize groups of JetBlue crewmembers."[62]

As can be expected from the general environment, JetBlue is exposed to the widespread attraction of media coverage and negative press. One recent major incident appearing in headlines is the mechanical failure of Flight 292 landing in Los Angeles.[63] On September 21, 2005, JetBlue Flight 292 left Burbank, California, bound for JFK in New York City. Soon after takeoff, the pilot acknowledged problems with the landing gear. The decision was made to have an emergency landing at Los Angeles International Airport and after circling Orange County for three hours, to burn off fuel, Flight 292 landed safely. None of the 139 passengers or six crew members was injured during the landing. Upon landing it became certain that the nose gear had rotated 90 degrees and was locked in the down position[64] (see Exhibit 8). Although the outcome was ultimately favorable, had Flight 292 crashed or lives been lost, JetBlue's image would have

Exhibit 8 JetBlue Airbus A-320 Flight 292 with Its Nose Landing Gear Jammed

Source: JetScott, 2005, http://www.aerospaceweb.org/question/planes/q0245a.shtml, October 2.

suffered drastically. The perceived safety of air travel is important for all airlines.

Airlines also face a heightened sense of consumer information privacy. In 2002, JetBlue offered extensive passenger data to a data mining company, Torch, who in conjunction with the U.S. Army, tested a customer profiling system to identify high risk passengers that might threaten military installations.[65] According to the District Court, Eastern New York, Memorandum & Order 04-MD-1587, JetBlue was responsible for the release of "each passenger's name, address, gender, home ownership or rental status, economic status, social security number, occupation, and the number of adults and children in the passenger's family as well as the number of vehicles owned or leased."[66] With increased online purchases, all airlines are publicly pressured to protect passengers' identity.

JetBlue must make a conscious effort to rise above all of the setbacks associated with the general environment and ensure that all actions are in alignment with its corporate and business strategies.

JetBlue Strategies

Because many of the other airlines play a significant role in the low-cost carrier segment within the airline industry, JetBlue competes by differentiation. The goal is to achieve an image of far superior customer service.

Superior Customer Service

JetBlue delivers this service by offering additional pre-flight and on-board conveniences that other low-cost carriers do not provide as a whole package. Before traveling, customers benefit from JetBlue's simple-to-use reservation system, ticketless travel, and preassigned seating. The cabin features leather seats and an additional two inches of leg room than most carriers. As previously mentioned, on board JetBlue passengers receive free DIRECTV service, and its Embraer E190 planes have XM Satellite Radio.[67] To improve the customer experience, JetBlue added healthier snacks and, as of November 2006, offers a 100 percent transfat-free selection. All snacks are complementary and unlimited.

All passengers on "shut eye" flights receive a comfort kit from Bliss, which includes earplugs, lip balm, an eye mask, and hand lotion. Crewmembers wake customers with the smell of Dunkin' Donuts coffee and offer a hot towel service.[68]

It is valuable to customers to have their flight depart as planned. To provide customers with confidence, JetBlue focuses on its completion rate, even at the expense of its on-time rate. At the end of third quarter 2006, JetBlue had a 99.6 percent completion rate. In addition, customers want to be confident that they will have their bags at the end of the flight. At 2006 year-end, JetBlue was ranked number 1 out of the 15 busiest airlines in regard to the least number of lost or mishandled bags.[69]

A critical factor in achieving superior service is employee moral. As Neeleman has stated, the crewmembers are the "real secret weapon."[70] His philosophy is that if crew members are treated well, they will in turn treat the customers well.

Culture

Currently, David Neeleman, chairperson, and Dave Barger, CEO, are hands-on people who like to interact with employees and customers. Each week members of top management fly with 8 to 12 crew members and almost always attend new hire training to teach new crewmembers about JetBlue's brand, how the company makes money, and how crewmembers contribute to the bottom line. Whenever they fly, they help the crew clean the plane after the flight to ensure a quick turnaround time. In addition they have informal meetings with crewmembers to learn about issues and problems as crewmembers see them.[71] This management style continues to attract motivated new hires; JetBlue has a reputation as a great place to work, company profit sharing, high productivity of planes and people, and rapid advancements. In 2004 alone, JetBlue hired 1,700–1,800 people.[72]

The combined effort to provide exceptional service and instill a valued-employee culture will fulfill Neeleman's hope that JetBlue can "keep our folks fresh and keep our customers coming back."[73]

However, as proven by Delta's Song and the installation of leather seats in its planes, the "superior service" attributes can be imitated by competitors. What has also allowed JetBlue to remain one step ahead in its competitive environment is cost management.

Cost Management

JetBlue's cost-saving initiative includes electronic ticketing, paperless cockpits, and online check-in.[74] In order to achieve paperless cockpits, JetBlue supplied pilots and first officers with laptops to retrieve electronic flight manuals and make preflight load and balance calculations.[75] In the year following implementation of paperless cockpits, the company saved approximately 4,800 hours of labor.[76] One of JetBlue's more original strategies to cut costs is its telephone reservation system. Reservation agents work from their homes in Salt Lake City, using personal computers equipped with VoIP technology. VoIP stands for Voice over Internet Protocol and utilizes the Internet to make free phone calls.[77] This system gives JetBlue flexibility to handle varying call volumes without needing a costly call center.[78]

JetBlue also uses technology to manage its marketing costs. JetBlue employs Omniture software to increase efficiency of Internet searches, decreasing associated search conversion costs by 94 percent.[79] By using animation in its television ads with its advertising agency, JetBlue produced eight ads for the standard price of one.[80]

Another value-adding initiative is BlueTurn, the name for JetBlue's ground operations. In an effort to improve the overall on-time performance statistics, BlueTurn allows crewmembers to minimize ground time and decrease the turnaround time for aircraft.[81]

JetBlue operates two aircraft types and a single travel class. This simplicity reduces training, maintenance, and operating costs relative to competitors that operate multiple aircraft types.

These cost-cutting strategies follow the standard low-cost, low-fare business model, without sacrificing the ultimate strategy of providing superior customer service with happy employees.

In order to best market its services, JetBlue has carefully considered its marketing approach.

Marketing Strategy

Neeleman believes that marketing is best accomplished by word of mouth; therefore top management aims to make sure that customers are treated well and employees feel valued.[82] Yet, they have made concerted efforts to market in other ways. To establish a media campaign, JetBlue hired J. Walter Thompson (JWT) as its advertising agency.[83] To create a fresh identity, JWT found candid statements by customers on JetBlue service. Online sources were consulted such as Craigslist and Epinions. The statements, written as short stories, were used to create eight different animated ads as testimonials to JetBlue's customer service. Other forms of direct marketing were used such as leather benches and snack bins in serviced airports. JetBlue also created comical postcards and distributed to customers to mail back their comments.[84]

In order to record customers' opinions on JetBlue service, an interactive video installation called the "JetBlue Story Booth" was set up in Rockefeller Center, and is traveling around the country to other cities served by JetBlue.[85] In the one-week New York exhibit, an estimated 20,000 people participated in the installation.[86] A vehicle called Blue Betty was created to simulate an airplane cabin and showcase in-flight amenities. As it traveled to various events across the country, visitors could enter a contest (or lottery) for ticket giveaways. JetBlue also used direct marketing to target college students with a public relations team called CrewBlue. This group used unconventional methods of posters, flyers, and chalk art to educate students about various aspects of the airline's services. Other marketing efforts include "Blue Days," where students were encouraged to wear blue and were rewarded with airline tickets through drawings. A 2005 survey indicated this marketing campaign was successful and increased JetBlue awareness by 41 percent.[87]

In addition to marketing initiatives, JetBlue on a consistent basis updates its business strategy to increase growth and revenue.

Current Strategies

In the first quarter of 2006, due to operating losses, JetBlue executives announced a turnaround plan called "Return to Profitability." Items included in this initiative were revisions to fare structures, corrections to flight capacity, and reprioritizing of flight segments (short, medium, and long haul).[88]

The growth rate has been slowed. The company expects to grow between 14 and 17 percent over the next year versus the 18 to 20 percent originally forecasted.[89]

JetBlue plans to fuel this growth by adding a number of flights on existing routes, connecting new city pairs among the destinations already served, and entering new markets usually served by higher-cost, higher-fare airlines. To determine which cities JetBlue should include in its flight pattern, executives study information made available from the Department of Transportation, which outlines the historical number of passengers, capacity, and average fares over time in all city-pair markets within North America.[90] This information along with JetBlue's historical data allows them to predict how a market will react to the introduction of JetBlue's service and lower prices.

JetBlue expects to use the new Embraer fleet to create demand in many midsized markets that could benefit from its point-to-point service.[91]

In addition, as mentioned previously, JetBlue is in the midst of some discussions about creating a partnership to enter the international market. Due to the limited type of aircraft in JetBlue's fleet, an alliance is the only way for JetBlue to capitalize on the international market opportunities, because its aircraft are not large enough to fly overseas.

The firm is also optimistic that recent moves to expand distribution channels will increase revenue. In August of 2006, the company signed a five-year agreement with Sabre Holdings and Galileo International. This arrangement will allow more than 52,000 travel agencies to purchase tickets for JetBlue travelers with a single connection. These deals are an attempt to reach a broader customer base, especially business travelers.[92]

Moreover, JetBlue is constantly striving to introduce new methods of providing superior customer service. As of March 2007 the first 11 rows in the cabin feature four inches of legroom between each row rather than the previous two inches.[93] To augment its flight services, JetBlue has established complementary products and services.

Associated Products and Services

In addition to air travel, JetBlue sells combined flight and hotel packages, which it terms "JetBlue Getaways." When JetBlue Getaways launched in November 2005, Tim Claydon, vice president of Sales and Marketing, commented, "By working with the hotels directly, rather than through an intermediary, we are able to offer our customers only the finest properties at great prices. Using the latest technology to combine the lowest JetBlue airfare with the best hotel or resort rate, we are able to offer our customers a new level of value with vacations beginning and ending on JetBlue Airways—something not available on any other online travel site."[94]

An American Express card was issued in 2005 called the "JetBlue Card," which earns TrueBlue points for members.[95] Customers earn TrueBlue points when purchasing flights, movie tickets, sporting event tickets, and gym memberships. When a customer amasses 100 TrueBlue points (equivalent to approximately five medium-length round trips), the customer earns a free round-trip valid for one year. In 2006, award travel accounted for only 2 percent of JetBlue's total revenue passenger miles.[96]

In order to sustain its business and corporate strategies, JetBlue monitors its financial situation regularly.

Financial Condition

JetBlue's current financial situation is highlighted by its short-term liquidity, long-term stability, and company profitability. Stockholder profitability signals whether JetBlue is meeting its stockholders' expectations.[97]

Short-Term Liquidity

JetBlue's balance sheet over the past five years is shown in Exhibit 2. JetBlue has struggled with financial performance since 2005. The growth of current liabilities from

Exhibit 9 Liquidity Ratios

	2006	2005	2004	2003	2002
Current ratio	1.1	0.94	1.05	1.75	1.05
Quick ratio	1.05	0.91	1.03	1.72	1.03

Source: JetBlue Airways Corporation 2006 Annual Report.

Exhibit 10 Receivables and Payables

Receivables	2006	2005	2004	2003	2002
Receivable turnover	30.6	26	47.1	69.7	38.8
Days to collect	11.9	14.1	7.8	5.2	9.4

Payables	2006	2005	2004	2003	2002
Payable turnover	16.4	13.8	12.9	11.5	9.5
Days to pay		26.4	28.3	31.7	38.5

Source: JetBlue Airways Corporation 2006 Annual Report.

Exhibit 11 Stability Ratios

	2006	2005	2004	2003	2002
Debt/Asset ratio	0.8	0.8	0.7	0.7	0.7
Asset/Equity ratio	5.1	4	3.5	3.3	3.5
Debt/Equity (financial leverage)	4.1	3.3	2.7	2.3	2.3
Interest coverage ratio	0.7	0.7	2.7	8.4	7.1

Source: JetBlue Airways Corporation 2006 Annual Report.

Exhibit 12 Fuel Expenses

	2006	2005	2004	2003	2002
Operating revenue	$2363	$1701	$1265	$998	$635
Aircraft fuel	752	488	255	147	76
Aircraft fuel %	31	29	20	15	12
Other Costs % Revenue					
Salaries and benefits %	23	25	27	27	26
Aircraft rent %	4	4	6	6	6
Sales and Marketing %	4	5	5	5	7
Maintenance %	4	4	4	2	1

Source: JetBlue Airways Corporation 2006 Annual Report.

2003 to 2006 is significant, compared to the growth of current assets. However, the payables turnover ratio has been increasing, which indicates that JetBlue has been able to pay its suppliers at a faster rate even though it has not been as efficient in collecting receivables as in years past. (Liquidity ratios are shown in Exhibit 9 and turnover ratios are shown in Exhibit 10.)

Long-Term Stability

Long-term financial stability will be an issue as JetBlue toils to consistently turn a profit. JetBlue has maintained

Exhibit 13 Profitability

	2006	2005	2004	2003	2002
Gross margins	20%	27%	33%	40%	45%
Operating margins	5.4%	3%	9%	17%	17%
Net profit margins	0.4%	−1%	4%	10%	9%
Return on equity	0.97%	−2%	6%	19%	19%
Return on assets	2%	2%	3%	6%	6%

Source: JetBlue Airways Corporation 2006 Annual Report; 2007; http://www.finance.yahoo.com.

a fairly consistent debt-to-asset mix as most of the cash received from issuances has been invested in capital assets. The majority of JetBlue's issuances are floating rate bonds, exposing the firm to increases in the Federal Reserve's prime rate.[98] JetBlue's first quarter 2007 assets/equity ratio stood at 5.4 compared to the industry average of 3.[99] (See Exhibits 3 and 11 for details.)

Company Profitability

JetBlue's gross margins continued to decline in recent years, which can be mainly attributed to increasing fuel charges as shown in Exhibit 12. Salaries, landing fees, and other expenses remain fairly stable as a percent of revenues (most have actually decreased, see Exhibit 1). For 2006, gross margins remained 23 percent (see Exhibit 13). As stated earlier, interest expense has a negative effect on profitability.

Stockholder Profitability

In July 2007, the stock was trading at $11.01 versus $14.90[100] at the end of April 2002. In addition to the lackluster stock movement, JetBlue has never paid dividends, so the overall return for the past four years is 5.5 percent. According to moneycentral.com and Yahoo! Finance, the average analyst recommendation is "Hold" for JetBlue. The declining return on equity and inconsistency of net income appears to be having negative implications for JetBlue.

Strategic Challenges

JetBlue faces many challenges as it continues to operate in the highly competitive airline industry. The main challenges are maintaining JetBlue's culture as it grows, dealing with the surfacing complexities of two fleet types, managing maintenance expenses as airplanes and engines begin to age, and dealing with an increasingly senior labor pool. Although fuel prices are a concern, they affect the industry in the same way, and airlines have opportunities to mitigate these risks. Southwest hedged its fuel position more effectively than other airlines, but these hedges will expire and everyone will have a more level playing field when it comes to fuel prices.[101]

Maintaining the JetBlue culture will be difficult to do as the airline grows. The explosive increase in employees may hinder the ability to sustain high utilization and maintain a positive work environment. The time that top management has to interact with individual crewmembers will decrease. Neeleman stated that he would no longer be able to respond to every crewmember's e-mail.[102] This change will hinder a popular cultural component because the chairperson and CEO may no longer be seen as accessible.[103]

Multiple Aircraft Types

JetBlue will have a challenge as it continues to integrate two different types of aircraft. The firm suffered a setback when it incorporated the Embraer E190 into its fleet. JetBlue wanted to fly the new planes 14 hours a day, similar to its A-320s. However, the airplane characteristics were different from the Airbus.[104] Both pilots and mechanics needed additional time and training to understand the new plane. These factors caused flight delays and cancellations throughout the JetBlue system.[105] JetBlue had to reevaluate its plans.

Another issue associated with two types of aircraft is that JetBlue must staff two groups of pilots and flight attendants. The different aircraft require unique training and integration procedures. JetBlue will need separate inventories, training programs, and facilities to accommodate two fleet types.[106] In addition, the pay scales are different, which requires additional support from corporate employees.

Increased Maintenance Expenses

Maintenance expense will be a significant concern for JetBlue in coming years. As with a new car, new airplanes rarely need maintenance and when they do, they are covered under warranty. In 2004, JetBlue experienced a 94 percent increase in maintenance costs.[107] The increase in maintenance costs was not as significant in 2005 and 2006 at 36 percent and 42 percent, respectively (see Exhibit 1); however, as the large fleet of new planes comes due for heavy maintenance at the same time, JetBlue will experience a significant increase in maintenance costs.

Airplane operators have A, C, and D levels of scheduled maintenance and inspection intervals. A-checks occur every 400–500 hours and are similar to an oil change on a vehicle. C- and D-checks are more extensive, more expensive, and longer. The C-check schedule is every 18 months/6,000 hours/3,000 cycles.[108] Additionally, the fourth C-check consists of more inspections, and takes

10 days, compared to just 4 days for regular C-checks.[109] Furthermore, JetBlue decided to outsource maintenance to Air Canada Technical Services in Winnipeg, and Aeroman in El Salvador. Because these operations are not co-located with any of its scheduled service, JetBlue has to spend additional money ferrying planes and paying employees to work in these facilities. JetBlue spends "seven figures" each year in ferrying planes and as much as $700 per day extra for people to monitor the quality of work.[110] As JetBlue's planes enter more extensive service, the amount of time to ferry airplanes and actual maintenance will increase.

Engine expense is another huge maintenance cost for JetBlue. In July 2005, JetBlue signed a 10-year service agreement with a German company, MTU. It covers all scheduled and unscheduled repair for all A-320 engines.[111] At year-end 2006, JetBlue had more than 90 A-320 aircraft, and with two engines per plane and a healthy spares inventory, JetBlue has a significant number of engines to maintain (including its 23 E190 airplanes and engines).[112] Typical charges for a comparable engine overhaul range from $1 million to $1.5 million per heavy visit.

In addition to engines and airframes, airplane operators have additional equipment they must maintain and arrange for contract maintenance support. They have auxiliary power units, landing gear systems, environmental systems, avionics, and flight controls.

As the number of aircraft increases, the cost to maintain will increase. JetBlue may lose economies of scale because multiple aircraft types require multiple repair facilities, and they will have to employ and house multiple sets of inventory and people.

Increased Payroll Expenses

Payroll costs will multiply at JetBlue as the company ages. During 2006 salaries, wages, and benefits increased 29 percent, or $125 million, due primarily to an increased workforce (refer to Exhibit 1).[113] According to the Bureau of Transportation (see Exhibit 14), JetBlue experienced a 212 percent staff growth and ranks third among low-cost carriers for total number of employees in the United States.

Currently, all of the crewmembers are near the bottom of the pay scales, and JetBlue enjoys a relatively low-cost labor pool. However, as these people attain seniority with the company their pay level will increase.[114] Not only will salaried employees get annual pay raises, but crewmembers are paid for each hour flown, according to type of aircraft and depending on the number of years with the company (see Exhibit 15). A more senior staff means the company will start paying higher wages.

Exhibit 14 Low-Cost Carrier Full-Time Equivalent Employees, August 2002–2006

(Numbers in thousands)

Rank		2002	2003*	2004*	2005*	2006	Percent Change 2002–2006
1	Southwest	34	33	31	31	32	–4.5
2	America West	12	11	11	12	13	7.0
3	JetBlue	3	5	6	8	10	212.4
4	AirTran	5	5	6	6	7	56.9
5	Frontier	3	3	4	4	5	70.6
6	ATA	7	7	7	4	3	–61.5
7	Spirit	2	2	2	2	2	–14.4
8	Independence	N/A	4	4	3	N/A	N/A
	Total****	65	71	72	71	71	9.3

*Employment numbers in 2003, 2004, and 2005 for Independence Air, which changed its business model from a regional to low-cost carrier in mid-2004, are included with low-cost carriers. The carrier did not meet the standard for filing in previous years. The airline discontinued flights on January 5, 2006.

N/A = Not applicable because carriers did not meet the standard for filing.

Source: Bureau of Transportation Statistics.

Exhibit 15 Pay Scale Table

2004 Year	A-320 Captain	EMB190 Captain	A-320 FO	EMB190 FO
12	$126	$89	$76	$53
11	$126	$87	$76	$52
10	$126	$85	$76	$51
9	$125	$84	$75	$50
8	$124	$82	$74	$49
7	$123	$80	$74	$48
6	$122	$79	$73	$47
5	$121	$77	$72	$46
4	$118	$76	$67	$44
3	$116	$74	$61	$42
2	$113	$72	$56	$40
1	$110	$71	$51	$37

Note: Guarantee of 70 hrs/month; above 70 hours paid at 150%.

Source: 2006, Will fly for food, http://www.willflyforfood.cc/Payscales/PayScales.htm.

Because JetBlue desires to remain nonunionized, it will have to pay its employees well to ensure they do not become disgruntled and demand representation. Unions have not gained a foothold in JetBlue, but the Air Lines Pilot Association has JetBlue as a target. In addition to pilots, flight attendants, mechanics, ground crews, and gate agents will also receive pressure from other national unions for representation. If by chance the employees of JetBlue succumb to union pressure, union negotiators will then push for increased wages and other amenities—such as hotel requirements, time off, minimum number of flight hours per month, and so on—resulting in higher costs.

JetBlue's Challenge in Coming Years

David Neeleman started an airline based on previous experience and an entrepreneurial spirit. He knew what people wanted and how much they would pay for it. JetBlue attracted high-quality employees because of the unique culture that stressed customer service and differentiated offerings. Allowing at-home reservations agents, paperless cockpits, and crewmembers' easy access to executives has created an environment with which people want to associate. In addition, by purchasing brand new Airbus airplanes and having a junior staff, JetBlue has minimized labor and maintenance costs, both major operating expenses, for several years. As growth slows in the domestic market, its aircraft begin to age, and the workforce becomes more senior, the number of challenges will increase. Barger and Neeleman are faced with persistent questions about how to continue to grow the airline profitably. Does JetBlue attack Southwest, United, Delta, American, or Continental strongholds in the Midwest and/or smaller airports? Does it form an alliance in order to expand into international markets such as Europe and Asia? To minimize expenses related to airplanes, should JetBlue return to one airplane type? Finally, while unions are prevalent at every other airline, how can JetBlue maintain an environment where employees remain committed, dedicated, and satisfied?

NOTES

1. 2002, JetBlue Airways Corporation, *International Directory of Company Histories*, Vol. 44. St. James Press. 2006, Reproduced in Business and Company Resource Center. Farmington Hills, Mich.:Gale Group.

2. M. Trottman & S. Carey, 2006, Legacy Airlines may outfly discount rivals, *Wall Street Journal*, October 30, C1.

3. T. Fredrickson, 2006, Middle-aged JetBlue finds it's harder to fly; Ballooning fuel costs, intense competition turn it into a loser, *Crain's New York Business*, February 13, 22(7):4.

4. J. Bernstein, 2006, JetBlue posts quarterly loss, *Newsday*, October 25.

5. J. H. Dobrzynski, 2006, We're still a growth airline, *Wall Street Journal*, November 4, A6.

6. JetBlue Airways Corporation, http://galenet.galegroup.com. ezproxy1.lib.asu.edu/servlet/BCRC.

7. S. Overby, 2002, JetBlue skies ahead, *CIO Magazine*, http://www. cio.com, July 1.

8. 2006, Airbus, http://www.airbus.com/en/aircraftfamilies/a320/a320/.

9. S. Overby, JetBlue skies ahead.

10. Ibid.

11. 2002, JetBlue announces second quarter 2002 earnings—Low-fare carrier achieves record operating margin of 18.6%, JetBlue Airways Corporation press release, July 25.

12. 2002, JetBlue announces initial public offering of its common stock, JetBlue Airways Corporation press release, April 11.

13. 2005, JetBlue's New Terminal 5 will more than double airline's JFK capacity within three years, JetBlue Airways Corporation press release, December 7.

14. 2006, Fourth quarter of 2005, JetBlue Airways Corporation press release, February 1.

15. 2006, Third quarter of 2006, JetBlue Airways Corporation press release, October 24.

16. Ibid.

17. J. Bailey, 2007, JetBlue's C.E.O. is mortified after fliers are stranded, *New York Times*, http://www.nytimes.com, February 19; T. Keenan, 2007, JetBlue damage control, http://www.foxnews. com, February 27.

18. 2007, JetBlue announces the JetBlue Customer Bill of Rights, JetBlue Airways Corporation press release, February 20.

19. 2006, Air transportation, scheduled, *Encyclopedia of American Industries,* online ed., Thomson Gale.

20. 2006, Hoover's Company Records, JetBlue Airways Corporation, October 31.

21. R. M. Schneiderman, 2006, Legacy carriers fly back into favor, *Forbes*, http://www.forbes.com, October 20.

22. 2006, Air transportation, scheduled.

23. J. Schoen, 2006, Airline woes spark industry dogfight, http://www .msnbc.com, July 31.

24. 2006, Star Alliance, http://www.staralliance.com/en/travellers/index .html.

25. K. Iatrou & N. Skourias, 2005, An attempt to measure the traffic impact of airline alliances, *Journal of Air Transportation*, 10(3): 73–99.

26. C. Jones, 2006, JetBlue seeks international partnerships, *Deseret News*, Salt Lake City, March 16.

27. D. Rosato, 2006, How to score a cheap airline ticket, *CNNMoney*, http://www.cnnmoney.com, October 27.

28. 2007, US Airways withdraws offer for Delta Air Lines, press release, http://www.usairways.com, January 31.

29. C. Palmeri, D. Frost, & L. Woellert, 2006, Doug Parker wants to fly Delta, *BusinessWeek*, http://www.businessweek.com, November 16.

30. 2006, Southwest Airlines Co. Annual Report.

31. W. Zellner, 2005, Southwest: Dressed to kill . . . competitors, *BusinessWeek*, February 21.

32. R. E. Hoskisson, M. A. Hitt, & R. D. Ireland, 2003, *Competing for Advantage*, Mason, OH: South-Western, 24.

33. D. Reed, 2006, At 35, Southwest's strategy gets more complicated, *USA Today*, July 11.

34. 2006, Hoover's Company Reports: In-depth records, AMR Corporation, November 28.

35. 2006, AMR Corp Annual Report.

36. 2006, Hoover's Company Reports: In-depth records, UAL Corporation, November 28.

37. Ibid.

38. R. M. Schneiderman, 2006, Report: UAL looking to merge, *Forbes*, December 1.

39. C. Palmeri, D. Frost, & L. Woellert, 2006, Doug Parker wants to fly Delta.

40. 2006, USAirways Group, Inc. Annual Report.

41. 2006, Airline Domestic Market Share: September 2005–August 2006, *Bureau of Transportation Statistics—The Intermodal Transportation Database,* http://www.transtats.bts.gov/, December 6.

42. 2006, Hoover's Company Reports: In-depth records, Continental Airlines Inc., November 28.

43. R. Fozard, 2006, Continental's surprising ascent, *BusinessWeek*, July 31.

44. R. M. Schneiderman, 2006, Continental packs 'em in, *Forbes*, October 19.

45. 2006, Congressional testimony, *Congressional Quarterly, Inc.,* February 8.

46. Ibid.

47. Ibid.

48. E. Roston, 2005, Hedging their costs: Whether oil prices go up or down, smart airline companies are covered, *Time,* July 27.

49. 2005, Oil prices will prune revenue gains but Southwest, JetBlue look good, *Airline Business Report*, July 4, 23(12).

50. 2007, FAA aerospace forecast fiscal years 2007–2020, http://www .faa.gov/data_statistics/.

51. 2006, JetBlue Airways Corporation Form 10-K, Fiscal year ending December 31, 21.

52. C. Jones, 2006, JetBlue founder pushes for alternative fuel, http:// www.timesdispatch.com, November 15.

53. K. Johnson, 2005, Fuel hedging gets tricky, *Wall Street Journal,* May 19.

54. 2005, JetBlue Airways Corporation Form 10-K, Fiscal year ending December 31, 4.

55. Ibid, 9.

56. 2006, *Wall Street Journal* (Eastern edition), November 22.

57. 2005, JetBlue Airways Corporation Form 10-K, Fiscal year ending December 31, 2.

58. 2000, http://www.house.gov/transportation/aviation/hearing/ 12-05-00/12-05-00memo.html.

59. D. Bond, 2006, The FAA's demand-management plans for LaGuardia call for bigger aircraft, market-based slot turnover, *Aviation Week & Space Technology*, September 4.

60. 2005, JetBlue Airways Corporation Form 10-K, Fiscal year ending December 31, 69.

61. S. Overby, 2002, JetBlue skies ahead.

62. S. Lott, 2006, IAM fails in first attempt to organize JetBlue ramp staff, *Aviation Daily*, July 20.

63. 2006, Significant safety events since 2000 for JetBlue Airlines, AirSafe.com, LLC, http://www.airsafe.com, May 6.

64. J. Scott, 2005, http://www.aerospaceweb.org/question/planes/ q0245a.shtml, October 2.

65. R. Singal, 2003, Army admits using JetBlue data, Wired News, http://www.wired.com, September 23.

66. 2002, United States District Court Eastern District of New York, Memorandum & Order, JetBlue Airways Corp: Privacy Litigation: 04-MD-1587 (CBA), http://www.epic.org/privacy/airtravel/jetblue/ decision_0705.pdf.

67. 2005, JetBlue Airways Corporation Form 10-K, Fiscal year ending December 31, 2.

68. 2006, JetBlue Announces 6.6 Percent Operating Margin for Third Quarter 2006, JetBlue Airways Corporation press release, October 24.

69. J. Miner, 2006, http://luxuryresorttravel.suite101.com/article/cfm./ jetblue_airways_pros_and_cons, November 13.

70. S. Salter, 2004, And now the hard part, *Fast Company*, http://www .fastcompany.com, May, 82: 67.

71. Ibid.
72. Ibid.
73. B. Harrell, 2005, http://www.yaleeconomicreview.com/issues/fall2005/davidneeleman.
74. 2005, JetBlue Airways Corporation Form 10-K, Fiscal year ending December 31, 3.
75. S. Overby, JetBlue skies ahead.
76. Ibid.
77. R. Valdes, How VoIP works, http://electronics.howstuffworks.com/ip-telephony.htm.
78. S. Salter, 2004, Calling JetBlue, *Fast Company*, http://www.fastcompany.com, May, 82.
79. 2005, JetBlue soars with Omniture Research Center, Omniture, Inc., http://www.omniture.com, December 2.
80. D. Sacks, 2006, Rehab: An advertising love story, *Fast Company*, http://www.fastcompany.com, June, 106.
81. Ibid.
82. B. Harrell, http://www.yaleeconomicreview.com/issues/fall2005/davidneeleman.
83. 2005, JetBlue Airways Corporation Form 10-K, Fiscal year ending December 31, 3.
84. D. Sacks, Rehab: An advertising love story.
85. 2006, XS Lighting & sound lights JetBlue interactive kiosks, *Prism Business Media*, http://www.livedesignonline.com, June 7.
86. K. Prentice, Your client's ad, taking it to the streets, *Media Life Magazine*, Http://www.medialifemagazine.com, May 15.
87. Ibid.
88. 2005, JetBlue announces first quarter results, JetBlue Airways Corporation press release, April 1.
89. 2006, JetBlue announces 6.6 percent operating margin for third quarter, JetBlue Airways Corporation press release, October 24.
90. 2005, JetBlue Airways Corporation Form 10-K, Fiscal year ending December 31, 10.
91. Ibid.
92. R. M. Schneiderman, 2006, JetBlue courts Corporate America, *Forbes*, August 11.
93. D. Neeleman, 2006, http://www.jetblue.com/about/ourcompany/flightlog, December 14.
94. 2005, Introducing JetBlue getaways, JetBlue Airways Corporation press release, November 3.
95. 2005, JetBlue Airways Corporation Form 10-K, Fiscal year ending December 31, 1.
96. 2006, JetBlue Airways Corporation Form 10-K, Fiscal year ending December 31, 19.
97. Financial Accounting Module 3.
98. 2005, JetBlue Airways Corporation Form 10-K, Fiscal year ending December 31, 17.
99. 2006, Industry data from www.moneycentral.msn.com.
100. 2006, Yahoo! Finance, http://finance.yahoo.com/q/hp?s=JBLU&a=03&b=18&c=2001&d=10&e=30&f=2006&g=m.
101. K. Prentice, 2006, After backing away, some airlines turning to fuel hedging again, Associated Press State & Local Wire, September 4.
102. S. Salter, On the runway, *Fast Company*, http://www.fastcompany.com, May (82).
103. S. Salter, And now the hard part, 67.
104. D. Reed, 2006, Loss shifts JetBlue's focus to climbing back into black, http://www.usatoday.com, Feb 22.
105. Ibid.
106. M. Bobelian, 2003, JetBlue lands expansion plans, *Forbes*, http://www.forbes.com, June 10.
107. T. Reed, 2006, TheStreet.com, http://www.thestreet.com/stocks/transportation/10260392.html, January 6.
108. 2006, *Aircraft Technology, Engineering & Maintenance*, October/November, 99.
109. 2005, McGraw-Hill Companies *Overhaul & Maintenance*, Magazine for MRO Management, October 2.
110. Ibid, 5.
111. 2006, JetBlue Airways Corporation, Form 10-Q, October 24.
112. *Aircraft Technology Engineering & Maintenance*, 101.
113. 2006, JetBlue Airways Corporation Form 10-K, Fiscal year ending December 31, 41.
114. T. Reed, http://www.thestreet.com.

George Griffith, Tiffany Johnson, Rebecca Sebald,
Tracey Cowan, Nick Trotter, and Alfred Wong

Arizona State University

*It's customers that made Dell great in the first place, and
if we're smart enough and quick enough to listen to customer
needs, we'll succeed.*

—**MICHAEL DELL**

Dell Inc., founded in 1984 by present CEO and chairman
of the board Michael Dell, is a leading technology
provider that designs, develops, manufactures, and
supports PCs, software and peripherals, storage and
servers, and associated services. The public company is
headquartered in Round Rock, Texas, with operations
in three geographic regions: the Americas; Europe, the
Middle East, and Africa (EMEA); and Asia Pacific–
Japan (APJ). Additionally Dell has business centers and
manufacturing sites in more than 20 locations around
the world. Dell operates primarily on a direct customer
sales business model that provides it with in-depth
customer knowledge so that solutions can be effectively
tailored to meet customer needs. Since its founding, Dell
has expanded its core business model by broadening its
product portfolio and adding distribution partners (retail,
value-added resellers, and distributors) that allowed Dell
to reach more than 24,000 retail locations worldwide in
FY09.[1]

Over the past two decades, Dell has been very
successful with the direct customer sales business model,
with an average annual revenue growth of 10 percent
annually. Dell shipped 43 million units in FY09 and held
a 15.1 percent share of the worldwide computer systems
market, enjoying 11.1 percent growth, which exceeded
industry worldwide computer systems growth of
9.7 percent (in terms of sales). In April 2008, Dell was the top
PC provider in the United States and second worldwide in
terms of sales; however, the top position in the United States
was overtaken by Hewlett-Packard (HP) in the first quarter
of 2009.[2] Revenue growth has stalled, with fiscal year 2009
(FY09 ending January 30) revenues of $61.101 billion

compared to FY08 revenues of $61.133 billion. PCs,
their largest product revenue stream, experienced a
12 percent decline. Dell's average selling price (total
revenue per unit sold) also decreased 7 percent year-
over-year, which is attributed to changes in revenue mix
from commercial to consumers, lower selling prices in
retail, and an increasingly competitive environment.
Amidst the economic downturn, corporate IT spending
continues to weaken, with worldwide PC shipments
declining 6.5 percent in the first quarter of 2009. With 80
percent of Dell's sales coming from corporate buyers, the
scaled-back spending has directly impacted Dell's market
share, with Dell shipping 16.7 percent fewer computers
worldwide in Q1 2009 versus Q1 2008.[3]

On December 31, 2008, Dell announced it would reorganize its business units from regional segments to four
globally operated areas—large enterprise, public sector,
small and medium businesses, and global consumer—to
better align with customer needs for "faster innovation
and globally standardized products and services."[4]

History of Dell Inc.

In 1984, while still a student at the University of Texas and
with only $1,000 to his name, Michael Dell founded PCs
Limited, the original name of Dell Inc., and introduced its
first computer, the Turbo, the following year. The company
changed its name to Dell Computer Corporation in 1988
and ultimately to Dell Inc. in 2004 to recognize its expansion beyond a PC-only business. Dell's Web site began
selling computers in 1996, and the company overtook
Compaq as the largest seller of PCs in the United States in
1999. In 2006, Dell acquired computer hardware manufacturer Alienware and both ASAP Software Express Inc. and
EqualLogic in 2008. Since its founding in 1984, Dell Inc.
has grown to employ approximately 78,900 employees.

Note: This case was written to be used as a basis for class discussion rather than to illustrate either effective or ineffective handling of an administrative situation.
We would like to thank Robert E. Hoskisson and Robert E. White for useful feedback in writing this case. Data was collected from publically available sources.

The early business model (1984–1990) was to assemble computers comparable to those of the more widely known IBM and target the price-conscious but tech-savvy consumer segment with lower prices. Dell was able to purchase parts and build their products in house, selling them at a fraction of the price that IBM could offer. It then took orders directly from customers (keeping advertising costs low), built the products to order (keeping inventory costs low), and provided a high level of customer service when delivering the end product.[5] Dell quickly moved into the top position in the direct-mail computer market, specializing in inexpensive PCs.[6] In 1984, Dell grossed $6 million in sales, increasing to $40 million the following year.

In order to sustain growth, the company brought the Tandy Group as consultants in 1987 to create a sales force focused on diversifying their customer base. While profits rose initially, Dell was unwilling to modify its direct customer sales business model to a more traditional sales approach with higher advertising spending and larger sales force, so most of the Tandy Group employees were released within the year. Around the same time, Dell opened new offices in London and Canada, allowing them to garner the attention of corporations, government, and educational consumers. This provided the foundation for the company to go public in June 1988, when they sold 3.5 million shares at $8.50 a share.[7]

Shortly after going public, Dell faced severe competition from several Japanese manufacturers offering similar products at lower prices. In response, Dell increased R&D spending and hired a computer scientist from IBM to manage the R&D staff and increase the technological sophistication of their product offerings. Dell also faced massive holding costs due to underestimating the change in demand the Japanese competition brought. Dell, in fact, had increased capacity substantially to accommodate the previously increasing demand, which resulted in unsold inventory.

To improve its management processes, Dell increased its emphasis on the corporate customer which resulted in a large increase in sales from the corporate segment, from 15 percent of sales in 1987 to 40 percent in 1990.[8] From 1990 to 2000, Dell opened new offices in Italy, France, and Ireland, allowing them to serve Europe, the Middle East, and Africa's larger corporations, offering powerful server solutions. At this time, they also worked to diversify their sales channels by introducing their products in large computer retail stores. As a result, Dell became the sixth-largest PC producer in the United States, and the focus on customer service earned them a #1 rating in J.D. Power and Associates's first survey of PC customer satisfaction.[9] By 1991, Dell had their first laptop PC available for purchase to cater to the fastest-growing segment of the PC market.

In response to the recession and ongoing price wars with PC makers Compaq, IBM, and Apple, Dell made steep price cuts, lowering their profit margins dramatically. Compaq, in particular, had released a lower-end PC that was priced competitively while offering increased customer service, which appealed to Dell's target consumers. Within the next few years, Dell also expanded their product portfolio to include fax machines and compact discs.

In the mid 1990s, "Dell introduced a line of network servers and was soon the fastest-growing company in the server sector."[10] Shortly thereafter, the company implemented an online channel for consumers to place their orders directly. They also strengthened their market position by opening a manufacturing plant in Malaysia. In the late 1990s, they began producing workstations and storage products as well as offering a leasing program that allowed customers to avoid maintaining a system as it became older and more obsolete. In 1998, they built a production and sales facility in China, further extending their global presence. Their final undertakings in the 1990s were to offer Internet access, Dellnet, to their customers as well as adding manufacturing plants in the United States and Brazil.[11] For the fiscal year ending in January 2000, Dell reported net income of $1.86 billion on total revenues of $25 billion.

In the first decade of the twenty-first century, Dell's strategy continued to develop. In late 2001, Dell introduced a new line of products, PowerConnect, which allowed consumers to network within a small business environment. In 2003, they launched their Axim line of handheld computers to compete with competitors' PDAs. In efforts to retain and attract new consumers, Dell set up kiosks in retail shopping malls, opened their first Dell location within a Sears store, created an online music service, and introduced their first line of printers.[12] Dell's diversification, coupled with large increases in shipments of high-profit-margin products such as servers, notebook computers, and storage equipment, propelled the company to new heights in 2004.[13] This diversification allowed annual net income to increase to $2.65 billion. Dell also had an interest in the growing Chinese market and began increasing their presence in rural Chinese areas, capitalizing on subsidies farmers received and has allowed Dell to weather the current tough economic times and boost sales.[14]

Despite the success of the direct sales model, Michael Dell realized the company must keep pace with shifting consumer sentiment and market conditions. Dell told *Forbes* in 2007 that "the old model ran its course, now it's time for a new course."[15] With eyes on the consumer market offering new channels of distribution, Dell brought on a new executive group to accomplish this goal.

Competitive Situation

Key Competitors

Dell faces stiff competition within the computer hardware industry. According to IDC, for Q1 2009, the top five PC shipment vendors worldwide are (in rank order): HP, Dell, Acer, Lenovo, and Toshiba (for U.S. PC shipments, Apple replaces Lenovo as fourth place).[16] For the enterprise market, Dell's standardized desktops and laptops remain the most popular among North American and European enterprises and are a clear leader over HP and Lenovo.[17] Market share data can be found in Exhibits 1 through 3 and competitor revenues from geographic regions can be found in Exhibit 4. The following key competitors will be discussed in order: Acer, HP, Apple, and Lenovo.

Acer Group. Founded in 1977, Acer Group is a Taiwanese company competing with Dell in the desktop PC, notebook computer, server, displays, and information technology (IT) solutions segments. Acer's portfolio of brands includes Gateway and eMachines, which were acquired in October 2007, as well as Packard Bell.

In the first quarter of 2009, Acer had sales of US $3.4 billion, which was down from $3.9 billion in the same quarter in 2008.[18] Their strongest sales came from the EMEA (Europe, Middle East, Africa), where they earned 49 percent of their revenue in the first quarter of 2009. They are the leading manufacturer of notebook computers in the EMEA, with a 26.6 percent market share. In the United States, Acer is the third-ranked maker of both PCs and notebooks with 13.6 percent and 16.8 percent market shares, respectively. Worldwide, for PCs and notebooks, they rank third and second,

Exhibit 1 Worldwide PC Shipments in 2008—Market Share

PC OEM	Market Share	YoY Growth
HP	19.2%	12.7%
Dell	15%	11%
Acer	10.9%	53.3%
Lenovo	7.4%	8.3%
Toshiba	4.6%	25.1%
Others	43%	1.3%

WW PC Shipments 2008

Source: IDC

Exhibit 2 U.S. PC Shipments in 2008—Market Share

PC OEM	Market Share	YoY Growth
Dell	29.5%	3.3%
HP	24.9%	1.8%
Acer	9.1%	62.1%
Apple	7.7%	25.7%
Toshiba	5.5%	7.6%
Others	23.4%	−16%

U.S. PC Shipments 2008

Source: IDC

respectively, with 12.8 percent and 19.6 percent market shares. Notebook sales accounted for 68 percent of their revenue in FY 09 Q1, while PCs accounted for 17 percent, displays 12 percent, and other segments 3 percent.[19]

Acer Group CEO J. T. Wang defines Acer's corporate sustainability as, "A successful global IT company which achieves in triple bottom lines, meaning, outstanding and balanced performance in the economy, environment and society."[20] Most recently, Acer has launched a set of new core values as described by CEO Wang: "The pillars on which we must base our actions include: value-creating, customer-centric, ethical and caring. The way we must act should be: innovative, fast and effective." [21]

Acer has been focusing on the execution of the October 2007 acquisition of Gateway and eMachines by positioning and uniquely segmenting each brand. Acer, which is not known for its direct customer selling, has been evaluating this strategy. However, Gateway has long had a similar direct-selling strategy to Dell but has failed to execute it as effectively. Acer's strategy is to segment their customers based on their needs and tailor one of their brands to meet those needs. Gianfranco Lanci, Acer's president and CEO, stated, "Our channel strategy will be very different from our competitors. The market is changing where users have different needs for our products. We do not want to confuse our customers and think that multiple branding is the future."[22]

Hewlett-Packard. Hewlett-Packard (HP), founded in 1936 and based in the United States, competes directly with Dell in almost every category.[23] HP holds the top position globally in the PC segment with 19 percent market share and recently overtook the top spot in the United States. HP's highest margin business

Exhibit 3 Enterprise Laptop and Desktop Market

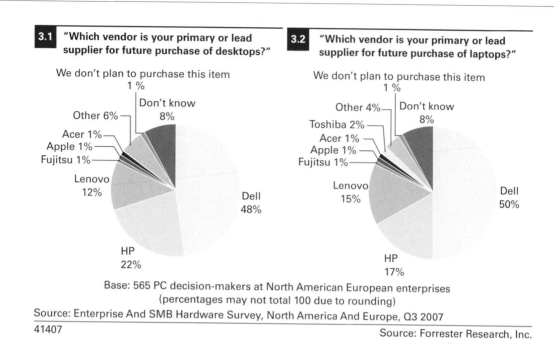

3.1 "Which vendor is your primary or lead supplier for future purchase of desktops?"

We don't plan to purchase this item 1%
Don't know 8%
Other 6%
Acer 1%
Apple 1%
Fujitsu 1%
Lenovo 12%
Dell 48%
HP 22%

3.2 "Which vendor is your primary or lead supplier for future purchase of laptops?"

We don't plan to purchase this item 1%
Other 4%
Don't know 8%
Toshiba 2%
Acer 1%
Apple 1%
Fujitsu 1%
Lenovo 15%
Dell 50%
HP 17%

Base: 565 PC decision-makers at North American European enterprises
(percentages may not total 100 due to rounding)
Source: Enterprise And SMB Hardware Survey, North America And Europe, Q3 2007

41407

Source: Forrester Research, Inc.

has been the imaging and printing business, which contributed 36 percent of earnings but only represented 25 percent of revenues.[24] Their 2008 revenues were $118.4 billion, up from $104 billion in 2007, and break down as follows among their core businesses: Personal

Exhibit 4 Percentage of Revenue by Global Regions and Competitor

	% Sales by Region (2008)		
Provider	**Americas**	**EMEA**	**APJ**
Dell[?]	47%	22%	12%
Lenovo	28%	22%	50%
HP	42%	42%	16%
Apple*	45%	23%	12%
Acer**	30%	49%	21%

[?]Dell's other operating segment, Global Consumer, accounts for 19% of sales and operates globally.

*Apple's other operating segment, Retail, accounts for 20% of sales and consists of locations in America and International.

**Acer figures based on Q1 2009 results and not annual due to limited availability of information.

Systems Group (PC and handheld devices segment) 35 percent, Imaging and Printing 25 percent, HP Services 19 percent, Enterprise Storage and Solutions 16 percent, HP Software 2 percent, HP Financial Services 2 percent, and Corporate Investments 1 percent.[25] By geographic regions, HP receives 42 percent of its revenue from the Americas (United States, Canada, Latin America), 42 percent from the EMEA, and 16 percent from Asia Pacific. EMEA shows the highest growth, with revenues up 22 percent in 2008 compared to 2007.[26]

In August 2008, HP acquired Electronic Data Services (EDS) for $13 billion, adding strength to their services business. EDS also expanded the breadth of products and services HP offers and gave potential customers, both businesses and at-home consumers, the ability to meet all of their needs. HP is currently going through a four-year restructuring project to improve its efficiency and seek financial savings through shared costs among its business units, and has released plans to cut 24,700 employees from its global workforce.[27]

HP's strategy moving forward is to serve as their corporate customers' only resource for everything IT related. As Mark V. Hurd, the chairman, CEO, and president of HP, stated in the 2008 annual report, "Enterprises are straining to meet ever-growing demand with aging, complex, proprietary and inefficient IT infrastructures. These dynamics are creating a massive disruption in the

IT marketplace and a massive opportunity for HP. With a comprehensive portfolio of hardware, software, and services, HP is well positioned to help customers manage and transform their IT environments."[28]

In their largest revenue business, the PC segment, they are trying to revamp stale sales by introducing new sleek touchscreen computers.[29] "HP is offering the assistance of hardware and software consultants from its services division to help customers come up with new uses for touch technology."[30] As part of this strategy, HP has partnered with Chicago's O'Hare airport and placed 50 touchscreens for patrons to use to access maps and local information. HP is hoping to increase sales from the 400,000 units sold in 2008.

Apple. Apple entered the computer industry in 1976 and has evolved its business strategies of brand loyalty, innovation, marketing advantage, and end-to-end user experience over the past 30 years. In 1998, Apple CEO Steve Jobs took note that their products integrated with very few of the industry standard peripherals, operating systems, and applications, threatening isolation. Jobs decided to adjust their business strategy to focus on product differentiation with offerings that were user friendly, attractively designed, well supported, and comprehensive using Apple products that address specific user needs. The iMac, introduced in 1998, had these qualities and was the catalyst for a turnaround in the company's performance.

While prices of Macs (Apple's computers) are generally more expensive than those of competitors, Apple's competitive strategy is basic: "make the best product possible, and rewards will follow."[31] Without the need to maintain a cost leadership position in the market, Apple is able to focus on differentiating its product, focusing on innovation to cater to the user experience.[32] On average historically, Apple spends 4 to 5 percent of its revenue on R&D, compared to 1 percent by competitors, including Dell.[33] Their current product portfolio now includes iPhones, Macs, notebooks, and iPods, as well as accessories for these core items. Diversification and user-centric design have allowed Apple to hedge the risk of substitutes and to enter markets without excessive marketing expenses traditionally required to target specific market segments or user groups. While Macs currently account for fewer than 5 percent of corporate desktops, many companies responding to an Information Technology Industry Council (ITIC) survey indicate that they are likely to let employees select Macs as business workstations within the next year.[34]

Apple continues to focus on controlling costs through efficient operations. In 2008, Apple outsourced much of its transportation and logistics management outside of the United States. This was done to control costs at the potential risk of losing direct control over production and distribution, potentially compromising quality and quantity of products, and limiting response flexibility to changing market conditions.[35] In 2008, Apple earned first place in the Supply Chain Top 25 ranking by AMR Research. AMR Research stated, "Behind-the-scenes moves like tying up essential components well in advance and upgrading basic information systems have enabled Apple to handle the demands of its rabid fan base without having to fall back on their forgiveness for mistakes."[36]

Apple's total net sales of domestic and international products increased 68 percent from FY06 to FY08 to $32.5 billion while cost of sales increased 50 percent to $4.8 billion.[37] The ratio between domestic and international sales has remained relatively consistent FY06 through FY08, with 43 percent of sales revenue being generated outside of the United States in 2008.[38] Despite strained economic times, Apple's earnings per common share continues to increase year over year. With 31,010 regular employees worldwide in 2008, Apple resource numbers continue to grow as well as research and development expenses (3 percent of net sales in 2008 which is below its historical average).[39]

Lenovo. Founded in 1984, Hong Kong–based Lenovo Legend Group is the largest computer producer in Asia and retains approximately 24,000 employees worldwide. Lenovo acquired IBM's personal computer business in 2005, creating the third-largest personal computer company in the world at the time. Lenovo has been listed on the Stock Exchange of Hong Kong since 1994 and currently controls 25 percent of the Asian computer market due to cost leadership and entry barriers to the Chinese market historically caused by high import tariffs.

Lenovo boasts a "worldsourcing" business model that distributes management, operations, and production into global "hubs of excellence." Strategies for growth in 2009 are outlined to include streamlining and improving the global supply chain and logistics network to control costs, growing customer intimacy to better understand consumer demands, PC focus on workstations and servers, increasing scale to appreciate benefits of economic efficiencies, and building brand recognition and loyalty.[40] Lenovo's product offerings are similar to Dell's (PCs, notebooks, servers, peripherals, and support services), however, it does not offer adjacent product lines (i.e., entertainment, telecommunications, TV), which competitors have begun to offer to hedge the risk of substitute products.

In 2008, Lenovo launched a backwards integration strategy into its supply chain in order to eliminate third parties from the manufacturing process.[41] This move into vertically shoring up its supply chain is aimed at reducing supplier power, thereby increasing control over quality and ability to implement design changes more quickly.

Lenovo sales decreased from FY07 to FY08 (FY ends March 31) by more than 20 percent while operating expenses decreased less than 9 percent.[42] Research and development expenses increased 17.1 percent, indicating a growing focus on innovation and product enhancements. The majority of sales, driven by China, account for nearly 40 percent of total sales while less than 30 percent of sales occur in the United States. Asia Pacific, Europe, Middle East, and Africa account for the remaining 30 percent of sales.

Customer Segments

As alluded to above, Dell serves four main customer segments—Home Users, Large Enterprise, Small and Medium Businesses (SMB), and Public Sector.[43] The segmentation is based on the different needs of each customer sector. As Michael Dell describes it, "Customer requirements are increasingly being defined by how they use technology rather than where they use it. That's why we won't let ourselves be limited by geographic boundaries in solving their needs."[44]

Home Users

The Home Users segment addresses all personal usage of computers and has traditionally been a smaller market than the commercial space. Of all computers shipped worldwide, approximately 75 percent are used professionally while 25 percent are for personal or home use.[45] Despite being a smaller market, the consumer segment "has the potential to expand faster than [Dell's] business with corporations and government agencies."[46]

Large Enterprise

Dell has identified Facebook, Microsoft, Amazon, Akamai, and Baidu as key customers in the corporate servers and data center business segment.[47] The needs of Large Enterprise customers vary from business to business across solutions for data storage, networking, security, or hardware procurement. Being the largest buyers in the IT industry, enterprise customers can demand customized solutions catered to their specific needs. However, with a large amount of resources invested with a specific IT vendor, it is not easy to switch to another vendor without incurring significant change and costs. Curiously, some of Dell's corporate customers also happen to be key vendors, which makes managing "these relationships [a] little challenging," according to

Dell's CIO Jerry Gregoire.[48] Enterprise IT spending is expected to remain flat for 2009.[49]

Small and Medium Business

Unlike large enterprises, SMBs do not have a large amount of resources dedicated for IT needs. In fact, the person responsible for IT is often "one of the founding members who is juggling many roles—CFO, sales manager, marketing guy, and so on."[50] Dell has traditionally been a strong player in the SMB market by comprehensively managing SMB's IT needs so the dedicated IT resource can focus on other roles. Dell understands that "SMBs are far more sensitive to cost issues because if their computers are down, that might be all of their systems," as opposed to large enterprises, which would have redundant backup systems with a dedicated IT staff resolving any issues.[51] By having multi-tier service offerings, Dell is able to potentially have more than 72 million SMB customers worldwide.[52] Analysts suggest that SMBs will spend double what big business spends in 2009. HP forecasts show that SMB is "one of the fastest growing IT market opportunities, with 4 to 7 percent growth expected in 2009 for a total available market opportunity of $68 billion."[53] Despite the economic slowdown, competitors such as HP, Lenovo, and Toshiba have all announced plans to target the SMB market in 2009.

Public Sector

In the Public Sector customer segment, Dell has identified government, education, and health care as areas of strategic focus.[54] For these customers, Dell is committed to providing simplified and standardized solutions to satisfy any of their IT requirements. Besides competing in the above segments, Dell is experiencing other competitive issues associated with these segments.

Additional Competitive Issues

Dell offers a broad range of product categories, including mobility products, desktop PCs, software and peripherals, servers and networking, services, and storage.[55] Due to the rapid technological innovations in computer electronics and the high level of dependency of many businesses and home users, there are no clear, direct substitute products for Dell's product portfolio.

While there are no imminent threats from substitute products, there is increasing competition from new entrants in the Home Users market segment. Witnessing the success of new entrants from Taiwan and Japan such as Acer, Asus, Toshiba, and Fujitsu in the late 1990s and early 2000s, many electronics manufacturers continue to attempt to enter the computer manufacturing market. For example, Micro Electronics Inc., the parent company of the computer retailer Micro Center, started selling an in-house line of laptops known as Winbook in 2004.[56,57] Other electronics manufacturers such as Archos, maker of portable DVD players, made its entry into the portable computing market in 2009 with its Archos 10 netbook.[58] Bigger brands such as Samsung, which is famous for its cell phones, LCD monitors, and TVs, also entered the Home User market with its line of laptops. It is expected that more electronics makers will try to leverage their brand name and enter the home computing market. Furthermore, as the younger population becomes more tech savvy, possible "new entrants" are home or small PC makers that purchase stock parts directly and assemble a customized machine themselves or for a small fee. Ironically, this is how Dell was first founded 25 years ago.[59]

On the other hand, the commercial and public sector markets are experiencing a wave of consolidation. This is evident through major strategic decisions in the industry such as HP's merger with Compaq, Acer's acquisition of Gateway, and IBM's decision to exit the hardware market and focus on IT services. However, there are new competitors in the server market, including producers of supplier products. For example, Cisco systems has signaled that it will enter the server market to more fully serve corporate data centers, which often require integrated solutions based on multiple products.[60]

Economic Downturn and Other Challenges

Dell faces significant challenges in the midst of the current economic recession. Gartner Research predicts the worst-case scenario for IT spending in 2009 will be no growth in the United States, and IT expenditures are expected to shrink in Europe.[61] Forrester Research analyst Andrew Bartels further predicts "the brunt of the slowdown in IT spending will hit servers and PCs,"[62] which is Dell's primary market. In the Home User market, households are reducing their discretionary spending and will opt for low cost PCs with the bare minimum number of features, which may impact Dell's product lineup.

In this difficult economic environment, supplier and customer insolvency is plausible and may result in product delays and reduced demand. Dell also faces risks on the global front due to its international exposure. In FY09, "sales outside the U.S. accounted for approximately 48 percent of [Dell's] consolidated net revenue." Changes in the U.S. monetary policy as well as economic policies around the world may lead to volatile exchange rates, exposing Dell to currency risks despite its foreign currency hedging program.

Also, government and environmental groups have called for corporations to become more "green" and energy efficient. Dell is an industry leader in this area, as it announced in August 2008 that it has "reached its goal of becoming 'carbon neutral' five months ahead of schedule."[63] While Dell's claim of "carbon neutrality" has been questioned by journalists, Dell is at least taking proactive steps to "set an example by reducing its environmental impact as responsibly and aggressively as it can."[64] Dell's reliance on renewable energy as well as being more energy efficient are estimated to save the company $3 million a year. Dell has also demonstrated itself to be a responsible corporate citizen by participating in programs such as (PRODUCT)RED™, where Dell contributes a part of the proceeds for each product sold associated with the program to a global fund to combat AIDS in Africa.[65]

Other regulatory and legal challenges remain. While Dell is not currently involved in any antitrust lawsuits, its suppliers, such as Microsoft and more recently Intel, have been fined for anti-competitive practices.[66] This can present challenges to Dell as these rulings may affect its pricing arrangements with suppliers as well as how Dell conducts its operations, particularly in Europe.

Finally, on the technological front, computer companies are watching the trend towards mobile computing. Analysts at IDC report that "laptops will overtake desktop PCs as the dominant form of computer in 2011."[67] Despite the economic downturn, IDC expects strong growth in the market of low-cost, small form-factor laptops known as netbooks. The proliferation of wireless infrastructure will also make "Portable PCs as part of a digital lifestyle, rather than just computing device, [which will] sustain growth in both Consumer and Commercial segments."[68] While Dell introduced the Dell Inspirion Mini series in the netbook market in September 2008, it is a follower in this market behind other companies such as Asus's EeePC and Acer's Aspire One.[69]

Dell's Segment Growth Strategies

Upon returning to Dell as CEO in January 2007, Michael Dell resumed control of a company showing signs of struggle in multiple areas including customer service, product quality, and the overall effectiveness of its direct sales model.[70] These issues caused Dell to lose market share to its major rivals. As a first step, Michael Dell identified five large growth areas with at least $5 billion of potential new revenue and reorganized the company around them.[71] The five focus areas for Dell's operations are "consumer business, mobile computers, emerging countries, enterprise, and small/medium business."[72] Dell has also identified and implemented additional company-wide strategic and cost cutting initiatives.

Dell's current strategic initiatives within the consumer market include providing technologically advanced differentiated products that can support price premiums in order to increase profit margins, rapidly detecting shifts in consumer preferences in order to reduce product development time, and increasing distribution via retail channels.

Within the consumer market, Dell is actively seeking to move upmarket to attract technologically savvy customers who are willing to pay a premium to have the newest and best technologies.[73] To support this migration, Dell's products must provide technological superiority compared to its competitors. Dell has increased research and development spending 39.1 percent in 2008 ($693M) versus 2007 ($495M) to facilitate the development of differentiated products.

Dell's historical direct sales model has provided the company with the potential to gather consumer sentiment information directly from consumers rather than through a third-party reseller. Dell is seeking to leverage its direct sales model to detect shifts in consumer preferences earlier than competitors in order to reduce new product development time. Both benefits increase Dell's pricing power and competitive advantage. CEO Michael Dell sees Dell's ability to sense rapidly changing consumer preferences as one of the company's largest potential strategic advantages.[74]

Dell is also seeking to diversify its distribution channels beyond direct sales in an effort to remain competitive as consumers increasingly show preference for shopping for computers at retailers where they can directly compare multiple models.[75] In addition, Dell is able to reach more customers worldwide than would otherwise be possible with a direct-only model. In 2007, Dell began offering its computers at retail outlets ranging from domestic retailers (i.e., Wal-Mart and Staples) to chains in Japan, China, Russia, and the United Kingdom. By 2009, Dell had expanded its retail operations to include 24,000 outlets worldwide. Dell's efforts have led to an 11 percent revenue growth within this segment from 2007 to 2008, a reversal from the 6 percent decrease Dell experienced in 2007. This turnaround in revenue suggests that Dell's efforts directed at the consumer market are having early success.

In regard to mobile computing, the entire computer market is undergoing a gradual transition to more mobility-based computing products. In Q3 of 2008, laptops outsold traditional desktop computers for the first time.[76] Dell's strategic efforts within the mobile computing market include creating new platforms to better meet new consumer and business-user needs in terms of performance, size, weight, and price. To do this, it has separated the product design function for consumer and commercial markets. This strategic change has enabled Dell to produce multiple new product platforms specialized for both consumer and commercial markets, including the Inspirion Mini 3G that targets the rapidly expanding netbook consumer market, and the Latitude XT-2 tablet PC and new thinner and lightweight E-series Latitude laptop for the commercial markets.

In emerging markets, Dell's strategy is to focus on providing region-specific products to meet the needs of emerging markets, particularly in Brazil, Russia, India, and China (BRIC countries). Typically, customers in these markets need a low-cost PC that provides the basic PC functionality, including web-surfing, e-mail, and word processing.[77] Dell has introduced the Vostro-A line of desktop and laptop computers that are specifically focused on the needs of price-sensitive customers within the BRIC market. Dell's marketing and product development efforts targeting BRIC customers have led to 20 percent sales growth within the BRIC market.[78]

Dell provides value to its largest customers by helping them to "simplify their IT environments."[79] To reduce the cost and complexity of large enterprise IT systems, Dell seeks to partner with customers to provide customized solutions including servers, storage, software, and support services. In this way, Dell is potentially building long-term relationships with its most important customers. These complementary products, solutions, and services provide a consistent revenue stream in addition to Dell's traditional hardware lines.

Dell is also seeking to be an innovator in hardware and software products that enable Net 2.0 companies, such as Microsoft, Amazon.com, and Google, as well as "cloud computing" initiatives where companies deliver hosted services over the Internet, usually on a subscription or license basis.[80] These companies are building massive computer networks that require a significant number of servers and IT infrastructure to support their businesses.[81] Michael Dell believes that Dell has "created a whole new business just to build custom products for those customers."[82] He also goes on to state that "now it's a several-hundred-million-dollar business and it will be a billion-dollar business in a couple of years."[83] Supporting these companies with technologically advanced solutions is strategically important to Dell maintaining its leadership in this market.

Similar to the strategy for large enterprise, Dell's small/medium business strategy is to provide the "simplest and most complete IT solution customized for their [specific] needs."[84] To do this, Dell offers a complete line of fully customizable desktop and laptop computers and servers as well as consulting and support services for this market which provide additional revenue streams beyond traditional hardware lines.

In 2008, Dell acquired EqualLogic, Inc. an industry leader in iSCSI SAN storage devices, a key technology for small and medium business customers.[85] Dell executives expect this acquisition to allow them to offer a broader array of storage products specifically tailored for this market. Dell also launched the "Dell Download Store" to enable small and medium-sized businesses to directly obtain third-party software solutions from Dell's Web site.[86]

Dell offers a full set of consulting and support services to support small and medium businesses throughout the product life cycle, including "Dell Pro-Manage" services, which provide "a team that proactively monitors your entire Dell or non-Dell IT infrastructure to prevent downtime before it starts."[87] Dell also makes "a la carte" services available, including services to prevent or address technical problems or hardware failures, protection services for both hardware and data theft, and pre-sale consulting services and IT infrastructure installation.

Cost Initiatives

In addition to strategic efforts aimed at growth, Dell has undertaken a massive cost-cutting campaign to drive down costs while maintaining its supply chain and production cost advantages over its competitors. Dell's current cost-cutting initiative seeks to cut $4 billion in costs by end of FY 2011. They are focused on costs of goods sold (COGS) and Operating Expenses (OpEx), specifically "design-to-value" or designing products that optimize their manufacturing and logistics supply chain as well as reducing total headcount in its sales organization as more and more of its sales are originating from third-party retailers.[88] In design-to-value, "33 percent of the business client and 57 percent of the consumer platforms have been redesigned and cost optimized which now equates to more than 50 percent of [Dell's] total [product] volume."[89] These redesigns led to a 10 percent reduction in average cost per unit in the past 12 months. As Dell's competitors provide pressure to drive down prices, cost initiatives are critical to its competitiveness in the global market for computers and IT equipment.[90]

Changes in Supply Chain Management and Manufacturing

As a computer manufacturer, Dell's manufacturing plants perform computer assembly operations on parts supplied by other companies. These parts could range from instruction manuals to optical drives, which Dell procures and assembles into a final product for its customers. To provide a quality product to its customers, Dell interacts with a large number of suppliers for its many different needs.

To maintain supplier flexibility and manage supplier bargaining power, Dell maintains strategic partnership with a large number of suppliers, procuring parts from multiple sources. While some parts can be easily shipped, Dell requires suppliers of some parts, such as computer motherboards, to be located nearby.[91] Because Dell is often one of their largest customers, Dell's suppliers often open facilities within a 20-mile radius of Dell manufacturing plants. These include Eagle Global Logistics and Cerqa Copyright, which handle computer parts and components and manuals and software, respectively. Due to the oligopolistic/monopolistic nature of the high-tech industry, Dell is forced to contract exclusively with a few suppliers who have control over key capabilities in the value chain. For example, Dell deals almost exclusively with Intel and Microsoft as its suppliers of microprocessors and operating systems. However, Dell is also investigating opportunities with other suppliers. Dell has begun shipping servers equipped with the Linux operating system rather than Microsoft Windows, and while currently Dell only offers "one AMD (Advanced Micro Devices) desktop but no AMD notebooks … a year from now, it's probably going to be different," states Darrel Ward, Dell's director of product management for its business client product group.[92]

As part of its business strategy, Dell has a Supplier Diversity program where "Dell relies on the diversity of its personnel, suppliers … to maximize innovation, growth, competitiveness, and customer satisfaction."[93] This program has earned Dell the number two ranking on DiversityBusiness.com's list of Top 50 Organizations for Multicultural Business Opportunities, which cites, "supplier diversity is a global concern as the leading global systems and services company relies on a worldwide network of quality suppliers to help it build all the products it ships around the globe."[94] Dell also exemplifies industrial leadership in managing supplier relationship by recognizing and rewarding its top suppliers at its annual Worldwide Procurement Supplier Awards. Each year, six suppliers receive awards across the categories of Best Quality, Global Citizenship, Service, Diversity, General Procurement, and Best Overall Supplier.[95]

As noted, Dell has historically utilized a build-to-order approach to supply chain management with a just-in-time manufacturing model where unit pieces were manufactured and stored in inventory but were not pieced together until a consumer request was issued. While this methodology rarely affords the opportunity to maximize economies of scale, it does maintain a low inventory holding cost. In May 2007, Dell began its transition into the retail market when it began selling PCs through Wal-Mart and Sam's Club. Early in 2009, Mike Gray, supply chain director for Dell, made the decision to transition the build-to-order model over to an industry standard build-to-stock methodology to offset increasing manufacturing costs and logistical complexities.[96] This meant that PC units would be put together prior to a custom order in an attempt to decrease costs and compete with other companies selling stock items.

Dell is in the process of moving manufacturing operations from Ireland to Poland in order to better serve customers in Europe, the Middle East, and Africa. With the transition they will be able to automate work and reduce the necessary labor force by 1,900 employees.[97] Pieces of the historically integrated and tightly controlled manufacturing and supply chain process are being outsourced to continue to maintain profits as the profit margin decreases.

Product Lines and Services

Dell offers solutions for PCs, mobility, software, peripherals, storage, and networking servers as well as services. Dell's service offerings include infrastructure consulting, deployment service, asset recovery and recycling, product training, support, and IT management outsourced services. Dell also offers financial services for training and advising on consumer and enterprise financing opportunities. Exhibits 5 through 7 provide a detailed description of Dell's product and service offerings.

The desktop Personal Computer (PC), the flagship product line for Dell since 1984, has traditionally been their largest product revenue stream. Throughout the 1990s, Dell continued to reinvent its PC line with bigger hard drives, faster processors, and better user experiences that cater to several different target market groups. Today, the PC product line includes:

Exhibit 5 Home Office/Consumer Product Comparison

Product Offering	Description	Target Market	Notebooks	Retail Price	Desktops	Retail Price (excludes monitors)	Sales Rep Notes
Inspiron Mini	Consumer Notebook	Cost Leadership, Travel and Portability	Mini9, Mini10, Mini12	$250–$400	None	—	Good for travel and highly portable. Very small screen with small memory but lightweight with good processing speed.
Inspiron	Consumer Desktop and Notebook	Mainstream Consumers	Inspiron13, Inspiron 14, Inspiron15	$350–$700	Inspiron530s, Inspiron 530, Inspiron 531, Inspiron 537s, Inspiron 537	$260–$350	Significantly slower than XPS and more for home use than office.
Studio	High Performance Desktop and Notebook	Enthusiast-Hi Tech Consumer	Studio15, Studio17	$600–$700	Studio Hybrid, Studio Slim, Studio Desktop, Studio One 19	$400–$500	Pre-loaded with antivirus and anti-spyware software.
XPS & Alienware	High end design with unique multimedia capability, high performance gaming systems rivaling HPs gaming division.	Gamers and Innovation Seekers	XPS M1730, XPS 1530, XPS M1330, Studio XPS 13, Studio XPS 16, M17, M15x	$750–$2,000	Studio XPS, XPS ONE, Studio XPS 435, XPS 625, XPS 630, XPS 730x, Alienware ALX X-58	$700–$3,700	Popular with gamers who especially respect the Alienware line. Very competitive against any Gateway and HP products. Great video cards with RunFast software. The newer XPS systems run the latest I7 processor technology.

Source: Dell Web site, http://www.dell.com/; Best Buy Interview performed May 26, 2009, with two customer specialists.

Exhibit 6 Business/Corporate Product Comparison

Product Offering	Description	Target Market	Notebooks	Retail Price	Desktops	Retail Price (excludes monitors)
OptiPlex	Office Desktop	Business, Government, Institutional Users	None	—	360, 740, 760, 960, 160	$300–$850
Vostro	Small Business Desktop and Notebook	Small Business	A90, A860, 1520, 1720, 1320, E5400	$300–$730	220 Mini Tower, 220s Slim Tower, 420 Tower	$300–$530
Latitude	Commercial Enterprise Notebooks	Business, Government, Institutional Users	E5400, E5500, D630, E6400, E6500, E4200, E4300, XT2, E6400 ATG, E6400 XFR	$750–$1,800	None	—
Precision	High performance Notebooks and Desktops	Working Professionals	M2400, M4400, M6400, M6400 Covet	$1,400–$3,400	T3500, T3400, T5500, T5400, T7500, T7400	$750–$1,800

Source: Dell Web site, http://www.dell.com/.

Exhibit 7 Network Server and Storage Solution Comparison

Product Offering	Description	Target Market	Model	Retail Price
PowerEdge Tower Server	Business Server	Cost Leadership	T105, T100, 840, T300, T605, 2900 III, T1610	$400–$1,000
PowerEdge Rack Server	Business Server	Cost Leadership	R200, R300, SC1435, 1950 III, R805, 2950 III, 2970, R905, R900, R710, R610	$650–$3,800
PowerEdge Blade Server	Business Server	Cost Leadership	M605, M600, M805, M905, M1000e, M710, M610	$1,000–$1,800
PowerEdge Rack Infrastructure	Business Server	Cost Leadership	2410, 2420, 4220	$600–$1,000
PowerVault	Direct Attach Storage and Some Network-Attached Storage	Limited Storage, Cost Advantage	MD 1000, MD 1120 DAS, MD 3000 DAS	$2,600–$5,500
PowerConnect	Network Switches	High Quality, Product Differentiation	>51 models	$300–$3,000
Dell/EMC	Storage Area Networks	Mid-level Enterprise Storage	>51 models	$2,000–$4,000

Source: Dell Web site, http://www.dell.com/.

- The **XPS™** and **Alienware** lines targeted at customers seeking innovative designs that cater to user experience.
- The **OptiPlex™** line, which was developed for business, government, and institutional users that are concerned with controlling costs while maintaining security.
- The **Inspiron™** line, which is designed for "mainstream PC users requiring the latest features for their productivity and entertainment needs."
- The **Vostro™** line, launched in July 2007, which caters to the needs of small businesses.
- **Precision™** workstations created for working professionals who demand exceptional performance from hardware platforms and software and application offerings. These professional users are less concerned with cost and are more interested in "three-dimensional computer-aided design, digital content creation, geographic information systems, computer animation, software development, computer-aided engineering, game development, and financial analysis."[98]

In mobile computing, two years after the first Dell laptop debuted in 1989, Dell jumped into the top five computer companies in the world in terms of unit shipments, sending shares skyrocketing. Apple PowerBook designer John Medica led the efforts to create the enhanced Dell Latitude notebook offering. As the industry frontrunner of lithium-ion battery production and the first to introduce a rapid notebook charger, Dell enjoyed financial benefits of a first-mover advantage. Today, the mobility product line includes:

- **XPS™** and **Alienware** laptop lines, which provide customers with the best design and user experience with a high level of gaming capacity. In 2008, the XPS M1330 was introduced with a 13-inch high-definition display with ultra-portable features that earned numerous awards for its unique design.
- **Inspiron™** laptops, which meet customer needs for innovation, style, and high performance at an affordable cost.
- **Latitude™,** developed for business, government, and institutional customers that are interested in security, product lifecycle management, and cost control.
- **Vostro™,** which serves small businesses, was introduced in July 2007.
- **Precision™** serves professionals with exceptional performance in running sophisticated applications that are offered within the line of mobile workstations.

Dell offers "a wide range of third-party software products, including operating systems, business and office applications, antivirus and related security software, entertainment software, and products in various other categories."[99] The primary third-party software provider, ASAP Software Express Inc., historically licensed their software innovations to Dell. In 2008, Dell acquired ASAP and has since released products from more than 2,000 software publishers. Dell packages antivirus and antispyware software from McAfee, Webroot Software, Norton, PC Mover, and other third-party software solutions preloaded with their personal computer units using these software solutions to differentiate the notebooks and desktops.

In 2002, Dell chose to expand its product portfolio to include peripherals that could be value-added components for personal computers. Today, Dell's primary peripherals include printers, projectors, and displays. They first entered the projector segment, shortly followed by entrance into the printer market in 2004, and started using Blu-ray disc technology in 2006. Currently, Dell offers a variety of printers ranging from ink-jet to large multifunction devices for enterprise solutions. Their printers are differentiated by the Dell Ink and Toner Management System™ that streamlines the purchase process by displaying the ink levels of color and non-color cartridges during each print job. Dell offers both branded and non-branded display solutions. To maintain the same level of innovation as Acer and HP, in 2008 Dell introduced cameras and microphones into the external monitors. Since then, Dell has won several awards for "quality, performance, and value" for their monitors.

Dell also offers both network attached storage and peripheral storage. By offering "a comprehensive portfolio of advanced storage solutions, including storage area networks, network-attached storage, direct-attached storage, disk and tape backup systems, and removable disk backup," data can be stored and transitioned over to a new PC or network unit at the end of the prior unit's life cycle. The diversity in the storage options between Dell PowerVault™, Dell EqualLogic, and Dell/EMC storage systems caters to a wide variety of target segments. The options vary based on use, modularity, scalability, encryption options, and backup storage solutions.[100]

In 1994, both Dell and rival HP entered the network and server markets. Throughout the 1990s, Dell expanded their data center offerings to an enterprise solution utilizing the "high-end, fiber channel-based PowerVault™ 650F storage subsystem."[101] In 2004, Dell led a pioneering effort to develop the first Disk Data Format (DDF), a first attempt at a corporate data center server storage solution. By staying at the forefront of the industry and focusing on ease of use, Dell maintains a leadership position in the market. The products are known to be affordable, reliable, scalable, and customizable to meet client needs, demands, and level of understanding and requirement for use. The Dell networking solutions offer both managed and unmanaged connectivity. Current products include:

- The **PowerEdge™** line of servers competes in cost leadership and emphasizes scalability and reliability.
- **PowerConnect™** offers many high-quality features for very large data center customers, with switches that connect computers and servers in small to medium-sized networks.
- **PowerVault™** provides direct attached storage, common interfaces for internal and external storage, high capacity, and possible expansion.

From the time the first PC was introduced in 1985, Dell has relied on customer service as a corporate cornerstone and attributes its consistent success to this focus. In fact, in 2008, every *Fortune* 100 company did business with Dell.[102] Dell caters specifically to user needs in the areas of customer service, financing support, sales support, product support, and international

support. In the 2008 annual report, Dell outlined the importance of customer service—to listen to their customers, innovate, and then make the necessary changes In this way, Dell can drive innovation to meet market demands.[103] Businesses and users can call, chat, or e-mail service requests.

Financials

While operating in a very competitive industry, Dell has remained a fiscally stable company. In the last decade, Dell has increased revenues by 142 percent, with recent revenues of $61.1 billion in 2008 with a 10 percent compound annual growth rate (CAGR), and currently has roughly $9 billion in cash.[104] From 1999 to 2008, Dell's net income reached a high of $3.6 billion in 2005 and a low of $1.2 billion in 2001. However, as noted in the introduction, revenue growth has slowed with FY09 revenues of $61.101 billion compared to FY08 of $61.133 billion, with desktop PCs, their largest product revenue stream, experiencing

Exhibit 8 Dell Financial Performance (FY00–FY09)

Select Financial Details from Dell's Balance Sheet and Income Statement										
Income Statement ($M)	FY09	FY08	FY07	FY06	FY05	FY04	FY03	FY02	FY01	FY00
Revenue	$61,101	$61,133	$57,420	$55,908	$49,205	$41,444	$35,404	$31,168	$31,888	$25,265
Operating Income	$4,193	$4,344	$3,541	$4,740	$4,588	$3,807	$3,055	$2,510	$3,008	$2,613
Net Income	$2,478	$2,947	$2,583	$3,572	$3,043	$2,645	$2,122	$1,246	$2,236	$1,666
Effective Tax Rate	25.5%	22.8%	22.8%	21.9%	31.5%	29%	29.9%	28%	30%	32%
Balance Sheet ($M)	FY09	FY08	FY07	FY06	FY05	FY04	FY03	FY02	FY01	FY00
Cash	$9,092	$7,972	$9,546	$7,042	$4,747	$4,317	$4,232	$3,641	$4,910	$3,809
Total Assets	$26,500	$27,561	$17,791	$23,190	$23,215	$19,311	$15,470	$13,535	$13,435	$11,471
Current Liabilities	$14,859	$18,526	$17,791	$15,927	$14,136	$10,896	$8,933	$7,519	$6,543	$5,192
Long-Term Debt	$1,898	$362	$569	$504	$505	$505	$506	$520	$509	$508
% Long-Term Debt of Capitalization	30.8	8.6	11.4	10.9	7.2	7.4	9.4	10.0	8.3	8.7

Source: Dell Annual FY10 1Q Financial Tables, disclosed May 28, 2009.

Exhibit 9 Dell Revenue by Product Line (FY07–FY09)

Annual Revenue by Product Line (in millions, except %)								
	FY09 Fiscal Year Ending: 30 Jan 2009			FY08 Fiscal Year Ending: 1 Feb 2008			FY07 Fiscal Year Ending: 2 Feb 2007	
Product Line	Dollars	% of Revenue	% Change	Dollars	% of Revenue	% Change	Dollars	% of Revenue
Mobility	18,638	31%	7%	17,423	28%	13%	15,480	27%
Desktop PCs	17,244	29%	–12%	19,573	32%	–1%	19,815	34%
Software and Peripherals	10,603	17%	7%	9,908	16%	10%	9,001	16%
Servers and Networking	6,275	10%	–3%	6,474	11%	12%	5,805	10%
Services	5,715	9%	7%	5,320	9%	5%	5,063	9%
Storage	2,626	4%	8%	2,435	4%	8%	2,256	4%
Net Revenue	61,101	100%	0%	61,133	100%	6%	57,420	100%

Source: Dell Annual 10-K Report for FY2009, filed March 26, 2009.

a 12 percent decline. A breakdown of Dell's sales by product segment can be found in Exhibits 9 and 10.

In first quarter 2009 (reported as FY10 Q1), Dell released performance in the reorganized globally operating business segments. Large Enterprise, their largest commercial revenue stream, saw quarterly revenues down 31 percent to $3.4 billion (year to year) and operating margins of 5.7 percent. The public sector segment, which includes government, education, and health care, saw revenues down 11 percent to $3.2 billion from the previous year and operating margins of 9.2 percent. Growth in federal and national accounts was offset by the weak performance of remaining accounts. For SMB, revenue fell 30 percent from the previous year to $3 billion, with the strongest demand continuing to be from Asia. Operating margins remained relatively flat at 7.7 percent. The consumer segment saw growth in unit volume (a 12 percent increase) with notebook volume up 32 percent offset by desktop units, which were down 20 percent year to year. Revenues for the consumer segment were down 16 percent to $2.8 billion with operating margins at 0 percent.[105] Detailed financial results for Q1 FY10 can be found in Exhibits 10, 12, and 13.

Publicly traded on the NASDAQ, Dell has been a volatile stock over the past year with a high of $26.04 and a low of $7.84 per share. Dell's 12-month stock performance is –48.29%, which is due in large part to the global recession.[106] At the end of FY09, Dell had 29,542 stockholders, of which 69 percent were institutional owners. Dell has never paid a dividend in its history. In FY09, Dell's percentage of long-term debt to capitalization rose from a decade average of 11.3 percent up to 30.8 percent, earning Dell an A– S&P credit rating.

Dell continues to increase its investment in research and development to improve and expand their product lines in their five key areas (PCs, software and peripherals, servers and networking, services, and storage), spending $693 million in 2008. With the company expanding rapidly in international markets, their customer base is broad and no single customer accounted for more then 10 percent of their sales the last three fiscal years. Dell's sales breakdown by geographic region is available in Exhibit 11.

Key Strategic Leaders

Michael Dell is the youngest CEO ever to earn a ranking on the *Fortune* 500.[107] Dell has held the title of chairman since he founded Dell Inc. in 1984, and served as its CEO for the first 20 years of company history. Dell left his CEO role to Kevin Rollins in July 2004 to work with

Exhibit 10 Dell Revenue by Product Line (Quarterly Results–FY10 & FY09)

Product Line	Quarterly Results by Product Line (After Dec. 31st Organizational Announcement)													
	FY10			FY09										
	May 1, 2009			January 30, 2009		October 31, 2008		August 1, 2008		May 2, 2008				
	Dollars	% of Revenue	% Change Y over Y	Dollars	% of Revenue	Dollars	% of Revenue	Dollars	% of Revenue	Dollars	% of Revenue
Mobility	$3,875	31.4%	–20%	$3,999	30%	$4,861	32%	$4,895	30%	$4,849	30%
Desktop PCs	$3,163	25.63%	–34%	$3,538	26%	$4,091	27%	$4,954	30%	$4,781	30%
Software & Peripherals	$2,246	18.2%	–18%	$2,487	19%	$2,585	17%	$2,790	17%	$2,741	17%
Servers & Networking	$1,286	10.42%	–25%	$1,431	11%	$1,630	11%	$1,733	11%	$1,718	11%
Enhanced Services	$1,238	10.03%	–8%	$1,270	9%	$1,365	9%	$1,372	8%	$1,344	8%
Storage	$534	4.33%	–17%	$703	5%	$630	4%	$690	4%	$644	4%
Net Revenue	$12,342	100%	–23%	$13,428	100%	$15,162	100%	$16,434	100%	$16,077	100%

Source: Dell Annual FY10 1Q Financial Tables, disclosed May 28, 2009.

Exhibit 11 Revenue by Global Segments (FY07–FY09)

| Business Unit | Annual Revenue by Business Unit (Prior to Dec. 31st Organizational Announcement) | | | | | | | | |
| | FY09 Fiscal Year Ending: 30 Jan 2009 | | | FY08 Fiscal Year Ending: 1 Feb 2008 | | | FY07 Fiscal Year Ending: 2 Feb 2007 | | |
	Dollars	% of Revenue	% Change	Dollars	% of Revenue	% Change	Dollars	% of Revenue
Americas Commercial	$28,614	47%	–4.56%	$29,981	49%	5.98%	$28,289	49%
EMEA Commercial	$13,617	22%	0.07%	$13,607	22%	14.9%	$11,842	21%
APJ Commercial	$7,341	12%	2.43%	$7,167	12%	15.17%	$6,223	11%
Global Consumer	$11,529	19%	11.09%	$10,378	17%	–6.22%	$11,066	19%
Net revenue	$61,101	100%	–0.05%	$61,133	100%	6.47%	$57,420	100%

Source: Dell Annual 10-K Report for FY2009, filed March 26, 2009.

Exhibit 12 Revenue by Global Segments (Quarterly Results–FY10 & FY09)

	Quarterly Results by Global Segment (After Dec. 31st Organizational Announcement)													
	FY10			**FY09**										
Global Segment	**May 1, 2009**			**January 30, 2009**		**October 31, 2008**		**August 1, 2008**		**May 2, 2008**				
	Dollars	**% of Revenue**	**% Change Y over Y**	**Dollars**	**% of Revenue**	**Dollars**	**% of Revenue**	**Dollars**	**% of Revenue**	**Dollars**	**% of Revenue**			
Large Enterprise	$3,400	27.55%	–31%	$3,889	29%	$4,395	29%	$4,806	29%	$4,921	31%			
Public	$3,171	25.69%	–11%	$3,287	24%	$3,960	26%	$4,510	27%	$3,581	22%			
SMB	$2,967	24.04%	–30%	$3,043	23%	$3,647	24%	$3,958	24%	$4,244	26%			
Consumer	$2,804	22.72%	–16%	$3,209	24%	$3,160	21%	$3,160	19%	$3,331	21%			
Net Revenue	$12,342	100%	–23%	$13,428	100%	$15,162	100%	$16,434	100%	$16,077	100%			

Source: Dell Annual FY10 1Q Financial Tables, disclosed May 28, 2009.

the Michael and Susan Dell Foundation, which manages the family's philanthropic efforts. Amidst poor performance and scandals with accounting practices, Michael Dell returned as CEO in January 2007.

Dell attended the University of Texas but, much like other titans of the computer industry, dropped out of college and went on to found a company based on the idea of selling custom-made computers directly to customers, revolutionizing the way computers were sold.[108] Dell was the first company in the PC business services to offer toll-free technical support and on-site service, which is now considered standard practice throughout the industry. Dell also was able to reduce its inventory costs by ordering the computer parts from nearby suppliers only once an order has been received.

Steven Schuckenbrock joined Dell in January 2007 as Senior Vice President of Global Services, expanded his role to include CIO in September 2007 and currently serves as the president of the division. Schuckenbrock is responsible for all aspects of Dell's support services, which is a potentially quick-growing unit that is responsible for worldwide enterprise service offerings and technology infrastructure.[109] Schuckenbrock is responsible for pioneering Dell's recent "cradle-to-grave policy," offered to enterprise customers, where their systems are updated and maintained for them from the time the machines are purchased until they are retired.

Prior to Dell, Schuckenbrock was a client and competitor as co-COO and Executive VP of Global Sales and Services for Electronic Data Systems Corporation (EDS), one of the largest IT consulting firms. He also brings previous experience as the COO of The Feld Group, an IT consulting organization, from 2000 to 2003 and the CIO for PepsiCo prior to that.

Prior to joining Dell, Ronald G. Garriques worked in Motorola through a number of executive positions, including Executive VP and President of the Mobile Devices Division. As the president of Dell's Global Consumer Group, Garriques is responsible for Dell's portfolio of consumer desktops, laptops, software, and accessories. Garriques is credited with the design of the Motorola RAZR that revived Motorola's line of cell phones in the North American market, and analysts expect Garriques to continue to design revolutionary products for the consumer market for Dell. Garriques holds an MBA degree from The Wharton School of Business at the University of Pennsylvania as well as a master's degree in Mechanical Engineering from Stanford University.

Alan Lafley is the Chairman and CEO of Procter & Gamble (P&G) and has served on the board of Dell since July 2006. When Michael Dell returned as CEO, he recognized the company had issues marketing its products to a consumer market, and utilized this board member connection to learn about consumer marketing from P&G. After spending a day with P&G's marketing group at its Cincinnati headquarters, Michael Dell recalled thinking, "We were doing everything wrong."[110]

Exhibit 13 Operating Performance by Global Segments (Quarterly Results – FY10 & FY09)

	Quarterly Results by Global Segment (After Dec. 31st Organizational Announcement)									
	FY10				FY09					
	May 1, 2009		January 30, 2009		October 31, 2008		August 1, 2008		May 2, 2008	
Global Segment	Operating Income ($M)	Operating Margin	Operating Income ($M)	Operating Margin	Operating Income ($M)	Operating Margin	Operating Income ($M)	Operating Margin	Operating Income ($M)	Operating Margin
Large Enterprise	$192	5.7%	$259	6.7%	$254	5.8%	$259	5.4%	$386	7.8%
Public	$293	9.2%	$289	8.8%	$361	9.1%	$331	7.3%	$277	7.7%
SMB	$230	7.7%	$239	7.9%	$374	10.3%	$330	8.3%	$330	7.8%
Consumer	–($1)	0.0%	$47	1.5%	$142	4.5%	$29	0.9%	$88	2.7%

Source: Dell Annual FY10 1Q Financial Tables, disclosed May 28, 2009.

Strategic Challenges

Michael Dell, with his newly reorganized business and five key areas of growth, is seeking to overcome the issues preventing its continued financial success. Shareholders and the technology world will be carefully watching how Dell and his leadership team deal with these issues. Internally, Dell will need to address operating costs while balancing the expansion into retail distribution channels other than through its traditional direct sales model. The corporate market, which Dell is accustomed to as its core source of revenue, is experiencing little to no growth worldwide, while the consumer market is growing slowly. Externally, the industry is reacting to the current economic downturn and price competition is intensifying. Competitors are aggressively taking market share by providing solutions that match or exceed Dell's technological offerings while meeting evolving customer needs. The globalization of the market is introducing opportunities to move manufacturing and operations to offset costs and open new potential customer markets, but it also exposes Dell to additional competition and risk associated with such emerging markets. With the success of competitors rising and growth in the corporate market declining, how should Dell change its corporate- and business-level strategies to enable growth and meet these challenges?

NOTES

1. 2009, Dell Inc Form 10-K for Fiscal Year 2009, http://i.dell.com/sites/content/corporate/secure/en/Documents/FY09_SECForm10K.pdf, filed March 26, 2009.
2. 2009, B. Charny, H-P dethrones Dell for top sales spot in U.S. Market, *Wall Street Journal* Online, April 16.
3. 2009, Gartner says Worldwide PC shipments declined 6.5 percent in first quarter of 2009, Gartner press release, http://www.gartner.com/it/page.jsp?id=939015, April 15.
4. 2008, Dell globalizes business groups around major customer segments, Dell press releases, http://content.dell.com/us/en/corp/d/press-releases/2008-12-31-00-global-business.aspx, December 31.
5. 2004, *International Directory of Company Histories*, Vol. 63, St. James Press, http://www.fundinguniverse.com/company-histories/Dell-Inc-Company-History.html.
6. 2003, BBC News Channel, Dell's diversification pays off, http://news.bbc.co.uk/1/hi/business/3269299.stm, November 13.
7. *International Directory of Company Histories*, Vol. 63, 2004, St. James Press, http://www.fundinguniverse.com/company-histories/Dell-Inc-Company-History.html.
8. Dell Inc., FY94, Form 10-K for year ending January 30, 1994, http://www.sec.gov.
9. Dell Company History, http://www.referenceforbusiness.com/history2/21/Dell-Computer-Corporation.html.
10. *International Directory of Company Histories*.
11. http://www.fundinguniverse.com/company-histories/Dell-Inc-Company-History.html.
12. 2007, B. Stokes, The history of Dell, http://www.articlealley.com/article_175455_10.html, June 16.
13. *International Directory of Company Histories*.
14. 2009, Bloomberg, Dell to push PCs to China rural areas to boost sales, http://www.bloomberg.com/apps/news?pid=20601080&sid=aJ3XJU_EvYzk&refer=asia, March 26.

15. C. Helman, 2007, The second coming, *Forbes*, December 10, 79–86.
16. http://www.idc.com/getdoc.jsp?containerId=prUS21797609.
17. B. Gray, 2007, How enterprise buyers rate their PC suppliers and what it means for future purchases, Forrester Research, http://www.dell.com/downloads/global/corporate/iar/2007112_Forrester_HowEnterpriseBuyersRate.pdf,_November 12.
18. 2009, Acer Inc. 2009 Q1 Investor Conference Presentation, http://www.acer-group.com/public/Investor_Relations/pdf/2009-4-29AcerQ1-2009-E.pdf, Presented April 29.
19. Acer Inc. 2009 Q1 Investor Conference Presentation.
20. Declaration from Management, http://www.acer-group.com/public/Sustainability/sustainability02.htm.
21. Acer Inc. 2009 Q1 Investor Conference Presentation.
22. Softpedia, 2007, Acer talks about its global strategy, http://news.softpedia.com/news/Acer-Talks-About-Its-Global-Strategy-66563.shtml, September.
23. Hewlett-Packard Web site, http://www.hp.com/hpinfo/abouthp/.
24. 2008, Standard and Poor's, Hewlett-Packard Stock Report, May 9.
25. 2008, Hewlett-Packard, 10-K Annual Report
26. Hewlett-Packard Web site, http://www.hp.com/hpinfo/abouthp/.
27. Ibid.
28. Ibid.
29. J. Scheck, 2009, H-P tries to revive PC sales with touch screens, *Wall Street Journal*, http://online.wsj.com/article/SB124234971369322195.html, May 15.
30. Ibid.
31. 2007, Welcome to planet Apple, *BusinessWeek* Online. http://www.businessweek.com/magazine/content/07_28/b4042058.htm, July 9.
32. L. Grossman, 2007, Invention of the year: The iPhone, http://www.time.com/time/specials/2007/article/0,28804,1677329_1678542,00.html.
33. D. B. Yoffie, 2004, Where does Apple go from here? Harvard Business School Working Knowledge, http://hbswk.hbs.edu/item/3877.html, February 2
34. J. Brodkin, 2009, Apple lacks broad corporate strategy but still sees gains, http://www.networkworld.com/news/2009/010609-apple-corporate-strategy.html, January 6.
35. 2008, Apple Inc, Form 10-Q, http://phx.corporate-ir.net/External.File?item=UGFyZW50SUQ9MzA4OHxDaGlsZElEPS0xfFR5cGU9Mw==&t=1.
36. S. Murphy, 2008, Apple's supply chain is tops, *Modenr Materials Handling*, http://www.mmh.com/article/CA6574253.html, July 1.
37. 2008, Apple 2008 Annual Report (10-K) filed November 5, http://www.apple.com/investor/.
38. Apple Inc., 2-Year Financial History, FY08/FY06, http://library.corporate-ir.net/library/10/107/107357/items/314467/AAPL_3YR_Q4FY08.pdf.
39. Apple 2008 Annual Report (10-K).
40. Lenovo 2007/2008 Annual Report, http://www.pc.ibm.com/ww/lenovo/pdf/07_08/Lenovo_2007-08_Annual_Report_Final_E.pdf.
41. A. All, 2008, Lenovo's strategy includes no global HQ, more vertical supply chain, *ITBusinessEdge*, http://www.itbusinessedge.com/cm/blogs/all/lenovos-strategy-includes-no-global-hq-more-vertical-supply-chain/?cs=10312, March 3.
42. 2009, Lenovo Interim Report 2008/2009. http://www.pc.ibm.com/ww/lenovo/annual-interim_report.html.
43. Dell Inc., 2009, Dell laptops, desktop computers, monitors, printers and PC accessories, http://www.dell.com/, May 13.
44. Dell globalizes business groups around major customer segments.
45. M. Kanellos, 2002, PCs: More than 1 billion served, CNET News, http://news.cnet.com/2100-1040-940713.html, June 30.
46. Ibid.
47. I. Fried, 2008, Dell racks up Microsoft as data center customer, CNET News, http://news.cnet.com/8301-13860_3-10111860-56.html, December 3.
48. R. Finney, 1999, Dell business strategy secrets (Part 1), The itmWEB Site, http://www.itmweb.com/f031099.htm, February 14.
49. S. Swoyer, 2009, IT spending to hold the line in 2009, Enterprise Systems, http://esj.com/articles/2009/01/20/it-spending-to-hold-the-line-in-2009.aspx, January 20.
50. 2009, Dell: Services targeting SMBs, seeking alpha, http://seekingalpha.com/article/130899-dell-services-targeting-smbs, April 14.
51. A. Patrizio, 2009, Dell targets SMBs with managed service, http://www.internetnews.com/infra/article.php/3815376/Dell+Targets+SMBs+With+Managed+Services.htm, April 15.
52. Dell Inc., 2008, Dell globalizes business groups around major customer segments, http://content.dell.com/us/en/corp/d/press-releases/2008-12-31-00-global-business.aspx, December 31.
53. J. Davis, 2009, More PC makers target SMBs as SMBs pull back IT spending, Channel Insider, http://www.channelinsider.com/c/a/News/More-PC-Makers-Target-SMBs-as-SMBs-Pull-Back-IT-Spending/, March 12.
54. 2008, Simplifying information technology, http://www.egovonline.net/interview/interview-details.asp?interviewid=321, January 3.
55. Ibid.
56. 2004, WinBook W360 Laptop Reviews, CNET Reviews, http://reviews.cnet.com/laptops/winbook-w360/4505-3121_7-30880951.html, May 10.
57. Wikipedia, 2008, Micro Electronics Inc., http://en.wikipedia.org/wiki/Micro_Electronics,_Inc., October 3.
58. J. Stern, 2009, Hands-on with the Archos 10 netbook, http://blog.laptopmag.com/hands-on-with-the-archos-10-netbook, January 14.
59. Wikipedia, 2009, Dell, http://en.wikipedia.org/wiki/Dell, May 12.
60. B. Worthen & J. Scheck, 2009, As growth slows, ex-allies square off in a turf war, *Wall Street Journal*, March 16, A1.
61. C. D. Marsan, 2008, 8 reasons tech will survive the economic recession, CIO.com, http://www.cio.com/article/462919/_Reasons_Tech_Will_Survive_the_Economic_Recession, November 13.
62. PC market continues to resist economic pressures with a boost from low cost portable PCs.
63. K. Johnson, 2008, Dell's green payday: Going carbon-neutral helps bottom line, *Wall Street Journal*, http://blogs.wsj.com/environmentalcapital/2008/08/06/dells-green-payday-going-carbon-neutral-helps-bottom-line/, August 6.
64. J. Ball, 2008, Green goal of "carbon neutrality" hits limit, *Wall Street Journal*, http://online.wsj.com/article/SB123059880241541259.html, December 30.
65. 2008, Introducing (RED) inspired Dell studio laptops, Product (RED), http://www.joinred.com/News/Articles/ArticleDetail/08-11-13/Introducing_RED_inspired_Dell_Studio_laptops.aspx, November 13.
66. Europa Press Release RAPID, 2009, Antitrust: Commission imposes fine of EU1.06Bn on Intel for abuse of dominant position; orders Intel to cease illegal practices, http://europa.eu/rapid/pressReleasesAction.do?reference=IP/09/745&type=HTML&aged=0&language=EN&guiLanguage=en, May 13.
67. BBC News, 2007, Laptops set to outsell desktops, http://news.bbc.co.uk/2/hi/technology/6474581.stm, Mar 21.
68. IDC, 2008, PC market continues to resist economic pressures with a boost from low cost portable PCs, http://www.idc.com/getdoc.jsp?containerId=prUS21420408, September 10.
69. Wikipedia, 2009, Dell Inspiron Mini Series, http://en.wikipedia.org/wiki/Dell_Inspiron_Mini_Series, May 12.
70. L. Lee & P. Burrows, 2007, Is Dell too big for Michael Dell?, *BusinessWeek*, http://www.businessweek.com/magazine/content/07_07/b4021052.htm, February 12.
71. O. Malik, 2008, GigaOM Interview: Michael Dell. Reprinted at Businessweek.com, http://www.businessweek.com/technology/content/jul2008/tc20080727_306498.htm, July 28.
72. PC market continues to resist economic pressures with a boost from low cost portable PCs.
73. A. Ricadela, 2009, Will this bold shakeup save Dell?, *BusinessWeek*, wwwbusinessweek.com, January 1.
74. PC market continues to resist economic pressures with a boost from low cost portable PCs.
75. 2009, Why the big dip at Dell in the first quarter, *Wall Street Journal*, http://blogs.wsj.com/digits/2009/04/15/why-the-big-dip-at-dell-in-the-first-quarter/?mod=crnews, April 15.
76. Suppli.com, 2008, Notebook PC shipments exceed desktops for first time in Q3, http://www.isuppli.com/NewsDetail.aspx?ID=19823, December 23.
77. C. Thompson, 2009, The netbook effect, *Wired*, http://www.wired.com/gadgets/wireless/magazine/17-03/mf_netbooks?currentPage=4, February 23.
78. Dell Inc Form 10-K for Fiscal Year 2009.

79. Ibid.
80. 2008, Michael Dell: A big second half, *BusinessWeek*, wwwbusinessweek.com, July 28.
81. J. Brandon, 2008, What does cloud computing mean for you? *PC Magazine*, http://www.pcmag.com/article2/0,2817,2320619,00.asp, June 23.
82. Why the big dip at Dell in the first quarter?
83. Ibid.
84. Dell Inc Form 10-K for Fiscal Year 2009.
85. Ibid.
86. Ibid.
87. 2009, Dell Web site, http://www.dell.com/content/topics/global.aspx/services/managed/managed_services_overview?c=us&cs=04&l=en&s=bsd.
88. A. Gonsalves, 2009, Dell cost cutting 1 billion as profits fall 48%, http://www.informationweek.com/news/hardware/desktop/showArticle.jhtml?articleID=214700011, February 26.
89. 2009, FY10 Q1 earnings call transcript, http://www.dell.com, May 28.
90. B. Einhorn, 2009, Acer boss Lanci takes aim at Dell and HP, *BusinessWeek*, www.businessweek.com, April 13.
91. M. Harrington, 2004, "Dell Suppliers could be key to deal," *The Business Journal*, http://www.bizjournals.com/triad/stories/2004/10/04/story1.html, October 1.
92. B. Crothers, 2009, Dell offers lesson in Intel-AMD rivalry, CNET News, http://news.cnet.com/8301-13924_3-10240294-64.html, May 13.
93. Dell Inc., 2009, Dell supplier diversity, http://www.dell.com/content/topics/global.aspx/corp/sup_diversity/en/index?c=us&l=en&s=corp, May 13.
94. J. Bowles, 2008, Supplier diversity in action: Best practices of the top organizations for multicultural business opportunities, *BusinessWeek*, advertisement.
95. 2005, Dell recognizes six suppliers in annual awards program, Servigistics press release, http://www.servigistics.com/news/press/2005/04-141.html, April 14.
96. M. Gray, 2008, Dell supply chain director, speaker introduction, http://www.supplychain.eu.com/speakers.asp, June 8.
97. 2009, Limerick, Dell to migrate manufacturing operations from Ireland to Poland and partners by early 2010, http://www.dell.com/content/topics/global.aspx/corp/pressoffice/en/2009/2009_01_08_rr_000?c=us&l=en&s=corp, January 8.
98. Dell Inc. Form 10-K for Fiscal Year 2009.
99. 2009, Dell, Inc. (DELL) description of business, http://www.hotstocked.com/companies/d/dell-inc-DELL-description-52599.html, May 26.
100. 2009, Dell Web site, Data storage and backup, http://www.dell.com/business/storage.
101. 2009, Dell Web site, History, Dell takes on servers and storage, http://www.dell.com/content/topics/global.aspx/about_dell/company/history/history?c=us&l=en&s=corp.
102. Dell Inc. Form 10-K for Fiscal Year 2009.
103. 2008, Dell fiscal year 2008 in review, http://content.dell.com/us/en/corp/d/corp-comm/ir-FY08-in-Review.aspx?c=us&l=en&s=corp&redirect=1, June 1.
104. Standard & Poor's, 2009, Dell stock report, May 9.
105. 2009, FY10 Q1 earnings call transcript.
106. Yahoo Finance, http://www.yahoo.com/finance.
107. Dell, 2009, Michael Dell, Dell executive team, http://content.dell.com/us/en/corp/d/bios/michael-dell-bio.aspx.
108. 2009, Michael Dell biography, A&E Television Networks, http://www.biography.com/articles/Michael-Dell-9542199.
109. Reuters, 2009, Officers and directors for Dell Inc., http://www.reuters.com/finance/stocks/companyOfficers?symbol=DELL.O&viewId=bio.
110. Helman, The second coming.

Dan Phillips, Bo Young Hwang, Sarah Sheets, Tristan Longstreth

Arizona State University

Introduction

The succession of CEOs, presidents, and board of directors provides a challenge for businesses as they reform, reposition, and restructure. Although these successions may provide a company with beneficial results, many experience hardship. Top company officials leave due to a variety of reasons, but a common reason is conflict with employees related to executive leadership style and the culture it creates.

Robert Nardelli, former CEO of Home Depot Inc., resigned in January 2007. Numerous factors led to Nardelli's resignation: Shareholders experienced dissatisfaction with the performance of Home Depot's stagnating stock prices; Nardelli's militaristic leadership style and centralized organizational structure affected the performance of employees resulting in excessive layoffs; and the expansion of retail stores became unmanageable. The once successful and highly valued Home Depot culture had changed, affecting Home Depot's sales and customer loyalty. Along with the change in Home Depot's business culture, it faced challenges associated with the dramatic boom and fall in the housing market. These problems affected Home Depot's employee morale, stockholders, and customers. CEO successor Frank Blake has much to address in order to reposition Home Depot as the industry giant it has been for 20 years.

History

Bernie Marcus and Arthur Blank cofounded Home Depot on June 29, 1978, after being fired from Handy Dan, a small chain of home improvement stores. Their vision was to offer "warehouse stores filled from floor to ceiling with a wide assortment of products at the lowest prices" along with superior customer service provided by a knowledgeable staff.[1] This vision became a reality after acquiring sufficient capital from a New York investment banker. They opened two Home Depot stores on June 22, 1979, in the company headquarters, Atlanta, Georgia. Home Depot grew rapidly in a short period of time and went public in 1981. In 1986 Home Depot broke the $1 billion mark in sales with 50 stores that expanded into eight markets.

Home Depot revolutionized the home improvement industry by offering a wide selection of merchandise, low prices, and superior customer service to both the professional contractor as well as the do-it-yourself patron. In-store inventory contains premium products imported from more than 40 countries, including 40,000–50,000 different types of building materials, home improvement supplies, and lawn and garden products. An additional 250,000 products are available upon special order. In addition, merchandise is localized throughout each store to match the area's specific market needs.

Today Home Depot is the largest home improvement retailer in the world.[2] The 2,100 stores located throughout the United States, Canada, China, and Mexico employ roughly 335,000 people. Home Depot also operates 34 EXPO design centers, 11 landscape supply stores, and two floor stores.[3] In addition, Home Depot has become one of the leading diversified wholesale distributors in the United States due to its former HD Supply division. HD Supply Centers caters to the professional contractor for home improvement and municipal infrastructures with nearly 1,000 locations in the United States and Canada.[4]

Marcus and Blank implemented a decentralized structure with an entrepreneurial style of management, which consisted of a laid-back organization known for

The authors would like to thank Professor Robert E. Hoskisson for his support under whose direction the case was developed. The authors do not intend to illustrate either effective or ineffective handling of a managerial situation. The case solely provides material for class discussion. This case was developed with contributions from Kevin Holmberg.

the independence of its store managers.[5] Over time the changes in leadership, structure, and management style diverged from what the originators intended.

Strategic Leaders

Robert L. Nardelli acted as president, CEO, and chairperson of the board from December 2000 until January of 2007. Nardelli received his BS in business from Western Illinois University and earned his MBA from University of Louisville. Nardelli joined General Electric in 1971 as an entry-level manufacturing engineer and by 1995 became president and CEO of GE Power Systems.

After leaving GE he was quickly hired as CEO of Home Depot despite the fact that he lacked any retail experience. From GE he brought a new management strategy based on Six Sigma to Home Depot. Using Six Sigma principles he centralized the management structure of the company by eliminating and consolidating division executives, he initiated processes and streamlined operations, such as the computerized automated inventory system, and centralized supply orders at the Atlanta headquarters. He took the focus off the retail stores, moving beyond the core U.S. big-box business to conquer new markets by building up its Home Depot Supply division, and expanded into China.[6] Under Nardelli, Home Depot's sales over a five-year period went from $45.7 in 2000 to $81.5 billion in 2005,[7] and stock prices stagnated during Nardelli's six-year reign at just over $40 per share.[8] The weak financial profits and his results-driven management style, which allegedly affected the cherished culture of the company, led to a backlash and push for his resignation in January 2007.

Frank Blake succeeded Nardelli as chair and CEO of Home Depot in January of 2007. He earned his bachelor's degree from Harvard College and a jurisprudence degree from Columbia Law School. Blake originally joined the company in 2002 as executive vice president of Business Development and Corporate Operations.[9] His responsibilities included real estate, store construction and maintenance, credit services, strategic business development, special orders and service improvement, call centers, and installation services business. Prior to this role, Blake was deputy secretary for the U.S. Department of Energy and also a former GE executive. Blake also has public sector experience, serving as general counsel for the U.S. Environmental Protection Agency, deputy counsel to Vice President George Bush, and as a law clerk to Justice Stevens of the U.S. Supreme Court.[10] As Home Depot's new leader, Blake faces significant challenges, especially when it comes to rising above competition.

Competition

Competition fuels businesses to be efficient in almost every way. Competition forces companies to control their costs, develop new products, and stay at the forefront of technology. Companies that provide similar services are required to differentiate from the rest of the pack. All of these facets of competition exist in the home improvement industry. Home Depot has more than 25 direct competitors including Lowe's, Menards, True Value, Ace Hardware, Do It Best, Sears, Target, and Wal-Mart.[11] Only a select few pose a true threat to Home Depot.

Lowe's

Lowe's is Home Depot's largest competitor and holds a significant market share. Founded in 1946, Lowe's grew from a small hardware store in North Carolina to the second largest home improvement wholesaler in the world. It currently operates 1,375 stores in 49 states and ranks 42 on the *Fortune* 500 list. Lowe's can attribute its success to a philosophy similar to Home Depot's: "Providing customers with the lowest priced and the highest quality home improvement products."[12] However, Lowe's distinguished itself from Home Depot by targeting the individual customer, especially women, as Home Depot began to focus on contractors. Lowe's will continue to differentiate from competitors by promoting and expanding through exclusive private labels or select brands. Premium kitchen cabinets and stone countertops are a few new product lines that Lowe's is implementing within their stores. Much like Home Depot, Lowe's is looking to expand by pursuing interest in installing services, special orders, and commercial sales.[13]

Menards

Menards is Home Depot's second biggest competitor.[14] Although most competitors construct their stores in a compact fashion in order to adhere to real estate constraints, Menard's is moving ahead with an opposing strategy. The midwestern home center chain has started to build two-story urban stores. "We might be No. 3 as far as store counts go, but we are a regional player and we are innovative," said Menards spokeswoman Dawn Sands. Customers navigate the two-story stores using escalators that accommodate both the customer and their shopping cart. The stores also brag a unique customer experience, including a baby grand piano that provides in-store music, new boutique departments, upscale merchandise, specialty departments, wider aisles, and lower, more convenient merchandise shelves.[15]

Home Depot's competitive position is not only affected by the strategies used by the top two competitors, but also by the relationships it maintains with suppliers.

Suppliers

Home Depot relies on 10,000 to 12,000 suppliers to keep its shelves stocked, creating a tremendous challenge in regard to the process and coordination of the logistics.[16] During the reign of CEO Robert Nardelli, Home Depot expanded at a rapid rate and failed to take the additional supply requirements into consideration,[17] and thus found its brand image in jeopardy when suppliers were unable to keep up with the increased production demands.

When Robert Nardelli became CEO, he inherited a disorganized system of suppliers that relied on archaic accounting practices, including individual product order forms and fax-only lines of communication.[18] Nardelli placed increased emphasis on renovating the Home Depot supplier networks. The first thing he did was to gradually implement the Home Depot Online Supplier Center and the Cognos 8 Scorecarding software. The Center "features continuously updated information on how to do business with Home Depot, including the corporate performance policy, updates, news, information on events and training and scorecards."[19] The Cognos 8 system gathers data from warehouse management sources, purchase orders, and contract terms, and condenses it. The data is then analyzed and each supplier is rated on various aspects of the transaction. All the information is available online via the supplier center, allowing suppliers to see what areas they should improve to become more efficient.[20]

Nardelli also held workshops for specific groups of Home Depot suppliers. For instance, Nardelli hosted meetings with Home Depot's top 15 strategic suppliers four times a year to discuss plans for new products and store promotions. The suppliers toured a Home Depot Store and gave Nardelli input on product placement.[21] Because Home Depot has such a wide variety of suppliers, including suppliers from many different countries, it offers overseas workshops to educate prospective suppliers. The latest workshop took place in Shanghai and was conducted by native speakers in an effort to educate vendors on "how to do business with Home Depot, and be a better supplier overall."[22]

Another area of innovation is Home Depot's inventory and warehousing procedure. Home Depot prefers to receive products directly from their suppliers, eliminating the need for distribution centers, which are popular with many other retail organizations.[23] This system has serious benefits and drawbacks. First, it allows Home Depot to leverage the space it has and display a multitude of products in a warehouse setting. This capability is beneficial because customers are able to see the products available and purchase them in the same visit. The major drawback to this system is that each store must have an extremely efficient and organized warehouse supply chain operation. If a store runs out of a particular item, the customer will have to wait until the supplier can produce more of that item, which can take more time than transporting an out-of-stock item from a distribution center to a local store.[24] Finally, Home Depot has utilized a system of "less than truck load" store deliveries, which allows its trucking partners to carry inventories to Home Depot stores along with products destined for other customers to save on transportation costs. But as Home Depot expands, it may switch to a dedicated trucking system with full truck loads servicing multiple stores in a specific region.[25] Home Depot has developed many innovations to help make transactions with suppliers more efficient. One of Home Depot's biggest challenges is ensuring good interactions with its customer base.

Customers

Although Home Depot was originally designed as a home improvement superstore that would cater to both individual consumers and building contractors, throughout its tumultuous history, Home Depot has changed its focus a number of times. During Nardelli's reign, cost cutting was a key focus and the individual customer was neglected in lieu of professional contractors who purchased materials in bulk amounts. Many long-time Home Depot customers have switched to competitors, mainly Lowe's, because of constant inefficiencies at Home Depot. One customer explained that he had to wait three months to get his kitchen remodeled due to errors on Home Depot's behalf and he will now "go out of [his] way to go to Lowe's."[26] This customer's experience is not unique and new CEO Frank Blake has acknowledged the magnitude of this issue. Home Depot has sold its contractors supply division, which will allow them to resume the focus on the individual customer.[27] Due to the wide range of customers it caters to, Home Depot will likely face significant competition from other firms selling substitute services that match the information provided by Home Depot in the do-it-yourself segment.

Substitute Information Services for Do-It-Yourself Customers

Most companies focus on differentiating their products and services in order to combat rivalry, but also obtain enough loyalty to dissuade customers from switching to a substitute product. Not many substitutes can realistically threaten the success of Home Depot's product sales because they offer such a wide variety of products and people will always need to build houses and desire to improve existing homes. However, Home Depot's services, such as installation, may be hampered by substitutes. Today numerous Internet sites offer "How to" information as well as structured plans for various types of home improvement projects. HGTV and other home improvement shows may also deter customers away from Home Depot's services. One way to fend off threats from rivalry and possible substitutes is for Home Depot to expand its operations internationally.

International Operations

Home Depot is the largest home improvement retailer in the world and employs 335,000 people. In light of the industry trends that are occurring, Home Depot is reaching out to new markets, which may give them additional sources of revenue as well international business experience. Stores are opening in Canada and Mexico. In Canada, Home Depot acquired Canadian hardware store Aikenhead Hardware, and has ambitions to take over its biggest Canadian competitor Rona Hardware.[28] The most recent stage of expansion includes 12 stores in China, called "The Home Way."[29] This foothold in Asia will allow them access to markets that were previously inaccessible.

The Chinese home improvement industry is a refreshing niche market with a lot of potential for new sales for Home Depot. In China, when a consumer purchases a home from a contractor, they purchase an unfinished shell. The house itself is little more than four walls and floor.[30] In order to make the house livable, Chinese consumers must pay contractors, including electricians, plumbers, and drywall experts, to renovate the house. Home Depot plans to provide Chinese consumers with the hardware and skills to do much of the renovation work themselves. In order to meet this goal Home Depot will need to train an army of knowledgeable salespeople who can provide assistance and workshops for consumers.[31] Home Depot will face a number of challenges as they expand into China. It must contend with the bureaucratic communist government that rules China. There are relatively few safeguards against nationalization, if the government decides to appropriate Home Depot assets or property. In addition the Chinese consumers may not have the desire to renovate their homes by themselves. Upper management must decide which method of entry would be most appropriate, and the most effective way to appeal to the average Chinese consumer. In addition, given the recent domestic housing recession, upper management must decide whether expansion into China is the most effective use of the firm's money. Because of the diverse ventures Home Depot is involved in, Nardelli

and more recently Frank Blake adopted some basic strategies that can be applied in order to maintain the company's viability.

Strategies Used

As previously mentioned Home Depot historically used a decentralized organizational structure with an entrepreneurial management style, focusing on the retail stores. Store managers were given immense autonomy, and its stores were staffed with well-trained and knowledgeable employees who could offer advice and help customers find items they wanted quickly.[32] Home Depot used to place a huge emphasis on creating a customer-friendly atmosphere with clean aisles, organized shelves, and well-stocked inventory.

However, profit from the retail stores began to decrease as the home improvement retail industry matured and became saturated. Home Depot needed to find its next great idea that would sustain growth. Nardelli believed that the key to Home Depot's success was the acquisition and incorporation of existing business into Home Depot Supply, while simultaneously squeezing efficiencies out of its retail stores.[33]

Home Depot Retail

A critical part of Nardelli's strategy was to reshape Home Depot into a more centralized organization.[34] The centralization effort was evident in the management system that one journalist referred to as a "Command and Control Management system," with a goal to replace the old, sometimes random, management style with a strict one.[35] Management in corporate headquarters started to rank every employee on the basis of four performance metrics: financial, operational, customer, and people skills. Nardelli created an equation to measure effective performance. The equation is $VA = Q \times A \times E$: the value-added (VA) of an employee equals the quality (Q) of what the employee does, multiplied by its acceptance (A) in the company, times how well the employee executes (E) the task.[36]

Influenced by his military background, Nardelli often hired employees who had military experience. Of the 1,142 people who were hired into Home Depot's store leadership program, which consisted of a two-year training program for future store managers, 528 were junior military officers.[37] He also brought many militaristic ideas into managing Home Depot, which required his employees to carry out his "command." Home Depot began to measure everything from gross margin per labor-hour to the number of greets at its front doors to maintain better information, allowing the CEOs to improve control of the Home Depot operation. However, this lead to many underperforming executives being routinely pushed out of their positions. Since 2001, 56 percent of job changes involved bringing new managers in from outside the company.[38] This hiring trend is quite different from the past, when managers ran Home Depot stores based on the knowledge built through the years of internal experience in Home Depot operations.

In an effort to drive down labor costs, many full-time employees were replaced by part-time employees. But this approach did more than just cut costs; it damaged employee morale, diminished the knowledgeable staff available to customers, and led to many complaints about poor customer service and understaffing. As one customer from San Fernando, California, stated:

The Home Depot at 12960 Foothill Boulevard, San Fernando, California 91342, has virtually no customer service. First I thought I couldn't find any employees to help me because I used to go after work at around 5:00 P.M. Then I tried going during my lunch hour, then during off-work week days. To my surprise, no matter what time I go, there are no present employees out on the floor. The one or two that I've seen are obtained by hassling the cashiers. Try getting help from the guy out in the garden department and he answers with "I don't know, I'm not an expert. They didn't train me." What kind of answer is this, what kind of store is this? The commercials on TV make it almost seem like a mom and pop candy store. You go in and you're by yourself. You need a refrigerator? Tough. There's nobody there to sell it to you. You need a chandelier? Tough—no one in this department to help you. What about the next department? Oh, he replies he knows nothing about the department next door. Customers beware: shop elsewhere.[39]

According to the University of Michigan's annual American Customer Satisfaction Index released on February 21, 2006, with a score of 67, down from 73 in 2004, Home Depot scored 11 points behind Lowe's. Claes Fornell, a professor at University of Michigan, stated that the drop in satisfaction was one reason why Home Depot's stock price has declined at the same time Lowe's has improved.[40]

The general appearance of Home Depot retail stores was becoming a drawback for customers. They often complained that Home Depot had become more like a "warehouse" that was unclean, unorganized, and far from the enjoyable shopping experience it had been in the past.[41] This neglect of the Home Depot's retail stores may have been the result of Nardelli shifting his focus toward new ventures, including Home Depot Supply.

Home Depot Supply

The building supply market during the early 1990s was a growing yet fragmented market segment worth $410 billion per year.[42] Nardelli saw an opportunity to enter this new market because there were few large competitors. To reduce the cannibalization of sales from its existing retail stores, he announced that Home Depot would cut retail store openings by nearly half over a five-year period.[43] Using the money saved from cutting retail store construction, Home Depot spent about $6 billion acquiring more than 25 wholesale suppliers to build up Home Depot Supply (HDS). HDS was a wholesale unit that sold pipes, custom kitchens, and building materials to contractors and municipalities.

Because Home Depot had acquired so many wholesalers, HDS became one of the leaders in the building supply industry. For example, in 2005 Home Depot purchased National Waterworks and entered the municipal water pipe market. Home Depot's biggest purchase was that of the $3.5 billion acquisition of Hughes Supply in 2006, which made Home Depot a leading distributor of electrical and plumbing supplies. HDS expected to have 1,500 supply houses with revenues of $25 billion annually by 2010.[44]

Due to the fragmentation of the building supply market, many contractors were associated with their regional suppliers based on long-standing relationships. Those regional suppliers offered a highly trained sales staff and specialized service, whereas HDS stores worked much like the standard warehouse format.[45] Home Depot was challenged to satisfy a new range of customers' needs, which were different from do-it-yourself customers. Therefore, HDS encouraged its sales employees by rewarding them, primarily in commissions, to win contracts. Furthermore, Home Depot retained most of the management of acquired suppliers, realizing the importance of cultural continuity. Nardelli insisted that top management, salespeople, and internal cultures of the acquired companies maintain their corporate names and colors on stores and delivery trucks.[46] He believed that these efforts would help them keep existing long-term relationships with contractors. HDS was expected to earn 20 percent of the company's overall sales.

As mentioned, when Blake took over as CEO he saw the need to refocus Home Depot's vision and again cater to the retail market. Therefore, in June 2007 Home Depot announced the sale of Home Depot Supply for $10 billion to a group of private equity firms (Brian Capital Partners, Carlyle Group, and Clayton, Dubilier, and Rice).[47] The proceeds from the sale will be used to implement necessary changes in Home Depot such as increased capital spending, upgrading merchandise, and hiring trained and qualified staff and sales associates.[48] The latter is especially important because many employees were beginning to feel dissatisfied with their positions, leading to a dangerously volatile corporate culture.

Corporate Culture

Home Depot's corporate culture has changed drastically as a result of Nardelli's leadership style. Due to Nardelli's military background, many of the changes he implemented were designed to create a more vertically oriented management structure. Originally each Home Depot store enjoyed a sense of autonomy, as each store director was able to set prices and promote products within that store to match the needs of the community in which it was located. Under Nardelli, each executive and store director was responsible for various financial targets, and if these targets were not met, they were immediately terminated. This expectation created a general atmosphere of fear and distrust. Throughout Nardelli's tenure as CEO, 97 percent of top executives were removed and replaced.

To further cut costs, Nardelli implemented a part-time workforce and eliminated many of the full-time employee positions. This trend caused a great deal of resentment from employees who had previously worked full time for Home Depot, because they could no longer receive medical and dental benefits. When the part-time workforce was combined with a management system that only focused on the bottom line, no time was left for taking care of the customer.

The advent of new technology had a big impact on corporate culture, and ultimately customer service. Nardelli believed that by implementing automated checkout lines, customers would be able to pay for their purchases quickly and save time. This innovation would also cut down on employee hours, and checkout personnel would no longer be used. However, this plan backfired when the automated checkout machines malfunctioned more often than they worked correctly, and the few employees who were not laid off as a result of the innovation experienced a significant amount of stress due to having to fix the checkout machines, and answer customer questions at the same time. This frustration was mirrored by customers who were unable to find sales associates when they had specific questions. In addition to significant corporate culture problems, Home Depot's financial statements were beginning to show signs of trouble for the home improvement giant.

Financial Issues

Due to the housing and home improvement boom, sales soared from $46 billion in 2000, the year Nardelli took over, to $81.5 billion in 2005, with an annual average growth rate of 12 percent.[49] The Home Depot's gross margins increased 3.5 percent from 2000 to 35.5 percent in 2005.[50]

For fiscal 2006, net sales were $90.8 billion with earnings of $5.8 billion, an 11.4 percent increase from fiscal 2005. Fiscal 2006 net sales in the retail segment were $79.0 billion, a 2.6 percent increase from 2005, which was driven by the opening of new stores. The Home Depot Supply segment contributed $12.1 billion, an increase of 161.6 percent from 2005. This increase was driven by solid organic growth and sales from acquired businesses.[51] Although Home Depot remains one of the world's largest home improvement retailers in the world, results for fiscal 2006 were disappointing, according to Frank Blake, current chair and CEO.[52] Housing slowdowns have hurt the financial goals for the retail segment of Home Depot. In the third quarter of 2006, same-store sales at Home Depot's 2,127 retail stores declined 5.1 percent.[53]

Economic and current market conditions caused a slowdown in the residential and housing market and an overall market share decline. Analysts do not expect an improvement until late 2007 or early 2008. The company's main focus for fiscal 2007 will be on the retail segment of their business, with total investments of $2.2 billion of capital spending and investments.[54] For Home Depot's income statement, balance sheet, statement of cash flows, and key ratios, see Exhibit 1. For a comparison of January 2006 and January 2007 consolidated statement of earnings, balance sheet, and segment information, see Exhibits 2, 3, and 4, on pages 160, 161, and 162, respectively.

Shareholders

Even though Nardelli was helping Home Depot achieve drastic structural changes, stock prices were affected by the lack of focus of this retail organization. Home Depot's shares were down 7 percent while archrival Lowe's stock prices had soared more than 200 percent since 2000. The poor stock performance led to anger among many of the shareholders.[55] (For a comparison of Home Depot's top competitors and their industry and market, see Exhibit 5, on page 162.)

Investment bankers are currently working on different ways to solve the share price problem such as returning $1.4 billion in cash to shareholders through dividends paid.[56] The company's dividend payout ratio is now approximately 24 percent.[57] In addition, during fiscal year 2006, Home Depot returned cash to shareholders by spending $6.7 billion to repurchase 174 million shares, or 19 percent of its outstanding shares. A stock chart is provided in Exhibit 6, on page 163, which illustrates share prices between March 27, 2006, and March 27, 2007.

Exhibit 1 Highlights of Key Financial Statements and Ratios for Home Depot

Income Statement (in US$ millions, except for per-share items)	01/28/07	01/29/06	01/30/05 Restated 01/29/06	02/01/04 Restated 01/29/06	02/02/03
Net Sales	90,837.00	81,511.00	73,094.00	64,816.00	58,247.00
Cost of Goods Sold	29,783.00	27,320.00	24,430.00	20,580.00	18,108.00
Income Before Tax	9,308.00	9,282.00	7,912.00	6,843.00	5,872.00
Net Income	5,761.00	5,838.00	5,001.00	4,304.00	3,664.00

Balance Sheet	01/28/07	01/29/06 Restated 01/28/07	01/30/05 Restated 01/29/06	02/01/04 Restated 01/30/05	02/02/03
Assets					
Total Current Assets	$18,000.00	$15,269.00	$14,273.00	$13,328.00	$11,917.00
Net PP&E	26,605.00	24,901.00	22,726.00	20,063.00	17,168.00
Total Assets	52,263.00	44,405.00	39,020.00	34,437.00	30,011.00
Liabilities and Shareholders' Equity					
Total Current Liabilities	$12,931.00	$12,706.00	$10,455.00	$ 9,554.00	$ 8,035.00
Long-Term Debt	11,643.00	2,672.00	2,148.00	856.00	1,321.00
Total Liabilities	27,233.00	17,496.00	14,862.00	12,030.00	10,209.00
Total Shareholders Equity	25,030.00	26,909.00	24,158.00	22,407.00	19,802.00
Total Liabilities & Shareholders Equity	52,263.00	44,405.00	39,020.00	34,437.00	30,011.00

Cash Flow Statement	01/29/06	01/30/05	02/01/04 Restated 01/30/05	02/02/03 Restated 01/30/05	02/03/02
Net Cash Flows from Operations	$ 6,484.00	$ 6,904.00	$ 6,545.00	$ 4,802.00	$ 5,963.00
Net Cash Flows from Investing	(4,586.00)	(4,479.00)	(4,171.00)	(2,601.00)	(3,466.00)
Net Cash Flows from Financing	(1,612.00)	(3,055.00)	(1,931.00)	(2,165.00)	(173.00)

Key Ratios	As of 03/26/07
Price/Earnings (TTM)	$13.64
Annual Dividend	.90
Annual Yield %	2.36
Quick Ratio (MRQ)	.40
Current Ratio (MRQ)	1.39
Return on Equity (TTM)	16.22
Return on Assets (TTM)	11.92
Return on Investment (TTM)	16.22

Data provided by Marketguide. Shareholder.com, the producer of this site, and The Home Depot, Inc. do not guarantee the accuracy of the information provided on this page, and will not be held liable for consequential damages arising from the use of this information.

Source: Home Depot, 2007, http://ir.homedepot.com/summary_financials.cfm.

Exhibit 2 Statement of Earnings for Home Depot

THE HOME DEPOT, INC. AND SUBSIDIARIES
CONSOLIDATED STATEMENTS OF EARNINGS
FOR THE THREE MONTHS AND YEARS ENDED JANUARY 28, 2007 AND JANUARY 29, 2006

(Unaudited)
(Amounts in Millions Except Per Share Data and as Otherwise Noted)

	% Three Months Ended		Increase (Decrease)	% Years Ended		Increase (Decrease)
	1-28-07	1-29-06		1-28-07	1-29-06	
NET SALES	$20,265	$19,489	4.0 %	$90,837	$81,511	11.4 %
Cost of Sales	13,627	12,896	5.7	61,054	54,191	12.7
GROSS PROFIT	6,638	6,593	0.7	29,783	27,320	9.0
Operating Expenses:						
Selling, General and Administrative	4,594	4,132	11.2	18,348	16,485	11.3
Depreciation and Amortization	442	413	7.0	1,762	1,472	19.7
Total Operating Expenses	5,036	4,545	10.8	20,110	17,957	12.0
OPERATING INCOME	1,602	2,048	(21.8)	9,673	9,363	3.3
Interest Income (Expense):						
Interest and Investment Income	4	8	(50.0)	27	62	(56.5)
Interest Expense	(127)	(35)	262.9	(392)	(143)	174.1
Interest, net	(123)	(27)	355.6	(365)	(81)	350.6
EARNINGS BEFORE PROVISION FOR INCOME TAXES	1,479	2,021	(26.8)	9,308	9,282	0.3
Provision for Income Taxes	554	736	(24.7)	3,547	3,444	3.0
NET EARNINGS	$ 925	$ 1,285	(28.0)%	$ 5,761	$ 5,838	(1.3)%
Weighted Average Common Shares	1,993	2,119	(5.9)%	2,054	2,138	(3.9)%
BASIC EARNINGS PER SHARE	$0.46	$0.61	(24.6)%	$2.80	$2.73	2.6%
Diluted Weighted Average Common Shares	2,004	2,128	(5.8)%	2,062	2,147	(4.0)%
DILUTED EARNINGS PER SHARE	$0.46	$0.60	(23.3)%	$2.79	$2.72	2.6%

SELECTED HIGHLIGHTS

	% Three Months Ended		Increase (Decrease)	% Years Ended		Increase (Decrease)
	1-28-07	1-29-06		1-28-07	1-29-06	
Number of Customer Transactions (1)	304	308	(1.3)%	1,330	1,330	– %
Average Ticket (1)	$56.27	$57.20	(1.6)	$58.90	$57.98	1.6
Weighted Average Weekly Sales per Operating Store (000's) (1)	$617	$676	(8.7)	$723	$763	(5.2)
Square Footage at End of Period (1)	224	215	4.2	224	215	4.2
Capital Expenditures	$1,032	$1,028	0.4	$3,542	$3,881	(8.7)
Depreciation and Amortization (2)	$476	$445	7.0%	$1,886	$1,579	19.4%

(1) Includes retail segment only.
(2) Includes depreciation of distribution centers and tool rental equipment included in Cost of Sales and amortization of deferred financing costs included in Interest Expense.
Source: Home Depot, 2007, http://www.homedepot.com.

Exhibit 3 Consolidated Balance Sheets for Home Depot

THE HOME DEPOT, INC. AND SUBSIDIARIES
CONSOLIDATED BALANCE SHEETS
AS OF JANUARY 28, 2007 AND JANUARY 29, 2006
(Amounts in Millions)

	1-28-07 (Unaudited)	1-29-06 (Audited)
ASSETS		
Cash and Short-Term Investments	$ 614	$ 807
Receivables, net	3,223	2,396
Merchandise Inventories	12,822	11,401
Other Current Assets	1,341	665
Total Current Assets	18,000	15,269
Property and Equipment, net	26,605	24,901
Goodwill	6,314	3,286
Other Assets	1,344	949
TOTAL ASSETS	$52,263	$44,405
LIABILITIES AND STOCKHOLDERS' EQUITY		
Short-Term Debt	$ –	$ 900
Accounts Payable	7,356	6,032
Accrued Salaries and Related Expenses	1,295	1,068
Current Installments of Long-Term Debt	18	513
Other Current Liabilities	4,262	4,193
Total Current Liabilities	12,931	12,706
Long-Term Debt	11,643	2,672
Other Long-Term Liabilities	2,659	2,118
Total Liabilities	27,233	17,496
Total Stockholders' Equity	25,030	26,909
TOTAL LIABILITIES AND STOCKHOLDERS' EQUITY	$52,263	$44,405

Source: Home Depot, 2007, http://www.homedepot.com.

What Should Happen to Improve Home Depot?

Home Depot has been plagued by many problems in its recent history. Robert Nardelli's strategic approach of focusing on suppliers and improving efficiency demoralized much of the human capital in its retail business, and as a result seemingly reduced the effectiveness of Home Depot's cherished organizational culture. The approach left employees afraid of their own executives, which forced them to focus on maintaining their current positions through hyperefficiency and in effect to fall short in customer service. This bottom-line thinking had drastic implications for Home Depot's customer base as more customers left Home Depot to shop at other stores such as Lowe's and Wal-Mart to meet their home improvement needs. In addition, a cyclical market and international expansion are issues that will need to be addressed. Frank Blake as the new CEO faces the monumental task of making the home improvement giant profitable again and restructuring to repair the damaged aspects of the corporation. With Blake in command, Home Depot has a good chance of leveraging its core competencies in the retail market and becoming an excellent corporation for customers and shareholders. Shareholders and employees alike anxiously await the future to see what lies in store for Home Depot.

Exhibit 4 Segment Financial Information for Home Depot

THE HOME DEPOT, INC. AND SUBSIDIARIES
SEGMENT INFORMATION
FOR THE YEARS ENDED JANUARY 28, 2007, AND JANUARY 29, 2006
(Unaudited)
(amounts in $ millions)

Year Ended January 28, 2007

	HD Retail (a)	HD Supply	Eliminations/ Other (b)	Consolidated
Net Sales	$79,027	$12,070	$(260)	$90,837
Operating Income	9,024	800	(151)	9,673
Depreciation and Amortization	1,679	197	10	1,886
Total Assets	42,094	10,021	148	52,263
Capital Expenditures	3,321	221		3,542
Payments for Businesses Acquired, net	305	3,963	–	4,268

Year Ended January 29, 2006

	HD Retail (a)	HD Supply	Eliminations/ Other (b)	Consolidated
Net Sales	$77,022	$4,614	$(125)	$81,511
Operating Income	9,058	319	(14)	9,363
Depreciation and Amortization	1,510	63	6	1,579
Total Assets	39,827	4,517	61	44,405
Capital Expenditures	3,777	104	–	3,881
Payments for Businesses Acquired, net	190	2,356	–	2,546

(a) Includes all retail stores, Home Depot Direct and retail installation services.

(b) Includes elimination of intersegment sales and unallocated corporate overhead. Operating Income for the year ended January 28, 2007, includes $129 million of cost associated with executive severance and separation agreements.

Source: Home Depot, 2007, http://www.homedepot.com.

Exhibit 5 Industry Statistics and Comparisons

	Home Depot	Lowe's	Menard	True Value
Annual Sales	$81,511	$43,243	$6,500	$2,043
Employees	345,000	185,000	35,000	2,800
Market Cap ($ millions)	$77,488	$48,852.8	0	0

Comparison of Home Depot to Industry and Stock Market

Valuation	Company	Industry[1]	Stock Market[2]
Price/Sales Ratio	0.83	0.83	2.22
Price/Earnings Ratio	12.51	12.51	18.98
Price/Book Ratio	2.70	2.93	2.16
Price/Cash Flow Ratio	12.02	12.02	13.44

[1]**Industry:** Building Materials, Hardware, Garden Supply, and Mobile Home Dealers

[2]**Market:** Public companies trading on the NYSE, AMEX, and NASDAQ

Source: © 2007, Hoover's, Inc., All Rights Reserved, http://www.hoovers.com/home-depot/—ID__11470,ticker__—/free-co-fin-factsheet.xhtml.

Exhibit 6 Home Depot Stock Chart

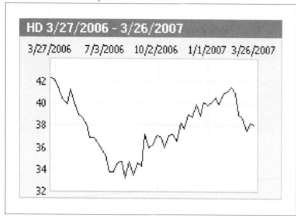

Source: Home Depot, Inc. (HD), http://moneycentral.msn.com/stock_
quote?Symbol=HD.

NOTES

1. 2007, Home Depot, http://corporate.homedepot.com/wps/portal,
   March 28.
2. Ibid.
3. Ibid.
4. Ibid.
5. R. Farzad, D. Foust, B. Grow, E. Javers, E. Thornton, & R.
   Zegel, 2007, Out at Home Depot, *BusinessWeek*, http://www.
   businessweek.com, January 15.
6. Ibid
7. 2007, Home Depot, http://ir.homedepot.com/releaseDetail
   .cfm?ReleaseID=194738&ShSect=E, July 3.
8. Ibid.
9. 2007, Home Depot, http://corporate.homedepot.com/wps/portal,
   March 28.
10. Ibid.
11. 2007, http://www.hoovers.com, April 1.
12. 2007, Lowe's , http://www.Lowe's.com, April 1.
13. D. Howell, 2005, Lowe's hammers home growth objective: National
    in a year, http://findarticles.com/p/articles/mi_m0FNP/is_6_44/
    ai_n13726491.
14. 2007, HD: Competitors for Home Depot, *Yahoo! Finance*, July 10.
15. Ibid.
16. R. Bowman, 2006, Home Depot turns its attention to supplier
    performance management, *Global Logistics & Supply Chain Strategies*,
    http://www.glscs.com/archives/06.06.casestudy.htm?adcode=5, June.
17. Ibid.
18. Ibid.
19. Ibid.
20. Ibid.
21. Ibid.
22. Ibid.
23. R. Bowman, 2001, Global supply chain partnerships, *Global
    Logistics & Supply Chain Strategies*, http://www.glscs.com/
    archives/7.02.homedepot.htm?adcode=5, July.
24. Ibid.
25. Ibid.
26. B. Grow & S. McMillan, 2006, Home Depot: Last among shoppers,
    BusinessWeek Online, http://www.businessweek.com, June 19.
27. H. Weber, 2007, Home Depot undecided on supply business,
    BusinessWeek Online, http://www.businessweek.com, March 22.
28. 2007, Home Depot, http://en.wikipedia.org/wiki/Home_depot,
    accessed on April 17.
29. Ibid.
30. B. Grow & F. Balfour, 2006, Home Depot: One foot in China,
    BusinessWeek Online, http://www.businessweek.com, May 1.
31. Ibid.
32. D. Brady & B. Grow, 2006, Renovating Home Depot,
    BusinessWeek, http://www.businessweek.com, March 6, 50–56.
33. Ibid.
34. Ibid.
35. Ibid.
36. R. Farzad, D. Foust, B. Grow, E. Javers, E. Thornton, & R. Zegel,
    2007, Out at Home Depot.
37. D. Brady & B. Grow, Renovating Home Depot.
38. Ibid.
39. 2004, http://www.complaints.com/directory/2004/june/14/15.htm.
40. D. Brady & B. Grow, Renovating Home Depot.
41. H. Weber, 2006, Home Depot needs makeover, *Washington Post*,
    http://www.washingtonpost.com, January 6.
42. 2006, Home Depot will buy building supply chain, *Winston-Salem
    Journal*, http://www.journalnow.com/servlet/Satellite?pagename=W
    SJ%2FMGArticle%2FWSJ_BasicArticle&c=MGArticle&cid=1128769
    238504&path=!business&s=1037645507703%20, January 11.
43. C. Terhune, 2006, Home Depot knocks on contractors' doors, *Wall
    Street Journal*, August 7.
44. P. Bond, 2006, Commercial wholesale division doubles Home
    Depot's supply business, *The Atlanta Journal-Constitution*,
    August 6.
45. C. Terhune, 2007, Home Depot knocks on contractors' doors,
    Wall Street Journal Online, http://online.wsj.com/article/
    SB115491714152328447.html, July 13.
46. Ibid.
47. M. Flaherty & K. Jacobs, 2007, Bids for Home Depot Supply due
    Friday, *BNET Today*, http://www.bnet.com/2407-13071_23-88489.
    html, July 5.
48. Ibid.
49. D. Brady & B. Grow, Renovating Home Depot.
50. Ibid.
51. Home Depot, 2007, The Home Depot announces fourth quarter
    and fiscal 2006 results, http://ir.homedepot.com, February 20.
52. Home Depot, 2007, The Home Depot announces fourth quarter
    dividend, http://ir.homedepot.com, February 22.
53. R. Farzad, D. Foust, B. Grow, E. Javers, E. Thornton, & R. Zegel,
    2007, Out at Home Depot.
54. Home Depot, 2007, The Home Depot presents 2007 key priorities
    and financial outlook, http://ir.homedepot.com,February 28.
55. D. Brady & B. Grow, Renovating Home Depot.
56. Home Depot, 2007, The Home Depot announces fourth quarter
    dividend, http://irhomedepot.com, February 22.
57. Ibid.

Marit Loewer

Otto Beisheim School of Management

It was a Friday morning in May 2008 when Andreas Welsch, General Manager of the German department of Henkel Adhesives Technologies for Consumers and Craftsmen, arrived early at the Henkel site in Düsseldorf-Holthausen, Germany (see Exhibit 1).

The chimneys at the enormous production site were already bellowing smoke, even at this early hour. As Welsch walked to the impressive glass building where his office was located, he thought about his upcoming meeting with company marketing executives. A

Exhibit 1 Henkel site in Düsseldorf-Holthausen

gloomy forecast awaited him in the latest consumer report: Gasoline prices kept rising and further looming price increases caused German consumers to worry about their purchasing power. Concerns about price stability and uncertainty resulting from the financial crisis and the flagging U.S. economy fueled economic fears among German consumers. This news would certainly influence Henkel's business and increase the importance of today's meeting.

Upon his arrival at the conference room, he spoke to his marketing managers:

We are facing a challenging situation. As we already know, the growth of our markets has slowed down in recent years and the raw material price increase puts pressure on our margins. But even worse now, one of our competitors in the adhesives business is just about to enter one of our core categories with very low prices. This will certainly affect our sales numbers. The time has come where we have to develop a long-term strategy in order to escape the constant war for market share with our competitors. Competing for an ever smaller market is not a solution. This new strategy is of utmost importance for the adhesives business, if we want to stay put as market leaders in the long run. It has to be developed quickly as senior management expects it in two days!

Company Profile: Henkel AG & Co. KGaA

Based in Düsseldorf, Germany, Henkel AG & Co. KGaA was an international group with worldwide presence and listed on the London Stock Exchange. Its sales were €13,074 million (see Exhibit 2) and employed approximately 53,000 people in the fiscal year 2007. Henkel was among the most internationally aligned German-based companies in the global marketplace. Consumers in approximately 125 countries around the world trusted in brands and technologies that originated on the Henkel production line. The company was organized into three operational business sectors: Laundry & Home Care, Cosmetics/Toiletries, and Adhesives Technologies (see Exhibit 3). It was the umbrella company for well-known brands such as Persil, Schwarzkopf, Pritt, and Pattex.

History of Henkel

Founded in 1876 as Henkel & Cie in Aachen by 28-year-old merchant Fritz Henkel (see Exhibit 4), the company's first successful product was a washing powder based on water-glass. In contrast to all similar products, which were at that time sold loose, this heavy-duty detergent

Exhibit 2 Key Financial Data of Henkel AG & Co. KGaA for 2006–2007

Key Financials

Figures in mill. euros		2006	2007	Change
Sales		12,740	13,074	+2.6%
Operating profit (EBIT)		1,298	1,344	+3.5%
Return on sales (EBIT)	in %	10.2	10.3	+0.1 pp
Net earnings		871	941	+8.0%
Earnings after minority interests		855	921	+7.7%
Earnings per preferred share [1]	in euros	1.99	2.14	+7.5%
Return on capital employed (ROCE)	in %	14.5	15.4	+0.9 pp
Capital expenditures on property, plant, and equipment		431	470	+9.0%
Research and development expenses		340	350	+2.9%
Employees (annual average)	number	51,716	52,303	+1.1%

[1] basis: share split (1:3) of June 18, 2007

pp = percentage points

© Henkel 2008   1

Exhibit 3 Henkel Business Sectors

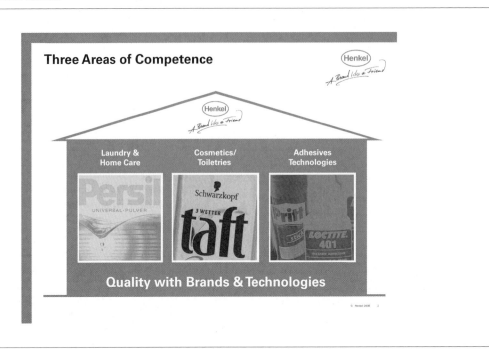

Exhibit 4 The Founder of the company

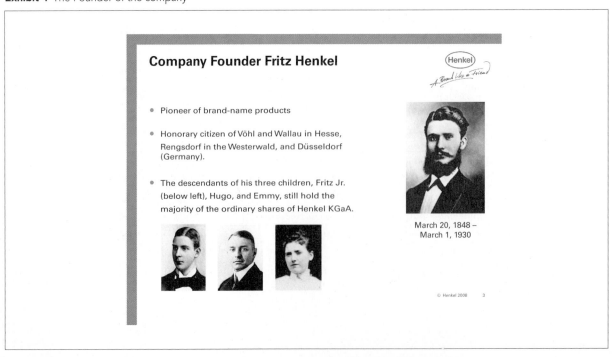

was marketed in handy packets. It was a huge success, and, two years later, Henkel relocated his company to Düsseldorf by the Rhine to take advantage of logistics and better sales opportunities. In the years to come, many innovations were developed at Henkel. In 1907,

Persil, the first self-acting laundry detergent, became the pillar for the company's growth and helped radically simplify the laborious and time-consuming household chore of doing laundry. However, Fritz Henkel did more than revolutionize laundry care. He was also a pioneer of modern brand management. He systematically raised awareness about Persil in the general public by means of innovative and sensational advertising campaigns. Ever since then, the combination of outstanding product quality and intelligent brand management has been the cornerstone of Henkel's success. In 1922, the product range was extended to adhesives, and, in 1950, Henkel entered the cosmetics markets with the acquisition of TheraChemie (hair colorants). The Henkel brand grew very quickly as a result of international expansion.

Henkel's diverse product range and strengths that ranged from modern consumer products for everyday use to complex chemical and technical system solutions for industrial consumers influenced the company to concentrate on its corporate identity. Branded products and technologies were identified as strategic pillars for the future, and four business sectors were defined: Laundry and Home Care, Cosmetics/Toiletries, Consumer and Craftsmen Adhesives, and Henkel Technolgies (industrial and engineering adhesives, sealants, and surface treatments). The slogan "A Brand Like a Friend" was introduced to convince consumers to embrace the broad variety of Henkel products and facilitate the perception of Henkel as a brand, not a corporation. Henkel's intention was to suggest proximity to the customer and foster their trust in Henkel quality.

The latest major acquisition was completed in March 2008: Henkel took over the Adhesives and Electronic Materials business from Akzo Nobel, previously owned by National Starch. Following the integration, Henkel's Adhesive Technologies business sector was expected to increase to around €7.5 billion in annualized sales in 2008. By completing this acquisition, Henkel further strengthened its leading position in the global adhesives markets, particularly in the industrial segment.

Adhesive Technologies Business Sector

Effective April 1, 2007, the previously separately managed business sectors of "Consumer and Craftsmen Adhesives" and "Henkel Technologies" were merged to form the Adhesive Technologies sector. This enabled the adoption of a unified market approach with better utilization of core competencies of both businesses. The Adhesive Technologies business sector offered adhesives, sealants, and surface treatment products for use in household and office applications for the do-it-yourself populace, professional craftsmen, and for industrial and engineering applications. The new sector was the world leader in its segment, with about €5,711 million in sales in 2007, accounting for 43 percent of Henkel revenues overall (see Exhibit 5). In view of the heavily fragmented competitor landscape with over 1,500 vendors and a relatively small number of global players offering a comparable product portfolio, the business sector saw itself as market leader in each

Exhibit 5 Sales and EBIT by Business Sector

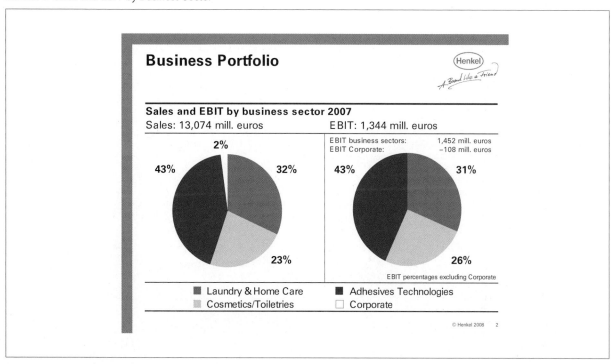

of its product categories. The variety of markets for adhesives was unmatched: the packaging industry, auto manufacturers, aircraft building, power plants, steel-mills, tin-can producers, and powerhouses were all customers of Henkel adhesives. Different competitors existed in each of these markets, and often each competitor only served a special niche and sector. Only very few companies were active in as many segments as Henkel, and this was the reason that Henkel was almost triple the size of its next best competitor.

Adhesive Technologies for Consumers and Professionals in Germany

The market catering to consumers and professionals for adhesive technology in Germany was also complex, with many different segments and sub-segments. Henkel was exceptional in that it offered so many different products under one corporate umbrella (see Exhibit 6).

Products were available for different customer segments. Consumers were divided into the two subgroups of households/offices, which were offered products for repair jobs and handcrafts, and "do-it-yourself" customers with products for renovation and repairing. On the other hand, there were professionals to whom Henkel offered products for construction and intensive usage, such as External Thermal Insulation Composite Systems. Sales channels for the customer segments were very different: products for consumers were sold in do-it-yourself (DIY) stores, specialist shops, drugstores, and food retailing shops. Driven by the ever-growing discount channel, price had become a key parameter in all trade negotiations and even in the communication of the trade itself.

The products for professionals were sold in specialist stores, and producers had to follow a completely different approach in this channel. Sales representatives would contact the relevant craftsmen—painters, tilers, floorers, and so on—individually, as each one of them chose the products they would use and had to be convinced about the advantages of new products. The craftsmen were a rather conservative group who mostly trusted in products they already knew and worked with for a long time. Thus, they were difficult to convince about the advantages of new products, and it took the sales representatives about five to six visits per person to gain a new customer. Therefore, the quantity and quality of sales representatives were, understandably, key factors in how well a product sold. Professionals tended to stick with products with which they were familiar in order to avoid customer complaints. Craftsmen faced several challenges in earning new customers, including their high hourly wages and the challenge of showing, in advance, that their work was superior to that of others in the field and, as such, worthy of a higher salary. The most common way for customers to make their choice was through looking at ads for craftsmen in the Yellow Pages. No ranking system of any kind existed for craftsmen, and customers were often very hesitant

Exhibit 6 Sub-brands under the Henkel Brand

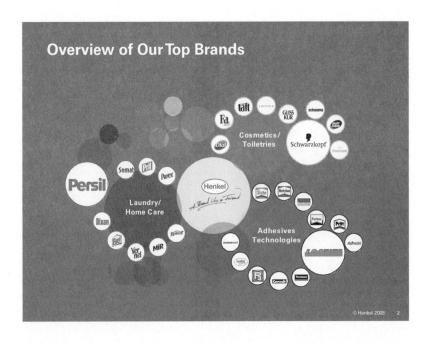

to order such professional services because they were unsure of the quality they would receive in return.

Henkel offered its customers (the do-it-yourself category and professionals) high-quality products (see Exhibit 7), as this was traditionally the way to differentiate the firm's products from the competition. Many customers were not familiar with Henkel brands, but instead knew the sub-brands, as Henkel did not invest in the overall Henkel name. The Henkel organization was built on these sub-brands because product managers for each sub-unit developed their own marketing strategy for the products of their sub-brand. Therefore, customer confidence had to be established for each sub-brand, and only some were already well known. Brands like Pritt, Pattex, and Ponal were the most popular brands in the DIY segment.

Adding new features to improve their products was another method Henkel used to outperform its competitors. Their product range was constantly expanding and different products had been developed for every possible area of application. However, in the DIY segment, this complexity did not make the task of choosing the "right" product easy for consumers. Information about renovation products in the DIY stores was not always sufficient, and qualified store personnel were sometimes difficult to find. Also, other supplementary information sources were rare. Customers could not access sufficient information about the proper application of a product, the required quantity for a certain renovation job, or new product information. Most women avoided DIY stores completely because the brand image and product descriptions were very technical. Traditionally, it was a man's task to maintain the house, and although many women were doing craftwork to decorate their homes, they felt less comfortable with renovation work. In addition, women preferred models and concrete samples of how a house would look after renovation so as to get some inspiration, but these samples were hard to come by. Even in the professional segment, the broad product range was not appreciated by all customers: some preferred to have a "universal" product for a certain task, since, from their point of view, many new products did not offer additional value.

Overall, it was difficult for Henkel to increase the number of products sold as its products had already achieved solid market positions. On the other hand, it was difficult to meaningfully influence the size of different markets in that each market was affected by trends associated with primary materials, such as tiles and wallpaper, as well as individuals' overall inclination to build and renovate.

The entire market had undergone a drastic downturn over the past 10 years. The reunion of East and West Germany in 1989 led to several years of strong growth. First, the population of East Germany entered the market and added another 13 million consumers. Second, East Germany was under-served by distribution channels for renovation products and many new DIY

Exhibit 7 Products of Henkel Adhesives Technologies

stores had to be set up. Third, the foundations of most houses in East Germany were very old and in need of renovation. Moreover, many new buildings were erected after the reunion, sponsored by the government through tax incentives. All these factors caused a boom in the industry that lasted until the late 1990s. There were few new competitors because of the entry barriers created by the need for significant capital investments to enter the industry. During the boom, many existing competitors built new capacities to be able to respond quickly and adequately to the high demand.

After 10 years of prosperity in the industry, the German DIY market became saturated with the 3,300 DIY stores that were built over the years and saw a decrease in public building licenses, which in turn reduced the demand for renovation material. Also, the percentage of homeowners in Germany was one of the lowest in Europe. Eventually the market began to shrink and competition intensified to secure and gain larger shares of a declining market.

The competition in the adhesives market for consumers and craftsmen was diversified among different product segments and target groups. In the adhesives segment for households and offices, UHU was the largest competitor in Germany. The company was part of the Bolton Group, a privately owned Italian business. UHU's product range was comparable to Henkel's in this segment. But UHU had one specific advantage—their adhesive "Alleskleber" was well known to every German since childhood and nearly synonymous with household adhesives. It was widely available and sold in supermarkets as well as stationery shops and malls, and, therefore, had the largest market share.

For the professional craftsmen target group, it was important to offer direct contact between the producer and client for support and product enhancements, technical advice, addressing complaints, and warranty support. Product innovations were another factor that companies used to attract customers. Henkel saw itself as an innovator in the industry and built its strategy around innovation. This positioned Henkel in the premium segment, but the strategy often deployed by competitors was to battle over price—the tighter the market, the fiercer the price war. This hurt every competitor. Henkel was very proud of its broad product range, which accentuated its unique image in the competitive landscape. Often, other companies tried to emulate Henkel's advantage by expanding their product portfolio to capture a share of the shrinking market, so as to reduce the factor of differentiation in competition.

Besides shrinking markets, increasing energy prices also cut into profitability. Henkel was highly dependent on energy prices in terms of product manufacturing and transportation. Since oil was the base for many of Henkel's products, oil prices directly influenced Henkel's profit margins. Employee salaries were also continuously rising. Henkel was a member of the IG Chemie, the industrial union for chemical companies that was very successful in negotiating higher wages.

In the long run, consumer markets were projected to stagnate. Low birth rates in Germany would lead to a lower population and a higher average age in the future. The typical age limit for doing DIY work was just 50 years, and this demographic development would lead to a shrinking target customer group.

The Business Situation for the Adhesives Technologies Department

The overall adhesives market influenced the business situation of Henkel's Adhesives Technologies department. Even if it was able to hold profits at the same level as the previous year, its profitability would be below expectations. In addition to the impact of high raw material costs and increasing salaries negotiated by the IG Chemie, it also had to compete successfully against its competitors in each business segment.

For example, in the tiler segment, the company PCI—a subsidiary of BASF—held a 28 percent market share and was the market leader, while Henkel's market share was at single digits. Even though PCI was the major player, it was not the most aggressive on price. These international companies entered the local market from outside Germany because Germany was still attractive: Requirements for quality standards for renovation work were comparably high. Local professional craftsmen appreciated high-quality products and product innovations offered by these international companies, as compared to other countries, in order to avoid customer complaints.

Italian producer Mapei entered the German market in 2006. It was number one internationally in the tiler segment with €1.3 billion turnover. It acquired several companies, including Soppro, which were already active in the German market and had local knowledge. These companies then received orders at such low prices that none of the local producers could compete with them. For these projects, they then assigned sub-contracts to tilers who had to use Mapei's products for their work. Henkel's strategy was different. It tried to gain market share by developing superior products. Henkel tried to convince tilers of the quality of its products with incremental product innovations. Henkel's developers had produced a "low dust" tile adhesive, which was healthier for tilers to work with. Another innovation was a "lightweight" tile adhesive. The product usage results of 25 kg

(55 lb) were comparative to jobs done with 80 kg (176 lb) of a conventional tile adhesive.

Nevertheless, Henkel's product innovations were not systematically based on current customer needs, but rather on technical feasibility. Market research completed by other departments recognized new trends in consumer behavior, such as the preference for wellness and health products and the awareness for eco-friendly goods. However, these trends were not incorporated during development of new adhesives products. Research and development was laboratory-driven rather than customer-driven. Therefore, products became increasingly specialized and equipped with new features that would allow them to be used with all possible materials and situations. The product range that served the same purpose widened.

In all, products became increasingly comparable throughout the industry. In the long run, incremental improvements would not assure business success because of the saturated market for adhesives. A further specialization in adhesives would not increase demand, but would only take away some market share from an existing product. It was a spiraling race with competitors trying to gain some temporary market share.

As a response to this development, Henkel's strategy was two-fold. First, Henkel strived to be better than its competition. It aimed to gain market share through innovation, POS excellence, distribution expansion, and better marketing concepts. Second, profitability was to be secured by cost-saving projects, simplification of processes, and improvements in the organization.

Andreas Welsch's introductory speech to his marketing executives included a presentation on the current business situation and the latest consumer report. It caused a lively discussion in the room about how to develop a long-term strategy for the department of Adhesives Technologies for Consumers and Craftsmen. Different possibilities were debated, which led to the conclusion that in the long run, the competition could not be beaten by incremental improvements of the existing products. A promising alternative would be to expand the existing market by creating new and uncontested market space where competition would be irrelevant. New target groups would expand the customer pool and alleviate the pressure of fighting with the competitors over the same customers.

Welsch was pleased with the direction the discussion was taking and announced that this meeting should be the kickoff for a Blue Ocean Strategy implementation. A creative but structured process to develop ideas for new markets and customer groups had to be started—and there was no time to lose.

Dr. Minyi Huang, Ali Farhoomand

The University of Hong Kong

In 2000, in response to intense competition and the dot-com boom, Citibank made a serious push to deliver integrated solutions that enabled its corporate customers to conduct business online. Citibank's e-business strategy ("connect, transform, and extend") was to Web-enable its core services, develop integrated solutions, and reach new markets. Citibank aimed to build a single Web-enabled platform for all customers with similar needs. Following the success of CitiDirect, a corporate banking platform which was developed in 2000 and strengthened in 2003, Citibank started to develop Treasury Vision as a replacement to suit the changing marketplace.

When developing its e-business, Citibank faced constant challenges in serving corporate customers with diverse needs. Sophisticated clients, such as multinational companies (MNCs), required custom-built host-to-host product interfaces. Other customers, such as small and medium-sized enterprises (SMEs), were more conservative and not ready for Web-based solutions. Meanwhile, Citibank was under increasing pressure to cut costs and improve efficiency. Following the outcry over subprime mortgages in October 2007, Citibank faced a very tough business environment.

How could Citibank build a flexible and agile e-business product that could capture its clients' total cash-management and trade-service needs, yet still lower costs and improve efficiency? Given Citibank's enormous global reach, how could it integrate Internet initiatives into its overall strategy and create sustainable competitive advantages?

Global Corporate Banking at Citibank

Citibank was incorporated in 1812 as City Bank of New York. The bank experienced several mergers after its inception. The name Citibank N.A. was adopted in 1976. Following its merger with Travelers Group in 1998, the holding company changed its name to Citigroup Inc. ("Citigroup"). In 2006, Citigroup employed 325,000 staff serving 200 million customers in over 100 countries and had an information technology expenditure of US$3,762 million.

Starting in the 1990s, Citibank's corporate banking activities became more centralized, with more attention focused on 1,400 large global corporations and institutional investors.[1] Citibank transformed from a geography-based organization into a multidimensional one. Customer needs became its first priority, while product types were given second priority.[2]

By most measures, Citibank was the most global U.S. bank. In 1997, Citibank was also one of the most profitable banks in the United States, with an annual profit of US$3.59 billion, of which global corporate banking accounted for US$2.56 billion. Citibank's global corporate banking business continued its healthy growth. The bank's Cash and Trade service was a core product offered to corporate customers. By 2000, Citibank's Cash and Trade division had already exceeded US$1 trillion in financial transactions for customers and counterparts around the world daily. These included foreign exchange transactions, equities, deposits, settlements of trade transactions, and payment of insurance policies. In 2006, the income from its global corporate and investment banking activities reached US$7.127 billion, a three percent increase over 2005.[3]

Citibank's target corporate client base included MNCs, financial institutions, government sectors, local corporations, and SMEs. Citibank differentiated itself from other banks through customer service by offering telephone hotlines, relationship managers who understood clients' needs, and product consultants who

Dr. Minyi Huang prepared this updated version of the case with the same title published in 2001 under the supervision of Professor Julie H. Yu and Professor Ali Farhoomand for class discussion. This case is not intended to show effective or ineffective handling of decision or business processes.

provided service expertise. Most importantly, Citibank made continuous investment in technology to support both the front-end and back-end electronic banking system.

For corporate customers, Citibank provided a full range of financial services, except for investment banking services in the United States. The core products were broadly grouped into three categories:[4]

- Transaction services, such as cash management, trade, and custody services
- Corporate finance services, such as working-capital finance, trade finance, and asset-based financing
- Treasury market services, such as hedging and foreign exchange

Citibank aimed to make the organization accessible to its corporate customers by using its unified platform and group-wide expertise. It used a team coverage approach, which allowed Citigroup to work closely with each function in a client's organization.

Cash Management[5]

The main focus of cash management was to find ways to move money around in the most efficient manner possible in order to meet customers' requirements. Two crucial aspects of a corporate treasurer's needs were accounts payable and accounts receivable. In 2000, Citibank focused on developing solutions to address three process areas: accounts receivable process management, accounts payable process management, and

liquidity management (Exhibit 1). By 2007, after continuous developments, Citibank's cash management products included Web-enabled payment and receivables solutions, vendor financing, commercial card solutions, and liquidity products designed to help customers to reduce financing costs and achieve greater returns on assets.

To help customers make payments, WorldLink Payment Services had been Citibank's cross-border banking solution for more than 20 years. Using WorldLink Payment Services, payments can be made in more than 135 currencies through a range of payment options including cash, cross-border Automated Clearing House (ACH)[6], checks, or electronic funds transfers. There was no need for multiple foreign currency accounts, and transactions were protected by sophisticated encryption technologies, access restrictions, and authentication procedures. Citibank's QuikRemit Service, a newer service, offered a robust software platform and global distribution network to process fund transfers effortlessly across borders. QuikRemit allowed corporate customers to offer both in-branch and Web-based money transfers to their own customers.

In terms of receiving payments, Citibank's Customer Initiated Payments offered an integrated solution enabling corporate customers to offer Web and telephone payment capabilities to their clients. Corporate customers were able to develop a tailor-made Internet payment application hosted on the Citibank Customer Initiated Payments system that provided one-time or automated

Exhibit 1 Citibank's Treasury and Cash Management Objectives

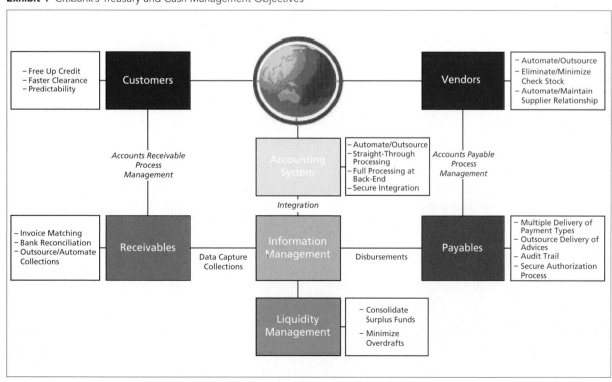

recurring payment initiation. This solution also included a touch-tone telephone payment application for one-time payment initiation as well as a customer service console to enable payment initiation by an operator.

Citibank's commercial cards offered a wide array of Web-based program management tools designed to streamline payment, reporting, spend analysis, global data consolidation, and other critical day-to-day processes. In Asia, commercial cards enabled corporate customers to receive consolidated spend data for all countries within Asia which could be easily leveraged during supplier negotiations. Corporate customers could also work with a single Citibank sales manager responsible for program implementation across all participating Asian countries. Therefore, clients could benefit from consistency in products, delivery, and services. By the end of 2007, Citibank remained the only bankcard issuer that was able to deliver local-currency and local-language programs to clients worldwide by using its own proprietary systems and customer service operations.

Citibank also offered an array of integrated investment options through multiple channels, including automatic orders, branch services, and online services. Through its network of Liquidity Desks, Citibank provided a central point of contact to facilitate investment transactions in every major region. Citibank's Online Investments was a global, secure, Web-based system allowing customers to access a variety of short-term investments using its award-winning electronic banking platform, CitiDirect Online Banking (which was later replaced by Treasury Vision) allowed customers to actively manage their short-term investment portfolios conveniently and efficiently.

Citibank also offered Target Balancing and Notional Pooling as integrated parts of its Global Liquidity and Investments product suite. Target Balancing was an automated process that concentrated end-of-day balances from a source account to a target account, while these services were maintained in-country, regionally, and globally, and encompassed structures operating within a single branch or multiple branches throughout the Citibank network. Notional Pooling was ideal for corporations with decentralized operational structures that wanted to preserve the autonomy of their subsidiaries and accounts. Pool participant accounts in a single currency were aggregated for interest compensation purposes. Funds were not physically moved, but were instead notionally combined. Notional Pooling enabled corporate customers to minimize interest expenses by offsetting debit and credit positions while preserving autonomy, control, and record-keeping. Customers were also able to benefit from offsetting without movement of funds, automating interest reallocation, reducing operating expenses, and concentrating balances. Notional Pooling was used

in conjunction with Target Balancing and Automated Investments to enable corporate customers to fully realize the benefits of a global liquidity structure.

Securities and Fund Services[7]

By 2008, Citibank had developed the financial industry's largest proprietary network, covering 49 markets with more than US$12.5 trillion in assets under custody. Citibank offered international securities trading and investment services to intermediaries. Citibank's Agency and Trust could provide support to help issuers raise short-, medium-, and long-term debts in all major markets. Additionally, Citibank's Depositary Receipts (DR) could provide a wide range of pre- and post-DR program services.

Trade Services and Finance[8]

Back in 2000, Citibank already offered Trade Finance, Trade Services, and Trade Support Services. These product offerings covered the banking service and financing needs of customers who conducted import or export trade transactions (Exhibit 2).

In 2007, Citibank was able to offer efficient services to both importers and exporters due to its global reach and ability to offer secure transactions. For importers, Citibank also provided an array of products to help conduct, monitor, and control international commercial transactions as well as mitigate the associated risks.

Citibank's global electronic banking service was a comprehensive system for initiating transactions and managing financial data activities. Customers could access information and manage all their banking transactions, trade services, cash management, and foreign exchange data from the multiple locations around the world where they conducted their business. They could control the entire trade process, including advising and confirming letters of credit, establishing direct export collections, initiating and tracking payments, retrieving timely status reports, communicating via an online customer service facility, retrieving real-time data worldwide, and customizing reports using data from different systems.

Pricing and Customer Service

Citibank set a standard price for each service, but price discrimination was discretionary based on client volume and value. While some banks competed on price, Citibank emphasized customer service (e.g., response time, technology and support), which gave customers more confidence. Citibank had moved beyond traditional boundaries of banking services by taking over some of the back-office functions of its customers. Customers could move away from the paper-based, labor-intensive payment and collection process, and instead focus resources on their core business of

Exhibit 2 Citibank's Trade Service Products

generating sales and revenue. The value to Citibank in offering outsourcing services was to lock in its corporate customers; when a customer outsourced all of its back-end processes to Citibank, Citibank not only secured all the businesses from the customer, but also gained a deeper relationship with the customer. Managing processes for a large number of customers also provided Citibank with economies of scale.

We have the economy of scale and it is viable for us to do all the back-end processes—because the more processes we do for more customers, the lower the unit cost. So our strategy is to get as many outsourcing customers as we can, and by providing the outsourcing, we get the total wallet of the client.

—Caroline Wong, Head of E-Business Group (Cash & Trade), Citibank Hong Kong[9]

Citibank also used technology to provide customers with better services at lower costs.[10] In 2006, for example, it invested in an electronic communications network that provided state-of-the-art technology for immediate access to liquidity.

A Changing Global Environment

Banks are always under the pressure of revenue and earnings growth to intensify cost-reduction efforts. In an era of tough competition, banks could not simply use head-count reduction and belt-tightening efforts and needed to find ways to increase operating efficiency while maintaining or even improving services to customers.[11]

Like most other businesses, banks need to increase their profit margins. Net interest margins were falling and fee income growth did not increase as expected. For example, for the 70 largest European banks, net interest margins fell from 2 percent in 2004 to about 1.8 percent in 2006.[12] Meanwhile, competition kept charges for credit cards relatively low; bank customers did not embrace brokerage or life insurance services. Moreover, regulators had made an effort to cap fees or require greater transparency of bank charges.

Between 2005 and 2006, Citigroup's revenue grew 8 percent; however, its operational expenses grew by nearly 15 percent. Therefore, in April 2007, Citibank announced an overhaul of its IT operations and cut 17,000 positions in order to save the company more than US$10 billion over the next three years. Charles Prince, then the company's chairman and chief executive, said that the goal was to identify and eliminate "organizational, technology, and administrative costs that do not contribute to our ability to efficien[t...] and services to our clients."[13]

Moreover, as a result of the su[...] crisis in the United States, a credit [...] in October 2007. The subprime mark[...]

providing loans to those with limited or poor credit histories. During the U.S. housing boom between 2000 and 2006, this market expanded significantly, but a series of interest rate increases in 2006 and 2007 meant that many subprime borrowers could no longer afford their monthly payments, causing them to default on loans.

In November 2007, Prince had to resign after the full extent of Citigroup's subprime mortgage losses began to emerge. Vikram Pandit took up the top job at Citigroup in December 2007. Then, on January 15, 2008, Citigroup announced a US$9.83 billion net loss for the last quarter of 2007. Pandit explained that this loss was due to a US$18.1 billion exposure to bad mortgage debt and was "clearly unacceptable." The group announced that revenues during the fourth quarter had fallen 70 percent from a year earlier to US$7.2 billion.

Smarter and Tougher Customers

Citibank developed expertise and had specific coverage models to serve different market segments. However, as more of Citibank's clients expanded their businesses globally and became e-enabled, it became necessary for Citibank to shift to e-space. In particular, corporations that historically dealt largely through wholesale channels had found that the Internet allowed them to sell directly to customers. Sophisticated corporate customers began to look for an additional range of services. They wanted to collect payments online and have access to more efficient Web-enabled financial processes.[15]

Middle markets were also driving the growing need for Internet banking capabilities. A study by Greenwich Associates in May–June 2001 showed that over half of the middle-market companies in the United States and Canada were using their financial institutions' online banking facilities more often. Nearly 50 percent of respondents said online offerings represented an important component of their banking relationships, and cash management had the steepest gain in usage among mid-size companies.[16] Banks were therefore compelled to identify what companies were looking for and to keep up with the customers with whom they were supposed to develop consultative relationships.

The Business-to-Business (B2B) Market

Sophisticated clients were looking for ways to streamline and improve their traditional payment processes. They demanded electronic invoicing, automatic application of payments to accounts receivable, online payment guarantees, and non-repudiation of transactions that could be enabled by digital receipts stored in archives. On the payment side of transactions, businesses required multi-currency payment management and payment aggrega-… by invoice and currency. Most companies were …ested in technological solutions that allowed them

to avoid paper disputes, which meant that the information flowing with a payment was deemed to be as important as the payment itself.[17]

TowerGroup, a research and consulting firm, predicted that payment activities would migrate to the Internet and that there would be US$4 trillion in B2B e-payment activities by 2010. TowerGroup also reported that in 2000, more than 90 percent of all B2B payments were made by check, with 7 percent occurring over the automated clearinghouse (ACH) network, a non-Internet system designed to handle large payments, and the rest using financial Electronic Data Interchange (EDI) services such as Fedwire.[18] The majority of small businesses used traditional payments such as checks; large companies that used ACH did not have the complete data that were necessary for a B2B payment. In addition to checks, various payment methods were available, with clearance time varying according to the method:

- Notes and coins: Notes and coins paid into an account did not require clearing; they had no particular attraction for banks, especially in large volumes, because they were a non-interest-bearing item.
- Banker's draft: This was a check drawn on a bank. Payment by banker's draft was guaranteed.
- Credit cards: Made by voucher or electronically, voucher payments were processed in a way similar to checks.
- Special presentation of checks: This payment method was taken only in cases of extreme doubt about a customer. For example, a payee company could ask its bank to make a special presentation of the check by posting the check to the paying customer's bank.
- Transfers: Funds were transferred from one bank account to another on receipt of instructions (through telephone, subsequently confirmed by writing, on paper, or sent by cable, telex, or an electronic processing center) by the paying bank to make the payment.

Bank-to-corporate connectivity was the biggest hurdle in enabling straight-through processing in treasury- and cash-management across borders.[19] In 1999, corporate customers could access SWIFTNet[20] to exchange confirmations with their banks through Treasury Counterparties. In 2002, access was enhanced by the Member Administrated Closed User Croup, where a company could join SWIFTNet if a member bank sponsored it. Though there were no limits on the messages that the corporate customer could exchange with the sponsoring bank, the communication was limited to the sponsoring bank and it was expensive and troublesome for corporate customers to reach an agreement with the banks.

Since the beginning of 2007, most large corporate customers had begun using a new legal model for accessing SWIFTNet: Standardized CORporate Environment (SCORE). Using the SCORE model, a corporate customer could access all participating banks with only one agreement in place. SCORE also laid down rules for the messages that could be sent within the SCORE framework. The only exception was for FileAct message, where the body of a FileAct message could contain any type of messages, such as an EDIFACT[21] or ISO 20022[22] format message. The introduction of SCORE was intended to make it easier, cheaper, and less risky for corporate customers to switch between banks because no technical or format changes were needed for corporate customers in switching banks.[23]

Many banks openly admitted that formats and connectivity were no longer a competitive space but instead a place for cooperation, using standards to reduce costs for their customers as well as themselves. The competition would be in the value-added services that banks sold to customers.[24]

Competition

Some MNCs could not wait for banks to develop Web-enabled financial products, so they started building their own systems and looking for ways to disintermediate banks. Other corporations approached the banks and announced their interest in participating in future developments. New technology, however, required major investments in people, risk, and technological services that some banks were not ready to make. The banking industry's trend toward consolidation meant that fewer banks were competing in the global transaction services marketplace. Deutsche Bank and Citibank were two leading banks that invested hundreds of millions of dollars in the infrastructure required to move and monitor cash balances online. ABN AMRO was also making a serious push to develop its product range.

In early 2001, Deutsche Bank sought to outdo its competitors by building a global payment system capable of accommodating many currencies, languages, and local business practices through its e-bills service. More large banks sought partnerships to provide global business solutions. In international cash management (ICM), companies either partnered with a lead bank that put together a solution for them, or dealt directly with local banks. The majority of companies used a lead bank to provide a solution in four ways: using correspondent banks, acting as an overlay bank, becoming a member of a banking club, or bringing together a network of standardized service providers (Exhibit 3).

Exhibit 3 The Main Trends in ICM in 2000 and 2008

Trends in 2000

- The centralization of cash management and the introduction of shared service centers continued in large companies and were spreading to medium-sized and small companies.
- There was a growing acceptance of the need to outsource ICM operations.
- Companies were realizing that the company-bank relationship was more important than whether or not a bank could offer Internet-based or e-commerce services.
- Companies increasingly wanted to understand and be comfortable with a bank's e-commerce strategy before they were prepared to award them business.
- The use of cross-border zero-balance accounts grew much faster than notional pooling because many companies had sophisticated in-house cash- and treasury-management systems to run them.
- There was a growing realization among some of the major banks that a network of standardized service-provider banks was not always enough; it was also important to have a local branch or branches in countries around the world.
- Banks were walking away from the ICM business where it had ceased to be profitable, producing a growing understanding and acceptance among large companies that banks needed to make reasonable returns; otherwise the standard and quality of services would inevitably suffer.
- As banks' ICM products and memberships of local clearings became similar, the key differentiator in the business became delivery.

Source: D. Danko, J. H. Godwin & S. R. Goldberg, 2002, How to profit from new trends in treasury management, *Journal of Corporate Accounting and Finance,* 14(1): 3–10.

Trends in 2008

- Banks and corporate treasurers were driving the move toward electronic payments in order to better integrate money and information flows.
- Corporate treasury was pushing to integrate the physical and financial supply chains, and there was a parallel convergence in international trade toward open-account, electronic financial supply chains.
- Corporate treasury was focusing on standardizing processes and strengthening internal controls in order to create transparency across a range of business activities to manage risk and ensure financial reporting integrity in compliance with Sarbanes-Oxley.[25]

Source: S. Wilder, 2008, The latest trends in North American cash management, JPMorgan Chase & Co.

Most Fortune 500 companies preferred Citibank when making international e-payments.[26] Although Citibank established itself as a strong contender, technology companies competed heavily by using their technological expertise and interests in providing new services.

Regulatory Scrutiny

Risk management and legal compliance were priorities for banks in 2008.[27] Regulators took an increasingly cross-platform view of risk and therefore expected banks to increasingly connect exposures across channels and payments, which put more pressure on bank architectures where risk management was usually buried at the platform level. For example, the implementation of Basel II[28] increased the pressure on information systems functions and encouraged banks to develop integrated information systems strategies and consequently amend their existing IT infrastructures.[29]

Regulators were also more cautious about privacy issues. They expected banks to be able to identify specific data breaches quickly in order to limit any damage as a result of fraud. In addition, with the growing number of nonbank processors in the marketplace who were generating numerous transactions within the banking systems, regulators scrutinized third-party arrangements much more closely to ensure that banks understood the underlying commercial purpose and ensure that a bank's operations were not hijacked for fraudulent purposes.

Citibank's E-Business Strategy

We are here to serve our clients: whatever our clients want us to do we'll do it for them. We're into e-business not because we're into the dot-com business; we're here because our clients want us to continue performing the basic banking functions for them on the web.

— *CAROLINE WONG, HEAD OF E-BUSINESS GROUP (CASH & TRADE), CITIBANK HONG KONG*[30]

Citibank's vision was to become the world's leading e-business enabler. It wanted to empower local, regional, and global customers and the business-to-business-to-consumer marketplace and provide solutions to help them take advantage of the efficiencies and opportunities created by e-commerce. Citibank's e-business strategy to "connect, transform and extend" was a means to deliver on its vision.

Meanwhile, with technology investments in the global financial service industry growing at a rate of 4.2 percent per year, Citibank tried to manage the overall costs of IT investments. The plan announced in April 2007 to overhaul IT operations included the consolidation of data centers; better use of existing technologies; optimization of global voice and data networks; standardization of its application-development processes; and vendor consolidation. As Citibank stated, "simplification and standardization of Citibank's information technology platform will be critical to increase efficiency and drive lower costs as well as decrease time to market."[32]

Citibank's E-Business Structure

In March 2000, Citigroup chief executive Sanford Weill announced the formation of the Internet Operation Group, a high-level committee charged with spreading

Citibank's E-Business Strategy[31]

CONNECT	TRANSFORM	EXTEND
Web-enable its core services to connect with its customers	Draw on the full range of Citibank's capabilities to deliver integrated solutions	Reach new markets, new customers, and new products

The Six Key Elements of Citibank's E-Business Strategy

Embed Citibank as the trusted brand within communities
Build a network of strategic partners
Help customers to serve themselves
Web-enable core services
Create knowledge-based e-services
'e-Us'

Exhibit 4 Citibank's Global Transaction Services Awards in Asia, 2007

- Best Custodian in Asia; Best Fund Administrator in Asia (*Asia Asset Management*)
- Best Overall Cash Management Bank across all categories as voted by corporations; Best Electronic Banking Platform; Best at Understanding Business Strategies, Objectives, and Requirements as voted by financial institutions (*Asiamoney*)
- Best Transaction Bank in Asia; Best Cash Management Bank in Asia; Best Corporate Specialist in Asia (*The Asset*)
- Best Cash Management Bank; Best Cash Management Solutions (*FinanceAsia*)
- Asia's Best Investment Management Services; Best Corporate/Institutional Internet Bank in Asia (*Global Finance*)

responsibility for Internet activities more evenly between e-Citi, an incubator for Internet initiatives, and the bank's business units. In April 2000, the group announced the second phase of Citigroup's Internet activity, which involved the creation of two units aimed at infusing the Internet into all consumer and corporate banking activities: e-Consumer and e-Business. Both units were intended to complement e-Citi.[33] In May 2000, two new business units, e-Capital Markets and e-Asset Management, were added.

Jorge Bermudez, executive vice-president and head of Global Cash Management and Trade Services, was appointed to lead the e-Business unit.[34] Bermudez's e-Business unit was responsible for developing Internet software for corporate clients setting up B2B electronic commerce exchanges.

The new business units brought people from the business lines together with people from the Internet side of operations, which combined resources and eliminated duplication and competition. The new strategy of forming high-level committees reversed the centralized approach that Citigroup had pursued under John Reed, the driving force behind the formation of e-Citi.[35] Citigroup's new structure involved traditional business units in formulating Internet strategies and forming committees to coordinate and synthesize an approach that mirrored that of other banks.[36]

In 2002, Global Transaction Services was created as a division of Citibank's Markets and Banking to integrate Cash, Trade, and Treasury Services and Global Securities Services. It offered integrated cash management, fund services, securities services, trade services, and finance to MNCs, financial institutions, and the public sector around the world (Exhibit 5). The objective was to help corporate customers gain greater control over financial positions both locally and globally, increase efficiency, and reduce costs.

Within just one year, Global Transaction Services was already tapped by 95 percent of Fortune 500 companies and profits grew 38 percent. With a global reach and local presence, Global Transaction Services had assets and businesses in several countries and regions. Its Internet-based cash management, electronic bill payment and online statements, reporting and analytics, securities processing, and other capabilities enabled corporate customers to re-engineer processes, manage working capital more effectively, and improve straight-through processing.

In 2006, Global Transaction Services already supported 65,000 clients, cleared an average of 752,000

Exhibit 5 Citigroup Organizational Structure

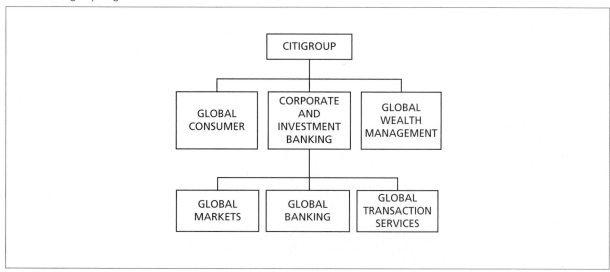

securities trades every week, and processed more than US$3 trillion in payments every day. On average, it held US$189 billion in liability balances under administration and US$10.4 trillion in assets under custody and trust, and had the world's largest commercial letter-of-credit portfolio, worth over US$7 billion.

Citibank's Alliance Strategy

Before 2000, Citibank had tried to excel at all facets of e-business—a strategy that failed. The company invested millions of dollars and tried to specialize in each area, including software development, systems development, and front-end services; however, clients and software technology were constantly changing and Citibank was struggling to keep pace with client needs. By 2000, Citibank's strategy focused on alliances and the use of its partners' strengths. Specifically, Citibank partnered with companies that had complementary technology, infrastructure, or access to markets. As Tom Edgerton, head of alliance for Citibank e-business, said, "In the future, it won't be what your company can do, but what the network of companies you work with can provide."[37]

Citibank's key technology players included Oracle, Commerce One Inc., SAP AG, Wisdom Technologies, and Bolero.net. In August 2000, four companies teamed up with Citibank to form FinancialSettlementMatrix .com, a company that connected buyers and sellers in e-marketplaces with payment processing, credit, and other services through multiple participating banks and financial service companies.[38] Citibank's challenge was managing the vendors and suppliers and ensuring that they understood Citibank's strategy and would not exploit the bank's existing strengths in the banking industry. Edgerton said of companies that had approached Citibank to partner with it: "Citibank brings considerable value to potential alliance partners. They're interested in our brand, our financial services expertise, our global presence, our strong customer relationships and position as a trusted provider, as well as our knowledge of specific industries and international markets."[39]

In 2004, Citibank acquired Lava Trading, a leader in electronic execution and sell-side order management systems. This acquisition enabled Citibank to offer institutional clients the benefits of the most sophisticated and robust electronic trading system in the market, with technology that complemented and enhanced their existing platforms and product ranges.

"Connect" in Citibank's E-Business Strategy

Customer convenience was the thrust of the continuous evolution of Citibank's products and services. Key to this goal was providing clients with more channels to access Citibank, and the Internet provided Citibank the flexibility to meet this demand. Jorge Bermudez, Citibank executive vice-president and head of e-Business, stated: "A core part of our e-business strategy is Web-enabling our current services. With CitiDirect, we are building the infrastructure that will serve as the foundation for many of the value-added services we are developing on the Internet."[40]

CitiDirect was designed for corporate customers to do full transactions online anywhere around the world.[41] It was a browser-based delivery channel designed to deliver all of Citibank's cash management and trade products and services online, enabling customers to make inquiries about their account balances, request statements, provide transaction initiation details, and request statement transaction reports online and in real time. CitiDirect allowed customers to perform these functions at any location with Internet access. This was particularly useful for global companies with operations spread out in many countries but wishing to maintain control at regional or global treasury centers.

CitiDirect was piloted in October 2000. In Asia, it was piloted in Singapore, Hong Kong, Australia, Japan, and Malaysia.[42] In 2000, CitiDirect was operating in 36 countries and available in five languages and was expected to be operating in 80 countries and 20 languages and doing a trillion U.S. dollars of business per day by 2002.[43] In May 2001, CitiDirect was already serving 1,000 corporate customers worldwide.

In 2003, Citibank upgraded CitiDirect Online Banking to offer complete payment, receivables, and trade capabilities in emerging markets. The service was made available in 90 countries and in 20 languages, and was awarded Best of the Web for 2003 by Forbes.com in the financial services category. In 2004 alone, this corporate banking platform processed more than 39 million transactions around the world. CitiDirect linked the back-office systems of 90 countries and allowed Citibank to replace its outdated and less-powerful systems and move training and customer services online.

In 2006, Citibank developed TreasuryVision, which was similar to CitiDirect. As Paul Galant, head of Global Cash Management for Citibank, noted, "We are putting a lot of energy behind it and TreasuryVision essentially meets the trends in the marketplace. It connects our clients not only to their internal systems, but it also connects to their enterprise resource planning systems."

TreasuryVision was staffed by world-class employees with expert knowledge of financial data. Once the data were proved by these experts, they would be put into a knowledge warehouse and provided to clients (i.e., corporate treasuries). Therefore, TreasuryVision would not only be an effective way of managing liquidity, but also be a useful channel for knowledge management.

"Transform" in Citibank's e-Business Strategy

Transaction processing, such as cash management, trade finance, and derivatives, was a back-office activity that was not at the forefront of customers' minds. Traditionally, transaction processing for a corporate customer (e.g., the transactional work involved in loan processing) was a function of the bank-customer relationship. Citibank's global presence translated to a huge transactional business and required supporting more than 200 data centers, which did basic, repeatable processes. In 1998, Citibank realized that, similar to any other factory product, this could be commoditized. At that point, Citibank began the transformation.

Regionalization

The transformation process involved consolidating all the data centers within each country and moving them to Singapore. Data were centralized and systems were developed to manage the automatic processing of transactions. By May 1999, the data centers were consolidated down to 60. On the operations side, Citibank began with the regionalization of cash and trade, which afforded Citibank a complete focus on the process. Approaches that Citibank used to decide the location for the regionalized centers were not mutually exclusive. It had considered the following in various combinations:

- Take the biggest infrastructure already existing (i.e., Singapore) and build it up to replace all the smaller centers.
- Ask where to get the best balance of all factors of production and start there from scratch (e.g., Penang)—Greenfield Approach.
- Rely on locally available people and skills (e.g., Sydney).
- Consider the pure cost of labor for lower-skilled areas such as voucher processing.

Singapore, which had back-office operations in several of the bank's business units, was the first processing center that was regionalized, followed by Penang[44] and Sydney's foreign-exchange and derivatives centers. The centers were time-zone-centric, so that decisions were based on the three continental time zones of Europe, Asia, and the Americas.

As a way to lower costs and improve efficiency, in 2006, Citibank reduced the number of data centers by 20 percent. In April 2007, in order to save the company more than US$10 billion, Citibank introduced a plan to overhaul its IT operations. It planned to further consolidate its existing data centers, better use its existing technologies, optimize its global voice and data networks, standardize its application development processes, and consolidate its vendor networks.

The regionalized and specialized processing centers provided Citibank scale and continual improvement opportunities. They reduced the cycle time for transactions, reduced error rates to nearly zero, and yielded new efficiencies for Citibank and its customers. As one manager noted:

We're now able to fragment the process and focus on the little pieces that make the difference, this also means that there's a lot of exchange of information and standardization of processes.

—VENRY KRISHNAKUMAR, CITIBANK VICE-PRESIDENT AND REGIONAL DIRECTOR, OPERATION AND TECHNOLOGY, ASIA-PACIFIC AND JAPAN[45]

Internalizing the Web

Within Citibank, there was a program to promote the e-workplace. The processing centers in particular had taken off through integrating the Web into their business processes. The transformations in the processing cycle focused on workflow automation; employees now had access to information without the need to make phone calls, check paper files, or send faxes. Processing centers had previously required millions of checks and huge reconcilement departments, which were paper-based and labor-intensive. The centralized and specialized processing locations made it easier for Citibank to integrate secure databases into the processing of a transaction. For example, signature-verification and digital-imaging systems were linked with the funds-transfer system.[46]

Straight-Through Automation

Citibank was continuously pushing the limits of straight-through automation by constantly deploying various initiatives. For example, Citibank conducted some artificial intelligence projects, such as prepopulating forms with historical data, which dramatically reduced error rates. It could select rejected transactions and take a look at a customer's history with similar transactions and try to predict what the customer would try to do.[47] The effective implementation of such projects was attributable to the qualified and experienced staff at Citibank.

The benefits of efficiency and cost savings also trickled down to Citibank's customers. In traditional transactions, customers deposited checks into ATMs or opened Letters of Credit by submitting the paperwork to banks, but they did not know when the banks would actually perform the task. With Citibank's straight-through processing, customers' expectations and need to know were matched because the processes took place online and in real time.

Achievements

Proof that Citibank was at the top of its league was the awards it received (Exhibit 4). Citibank was the first company in the financial services industry to receive a quality award for its cash-processing center or regional cash-process management unit (RCPMU).[48] Customer surveys showed that Citibank's RCPMU was rated higher than those of its competitors in the areas of accuracy, timeliness, accessibility, and responsiveness several years in a row. Processing was fast becoming one of Citibank's unique selling propositions. Citibank's commitment to excellence in its processing business translated to greater transparency of the process for customers, allowing them full access to information about the status of their transactions.

"Extend" in Citibank's E-Business Strategy

CitiDirect's roll-out was evidence of Citibank's vision of delivering transaction services online anywhere in the world at any time. Building a new global infrastructure gave Citibank the opportunity to deliver e-products at scale more quickly and efficiently, and any capability improvements in one region would be seamlessly deployed worldwide. Citibank expected CitiDirect to evolve constantly, which would give Citibank the flexibility to continuously enhance the system according to the changing needs of its customers. Other European banks focused mainly on providing pan-European solutions; very few banks wanted to deliver global services.

Citibank's priority was to move all its corporate customers onto CitiDirect because its main goal was to retire the legacy systems of electronic banking. Citibank had to contend, however, with difficulties in migrating customers from using traditional means to using the new products and services. Citibank's corporate clients included top-tier MNCs as well as SMEs. Previously, Citibank had not focused on SMEs; it was in 1997 that it started to consider the SME segment and introduced CitiBusiness.[49] While MNCs dealing in e-business knew what they wanted, SMEs that wanted an e-business presence were unsure how to move forward. Some were not even e-enabled and were still tied up with the legacy systems of the 1970s, 1980s, and 1990s. The greatest concern among most customers was security. Some resisted making the transition because they were skeptical about security, and such behavior was entrenched. CitiDirect had already developed sophisticated security procedures using the latest encryption techniques. Its multilayered security architecture included public and private access keys, single-use passwords, and multiple authorization controls. Despite Citibank's readiness, customer concerns about security did somewhat hinder Citibank's roll-out of Web-based applications.

In 2001, Citibank still provided services using legacy systems for conservative SME customers, while at the same time serving global customers such as MNCs that demanded to transact through the Internet. Citibank was aware that building customers' trust in the Web took years of education. To encourage conservative customers to embrace CitiDirect, Citibank's plan was to build a strategy that included a pricing incentive scheme.

The Citibank Advantage

Global Reach

As part of a global financial institution that employed over 268,000 employees in 100 countries, Citibank was uniquely positioned to serve its customers' global needs. In emerging markets, where 86 percent of the world's population lived and which accounted for 43 percent of the world's purchasing power, Citibank implemented an "embedded bank" strategy. Through this strategy, Citibank established roots in a country as deep as those of any local indigenous bank by building a broad customer base, offering diverse products, actively participating in the community, and recruiting staff and senior management from the local population. This local commitment and history, together with Citibank's global reach and expertise, was a powerful combination that set Citibank apart from its competition. In 2002, Citibank celebrated its 100th year of operations in China, Hong Kong, India, Japan, the Philippines, and Singapore.

Continuous Investment in Technology

Citibank was committed to upholding its position as a premier supplier of cash-management and transactional banking services and invested heavily in technology to improve its services. The main goal was to provide corporate customers the most cost-effective, cutting-edge, reliable, and secure solutions. As a Citibank senior executive explained, "We continuously invest in technology and it's one of our competitive advantages. We've been around a long time, we have been able to invest year after year, and we have seen compounded value from that. A new entrant would have a difficult time investing all at once, but by spending money on infrastructure— not on salespeople or front ends—I think that's how you stay in the position we're in."[50]

Technology was used as a means to achieve a strategic objective for Citibank. With the need to lower costs and improve efficiency, its investment in IT provided better client services at a lower cost. Chuck Prince, former chief executive of Citigroup, said, "One of our goals is to have more common systems and standards across Citigroup so clients can transact with us more easily, no matter what business is serving them or where they're conducting business."[51]

Conclusion

The Internet affected many areas of banking and changed how institutions make strategic decisions. At the same time, technology changed customers' expectations and needs. It was a challenge for Citibank to translate its traditional strengths to the Internet in a way that would add value for its customers. Citibank responded to this challenge by:

- Deploying Web-enabling access points to allow customers to connect seamlessly to Citibank.

- Building a new global infrastructure to deliver products and services online.
- Integrating products in new ways.

In a business environment where change was inevitable and competition was tough, Citibank needed a distinctive strategic direction that would create competitive advantages that would not be easily replicated by its competitors. Citibank also needed to make transformations on a global scale to deliver its e-business strategy and create a business culture that would embrace the e-banking concept, a key element of a highly integrated e-business, within a reasonable budget.

A key question for Citibank is how can it continue to be successful and stay ahead of the competition as Web-enabled technology diffuses through the banking industry? Also, what future trends will emerge that Citibank will need to address in order to continue to be in the lead?

NOTES

1. D. Baron & D. Besanko, 2001, Strategy, organization and incentives: Global corporate banking at Citibank, *Industrial and Corporate Change*, 10(1): 12–14.
2. Ibid.
3. Citigroup 2006 Annual Report.
4. D. Baron & D. Besanko, 2001, Strategy, organization and incentives: Global corporate banking at Citibank, *Industrial and Corporate Change*, 10(1): 12–14.
5. This section adapted from Citigroup, 2008, Global Transaction Services: Cash Management, http://www.transactionservices.citigroup.com/transactionservices/homepage/cash/cash_mgmt.htm (accessed February 18, 2008).
6. Introduced in the 1970s as an alternative to traditional check payments, ACH is a secure network connecting banks to each other. Direct deposits, electronic payments, money transfers, debit-card payments, business-to-business payments, and even tax transactions may be processed through the ACH network.
7. This section adapted from Citigroup, 2008, Global Transaction Services: Securities and Fund Services, "http://www.transactionservices.citigroup.com/transactionservices/homepage/securitiesfunds.htm (accessed February 18, 2008).
8. This section adapted from Citigroup, 2008, Global Transaction Services: Trade Services and Finance, http://www.transactionservices.citigroup.com/transactionservices/homepage/trade/index.htm (accessed February 18, 2008).
9. Company interview in July 2001.
10. Citigroup 2006 Annual Report.
11. Deloitte, 2007, Global banking industry outlook: Issues on the horizon 2007, http://www.deloitte.com/cda/content/banking.pdf (accessed February 20, 2008).
12. Ibid.
13. J. Vijayan, 2007, Citigroup to lay off 17,000, overhaul IT operations, *ComputerWorld*, April 11.
14. A credit crunch is "a state in which there is a short supply of cash to lend to businesses and consumers and interest rates are high." Princeton University, 2008, Credit crunch, http://wordnet.princeton.edu/perl/webwn (accessed February 20, 2008).
15. C. Cockerill, 2001, Cash management takes to the Internet, *Euromoney*, 381(January): 105.
16. Greenwich Associates was an international research and consulting firm specializing in financial services. Greenwich Associates interviewed 500 corporate treasurers and other executives at middle-market companies in the United States and Canada in May–June 2001. See also: D. Rountree, 2001, Importance of on-line banking, *Bank Technology News*, 14(11): 86.
17. For example, if a company shipped a buyer 100 products at US$10 per piece, but five of the products were defective, the company might simply remit US$50 electronically without any information about the defective products. In such a case, there would be greater possibility of costly payment processes because of back-and-forth inquiries. The solution would be to send a paper explanation; however, this could translate to additional billing inquiries and disputes.
18. To use the ACH network, a company was required to have between US$10 million and US$50 million in annual revenues.
19. J. Jensen, 2007, Bank-to-corporate connectivity: The next stage, http://www.gtnews.com/article/6878.cfm, August 16 (accessed February 13, 2008).
20. SWIFTNet is a general-purpose, industry-standard solution for the financial industry. It provides an application-independent, single window interface to all the financial institutions around the globe.
21. EDIFACT is the international EDI standard developed by the United Nations.
22. ISO is a worldwide federation of National Standards Bodies. ISO20022 (UNIversal Financial Industry [UNIFI] message scheme) provides the financial industry with a common platform for the development of messages in a standardized XML syntax.
23. Ibid.
24. Ibid.
25. The Sarbanes-Oxley Act of 2002 is a U.S. federal law enacted in response to a number of major corporate and accounting scandals, which establishes new or enhanced standards for all U.S. public company boards, management, and public accounting firms.
26. P. Clark, 2001, No longer banking on exchanges, *B to B*, 86(13): 13.
27. S. DeZoysa, 2007, A strategy for future growth: Banking challenges and trends, http://www.gtnews.com/feature/201.cfm, August 16 (accessed February 12, 2008).

28. The Basel Accords are issued by the Basel Committee on Banking Supervision to make recommendations on banking laws and regulations. Basel II is the second of the Basel Accords, discussing how much capital banks need to put aside to prepare for the types of financial and operational risks they face.

29. A. Papanikolaou, 2007, Impact of Basel II on bank's IT strategies, http://www.gtnews.com/article/6875.cfm, August 16 (accessed February 13, 2008).

30. Company interview in July 2001.

31. 2001, CitiDirect online banking—a new era in business banking, *Asiamoney*, May, 84.

32. J. Vijayan, 2007, "Citigroup to lay off 17,000, overhaul IT operations, *Computerworld*, April 11.

33. Robert Willumstad was head of e-Consumer while Edward Horowitz was head of e-Citi.

34. Bermudez reported to Victor Menezes, chairman and chief executive of Citibank, and to the IOG.

35. Reed resigned from his co-CEO post on April 18, 2000.

36. For example, Wells Fargo & Co. and Chase Manhattan Corp. integrated their efforts on using the Internet more closely with their business units.

37. Citibank, 2000, Citibank seeks alliances to accelerate into the e-space, *The Citibank Globe*, http://www.citibank.com/e-business/, November–December (accessed December 3, 2001).

38. Citibank partner companies were Enron Broadband Services (a delivery platform), i2 Technologies (an integrated open-architecture solution), S1 Corporation (a provider of Internet-based payment processing), and Wells Fargo & Company (a provider of complementary services to the entire e-business market).

39. Citibank, 2000, Citibank seeks alliances to accelerate into the e-space, *The Citibank Globe*, http://www.citibank.com/e-business/, November–December (accessed December 3, 2001).

40. Ibid.

41. During the development of CitiDirect, Citibank asked its customers what they wanted from e-commerce and the Internet. Customers put a premium on security, stability, speed, accuracy, and user-friendliness.

42. 2001, CitiDirect online banking—a new era in business banking, *Asiamoney*, May, 83.

43. C. Power, 2000, Citibank deploys its Web troops into business lines, *American Banker*, 165(230), 1.

44. In Singapore, front-end securities processing was also regionalized; however, due to local settlement issues, the back-end processing of securities transactions still needed to be done in individual countries.

45. 2001, Processing comes to the fore, *Finance Asia*, May, 83.

46. A system similar to SWIFT and Forex systems.

47. 2001, Processing comes to the fore, *Finance Asia*, May, 83.

48. The center processed up to US$20 billion worth of transactions daily.

49. CitiBusiness was a one-stop financing solution offered to SME entrepreneurs. Products and services included: CitiBusiness Direct (Internet banking); Cash Management; Trade Services and Trade Finance (trade products); CitiCorp Commercial Finance (asset-based finance); treasury products such as Spot and Forward Foreign Exchange, Interest Rate Hedging, and Yield Enhancement Investment Products; and a customer center. The customer center provided CitiService (an integrated customer inquiry line for after-sales services), Document Collection (an express collection service), CitiFax (a convenient way to update account information) and CitiBusiness Direct (providing online access to account information and transaction initiation).

50. *Finance Asia*, 2001, Processing comes to the fore, May, 83.

51. Citigroup 2005 Annual Report.

Frank C. Barnes

University of North Carolina-Charlotte, Belk College of Business

Beverly B. Tyler

North Carolina State University, College of Management

Nucor was the classic American success story, rising on the world stage while "old steel" gave up. However, in 2009, Nucor and its CEO, Daniel DiMicco, faced challenges as great as any in the company's 54-year history. In December 2008, DiMicco announced earnings for the fourth quarter of 2008 would plunge and told Jim Cramer on CNBC how sales for the steel industry "went off the edge of a cliff." After three record quarters, capacity utilization "immediately" fell to 50 percent. The U.S. mortgage crises led to a global financial meltdown that affected the growth and economic health of both developed and developing economies. Iron ore and scrap metal prices, which had soared only months before due to the voracious demand for infrastructure projects in China and India, plummeted to bargain basement prices along with demand for steel and steel products. With the financial markets in disarray and governments working to bail out financial institutions, consumers who had spent freely on big ticket items suddenly became risk averse. Nucor, which had become the world's tenth largest steelmaker by 2005, dropped to the twelfth largest by 2007, as it and its competitors completed acquisitions around the world. DiMicco, who had led the company during the downs and ups of 2001 and 2005, had a big job ahead—to assess the threats and opportunities facing Nucor and to select the best strategies and structure for the company as it moved into the twenty-first century.

Background

The solid foundation of Nucor was built on the failure of several companies. The first failure involved Nuclear Consultants, a company formed after World War II to ride the wave of growth in "nuclear" technology. When this didn't happen, the renamed Nuclear Corp. of America moved on to the "conglomerate" trend popular at the time. Nuclear acquired various "high-tech" businesses, such as radiation sensors, semi-conductors, rare earths, and air-conditioning equipment. However, the company still lost money, and a fourth reorganization in 1966 put 40-year-old Ken Iverson in charge. The building of Nucor began.

Ken Iverson joined the Navy after high school and transferred from officer training school to Cornell's aeronautical engineering program. After graduation, he selected mechanical engineering/metallurgy for a master's degree to avoid the long drafting apprenticeship in aeronautical engineering. His college work with an electron microscope earned him a job with International Harvester. After five years in that company's lab, his boss and mentor prodded him to expand his vision by going with a smaller company.

Over the next 10 years, Iverson worked for four small metals companies, gaining technical knowledge and increasing his exposure to other business functions. He enjoyed working with the presidents of these small companies and admired their ability to achieve outstanding results. Nuclear Corp., after failing to buy the company Iverson worked for, hired him as a consultant to locate another metals business the firm could purchase. In 1962, Nuclear Corp. acquired a small joist plant in South Carolina that Iverson found. The purchase was completed with the condition that Iverson be allowed to run the operation.

Over the next four years, Iverson built up the Vulcraft division as Nuclear Corporation struggled. The president, David Thomas, was described as a great promoter and salesman but a weak manager. A partner with Bear Stearns actually made a personal loan to the company to keep it going. In 1965, when the company was on the edge of bankruptcy, Iverson, who headed the only successful division, was named president and moved the company's headquarters to Charlotte, North Carolina. He immediately began getting rid of the esoteric, but unprofitable, high-tech divisions and concentrated on the successful steel joist business. The company built more joist plants, and, in 1968, began building its first steel mill in South Carolina to "make steel cheaper than they were buying from importers." By 1984, Nucor had six joist plants and four steel mills, using the new "mini-mill" technology.

The original owner of Vulcraft, Sanborn Chase, was known at Vulcraft as "a scientific genius." He was a man of great compassion who understood the atmosphere necessary for people to be self-motivated. Chase, an engineer by training, invented a number of products in diverse fields. He also established the incentive programs for which Nucor later became known. With only one plant, he was still able to operate in a "decentralized" manner. Before his death in 1960, the company was studying the building of a steel mill using newly developed mini-mill technology. His widow ran the company until it was sold to Nucor in 1962.

Dave Aycock met Ken Iverson when Nuclear purchased Vulcraft and they worked together closely for the next year and a half. Located in Phoenix at the corporate headquarters, he was responsible to Iverson for all the joist operations and was given the task of planning and building a new joist plant in Texas. In late 1963, he was transferred to Norfolk, where he lived for the next 13 years and managed a number of Nucor's joist plants. In 1977, he was named the manager of the Darlington, South Carolina, steel plant. In 1984, Aycock became Nucor's president and chief operating officer, while Iverson became chairman and chief executive officer.

Aycock had this to say about Iverson: "Ken was a very good leader, with an entrepreneurial spirit. He is easy to work with and has the courage to do things, to take lots of risks. Many things didn't work, but some worked very well." For some companies, failure to take a risk is failure—this was the belief of the company's founder and reinforced by Iverson during his time at the helm. Nucor was very innovative in steel and joists. The firm's plant at Norfolk was years ahead of its time in wire rod welding. In the late 1960s, they had one of the first computer inventory management systems and design/engineering programs. They were very sophisticated in purchasing, sales, and managing, and they often beat their competition through the speed of their design efforts.

By 1984, the once-bankrupt conglomerate had become a leading U.S. steel company. It was a fairytale story. Tom Peters used Nucor's management style as an example of "excellence" while the barons of old steel ruled over creeping ghettos. NBC did a feature about Nucor, and *The New Yorker* serialized a book about how a relatively small American steel company built a team that led the whole world into a new era of steelmaking. Iverson was rich, owning $10 million in stock, but with a salary that rarely reached $1 million, a fraction of some other U.S. executives made. The 40-year-old manager of the South Carolina Vulcraft plant had become a millionaire. Stockholders chuckled and non-unionized hourly workers, who hadn't seen a layoff in 20 years, earned more than the unionized workers of old steel and more than 85 percent of the people in the states where they worked.

Nucor owed much of its success to its benchmark organizational style and the empowered division managers. There were two basic lines of business, the first being the six steel joist plants that made the steel frames seen in many buildings. The second line included four steel mills that utilized innovative mini-mill technology to supply the joist plants at first and, later, outside customers. In 1984 Nucor was still only the seventh-largest steel company in America, but it had established the organization design, management philosophy, and incentive system that led to the firm's continued success.

Nucor's Formula for Success, 1964–1999

In the early 1990s, Nucor's 22 divisions, one for every plant, had a general manager, who was also a vice president of the corporation. There were three divisions: joist plants, steel mills, and miscellaneous plants. The corporate staff consisted of less than 25 people. In the beginning, Iverson had chosen Charlotte "as the new home base for what he had envisioned as a small cadre of executives who would guide a decentralized operation with liberal authority delegated to managers in the field," according to *South* magazine. The divisions did their own manufacturing, selling, accounting, engineering, and personnel management, and there were only four levels from top to bottom (see Exhibit 1).

Iverson gave his views on keeping an organization lean:

Each division is a profit center and the division manager has control over the day-to-day decisions that make that particular division profitable or not profitable. We expect the division to provide a contribution, which is earnings before corporate expenses. And we expect a division to earn 25 percent return on total assets employed, before corporate expenses, taxes, interest or profit sharing. And we have a saying in the company—if a manager doesn't provide that for a number of years, we are either going to get rid of the division or get rid of the general manager, and it's generally the division manager.

Nucor strengthened its position by developing strong alliances with outside parties. It did not engage in internal research and development. Instead, it monitored others' work worldwide and attracted investors who brought them new technical applications at the earliest

Exhibit 1 Nucor Organization Chart, 1991

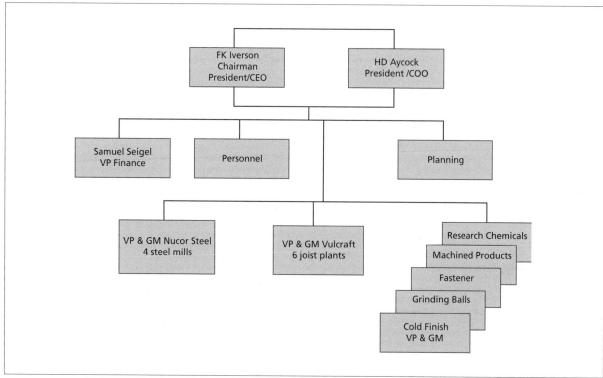

possible dates. Though Nucor was known for economically constructing new facilities, its engineering and construction team consisted of only three individuals. They did not attempt to specify exact equipment parameters, but asked the equipment supplier to provide this information and then held the manufacturer accountable. They had alliances with selected construction companies around the country who knew the kind of work Nucor wanted. Nucor bought 95 percent of its scrap steel from an independent broker who followed the market and made recommendations regarding scrap purchases. Nucor did not have a corporate advertising department, corporate public relations department, or a corporate legal or environmental department; however, it did have long-term relationships with outsiders to provide these services.

The steel industry had established a pattern of absorbing the cost of shipments so that, regardless of the distance from the mill, all users paid the same delivered price. Nucor broke with this tradition and stopped equalizing freight. It offered all customers the same sales terms—price plus actual shipping costs. Nucor gave no volume discounts, feeling that with modern computer systems, there was no justification. Customers located next to the plant guaranteed themselves the lowest possible costs for steel purchases. Two tube manufacturers, two steel service centers, and a cold-rolling facility were located adjacent to the Arkansas plant. These facilities accounted for 60 percent of the shipments from the mill.

The plants were linked electronically to each other's production schedules, thereby allowing them to function in a just-in-time inventory mode. All new mills were built on large enough tracts of land to accommodate collaborating businesses.

Iverson didn't feel greater centralization would be good for Nucor. Hamilton Lott, a Vulcraft plant manager, commented in 1997: "We're truly autonomous; we can duplicate efforts made in other parts of Nucor. We might develop the same computer program six times. But the advantages of local autonomy make it worth it." Joe Rutkowski, manager at Darlington steel, agreed: "We're not constrained; headquarters doesn't restrict what I spend. I just have to make my profit contribution at the end of year."

South magazine observed that Iverson had established a characteristic organizational style described as "stripped down" and "no nonsense." "Jack Benny would like this company," observed Roland Underhill, an analyst with Crowell, Weedon and Co. of Los Angeles, "so would Peter Drucker." Underhill pointed out that Nucor's thriftiness didn't end with its "spartan" office staff or modest offices. "There are no corporate perquisites," he stated, "No company planes, No country club memberships. No company cars."

Fortune noted, "Iverson takes the subway when he is in New York, a Wall Street analyst reports in a voice that suggests both admiration and amazement." The general managers reflected this style in the operation of their individual divisions. Their offices were more like plant offices or the offices of private companies built around manufacturing rather than for public appeal. They were simple, routine, and businesslike.

Division Managers

The corporate personnel manager described management relations as informal, trusting, and not "bureaucratic." There was a minimum of paperwork, a phone call was more common than memos, and no confirming memo was thought to be necessary.

A Vulcraft manager commented: "We have what I would call a very friendly spirit of competition from one plant to the next. And, of course, all of the vice presidents and general managers share the same bonus systems, so we are in this together as a team even though we operate our divisions individually."

The divisions managed their activities with a minimum of contact with the corporate staff. Each day disbursements were reported to corporate office. Payments flowed into regional lockboxes. On a weekly basis, joist divisions reported total quotes, sales cancellations, backlogs, and production. Steel mills reported tons rolled, outside shipments, orders, cancellations, and backlog.

Each month, the divisions completed a brief operations analysis, which was sent to all the managers. Its three main purposes were (1) financial consolidation, (2) sharing information among the divisions, and (3) corporate management examination. The summarized information and the performance statistics for all the divisions were then returned to the managers.

The general managers met three times a year. In late October they presented preliminary budgets and capital requests. In late February they met to finalize budgets and deal with miscellaneous matters. Then, at a meeting in May, they handled personnel matters, such as wage increases and changes of policies or benefits. The general managers, as a group, considered the raises for the department heads, the next lower level of management for all the plants.

Vulcraft: The Joist Divisions. One of Nucor's major businesses was the manufacture and sale of open web steel joists and joist girders at Vulcraft divisions located in Florence, South Carolina; Norfolk, Nebraska; Ft. Payne, Alabama; Grapeland, Texas; St. Joe, Indiana; Brigham City, Utah; and Chemung, New York. Open web joists, in contrast to solid joists, were made of steel angle iron separated by round bars or smaller angle iron (see Exhibit 2). These joists cost less, were of greater

Exhibit 2 Nucor's Vulcraft Group

BARTLE HALL CONVENTION CENTER

Kansas City, Missouri

NUCOR VULCRAFT - GROUP

strength for many applications, and were used primarily as the roof support systems in larger buildings, such as warehouses and shopping malls.

The joist industry was characterized by high competition among many manufacturers for many small customers. With a large percentage of the market, Nucor had been the largest supplier of joists in the United States since 1975. It utilized national advertising campaigns and prepared competitive bids on 80 to 90 percent of the buildings using joists. Competition was based on price and delivery performance. Nucor had developed computer programs to prepare designs for customers and to compute bids based on current prices and labor standards. In addition, each Vulcraft plant maintained its own engineering department to help customers with design problems or specifications. The Florence manager commented, "Here on the East Coast we have six or seven major competitors; of course none of them are as large as we are." He added, "It has been said to us by some of our competitors that in this particular industry we have the finest selling organization in the country."

Nucor aggressively sought to be the lowest-cost producer in the industry. Materials and freight were two important elements of cost. Nucor maintained its own fleet of almost 150 trucks to ensure on-time delivery all over the country, although most business was regional due to transportation costs. Plants were located in rural areas near the markets they served. Nucor's move into steel production was a move to lower the cost of steel used by the joist business.

On the basic assembly line used at the joist divisions, three or four of which might make up any one plant, about six tons of joists per hour would be assembled. In the first stage, eight people cut the angles to the right lengths or bend the round bars to the desired form. These were moved on a roller conveyer to six-man assembly stations, where the component parts would be tacked together for the next stage, which was welding. Drilling and miscellaneous work were done by three people between the lines. The nine-man welding station completed the welds before passing the joists on roller conveyers to two-man inspection teams. The last step before shipment was the painting.

The workers had control over and were responsible for quality. There was an independent quality control inspector who had the authority to reject the run of joists and cause them to be reworked. The quality control people were not under the incentive system and reported to the engineering department.

Daily production might vary widely, since each joist was made for a specific job. The wide range of joists made control of the workload at each station difficult; bottlenecks might arise anywhere along the line. Each workstation was responsible for identifying such bottlenecks so that the foreman could reassign people promptly to maintain productivity. Because workers knew most of the jobs on the line, including the more skilled welding jobs, they could be shifted as needed to avoid bottlenecks.

There were four lines of about 28 people each on two shifts at the Florence division. The jobs on the line were rated on responsibility and assigned a base wage, from $11 to $13 per hour in 1999. In addition, a weekly bonus was paid on the total output of each line. Each worker received the same percentage bonus based on their base wage. The Texas plant had a typical bonus of 225 percent, giving workers an average wage of $27 an hour.

The amount of time required to make a joist had been established over time. As a job was bid, the cost of each joist was determined through the computer program. The time required depended on the length, number of panels, and depth of the joist. At the time of production, the labor value of production, the standard, was determined in a similar manner. The general manager of the South Carolina plant stated, "In the last nine or ten years, we have not changed a standard." The Grapeland plant maintained a time chart based on the time jobs usually take, which was used to estimate the labor required on a job. The plant teams' bonuses were measured against this time.

Steel Divisions. Nucor moved into the steel business in 1968 to provide raw material for the Vulcraft plants. Iverson said, "We got into the steel business because we wanted to build a mill that could make steel as cheaply as we were buying it from foreign importers or from offshore mills." Thus, they entered the industry using the new mini-mill technology after they took a task force of four people around the world to investigate new technological advancements. A case writer from Harvard recounted the development of the steel divisions:

By 1967 about 60 percent of each Vulcraft sales dollar was spent on materials, primarily steel. Thus, the goal of keeping costs low made it imperative to obtain steel economically. In addition, in 1967 Vulcraft bought about 60 percent of its steel from foreign sources. As the Vulcraft Division grew, Nucor became concerned about its ability to obtain an adequate economical supply of steel and, in 1968, began construction of its first steel mill in Darlington, South Carolina. By 1972 the Florence, South Carolina, joist plant was purchasing over 90 percent of its steel from this mill. The Fort Payne, Alabama plant bought about 50 percent of its steel from Florence. Since the mill had excess capacity, Nucor began to market its steel products to outside customers. In 1972, 75 percent of the shipments of Nucor steel were to Vulcraft and 25 percent were to other customers.

Between 1973 and 1981, Nucor built three more bar mills and their accompanying rolling mills to convert the billets into bars, flats, rounds, channels, and other products. Iverson explained in 1984:

In constructing these mills we have experimented with new processes and new manufacturing techniques. We serve as our own general contractor and design and build much of our own equipment. In one or more of our mills, we have built our own continuous casting unit, reheat furnaces, cooling beds, and, in Utah, even our own mill stands. All of these to date have cost under $125 per ton of annual capacity—compared with projected costs for large integrated mills of $1,200-1,500 per ton of annual capacity, ten times our cost. Our mills have high productivity. We currently use less than four man-hours to produce a ton of steel. Our total employment costs are less than $60 per ton compared with the average employment costs of the seven largest U.S. steel companies of close to $130 per ton. Our total labor costs are less than 20 percent of our sales price.

In 1987, Nucor was the first steel company in the world to begin to build a mini-mill to manufacture steel sheet, the raw material for the auto industry and other major manufacturers. This project opened up another 50 percent of the total steel market. The first plant in Crawfordsville, Indiana, was successful, and three additional sheet mills were constructed in 1989 and 1990. During the next several years, these steel plants were significantly modernized and expanded. By 1999, their total capacity was three million tons per year at a capital cost of less than $170 per ton. Nucor's total steel production capacity was 5.9 million tons per year at a cost of $300 per ton of annual capacity. The eight mills sold 80 percent of their output to outside customers and the balance to other Nucor divisions.

The Steelmaking Processing

A steel mill's work is divided into two phases, preparation of steel of the proper "chemistry" and the forming of the steel into the desired products. The typical mini-mill utilizes scrap steel, such as junk auto parts, instead of the iron ore, which would be used in larger, integrated steel mills. The typical bar mini-mill had an annual capacity of 200 to 600 thousand tons, compared with the seven million tons of Bethlehem Steel's integrated plant in Sparrow's Point, Maryland.

In the bar mills, a charging bucket fed loads of scrap steel into electric arc furnaces. The melted load, called a "heat," was poured into a ladle to be carried by overhead crane to the casting machine. In the casting machine, the liquid steel was extruded as a continuous red-hot solid bar of steel and cut into lengths weighing some 900 pounds called "billets." In the typical plant the billet,

about four inches across and about 20 feet long, was held temporarily in a pit where it cooled to normal temperatures. Periodically, billets were carried to the rolling mill and placed in a reheat oven to bring them up to 2,000°F at which temperance they would be malleable. In the rolling mill, presses and dies progressively converted the billet into the desired round bars, angles, channels, flats, and other products. After cutting to standard lengths, they were moved to the warehouse.

Nucor's first steel mill, which employed more than 500 people, was located in Darlington, South Carolina. The mill, with its three electric arc furnaces, operated 24 hours per day, five-and-a-half days per week. Nucor made a number of improvements in the melting and casting operations. Thus, less time and lower capital investment were required at Darlington than at older mini-mills The casting machines were "continuous casters," as opposed to the old batch method.

Not all of Nucor's research projects were successful. The company spent approximately $2,000,000 in an unsuccessful effort to utilize resistance heating. Even more was lost from an effort at induction melting. As Iverson told *Metal Producing*, "That costs us a lot of money. Time wise it was very expensive. But you have got to make mistakes and we've had lots of failures."

The Darlington design became the basis for plants in Nebraska, Texas, and Utah. The Texas plant cost less than $80 per ton of annual capacity. Whereas the typical mini-mill at the time cost approximately $250 per ton, the average cost of Nucor's four mills was under $135. An integrated mill was expected to cost between $1,200 and $1,500 per ton.

The Darlington plant was organized into 12 natural groups for the purpose of incentive pay. Two mills each had two shifts with three groups: melting and casting, rolling mill, and finishing. In melting and casting there were three or four different standards, depending on the material. These standards had been established by the department manager years ago based on historical performance and were never adjusted. The caster, the key to the operation, was used at a 92 percent level—greater than the claims of the manufacturer. For every good ton of billet above the standard hourly rate for the week, workers in the group received a 4 percent bonus. Workers received a 4 to 6 percent bonus for every good ton sheared per hour for the week over the computed standard. A manager stated: "Meltshop employees don't ask me how much it costs Chaparral or LTV to make a billet. They want to know what it costs Darlington, Norfolk, Jewitt to put a billet on the ground—scrap costs, alloy costs, electrical costs, refractory, gas, etc. Everybody from Charlotte to Plymouth watches the nickels and dimes."

Management Philosophy

Aycock, while still the Darlington manager, stated:

The key to making a profit when selling a product with no aesthetic value, or a product that you really can't differentiate from your competitors, is cost. I don't look at us as a fantastic marketing organization, even though I think we are pretty good; but we don't try to overcome unreasonable costs by mass marketing. We maintain low costs by keeping the employee force at the level it should be, not doing things that aren't necessary to achieve our goals, and allowing people to function on their own and by judging them on their results.

To keep a cooperative and productive workforce you need, number one, to be completely honest about everything; number two, to allow each employee as much as possible to make decisions about that employee's work, to find easier and more productive ways to perform duties; and number three, to be as fair as possible to all employees. Most of the changes we make in work procedures and in equipment come from the employees. They really know the problems of their jobs better than anyone else.

To communicate with my employees, I try to spend time in the plant, and, at intervals, have meetings with the employees. Usually, if they have a question, they just visit me. Recently a small group visited me in my office to discuss our vacation policy. They had some suggestions and, after listening to them, I had to agree that the ideas were good.

In discussing his philosophy for dealing with the workforce, the Florence manager stated:

I believe very strongly in the incentive system we have. We are a non-union shop and we all feel that the way to stay so is to take care of our people and show them we care. I think that's easily done because of our fewer layers of management…I spend a good part of my time in the plant, maybe an hour or so a day. If a man wants to know anything, for example an insurance question, I'm there and they walk right up to me and ask me questions, which I'll answer the best I know how.

We don't lay our people off and we make a point of telling our people this. In the slowdown of 1994, we scheduled our line for four days, but the men were allowed to come in the fifth day for maintenance work at base pay. The men in the plant on an average running bonus might make $17 to $19 an hour. If their base pay is half that, on Friday they would only get $8 to $9 an hour. Surprisingly, many of the men did not want to come in on Friday. They felt comfortable with just working four days a week. They are happy to have that extra day off. About 20 percent of the people took the fifth day at base rate, but still no one had been laid off, in an industry with a strong business cycle.

In an earlier business cycle, the executive committee decided in view of economic conditions that a pay freeze was necessary. The employees normally received an increase in their base pay on the first of June. The decision was made at that time to freeze wages. The officers of the company, as a show of good faith, accepted a 5 percent pay cut. Management held meetings with the production workers to explain the economic crisis the company faced and to address any employee questions.

Personnel Policies

Nucor provided an incentive plan and job security. All employees at Nucor received the same fringe benefits and there was only one group insurance plan. Holidays and vacations did not differ by job. Every child of every Nucor employee received up to $1,200 a year for four years if they chose to go on to higher education, including technical schools. The company had no executive dining rooms or restrooms, no fishing lodges, company cars, or reserved parking places.

Jim Coblin, Nucor's vice president of human resources at the time, described Nucor's systems for *HR Magazine* in a 1994 article, "No frills HR at Nucor: a lean, bottom-line approach at this steel company empowers employees." Coblin, as benefits administrator, received part-time help from one of the corporate secretaries in the corporate office. The plants typically used someone from their finance department to handle compensation issues, although two plants had personnel generalists. Nucor plants did not have job descriptions, finding they caused more problems than they solved, given the flexible workforce and non-union status of Nucor employees. Surprisingly, Coblin found performance appraisal a waste of time. If an employee was not performing well, the problem would be dealt with directly. The key, he believed, was not to put a maximum on what employees could earn and pay them directly for productivity. Iverson firmly believed that the bonus should be direct and involve no discretion on part of a manager.

Employees were kept informed about the company. Charts showing the division's results in return-on-assets and bonus payoff were posted in prominent places in the plant. The personnel manager commented that as he traveled around to all the plants, he found everyone in the company could tell him the level of profits in their division. The general managers held dinners at least once a year with their employees. The dinners were held with 50 or 60 employees at a time, resulting in as many as 20 dinners per year for the general managers. After introductory remarks, the floor was opened for discussion of any work-related problems. There was a new employee orientation program and an employee handbook that contained personnel policies and rules. The corporate office sent all news releases to each division where they were posted on bulletin boards. Each employee in the company also received a copy of the annual report. For the last several years, the cover of the annual report contained the names of all Nucor employees.

Absenteeism and tardiness were not a problem at Nucor. Each employee had four days of absences before pay was reduced. In addition to these, missing work was allowed for jury duty, military leave, or the death of close relatives. After this, a day's absence cost the employee bonus pay for that week and lateness of more than a half-hour meant the loss of bonus for that day.

Safety was a concern of Nucor's critics. Nucor plants had 10 fatalities in the 1980s, but after safety administrators were appointed at each plant, safety improved in the 1990s. The company also had a formal grievance procedure, although the Darlington manager couldn't recall the last grievance he had processed.

The average hourly worker's pay was more than twice the average paid by other manufacturing companies in the states where Nucor's plants were located. In many rural communities, Nucor provided better wages than most other manufacturers. The plant in Hertford County illustrated this point. A June 21, 1998, article in *The Charlotte Observer* entitled "Hope on the Horizon: In Hertford County, Poverty Reigns and Jobs are Scarce" reported, "In North Carolina's forgotten northeastern corner, where poverty rates run more than twice the state average, Nucor's $300 million steel mill is a dream realized." The plant on the banks of the Chowan River saw employees earning up to three times the average local manufacturing wage. Nucor's desire to have other companies in the field close by to save on shipping costs led to four companies announcing they would locate close to Nucor's property, adding another 100 to 200 jobs. People couldn't believe such wages, but the average wage for these jobs at the Darlington plant was $70,000 and it was thought that this plant paid similarly. The plant CFO added that Nucor didn't try to set its pay "a buck over Wal-Mart" but instead went for the best workers. The article noted that steelwork is hot and often dangerous, and that turnover at the plant may be high as people adjust to the nature of the work and Nucor's hard-driving team system. He added, "Slackers don't last." The local preacher said, "In 15 years, Baron (a local child) will be making $75,000 a year at Nucor, not in jail. I have a place now I can hold in front of him and say 'Look, right here. This is for you.'"

In early 2009, Nucor's unique policies with its employees were still evident. Despite the economic crisis, performance in 2008 was excellent and $40 million in bonuses were distributed, with an extra bonus on top because of the extraordinary year. The company paid $270 million in profit sharing. Gail Bruce, the new vice president of human resources, explained how Nucor had avoided the layoffs other plants experienced. First, there was a history of open communications and a system designed to deal with the nature of the industry and educate workers about it. If plants were idled, pay automatically went to base pay, which was about half the usual total income with bonuses. No one was laid off and the well-paid workers could adapt, just like the company. He marveled, "The spirit in the operations is extraordinary." The cooperation extended to other solutions. *BusinessWeek* reported, "Work that used to be done by contractors, such as making special parts, mowing the lawns, and even cleaning the bathrooms, is now handled by Nucor staff. The bathrooms, managers say, [were] an employee suggestion." *BusinessWeek* reported that DiMicco and other managers received hundreds of cards and e-mails thanking them for caring about workers and their families.

The Incentive System

There were four incentive programs at Nucor, one each for (1) production workers, (2) department heads, (3) staff people, such as accountants, secretaries, or engineers, and (4) senior management, which included the division managers (VP/general managers of each division). All of these programs were based on group performance.

Within the production program, groups ranged in size from 25 to 30 people and had definable and measurable operations. The company believed that a program should be simple and that bonuses should be paid promptly. "We don't have any discretionary bonuses—zero. It is all based on performance. Now we don't want anyone to sit in judgment, because it never is fair…" said Iverson. Bonuses are based on roughly 90 percent of the historical time it takes to make a particular joist. If, for example, that week the joists are produced 40 percent faster than the standard time, workers get a 40 percent bonus in their pay the following week. The complete paycheck amount, including overtime, was multiplied by the bonus factor. A bonus was not paid when equipment was not operating. The foremen were also part of the group and received the same bonus as the employees they supervised.

The second incentive program was for department heads in the various divisions. The incentive pay here was based on division contribution, defined as the division earnings before corporate expenses and profit sharing are determined. Bonuses were reported to run between 0 and 90 percent (averaging more than 50 percent) of base salary. The base salaries at this level were set at 75 percent of industry norms.

There was a third plan for people who were not production workers, department managers, or senior managers. Their bonuses were based on either the division return-on-assets or the corporate return-on-assets, depending on their unit. Bonuses were typically 30 percent or more of a person's base salary for corporate positions.

The fourth program was for the senior officers. This group had no employment contracts, pension or retirement plans, or other perquisites. Their base salaries were set at about 75 percent of what an individual doing similar work in other companies would receive. Once return-on-equity reached 9 percent (slightly below the average for manufacturing firms) 5 percent of net earnings before taxes went into a pool, which was divided among the officers based on their salaries. For example, if the return-on-equity for the company reaches 20 percent, then senior officers can wind up with as much as 190 percent of their base salaries and 115 percent on top of that in stock. Half of the bonus was paid in cash and half was deferred. Individual bonuses ranged from zero to several hundred percent, averaging 75 to 150 percent.

However, the opposite was true as well. In 1982 the return was 8 percent and the executives received no bonus. Iverson's pay in 1981 was approximately $300,000 but dropped the next year to $110,000. "I think that ranked by total compensation I was the lowest paid CEO in the *Fortune* 500. I was kind of proud of that, too." In his 1997 book *Plain Talk: Lessons from a Business Maverick*, Iverson said, "Can management expect employees to be loyal if we lay them all off at every dip of the economy, while we go on padding our own pockets?" Even so, by 1986 Iverson's stock was worth over $10 million, and the former Vulcraft manager was a multimillionaire.

In lieu of a retirement plan, the company had a profit-sharing plan with a deferred trust. Each year 10 percent of pretax earnings were put into profit sharing for all employees below officer level. Twenty percent of this was set aside to be paid to employees the following March as a cash bonus, and the remainder was put into trust for each employee on the basis of a percentage of their earnings as a percentage of total wages paid within the corporation. The employee was vested after the first year. Employees received a quarterly statement of their balance in profit sharing.

The company had an Employer Monthly Stock Investment Plan into which Nucor added 10 percent to the amount the employee contributed to the purchase of any Nucor stock and paid the commission. For each five years of service with the company, the employee received a service award consisting of five shares of Nucor stock. Moreover, if profits were good, extraordinary bonus payments would be made to the employees. For example, in December 1998 each employee received an $800 payment.

According to Iverson:

I think the first obligation of the company is to the stockholder and to its employees. I find in this country too many cases where employees are underpaid and corporate management is making huge social donations for self-fulfillment. We regularly give donations, but we have a very interesting corporate policy. First, we give donations where our employees are. Second, we give donations that will benefit our employees, such as to the YMCA. It is a difficult area and it requires a lot of thought. There is certainly a strong social responsibility for a company, but it cannot be at the expense of the employees or the stockholders.

Having welcomed a parade of visitors over the years, Iverson became concerned with the pattern apparent at other companies' steel plants: "They only do one or two of the things we do. It's not just incentives or the scholarship program; it's all those things put together that results in a unified philosophy for the company."

Building on Their Success

Throughout the 1980s and 1990s, Nucor continued to take the initiative and be the prime mover in steel as well as the industries vertically related to steel. For example, in 1984 Nucor broke the industry pattern of basing the price of an order of steel on the quantity ordered. Iverson noted, "Some time ago we began to realize that with computer order entry and billing, the extra charge for smaller orders was not cost justified." In a seemingly risky move, in 1986 Nucor began construction of a $25 million plant in Indiana to manufacture steel fasteners. Imports had grown to 90 percent of this market as U.S. companies failed to compete. Iverson said "We're going to bring that business back; we can make bolts as cheaply as foreign producers." A second plant, which opened in 1995, gave Nucor 20 percent of the U.S. market for steel fasteners. Nucor also acquired a steel bearings manufacturer in 1986, which Iverson called "a good fit with our business, policies, and our people."

In early 1986, Iverson announced plans for a revolutionary plant at Crawfordsville, Indiana, that would be the first mini-mill in the world to manufacture flat-rolled or sheet steel, the last bastion of the integrated manufacturers. This market alone was twice the size of the existing market for mini-mill products. It would be a $250 million gamble on new technology. The plant was expected to halve the integrated manufacturer's labor cost of $3 per ton and save $50 to $75 on a $400-per-ton selling price. If it worked, the profit from this plant alone would come close to the profit of the whole corporation. *Forbes* commented, "If any mini-mill can meet the challenge, it's Nucor. But expect the going to be tougher this time around." If successful, Nucor would have the licensing rights to the next two plants built in the world with this technology. Nucor had spent millions trying to develop the process when it heard of some promising developments at a German company. In the spring of 1986, Aycock flew to Germany to see the pilot machine at SMS Schloemann-Siemag AG. In December the Germans came to Charlotte for the first of what they thought would be many meetings to hammer out a deal with Nucor. Iverson shocked them when he announced Nucor was ready to build the first plant of its kind.

Keith Busse was named general manager and put in charge of building the Crawfordsville steel sheet plant. The process of bringing this plant online was so exciting it became the basis for a best-selling book by Robert Preston, which was serialized in *The New Yorker*. Preston reported on a conversation during construction between Iverson and Busse. Thinking about the future, Busse was worried that Nucor might someday become like Big Steel. He asked, "How do we allow Nucor to grow without expanding the bureaucracy?" He didn't want to see Nucor end up like other companies with overlapping people doing the same job. Iverson agreed. Busse seriously suggested, "Maybe we're going to need group vice-presidents." Iverson's heated response was, "Do you want to ruin the company? That's the old Harvard Business School thinking. They would only get in the way, slow us down." He said the company could at least double in size before it added a new level of management. "I hope that by the time we have group vice-presidents I'll be collecting Social Security," he said.

The gamble on the new plant paid off, and Busse became a key man at Nucor. The new mill began operations in August 1989 and reached 15 percent of capacity by the end of the year. In June 1990 it had its first profitable month and Nucor announced the construction of a second plant in Arkansas.

The supply and cost of scrap steel to feed the mini-mills were an important future concern to Iverson. In 1993 Nucor announced the construction of plant in Trinidad to supply its mills with iron carbide pellets. The innovative plant would cost $60 million and take a year and a half to complete. In 1994 the two existing sheet mills were expanded and a new $500 million, 1.8-million-ton sheet mill in South Carolina was announced, to begin operation in early 1997.

In 1987, in what *The New York Times* called their "most ambitious project yet," Nucor began a joint venture with Yamato Kogyo, Ltd. to make structural steel products in a mill on the Mississippi River in direct challenge to the Big Three integrated steel companies. John Correnti was put in charge of the operation. Correnti built and then became the general manager of Nucor-Yamato when it started up in 1988. In 1991 he surprised

many people by deciding to double Nucor-Yamato's capacity by 1994. It became Nucor's largest division and the largest wide-flange producer in the United States. By 1995, Bethlehem Steel was the only other wide-flange producer of structural steel products left and had plans to leave the business.

Nucor started up its first facility to produce metal buildings in 1987. A second metal buildings facility began operations in late 1996 in South Carolina and a new steel deck facility in Alabama was announced for 1997. At the end of 1997, the Arkansas sheet mill underwent a $120 million expansion to include a galvanizing facility.

In 1995, Nucor became involved in its first international venture, an ambitious project with Brazil's Companhia Siderurgica National to build a $700 million steel mill in the state of Ceara. While other mini-mills were cutting deals to buy and sell abroad, Nucor was planning to ship iron from Brazil and process it in Trinidad.

Nucor set records for sales and net earnings in 1997. Although sales for 1998 decreased 1 percent and net earnings were down 10 percent, the management made a number of long-term investments and closed draining investments. Startup began at the new South Carolina steam mill and at the Arkansas sheet mill expansion. The plans for a North Carolina steel plate mill in Hertford were announced. This would bring Nucor's total steel production capacity to 12 million tons per year. Moreover, the plant in Trinidad, which had proven much more expensive than was originally expected, was deemed unsuccessful and closed. Finally, directors approved the repurchase of up to five million shares of Nucor stock.

Still, the downward trends at Nucor continued. Sales and earnings were down 3 percent and 7 percent, respectively, for 1999. However, these trends did not seem to affect the company's investments. Expansion was under way in the steel mills and a third building systems facility was under construction in Texas. Nucor actively searched for a site for a joist plant in the Northeast. A letter of intent was signed with Australian and Japanese companies to form a joint venture to commercialize the strip casting technology. To understand the challenges facing Nucor, industry, technology, and environmental trends in the 1980s and 1990s have to be considered.

Evolution of the U.S. Steel Industry

The early 1980s were the worst years in decades for the steel industry. Data from the American Iron and Steel Institute showed shipments falling from 100 million tons in 1979 to around 85 million tons in 1980 and 1981.

A slackening in the economy, particularly in auto sales, led the decline. In 1986, when industry capacity was at 130 million tons, the outlook was for a continued decline in per-capita consumption and movement towards the 90 to 100 million-ton range. The chairman of Armco saw "millions of tons chasing a market that's not there: excess capacity that must be eliminated."

The large, integrated steel firms, such as U.S. Steel and Armco, which made up the major part of the industry, were the hardest hit. The *Wall Street Journal* stated, "The decline has resulted from such problems as high labor and energy costs in mining and processing iron ore, a lack of profits and capital to modernize plants, and conservative management that has hesitated to take risks." These companies produced a wide range of steels, primarily from ore processed in blast furnaces. They found it difficult to compete with imports, usually from Japan. They sought the protection of import quotas.

Imported steel accounted for 20 percent of the U.S. steel consumption, up from 12 percent in the early 1970s. The U.S. share of world production of raw steel declined from 19 percent to 14 percent during the period. *Iron Age* stated that exports, as a percentage of shipments in 1985, were 34 percent for Nippon, 26 percent for British Steel, 30 percent for Krupp, 49 percent for USINOR of France, and less than 1 percent for every American producer on the list. The consensus of steel experts was that imports would average 23 percent of the market in the last half of the 1980s.

By the mid-1980s, the integrated mills were moving fast to get back into the game: they were restructuring, cutting capacity, dropping unprofitable lines, focusing products, and trying to become responsive to the market. The industry made a pronounced move toward segmentation. Integrated producers focused on mostly flat-rolled and structural grades; reorganized steel companies focused on a limited range of products; mini-mills dominated the bar and light structural product areas; and specialty steel firms sought niches. There was an accelerated shutdown of older plants, elimination of products by some firms, and the installation of new product lines with new technologies by others.

The road for the integrated mills was not easy. As *Purchasing* pointed out, tax laws and accounting rules slowed the closing of inefficient plants. Shutting down a 10,000-person plant could require a firm to hold a cash reserve of $100 million to fund health, pension, and insurance liabilities. The chairman of Armco commented: "Liabilities associated with a planned shutdown are so large that they can quickly devastate a company's balance sheet."

Joint ventures were formed to produce steel for a specific market or region. The chairman of USX called them "an important new wrinkle in steel's fight for survival" and stated, "If there had been more joint ventures like these two decades ago, the U.S. steel industry might have built only half of the dozen or so hot-strip mills it put up in that time and avoided today's over-capacity."

The American Iron and Steel Institute reported steel production in 1988 of 99.3 million tons, up from 89.2 in 1987 and the highest in seven years. As a result of modernization programs, 60.9 percent of production was from continuous casters. Exports for steel increased and imports fell. Some steel experts believed the United States was now cost competitive with Japan. However, 1989 proved to be a year of "waiting for the other shoe to drop," according to *Metal Center News*. U.S. steel production was hampered by a new recession, the expiration of the voluntary import restraints, and labor negotiations in several companies. Declines in car production and consumer goods hit flat-rolled steel hard. AUJ Consultants told MCN, "The U.S. steel market has peaked. Steel consumption is trending down. By 1990, we expect total domestic demand to dip under 90 million tons."

The economic slowdown of the early 1990s did lead to a decline in the demand for steel through early 1993, but by 1995 America was in its best steel market in 20 years and many companies were building new flat-roll mini-mills. A *BusinessWeek* article at the time described it as "the race of the Nucor look-alikes." Six years after Nucor pioneered the low-cost German technology in Crawfordsville, competitors were finally gearing up to compete. Ten new projects were expected to add 20 million tons per year of the flat-rolled steel, raising U.S. capacity by as much as 40 percent by 1998. These mills opened in 1997, just as the industry was expected to move into a cyclical slump. It was no surprise that worldwide competition increased and companies that had previously focused on their home markets began a race to become global powerhouses. The foreign push was new for U.S. firms who had focused on defending their home markets. U.S. mini-mills focused their international expansion primarily in Asia and South America.

Meanwhile, in 1994, U.S. Steel, North America's largest integrated steel producer, began a major business process re-engineering project to improve order fulfillment performance and customer satisfaction on the heels of a decade of restructuring. According to *Steel Times International*, "U.S. Steel had to completely change the way it did business. Cutting labor costs and increasing reliability and productivity took the company a long way towards improving profitability and competitiveness. However, it became clear that this leaner organization still had to implement new technologies and business processes if it was to maintain a competitive advantage." The goals of the business process re-engineering project included a sharp reduction in cycle time, greatly decreased levels of inventory, shorter order lead times, and the ability to offer real-time promise dates to customers. In 1995, they successfully installed integrated planning/production/order fulfillment software, and results were very positive. U.S. Steel believed that the re-engineering project had positioned it for a future of increased competition, tighter markets, and raised customer expectations.

In late 1997 and again in 1998, the decline in demand prompted Nucor and other U.S. companies to slash prices in order to compete with the unprecedented surge of imports. By the last quarter of 1998, these imports had led to the filing of unfair trade complaints with U.S. trade regulators, causing steel prices in the spot market to drop sharply in August and September before they stabilized. A press release from William Daley, the U.S. Secretary of Commerce, stated, "I will not stand by and allow U.S. workers, communities and companies to bear the brunt of other nations' problematic policies and practices. We are the most open economy of the world. But we are not the world's dumpster."

The Commerce Department concluded in March 1999 that six countries had illegally dumped stainless steel in the United States at prices below production costs or home market prices. The Commerce Department found that Canada, South Korea, and Taiwan were guilty only of dumping, while Belgium, Italy, and South Africa also gave producers unfair subsidies that effectively lowered prices. However, on June 23, 1999, the *Wall Street Journal* reported that the Senate decisively shut off an attempt to restrict U.S. imports of steel despite industry complaints that a flood of cheap imports were driving them out of business. Reportedly President Clinton would have vetoed the bill anyway because it would violate international trade law and leave the United States vulnerable to retaliation.

The American Iron and Steel Institute reported that in May 1999, U.S. steel mills shipped 8,330,000 net tons, a decrease of 6.7 percent from the 8,927,000 net tons shipped in May 1998. They also stated that for the first five months of 1999, shipments were 41,205,000 net tons, down 10 percent from the same period in 1998. AISI president and CEO Andrew Sharkey III said, "Once again, the May data show clearly that America's steel trade crisis continues. U.S. steel companies and employees continue to be injured by high levels of dumping and subsidized imports … In addition, steel inventory levels remain excessive, and steel operating rates continue to be very low."

As the 1990s ended, Nucor was the second-largest steel producer in the United States, behind USX. The company's market capitalization was about two times that of the next smaller competitor. Even in a tight industry, someone can win. Nucor was in the best position because

the industry was very fragmented and there were many marginal competitors.

Steel Technology and the Mini-Mill

A new type of mill, the mini-mill, emerged in the United States in the 1970s to compete with the integrated mill. The mini-mill used electric arc furnaces initially to manufacture a narrow product line from scrap steel. The leading U.S. mini-mills in the 1980s were Nucor, Florida Steel, Georgetown Steel, North Star Steel, and Chaparral. Between the late 1970s and 1980s, the integrated mills' market share fell from about 90 percent to about 60 percent, with the integrated steel companies averaging a 7 percent return on equity, the mini-mills averaging 14 percent, and some, such as Nucor, achieving about 25 percent. In the 1990s, the integrated mills' market share fell to around 40 percent while mini-mills' share rose to 23 percent, reconstructed mills increased their share from 11 percent to 28 percent, and specialized mills increased their share from 1 to 6 percent.

Some experts believed that a relatively new technology, the twin shell electric arc furnace, would help mini-mills increase production and lower costs and take market share. According to the *Pittsburgh Business Times*, "With a twin shell furnace, one shell—the chamber holding the scrap to be melted—is filled and heated. During the heating of the first shell, the second shell is filled. When the heating is finished on the first shell, the electrodes move to the second. The first shell is emptied and refilled before the second gets hot." This increased production by 60 percent. Twin shell production had been widely adopted. Nucor Steel began running a twin shell furnace in November 1996 in Berkeley, South Carolina, and installed another in Norfolk, Nebraska, which began operation in 1997. "Everyone accepts twin shells as a good concept because there's a lot of flexibility of operation," said Rodney Mott, vice president and general manager of Nucor-Berkeley. However, this move toward twin shell furnaces was destined to affect scrap availability. According to an October 1997 quote in *Pittsburgh Business Times* by Ralph Smaller, vice president of process technology at Kvaerner, "Innovations that feed the electric furnaces' production of flat-rolled (steel) will increase the demand on high quality scrap and alternatives. The technological changes are just beginning and will accelerate over the next few years."

According to a September 1997 *Industry Week* article, steelmakers around the world were now closely monitoring the development of continuous "strip casting" technology, which many thought would prove to be the next leap forward for the industry. "The objective of strip casting is to produce thin strips of steel (in the 1-mm to 4-mm range) as liquid steel flows from a tundish—the stationary vessel which received molten steel from the ladle. It would eliminate the slab-casting stage and all of the rolling that now takes place in a hot mill." Strip casting was reported to have some difficult technological challenges but companies in Germany, France, Japan, Australia, Italy, and Canada had strip-casting projects under way. In fact, all of the significant development work in strip casting was taking place outside the United States.

Larry Kavanagh, American Iron and Steel Institute vice president for manufacturing and technology, said, "Steel is a very high-tech industry, but nobody knows it." The most-productive steelmaking facilities incorporate advanced metallurgical practices, sophisticated process-control sensors, state-of-the art computer controls, and the latest refinements in continuous casting and rolling mill technology. Michael Shot, vice president of manu-facturing at Carpenter Technology Corp., a maker of specialty steels and premium-grade alloys, said, "You don't survive in this industry unless you have the tech-nology to make the best products in the world in the most efficient manner."

Environmental and Political Issues

Not all stakeholders were happy with the way Nucor did business. In June 1998, *Waste News* reported that Nucor's mill in Crawfordsville was cited by the Environmental Protection Agency for alleged viola-tions of federal and state clean-air rules. The Pamlico-Tar River Foundation, the North Carolina Coastal Federation, and the Environmental Defense Fund had concerns about the state's decision to allow the com-pany to start building the plant before the environmen-tal reviews were completed. According to the Charlotte *News & Observer,* "The environmental groups charge that the mill will discharge 6,720 tons of pollutants into the air each year."

Moreover, there were other concerns about the fast-track approval of the facility being built in Hertford County. This plant was to be located on the banks of one of the most important and sensitive stretches of the Chowan, a principal tributary to the Albemarle Sound and the last bastion of the state's once-vibrant river-herring fishery. North Carolina passed a law in 1997 that required the restoration of this fishery through a combination of measures designed to prevent overfish-ing, restore spawning and nursery habitats, and improve water quality in the Chowan. Another issue regarded the excessive incentives the state of North Carolina gave Nucor to build a $300 million steel mill there. Some questioned whether the promise of 300 well-paying jobs

in Hertford County was worth the $155 million in tax breaks the state was giving Nucor.

Management Evolution

Only five members of the board of directors were in attendance during their meeting in January 1999 due to the death of Jim Cunningham. Near the end of the meet-ing, Aycock read a motion, drafted by Siegel, that Ken Iverson be removed as chairman. It was seconded by Hlavacek and passed. This came as a surprise to Iverson. Prior to this time, in the spring of 1998, as Iverson approached his seventy-third birthday, he commented, "People ask me when I'm going to retire. I tell them our mandatory retirement age is 95, but I may change that when I get there." Now he was being forced out. It was announced that Iverson would be a chairman emeritus and a director, but after further disagreements, Iverson left the company completely. It was agreed, Iverson would receive $500,000 a year for five years. John Correnti succeeded Iverson in January 1999; but, he was voted out of this position in June 1999. At that time, David Aycock came out of retirement to become chairman, CEO, and president of Nucor.

All of this was a complete surprise to investors and brought the stock price down 10 percent. Siegel com-mented, "The board felt Correnti was not the right per-son to lead Nucor into the twenty-first century." Aycock assured everyone he would be happy to move back into retirement as soon as replacements could be found.

Aycock moved to increase the corporate office staff by adding a level of executive vice presidents over four areas of business and adding two specialist jobs in stra-tegic planning and steel technology. When Siegel retired, Aycock promoted Terry Lisenby to CFO and treasurer and hired a director of IT to report to Lisenby (see Exhibit 3 for the organizational chart in 2000).

Jim Coblin, vice president of human resources, believed the additions to management were necessary, "It's not bad to get a little more like other companies." He noted that the various divisions did their business cards and plant signs differently; some did not even want a Nucor sign. Sometimes six different Nucor salesmen would call on the same customer. "There is no manager of human resources in the plants, so at least we needed to give additional training to the person who does most of that work at the plant," he stated. With these new additions there would be a director of information tech-nology and two important committees, one for environ-mental issues and the second for audit.

Coblin believed the old system might have worked well when there was less competition. Aycock considered it "ridiculous." "It was not possible to properly manage,

Exhibit 3 Nucor Organization Chart, 2000

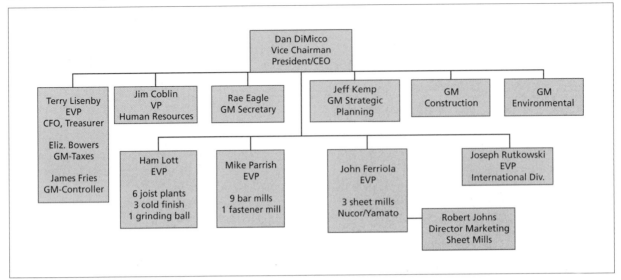

to know what was going on. The top managers have totally lost contact with the company." Coblin was optimistic the use of executive vice presidents would improve management. The three meetings of the general managers had slowly increased in length from about a day and a half to two-and-a-half days and became more focused. The new executive vice presidents would bring a perspective above the level of the individual plants. Instead of 15 individual detailed presentations, each general manager would give a short, five-minute briefing and then there would be an in-depth presentation on the group, with team participation. After some training by Lisenby, the divisions became pretty good with SWOT analysis. Coblin thought these changes would make Nucor a stronger global player.

To Jeff Kemp, the new general manager of strategic planning and business development, the big issue was how to sustain earnings growth. In the U.S. steel industry there were too many marginal competitors. The U.S. government had recently added to the problem by giving almost a billion dollars to nine struggling mills, which simply allowed them to limp along and weaken the industry. He was looking for Nucor's opportunities within the steel industry. His experience in the chemical industry suggested a need for Nucor to establish a position of superiority and grow globally, driving industry competition rather than reacting. He argued that a company should protect its overall market position, which could mean sacrifices for individual plants. Aycock liked Kemp's background in law and accounting and had specifically sought someone from outside the steel industry to head up Nucor's strategic planning. By June 2000, Kemp had conducted studies of other industries in the

U.S. market and developed a working document which identified opportunities worthy of further analysis.

"Every company hits a plateau," Aycock observed, "You can't just go out and build plants to grow. How do you step up to the next level? I wouldn't say it's a turning point, but we have to get our strategic vision and strategic plans." Nucor had its first-ever strategic planning sessions. Aycock believed Nucor needed to be quick to recognize developing technology in all production areas. He noted the joint venture to develop a new strip caster. This new product could allow Nucor to build smaller plants closer to markets. This would be particularly helpful on the West Coast. Nucor would own the U.S. and Brazilian rights, their partners the rest. He was also looking forward to the next generation of steel mills and wanted to own the rights to them. He praised Iverson's skill at seeing technology and committing to it.

Aycock was very interested in acquisitions, but felt they must fit the company's strategic plans. A significant opportunity existed in pre-engineered buildings. Aycock intended to concentrate on steel for the next five to six years, achieving an average growth rate of 15 percent per year. In about seven years he wanted Nucor to be ready to move into other areas. He said Nucor had already "picked the low hanging grapes" and must be careful in its next moves.

Daniel DiMicco assumed the role of Nucor's president and chief executive officer in September 2000, when Aycock stepped down as planned. Peter Browning was elected chairman of the board of directors. Aycock retired from the board a year later.

Sales for 2000 increased 14 percent over 1999 to reach a record level. Earnings were also at record levels, up 27 percent over 1999. The year began strongly but business weakened by year's end. The good news was that Nucor had record profits while other steel companies faced bankruptcy. A Vulcraft plant was under construction in New York, their first northeastern operation. They were also attempting a breakthrough technological step in strip casting at Crawfordsville known as the Castrip process. They sold their Grinding Ball process and the Bearing Products operation because they were not a part of their core business.

In the company's annual report, DiMicco laid out their plans for 2000 and beyond: "Our targets are to deliver an average annual earnings growth of 10–15 percent over the next 10 years, to deliver a return well in excess of our cost of capital, to maintain a minimum average return on equity of 14 percent, and to deliver to return on sales of 8–10 percent. Our strategy will focus on Nucor becoming a 'Market Leader' in every product group and business in which we compete. This calls for significant increases in market share for many of our core products and the maintenance of market share where we currently enjoyed a leadership position." While pointing out that it would be impossible to obtain this success through the previous strategy of greenfield construction, he added, "There will now be a heavy focus on growth through acquisitions. We will also continue growing through the commercialization of new disruptive and leapfrog technologies."

Steel and Nucor in the Twenty-First Century

In early 2009, DiMicco reflected back on his nine-year tenure as CEO of Nucor with pride. These had been some of the steel industry's rockiest times, and yet under his leadership, Nucor had almost doubled in size (see Appendices 1, 2, and 3).

By October 2001, more than 20 steel companies in the United States, including Bethlehem Steel Corp. and LTV Corp., the nation's third- and fourth-largest U.S. steel producers, respectively, had filed for bankruptcy protection. Over a dozen producers were operating under Chapter 11 bankruptcy-law protection, which allowed them to maintain market share by selling steel cheaper than non–Chapter 11 steelmakers. On October 20, 2001, *The Economist* noted that of the 14 steel companies followed by Standard & Poor's, only Nucor was indisputably healthy. In the fall of 2001, 25 percent of domestic steel companies were in bankruptcy proceedings, although the United States was the largest importer of steel in the world. Experts believed that close to half of the U.S. steel industry might be forced to close before conditions improved.

In 2001, the world steel industry found itself in the middle of one of its most unprofitable and volatile periods ever, in part due to a glut of steel that had sent prices to 20-year lows. While domestic steel producers were mired in red ink, many foreign steelmakers desperately needed to continue to sell in the relatively open U.S. market to stay profitable. The industry was hovering around 75 percent capacity utilization, a level too low to be profitable for many companies. Three European companies—France's Usinor SA, Luxembourg's Arbed SA and Spain's Aceralia Corp.—merged to form the world's largest steel company. Two Japanese companies—NKK Corp. and Kawasaki Steel Corp.—merged to form the world's second-biggest steelmaker. These new mega-steelmakers could outmuscle U.S. competitors, which were less efficient, smaller, and financially weaker than their competitors in Asia and Europe. At this time, the largest U.S. steelmaker, USX-U.S. Steel Group, was only the eleventh-largest producer in the world. Furthermore, while in 1990 mini-mills accounted for 36 percent of the domestic steel market, by 2000 the more efficient mini-mill had seized 50 percent of the market and the resulting competition had driven prices lower for integrated steel as well as mini-mills.

The year 2001 turned out to be one of the worst ever for steel. There were the September 11th attacks, a recession, and a surge of imports. DiMicco broke with Nucor's traditional opposition to government intervention to make a major push for protective tariffs. He stated, "The need to enforce trade rules is similar to the need to enforce any other law. If two merchants have stores side by side, but one sells stolen merchandise at a vast discount, we know that it's time for the police to step in." In March 2002, President Bush, after an investigation and recommendation by the ITC, imposed anti-dumping tariffs under section 201 of the Trade Act of 1974. This restricted some imports of steel and placed quotas of up to 30 percent on others. The move was opposed by many, including steel users. Some criticized the president for abandoning free trade and pointed out that protection would hamper the necessary actions to restructure the steel industry in America by reducing excess capacity. The European Union immediately threatened reprisals and appealed to the WTO. In December, China imposed its own three-year program of import duties. Steel prices rose 40 percent in 2002 after the tariffs. Within a year, the price of hot-rolled steel increased to $260 per ton over the 20-year low of $210 during 2002. In November 2003, the WTO ruled against the tariffs and, under increasing pressure of retaliation, Bush withdrew them.

While many steel companies floundered, Nucor was able to take advantage of these conditions. In March 2001, Nucor made its first acquisition in 10 years, purchasing a mini-mill in New York from Sumitomo Corp. DiMicco commented, It's taken us three years before our team has felt this is the right thing to do and get started making acquisitions." In this challenged industry, he argued it would be cheaper to buy than build plants. Nucor made more purchases. They purchased the assets of Auburn Steel, which gave them a merchant bar presence in the Northeast and helped the new Vulcraft facility in New York. They acquired ITEC Steel, a leader in the emerging load-bearing light-gauge steel-framing market, and saw an opportunity to aggressively broaden its market. Nucor increased its sheet capacity by roughly one third when it acquired the assets of Trico Steel Co. in Alabama for $120 million. In early 2002, they acquired the assets of Birmingham Steel Corp. This $650 million purchase of four mini-mills was the largest acquisition in Nucor's history. However, 2002 also proved to be a difficult year for Nucor. While they increased their steelmaking capacity by more than 25 percent, revenue increased 11 percent, and earnings improved 43 percent over their weak numbers of 2001, their other financial goals were not met.

This did not stop Nucor from continuing its expansion through acquisitions to increase their market share and capacity in steel and by actively working on new production processes that would provide them with technological advantages. They acquired the U.S. and Brazilian rights to the promising Castrip process for strip casting. After development work on the process in Indiana, they began full-time production in May 2002 and produced 7,000 tons in the last 10 months of 2002. Moreover, in April, Nucor entered into a joint venture with a Brazilian mining company, CVRD, the world's largest producer of iron-ore pellets, to jointly develop low-cost iron-based products. Success with this effort would give them the ability to make steel by combining iron ore and coke rather than using scrap steel, which was becoming less available (as was once feared).

During 2003, prices of steel rose in the United States and Asia as global demand outpaced supply. China, with its booming economy, drove the market. World prices did not soar dangerously because the steel industry continued to be plagued by overcapacity, but steel-hungry China and other fast-growing nations added to their steel capacity to balance supply and demand.

In August 2003, imports of steel commodities into the United States fell 22 percent. A weakened dollar, the growing demand from China, and tariffs imposed in 2002 limited imports. Domestic capacity declined as producers consolidated, idled plants, or went out of business, which increased capacity utilization from 77.2 to 93.4 percent. Prices for iron ore and energy rose, affecting integrated producers. Mini-mills saw their costs rise as worldwide demand for scrap rose. Thus, U.S. steelmakers boosted their prices. By February 2004, a growing coalition of U.S. steel producers and consumers was considering whether to petition to limit soaring exports of scrap steel from the United States, the world's largest producer of steel scrap. The United States had exported an estimated 12 million metric tons of steel scrap in 2003, a 21 percent increase from 2002. Moreover, the price of scrap steel had risen to $255 a ton. At the same time the price of hot-rolled sheet steel rose to $360 a ton. One result was that the International Steel Group (ISG) replaced Nucor as the most profitable U.S. steel producer. ISG was created when investor Wilbur Ross acquired the failing traditional steel producers in America, including LTV, Bethlehem, and Weirton. These mills used iron ore rather than scrap steel.

When 2003 ended, Nucor struck a positive note by reminding their investors that they had been profitable every single quarter since beginning operations in 1966. But, while Nucor set records for both steel production and steel shipments, net earnings declined 61 percent. While the steel industry struggled, Nucor increased its market share and held on to profitability. They worked on expanding their business with the automotive industry, continued their joint venture in Brazil to produce pig iron, and pursued a joint venture with the Japanese and Chinese to make iron without the usual raw materials. In February 2004, they were still "optimistic about the prospects for obtaining commercialization" of their promising Castrip process for strip casting in the United States and Brazil. The mini-mills could not produce sheet steel, a large share of the market. Moreover, Nucor was optimistic because trade laws were curtailing import dumping and Nucor expected higher margins.

Global competition continued. According to the *Wall Street Journal*, Posco Steelworks in Pohang, South Korea, enjoyed the highest profits in the global steel industry as of 2004. Moreover, *BusinessWeek* reported that the company had developed a new technology called Finex, which turned coal and iron ore into iron without coking and sintering and was expected to cut production costs by nearly a fifth and harmful emissions by 90 percent. They had also expanded their 80 Korean plants by investing in 14 Chinese joint ventures. By December 2004, demand in China had slowed and it had become a net steel exporter, sparking concerns of global oversupply.

Global consolidation also continued. In October 2004, London's Mittal family announced that they would merge their Ispat International NV with LNM Group and ISG, to create the world's largest steelmaker, with estimated annual revenue of $31.5 billion and output of 57 million tons. This would open a new chapter for the industry's consolidation, which had been mostly regional. Although the world's steel industry remained largely fragmented with the world's top 10 steelmakers supplying less than 30 percent of global production, Mittal Steel would have about 40 percent of the U.S. market in flat-rolled steel. Mittal, which had a history of using its scale to buy lower-cost raw materials and importing modern management techniques into previously inefficient state-run mills, was buying ISG, a U.S. company which already owned the lowest-cost, highest profit mills in the United States. In January 2005, Mittal also announced plans to buy 37 percent of China's Hunan Valin Iron & Steel Group Co.

In 2004 and 2005, Nucor continued its aggressive geographic expansion and introduction of new products. For example, Nuconsteel ("Nucon"), a wholly owned subsidiary of Nucor which specialized in load-bearing light-gauge steel-framing systems for commercial and residential construction markets, introduced two new low-cost automated fabrication systems for residential construction. In March 2005, Nucor formed a joint venture with Lennar Corporation, named Nextframe LP to provide comprehensive light-gauge steel framing for residential construction. Nucor's 25 percent joint venture with the Rio Tinto Group, Mitsubishi Corporation, and Chinese steelmaker Shougang Corporation for a HIsmelt commercial plant in Kwinana, Western Australia, started up in 2005. In 2004, Nucor acquired the assets of an idled direct-reduced iron (DRI) plant in Louisiana and moved them to Trinidad. By December 2006, construction was completed, and, in 2008, Nu-Iron Unlimited produced 1,400,000 metric tons of DRI from Brazilian iron ore for the United States.

By 2005, Nucor had 16 steel facilities producing three times as much as in 1999. The number of bar mills had grown to nine with capacity of 6,000,000 tons through the addition of Birmingham's four mills with 2,000,000 tons and Auburn's 400,000 tons. The sheet mills grew to four and increased capacity by one-third with the acquisition of Trico. Nucor–Yamato's structural steel capacity was increased by half a million tons from the South Carolina plant. A new million-ton plate mill, their second, had opened in North Carolina in 2000. Ninety-three percent of production was sold to outside customers.

By 2006, DiMicco had made many acquisitions while still managing to instill Nucor's unique culture in the new facilities. A May 2006 *BusinessWeek* article revealed that Nucor's culture and compensation system had changed very little since the 1990s. Michael Arndt reported that "Nucor gave out more than $220 million in profit sharing and bonuses to the rank and file in 2005. The average Nucor steelworker took home nearly $79,000 last year. Add to that a $2,000 one-time bonus to mark the company's record earnings and almost $18,000, on average, in profit sharing." He also noted that executive pay was still geared toward team building as "The bonus of a plant manager, a department manager's boss, depends on the entire corporation's return on equity. So there's no glory in winning at your plant if the others are failing."

Globally, steel mergers and acquisitions boomed during this time. This merger activity was due to a combination of low borrowing costs, high stock prices, and large amounts of cash. Another factor prompting mergers was a rise in the cost of raw materials. Despite all the transactions in 2006, 2007, and 2008, the industry remained fragmented, both domestically and internationally, and more mergers were expected.

Future merger activity was expected to differ slightly as steel companies attempted to become more vertically integrated. Examples included forward integration, such as combining Esmark's service center with Wheeling-Pittsburgh's steel production; and integration backward into scrap, such as the takeover of OmniSource by Steel Dynamics in 2007 and Nucor's acquisition of David J. Joseph Co. in 2008. These moves represented a trend toward becoming less dependent on outside vendors. This was due to the rising cost of scrap, which jumped from $185/ton in January 2006 to $635/ton in June 2008, and the highly concentrated nature of iron ore sources. BHP Billiton Ltd. based in Australia, Rio Tinto plc, headquartered in London, and Brazil-based Vale accounted for 75 percent of iron ore shipments worldwide.

Nucor was also active in mergers. In March 2007, Nucor acquired Harris Steel Group Inc. of Canada for $1.06 billion in cash, adding 770,000 tons of rebar fabrication capacity and over 350,000 tons of capacity in other downstream steel products. This acquisition showed that Nucor saw growth opportunities in finishing steel products for its customers and in distribution rather than additional steelmaking capacity. While many large steel companies were buying other primary steelmakers around the world, Nucor was focusing its investments largely in North America's manufacturing infrastructure such as reinforced steel bars, platform grating, and wire mesh for construction products ranging from bridges to airports and stadiums. According to Dan DiMicco, these moves "significantly advanced Nucor's downstream growth initiatives." Through the acquisition of Harris, Nucor also acquired a 75 percent interest in Novosteel S.A., a Swiss-based steel trading company that matched buyers and sellers of steel products on a global basis and offered its customers logistics support, material handling, quality certifications, and schedule management.

For the previous three years, Nucor had a joint venture with Harris, and in fact already owned a 50 percent stake in the company. Harris kept its name, as a Nucor subsidiary, and was led by the former chairman and CEO John Harris. However, the Harris board consisted of Harris and three Nucor representatives. This was the first time Nucor had broken from its non-union tradition, as about half of Harris's 3,000 employees were unionized. As steel analyst Timna Tanners said, "It's definitely a stretch for Nucor, culturally, since they have managed to keep its other operations non-union by offering higher salaries and production incentives. But there are not many non-union options left in North America when it comes to acquisitions and expansion."

The Harris team was operating as a growth platform within Nucor and had completed several acquisitions, including rebar fabricator South Pacific Steel Corporation in June 2007; Consolidated Rebar, Inc. in August 2007; a 90 percent equity interest in rebar fabricator Barker Steel Company, Inc. in December 2007; as well as smaller transactions. Nucor made several other acquisitions, which combined with the Laurel Steel, Fisher & Ludlow, and LEC businesses that came with the Harris acquisition and some internal organic growth, increased Nucor's cold finish and drawn products' capacity by more than

75 percent from 490,000 tons in 2006 to 860,000 tons at the end of 2007. In addition, it resulted in 90,000 tons of steel-grating capacity, and steel mesh capacity almost tripled, to 233,000 tons per year.

Nucor continued to invest in other downstream and upstream businesses (see Exhibit 4 for the organization chart in 2009). In the third quarter of 2007, they completed the acquisition of Magnatrax Corporation, a leading provider of custom-engineering metal buildings, for $275.2 million. The Magnatrax acquisition, when combined with their existing Building Systems divisions and a newly constructed Buildings Systems division in Brigham City, Utah, made Nucor the second-largest metal building producer in the United States, more than doubling their annual capacity to 480,000 tons of pre-engineered metal buildings.

In 2007, Nucor's seven Vulcraft facilities supplied more than 40 percent of all domestic buildings built using steel joists and joist girders. In both 2006 and 2007, 99 percent of its steel requirements were obtained from Nucor bar mills. Nucor's nine steel deck plants supplied almost 30 percent of total domestic sales in decking; six of these plants were constructed by Nucor adjacent to Vulcraft joist facilities and three were acquired in November 2006 as a wholly owned subsidiary called Verco Decking. These decking plants obtained 99 percent of their steel requirements from

Exhibit 4 Nucor Organization Chart, 2009

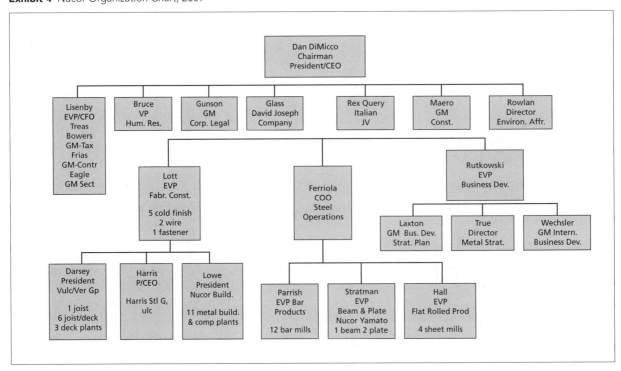

Nucor sheet plants in 2006, but only 76 percent in 2007.

In March 2008, Nucor completed the acquisition of the David J. Joseph Company (DJJ), the largest broker of ferrous and non-ferrous scrap in the United States and one of the nation's largest processors of ferrous scrap, for $1.44 billion. The company had been a supplier of scrap to Nucor since 1969. DJJ operated over 30 scrap-processing facilities. This acquisition expanded Nucor's scrap-processing capabilities from 500,000 to 4,000,000 short tons and provided them additional steelmaking raw materials through their brokerage operations, and rail services and logistics through its private fleet of some 2,000 scrap-related railcars. This allowed them to capture further margins in the steelmaking supply chain and to more closely control their raw-materials inputs. In May, they announced a plan to raise $3 billion for expansions and acquisitions, two-thirds to come from selling 25 million new shares.

U.S. steelmakers saw a major transition in 2008. In the first quarter, the combination of higher volume and increased prices led to a sizable gain in profits. Furthermore, data showed that the four leading domestic steel companies, AK Steel Holding Corp., Nucor Corp., Steel Dynamics Inc., and United States Steel Corp., which Standard & Poor's followed as a proxy for industry performance, collectively accounted for 45.5 percent of industry shipments in 2007. The rise in revenues for this proxy group reflected a 9.3 percent increase in revenue per ton, volume gained at the expense of imports, and the impact of acquisitions. At the end of July, major U.S. steelmakers' results were still supported by months of steel-price increases, which eased the burden of rising raw materials prices, as demand from emerging markets kept global steel supplies tight.

However, in September 2008, steelmakers in the United States experienced a sharp pullback from buyers who were concerned with the credit crisis and a slowdown in automobile and construction markets. This caused inventories to rise and prices on some key products to drop by 10 percent. The *Wall Street Journal* reported on November 17 that "Metals prices fell 35% in just four weeks last month—the steepest decline ever recorded, according to Barclays Capital." They also reported that big steelmakers worldwide were cutting production as much as 35 percent and that U.S. Steel planned to lay off 2 percent of its workforce. Chinese demand also slowed. This was a swift reversal in an industry that saw its profits increase 20-fold in five years. The pricing volatility was intensified by the global financial crisis as many hedge funds, pension funds, and other investors desperate to raise cash rapidly sold their commodities holdings. Still, the article said that ultimately the industry's problems were rooted in weakened demand, particularly in China, rather than the financial crisis.

So as 2009 began, with prices for steel, iron ore, and scrap metal plummeting, competition in the global steel industry was expected to increase. And further consolidation was expected as the major players sought to maintain their dominant positions (see Exhibit 5). In a December 2008 interview on CNBC, Cramer said to DiMicco, "Nucor's great CEO," that it was "amazing you can be profitable" with an overnight 40 percent drop in sales. DiMicco said it showed the success of their business model. He believed Nucor's acquisitions over the past 10 years, with their integration into steel products markets and raw materials, would position them to survive and even prosper—where there were threats there were also opportunities.

Exhibit 5 Top 12 Global Steel Producers, end 2007

2007 Rank	mmt	2006 Rank	mmt	Company Name
1	116.4	1	117.2	ArcelorMittal
2	35.7	2	34.7	Nippon Steel
3	34.0	3	32.0	JFE
4	31.1	4	30.1	POSCO
5	28.6	6	22.5	Baosteel
6	26.5	45	6.4	Tata Steel*
7	23.6	5	22.6	Anshan-Benxi
8	22.9	17	14.6	Jiangsu Shagang
9	22.8	9	19.1	Tangshan
10	21.5	7	21.2	U.S. Steel
11	20.4	16	15.1	Wuhan
12	20.0	8	20.3	Nucor

Note: *2007 figure includes Corus.
mmt = million metric tons.

Source: International Iron and Steel Institute, September 21, 2008.

Appendix 1 Balance Sheet 2000–2008 (in millions of U.S.[$])

As of 12/31	2008	2007	2006	2005	2004	2003	2002	2001	2000
Assets									
Cash	2,355	1,394	786	980	779	350	219	462	491
Receivables	1,229	1,612	1,067	1,001	963	572	484	331	350
Total Inventories	2,408	1,602	1,141	945	1,240	560	589	467	461
Other Current Assets	405	283	270	288	193	137	157	134	80
Total Current Assets	6,397	5,073	4,675	4,072	3,175	1,621	1,449	1,394	1,381
Property, Plant, & Equip.	4,132	3,233	2,856	2,856	2,818	2,817	2,932	2,366	2,329
Deposits & Other Assets	667	202	354	212	140	55	n/a	n/a	n/a
Goodwill, Other Intang.	2,679	1,318	n/a	n/a	n/a	n/a	n/a	n/a	n/a
Total Assets	13,874	9,826	7,885	7,139	6,133	4,492	4,381	3,759	3,711
Liabilities									
Accounts Payable	534	692	517	502	472	330	247	189	203
Curr. Long-Term Debt	180	n/a	n/a	n/a	n/a	n/a	n/a	n/a	n/a
Accrued Expense	352	431	478	384	565	300	319	295	355
Income Taxes	199	n/a	n/a	n/a	29	n/a	9	n/a	n/a
Other Cur. Liab., Salaries	580	436	455	369	n/a	n/a	n/a	n/a	n/a
Total Current Liabilities	1,854	1,582	1,450	1,256	1,066	630	592	484	558
Deferred Charges/Inc.	677	593	448	487	515	440	371	329	260
Long-Term Debt	3,086	2,250	922	922	924	904	879	460	460
Total Liabilities	5,945	4,713	2,820	2,665	2,504	1,973	1,841	1,274	1,279
Shareholder Equity									
Minority Interest	327	287	239	194	173	177	217	284	301
Preferred Stock	n/a	n/a	n/a	n/a	n/a	n/a	n/a	n/a	n/a
Common Stock	150	149	149	74	74	36	36	36	36
Capital Surplus	1,630	256	196	192	147	117	99	81	71
Retained Earnings	7,861	6,622	5,809	5,709	3,689	2,642	2,642	2,539	2,479
Treasury Stock	−1,521	−2,078	−1,332	−739	452	453	454	455	455
Total Shareholder Equity	7,929	5,113	4,826	4,280	3,456	2,342	2,323	2,201	2,131
Total Liability & Shareholder Equity	13,874	9,826	7,885	7,139	6,133	4,492	4,381	3,759	3,711

Source: Nucor annual reports.

Appendix 2 Income Statement 2000–2008

Period Ended	12/31/2008	12/31/2007	12/31/2006	12/31/2005	12/31/2004	12/31/2003	12/31/2002	12/31/2001	12/31/2000
Net Sales	23,663,324	16,592,926	14,751,270	12,700,999	11,376,83	6,265.82	4,801.78	4,333.71	4,756.52
Cost of Goods Sold	19,612,283	13,462,927	11,283,123	10,119,496	9,128.87	5,996.55	4,332.28	3,914.28	3,929.18
Gross Profit	4,051,041	3,130,049	3,468,147	2,581,503	2,247.96	269.28	469.5	419.43	827.34
R & D Expenditure	n/a	n/a	n/a	n/a	n/a	n/a	n/a	n/a	n/a
Selling G & A Exps	750,984	577,764	592,473	459,460	415.03	165.37	175.59	150.67	183.18
Depreciation & Amort.	n/a	n/a	n/a	n/a	n/a	n/a	n/a	n/a	n/a
Non-Operating Inc.	n/a	n/a	−37,365	−9,200	−79.3	−12.4	−49.57	−82.87	−150.65
Interest Expense	90,483	5,469	n/a	4201	22.35	24.63	14.29	6.53	n/a
Income Before Taxes	2,790,470	2,253,315	2,693,818	2,016,368	1,731.28	66.88	230.05	179.37	493.52
Prov. For Inc. Taxes	959,480	781,368	936,137	706,084	609.79	4.1	67.97	66.41	182.61
Minority Interest	313,921	293,501	219,121	110,650	80,840	n/a	n/a	n/a	n/a
Realized Investment	n/a	n/a	n/a	n/a	n/a	n/a	n/a	n/a	n/a
Other Income	n/a	n/a	n/a	n/a	n/a	n/a	n/a	n/a	n/a
Net Income	1,830,990	1,471,947	1,757,681	1,310,284	1,121.49	62.78	162.08	112.96	310.91

In thousands of USD

Source: Nucor annual reports.

Appendix 3 Nucor Valuation Rations, 2005–2008

	2008	2007	2006	2005
P/E(TTM)	7.38		11.76	7.38
Per Share Rations				
Divdend Per Share	1.31		0.67	0.47
Book Value Per Share	25.18		21.54	21.54
EPS Fully Diluted	5.98	4.94	5.68	7.02
Revenue Per Share	77.31		48.1	71.21
Profit Margins				
Operating Margin	13.95		18.26	16.23
Net Profit Margin	7.74	8.9	11.90	9.86
Gross Profit Margin	17.12		23.51	19.88
Dividends				
Dividend Yield	3.17		0.66	1.13
Dividend Yield -5-Year Avg.	3.21		2.17	1.28
Dividend Per Share (TTM)	1.31		0.6	0.52
Dividend Payout Ratio	35.94		37.32	6.66
Growth (%)				
5-Year Annual Growth	96.32		27.76	35.6
Revenue – 5-Year Growth	30.44		27.8	23.19
Div/Share – 5-Year Growth	45.63		71.5	12.57
EPS – 5-Year Growth	97.3		73.34	32.58
Financial Strength				
Quick Ratio	1.93		2.44	1.63
Current Ratio	3.45	3.2	3.22	2.98
LT Debt to Equity	38.92	44.01	19	26.72
Total Debt to Equity	42.09		19	26.72
Return on Equity (ROT) Per Share	27.91		38.61	38.57
Return on Assets (ROA)	16.19	16.62	23.4	25.4
Return on Invested Capital (ROIC)	19.91		29.58	33.33
Assets				
Assets Turnover	1.71		1.96	1.85
Inventory Turnover	9.51		10.82	9.7

Source: Thomson-Reuters Financial.

Jinxuan Zhang

We've been the No. 1 Web site in China for a number of years, and in fact we are the largest Web site outside of the U.S. When people get to know about the Internet, the first Web site they learn is about Baidu in China.

—ROBIN YANHONG LI, COFOUNDER, CHAIRMAN, & CEO, BAIDU[i]

We were late entering the China market, and we're catching up . . . . Our investment is working and we will eventually be the leader.

—ERIC SCHMIDT, CHAIRMAN & CEO, GOOGLE[ii]

By far China's most popular search engine, Baidu.com Inc. (Baidu) continued to dominate that market with a 60.4 percent market share in 2007,[iii] more than double that of Google Inc. (Google). In 2005, Google, the world's leading search engine, entered the Chinese market. While Google was catching up, Baida continued to grow. BNP Paribas observed: "Baidu and Google are winning at the expense of other search engines [in China] . . . Baidu gained market share at the expense of all players except for Google."[iv]

According to *BusinessWeek's* list of "The Best (and) Worst Leaders of 2006," Li was ranked third and his company was described as the "Best Answer to Google." Bill Gates and Steve Ballmer might want to have a sit-down with Chinese entrepreneur Robin Li. The founder and CEO of Baidu.com has achieved something that Microsoft's top brass have yet to manage—beating Google.[v]

On January 31, 2008, Ballmer made a proposal to Yahoo! to acquire outstanding shares of the company's common stock for per-share consideration of $31 in the hope of rapidly expanding Microsoft's presence in the online search advertising market dominated by Google.[vi]

On May 20, 2008,[vii] Baidu traded at a price to earnings ratio of 153. This is four times more than Google, over seven times more than Microsoft, and almost three times more than Yahoo! Was the price justified? Would it last?

Global vs. Local

Embarking on a Journey for Search

Google is a leading global Internet search and online advertising company. In January 1996, the company was founded by Larry Page and Sergey Brin, who started it as a research project when they were doctoral students at Stanford University. On September 7, 1998, it was formally incorporated as Google Inc. Google was able to win its audience because of the quality of its search results. Google's search algorithm[1] took into account relevance and other qualitative elements that other search engines did not.

Baidu—often referred to as "China's Google"—was incorporated in the Cayman Islands on January 18, 2000, by cofounders Robin Yanhong Li and Eric Yong Xu.[2] Both were Chinese nationals who had studied and worked overseas before returning to China. Baidu began as a provider of Internet search solutions to other Chinese portals. Then, it tapped into the unexplored Chinese online search market and gained a first-mover advantage by coming up with a search engine that provided information in local Chinese languages. Baidu initially became popular because of its multimedia content,

Research Associate Jinxuan (Ann) Zhang prepared this case under the supervision of Professor Didier Cossin as a basis for class discussion rather than to illustrate either effective or ineffective handling of a business situation.

[1] In computer science, a search algorithm is an algorithm that takes a problem as input and returns a solution to the problem, usually after evaluating a number of possible solutions.

[2] Li earned a master's degree in computer science from the State University of New York at Buffalo and worked at search engine Infoseek for more than two years before returning to China. Xu, a biochemist who was well connected in the Silicon Valley, was not involved in the management of the company.

including MP3 music and movies, but was criticized for being "weak on piracy, strong on censorship."[viii]

A "1 followed by 100 zeros" vs. "Hundreds of Times"

The name Google originated from the mathematical term "Googol" for a 1 followed by 100 zeros. It reflected Google's mission "to organize the world's information and make it universally accessible and useful."[ix]

The literal meaning of Baidu is "hundreds of times." It was inspired by an ancient Chinese poem and represented a persistent search for the ideal. The name was chosen so that the world would remember Baidu's Chinese heritage. By focusing on what it knew best, Baidu aimed "to provide the best way for people to find information"[x] by applying an avant-garde technology to the world's most ancient and complex language.

Growing, But Not Yet on the Same Scale

Even though Baidu is growing quickly, it still remains tiny in comparison to Google's global size. Baidu earned about $86 million in net income in 2007 on $239 million in revenue,[xi] compared with Google's $4.2 billion in net income on $16.6 billion in revenue.

Products & Services

Baidu's homepage was strikingly similar to Google's—a search bar at the center of a mostly empty page (see Exhibit 1). Both Baidu and Google provided a wide range of products and services that gave users a better search experience with a view to increasing traffic and user stickiness. Their offerings could be placed into three categories: search, community, and other enhancements. While Google has started to experiment with other markets, such as radio and print publications, Baidu looked towards consumer-to-consumer (C2C) and mobile search.

Business Model

Baidu and Google essentially utilized the same business model—selling ads tied to user searches (see Exhibit 2). Both companies primarily derived their revenues from online marketing activities on their Web sites, principally auction-based pay-for-performance (P4P)[3] search advertisements.

Baidu introduced "pay-for-placement," which allowed companies to bid for search-result placement based on relevant keywords. Google believed that "you can make money without doing evil"[4,xiii] and did not allow ads to be displayed on its results pages. Advertising produced by certain searches was clearly identified as a "sponsored link" and displayed above or to the right of the results.

In addition, Baidu and Google also expanded their search platforms to include a network of third-party Web sites that incorporated their search box or toolbar in a revenue-sharing model. This enabled both companies to use their advertising platforms to generate user traffic and enlarge their paid-search networks. According to BNP Paribas estimates, Baidu already derived 25 percent of its revenue from its partner Web sites,[xiv] while Google about 10% to 15% from such partner Web sites (see Exhibit 3 for the Google revenue breakdown).[xv]

Growth Strategy

Since 2001, Google has acquired some small startup companies with innovative teams and products—for example, Deja, Pyra Labs, and Sprinks. Since its IPO[5] in 2004, it also has entered into a wide array of products and services outside its sponsored-search domain. Google has attempted to keep pace with changing times and identify future growth opportunities both organically, by launching Gmail and Orkut,[6] and by acquiring YouTube and DoubleClick (see Exhibit 4 for a list of Google's major acquisitions). In April 2004, Google knocked on Baidu's door. Two months later, Google acquired a 2.6 percent stake in Baidu for $5 million (at the time, Baidu was not well known outside its homeland).

For its part, Baidu pursued strategic acquisitions of businesses, assets, and technologies that complemented its existing capabilities and business. In August 2004, it acquired the domain name hao123.com. Headquartered in Shanghai, hao123.com was Baidu's largest traffic contributor and its largest distributor of its P4P services.[7] Both companies also actively formed strategic alliances with market leaders in other business sectors to further broaden their customer bases and product and service offerings.

Geographic Expansion

Google has built up its international presence to the point that international revenues accounted for approximately 48 percent of Google's total revenue in 2007 and surpassed its domestic revenues in Q1 2008 (see Exhibit 3). More than half of its user traffic also came from outside the United States (see Exhibit 5 for a user traffic breakdown). Baidu, for its part, focused on offering searches in Chinese. However, on January 24, 2008, Baidu made

---

[3] P4P customers bid for priority placements of links to their Web sites among relevant search results.

[4] "Don't be evil" was the informal corporate motto or slogan for Google.

[5] Initial Public Offering.

[6] A social networking service run by Google and named after its creator—a Google employee.

[7] Baidu's ability for acquiring local companies was subject to foreign exchange regulations on mergers and acquisitions in China.

Exhibit 1 Homepages of Baidu and Google

Exhibit 2 Business System of a Search Engine

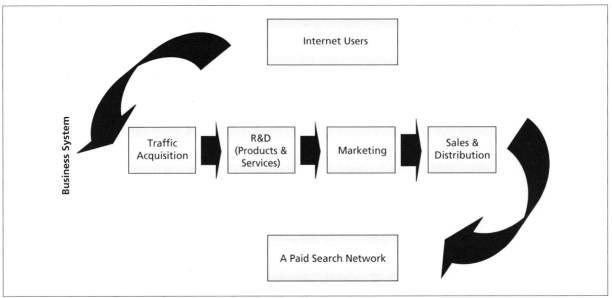

Source: IMD Research.

Exhibit 3 Google's Revenue Breakdown

By Source	2003	2004	2005	2006	2007	2008Q1
Revenues (in $ million)						
Google sites' advertising revenues	$792	$1,589	$3,377	$6,333	$10,625	$3,400
Google network advertising revenues	629	1,554	2,688	4,160	5,788	1,686
Total advertising revenues	1,421	3,143	6,065	10,493	16,413	5,087
Licensing and other revenues	45	46	74	112	181	99
Total revenues	$1,466	$3,189	$6,139	$10,605	$16,594	$5,186
As % of total revenues						
Google sites' advertising revenues	54%	50%	55%	60%	64%	66%
Google network advertising revenues	43%	49%	44%	39%	35%	33%
Total advertising revenues	97%	99%	99%	99%	99%	98%
Licensing and other revenues	3%	1%	1%	1%	1%	2%

Exhibit 3 Google's Revenue Breakdown *(Continued)*

By Source	2003	2004	2005	2006	2007	2008Q1
By Location (in $ million)						
U.S.	$1,038	$2,119	$3,757	$6,030	$8,629	$2,541
International	428	1,070	2,382	4,575	7,965	2,645
Total revenue	$1,466	$3,189	$6,139	$10,605	$16,594	$5,186
As % of total revenues						
U.S.	71%	66%	61%	57%	52%	49%
International	29%	34%	39%	43%	48%	51%

Source: Google's annual reports and quarterly results, dollar value in millions.

Exhibit 4 Google's Major Acquisitions

Acquisition Date	Company	Business	Country	Value	Derived Services
February 12, 2001	Deja	Usenet	USA		Google Groups
September 2001	Outride	Web search engine	USA		Google Personalized Search
February 2003	Pyra Labs	Web software	USA		Blogger
April 2003	Neotonic Software	Customer relationship management	USA		Google Groups, Gmail
April 2003	Applied Semantics	Online advertising	USA	$102 million	AdSense, AdWords
September 30, 2003	Kaltix	Web search engine	USA		iGoogle
October 2003	Sprinks (a division of Primedia)	Online advertising	USA		AdSense, AdWords
October 2003	Genius Labs	Blogging	USA		Blogger
May 10, 2004	Ignite Logic	HTML editor	USA		Google Page Creator
June 23, 2004	Baidu	Chinese language search engine	CHN	$5 million	Sold in 2006
July 13, 2004	Picasa	Image organizer	USA		Picasa, Blogger
September 2004	ZipDash	Traffic analysis	USA		Google Ride Finder
October 2004	Where2	Map analysis	USA		Google Maps

(Continued)

Exhibit 4 Google's Major Acquisitions *(Continued)*

Acquisition Date	Company	Business	Country	Value	Derived Services
October 27, 2004	Keyhole, Inc.	Map analysis	USA		Google Maps, Google Earth
March 28, 2005	Dodgeball	Social networking service	USA		Google Mobile, Google SMS
March 12, 2005	Urchin Software Corporation	Web analytics	USA		Google Analytics
July 2005	Reqwireless	Mobile browser	CAN		Google Mobile
July 7, 2005	Communications Group	Broadband Internet access	USA	$100 million	Internet Backbone
August 17, 2005	Android	Mobile software	USA		Google Mobile, Google SMS
November 2005	Skia	Graphics software	USA		Picasa
November 17, 2005	Akwan Information Technologies	Broadband Internet access	BRA		Internet Backbone
December 20, 2005	AOL	Broadband Internet access	USA	$1,000 million	
December 27, 2005	Phatbits	Widget engine	USA		Google Desktop
December 31, 2005	allPAY GmbH	Mobile software	GER		Google Mobile
December 31, 2005	bruNET GmbH dMarc	Mobile software	GER		Google Mobile
January 17, 2006	Broadcasting	Advertising	USA	$102 million	AdSense
February 14, 2006	Measure Map	Weblog software	USA		Google Analytics
March 9, 2006	Upstartle	Word processor	USA		Google Documents
March 14, 2006	@Last Software	3D modeling software	USA		Google Sketchup
April 9, 2006	Orion	Web search engine	AUS		Google Search
June 1, 2006	2Web Technologies	Online spreadsheets	USA		Google Spreadsheet
August 15, 2006	Neven Vision	Computer vision	USA		Google Maps
October 9, 2006	YouTube	Video sharing	USA	$1,650 million	Google Video
October 31, 2006	JotSpot	Web application	USA		Google Sites
December 18, 2006	Endoxon	Mapping	CHE	$28 million	Google Maps

Exhibit 4 Google's Major Acquisitions (Continued)

Acquisition Date	Company	Business	Country	Value	Derived Services
January 4, 2007	Xunlei	File sharing	CHE	$5 million	
February 16, 2007	Adscape	In-game advertising	USA	$23 million	AdSense
March 16, 2007	Trendalyzer	Statistical software	SWE		Google Analytics
April 13, 2007	Double Click	Online advertising	USA	$3,100 million	AdSense
April 17, 2007	Tonic Systems	Presentation program	USA		Google Documents
April 19, 2007	Marratech	Videoconferencing	SWE		Google Talk
May 11, 2007	GreenBorder	Computer security	USA		Internal Use
June 1, 2007	Panoramio	Photo sharing	ESP		Blogger
June 3, 2007	FeedBurner	Web feed	USA	$100 million	Google Reader
June 5, 2007	PeakStream	Parallel processing	USA		Server (computing)
June 19, 2007	Zenter	Presentation program	USA		Google Documents
July 2, 2007	GrandCentral	Voice over Internet Protocol	USA	$45 million	Google Mobile
July 9, 2007	Postini	Communications security	USA	$625 million	Gmail
July 20, 2007	Image America	Aerial photography	USA		Google Maps
September 27, 2007	Zingku	Social network service	USA		Google Mobile
October 9, 2007	Jaiku	Micro-blogging	FIN		Google Mobile

its first international move by launching its Japanese version—Baidu.jp[8]—with the primary objective of serving Chinese small and medium-sized enterprises (SMEs) doing business in Japan. Its focus remained on product development to meet the needs of Japanese users and operating costs and expenses of RMB30 million ($4.3 million) were incurred for Q1 2008 (no revenue was expected for fiscal year 2008).[xvii]

Google in China vs. "China's Google"

Google's Answer to Its Chinese Question
Google launched its Chinese language version in 2000 and its popularity quickly grew through word

of mouth among Chinese Internet surfers. The company did well until September 2002, when Google was blocked by the "Great Firewall of China"[9]—a political rift over censorship with the Chinese government—and was denied rights to China. While Google's company Web site proclaimed, "Google—the closest thing the Web has to an ultimate answer machine," it did not have an answer to its one big China question: how can we go into China and yet not do evil?[xviii]

"They [Google] can't afford to not be in China . . . They are facing a hard choice. They really don't want to be seen as doing something that is evil, but no one goes into China on their own terms."[xix]

According to Eric Schmidt, Google actually did "an evil scale" and finally reached the decision that "not to serve [users in China] at all was a worse evil."[xx] It

[8] With four products only: a Web page, images, videos, and blogs.

[9] Also referred to as the "Golden Shield Project," a censorship and surveillance project operated by the Ministry of Public Security of China.

Case 19: Baidu: Beating Google at Its Own Game

Exhibit 5 User Geographic Breakdown & Traffic Rank

User Geographic Breakdown				Traffic Rank			
Baidu.com		Google.com		Baidu.com		Google.com	
Market	%	Market	%	Market	Rank	Market	Rank
China	89.1%	U.S.	43.0%	China	1	U.S.	1
South Korea	2.8%	India	8.2%	South Korea	9	Algeria	1
U.S.	1.6%	Brazil	3.7%	Macao	9	Iran	2
Japan	1.0%	U.K.	3.2%	Hong Kong	14	India	3
U.K.	0.7%	Germany	3.0%	Singapore	14	South Africa	3
Taiwan	0.7%	Iran	2.8%	New Zealand	19	U.K.	4
Canada	0.6%	China	2.3%	Taiwan	22	Germany	4
Hong Kong	0.5%	Japan	2.3%	Malaysia	22	Spain	4
Australia	0.4%	Canada	1.8%	Australia	40	Australia	4
Malaysia	0.3%	Italy	1.7%	Canada	47	Indonesia	4
Germany	0.3%	Spain	1.4%	Nigeria	47	Pakistan	4
Singapore	0.3%	France	1.3%	U.K.	71	Saudi Arabia	4
Italy	0.1%	Australia	1.1%	Japan	125	Brazil	5
New Zealand	0.1%	Mexico	1.1%	U.S.	225	Italy	5
Indonesia	0.1%	Turkey	1.1%	Thailand	255	Turkey	5
Thailand	0.1%	Indonesia	1.0%	Indonesia	260	Netherlands	5
Macronesia	0.1%	Russia	0.9%	Germany	283	Canada	6
Spain	0.1%	Pakistan	0.8%	Netherlands	401	South Korea	6
Nigeria	0.1%	Algeria	0.7%	Italy	445	Mexico	9
India	0.1%	Saudi Arabia	0.7%	Spain	920	France	10
France	0.1%	South Africa	0.7%	France	1,024	Poland	10
Netherlands	0.1%	Netherlands	0.7%	Russia	1,226	Japan	11
Russia	0.1%	South Korea	0.7%	India	1,603	Russia	11

Exhibit 5 User Geographic Breakdown & Traffic Rank *(Continued)*

| User Geographic Breakdown | | | | Traffic Rank | | | |
| Baidu.com | | Google.com | | Baidu.com | | Google.com | |
Market	%	Market	%	Market	Rank	Market	Rank
Other markets	0.6%	Poland	0.5%			China	12
	100.0%	Argentina	0.4%			Argentina	12
		Other markets	14.9%				
			100.0%				

was finally granted the rights to open offices in China in January 2005, headed by Taiwan-born Kaifu Lee, a former Microsoft executive, who in 1998 was a founder of Microsoft Research Asia.[10] Several months later, Google introduced a new version of its search engine for the Chinese market by purging its search results of any Web sites of which the Chinese government did not approve.

"Gu Ge" in China

Consumer surveys showed that Chinese Internet users had a wide range of imaginative pronunciations of Google in English, including "gougou" (dog dog), "gugou" (ancient dog), "guoguo" (fruit fruit), and "gougou" (check check).[xxi] In fact, Google had been working on a Chinese name since 2002. After extensive internal debates, external consultations, and consumer surveys, in spring 2006 Google finally announced its Chinese name: Gu Ge. "Gu Ge" meant "song of the grain," expressing the abundance of harvest, or "song of the valley," a reference to the company's Silicon Valley roots.[xxii] This was the first time Google used a non-English name.

Because Google had now been able to enter China using its own name (or something like it), it decided to create on its own Web site there. In June 2006, Google sold its stake in Baidu for more than $60 million. Google spokeswoman Debbie Frost commented: "We have disposed of our modest investment in Baidu … It has always been our goal to grow our own successful business in China and we are very focused on that."[xxii]

Being Local, Understanding Local

Unlike Google, which offered multi-language search, Baidu focused on searches in Chinese. Interestingly, Chinese is one of the Asian languages based on syllables requiring two bytes to store each character while English only requires one byte. There were fundamental differences in algorithms and behavior between single-byte and double-byte searches. In addition, regular changes necessitated by these algorithms required manpower trained in the local language, which took time for outside companies to develop. CEO Robin Yanhong Li believed that Baidu's understanding of the Chinese language and culture gave it an advantage in that market over Google.[xxiv] On the other hand, Kaifu Lee, Vice President over Google's China operations, felt that his challenge was to help the leadership of Google understand the Internet in China—specifically, Chinese users.[xxv]

Channels

In China, most SME customers[11] were not accustomed to conducting business online. In addition, the payment and logistic infrastructure of e-commerce was far from perfect and required a lot of user education and support, at least initially, especially on how to navigate the Internet. Baidu had built up a direct sales force of more than 3,000 people located in seven major cities[12,xxvi] to better serve its customers and assist in these areas. It also had a much higher penetration of distributors than Google (see Exhibit 6 for a comparison of channel strength in China), who only had one Chinese distributor in mid-2005 and also generally adopted its global model of customer self-service for China.

---

[10] Microsoft sued Google and Kaifu Li for the move but the case was resolved in a confidential settlement.

[11] Only 100 out of 161,000 of Baidu's online marketing customers were big advertisers as of Q1 2008, but their spending started to outpace its traditional SME customers, especially the financial services, IT, electronics, and automobile industries.

[12] Beijing, Shanghai, Guangzhou, Shenzhen, Taiyuan, Tianjin, and Pooshan by the end of 2007.

Exhibit 6 Comparison of Channel Strength in China

	Baidu	Google China
Number of distributors	~200[20]	24
Number of provinces covered	24	8
Number of direct sales force employees	~3,000	0
Revenue from distributors in Q3 2007 (%)	32	48
Number of paid advertisers in Q3 2007	143,000	38,00
Revenue from top 10 channel partners (%)	10	93

Source: BNP Paribas estimates according to industry sources.[xxxix]

Corporate Structure, Financial Performance, and Valuation

Corporate Structure

To comply with the foreign ownership restrictions on providing Internet content and advertising services in China, from the outset, Baidu operated its Web sites and provided online advertising services in China through contractual arrangements with its local subsidiary, Baidu Netcom. Baidu Netcom, set up on June 5, 2001, was wholly owned by Li and Xu[13] and had the necessary licenses and approvals to operate in China[14] (see Exhibit 7). Google.com operated under a license owned by Google's local partner, Ganii.com.[xxvii]

Financial Performance

Exhibits 8a through 9c provide detailed financial information for Baidu and Google for fiscal years 2003 to 2007. Exhibit 10 contrasts the financial performance and valuation of Baidu and Google across several indicators for fiscal year 2007.

Revenue Drivers

Exhibit 11 shows that Baidu's revenue growth was mainly driven by an enlarged active online marketing customer base effectively served by its direct sales force and third-party distributors and through increasing revenue per online marketing customer. Baidu started to improve its monetization algorithm in 2006 by implementing dynamic bidding and dynamic starting bid prices, and incorporating quality factors in ordering sponsored links as a way of improving its revenue per search.

Breakdown of Costs

Traffic acquisition costs (TAC) remained a key component of Baidu's and Google's cost of revenues. Baidu's TAC continued to rise, reflecting continued growth of revenue contribution from Baidu Union[15] member partners (faster growth than from its own platform).[16] About 70 percent of Google's cost of revenue was TAC. BNP Paribas estimated that Baidu's TAC would continue its upward trend and close the gap with Google worldwide (see Exhibit 12).[xxviii]

Impact of RMB Revaluation

Baidu's reporting currency was the RMB (China's currency). Its revenues and costs were mostly denominated in RMB while a significant portion of its financial assets were denominated in U.S. dollars. Considerable international pressure on the Chinese government to permit the free floatation of the RMB resulted in a significant appreciation of the RMB against the U.S. dollar (see Exhibit 13).

Taxation

As a foreign-invested enterprise registered in a high-tech zone and a "new or high-technology enterprise," Baidu enjoyed preferential tax benefits[17] and a much lower effective tax rate (in the single-digit range, around 4 percent in fiscal years 2004 to 2007 and 7 percent for Q1 2008[xxix]) than Google.

Financial Policies

Baidu relied entirely on dividends and other fees paid by its subsidiaries and affiliates in China. Like Google, it did not pay dividends to its common shareholders.[18]

---

[13] Baidu funded the initial capitalization of Baidu Netcom in the form of a long-term shareholder loan of RMB 2 million ($0.24 million) to Li and Xu.

[14] Under the current Chinese laws and regulations on advertising, P4P was not classified as a form of advertising. The company may not be operated through Baidu Netcom and/or would be subject to higher effective taxation if the laws and regulations were to be changed.

[15] Baidu Union was the network of third-party Web sites and software applications, with five categories: proprietary Web sites, software, Internet cafes, carriers, and other ad networks.

[16] Baidu had the flexibility to turn on or off of the Union traffic and partnerships based on its assessment of the ROI for customers and advertisers, and the return for its profitability and revenue growth.

[17] An exemption from enterprise income tax: 7.5 percent for the first three years and a further 15 percent as long as it maintained its status as a "new or high-technology enterprise." Eligibility for potential tax refunds for Baidu Online on revenues derived from its technology consulting services.

[18] In China, offshore remittance of dividends was also subject to foreign exchange control by the State Administration of Foreign Exchange (SAFE).

Exhibit 7 Ownership and Corporate Structure of Baidu

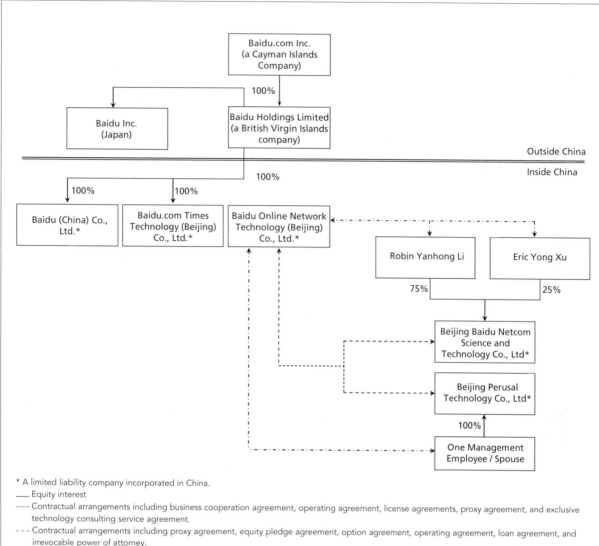

* A limited liability company incorporated in China.
⎯ Equity interest
····· Contractual arrangements including business cooperation agreement, operating agreement, license agreements, proxy agreement, and exclusive technology consulting service agreement.
- - - Contractual arrangements including proxy agreement, equity pledge agreement, option agreement, operating agreement, loan agreement, and irrevocable power of attorney.

Source: Developed from Baidu IPO prospectus and SEC filings.

Valuation

IPO

While Baidu regarded its IPO more as a branding event to raise company profile, the outcome far exceeded expectations. When Baidu completed its IPO on NASDAQ on August 5, 2005, its share price soared to $122.54, up 354 percent from its IPO price of $27 on the first trading day, which made it immensely popular among investors. As one investor remarked:

"It's just been amazing. It could be over-enthusiasm, it could be the way Google charted, but there is obviously a lot of speculative buyers who think this could be an Asian Google."[xxx]

In December 2007 Baidu became the first Chinese company to join the NASDAQ 100 Index. Baidu traded at a much higher premium than Google—three times Google's P/E ratio (see Exhibit 14).

Equity Share Ownership

At the end of fiscal year 2006, Li still retained 21.5 percent ownership of the common stock of Baidu. Other directors and officers together owned 6.7 percent of the common stock shares.[xxxi]

Dual-Stock Structure

Like Google, Baidu had a dual-stock structure—two classes of ordinary shares with identical rights except for voting and conversion rights. As a result, it was reported that Baidu may not be in compliance with the listing rules in Hong Kong.[xxxii]

Secondary Listings

There was no clear timeline for Baidu's initial listing in Hong Kong after it was postponed. The goal of listing in Hong Kong would be to help raise the company profile and fund expansion into new areas, such as online auctions. Its plan for an IPO in Shanghai was unlikely due to regulatory huddles that effectively blocked foreign-owned firms (due to its listing on the NASDAQ) from selling stocks on Chinese exchanges.

Still Too Early to Declare A Winner...

On May 3, 2008, Microsoft withdrew its offer to acquire Yahoo! and chose not to pursue a hostile bid (see Exhibit 15). Microsoft had increased its offer to $33 per share (about $47.5 billion) but the two parties still could not reach an agreement. In addition, a recent successful Google–Yahoo! paid-search test and potential deal made the acquisition even more complicated for Microsoft. Two weeks after withdrawing its offer to purchase Yahoo!, Microsoft reopened the door to the possibility of a potential new investment in Yahoo! (not a total acquisition) while discussions were still ongoing between Yahoo! and Google.

Robin Yanhong Li, cofounder, chairman, and CEO of Baidu,[xxxiii] feels that Baidu will someday pose a similar threat, saying, "If he [Bill Gates] is worried about Google he will probably be more worried about Baidu somewhere down the road. . . . When the Chinese market stops growing faster than other countries in world, we will look outside. The reason we focus here now is that this is the fastest growing market we can access."

In recent years, the Chinese search ad market has grown quickly (see Exhibits 16a and 16b) and is also becoming more concentrated. The combined market share of the top three search engines increased from 78 percent in Q1 2006 to 95 percent in 2007 (with Baidu 60.4 percent, Google 21.2 percent, and Yahoo! China/Alibaba 13.8 percent[19]).[xxxiv] In November 2007 the Chinese search market already exceeded the United States in the number of search requests, and by February 2008 in the number of internet users. As Sukhinder Singh Cassidy, the vice president for Asia Pacific and Latin American Operations for Google has said, "We're in sort of inning one of a nine-inning game. . . . It is very early to call a winner in the China search market."[xxxv]

I had no intention of keeping Baidu inside China from the start. Now that we have won over 60 percent share [Q4 2007] in China, I think it's natural that we turn to overseas markets.

—**Robin Yanhong Li, Co-Founder, Chairman & CEO, Baidu** [xxxvi]

Whatever Baidu does, it does not matter to us. The internet is not the same as other IT businesses. [Between] Google and users will turn to whoever does the better, and they will change again when they find someone even better.

—**Kaifu Lee, VP and President for Greater Google China** [xxxvii]

Is it just a matter of time before there is a Baidu.us portal? In this regard Russia's search engine, Yandex, has operations in the United States near Google's headquarters. What will happen if Microsoft acquires (or fails to acquire) Yahoo!? What will Baidu's considerations be for its next choice of secondary listing? How should investors evaluate the stock? These decisions and events will help determine the global, regional, and country battle shaping up in the search engine markets.

---

[19] Alibaba, a leading Chinese e-commerce company, acquired the entire assets of Yahoo! China in 2005, including its search technology, the Web site, its communications and advertising business, and 3721.com (a real-name search engine) Web site. Alibaba also received a $1 billion investment from Yahoo! as well as the exclusive right of using the Yahoo! brand. In return, Yahoo! took 40 percent of Alibaba's shares but only 35 percent of voting rights.

Exhibit 8a Baidu: Consolidated Income Statement (Fiscal Year Ending December 31, 2007)

BAIDU FINANCIALS	RMB Million (except for share, per share information)					$ Million (except for share, per share information)				
INCOME STATEMENT	2003	2004	2005	2006	2007	2003	2004	2005	2006	2007
Exchange rate	8.2767	8.2765	8.072	7.8051	7.3041	8.2767	8.2765	8.072	7.8051	7.3041
Revenues										
Online marketing services	31.8	106.9	307.4	828.5	1,741.0	3.8	12.9	38.1	106.1	238.4
Other services	8.8	10.6	11.9	9.4	3.4	1.1	1.3	1.5	1.2	0.5
Total Revenues	**40.6**	**117.5**	**319.2**	**837.8**	**1,744.4**	**4.9**	**14.2**	**39.5**	**107.3**	**238.8**
Operating costs and expenses										
Cost of revenues	23.3	41.2	104.4	245.5	645.4	2.8	5.0	12.9	31.5	88.4
Business tax and surcharges	1.9	6.5	20.8	51.8	108.8	0.2	0.8	2.6	6.6	14.9
Traffic acquisition costs	10.6	10.9	21.2	75.2	204.7	1.3	1.3	2.6	9.6	28.0
Bandwidth costs	2.2	8.5	21.3	40.0	117.6	0.3	1.0	2.6	5.1	16.1
Depreciation costs	4.1	7.1	25.3	51.6	147.1	0.5	0.9	3.1	6.6	20.1
Operational costs	3.7	6.5	14.9	25.5	65.5	0.4	0.8	1.8	3.3	9.0
Share-based compensation expenses	0.6	1.7	1.0	1.4	1.7	0.1	0.2	0.1	0.2	0.2
Selling, general and administrative	19.6	50.7	134.8	250.2	411.2	2.4	6.1	16.7	32.1	56.3

Exhibit 8a Baidu: Consolidated Income Statement (Fiscal Year Ending December 31, 2007) (Continued)

BAIDU FINANCIALS	RMB Million (except for share, per share information)					$ Million (except for share, per share information)				
INCOME STATEMENT	2003	2004	2005	2006	2007	2003	2004	2005	2006	2007
Research and Development	7.0	14.5	44.2	79.2	140.7	0.8	1.8	5.5	10.2	19.3
Total operating costs and expenses	49.9	106.4	283.4	575.0	1,197.3	6.0	12.9	35.1	73.7	163.9
Operating profit	(9.3)	11.0	35.8	262.9	547.2	(1.1)	1.3	4.4	33.7	74.9
Other income (and expenses)										
Interest income	0.3	1.1	13.6	42.4	49.0	0.0	0.1	1.7	5.4	6.7
Foreign exchange loss, net	–	–	(0.7)	(0.1)	–	–	–	(0.1)	(0.0)	–
Other, net	0.1	0.3	0.8	4.2	20.1	0.0	0.0	0.1	0.5	2.7
Total other income (and expenses)	0.4	1.5	13.7	46.5	69.1	0.0	0.2	1.7	6.0	9.5
Net income before income taxes and cumulative effect of change in accounting principle	(8.9)	12.5	49.5	309.4	616.2	(1.1)	1.5	6.1	39.6	84.4
Income taxes	–	0.5	1.9	12.3	(12.8)	–	0.1	0.2	1.6	(1.7)
Income before cumulative effect of change in accounting principle	(8.9)	12.0	47.6	297.2	629.0	(1.1)	1.5	5.9	38.1	86.1
Cumulative effect of change in accounting principle	–	–	–	4.6	–	–	–	–	0.6	–

Exhibit 8a Baidu: Consolidated Income Statement (Fiscal Year Ending December 31, 2007) (Continued)

BAIDU FINANCIALS	RMB Million (except for share, per share information)					$ Million (except for share, per share information)				
INCOME STATEMENT	2003	2004	2005	2006	2007	2003	2004	2005	2006	2007
Net income	(8.9)	12.0	47.6	301.8	629.0	(1.1)	1.5	5.9	38.7	86.1
Net income per Class A and Class B ordinary shares										
Basic (prior to cumulative effect of change in accounting principle)	(0.87)	1.09	2.40	8.92	18.57	(0.11)	0.13	0.30	1.14	2.54
Basic (cumulative effect of change in accounting principle)	–	–	–	0.14	–	–	–	–	0.02	–
	(0.87)	1.09	2.40	9.06	18.57	(0.11)	0.13	0.30	1.16	2.54
Diluted (prior to cumulative effect of change in accounting principle)	0.43	0.43	1.49	8.62	18.11	0.05	0.05	0.18	1.10	2.48
Diluted (cumulative effect of change in accounting principle)	–	–	–	0.13	–	–	–	–	0.02	–
	0.43	0.43	1.49	8.75	18.11	0.05	0.05	0.18	1.12	2.48
Weighted average number of Class A and Class B ordinary shares outstanding										
Basic	10,188,850	10,983,478	19,808,058	33,290,696	33,872,611	10,188,850	10,983,478	19,808,058	33,290,696	33,872,611
Diluted	10,188,850	28,124,327	32,042,888	34,506,594	34,724,364	10,188,850	28,124,327	32,042,888	34,506,594	34,724,364

*2007 results were unaudited results.

Source: Baidu annual reports and quarterly results.

(Continued)

Exhibit 8b Baidu: Consolidated Balance Sheet (Fiscal Year Ending December 31, 2007)

BAIDU FINANCIALS	RMB Million					$ Million				
BALANCE SHEET	2003	2004	2005	2006	2007	2003	2004	2005	2006	2007
Exchange rate						8.2767	8.2765	8.072	7.8051	7.3041
ASSETS										
Current assets										
Cash and cash equivalents	62.8	200.2	900.6	1,136.3	1,350.6	7.6	24.2	111.6	145.6	184.9
Short-term investments	–	–	–	85.3	242.0	–	–	–	10.9	33.1
Accounts receivable, net of allowance	1.9	9.6	22.4	23.1	64.3	0.2	1.2	2.8	3.0	8.8
Prepaid expenses and other current assets	0.9	2.4	11.0	32.3	66.0	0.1	0.3	1.4	4.1	9.0
Deferred tax assets, net of valuation allowance	–	–	1.4	1.7	2.6	–	–	0.2	0.2	0.4
Total current assets	65.7	212.3	935.4	1,278.7	1,725.5	7.9	25.6	115.9	163.8	236.2
Non-current assets										
Fixed assets, net	11.0	35.9	96.4	191.7	678.9	1.3	4.3	11.9	24.6	92.9
Prepayment for land use rights	–	–	77.2	92.4	96.5	–	–	9.6	11.8	13.2
Intangible assets, net	–	13.0	13.3	44.4	40.5	–	1.6	1.6	5.7	5.5
Goodwill	–	–	9.3	47.3	51.1	–	–	1.2	6.1	7.0
Investments, net	–	–	2.0	–	15.4	–	–	0.3	–	2.1

Exhibit 8b Baidu: Consolidated Balance Sheet (Fiscal Year Ending December 31, 2007) (Continued)

BAIDU FINANCIALS	RMB Million					$ Million				
BALANCE SHEET	2003	2004	2005	2006	2007	2003	2004	2005	2006	2007
Deferred tax assets, net	–	–	2.8	5.8	15.7	–	–	0.4	0.7	2.2
Other non-current assets	–	1.1	–	7.7	32.3	–	0.1	–	1.0	4.4
Total non-current assets	11.0	49.9	201.1	389.3	930.4	1.3	6.0	24.9	49.9	127.4
TOTAL ASSETS	76.7	262.2	1,136.4	1,668.1	2,655.9	9.3	31.7	140.8	213.7	363.6
LIABILITIES AND SHARE-HOLDERS' EQUITY										
Current liabilities										
Customers' deposits	8.4	26.0	70.3	141.2	257.6	1.0	3.1	8.7	18.1	35.3
Accrued expense and other liabilities	3.8	21.9	53.1	153.1	359.3	0.5	2.6	6.6	19.6	49.2
Deferred revenue	7.5	6.3	7.7	2.6	11.8	0.9	0.8	0.9	0.3	1.6
Deferred income	–	–	0.1	4.1	2.5	–	–	0.0	0.5	0.3
Total current liabilities	19.6	54.2	131.2	301.0	631.2	2.4	6.5	16.3	38.6	86.4
Non-current liabilities										
Long-term payable for acqui-sitions	–	–	–	7.0	3.0	–	–	–	0.9	0.4
Deferred income	–	–	0.1	2.8	0.3	–	–	0.0	0.4	0.0
Total non-current liabilities	–	–	0.1	9.8	3.3	–	–	0.0	1.3	0.5

(Continued)

Exhibit 8b Baidu: Consolidated Balance Sheet (Fiscal Year Ending December 31, 2007) (Continued)

BAIDU FINANCIALS	RMB Million					$ Million				
BALANCE SHEET	2003	2004	2005	2006	2007	2003	2004	2005	2006	2007
Total liabilities	19.6	54.2	131.4	310.8	634.5	2.4	6.5	16.3	39.8	86.9
Commitments	0	0				0	0	0	0	0
Redeemable convertible preferred shares	91.622	211.4				11.1	25.5	0	0	0
Shareholders' equity										
Class A ordinary shares outstanding at year-end	0.004	0.004	0.004	0.009	0.01	0.0005	0.0005	0.0005	0.0012	0.0014
Class B ordinary shares outstanding at year-end	0	–	0.01	0.005	0.004	–	–	0.0012	0.0006	0.0005
Additional paid-in capital	24.046	43.3	1,009.5	1,088.2	1,171.6	2.9	5.2	125.1	139.4	160.4
Accumulated other comprehensive income (loss)	0	–	(5.5)	(33.7)	(82.0)	0	–	(0.7)	(4.3)	(11.2)
Retained earnings (accumulated losses)	(58.6)	(46.6)	1.0	302.8	931.7	(7.1)	(5.6)	0.1	38.8	127.6
Total shareholders' equity	(34.6)	(3.3)	1,005.1	1,357.3	2,021.4	(4.2)	(0.4)	124.5	173.9	276.7
TOTAL LIABILITIES AND SHAREHOLDERS' EQUITY	76.7	262.2	1,136.4	1,668.1	2,655.9	9.3	31.7	140.8	213.7	363.6

* 2007 results were unaudited.

Source: Baidu annual reports and quarterly results.

Exhibit 8c Baidu: Consolidated Cashflow Statement (Fiscal Year Ending December 31, 2007)

BAIDU FINANCIALS	RMB Million					$ Million				
STATEMENT OF CASH FLOWS	2003	2004	2005	2006	2007	2003	2004	2005	2006	2007
Exchange rate						8.2767	8.2765	8.072	7.8051	7.3041
Cash flows from operating activities										
Net income	(8.9)	12.0	47.6	301.8	629.0	(1.1)	1.5	5.9	38.7	86.1
Adjustments to reconcile net income to net cash generated from operating activities						–	–	–	–	–
Depreciation of fixed assets	4.9	8.9	30.7	64.1		0.6	1.1	3.8	8.2	
Amortization of intangible assets	–	1.1	3.1	6.3		–	0.1	0.4	0.8	
Disposal of fixed assets	–	0.1	0.0	0.9		–	0.0	0.0	0.1	
Share-based compensation	5.1	16.5	33.6	48.3		0.6	2.0	4.2	6.2	
Provision for doubtful accounts	–	0.6	4.3	(0.3)		–	0.1	0.5	(0.04)	
Foreign exchange loss	–	–	0.6	0.1		–	–	0.1	0.01	
Impairment loss on investment		–	–	2.0		–	–	–	0.3	
Cumulative effect of change in accounting principle		–	–	(4.6)		–	–	–	(0.6)	
Change in operating assets and liabilities	n/a				n/a	–	–	–	–	n/a
Accounts receivable	(1.5)	(8.4)	(17.5)	(0.4)		(0.2)	(1.0)	(2.2)	(0.05)	
Prepaid expenses and other assets	0.3	(1.5)	(8.5)	(23.5)		0.0	(0.2)	(1.1)	(3.0)	
Customers' deposits	6.3	17.6	44.2	70.9		0.8	2.1	5.5	9.1	

Exhibit 8c Baidu: Consolidated Cashflow Statement (Fiscal Year Ending December 31, 2007) *(Continued)*

BAIDU FINANCIALS	RMB Million					$ Million				
STATEMENT OF CASH FLOWS	2003	2004	2005	2006	2007	2003	2004	2005	2006	2007
Accrued expenses and other liabilities	1.6	10.7	27.1	62.3		0.2	1.3	3.4	8.0	
Deferred tax assets, net	–	–	(4.3)	(3.2)		–	–	(0.5)	(0.4)	
Deferred revenue	5.0	(1.2)	1.4	(5.1)		0.6	(0.1)	0.2	(0.7)	
Deferred income	–	–	0.2	6.7		–	–	0.0	0.9	
Net cash generated from operating activities	12.7	56.5	162.4	526.1		1.5	6.8	20.1	67.4	
Cash flows from investing activities						–	–	–	–	–
Acquisition of fixed assets	(6.4)	(25.4)	(88.7)	(127.5)		(0.8)	(3.1)	(11.0)	(16.3)	
Acquisition of business	–	–	(10.5)	(43.3)		–	–	(1.3)	(5.6)	
Acquisition of intangible assets	–	(11.9)	(2.1)	(21.9)		–	(1.4)	(0.3)	(2.8)	
Capitalization of internal use software costs	(1.6)	(2.2)	(0.6)	(1.0)		(0.2)	(0.3)	(0.1)	(0.1)	
Acquisition of long-term investments	–	–	(2.0)	–		–	–	(0.3)	–	
Acquisition of marketable securities	–	–	–	(85.3)		–	–	–	(10.9)	
Prepayment for land use rights	–	–	(77.2)	(15.2)		–	–	(9.6)	(1.9)	
Net cash used in investing activities	(8.0)	(39.5)	(181.1)	(294.3)		(1.0)	(4.8)	(22.4)	(37.7)	
Cash flows from financing activities				n/a						n/a

Exhibit 8c Baidu: Consolidated Cashflow Statement (Fiscal Year Ending December 31, 2007) (Continued)

BAIDU FINANCIALS	RMB Million					$ Million				
STATEMENT OF CASH FLOWS	2003	2004	2005	2006	2007	2003	2004	2005	2006	2007
Issuance of Series C convertible preferred shares	–	119.7	–	–		–	14.5	–	–	
Proceeds from initial public offering (IPO), net of expenses	–	–	716.3	–		–	–	88.7	–	
Payments for expenses in connection with IPO	–	–	–	(0.6)		–	–	–	(0.1)	
Proceeds from exercise of share options	0.1	0.6	8.0	32.8		0.0	0.1	1.0	4.2	
Net cash generated from financing activities	0.1	120.3	724.3	32.2		0.0	14.5	89.7	4.1	
Effect of exchange rate changes on cash and cash equivalents	–	–	(5.2)	(28.4)		–	–	(0.6)	(3.6)	
Net increase in cash and cash equivalents	4.8	137.4	700.4	235.7		0.6	16.6	86.8	30.2	
Cash and cash equivalents at the beginning of the year	58.0	62.8	200.2	900.6		7.0	7.6	24.8	115.4	–
Cash and cash equivalents at the end of the year	62.8	200.2	900.6	1,136.3		7.6	24.2	111.6	145.6	–
Supplemental cash flow information	–									–
Cash paid during the year for income tax	–	–	4.7	24.2		–	–	0.6	3.1	–
Insurance of ordinary shares in purchase of intangible assets	–	2.1	–	–		–	0.3	–	–	–

* 2007 results not available.
Source: Baidu annual reports.

Exhibit 9a Google: Consolidated Income Statement

GOOGLE FINANCIALS INCOME STATEMENT	Year Ended 31 December				
$ Million (except for share, per share information)	2003	2004	2005	2006	2007
Revenues					
Advertising revenues	1,420.7	3,143.3	6,065.0	10,492.6	16,412.6
Licensing and other revenues	45.3	45.9	73.6	112.3	181.3
Total Revenues	1,465.9	3,189.2	6,138.6	10,604.9	16,594.0
Operating costs and expenses					
Cost of revenues	634.4	1,469.0	2,577.1	4,225.0	6,649.1
Research and Development	229.6	395.2	599.5	1,228.6	2,120.0
Sales and marketing	164.9	295.7	468.2	849.5	1,461.3
General and administrative	94.5	188.2	386.5	751.8	1,279.3
Contribution to Google Foundation	–	–	90.0	–	–
Non-recurring portion of settlement of disputes with Yahoo	–	201.0	–	–	–
Total costs and expenses	1,123.5	2,549.0	4,121.3	7,054.9	11,509.6
Income from operations	342.5	640.2	2,017.3	3,550.0	5,084.4
Interest income and other, net	4.2	10.0	124.4	461.0	589.6
Income before income taxes	346.7	650.2	2,141.7	4,011.0	5,674.0
Provision for income taxes	241.0	251.1	676.3	933.6	1,470.3
Net income	105.6	399.1	1,465.4	3,077.4	4,203.7
Net Income per share					
Basic	0.77	2.07	5.31	10.21	13.53
Diluted	0.41	1.46	5.02	9.94	13.29
Number of shares used in per share calculations					
Basic	137,697	193,176	275,844	301,403	310,806
Diluted	256,638	272,781	291,874	309,548	316,210

Source: Google annual reports.

Exhibit 9b Google: Consolidated Balance Sheet

GOOGLE FINANCIALS BALANCE SHEET	Year Ended 31 December				
$ Million	2003	2004	2005	2006	2007
ASSETS					
Current assets					
Cash and cash equivalents	149.0	426.9	3,877.2	3,544.7	6,081.6
Marketable securities	185.7	1,705.4	4,157.1	7,699.2	8,137.0
Accounts receivable, net of allowance	154.7	311.8	688.0	1,322.3	2,162.5
Income taxes receivable	–	70.5	–	–	145.3
Deferred income taxes, net	22.1	19.5	49.3	29.7	68.5
Prepaid revenue share, expenses and other assets	48.7	159.4	229.5	443.9	694.2
Total current assets	560.2	2,693.5	9,001.1	13,039.8	17,289.1
Prepaid revenue share, expenses and other assets, non-current	17.4	35.5	31.3	114.5	168.5
Deferred income taxes, net, non-current	–	11.6	–		33.2
Non-marketable equity securities	–	–	–	1,031.9	1,059.7
Property and equipment, net	188.3	378.9	961.7	2,395.2	4,039.3
Goodwill	87.4	122.8	194.9	1,545.1	2,299.4
Intangible assets, net	18.1	71.1	82.8	346.8	446.6
TOTAL ASSETS	871.5	3,313.4	10,271.8	18,473.4	25,335.8
LIABILITIES AND SHAREHOLDERS' EQUITY					
Current liabilities					
Accounts payable	46.2	32.7	115.6	211.2	282.1
Accrued compensation and benefits	33.5	82.6	198.8	351.7	588.4
Accrued expense and other liabilities	26.4	64.1	114.4	266.2	465.0
Accrued revenue share	88.7	122.5	215.8	370.4	522.0

(Continued)

Exhibit 9b Google: Consolidated Balance Sheet *(Continued)*

GOOGLE FINANCIALS BALANCE SHEET	Year Ended 31 December				
$ Million	2003	2004	2005	2006	2007
Deferred revenue	15.3	36.5	73.1	105.1	178.1
Income taxes payable	20.7	–	27.8	–	–
Current portion of equipment leases	4.6	1.9	–	–	–
Total current liabilities	235.5	340.4	745.4	1,304.6	2,035.6
Long-term portion of equipment leases	2.0	–	–	–	–
Deferred revenue, long-term	5.0	7.4	10.5	20.0	30.2
Liability for stock options exercised early, long-term	6.3	6.0	–	–	–
Deferred income taxes, net	18.5	–	35.4	40.4	–
Income taxes payable, long-term	–	–	–	–	478.4
Other long-term liabilities	1.5	30.5	61.6	68.5	101.9
Commitments and contingencies					
Redeemable convertible preferred stock warrant	13.9	–			
Shareholders' equity					
Convertible preferred stock, $0.001 par value, 100,000 shares authorized; no shares issued and outstanding	44.3	–	–	–	–
Class A and Class B common stock at 31 December of each year	0.2	0.3	0.3	0.3	0.3
Additional paid-in capital	725.2	2,582.4	7,477.8	11,882.9	13,241.2
Note receivable from officer/stockholder	(4.3)	–	–	–	–
Deferred stock-based compensation	(369.7)	(249.5)	(119.0)	–	–
Accumulated other comprehensive income	1.7	5.4	4.0	23.3	113.4
Retained earnings	191.4	590.5	2,055.9	5,133.3	9,334.8
Total shareholders' equity	588.8	2,929.1	9,419.0	17,039.8	22,689.7
TOTAL LIABILITIES AND SHAREHOLDERS' EQUITY	871.5	3,313.4	10,271.8	18,473.4	25,335.8

Source: Google annual reports.

Exhibit 9c Google: Consolidated Cashflow Statement

GOOGLE FINANCIALS CASHFLOW STATEMENT	Year Ended 31 December				
$ Million	2003	2004	2005	2006	2007
Operating activities					
Net income	105.6	399.1	1,465.4	3,077.4	4,203.7
Adjustments					
Depreciation and amortization of property and equipment	43.9	128.5	256.8	494.4	807.7
Amortization of intangibles and other	11.2	20.0	37.0	77.5	159.9
Stock-based compensation	11.6	11.3	200.7	458.1	868.6
Excess tax benefits from stock-based award activity	229.4	278.7	433.7	(581.7)	(379.2)
Deferred income taxes	–	191.6	21.2	(98.5)	(164.2)
Other, net	–	201.0	22.0	12.5	(39.7)
Changes in assets and liabilities, net of effects of acquisitions					
Accounts receivable	(90.4)	(156.9)	(372.3)	(624.0)	(837.2)
Income taxes, net	(6.3)	(125.2)	66.2	496.9	744.8
Prepaid revenue share, expenses and other assets	(58.9)	(99.8)	(51.7)	(289.2)	(298.7)
Accounts payable	36.7	(13.5)	80.6	95.4	70.1
Accrued expenses and other liabilities	31.1	86.4	166.8	291.5	418.9
Accrued revenues share	74.6	33.9	93.3	139.3	150.3
Deferred revenue	7.0	22.0	39.6	30.8	70.3
Net cash provided by operating activities	395.4	977.0	2,459.4	3,580.5	5,775.4
Investing activities					
Purchase of property and equipment	(176.8)	(176.8)	(838.2)	(1,902.8)	(2,402.8)
Purchase of marketable securities	(316.6)	(316.6)	(12,675.9)	(26,681.9)	(15,997.1)
Maturities and sales of marketable securities	219.4	219.4	10,257.2	23,107.1	15,659.5

(Continued)

Exhibit 9c Google: Consolidated Cashflow Statement *(Continued)*

GOOGLE FINANCIALS CASHFLOW STATEMENT	Year Ended 31 December				
$ Million	2003	2004	2005	2006	2007
Investments in non-marketable equity securities	–	–	–	(1,019.1)	(34.5)
Acquisitions, net of cash acquired and purchases of intangible and other assets	(40.0)	(40.0)	(101.3)	(402.4)	(906.7)
Net cash used in investing activities	(314.0)	(314.0)	(3,358.2)	(6,899.2)	(3,681.6)
Financing activities					
Net proceeds from stock-based award activity	2.3	15.5	85.0	321.1	23.9
Net proceeds from stock-based award activity	–	–	–	581.7	379.2
Net proceeds from public offerings	–	–	4,287.2	2,063.5	–
Payment of note receivable from office/stockholder	–	–	–	–	–
Payments of principal on capital leases and equipment loans	(7.4)	4.7	(1.4)	–	–
Net cash flow by financing activities	8.1	1,194.6	4,370.8	2,966.4	403.1
Effect of exchange rate changes on cash and cash equivalents	1.7	7.6	(21.6)	19.7	40.0
Net increase (decrease) in cash and cash equivalents	91.2	277.9	3,450.3	(332.5)	2,536.9
Cash and cash equivalents at beginning of year	57.8	149.0	426.9	3,877.2	3,544.7
Cash and cash equivalents at end of year	149.0	426.9	3,877.17	3,544.67	6,081.59
Supplemental disclosures of cash flow information					
Cash paid for interest	1.7	0.7	0.2	0.3	1.3
Cash paid for taxes	247.4	183.8	153.6	537.7	882.7
Acquisition-related activities					
Issuance of equity in connection with acquisitions, net	73.5	25.7	22.4	1,173.2	–

Source: Google annual reports.

Exhibit 10 Selected Financial Indicators (fiscal year ending 31 December 2007)

Key Facts	$ Million (except for per-share data)	
	Baidu	Google
Sales	230.1	16,594.0
Operating income	72.2	5,084.4
Net income	83.0	5,268.4
Total assets	361.5	25,302.6
Total liabilities	84.7	2,612.9
EBITDA	100.7	6,642.8
Enterprise value	13,087.0	175,662.0
Headcount	5,200	16,805
Stock price year end	389.8	691.5
Shares outstanding (million)	34.1	312.9
Year-end market cap	13,305.0	216,375.3
EPS	2.5	13.3
Return on assets		
Operating margin (%)	31.4	30.6
Return on assets (ROA) (%)	28.9	19.2
Asset turnover	0.64	0.66
Operating margin (%)		
Costing of goods sold to sales	28.6	34.2
Depreciation	8.7	5.8
Research and development	8.4	12.8
Selling, general and administrative expenses	24.5	16.5
Operating income	31.3	25.6

(Continued)

Exhibit 10 Selected Financial Indicators (fiscal year ending 31 December 2007) *(Continued)*

Key Facts	$ Million (except for per-share data)	
	Baidu	Google
Asset turnover		
Days accounts receivable (relative to sales)	n/a	39.9
Days inventoried (relative to net cost of sales and services)	n/a	n/a
Asset turnover	0.64	0.66
ROE (rate of return on equity)		
Profit margin	36.1	25.3
Asset turnover	0.64	0.66
Financial leverage	1.3	1.1
Return on equity (ROE) (%)	36.9	21.2
Financial risk indicators		
Days accounts payables	n/a	23.0
Current ratio	2.7	8.5
Debt/equity	–	–
Times interest earned (EBIT/Interest expenses)	n/a	4,717.5
Cash flow/debt	n/a	n/a
Per share data		
Common stock price (close)	389.8	691.5
Common stock price (high)	389.0	747.2
Common stock price (low)	388.0	437.0
Equity shares	34.1	312.9
Earning per share	2.5	13.3
Book value of equity per share (end of year)	8.1	70.8
Stock market acceptance		
MVE/BVE (price/book)	48.1	9.8

Exhibit 10 Selected Financial Indicators (fiscal year ending 31 December 2007) *(Continued)*

Key Facts	$ Million (except for per-share data)	
	Baidu	Google
Price/earnings	148.1	52.0
Price/sales	57.8	13.0
Price/cash flow	129.0	50.2
EV/EBITDA	130.0	30.4
EV/EBIT	161.0	35.6
EV/cash flow	127.8	37.0
Relative equity risk of company ('Beta')	3.31	2.42
Common stock price (end of year)	389.9	691.5
Equity shares (millions)	34.1	312.9
Market value of equity (end of year)	13,305.0	216,375.3
Book value of equity (end of year)	276.7	22,079.1
Stern Stewart Performance Indicators		
Market value added (MVA)	13,028.3	194,296.2
After-tax return on invested capital (ROIC) (%)	n/a	21.17
Weighted average cost of capital (WACC) (%)	25.42	21.16
Economic value added (EVA)	(12.7)	(1,187.4)

Note: Figures here were taken mainly from Thomson Financials for comparison purposes, certain figures may be subject to change once Baidu's annual report becomes available.
Source: Thomson Financials, Company annual reports.

Exhibit 11 Baidu: Revenue Drivers

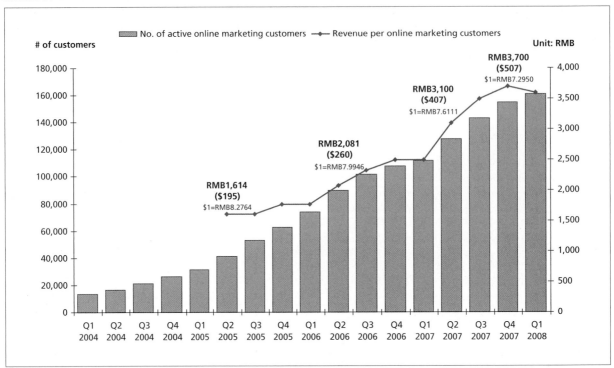

Source: Baidu's annual reports and quarterly results.

Exhibit 12 Comparison of Traffic Acquisition Costs

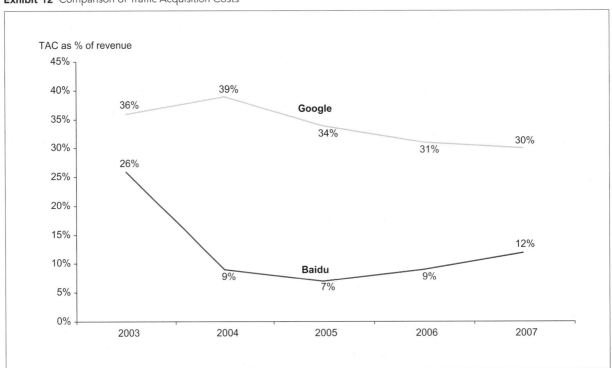

Source: Google's and Baidu's annual reports and quarterly results.

Exhibit 13 Evolution of USS vs. RMB Exchange Rate and Trend[xl] (forward quotation for indication purpose only)

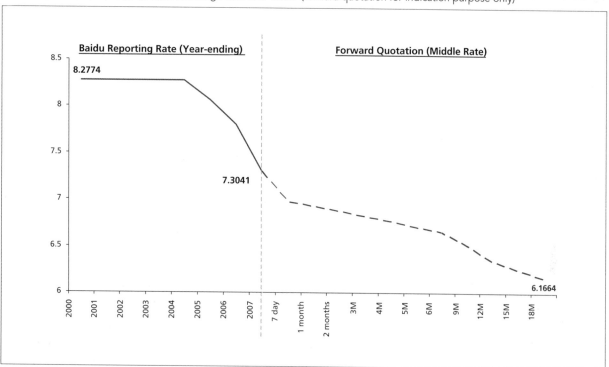

Source: Baidu's annual reports, quarterly results, and http://www.forex.com.

Exhibit 14 Share Performance and Selected Indexes

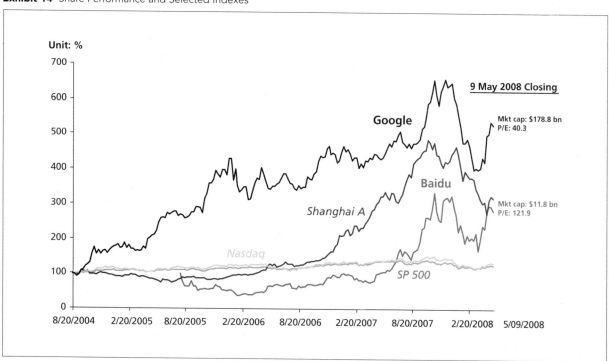

Source: Datastream.

Exhibit 15 U.S. Online Ad Market

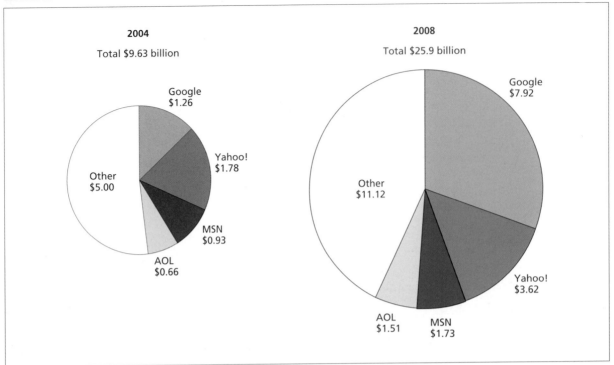

2004

Total $9.63 billion

Google
$1.26

Yahoo!
$1.78

Other
$5.00

MSN
$0.93

AOL
$0.66

2008

Total $25.9 billion

Google
$7.92

Other
$11.12

Yahoo!
$3.62

AOL
$1.51

MSN
$1.73

Source: *Wall Street Journal.*[xli]

Exhibit 16a China's Online Ad Market Size

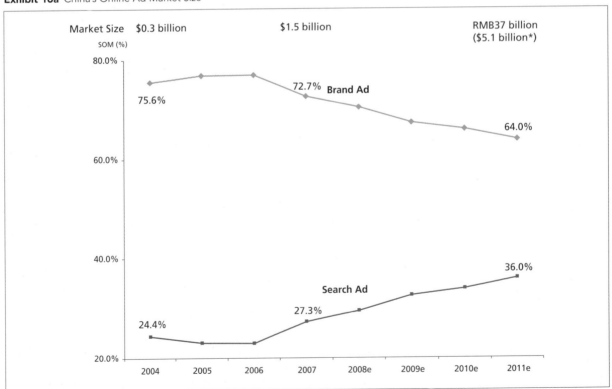

Market Size $0.3 billion $1.5 billion   RMB37 billion
                                                            ($5.1 billion*)

SOM (%)

80.0%

72.7% **Brand Ad**

75.6%

64.0%

60.0%

40.0%

36.0%

Search Ad

27.3%

24.4%

20.0%

2004   2005   2006   2007   2008e   2009e   2010e   2011e

Note: Converted at the 2007 year-end rate: $1 = 7.3041, did not take into consideration the effect of RMB revaluation.

Exhibit 16b China's Search Ad Market Size

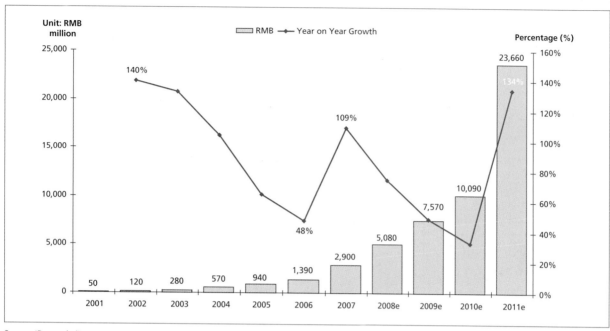

Source: iResearch.[xlii]

NOTES

i. L. Chao & E. Smith, New tune: Google aims to crack China with music push, *Wall Street Journal,* February 6, 2008.

ii. L. Chao & E. Smith, New tune: Google aims to crack China with music push, *Wall Street Journal,* February 6, 2008.

iii. iResearch China Online Search Annual Report 2007.

iv. BNP Paribas report, January 15, 2008.

v. Best Answer to Google, *BusinessWeek,* http://images.businessweek.com/ss/06/12/1207 bestleaders/source/4.htm (accessed May 17, 2008).

vi. Microsoft company press release. January 31, 2008, letter Microsoft sent to Yahoo! board of directors.

vii. Thomson Financials.

viii. Jonathan Watts in Beijing, 2005, Interview: Robin Li, founder of Baidu.com, *The Guardian,* December 8.

ix. Google company Web site.

x. Baidu company Web site.

xi. Baidu company press release.

xii. Google Web site.

xiii. Google Web site.

xiv. BNP Paribas report, January 15, 2008.

xv. Google annual reports.

xvi. BBC, 2006, Google offloads Baidu investment, http://news.bbc.co.uk/2/hi/asia-pacific/4715044.stm, February 15 (accessed May 12, 2008).

xvii. Preliminary Transcript: BIDU—Q1 2008 Baidu Earnings Conference Call, Thomson Street Events, April 24, 2008.

xviii. John Battelle, 2005, 2006, *The Search: How Google and Its Rivals Rewrote the Rules of Business and Transformed Our Culture,* London: Nicholas Brealey Publishing, 2005.

xix. John Battelle, *The Search: How Google and Its Rivals Rewrote the Rules of Business and Transformed Our Culture,* London: Nicholas Brealey Publishing, 2005, 208.

xx. Stacy Cowley, 2006, Google CEO on censoring: 'We did an evil scale,' IDG *News Service,* http://www.infoworld.com/article/06/01/27/74_874 HNgoogleceocensoring_ l html, January 27 (accessed May 16, 2008).

xxi. David Pescovitz, 2006, Chinese Google is song of the grain, http://www.boingboing.net/2006/04/14/chinese-google-is-so.html, April 14 (accessed May 11, 2008).

xxii. David Pescovitz, 2006, Chinese Google is song of the grain, http://www.boingboing.net/2006/04/14/chinese-google-is-so.html, April 14 (accessed May 11, 2008).

xxiii. A. Yeh, 2006, Google disposes of Baidu stake, *Financial Times,* http://www.ft.eom/cms/g/G/6756285a-026d-lldb-al41-0000779e2340.html7nclick_check=l, June 23 (accessed May 12, 2008).

xxiv. J. Watts, 2005, Interview: Robin Li, founder of Baidu.com, *The Guardian,* December 8.

xxv. Baidu 'not a great competitor," says Li Kaifu, *China Wire,* http://www.telecomasia.net/article.php?id article=6759 (accessed May 11, 2008).

xxvi. Baidu.com Q4 2007 Earnings Call Transcript—Seeking Alpha, http://seekingalpha.com/article/64687-baidu-com-q4-2007-earnings-call-transcript?page=-l (accessed May 17, 2007).

xxvii. 2006, Google defends China search site, BBC, http://news.bbc.co.Uk/2/hi/technology/4735662.stm, February 21 (accessed May 12, 2008).

xxviii. BNP Paribas report, January 15, 2008.

xxix. Preliminary Transcript: BIDU—Q1 2008 Baidu Earnings Conference Call, Thomson StreetEvents, April 24, 2008, and Baidu SEC Filings.

xxx. China's google Baidu soars in Nasdaq debut, ChinaDaily.com, http://www.chinadailY.com.cn/english/doc/2005-08/08/content_467140.htm (accessed May 12, 2008).

xxxi. Baidu annual report.

xxxii. 2008, Baidu was said not in compliance with the Hong Kong listing rules, Sina.com.cn, http://tech.sina.com.en/i/2008-05-20/l 1522205926.shtml, May 20.

xxxiii. J. Watts, 2005, Interview: Robin Li, founder of Baidu.com, *The Guardian*, December 8.

xxxiv. iResearch, China Online Search Annual Report 2007.

xxxv. Q. Leheng, 2006Baidu vs. Google, r 2006, http://web2.commongate.com/post/Baidu_vs_Google/, December 6 (accessed May 11, 2008).

xxxvi. C. Hui & H. Kaneko, 2008, Baidu CEO talks about Japanese market, Tech-On!, February 5.

xxxvii. Baidu 'not a great competitor,' says Li Kaifu, *China Wire*, http://www.telecomasia.net/article.php?id_article=6759 (accessed May 11, 2008).

xxxviii. http://www.alexa.com/data/details/trafficdetails/baidu.com, http://www.alexa.com/data/details/traffic_details/google.com (accessed May 12, 2008).

xxxix. BNP Paribas report, January 15, 2008.

xl. Baidu IPO Prospectus, annual reports, and forward quotation from http://forex.hexun.com/2008-04-23/105491657.html (accessed May 13, 2008).

xli. K. J. Delaney, M. Karnitschnig, & R. A. Guth, 2008, Giving up on Yahoo!, Microsoft rethinks its Internet options, *Wall Street Journal*, May 6, 2008.

xlii. K. J. Delaney, M. Karnitschnig, & R. A. Guth, 2008, Giving up on Yahoo!, Microsoft rethinks its Internet options, *Wall Street Journal*, May 6, 2008.

Andrew Inkpen, Michael Moffett

Thunderbird School of Global Management

In July 2008, BP was embroiled in a dispute with the Russian shareholders of its TNK-BP joint venture. The Russian shareholders, a group led by billionaires Mikhail Fridman, Viktor Vekselberg, and Len Blavatnik, were demanding the removal of TNK-BP Chief Executive Robert Dudley. The Russian shareholders maintained that BP was not adequately controlling costs and was blocking efforts to expand TNK-BP outside of Russia because that would compete with BP's own operations. They also claimed that BP was employing too many highly paid expatriates in Russia. BP's response was that the venture's main area of operation was always meant to be Russia and Ukraine. According to Dudley: "The company's corporate governance is being tested and the fate of the company is a bellwether for Russia's progress in improving the way its companies are run ... For five years, one of my roles has been trying to balance all the issues of shareholders. And I think the ability to keep this balance is important, and I will try to keep that balance."[1]

In comments made to the French newspaper, *Le Monde*, Russian Prime Minister Vladimir Putin said that he had warned both sides that the 50-50 structure would be problematic: "You shouldn't do this ... Work it out between yourselves so someone has a controlling stake...There needs to be a boss ... You see the result: There's always friction over who's in charge."[2]

With events escalating, Robert Dudley and BP senior management were faced with a challenging situation. Losing its stake in TNK-BP would have serious financial implications for BP. TNK-BP accounted for nearly one-quarter of BP's oil production, and close to one-fifth of its reserves. How the situation was resolved would have a lasting impact on BP and its presence in Russia. The resolution would also impact Russia's overall reputation for attracting and supporting foreign investment.

BP

BP, formerly British Petroleum, was the world's third-largest oil and gas supermajor. Originally founded as the Anglo-Persian Oil Company, BP went from a public company to a British state-owned entity, and then back to being publicly traded during the Thatcher years. BP made many acquisitions over the past century, including Standard Oil of Ohio, Amoco, Castrol, Aral, and Arco. BP's upstream business operated in various countries, including the United States, the United Kingdom, Australia, Angola, Azerbaijan, Canada, Egypt, Russia, Trinidad, Tobago, and Indonesia. The company also operated a diverse range of pipeline, refining, chemical, and retail assets around the world. In recent years, the company had adopted the tagline "Beyond Petroleum" as a way to distinguish itself from its hydrocarbon-based competitors.

Like its supermajor competitors, BP's biggest challenges were increasing oil and gas production and replacing reserves. Most host governments in oil-producing nations were looking for better contractual terms, and the so-called easy oil and gas discoveries were already made. Reserve replacement and equity ownership of new discoveries was becoming difficult. In 2003, then-CEO John Browne told analysts that BP's daily oil production would rise 1.0 million barrels to 4.5 million barrels per day by the end of 2007. The result was less than half the projection, and targets were scaled back to 4.3 million barrels per day by 2012. In 2008, the company planned to invest $15 billion in its upstream business. Relative to its competitors, BP's production growth was constrained by its mature oil fields. Thus, BP was aggressively looking for new reserves, and the stake in TNK-BP was a major part of expected production growth.

BP's financial performance in many areas lagged behind that of ExxonMobil and Shell, especially in the refining sector, which was planning 2,000 job cuts in 2008. The company was also planning about 2,500 head-office job cuts to eliminate bureaucracy and restructure the organization around global businesses rather than geographic sectors. In addition, BP's safety record was under close scrutiny after a recent series of incidents, the most serious being the 2005 explosion in Texas City (southeast of Houston, Texas) which killed 15 people.

The Oil and Gas Industry in Russia

Russia was the world's largest natural gas producer and second-largest crude oil producer. The share of oil and gas in Russia's GDP was believed by many analysts to have more than doubled since 1999 (although some reports, such as a 2007 report from Alfa Bank, said the oil and gas GDP share was declining). Oil and gas revenues made up about 50 percent of Russian budget revenues, 65 percent of exports, and 30 percent of foreign direct investment. According to *The Economist*, "The flow of petrodollars has created a sense of stability, masked economic woes, and given Russia more clout on the world stage."[3] Russia's proven reserves ranked number seven in the world, and there were huge opportunities for further exploration. To manage the windfall from high energy prices, the Russian government created a sovereign wealth fund that held almost $160 billion at the end of 2007.

The Russian oil and gas industry was dominated by six large firms: TNK-BP, Lukoil, Gazprom, Rosneft, Surgutneftegaz, and Tatneft (for comparable financial information see Appendix 4). The latter four were government controlled. Gazprom, with 436,000 employees, was Russia's largest company, the world's largest gas producer with about 93 percent of Russian gas production, and the dominant exporter of gas to Europe (Gazprom supplied about 25 percent of the European Union's gas). In recent years, Russia had been accused of using gas exports as a means of achieving foreign policy objectives. Gazprom had made many acquisitions of small Russian companies that had been privatized in the rigged auctions of the 1990s. Gazprom's oil subsidiary, Gazprom Neft, formerly the independent company Sibneft, was Russia's fifth-largest oil-producing company. Two oligarchs and former partners, Roman Abramovich and Boris Berezovsky, acquired Sibneft for US$100 million; in 2005, Gazprom paid $13 billion for majority control (an "oligarch" is a term for a small group of businessmen who acquired significant wealth and political influence in post-Soviet Russia). Gazprom announced that it planned to make major oil and gas investments outside Russia. Before becoming Russia's president, Dmitry Medvedev was chairman of Gazprom.

Rosneft, the largest oil producer, was a remnant of the Soviet Union's Ministry of Oil and Gas. Rosneft was broken up in the early 1990s and was left with few assets. After 2004, with the acquisition of assets from the now-defunct Yukos, Rosneft became a major firm. In 2006, Rosneft sold 15 percent of its shares in one of the world's largest IPOs. Surgutneftegaz was believed to be closely tied to the Kremlin. The controlling share-holder of Tatneft was the Russian Republic of Tatarstan. Ownership of Lukoil, the largest nongovernment-controlled oil company, included two oligarch share-holders with a 25 percent stake, and Conoco-Philips with 20 percent.

Despite the size and importance of the oil industry in Russia, all was not well. Production in 2008 was declining because of a combination of factors: (1) aging oil fields and poor maintenance; (2) a tax and regulatory regime that was increasingly viewed as confiscatory by oil companies; and (3) a dearth of Russian and foreign investment in exploration and development. The future of foreign investment was unclear. In May 2008, Russia's legislature approved a bill under which Gazprom and Rosneft would have exclusive rights to develop the country's offshore reserves in the Arctic and Far East (not the Caspian). This included the Sakhalin area, where Shell was forced in 2006 to transfer majority control of the Sakhalin II project to Gazprom. In May 2008, Russian President (and soon to be Prime Minister) Putin signed into law a bill limiting foreign investment in strategic industries, including major oil and gas fields. The law prohibited companies with less than 50 percent Russian ownership from bidding for strategic fields, allowing them to participate only as minority partners. The government retained the right to make a decision to issue a license to a foreign-controlled company in special cases.

BP's First Foray in Russia

In November 1997, BP paid $571 million to Uneximbank, one of Russia's most powerful financial and industrial groups, for a 10 percent ownership stake in Sidanco, Russia's fourth-biggest vertically integrated oil company. Sidanco owned three refineries and six production facilities. The deal gave BP 20 percent of the voting rights, a seat on the board, and the right to nominate chief operating and financial officers in the company. The intent was that BP and Sidanco would set up a joint venture to develop and operate Russian oil discoveries. The two companies would have an equal vote in how the venture was run. John Browne, CEO of BP, described the deal as a "major opportunity for BP in one of the great oil and gas provinces of the world … We believe the time is now right and, more importantly, that we have found in Sidanco a partner with a strong, established position at the heart of Russia's oil industry." Uneximbank said, "The agreement signed today is of great importance, both for Sidanco and the Unexim Group, which is the controlling shareholder of Sidanco. For successful development, Sidanco needs a strategic partner with considerable experience and a leading position in the international oil business. BP is this kind of partner."

In 1998, problems began to emerge with Sidanco's oil-producing subsidiary, Chernogorneft, in which Sidanco held 73 percent control. Although BP thought Chernogorneft was financially stable, oil sold to Sidanco had not been paid for, and large tax arrears had accumulated. This helped turn Chernogorneft's management against its parent, Sidanco. Also, the Russian financial crisis of 1998 undermined Uneximbank and sharply reduced oligarch Vladimir Potanin's political influence. Alfa, a rival conglomerate, became interested in Sidanco. As BP was drawn into daily management of Sidanco, Chernogorneft's debts continued to rise.

Alfa Access/Renova. In December 1998, Chernogorneft was driven into bankruptcy by Tyumen Oil Company (TNK), a company held 50–50 by a group known as Alfa Access/Renova, or AAR. TNK was created in 1997 from a cluster of 600 upstream and downstream companies in Russia and Ukraine acquired through various privatization auctions.

AAR was a complex alliance involving three private investment companies: Russia-based Alfa Group and Renova Group, and New York–based Access Industries. Each of the investment companies was headed by an oligarch:

- **Mikhail Maratovich Fridman**, president of Alfa Group Consortium, was born in 1964 in Lvov, on the western border of Ukraine. Fridman attended Moscow Institute of Steel and Alloys, where he had his first business ventures, including window washing, running a discotheque, and scalping Moscow theater tickets—all illegal under Soviet rule. In 1988, Fridman set up a photo cooperative, Alfa Foto, and subsequently ALFA/EKO, a commodities trading firm, which gave him the capital to establish Alfa Bank in 1991, which became one of Russia's largest banks. He hired a Russian foreign trade minister to head up the bank. As his wealth grew, Fridman was able to acquire significant oil interests in Russia. He was a member of a group that funded President Boris Yeltsin's 1996 re-election campaign. Alfa Group, one of Russia's largest privately owned financial-industrial groups, controlled Alfa Bank, Alfa Capital, several construction material firms (cement, timber,

glass), food processing businesses, and a supermarket chain. In 2008, *Forbes* listed Fridman's wealth as $20.8 billion, making him the twentieth richest person in the world.

- **Viktor Vekselberg** was born in 1957 in the Ukraine. He graduated from the Moscow Institute of Transportation Engineering and later went on to complete his master's degree and Ph.D. in mathematics. Vekselberg worked at the special design office of state-owned Rodless Pumps (OKB BN). He started as a technician and eventually became research manager. Vekselberg joined the world of business in 1990. In 1993, he became chairman of the board of directors of Renova Group, which became one of Russia's largest investment and business development companies. Through Renova, Vekselberg orchestrated Russia's first successful hostile takeover, acquiring the Vladimir Tractor Factory in 1994. He rose to prominence after Boris Yeltsin's re-election in 1996, when he started to purchase shares of oil companies, including Tyumen Oil (TNK). In 1997, he became a member of the board of directors of TNK. Vekselberg was ranked the sixty-seventh richest person in the world by *Forbes*, with a net worth of $11.2 billion.

- **Len Blavatnik** was born in Russia in 1958. After attending Moscow Institute of Transportation Engineering, he emigrated with his family to the United States in 1978. He received a master's degree in computer science from Columbia University and an MBA degree from Harvard Business School in 1989. In 1986, Blavatnik founded Access Industries, a privately held U.S.-based industrial group. After the fall of the Soviet Union, Access began making investments in Russia in industries such as oil, coal, aluminum, petrochemicals and plastics, telecommunications, media, and real estate. With his friend from university, Viktor Vekselberg, Access and Renova collaborated in various investments. Blavatnik was ranked the 113th richest person in the world by *Forbes* magazine with a net worth of $8.0 billion.

BP Writes off $200 Million. In February 1999, BP wrote off $200 million of its investment in Sidanco. In November 1999, Chernogorneft was sold out of bankruptcy for $176 million dollars to TNK. BP's director for external affairs in Russia commented: "The entire bankruptcy has been subject to major manipulations. We do not consider it to be valid. In many ways, this decision has damaging implications for foreign investors. BP Amoco will be very carefully reviewing its business position in Russia in the light of these events."[4]

Simon Kukes, chairman of TNK, said that his company had upheld "international standards of corporate governance and ethical behaviour," and stressed that "the purchase had been made in a competitive auction."[5] He offered BP the chance to enter a strategic alliance with him. Although TNK denied doing anything illegal, it appeared to most outside observers that the company used its political influence and the weaknesses of Russia's laws and judicial system to ensure that a succession of court cases went its way.

BP and TNK

In December 1999, TNK and BP announced an agreement under which Sidanco would regain Chernogorneft in return for TNK receiving a 25 percent stake in Sidanco. AAR, TNK's principal shareholder, would receive 25 percent plus one share in Sidanco. In exchange, TNK's shareholders would return Chernogorneft debt-free. The deal would cost TNK about $200 million, compared with $484 million paid by BP for its 10 percent stake. In 2000, after lengthy negotiations, AAR's controlling shareholders replaced Unexim Group as the dominant shareholders of Sidanco.

In February 2003, BP announced a major strategic alliance with the same companies with which it had battled for control of Sidanco. Under the terms of the alliance, BP and AAR would combine their interests in Russia to create the country's third-largest oil and gas business, in which both parties would have a 50 percent stake. The new company, TNK-BP, would be made up of various assets: TNK, Sidanco, and most of BP's Russian assets. BP's Russian assets included a retail network in the Moscow region, minority stakes in Sidanco Rusia Petroleum, and several other equity investments.

For its 50 percent stake, BP would pay AAR $3 billion in cash and three subsequent annual payments of $1.25 billion in BP shares. In describing the deal, BP CEO John Browne said that BP had instituted new governance mechanisms to protect the interests of all parties. He also said that changes in Russia's legal system and an increasing commitment to international rules of trade convinced BP that it was time to deepen its partnership with AAR. Browne called the experience with Chernogorneft and Sidanco a key learning experience in Russia. A BP executive said, "Of course, we had qualms, given the history. But sometimes you don't get the chance to choose your partners. It was the only deal available."[6]

When the JV was announced (see Exhibit 1), there was speculation that the Russian government had reservations about the desirability of foreign investment in energy reserves. There was also speculation that the speed with which the deal was done caught the government off guard.

Joint Venture Structure

The joint venture was legally created in August 2003. In 2004, a major restructuring simplified the complex TNK-BP holdings (a dozen subsidiaries and hundreds of legal entities). In 2005, further restructuring occurred. Three holding companies (TNK, Sidanco, and ONAKO) were merged into TNK-BP Holding. Approximately 70 percent (by value) of minority shareholders in 14 key TNK-BP subsidiaries exchanged their shares for shares in TNK-BP Holding through the voluntary share

Exhibit 1 Agreement on Structure of TNK-BP Holding Signed in London

TASS, Thursday, June 26, 2003

British Petroleum and the Russian Alfa Group (Access-Renova) signed an agreement in London on Thursday, determining the structure of a deal on establishing a TNK-BP joint venture. Under the agreement, all commercial and financial obligations of the sides are formalised, which opens a way for the final creation of a holding.

"The history of the TNK-BP Company starts from this moment," said chairman of the board of directors of the Alfa Group Mikhail Fridman. "I'm sure that this new unique entity will play a leading role in the Russian and, later, in the world oil industry." "We hope that merging trends in the Russian and world fuel and energy complex will not be limited to this deal," said, in turn, TNK board chairman Viktor Vekselberg. "This deal is an international recognition of rising political stability in Russia and its progress in the economic development," he noted.

Holding President Robert Dudley admitted in an interview with Tass that "it was not an easy thing" to take a decision on expanding BP business in Russia. The company carried out a painstaking assessment of assets over the past nine months, and spent enough time on making feasibility estimates. BP participated in a number of major deals over the past five years, and not a single one was concluded with greater carefulness than the present one: "this is true both of assets and obligations as well as legal formalities," the president said.

TNK-BP will have substantial assets in the most important oil-bearing areas of Russia: production will total 800,000 barrels a day in Western Siberia, and 370,000 barrels a day in the Volga-Ural area. Besides, Dudley continued, the company will continue the development of deposits, which was already conducted. There are now 8,000 mothballed wells, he went on to say, and the company mulls over a possibility of resuming their operation gradually. It will be necessary to restart several thousands of wells annually, the president stated. British Petroleum intends to use skilled Russian personnel and to bring machinery and methods from other areas of the world to organize production so as to optimize deposits, wells, and land infrastructure to boost efficiency of recovery, Dudley emphasized.

exchange program. Upon completion of the voluntary share exchange program, minority shareholders owned approximately 5 percent of publicly held TNK-BP Holding. An independent valuation by Deloitte & Touche put a value of $18.5 billion on TNK-BP Holding. See Exhibit 2 for the ownership structure in 2008.

Key elements of the joint venture agreement were as follows:

- Ten-member board with equal representation from BP and AAR.
- AAR nominates the chairman of the board and the chairman of the remuneration committee.
- BP nominates the vice chairman of the board and chairman of the audience committee.
- BP appoints the CEO and holds half the top management positions.
- The Russian shareholders have management control over government relations, legal affairs, and security.
- Dividends will be a minimum of 40 percent of TNK-BP's U.S. GAAP net income.
- The debt ratio must be kept at 25 to 35 percent.
- The business scope of TNK-BP is limited to oil and gas in Russia and Ukraine.
- Management is particularly focused on certain actions: to improve safety, focusing on reducing high-risk practices; to improve planning and forecasting, so that delivery can be assured and there are no surprises; to improve internal control systems and ethical conducts; to curb the chances of fraud,

illegal payments, and misjudgments; to improve the reporting of results, continuously diligent and appropriate disclosure; and, finally, to increase export and production, and reduce cost through the use of better technology.

- TNK-BP holds a 49.8 percent interest in Slavneft through TNK-BP International Ltd. Slavneft operates as a separate entity. TNK-BP and Gazprom Neft have equal representation on the Slavneft Board of Directors.
- The partners are not allowed to sell their interests in the venture until after December 31, 2007 (termed the "lock-in period").

BP appointed Robert Dudley as CEO. Dudley, an American and graduate of Thunderbird School of Global Management, was a veteran Amoco and BP executive. In the mid-1990s, Dudley worked for Amoco in Russia, and saw Amoco outmaneuvered on a deal by the Russian company Yukos.

Shareholder Comments about the JV Formation

At an analyst meeting in New York on October 17, 2003, BP Chairman John Browne made the following comments:

We regard this group of shareholders as one of the best in Russia, with a strong track record. We've built a strong relationship, tested by past difficulties, notably over Sidanco. We continued to build trust, and less and less viewed each other's motives with suspicion. AAR is a vital

Exhibit 2 TNK-BP Ownership Structure, 2008

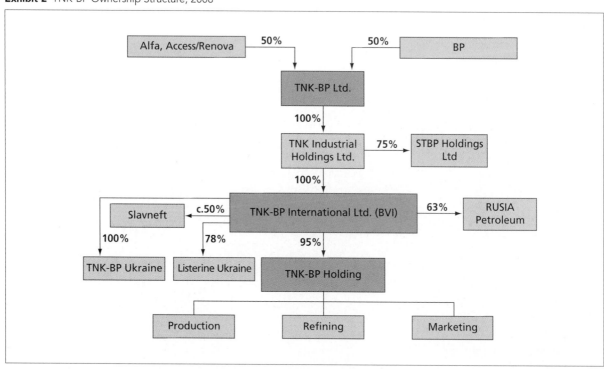

part of the future success of TNK-BP. It brings not only assets and people, but also experience and judgment on the right things to do in the Russian context. They've made it clear that they're committed to making TNK-BP not only a successful operation, but a company which can compare favorably with BP in terms of the quality of governance, transparency, safety, and ethics. In these matters, I know they are reinforcing President Putin's agenda for modernization. BP, as a powerful, globally connected company, brings not only technology to improve the business, but also credibility and experience in modern management. It is a partnership of mutual advantage. Finally, it's about people. And we've selected some of the very best people. Whether they've come from outside, or from TNK, or from Sidanco, or from BP.

At the same meeting, Mikhail Fridman (the lead oligarch shareholder) said:

Of course, we made quite significant profits from the deal but, frankly speaking, we've done this deal not because we just want to realize the profits, but because we do believe that the most important way for us as investors to increase our benefits and potential growth, we do believe that to create a joint venture with a company like BP at the end of the day, we'll benefit after all.

It is obvious to everybody here that the biggest challenge we have is probably the cultural gap between the Russian style of doing business and Western style of doing business. And it is not so easy to overcome that. And from this point of view, we are quite happy that we have a long story of relationship between us and BP. And this not very smooth story—not just, you know, [a] story of friendship and partnership that started from quite tough, you know, competition ... We do believe that there are only two things we need as a shareholder. I think it's trust and, second, probably patience.

And it seems to me that both sides have enough of that. So, that's why I'm quite optimistic about the future of our company.

TNK-BP Assets

In 2008, TNK-BP was Russia's third-largest oil and gas company in terms of liquids production, and accounted for almost 20 percent of Russia's total oil production. TNK-BP employed about 65,000 people, including 85 foreign managers, many of whom had formerly worked for BP. The main oil production assets of TNK-BP were located in West Siberia and the Volga-Urals region (Exhibit 3), with new provinces being opened in East Siberia via the planned development of the Verkhnechonskoye oil field (concurrently with the construction of the Transneft-operated East Siberia Oil Pipeline) and in the south of the Tyumen region. The main gas business assets included the Rospan project in Novy Urengoi, which is 100 percent owned by TNK-BP, and the Yugragazpererabotka gas processing joint venture with SIBUR Holding in Nizhnevartovsk. TNK-BP owned 49 percent of Yugragazpererabotka. Some specific data on TNK-BP assets are as follows:

Exhibit 3 TNK-BP's Asset Map, 2008

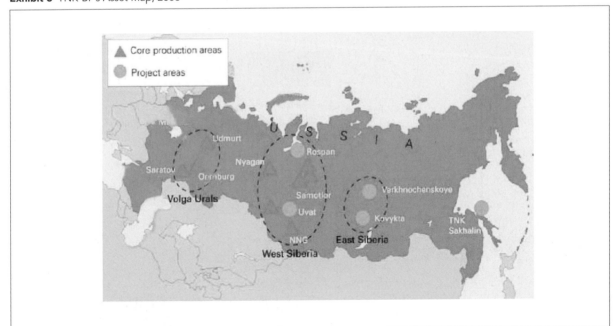

- TNK-BP held approximately 200 exploration and production licenses.
- Twenty-seven new licenses were acquired in 2007.
- TNK-BP's top 10 fields delivered two-thirds of its production.
- Top 20 fields held 80 percent of proved reserves.
- Average well productivity was 15 tons per day.
- Approximately 25,000 km of infield gathering pipelines (following divestment of assets).
- TNK-BP had four refineries located in Russia (Ryazan Refinery, Saratov Refinery, Nizhnevartovsk Oil Refining Enterprize, and Krasnoleninsk Refinery) and one refinery in Ukraine (Lisichansknefteorgsintez), all close to production areas and export routes.
- The company operated approximately 1,600 retail outlets branded either as BP or TNK in Russia and Ukraine.

JV Financial Results

TNK-BP's revenues, profitability, assets, and cash flow grew substantially over its brief life span (see Exhibit 4; also see the various appendices). However, the revenue structure was heavily constrained by export duties (the Russian government captured about 90 percent of crude prices), and the domestic market prices earned were complex combinations of contracts and regulated rates.

TNK-BP Strategic and Financial Objectives

TNK-BP's strategic objective was to "become a world-class oil and gas group that is an industry leader in Russia, with a clear focus on the sustainability and renewal of its resources and the efficiency of its operations." The company was committed to being an integrated oil and gas company, but the partners were not in agreement as to the level of non-Russian growth. The company was also committed to growing its gas business and was involved in various different discussions with Gazprom.

The joint venture's financial objectives were as follows:

- To maintain a strong balance sheet providing flexibility, liquidity, and cost-effective borrowing.
- To target a gearing range of 25 to 35 percent (net debt/net debt + equity, U.S. GAAP basis).
- To maintain a conservative debt structure with a significant percentage of long-term debt.
- To maintain a dividend policy of at least 40 percent of net income.
- To attain an investment grade credit rating over time.
- To improve the timeliness and quality of financial reporting based on centralized financial management.

In 2008, TNK-BP accounted for about one-quarter of BP's total production, one-fifth of its reserves, and about one-tenth of net income.

Key Joint Venture Events 2003–2007

June 2003—Uncertainty

According to Robert Dudley, TNK-BP CEO: "With all due respect for BP, it had a fairly vague idea about what was going on in Russia. It knew about Russian risks, but it had never had to deal directly with tax authorities, customs officers, monopolies, and relationships with regions …This is more than just an oil deal. And if we fail, it will be more than just a setback for one foreign investor. It will be a setback for the whole country—and the Russian government understands that very well … We will insist on the same level of transparency and governance as in BP."[7]

June 2003—Russians Say the Expatriate Costs Are Too High

Victor Vekselberg commented on expatriate costs: "Bonuses and entitlement for expatriates has been one of the most hotly debated issues. Foreigners who come to Russia want to bring a piece of their own life here."[8]

May 2004—The Russian Partners Want the Deal Changed

The Russian partners informed BP that they wanted the payments for their share of the JV to be made earlier. BP made the following statement:

We have an excellent set of agreements. We expect all partners to stick to those agreements. As we announced in February last year, BP, under the terms of the agreement, will pay three annual tranches on the anniversary of completion of dollars 1.25bn in BP shares valued at market prices prior to each annual payment. What our partners do with those agreements is a matter for them. The agreements provide for AAR to be 50 percent owners of TNK-BP through 2007.[9]

August 2004—Yukos Is Dismantled

The Russian government began the process that would see the bankruptcy and dismantling of oil company Yukos, and the jailing of its prominent and outspoken CEO, Mikhail Khodorkovsky. Yukos was charged with tax bills and other claims of about $28 billion.

April 2005—TNK-BP Faces a Huge Tax Bill

Russian tax authorities announced a $1 billion tax claim relating to 2001 earnings. Viktor Vekselberg said, "We cannot possibly have such liabilities, and will therefore dispute them … There can be no risks, no parallels with Yukos."[10] A few months later, the tax liability was reduced.

Robert Dudley made the following comments:

The significance of this (tax claim) goes far beyond our company. Everyone will watch this as a test of whether

Exhibit 4 TNK-BP's Financial Results, 2002–2007

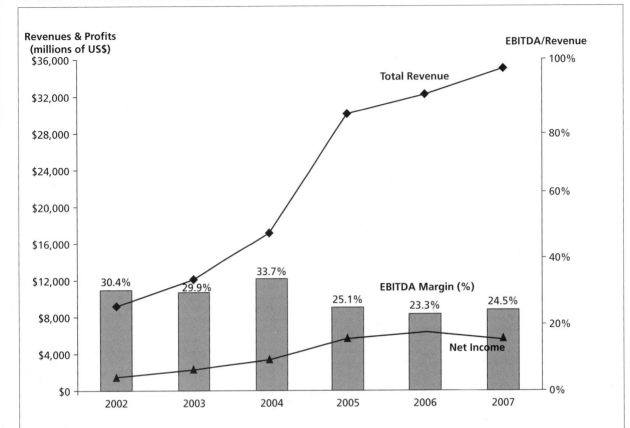

- Revenues grew from $9.2 billion in 2002 to $35 billion in 2007. Net income rose from $1.5 billion in 2002 (16.8 percent) to $5.7 billion in 2007 (16.1 percent).
- Total assets doubled between 2002 and 2007, from $12.6 billion in 2002 to $25.3 billion. The net debt/equity ratio (debt − cash/equity) decreased from 30.2 percent to almost zero in 2007 (0.1 percent). As a result, TNK-BP earned more in interest income than it paid in interest expenses in 2007.
- Operating cash flow grew from $1.385 billion in 2002 to $5.053 billion in 2007.
- The growth in cash flow was deployed between both the owners and the business. Capital expenditures (capex) rose from $595 million in 2002 to $2.23 billion in 2006, with another major jump to $3.285 billion in 2007.
- Dividends paid grew from $139 million in 2002 to $6.664 billion in 2006 and then down to $4.379 billion in 2007.
- Cash and liquid assets were $2.587 billion at end-of-year 2007.
- The share price for TNK-BP Holding fell from a high of $3.40/share in early 2006 to $2.00/share in mid-2008.

Russia can integrate with the world economy. I don't think it is in the interest of the Russian government to destroy TNK-BP. Russia is inadvertently becoming increasingly difficult to navigate for well-intentioned investors— Russian and foreign alike. The state has progressively asserted its influence over the commanding heights of the economy, and state-owned companies have begun to play an increasingly prominent role. At the time when Russia's economy is in need of knowledge and management skills, it is becoming increasingly difficult to bring in managers and executives.[11]

April 2005—TNK-BP May Not Be Allowed to Bid for New Oil Fields

A senior official in the Natural Resources Ministry said that that an auction for three major fields was canceled in March in order to exclude TNK-BP. Later in the month, Vladimir Putin told John Browne, BP CEO, "We were not mistaken when we supported your decision two years ago. The profits of the joint company have increased 20 times over. This is proof of the quality of management."[12]

October 2005—Foreign Oil Companies Cannot Participate in Auctions

Russia's natural resources minister announced that companies more than 50 percent foreign-owned will not be allowed to take part in 2006 auctions for new oil fields.

March 2006—TNK-BP in Major Dispute Over Gas Field

One of TNK-BP's most valuable assets was the Kovykta gas field in eastern Siberia. The license to develop Kovykta was held by Rusia Petroleum, 62.89 percent owned by TNK-BP and previously controlled by Sidanco. TNK-BP wanted to develop the gas for Asian markets, and Gazprom (the Russian government-owned natural gas company) said the gas should be developed for Russia. There was speculation that Rusia Petroleum's license for the field would be revoked. The Natural Resources Ministry accused TNK-BP of producing too little gas at the field. TNK-BP argued it could not produce the 9 billion cubic meters per year stipulated in the license since Gazprom had blocked construction of a pipeline to China, and local demand was insufficient. TNK-BP had been lobbying for years for the license to be amended.

October 2006—Robert Dudley Says TNK-BP Will Survive

Dudley stated, "We are confident there is a solid future for TNK-BP. Much has been written about the consolidation of the state … But I believe having companies like this is a good thing for the industry … As long as we continue to get good results, I think the company will more than survive, I think it will thrive. I have seen no evidence that they [the Russian partners] are working to sell their interest."[13]

An oil industry analyst had the following observation: "BP has found it is not only dancing with the wrong partner, but that the dance tune has changed, too. They got in at a good price, and they got in at a good time. It's better for the company to adjust rather than try to go against the tide."[14]

October 2006—TNK-BP Engineer Killed

The chief engineer for Rusia Petroleum, which held the license to develop the Kovykta gas field, was shot dead in Siberia. Rumors about a contract killing immediately began circulating.

June 2007—Putin Angry about the Kovykta Gas Field Dispute

In Germany for a G8 meeting, Putin said to reporters: "How long should we tolerate it if participants of that consortium do nothing to implement the license? This is not about BP, not about the foreign partner, but about all the shareholders that took the obligations to develop this field and, unfortunately, didn't meet the license terms … I won't even talk now about how the license was purchased. Let's leave this up to the conscience of those who did it a while ago, also in the early 1990s."[15]

Late June 2007—TNK-BP Sells Its Stake in the Kovykta Gas Field

TNK-BP sold its 62.89 percent stake in Rusia Petroleum to Gazprom for about $800 million, less than a third of its real value, according to some analysts. TNK-BP had invested about $450 million in developing the field. TNK-BP had the option to buy back 25 percent of the field at market price.

Gazprom Approaches BP about a Deal in 2007

In mid-2007, Gazprom initiated discussions with BP about a possible alliance. Gazprom's goal of becoming a global oil and gas company was being stymied by opposition from Western governments. Gazprom was interested in stakes in BP assets outside Russia. In return, Gazprom would contribute large stakes in its Russian oil business. A key element of the alliance would involve Gazprom buying AAR's TNK-BP stake, which would then allow BP and Gazprom to combine their various Russian oil assets and create the largest Russian oil producer.[16] Gazprom officials told BP privately that they believed AAR would sell. AAR said publicly that they had no intention of selling.

BP's country manager for Russia, James Dupree, handled most of the discussions with Gazprom. BP CEO Tony Hayward made several trips to Russia to meet with Gazprom CEO Alexei Miller. Based on the many meetings that were held, BP was confident that a deal would happen, and that the TNK-BP partner issues would be resolved.

2008: Can the JV Survive?

On March 19, 2008, Russian security services raided TNK-BP offices and detained an employee, Ilya Zaslavsky, on charges of espionage. On March 21, Russia's environmental agency announced an investigation of TNK-BP's largest oilfield. The investigation was to be led by the same official that investigated the Sakhalin II project operated by Shell. Shell was later forced to sell a stake in the project to Gazprom. On March 25, the Interior

Ministry said it was investigating a $40 million tax evasion case against Sidanco, a former TNK-BP subsidiary.

Expatriate Visa Problems for BP.

President Putin had complained about the dearth of Russians in top management positions in natural resource companies. In early 2008, BP had problems renewing visas for expatriate employees, allegedly because of a "lack of clarity." In May, a Siberian court refused to allow visas for 148 technology specialists seconded from BP. The court order was initiated by a Moscow brokerage, ZAO Tetlis, that owned a small stake in a publicly traded unit of TNK-BP, and alleged that the fees TNK-BP paid for the BP specialists amounted to an illegal dividend for BP. BP maintained that without the specialists, TNK-BP's production could be reduced. When the expatriates, already in the country, showed up for work, TNK-BP security refused to let them enter the office. Robert Dudley blamed a TNK-BP executive, German Khan (a billionaire investor and colleague of Mikhail Fridman), for orchestrating the visa issue, and sought his and two other executives' ouster from the venture for gross insubordination. BP said that Khan ignored instructions and applied for fewer than half the required visas. The Russian shareholders responded with a statement saying that TNK-BP should be allowed to expand outside Russia even if it would compete with BP's own operations, and called for reducing the venture's reliance on foreign specialists. The statement also called Dudley's recent comments about the visa issue deeply inappropriate.[17]

In July, immigration authorities approved only 71 visas, far fewer than the 150 BP requested. BP reassigned the 148 seconded employees to other BP units.

The Gazprom Deal Collapses.

Despite the various problems, BP remained hopeful that a deal with Gazprom would be worked out. In April 2008, BP CEO Tony Hayward visited Igor Sechin, a powerful Putin confidant and chairman of Rosneft (the following month, Sechin was promoted to deputy prime minister in charge of the energy industry). At the meeting, Hayward discussed BP's efforts to reach a deal with Gazprom. Sechin explained that Gazprom was not always able to deliver on its ambitions for making major international deals. In May, Hayward met with a former Kremlin official who informed him that his talks with Gazprom were "indecent" and that BP should be less confrontational with AAR. Hayward was also told that the Kremlin would not force AAR to sell. On May 14, 2008, Hayward met Gazprom officials in Manchester, England, at a football match. At this meeting, Gazprom was noncommittal and, in a surprise to BP, suggested holding off on any decisions for a month or so.

Partner Disagreements over JV Strategy.

In late May, the stakes escalated when the three Russian oligarchs met with Tony Hayward and demanded that Robert Dudley be removed as TNK-BP CEO. According to a statement released by the Russian shareholders, Dudley was favoring BP over the Russian shareholders. A spokesperson for the Russians said, "He [Dudley] is acting in the interests of only 50 percent of the shareholders. We want someone who will pursue the interests of all shareholders, not just run TNK-BP like a BP subsidiary."[18] The Russian shareholders were particularly upset with Dudley's five-year strategic plan forecasting lower shareholder returns in the coming years because of high taxes, increasing costs, and stagnant production. The Russian shareholders refused to approve the plan. They argued that Dudley was too focused on increasing reserves, and should be increasing the production of existing oil fields. They wanted the 2008 investment plan of $4.4 billion cut by $900 million and the money paid as dividends. BP argued that TNK-BP was the best-performing oil company in Russia. According to Mikhail Fridman: "There's a strategic conflict of interests between TNK-BP and BP itself. We had a company that was strong, energetic, and aggressive in the good sense of the word. BP turned it into a typical bureaucracy … We don't plan to leave, and I don't think that they plan to leave. So, ultimately, we're destined to come to some agreement.[19] The attempt to portray this conflict as a dispute between a respectable Western company and some Russian oligarchs who are trying to take control using dirty methods is completely cynical. It is our partners who are using methods from the 1990s. There is a good English word: arrogance … We sensed this condescending attitude towards what we were saying [for months] … This is about the type of foreign investors Russia needs. We don't need foreign investors who limit the development of the company."[20]

Hayward refused to remove Dudley. The Russian shareholders threatened legal action to strip BP-appointed directors of their powers. BP was contemplating its own lawsuit against the partners to recover a recently paid portion of back taxes. BP maintained that the taxes paid for the period prior to the formation of the JV should be borne entirely by the previous owners of TNK (which would include Fridman, Vekselberg, and Blavatnik) and its subsidiaries, and not BP.

BP Chairman Peter Sutherland expressed his frustration: "This is just a return to the corporate raiding activities that were prevalent in Russia in the 1990s. Prime minister has referred to these tactics as relics of the 1990s but, unfortunately, our partners continue to use them, and the leaders of the country seem unwilling or unable to step in and stop them. This is bad for us, bad for the company and, of course, very bad for Russia."[21]

"The Alfa Playbook." BP took several steps to deal with its partners. In early June, Tony Hayward met with Igor Sechin to discuss AAR's pressure tactics. BP moved Lamar McCay, an executive with Russia experience, from the United States to Russia to be executive vice president of TNK-BP. BP hired a consulting firm to study other foreign joint ventures involving AAR companies. The outcome of the study became known in BP as the "Alfa Playbook."[22] BP learned, for example, that other Alfa joint ventures had run into various difficulties. For example, Altimo, an Alfa subsidiary, had a joint venture with Norway's Telenor A/S. In 2007, Telenor accused Altimo of dirty tricks in the midst of a business dispute over a Ukrainian mobile phone company. Telenor accused Alfa of paying journalists in Ukraine to publish negative articles about Telenor. Altimo filed a lawsuit in Ukraine and received a favorable ruling. Telenor was never informed that the lawsuit was under way. The result of the lawsuit was sent to a Telenor address that was unoccupied, and by the time Telenor learned of the ruling, the Ukrainian judge on the case had disappeared (the day after giving the decision), and it was too late to appeal. According to BP officials, the Alfa Playbook was "playing out to the letter" in the TNK-BP dispute.

BP's Options

In late July 2008, it was looking increasingly likely that Robert Dudley would not be granted a visa and would have to leave Russia. There was also concern that Russia's Federal Labor and Employment Service would try to prosecute a group of TNK-BP managers for violating labor law. Because of the uncertainty, Dudley had not left Russia since March. The Russian partners maintained that his contract expired at the end of 2007, while BP said his contract was automatically renewed. In an interview, Dudley said: "Running the company now is like driving a car, and sometimes the brakes work and sometimes they don't. I spend a lot of time holding meetings out on the balcony of my office …. It's not me personally, it can't be performance; it's the role, the check and balance between the interests of the shareholders. I've got an obligation to hold the line for both sets of shareholders."[23]

Without a Gazprom deal to buy out AAR, Robert Dudley and his BP colleagues considered other options. One option was to take the dispute to the highest levels in the Russian government, perhaps even to Putin himself. The results of earlier meetings with Igor Sechin, deputy prime minister, suggested that this option would have limited value. A second option was to seek British government help, which had been offered. Prime Minister Gordon Brown was going to be in Russia in July for meetings with President Medvedev. A third option was legal action against AAR for violating the shareholder agreement. Finally, BP could sit tight, continue to run the business, and resist the Russian shareholders. Meanwhile, the Russian shareholders continued to push for Dudley's dismissal, with Victor Vekselberg calling for a July board meeting to discuss Dudley's infringement of Russian employment, immigration, and tax laws. Although BP said Dudley would keep his job, it was hard too see how he could remain CEO if he was outside Russia.

Appendix 1 TNK-BP Holding, Consolidated Statements of Income (millions of U.S. dollars)

	2002	2003	2004	2005	2006	2007
Sales revenue	$9,172	$12,114	$17,169	$30,106	$32,114	$34,995
Operating expenses	(6,381)	(8,497)	(11,390)	(22,536)	(24,684)	(26,399)
EBITDA	2,791	3,617	5,779	7,570	7,430	8,596
EBITDA margin	30.4%	29.9%	33.7%	25.1%	23.1%	24.5%
Depreciation & amortization	(580)	(814)	(1,039)	(1,206)	(1,250)	(1,341)
EBIT	2,211	2,803	4,740	6,364	6,180	7,255
Equity income					71	4
Net interest income					79	182
Interest expense	(273)	(177)	(29)	(111)	(210)	(167)

(Continued)

Appendix 1 TNK-BP Holding, Consolidated Statements of Income (millions of U.S. dollars) (*Continued*)

	2002	2003	2004	2005	2006	2007
Exchange gain (loss)					(104)	8
Gains on disposal of subsidiaries	133	189	—	766	2,677	105
Profit before tax	2,071	2,815	4,674	6,975	8,693	7,387
Income tax expense	(190)	(227)	(1,221)	(1,220)	(2,115)	(1,453)
Minority interest	(337)	(214)	(37)	(70)	(169)	(202)
Net profit	$1,544	$2,374	$3,416	$5,685	$6,409	$5,732
Return on sales	*16.8%*	*19.6%*	*19.9%*	*18.9%*	*19.9%*	*16.4%*
Weighted average shares (m)	15,448	15,448	15,448	15,448	15,448	15,448
EPS	$0.10	$0.15	$0.22	$0.37	$0.41	$0.37
DPS	$0.01	$0.04	$0.25	$0.25	$0.43	$0.16
Payout ratio	9.0%	25.0%	112.8%	68.6%	105.7%	42.2%
Export duties (part of operating expenses)					9,327	9,256

Source: TNK-BP Holding, TNK-BP, and author calculations.

Appendix 2 TNK-BP Holding, Consolidated Balance Sheet (millions of U.S. dollars)

	2002	2003	2004	2005	2006	2007
Cash and other liquid assets	1,083	869	477	485	827	635
Fixed assets	7,751	10,121	11,050	11,704	11,259	13,901
Long term investments	823	1,679	81	90	94	20
Other assets	2,948	3,445	4,826	6,609	9,530	13,348
Total Assets	12,605	16,114	16,434	18,888	21,710	27,904
Interest-bearing debt	3,167	2,755	1,669	1,811	1,515	1,859
Other liabilities	2,533	4,101	5,291	7,844	8,103	9,752
Total Liabilities	5,700	6,856	6,960	9,655	9,618	11,611
Shareholders' equity	5,099	8,530	8,958	8,606	11,488	15,585
Minority interest	1,806	728	755	866	604	708
Total Liabilities & Shareholders' Equity	12,605	16,114	16,434	18,888	21,710	27,904
Net debt	*2,084*	*1,886*	*1,192*	*1,326*	*688*	*1,224*
Net debt/equity	*30.2%*	*20.4%*	*12.3%*	*14.0%*	*5.6%*	*7.8%*
Change in working capital	*(327)*	*661*	*(499)*	*(214)*	*2,453*	*3,369*

Source: TNK-BP Holding and author calculations.

Appendix 3 TNK-BP Holding, Cash Flow (millions of U.S. dollars)

	2002	2003	2004	2005	2006	2007
Cash flow from operations	1,980	4,082	4,687	5,042	7,877	5,485
Net capital expenditures (capex)	(595)	(849)	(1,293)	(1,764)	(2,234)	(3,266)
Free cash flow	1,385	3,233	3,394	3,278	5,643	2,219
Dividends paid	(139)	(594)	(3,854)	(3,901)	(6,594)	(2,420)
Discretionary cash flow	1,246	2,639	(460)	(623)	(951)	(201)
Net change in borrowings	(472)	(807)	580	264	(2,026)	305
Equity capital raised, net	—	—	—	—	—	—
Other investing/financing activities	(72)	(2,111)	(338)	1,203	3,319	(296)
Net cash flow	702	(279)	(218)	844	342	(192)

Source: TNK-BP Holding.

Appendix 4 Public Comparables

Company	Country	Capitalization Million USD	Market Multipliers				Financial Multipliers				
			P/S	P/E	EV/ EBITDA	P/BV	ROE	ROA	ROIC	WACC	ROIC/ WACC
Gazprom	Russia	305,152	3.23	12.06	9.13	1.99	21.28%	12.70%	16.51%	8.89%	1.86
LUKOIL	Russia	64,090	1.06	8.50	5.62	1.69	25.07%	16.90%	21.97%	9.50%	2.31
Gazprom Neft	Russia	27,794	1.45	7.50	5.24	2.71	41.63%	29.59%	36.09%	10.15%	3.56
Surgut-neftegas	Russia	38,076	1.55	10.20	0.00	0.97	9.83%	9.15%	9.71%	10.84%	0.90
Tatneft	Russia	13,537	0.94	10.49	5.66	1.26	13.84%	9.90%	13.59%	11.30%	1.20
TNK-BP	Russia	29,634	1.27	4.38	0.00	2.44	73.96%	31.86%	60.87%	10.50%	5.80
Transneft	Russia	9,186	0.79	3.15	3.06	0.41	15.09%	10.38%	13.94%	9.86%	1.41
Rosneft	Russia	86,799	2.04	7.66	11.64	3.31	24.11%	9.20%	14.82%	9.86%	1.50
NOVATEK	Russia	23,531	9.91	34.44	21.34	7.20	22.42%	17.27%	20.78%	9.86%	2.11
Russia's Average			**2.47**	**10.93**	**6.85**	**2.44**	**27.47%**	**16.33%**	**23.14%**	**10.08%**	**2.29**
Petro-China	China	538,994	2.61	13.77	15.07	3.08	25.81%	17.24%	23.21%	17.20%	1.35
Petroleo Brasileiro SA	Brazil	253,141	2.29	17.58	9.83	3.39	29.39%	13.15%	19.85%	13.66%	1.45
Sasol	RSA	33,667	2.54	15.77		4.07	29.82%	15.33%	23.82%	14.09%	1.69
Sinopec	China	9,752	0.47	28.43	16.94	1.20	4.47%	3.11%	4.86%	17.49%	0.28

(Continued)

Appendix 4 Public Comparables (*Continued*)

Company	Country	Capitalization Million USD	Market Multipliers				Financial Multipliers				
			P/S	P/E	EV/EBITDA	P/BV	ROE	ROA	ROIC	WACC	ROIC/WACC
Emerging Markets Average			1.98	18.89	13.95	2.94	22.37%	12.21%	17.94%	15.61%	1.19
Murphy Oil	USA	15,409	0.83	18.85	11.15	3.16	16.99%	9.24%	14.32%	9.00%	1.59
Norsk Hydro	Norway	18,363	0.58	5.30		1.72	24.17%	11.16%	21.05%	13.13%	1.60
Occidental Petroleum	USA	64,736	3.48	14.91	6.29	2.85	25.67%	15.66%	24.14%	10.67%	2.26
Petro-Canada	Canada	24,295	1.11	9.96	3.66	2.00	24.50%	11.76%	19.69%	12.41%	1.59
Repsol YPF	Spain	42,498	0.54	8.73	4.37	1.51	18.54%	6.87%	12.30%	10.36%	1.19
Developed Markets Average			1.31	11.55	6.37	2.25	21.97%	10.94%	18.30%	11.11%	1.65
BP	Great Britain	205,892	0.73	10.03	5.94	2.20	23.38%	9.19%	18.64%	9.41%	1.98
Chevron Texaco	USA	186,271	0.92	10.25	5.68	2.49	26.04%	13.26%	22.56%	10.09%	2.24
Conoco-Phillips	USA	131,370	0.80	8.66	4.98	1.58	13.86%	6.94%	11.33%	10.09%	1.12
Exxon-Mobil	USA	488,394	1.36	12.28	6.91	4.12	35.11%	18.49%	33.43%	10.03%	3.33
Royal-Dutch	Holland	227,019	0.64	7.22	4.33	1.81	27.28%	12.41%	23.34%	9.18%	2.54
Total SA	France	182,004	0.83	8.61	4.33	2.52	30.95%	12.05%	22.81%	10.12%	2.25
Global Average			0.88	9.51	5.36	2.45	26.10%	12.06%	22.02%	9.82%	2.24

Source: Veles Capital, 2008, June 16, 17. Original data drawn from Bloomberg, Estimation, and Veles Capital.

NOTES

1. G. White, 2008, BP in Russia—plagued from start? Putin says venture structured poorly, clear boss is needed, *Wall Street Journal*, June 2, B2.
2. Ibid.
3. 2008, Trouble in the pipeline: Russia's oil industry, *The Economist*, May 10.
4. A. Jack, 1999, BP Amoco to review its Russian interests, *Financial Times*, November 27, 15.
5. Ibid.
6. G. White & G. Chazan, 2008, Boardroom brawl roils BP's Russia venture, talks break down; Kremlin's role murky, *Wall Street Journal*, June 12, A1.
7. C. Hoyas & A. Ostrovsky, 2003, Aiming to clean up in Russia with record deal: The success of BP's huge project will not only be judged in oil and money, *Financial Times*, June 26, 26.
8. Ibid.

9. C. Hoyas, A. Jack, & A. Ostrovsky, 2004, Russian partners seek to change BP deal, *Financial Times*, May 4, 1.

10. I. Gorst & A. Ostrovsky, 2005, TNK-BP hit by a dollars lbn tax bill, *Financial Times*, April 12, 21.

11. I. Gorst & A. Ostrovsky, 2005, TNK-BP chief attacks Russia's uncertain investment climate, *Financial Times*, April 13, 8.

12. C. Belton, 2005, Putin allays TNK-BP worries, *Moscow Times*, April 25.

13. C. Belton, 2006, Dudley dismisses talk of sale, *Moscow Times*, October 4.

14. Ibid.

15. A. Medetsky, 2007, An irritated president steps into Kovykta fray, *Moscow Times*, June 5.

16. G. White & G. Chazin, 2008, Misreading the Kremlin costs BP control in Russia venture, *Wall Street Journal*, December 16, A1, A6.

17. G. White & G. Chazan, 2008, BP venture is threatened as criticisms spill into the open, *Wall Street Journal*, May 28.

18. G. White & G. Chazan, 2008, Intrigue in Russia ensnares BP venture, *Wall Street Journal*, May 30, A1.

19. White & Chazan, Boardroom brawl roils BP's Russia venture.

20. C. Belton & E. Crooks, 2008, Fridman accuses BP of arrogance, *Financial Times*, June 17, 18.

21. R. Anderson, C. Belton, & E. Crooks, 2008, BP accuses Russians of corporate raiding, *Financial Times*, June 13, 1.

22. G. White & G. Chazan, 2008, BP is in the dark in struggle to save its Russian venture, *Wall Street Journal*, June 30, B4.

23. G. White, 2008, The bitter battle to lead TNK-BP: Dudley pushes back as Russian group seeks his ouster, *Wall Street Journal*, July 23, B1.

Mike Apostol, Jami Clement, Cory Edwards, Mairah Meller, Sam Park, Phil Rogers, Doug Trucha, Robin Chapman

Arizona State University

The New York Times Company

Arthur O. Sulzberger Jr., chairman and publisher for The New York Times Company, left work on November 5, 2008, reeling from amazement over the events of the day. Although since the 1980s[1] print circulation had rapidly declined in the newspaper industry, this day had been very different. Thanks to the post-election front page headline declaring, "OBAMA – Racial Barrier Falls in Decisive Victory," *The New York Times* had flown off shelves at a rate not seen since November 11, 1918, when the newspaper, then owned by Sulzberger Jr.'s grandfather, announced the end of World War I.[2] Even more significant is the fact that copies of the Obama-headlined newspaper were selling on eBay for more than $600.[3]

However, Sulzberger Jr. did not dwell on the good fortune of this particular day. The excitement in the newsroom over the paper's interest did not erase or even ease the current crisis at The New York Times Company. In September 2008 total company revenues from continuing operations decreased 8 percent compared with the same month in 2007, and advertising revenues decreased 13 percent.[4] Unlike the challenges that his forebears had faced, today's challenges could not be solved simply by investing money in the company with the hope that high-quality journalism would prove more profitable.[5] The company was fast approaching the point where it would have to manage its business primarily to conserve cash (with only $46 million in cash on the books) and avoid defaulting on its debt (approximately $1.1 billion). Furthermore, Sulzberger Jr. realized that the situation would only worsen as advertising revenue was widely projected to keep falling.[6]

According to The New York Times Company's policy on ethics in journalism, the core purpose of the company is to "enhance society by creating, collecting and distributing high-quality news, information and entertainment."[7] For 100 years the company had been able to fulfill this purpose and has set the standard for print publications in the United States as well as around the world by spending big money not only on the addition of new sections and color illustrations but also on a highly gifted editorial staff (salaries are thought to exceed $300 million a year[8]).

Sulzberger Jr. pondered on how great it would be if the company could return to the "good old days," when the newspaper was a profitable business simply due to subscriptions and advertising income.

History

Former banker George Jones and journalist/politician Henry Jarvis Raymond founded *The New York Times* on September 18, 1851.[9] From 1851 to 1860 the newspaper was published Monday through Saturday. However, demand for daily news became so great during the Civil War that *The New York Times*, along with other major dailies, began publishing Sunday issues.[10] In the 1880s the newspaper moved from supporting Republican candidates to a more politically independent position (although the newspaper supported Grover Cleveland, a Democratic presidential candidate, in 1884, a decision that temporarily damaged readership).[11]

In 1896 *The New York Times* was purchased by Adolph Ochs, publisher of *The Chattanooga Times*, thus beginning the Ochs-Sulzberger family ownership of the newspaper. In 1897 Ochs coined the newspaper's slogan "All the news that's fit to print."[12] This motto, which can still be found on the front page of each daily issue of *The New York Times*, was a shot by Ochs at competing newspapers, which were known for downplaying legitimate news in favor of eye-catching headlines that sold more newspapers.[13]

The authors would like to thank Professor Robert E. Hoskisson for his support and guidance during the development of this case. This case is not intended to illustrate either effective or ineffective handling of managerial situations. The case is solely intended for class discussion.

Entering the twentieth century there were many "firsts" which allowed *The New York Times* (now called the "*Gray Lady*" by some due to its staid appearance and style), under Ochs's guidance, to achieve international scope, circulation, and reputation. In 1904 the newspaper received its first wireless transmission from a battle at sea during the Russo-Japanese war. *The New York Times* began its first regular air delivery to Philadelphia in 1910. In 1920 the newspaper made its first trans-Atlantic delivery.[14]

In 1935, in the midst of the Great Depression, Ochs passed away, leaving his son-in-law, Arthur Hays Sulzberger, as the newspaper's publisher.[15] Sulzberger got to work right away, pushing the newspaper's editors to begin an editorial barrage on President Roosevelt's plan to pack the Supreme Court with hand-selected individuals. This editorial crusade is still remembered as one of the most intense periods in *The New York Times'* history, and cemented the newspaper's commitment to "hard-hitting, ground-breaking journalism."[16]

During the 1940s, *The New York Times* extended its reach by introducing daily crossword puzzles and a fashion section. An international edition was published for the first time in 1946, and continued until the following year when *The New York Times* collaborated with the *New York Herald Tribune* and *The Washington Post* to publish the *International Herald Tribune* in France. In 1946, the newspaper also purchased a radio station (WQXR).[17]

The 1960s are remembered for the paper's involvement in the 1964 libel case, *The New York Times v. Sullivan*. This case resulted in one of the key U.S. Supreme Court decisions supporting freedom of the press.[18] In 1967 *The New York Times* went public and founded The New York Times Company.[19]

The company experienced a period of substantial change after going public. In the 1970s it acquired magazine publications such as *Golf Digest* and *Tennis Magazine*, book publishing companies like Cambridge, various daily newspapers, and even television stations.[20] Throughout the 1980s the company continued to aggressively acquire media outlets, and in the late 1980s investors were rewarded by two stock splits and many repurchases.[21]

Early in the 1990s, The New York Times Company began to advance its digital strategy, and in 1995 the company launched its domain, nytimes.com, on the World Wide Web. The New York Times Company has tried to exploit the Internet by spending more than $500 million on acquisitions and investments in new media from 2005 to 2008. 2005 saw The New York Times Company acquisition of About.com (an online consumer information provider), and in 2007 it acquired consumeresearch.com (an online aggregator and publisher of product reviews).

The New York Times Company also owns 53 percent of BehNeem (a Web-based software package that supports the day-to-day learning activities of students and faculty, including networking, object/file sharing, and storage and blogging), 14 percent of Indeed (a vertical meta-search for help-wanted listings), and less than 10 percent in several other new media companies.

The company's revenue stream changed during the first decade of the twenty-first century as advertising revenues declined in traditional print operations. In 2007 they created a new alliance with Monster.com to promote jobs on nytimes.com as a supplement to its declining classified revenues.[22]

In 2008, The New York Times Company announced a joint venture called quadrantONE with the Tribune Company, the Gannett Company, and the Hearst Corporation as an attempt to make it simpler for advertisers to do business with any of the four media groups. The challenge being that Internet giants such as Google, Yahoo!, and Microsoft are increasingly stealing advertising dollars through simple online advertising programs such as Google AdWords.[23]

As of 2008, The New York Times Company is a leading media company. It holds sole ownership of *The New York Times* (the third largest daily newspaper in United States, with a circulation of 1.1 million on weekdays and 1.6 million on Sundays[24]), *The International Herald Tribune*, *The Boston Globe*, 16 other daily newspapers, and a radio station.[25] *The New York Times* syndicate sells columns, magazine and book excerpts, and feature packages to more than 2,000 newspapers and other media to clients in more than 50 countries. It is the largest syndicate in the world specializing in text, photos, graphics, and other noncartoon features.[26] The New York Times Company also co-owns Discovery Civilization Channel[27] and has a 17.5 percent stake in New England Sports Ventures, which owns the Boston Red Sox and 80 percent of New England Sports Network, a cable network that televises Red Sox games.[28]

The company has also strived to put the right people in top leadership positions in order to meet the challenges facing the industry, but certain aspects of leadership have created some additional challenges.

Key Strategic Leaders

Arthur Ochs Sulzberger, Jr., Chairman & Publisher

Sulzberger Jr. became a correspondent for *The New York Times* in 1978. After serving in various reporting and business positions he was promoted to assistant editor in 1987, became publisher in 1992, and succeeded his father, Arthur Ochs Sulzberger, as chairman of the board of The New York Times Company in 1997.[29]

Due to the dual stock structure using Class A and Class B stocks to limit voting power, the Ochs-Sulzberger family has been able to maintain control of The New York Times Company since it went public in 1967. Prominent stakeholders such as Harbinger and Firebrand have been trying to change the dual stock structure, but six trustees must vote in favor of the change, which will not occur as long as the Ochs-Sulzberger family controls eight of the seats.[30]

Janet L. Robinson, President & CEO

Janet Robinson joined The New York Times Company in 1983. She became president and general manager in 1996, and was elected to the company's board of directors in December 2004. At that time she was also appointed to be the company's president and CEO.[31]

Since Robinson's appointment as CEO, traditional print media and the U.S. economy have endured significant losses. In 2004 the stock price was $47, down from a high of $53.80 in 2002. The price tumbled even further to around $6.65/share in November 2008. Robinson has attempted to offset the losses of traditional print media by placing emphasis on and expanding the company's new media operations. According to Robinson, expanding the company's Internet businesses is an "absolute priority."[32] Under Robinson, the company has grown its Internet businesses, but it has not liquidated assets as quickly as desired by some investors.

James Follo, Senior Vice President and CFO

Prior to taking his post as senior vice president and CFO in January 2007, James Follo was chief of finance at both Martha Stewart Living Omnimedia and General Media International.[33] Given the financial difficulties The New York Times Company is currently facing, Follo has publicly stated that with the exception of The New York Times, The New York Times Company is willing to sell any of its assets.[34] However, Follo recognizes that in the current economy, selling assets would do little to alleviate long-term financial troubles and has been negotiating with bankers to secure loans for the company.[35]

Vivian Schiller, Senior Vice President and General Manager

Vivian Schiller has been with The New York Times Company since May 2002. She was appointed as senior vice president and general manager of nytimes.com in May 2006. In this role she has led the day-to-day operations of the The New York Times most significant Web site overseeing product technology, marketing, classifieds, strategic planning, and business development. Schiller previously served as senior vice president of television and video for The New York Times and also executive vice president and general manager for the Discovery Times. In November 2008, Shiller announced that she would be leaving the company for the post of CEO at National Public Radio. This is a critical loss at a time when strategic Internet leadership is needed more than ever.

Dissident Investors and Harbinger Capital Partners

After enduring a loss of $29 per share, Morgan Stanley sold its 7 percent stake in The New York Times Company. However, many dissident investors are still on board and plan to make changes to return The New York Times to its once proud and profitable state. One of these investors, Harbinger Capital Partners, has a 19 percent stake in the company.[36] Philip Falcone, lead at Harbinger Capital Partners, "has a long record of buying into troubled firms and then relentlessly pushing for change despite the odds."[37] The primary complaints of investors are the dual stock system that limits their access to controlling votes, slower than expected online expansion, and unprofitable holdings such as The Boston Globe. They also do not like the Company's stake in the Boston Red Sox because, though profitable, it is an unrelated business.

The Harbinger Group aims to transform the company in five years from one that does about 10 percent of its business in digital to one that does most of its business in digital. However, friction within the board of directors impedes the company's ability to make quick decisions, and since the Ochs-Sulzberger family owns the majority of shares, it is believed that "the company is going to do what the family wants it to do."[38]

The board is influenced not only by the Ochs-Sulzberger family, but also by the actions that competitors take.

Key Competitors

The New York Times Company's competitors are primarily in the publishing industry. The company also competes in the "information collection and delivery" and "Internet content provider" sectors. Top competitors include Gannett Co., Inc.; News Corporation; and The Washington Post Company.[39]

Gannett Co., Inc.[40]

Founded by Frank Gannett in 1906 and made public in 1967, Gannett is not only the largest newspaper publisher in the United States (as measured by total daily circulation), but a leading international news and information company. Approximately 8,900 shareholders in the United States and several foreign countries hold the company's more than 230 million outstanding shares of common stock. Total revenues in 2007 were $7.4 billion. (See Exhibit 1 for Gannett Financials 2005–2007.)

Exhibit 1 Gannett Financials 2005–2007

Gannett Income Statement	2007	2006	2005
Revenue ($ mil.)	7,439.5	8,033.4	7,598.9
Gross Profit ($ mil.)	3,275.4	3,595.1	3,537.7
Operating Income ($ mil.)	1,650.9	1,998.2	2,048.1
Total Net Income ($ mil.)	1,055.6	1,160.8	1,244.7
Diluted EPS (Net Income)	4.52	4.90	5.05

Gannett Quarterly Statements	Quarter Ending Jun 08	Quarter Ending Mar 08	Quarter Ending Dec 07
Revenue ($ mil.)	1,718.0	1,676.9	1,856.5
Gross Profit ($ mil.)	729.5	690.4	828.8
Operating Income ($ mil.)	(2,133.6)	327.6	372.7
Total Net Income ($ mil.)	(2,290.8)	191.8	245.3
Diluted EPS (Net Income)	(10.01)	0.84	1.06

Gannett Financial Ratios	Company	Industry Median	MarketMedian[1]
Price/Sales Ratio	0.32	0.45	1.04
Price/Earnings Ratio	—	9.00	10.88
Price/Book Ratio	0.34	0.82	0.98
Price/Cash Flow Ratio	1.84	4.14	6.46

[1] Public companies trading on the New York Stock Exchange, the American Stock Exchange, and the NASDAQ National Market.

Source: 2008, Gannett, *Hoover's*, November 13.

In the United States, Gannett publishes 85 daily newspapers with a total circulation of 6.9 million, as well as nearly 900 nondaily publications. Major U.S. newspapers owned by Gannett include *USA Today* (the largest daily newspaper with a circulation of more than 2.2 million), *The Arizona Republic,* and the *Detroit Free Press.* In addition, Gannett owns 23 television stations in the United States that reach more than 20 million households, publishes periodicals and inserts, and operates approximately 150 news and Internet advertising sites customized to the markets they serve. In January 2008, Gannett's total U.S. Internet audience was 25.8 million unique visitors, reaching about 15.9 percent of the Internet audience.

Gannett's newspaper publishing operations in the United Kingdom, through its subsidiary Newsquest, include 17 daily newspapers and approximately 300 weekly newspapers, magazines, and trade publications, as well as classified business Internet sites. In addition to its publishing and broadcasting businesses, in line with its mission "to successfully transform Gannett to the new environment,"[41] Gannett has also advanced in its digital strategy through business acquisitions including PointRoll (a provider of media marketing services to online advertisers) and Ripple6, Inc. (a social media services provider), partnerships with companies such as CareerBuilder (for employment advertising), ShopLocal (an online marketing solutions provider), and ShermansTravel (an online travel service).

Although Gannett has been aggressively cutting costs for some time and growing revenue from Internet sources, its newspaper advertising revenue decreased 14 percent in the first nine months of 2008 because of the movement of readers to the Internet as well as the weakening U.S. economy. In October 2008 Gannett reported that third-quarter profit fell 32 percent from the same quarter in 2007. In addition, the company announced that revenue and operating profit would likely experience double-digit percentage declines in 2009.[42] In response, Gannett planned to lay off 10 percent of its daily newspaper employees (up to 3,000 workers) by December 2008. These layoffs follow the elimination of more than 1,000 jobs since August 2008 in the company's most troubled division: U.S. publishing. However, Gannett is quick to point out that the layoffs amount to only 3 percent of the division's employees, and other publishers have made

much more drastic eliminations (for example, since June 2008, the *Miami Herald* has carried out two rounds of 10 percent layoffs).[43] To further emphasize the company's dedication to cut costs, Gannett's chairman, president, and CEO Craig Dubow recently announced that he is taking a voluntary salary cut of $200,000 from now through 2009 as well as freezing the 2009 salaries of all company and divisional officers.[44]

News Corporation[45]

Created in 1980 by Rupert Murdoch, News Corporation is the world's third largest media conglomerate with total revenues of $33 billion in 2008. (See Exhibit 2 for News Corporation Financials 2006–2008.) The company is publicly traded and listed on the New York Stock

Exhibit 2 News Corporation Financials 2006–2008

News Corp. Income Statement	2008	2007	2006
Revenue ($ mil.)	32,996.0	28,655.0	25,327.0
Gross Profit ($ mil.)	12,465.0	10,010.0	8,734.0
Operating Income ($ mil.)	5,381.0	4,452.0	3,868.0
Total Net Income ($ mil.)	5,387.0	3,426.0	2,314.0
Diluted EPS (Net Income)	1.80	1.14	0.76

News Corp. Quarterly Statement	Quarter Ending Jun 08	Quarter Ending Mar 08	Quarter Ending Dec 07
Revenue ($ mil.)	8,589.0	8,750.0	8,590.0
Gross Profit ($ mil.)	3,361.0	3,298.0	(1,261.0)
Operating Income ($ mil.)	1,478.0	1,438.0	1,418.0
Total Net Income ($ mil.)	1,129.0	2,694.0	832.0
Diluted EPS (Net Income)	0.42	0.88	0.27

News Corp. Financial Ratios	Company	Industry Median	Market Median[1]
Price/Sales Ratio	0.46	0.48	1.06
Price/Earnings Ratio	4.60	10.41	11.20
Price/Book Ratio	0.53	1.01	1.03
Price/Cash Flow Ratio	3.84	4.79	6.54

[1] Public companies trading on the New York Stock Exchange, the American Stock Exchange, and the NASDAQ National Market.

Source: 2008, NewsCorp, *Hoover's*, November 13.

Exchange, the Australian Securities Exchange, and the London Stock Exchange. Nearly 40 percent of the company is controlled by Murdoch and his family.

News Corporation's newspaper and information services include News International (which publishes four national newspapers in the United Kingdom), News Limited (which publishes more than 110 national, capital city, and suburban newspapers in Australia), the *New York Post* (the fifth largest daily in the United States), and the *Wall Street Journal* (an English-language daily with a worldwide circulation of more than 2 million). Its publishing businesses include HarperCollins (a global English-language book publisher) and Dow Jones & Co. (a provider of global business news and information services). Additionally, News Corporation has operations in film, television, cable network, and direct broadcast satellite television segments. It owns Fox Filmed Entertainment (a global film and television production and distribution operation), Fox Broadcasting Company (the largest broadcasting network in the United States with more than 200 affiliate stations), the more than 30 television stations in the Fox Television Stations group, 23 percent of Premiere AG (a German pay-television company), 35 percent of British Sky Broadcasting (the U.K.'s largest digital pay-television platform), and nearly 100 percent of SKY Italia (Italy's most popular pay-television company).

New media properties held by News Corporation include Fox Interactive Media (an interactive services company including MySpace, a lifestyle and social-networking site which attracts 230,000 new users per day), NDS Group (a supplier of open end-to-end digital pay-television solutions), and News Outdoor (the largest outdoor advertising company in Eastern Europe). In November 2008, News Corporation announced that despite strong increases in first-quarter cable network operating income (31 percent) as well as newspaper and information services income revenue (37 percent, driven by the company's December 2007 acquisition of Dow Jones & Company), first-quarter profit fell 30 percent from the same quarter the previous year due to declining television and newspaper advertising revenue, a weaker performance by Fox Filmed Entertainment, and investment losses in Premiere AG. Additionally, the company announced that revenue and operating profit would probably see double-digit percentage declines in 2009.[46]

Although Murdoch has not provided much detail on cost-cutting techniques that will be employed, he has said that he is considering merging the back-office operations of the *Wall Street Journal* and the *New York Post* as well as closing 10 of the 17 U.S. printing plants that produce the *Wall Street Journal*.[47] Additionally, Murdoch has said that more emphasis needs to be placed on the international expansion of Dow Jones & Company, as well as subscription-based businesses that have the benefits of twin revenues from subscribers and advertisers. "We will be looking to start new channels where there are opportunities, and we certainly see that on a big scale internationally."[48]

The Washington Post Company[49]

With a history dating back to 1877, The Washington Post Company is an education and media company publicly traded on the New York Stock Exchange since 1971. Apart from chairman Donald Graham and his family, who have voting control over the company, Warren Buffett and his Berkshire Hathaway corporation is also a substantial shareholder with 18 percent of the publicly traded shares. Total revenue in 2007 was $4 billion. (See Exhibit 3 for Washington Post Financials 2005–2007.)

Although The Washington Post Company is best known as the publisher of *The Washington Post*, the company also owns other media operations including *Newsweek*, six television stations, and the online publishing operations of Newsweek Interactive (WPNI) (a subsidiary whose products include washingtonpost.com, Newsweek.com, Slate, BudgetTravel.com, and Sprig.com). It owns nonmedia operations including Kaplan, Inc. (an international provider of educational and career services for individuals, schools, and businesses) and CableOne (a cable television and Internet service with approximately 700,000 subscribers in 20 U.S. markets).

In October 2008, The Washington Post Company reported an 86 percent decline in third-quarter profit compared with the same quarter in 2007. However, the company notes that if the $59.7 million goodwill impairment charge at some of its newspapers and the $12.5 million accelerated depreciation charge of *The Washington Post's* printing presses were to be excluded, its publishing division would be cash flow–positive with $3.8 million in profit for the quarter.[50]

At *The Washington Post*, advertising revenue fell 14 percent during the third quarter of 2008.[51] However, under Graham's leadership as well as that of his close advisors (namely Warren Buffet, who has publicly stated "The present model—meaning print—isn't going to work,"[52]) the company has been preparing for the industry's present crisis for some time. In addition to investing millions into its digital business (WPNI) since the mid-1990s, The Washington Post Company has labored to rebrand itself as a company associated with innovation in digital media and technology.

In March 2008 it announced that it would sponsor LaunchBox08, a global challenge for digital startups to submit innovative ideas in order to receive funding and

Exhibit 3 *Washington Post* Financials 2005–2007

Washington Post Income Statement	2007	2006	2005
Revenue ($ mil.)	4,180.4	3,904.9	3,553.9
Gross Profit ($ mil.)	2,297.4	1,862.5	1,644.3
Operating Income ($ mil.)	477.0	459.8	514.9
Total Net Income ($ mil.)	288.6	324.5	314.3
Diluted EPS (Net Income)	30.19	33.68	32.59

Washington Post Quarterly Statements	Quarter Ending Jun 08	Quarter Ending Mar 08	Quarter Ending Dec 07
Revenue ($ mil.)	1,106.2	1,063.1	1,125.5
Gross Profit ($ mil.)	598.2	572.0	596.9
Operating Income ($ mil.)	4.8	66.9	149.3
Total Net Income ($ mil.)	(2.7)	39.3	82.9
Diluted EPS (Net Income)	(0.31)	4.08	8.74

Washington Post Financial Ratios	Company	Industry Median	Market Median[1]
Price/Sales Ratio	1.17	1.44	1.56
Price/Earnings Ratio	31.16	19.02	15.82
Price/Book Ratio	1.51	2.99	1.52
Price/Cash Flow Ratio	8.84	13.62	9.88

[1] Public companies trading on the New York Stock Exchange, the American Stock Exchange, and the NASDAQ National Market.

Source: 2008, Washington Post Company, *Hoover's*, November 13.

participate in a business-building program with access to professional mentors and advisors.[53] Additionally, The Washington Post Company has steered away from investing in its print operations, but instead heavily investing in its nonmedia operations. Kaplan Inc. and CableOne now provide 53 percent and 16 percent, respectively, of total revenue.[54]

Nontraditional Media Competitors

While The New York Times Company has long fought its peers in the traditional print industry, the advent of the Internet created news opportunities for other companies beyond The New York Times Company and its traditional competitors. The second generation of the Internet brought with it new online mediums such as blogs, social networks, and online communities that allowed for anyone to self-publish for the world to see. With more than 112 million blogs now online, the avenues for advertisers to get their advertisements to niche audiences has risen dramatically. Bloggers add new blog entries with an astounding frequency of 1.6 million posts each day.[55] Recognizing the importance of the new online medium, *The New York Times* editor Bill Keller stated, "We must do whatever we can to strengthen our competitive position . . . [and ensure] among other things, that we are well equipped to navigate the passage to our digital future."[56]

Internet giants such as Google, Yahoo!, and Microsoft have increasingly encroached on the turf of traditional media by offering their own news sites. Sites such as Google News function without an editorial staff, instead leveraging an automated aggregation system that takes current, high-ranking stories and sorts them automatically into sections of the Google News page. "No human is involved in the altering of the front page or story promotion, beyond tweaking the aggregation algorithm.[57]"

The Google News site, which leverages more content from *The New York Times* than any other source (without paying for it), is said to be valued at more than $100 million, even though it generates no advertising revenue for Google directly.[58] Some have predicted a long drawn-out battle between Internet giants and the traditional print media.[59] The traditional print media has recognized this challenge and has suggested that perhaps partnering with Internet giants such as Google would be in their best interest. Jeff Jarvis, NYU journalist professor, and Edward Roussel, manager of digital content for *The Telegraph* said of print media's efforts to go online:

"It's hard to imagine a newspaper creating better technology than Google. And the service is proving to be brilliant at ad sales—so why not outsource those departments to Google so a paper can concentrate on its real job—journalism …. Ideally every newsroom would be able to think of Google and all its capabilities as their own.[60]"

Current Market Dynamics

Historically, The New York Times Company, like most of its primary competitors, has been deeply entrenched in the traditional print media industry where two consistent revenue streams exist: circulation unit sales and advertising related revenue. However, the Internet has truly become a disruptive technology in the information dissemination market. Internet subscriptions are replacing the daily newspaper expenditure in many households.

Unlike national newspapers such as *USA Today* and the *Wall Street Journal,* which have tended to hold their ground better, and for small-market dailies where competition from other media is not usually as intense, *The New York Times* has posted steep declines in circulation in recent years.[61] In October 2008 it was reported that its weekday circulation fell 3.6 percent from the previous year, and its Sunday circulation dropped 4.1 percent.[62] *The New York Times* has countered decreases in circulation with increases in subscription prices of more than 25 percent in recent years. As a result, it has not seen a decrease in circulation revenue. In fact, October 2008

circulation revenue increased 3.9 percent from the same period in 2007.[63]

As previously indicated, since the early 1990s the company has taken steps to profitably advance its digital strategy. In the past three years alone The New York Times Company has spent more than $500 million on acquisitions and investments in new media and the company's Internet operations. According to Nielsen Online, http://nytimes.com had 20 million unique visitors in September 2008, an increase of about 37 percent over the same period the previous year, and online advertising revenues climbed by approximately $10 million to $79 million. The popularity of the site stems not only from its content and format (which has benefited from the expertise of *The New York Times's* editorial staff), but also the reputation of *The New York Times* as a newspaper committed to "hard-hitting, ground-breaking journalism," something that cannot be easily replicated by competitors.

The New York Times Company also has the benefit of long-standing relationships with advertisers who may be wary of continuing a relationship with the company's traditional print media operations, but are eager to take advantage of the wide audience reached by the company's new media.

Despite the relationships *The New York Times* Company has maintained with advertisers and the reputation it has for employing great journalists, the financials indicate that the company has been more affected by its challenges than its assets.

Financials

Advertising revenues are typically elastic by nature. As the economy surges, companies advertising budgets expand. Unfortunately, economic challenges mean ad revenues generally decrease. Between October 2007 and October 2008, advertising revenues for The New York Times Company declined by 16.2 percent, with classified advertising revenue down 34.7 percent as offers for jobs, real estate, and automobiles each plunged at least 34 percent.[64]

The two major operating groups, News Media Group and the About Group, have seen divergent revenue paths during the past several years, with the About Group growing and becoming increasingly profitable while the News Media Group contracts and records net losses (see Exhibit 4 for New York Times Company Revenue Comparison by Segment).[65]

Advertising revenue for the About Group increased by 13.8 percent (see Exhibit 5) during the past year and has maintained double digit revenue growth since inception. However, this division of the company is

Exhibit 4 New York Times Company Revenue Comparison by Segment

Time Period	News Media Group Ad Revenue ($000s)	% Change	About Group Ad Revenue ($000s)	% Change	Circulation Revenue ($000s)	% Change
Q1–Q3 2008	1,231,411	–12.7	79,502	+16.5	676,486	+1.8
Q1–Q3 2007	1,410,208	–4.4	68,217	+28.2	664,539	+1.5
Q1–Q3 2006	1,474,408	–1.5	53,196	+102.4	654,994	+.01
Q1–Q3 2005	1,496,608		26,278		655,971	

Source: 2008, New York Times Company, http://morningstar.com, November 22.

Exhibit 5 New York Times Company Advertising Revenue Comparison 2007 v. 2008

The New York Times Company 2008 Q3 Advertising Revenues[a] ($ 000s)						
	September			Year to Date		
	2008	2007	% Change	2008	2007	% Change
News Media Group						
New York Times Media Group	$103,048	$116,753	–11.7	$781,607	$867,774	–9.9
New England Media Group	27,167	32,577	–16.6	240,591	289,414	–16.9
Regional Media Group	19,204	24,657	–22.1	209,212	253,020	–17.3
Total News Media Group	149,419	173,986	–14.1	1,231,410	1,410,208	–12.7
About Group[b]	8,739	7,878	+10.9	79,502	68,216	+16.5
Total Ad Revenues From Continuing Operations	$158,158	$181,864	–13.0	$1,310,912	$1,478,425	–11.3
Discontinued Operations: Broadcast Media Group[c]	0	0	N/A	0	45,745	N/A

(a) Numbers may not add due to rounding.
(b) Includes the Web sites of About.com, ConsumerSearch.com, UCompareHealthCare.com, and Calorie-Count.com.
(c) On May 7, 2007, the Company sold the Broadcast Media Group, consisting of nine network-affiliated television stations, their related Web sites and the digital operating center for approximately $575 million.

Source: 2008, New York Times Company, http:// www.nytco.com, November 22.

too small to make up for the decline in the traditional media group. As a result, total revenues for the company declined 8.9 percent in the third quarter of 2008, with circulation revenues up 1 percent because of the newspaper price increase (see Exhibits 6 and 7). Net income has decreased by 82.1 percent when compared to the same quarter in 2007, and net profit has decreased from $505 million in 1998 to $185 million in 2007 (Exhibit 8).

Total assets showed no growth at $3.5 billion in 2007, while total liabilities increased from $1.9 billion in 1998 to $2.4 billion in 2007 (see Exhibit 9). Debt-to-equity ratio increased from 0.39 in 1998 to 0.69 in 2007 (see Exhibit 10). At the end of third quarter in 2008, the company had $46 million in cash, $1.1 billion in debt, and a debt-to-equity ratio of 0.85. Of particular concern is the fact that $400 million of that debt is due in 2009.[66] Standard & Poor's threatened to downgrade the company's rating to junk status, causing insult to injury and raising the amount of interest expense The New York Times Company will be forced to pay on its debt.[67]

The company's quick ratio of 0.43 clearly shows the inability of the company to cover short-term cash needs. Further, the company's liquidity has decreased from the same period 2007, ironic given the fact that presidential election years typically create an advertising and circulation sales gain.

Exhibit 6 New York Times Company Revenue Comparison 2007 v. 2008

The New York Times Company 2008 Q3 Total Company Revenues[a] ($ 000s)			
	Third Quarter		
	2008	**2007**	**% Change**
Advertising Revenues			
News Media			
National	$188,666	$212,910	−11.4
Retail	86,507	97,191	−11.0
Classified	82,778	117,157	−29.3
Other Ad Revenue	13,658	14,423	−5.3
Total News Media Group	371,608	441,681	−15.9
About Group[b]	26,588	23,362	13.8
Total Ad Revenues from Continuing Operations	398,196	465,043	−4.4
Circulation Revenues	225,689	223,420	+1.0
Other Revenues[c]	63,157	65,896	−4.2
Total Company Revenues from Continuing Operations	$687,042	$754,359	−8.9
Discontinued Operations: Broadcast Media Group[d]	0	0	N/A

(a) Numbers may not add due to rounding.

(b) Includes the Web sites of About.com, ConsumerSearch.com, UCompareHealthCare.com, and Calorie-Count.com.

(c) Primarily includes revenues from wholesale delivery operations, news services/syndication, commercial printing, digital archives, direct mail advertising services, and rental income.

(d) On May 7, 2007, the Company sold the Broadcast Media Group, consisting of nine network-affiliated television stations, their related Web sites, and the digital operating center for approximately $575 million.

Source: 2008, New York Times Company, http://www.nytco.com, November 22.

Exhibit 7 New York Times Company Statement of Cash Flow 1998–2007

Cash Flow						As originally reported					
	1998	1999	2000	2001	2002	2003	2004	2005	2006	2007	TTM
Cash Flows from Operating Activities $Mil											
Net Income	278.9	310.2	397.5	444.7	299.8	302.7	292.6	259.8	(543.4)	208.7	(32.5)
Depr & Amort	135.2	197.5	228.0	194.0	153.4	47.8	146.8	143.8	169.9	189.6	155.1
Deferred Taxes	(12.6)	(44.6)	(28.2)	(52.9)	88.1	53.5	3.6	(29.6)	(139.9)	(11.6)	—
Other	49.9	138.1	(7.5)	(114.5)	(267.9)	(37.7)	1.1	(79.6)	935.8	(276.0)	103.2
Cash from Operations	451.5	601.1	589.9	471.2	273.3	466.3	444.0	294.3	422.3	110.7	225.8
Cash Flows from Investing Activities $Mil											
Cap Ex	(81.6)	(73.4)	(85.3)	(90.4)	(160.7)	(120.9)	(153.8)	(221.3)	(332.3)	(380.3)	(213.2)
Purchase of Business	0.0	—	(296.3)	(2.6)	(176.9)	(65.1)	0.0	(437.5)	(35.8)	(34.1)	(5.7)
Other	25.4	(9.5)	186.6	430.4	(23.3)	(60.0)	(38.4)	163.4	79.4	562.6	(2.7)
Cash from Investing	(56.2)	(82.9)	(195.0)	337.4	(360.9)	(245.9)	(192.2)	(495.5)	(288.7)	148.3	(221.6)
Cash Flows from Financing Activities $Mil											
Net Issuance of Stock	(441.9)	(395.8)	(543.1)	(591.4)	(62.7)	(175.3)	(252.1)	(43.0)	(52.3)	(4.0)	(2.7)
Net Issuance of Debt	222.5	103.9	331.3	—	195.1	49.9	107.4	658.6	61.1	0.0	—
Dividends	(69.6)	(72.0)	(75.4)	(77.0)	(80.3)	(85.5)	(90.1)	(94.5)	(100.1)	(125.1)	(133.1)
Other	(177.1)	(126.5)	(102.5)	(157.3)	20.5	(7.7)	(14.4)	(316.7)	(14.9)	(151.5)	122.8

(Continued)

Exhibit 7 New York Times Company Statement of Cash Flow 1998–2007 (Continued)

Cash from Financing	(466.1)	(490.4)	(389.7)	(825.7)	72.6	(218.7)	(249.2)	204.4	(106.2)	(280.5)	(13.0)
Currency Adj	—	—	—	—	—	—	—	—	—	—	—
Change in Cash	(70.8)	27.9	5.2	(17.1)	(15.0)	1.7	2.7	3.2	27.5	(21.6)	(8.7)
Free Cash Flow $Mil											
Cash from Operations	451.5	601.1	589.9	471.2	273.3	466.3	444.0	294.3	422.3	110.7	225.8
Cap Ex	(81.6)	(73.4)	(85.3)	(90.4)	(160.7)	(120.9)	(153.8)	(221.3)	(332.3)	(380.3)	(213.2)
Free Cash Flow	369.9	527.7	504.6	380.9	112.6	345.4	290.2	73.0	90.0	(269.6)	12.6

S&P Index Data: S&P 500 Copyright © 2008

Source: 2008, New York Times Company, http://morningstar.com, November 22.

Exhibit 8 New York Times Company Income Statement 1998–2007

Income Statement

As originally reported

	1998	1999	2000	2001	2002	2003	2004	2005	2006	2007	TTM
Revenue	2,936.7	3,130.6	3,489.5	3,016.0	3,079.0	3,227.2	3,303.6	3,372.8	3,289.9	3,195.1	3,042.6
COGS	1,461.6	1,378.8	1,458.1	1,362.9	1,352.6	1,428.8	1,475.6	1,540.4	1,529.5	1,341.1	1,325.4
Gross Profit	1,475.1	1,751.8	2,031.4	1,653.1	1,726.4	1,798.4	1,828.1	1,832.4	1,760.4	1,854.0	1,717.2
Operating Expenses $Mil											
SG&A	959.8	1,180.5	1,395.5	1,278.7	1,181.5	1,258.9	1,318.1	1,474.3	1,466.6	1,397.4	1,374.8
R&D	—	—	—	—	—	—	—	—	—	—	—
Other	0.0	NaN	0.0	0.0	NaN	0.0	(NaN)	(122.9)	814.4	229.1	194.7
Operating Income	515.2	571.3	635.9	374.4	544.9	539.6	510.0	481.1	(520.6)	227.4	147.7
Other Income and Expense $Mil											
Net Int Inc & Other	(9.70)	(32.80)	37.20	(34.60)	(53.50)	(31.50)	(33.60)	53.30	50.70	(39.80)	7.30
Earnings Before Taxes	505.50	538.50	673.10	339.90	491.40	499.90	476.70	446.10	(551.90)	185.00	(44.30)

(Continued)

Exhibit 8 New York Times Company Income Statement 1998–2007 (Continued)

Income Taxes	218.90	228.30	275.60	137.60	191.60	197.80	183.50	180.20	16.60	76.10	(3.40)
Earnings After Taxes	286.60	310.20	397.50	202.20	299.80	302.10	293.20	265.90	(568.50)	108.80	(40.80)
Acctg Changes	—	0.00	—	—	—	—	—	(5.90)	0.00	0.00	—
Disc Operations	—	—	—	242.50	0.00	0.00	—	—	24.70	99.80	8.70
Ext Items	(7.70)	0.00	0.00	—	—	—	—	—	—	—	—
Net Income	278.90	310.20	397.50	444.70	299.80	302.70	292.60	259.80	(543.40)	208.70	(32.50)
Diluted EPS, Cont Ops$	1.49	1.73	2.32	1.26	1.94	1.98	1.96	1.82	(3.93)	0.76	(0.29)
Diluted EPS$	1.45	1.73	2.32	2.78	1.94	1.98	1.96	1.78	(3.76)	1.45	(0.23)
Shares	192.00	179.00	171.00	160.00	154.00	152.00	149.00	145.00	144.00	144.00	143.00

S&P Index Data: S&P 500 Copyright © 2008

Exhibit 9 New York Times Company Balance Sheet 1998–2007

Balance Sheet									As originally reported		
Assets $Mil											
	1998	1999	2000	2001	2002	2003	2004	2005	2006	2007	Latest Qtr
Cash and Equiv	36.0	63.9	69.0	52.0	37.0	39.5	42.4	44.9	72.4	51.5	45.9
Short-Term Investments	—	—	—	—	—	—	—	—	—	—	—
Accts Rec	331.9	366.8	341.9	318.5	358.3	387.7	389.3	435.3	402.6	437.9	364.6
Inventory	32.3	28.7	35.1	31.6	23.3	29.0	32.7	32.1	36.7	26.9	27.5
Other Current Assets	121.8	155.7	164.8	157.8	144.5	147.2	149.6	145.5	673.3	148.1	139.3
Total Current Assets	522.0	614.9	610.8	559.9	563.1	603.3	613.9	657.8	1,185.0	664.5	577.3
Net PP&E	1,326.2	1,218.4	1,207.2	1,166.9	1,197.4	1,187.3	1,367.4	1,468.4	1,375.4	1,468.0	1,354.8
Intangibles	1,327.6	1,305.0	1,480.1	1,410.2	1,393.1	1,474.4	1,464.6	1,851.0	784.4	811.9	737.2
Other Long-Term Assets	289.4	357.5	308.7	301.7	480.3	539.8	504.0	555.9	511.2	528.7	552.4
Total Assets	**3,465.1**	**3,495.8**	**3,606.7**	**3,438.7**	**3,633.8**	**3,804.7**	**3,949.9**	**4,533.0**	**3,855.9**	**3,473.1**	**3,221.7**
Liabilities and Stockholders' Equity $Mil											
Accts Payable	163.8	191.7	178.3	171.0	177.7	176.6	190.1	201.1	242.5	202.9	160.7
Short-Term Debt	124.1	0.0	291.3	158.3	178.1	228.0	335.4	496.5	546.7	111.7	397.9
Taxes Payable	—	—	—	225.2	8.4	10.6	—	—	—	—	—
Accrued Liabilities	257.0	298.8	318.1	242.2	253.7	267.3	264.7	285.5	321.3	335.4	258.7
Other Short-Term Liabilities	82.9	183.0	89.7	64.2	117.9	77.9	329.6	83.5	187.5	325.7	131.8

Exhibit 9 New York Times Company Balance Sheet 1998–2007 (*Continued*)

Total Current Liabilities	627.8	673.5	877.4	860.9	735.7	760.4	1,119.8	1,066.5	1,298.0	975.7	949.1
Long-Term Debt	513.7	512.6	553.4	517.1	648.6	646.9	393.6	822.0	720.8	672.0	672.5
Other Long-Term Liabilities	792.1	861.0	894.7	911.1	980.2	1,005.2	1,036.0	1,128.3	1,017.3	847.1	803.0
Total Liabilities	1,933.6	2,047.1	2,325.5	2,289.0	2,364.5	2,412.5	2,549.3	3,016.8	3,036.1	2,494.9	2,424.6
Total Equity	1,531.5	1,448.7	1,281.2	1,149.7	1,269.3	1,392.2	1,400.5	1,516.3	819.8	978.2	797.1
Total Liabilities & Equity	3,465.1	3,495.8	3,606.7	3,438.7	3,633.9	3,804.7	3,949.9	4,533.0	3,855.9	3,473.1	3,221.7

S&P Index Data: S&P 500 Copyright © 2008

Source: 2008, New York Times Company, http://morningstar.com, November 22.

In comparison to industry competitors, The New York Times Company is underperforming in sales growth and net profit margin while capital spending is higher. Despite an effort to improve its financial situation, capital spending reached $213 million in 2008, up from $82 million in 1998 (see Exhibit 7).

Not unexpected with these financial results, the company's stock price has underperformed. In an effort to curb the steady stock devaluation, The New York Times Company announced in March 2007 that it would increase its dividend by 31 percent hoping that such a drastic increase in an already generous dividend

would help stabilize, if not increase, the stock price.[68] It did not work. Since then the stock dropped from $24/share to just over $5/share in November 2008, when the company announced that it would need to cut its dividend by 74 percent.[69] Financial analysts have favorably viewed this dividend reduction, upgrading the stock and commenting that the move alone should recoup $100 million in annual revenue.[70]

The New York Times Company's market cap is just under $1 billion, an astonishingly low figure given that far smaller media companies have sold for far more. Earlier this year for example, CBS acquired the consumer

Exhibit 10 New York Times Company Liquidity Ratios 1998–2007

Liquidity/Financial Health											
	1998	1999	2000	2001	2002	2003	2004	2005	2006	2007	Latest Qtr
Current Ratio	0.83	0.91	0.70	0.65	0.77	0.79	0.55	0.62	0.91	0.68	0.61
Quick Ratio	0.59	0.64	0.47	0.43	0.54	0.56	0.39	0.45	0.37	0.50	0.43
Financial Leverage	2.26	2.41	2.82	2.99	2.86	2.73	2.82	2.99	4.70	3.55	4.04
Debt/Equity	0.39	0.41	0.50	0.52	0.57	0.52	0.34	0.59	0.97	0.69	0.85

Source: 2008, New York Times Company, http://morningstar.com, November 22.

technology reviews company CNET Networks for $1.8 billion,[71] nearly twice The New York Times Company's market cap.

The company's financial condition makes it difficult for it to support growth at competitive rates, let alone to simply continue operations.

Strategic Challenges and the Future

The New York Times Company lacks any clear differentiators when compared to its market competitors. Moreover, its primary competitors are in stronger financial positions as the economy is in a period of turbulence and certain change is coming to the traditional print industry. In addition, the company lacks a defined strategic intent; clearly defined goals with respect to where

and how it intends to compete in the market. The New York Times Company will see significant headwinds as it enters various digital market segments. It will face a multitude of new (nontraditional) competitors, some with unique strategies and better capitalization to enter these markets and create new product offerings, vying for the same advertising dollars.

As Sulzberger Jr. looks beyond the momentary good fortunes of The New York Times owing to the Obama-headlined newspaper of November 5, 2008, he must address the serious challenges facing The New York Times Company. How can he influence the board of directors to act in unison? What long-term strategy should they implement? How can the company differentiate itself from competitors? How can it leverage the competencies of the new media outlets it has acquired to help improve its financial situation?

NOTES

1. L. Han, 2008, Newspaper circulation falls Again, Forbes, April 28.
2. 2008, Sulzberger Family, Wikipedia, November 20.
3. 2008, Guardian, November 6.
4. 2008, New York Times Company reports September revenue, Yahoo Finance, October 23.
5. 2005, The future of the New York Times, BusinessWeek, January 17.
6. H. Blodget, 2008, Cash crunch at the New York Times, Silicon Alley Insider, November 8.
7. 2008, New York Times Company: Press www.nytco.com, November 25.
8. A. Bianco, J. Rossant, & L. Gard, 2005, The future of the New York Times, BusinessWeek, January 17.
9. 2008, New York Times Company, Hoovers, November 18.
10. 2008, New York Times Company, Wikipedia, November 14.
11. Ibid.
12. New York Times Company, Hoovers.
13. New York Times Company, Wikipedia.
14. 2008, New York Times Company: Company Milestones 1981–1910, www.nytco.com, November 14.
15. 2008, New York Times Company: Company Milestones 1911–1940, www.nytco.com, November 14.
16. 2008, New York Times Company: Company Milestones 1941–1970, www.nytco.com, November 14.
17. 2008, New York Times Company: Company Milestones 1971–1980, www.nytco.com, November 14.
18. 2008, Times v. Sullivan, Cornell University, November 14.
19. New York Times Company: Company Milestones 1971–1980.
20. Ibid.
21. New York Times Company: Company Milestones 1981–1990.
22. R. Gavin, 2007, New York Times Co. partners with Monster, The Boston Globe, February 14.
23. L. Story, 2008, 4 news companies ally to sell ads on the Internet, New York Times, February 15.
24. New York Times, Wikipedia.
25. 2008, New York Times Company, www.nytco.com, November 20.
26. 2008, New York Times Company, www.answers.com November 25.
27. 2002, New York Times Company and Discovery Communications, Inc. announce joint venture in Discovery Civilization Channel, Business Wire, April 5.
28. L. Haul, 2008, New York Times CEO: Red Sox a good investment, Forbes, March 11.
29. 2008, Arthur Ochs Sulzberger, Jr., Wikipedia, November 15.
30. J. Yarow & J. Fine, 2008, How can the New York Times be worth so little?, BusinessWeek, July 25.
31. 2008, Janet L. Robinson, Wikipedia, November 15.
32. 2008, NY Times CEO: Focused on online growth, Forbes, March 11.
33. 2008, New York Times Company, www.nytco.com, November 20.
34. NY Times CEO: Focused on online growth.
35. C. Douglas, 2008, Globe shows red ink as Times faces cash crunch, Boston Business Journal, November 13.
36. R. Perez-Pena, 2008, Two funds raise their stake in Times Company to 19%, New York Times, February 26.
37. E. Hessel, 2008, Times Tussle, Forbes, February 15.
38. 2008, Dissident investors increase Times Co. stake, www.boston.com, February 21.
39. 2008, New York Times Company, Hoovers, November 13.
40. 2008, Gannett, www.gannett.com, November 14.
41. Ibid.
42. R. MacMillian, 2008, Gannett profit falls short on weak advertising, News Daily, October 24.
43. 2008, Gannett laying off 10% of newspaper staff; Dicky warns in memo: 'fiscal crisis is deepening,' http://Gannettblogspot.com, October 28.
44. 2008, Gannett Chairman Dubow takes $200,000 pay cut, Editor and Publisher, November 3.
45. 2008, NewsCorp, www.newscorp.com, November 13.
46. D. Wilkerson, 2008, News Corp shares plunge after outlook cut, MarketWatch, November 6.
47. R. MacMillian, 2008, News Corp slashes outlook, profits dive, Reuters, November 5.
48. D. Wilkerson, News Corp shares plunge after outlook cut.
49. 2008, Washington Post Company, www.washpostco.com, November 13.
50. F. Ahrens, 2008, Washington Post Co. earnings plummet in third quarter, washingtonpost, October 31.
51. A. Jesdanon, 2008, Ad sales drop squeezes 3Q earnings for Post, Belo, www.boston.com, October 31.
52. M. Gunther, 2007, Can the Washington Post survive?, http://money.cnn.com, July 26.
53. 2008, Washington Post Co. Sponsors LaunchBox08 Startup Competition, Business Wire, March 10.

54. Lin E., 2008, S&P: Washington Post Co. outlook negative, *Shaping the Future of the Newspaper*, October 28.

55. 2008, Technorati, www.technorati.com, November 26.

56. J. Koblin, 2008, Layoffs at The New York Times; Keller Says 'We Hope Worst is Behind Us,' *New York Observer*, May 7.

57. 2008, Google News, *Wikipedia*, November 18.

58. J. Fortt, 2008, What's Google News Worth? $100 Million, *Fortune Magazine*, July 22.

59. M. LaMonica, 2004, Googlezon: The Future of Media, *CNET*, December 27.

60. J. Jarvis, 2008, The Host With the Most, *Guardian*, July 21.

61. S. Sitel, 2008, New York Times Circulation Plummets, *The Huffington Post*, April 28.

62. R. Perez-Pena, 2008, Newspaper Circulation Continues to Decline Rapidly, *The New York Times*, October 27.

63. 2008, Internet Revenue At New York Times (NYT) Needs To Be Going Up 100%, But It's Not, *247wallst*, November 20.

64. 2008, New York Times Company: Investor Relations Financials, www.nytco.com, November.22.

65. Ibid.

66. C. Douglas, 2008, Globe Shows Red Ink as Times Faces Cash Crunch, *Boston Business Journal*, November 13.

67. J. Yarrow & J. Fine, How Can The New York Times Be Worth So Little.

68. Ibid.

69. D. Wilkerson, 2008, New York Times Co. Shares Tumble to New Low, *MarketWatch*, November 21.

70. M. Peer, 2008, NY Times' High Dividend Is Old News, *Forbes*, November 24.

71. M. Arrington, 2008, CBS to Acquire CNET for $1.8 Billion, *TechCrunch*, May 15.

Tesco versus Sainsbury's: Growth Strategies and Corporate Competitiveness

Markus Kreutzer, Christoph Lechner

University of St. Gallen

Introduction

In 2008, the UK-based international food and general merchandising retailer Tesco reached a market share of about 30 percent in the United Kingdom, roughly the same as its rivals Sainsbury's and ASDA combined. In recent years, Tesco has greatly diversified, extending its business lines from food into non-food, clothing, financial services, and telecommunications. It ranks sixth in the international retail market behind Wal-Mart (United States), Carrefour (France), Home Depot (United States), Metro (Germany), and Royal Ahold (Netherlands).[1]

Tesco was not always the dominant player it is today. In 1990, it was a mid-sized food chain far behind its rival, Sainsbury's. Starting in the 1990s, it pursued a broad set of growth initiatives, steadily increasing its market share and gaining importance. In 1995, Tesco surpassed Sainsbury's to become the U.K. market leader. Today, Tesco is the clear market leader. How did that happen? Why was Tesco so successful in growing sales and profits, while Sainsbury's could not keep pace? Where did the competitive actions of these firms differ? Let us start with a close look at their origins.

Sainsbury's, Tesco, and the U.K. Retail Market in 1990

Sainsbury's was established in 1869 by John James and Mary Ann Sainsbury, making it the oldest food retailing chain in Britain. In 1922, J Sainsbury became a private company, with J Sainsbury plc acting as parent company of Sainsbury's Supermarkets Ltd, commonly known as Sainsbury's, a chain of supermarkets in the United Kingdom. In 1973, the company was floated as J Sainsbury plc in what was at the time the largest flotation on the London Stock Exchange. The family currently retains about 14 percent of its shares. The group is also engaged in property and banking, owning real estate worth about £8.6 billion. For much of the twentieth century, Sainsbury's was the market leader in the U.K. supermarket sector, but in 1995 it lost its place to Tesco; in 2003, it was pushed to third place by ASDA.

Tesco was founded by Jack Cohen in London's East End. From a modest background, Cohen began selling groceries in Well Street market, Hackney, in 1919. In the aftermath of World War I, food supplies were low, so he bought damaged goods from other stores and re-sold them at reasonable prices. The Tesco brand first appeared in 1924. The name originated after Cohen bought a shipment of tea from TE Stockwell. He made new labels using the first three letters of the supplier's name and the first two letters of his surname. The first Tesco store opened in 1929 in Burnt Oak, Edgware, Middlesex. Tesco was floated on the London Stock Exchange in 1947 as Tesco Stores (Holdings) Ltd. During the 1950s and 1960s, Tesco grew slowly, until it owned more than 800 stores. The company purchased 70 Williamsons stores (1957), 200 Harrow Stores outlets (1959), 212 Irwins stores (1960), 97 Charles Phillips stores (1964), and the Victor Value chain (1968) (sold to Bejam in 1986). In 1973, Jack Cohen resigned and was replaced as chairman by his son-in-law, Leslie Porter. Porter and managing director Ian MacLaurin abandoned the "pile it high and sell it cheap" philosophy of Cohen, which had left the company stagnating with a bad image. In 1977, Tesco launched "Operation Checkout," which included price reductions and centralized purchasing for all its stores. As a result, its market share rose by 4 percent within two months.

At the beginning of the 1990s, the U.K. retail market slowly became more competitive. Three players dominated the food market: ASDA[2] (which became Wal-Mart's largest overseas subsidiary in 1999), Sainsbury's, and Tesco. ASDA positioned itself as the price leader and held this position for some time, closely followed by Tesco. Sainsbury's targeted the upper price segment, positioning itself between mass market and high end.

In the mid-1990s, competition intensified as a price war among these players emerged, resulting in squeezed margins and cost cutting. It is not surprising that this also had an adverse impact on the service level these corporations provided.

In general, prices of standard brands and private labels at both Sainsbury's and Tesco came closer, while the two firms differed slightly in their discounting policies. Tesco emphasized its low-price private label ("Value") and continued to cut prices, while Sainsbury's emphasized price reductions on the standard private labels. The price cuts were prompted by the increased price pressure from the market entry of discounters. For example, Aldi entered the market in 1990, followed by Lidl in 1994. In 2005, these two hard discounters had acquired a market share of 2.2 percent and 1.9 percent, respectively.

Store Formats

In 1975, Sainsbury's launched the "Sainsbury's SavaCentre" hypermarket format as a joint venture with British Home Stores. This was the first attempt in the United Kingdom to launch supermarkets with a large non-food range. SavaCentre became a wholly owned Sainsbury's subsidiary in 1989. As the hypermarket format became mainstream, with rivals such as ASDA and Tesco launching ever-larger stores, Sainsbury's decided that a separate brand was no longer needed. Over the following years, these stores were converted to the regular Sainsbury's superstore format and, subsequently, Sainsbury's retreated from hypermarkets and changed its store formats. Now, Sainsbury's operates three formats: regular Sainsbury's stores, Sainsbury's local stores (convenience stores), and Sainsbury's central stores (smaller supermarkets in urban locations). For an overview of Sainsbury's U.K. store portfolio at the end of fiscal year 2005–06, see Exhibit 1.

While Sainsbury's retreated from hypermarkets, Tesco expanded Tesco Extra and strengthened its hypermarket formats.[3] Its overarching store strategy is reflected in its core marketing slogan adopted when Terry Leahy became CEO in 1997. "The Tesco Way" implies a shift from a focus on the corporation to a focus on people, both employees and customers. Tesco stores are divided into five formats, differentiated by size and range of products, and are customized to specific segments: Tesco Extra, Tesco Superstores, Tesco Metro, Tesco Express, and One Stop (see Exhibit 2). The approximately 500 One Stop stores are the smallest units. They stay open in the late evening and feature a differentiated pricing and offer system. Tesco Extra, launched in 1997, is the largest format, consisting mainly of out-of-town hypermarkets that stock Tesco's entire product range and offer free parking. Their number has increased about 20 percent annually, mainly by conversions of other formats. Tesco Superstores are the standard large grocery supermarkets, with a much smaller range of non-food goods than Extra. They are referred to as "superstores" for convenience, but not as part of the name. It is the standard Tesco format. Most are located in suburbs of cities or on the edges of large- and medium-sized towns. Tesco Metro stores are sized between normal Tesco stores and Tesco Express stores. They are mostly located in city centers and on the high streets of small towns. The first Tesco Metro was opened in Covent Garden, London, in 1992. Tesco Express stores are neighborhood convenience stores, stocking mainly food, with an emphasis on high-margin products alongside everyday essentials. They are found in busy city center districts, in small shopping precincts in residential areas, and in petrol station forecourts. As CEO Terry Leahy remarked in the company's 2000 annual report:

This obsession with our customers, their needs, and how these must be changing, means that you should not expect us to go on opening large edge-of-town superstores long after the need for new ones has passed. Expect . . . continual evolution: expect us to provide a mix of formats in different locations . . . to meet special needs of customers in each location.

Exhibit 1 Sainsbury's Store Portfolio in the United Kingdom (at the end of 2006)

Format	Number	Area (ft²)	Area (m²)	Percentage of Space
Supermarkets	455	15,916,000	1,467,000	95.1%
Convenience stores	297	821,000	76,000	4.9%
Total	752	16,737,000	1,543,000	100%

Exhibit 2 Tesco's Store Portfolio in the United Kingdom (at the end of 2007)

Format	Number	Total Area (m²)	Total Area (sq ft)	Mean Area (m²)	Mean Area (sq ft)	Percentage of Space
Tesco Extra	147	952,441	10,252,000	6,479	69,741	36.89%
Tesco	433	1,227,434	13,212,000	2,834	30,512	47.55%
Tesco Metro	162	177,073	1,906,000	1,093	11,765	6.85%
Tesco Express	735	145,114	1,562,000	197	2,125	5.62%
One Stop	506	62,988	678,000	124	1,339	2.44%
Tesco Homeplus	5	16,258	175,000	3,251	35,000	0.62%
Total	1,988	2,581,310	27,785,000	1,298	13,976	100%

Much of Tesco's sales increases occurred through increases in total square footage with the opening of new stores, including new formats such as Metro and Express. From 1994 to 1996, selling areas increased by 22 percent for Tesco and 10 percent for Sainsbury's. At the same time, Tesco managed to increase sales per square foot by 14 percent, while Sainsbury's gained only 3 percent. In addition, acquisitions and alliances complemented the organic growth strategy. Tesco, for example, purchased Adminstore in 2004, owner of 45 Cullens, Europa, and Harts convenience stores in and around London. In late 2005, it purchased the 21 remaining Safeway/BP stores after Morrison's dissolved the Safeway/BP partnership. In 1997, Tesco formed an alliance with Esso Petroleum Company Ltd (now part of ExxonMobil Corp.). The agreement included several petrol filling stations on lease from Esso, where Tesco would operate the store under the Express format. In turn, Esso would operate the forecourts and sell their fuel via the Tesco store. Ten years later, over 600 Tesco/Esso stores can be found across the United Kingdom.

Sainsbury's also expanded by acquisition. As part of the acquisition of Safeway Group by Morrison's, Morrison's was to dispose of 53 of the combined group's stores. In May 2004, Sainsbury's announced that it would acquire 14 of these stores, 13 Safeway stores, and one Morrison's outlet, all located primarily in the Midlands and the north of England. The first of these new stores opened in August 2004. In 2004, Sainsbury's also expanded its share of the convenience store market through other acquisitions. Bell's Stores, a 54-store chain based in northeast England, was acquired in February 2004. Jackson's Stores, a chain of 114 stores based in Yorkshire and the North Midlands, was purchased in August 2004. JB Beaumont, a chain of six stores in the East Midlands, was acquired in November 2004. SL Shaw Ltd, which owned six stores, was acquired in April 2005 for £6 million. On September 29, 2004, Sainsbury's established Sainsbury's Convenience Stores Ltd to manage its Sainsbury's local stores and the Bell's and Jackson's chains. The latter two are to be rebranded as Sainsbury's local stores by 2009.

Service Offerings and Distribution Systems

"An inclusive offer" is how Tesco describes its aspiration to appeal to upper-, medium-, and low-income customers in the same stores. According to Citigroup retail analyst David McCarthy, "They've pulled off a trick that I'm not aware of any other retailer achieving. That is, to appeal to all segments of the market." One plank of this program has been Tesco's use of its private label products, including the upmarket "Finest" and low price "Value." Other examples include organic, kids, British specialty food, and "free from" brands. As Edward Garner, the communications director of the TNS Superpanel, remarks: "Tesco's winning formula is largely due to its ability to be all things to all people. According to TNS, over 60 percent of British households shop in Tesco every four weeks. That's 20 percent more than its nearest rival. The store appeals to wide-reaching demographics across the country and has built up a heritage of reliability and trustworthiness, which keeps shoppers returning to its stores. These factors have enabled Tesco to gain close to a third of the British grocery market."

Sainsbury's has also invested in private labels. A large Sainsbury's store typically stocks around 50,000 lines, of which about half are private labels. These lines include, for example, "Basics" (an economy range similar to

Tesco's "Values"), "Taste the Difference" (a premium range similar to Tesco's "Finest"), "Different by Design" (a smaller range of premium non-food lines), "Kids," "Be Good to Yourself" (products with reduced calorific and/or fat content), "Free from," "Sainsbury Organic," "Fair Trade," and "Super Naturals™" (a range of ready-made meals with healthy ingredients).

While service offerings today are quite similar, the rivals' distribution strategies differ significantly. In common with most other large retailers, Tesco decided to draw goods from suppliers into regional distribution centers for preparation and delivery to stores. Tesco is extending this logistic practice to cover collection from suppliers (factory gate pricing) and input to suppliers in a drive to reduce costs and improve reliability.

In contrast, Sainsbury's has heavily invested in fully automated depots. On January 14, 2000, Sir Peter Davis was appointed Sainsbury's CEO. This decision was well received by investors and analysts, as in his first two years he raised profits above targets. By 2004, however, the group had suffered a decline in performance relative to its competitors and fell to third in the U.K. food market. Davis oversaw an almost £3 billion upgrade of stores, distribution, and IT equipment. Part of this investment included the construction of four fully automated depots, which, at £100 million each, cost four times more than standard depots.

Loyalty Programs

Retailers try to gain the loyalty of their customers in various ways. Tesco was the first to launch a Clubcard system. It was introduced in 1995 and has become the most popular card in the United Kingdom, with around 13 million active Clubcard holders. Customers collect one Clubcard point for every £1 (€1 in Ireland) they spend in a Tesco store, Tesco Petrol, or at Tesco.com. Customers also collect points by paying with a Tesco credit card or by using Tesco Mobile, Tesco Homephone, Tesco Broadband, selected Tesco Personal Finance products, or by using its Clubcard partners, Powergen or Avis. Each point is worth 1p in-store when redeemed or 4p when used with Clubcard deals (offers for holidays, day trips, etc.). Every three months, holders receive a Clubcard statement offering discount coupons that can be spent in-store, online (if opted into eVouchers), or on various Clubcard deals. The program has numerous partners (e.g., hundreds of British pubs), but the Clubcard belongs to Tesco alone. Tesco implemented the Clubcard rewards program to gather customer information, which is then used to cater to specific potential customer needs and wants. When shoppers sign up for the card, they automatically submit their ages, genders, and incomes.

Tesco segments their shoppers on the basis of these factors. As soon as the shopper uses the card online or in-store, product information is automatically uploaded into the Tesco database. Product information is used to cross-sell additional products and services, such as food delivery.

Tesco is the most customer-focused business that I have ever worked for. They are absolutely obsessed with the customer.

—JOHN HOERNER, NON-FOOD DIRECTOR, TESCO

Sainsbury's was "wrong-footed" in its original reaction to the Tesco Clubcard, showing "no immediate response apart from disdain."[4] It lost market share in subsequent years. In 2004, the *London Times* quoted a former executive and others who viewed this event as the start of the company's downturn due to management failures by David Sainsbury and his successors, Dino Adriano and Peter Davis. David Sainsbury, who in 1992 replaced his cousin, the long-time CEO John Sainsbury, first dismissed Tesco's Clubcard. After long internal debates, Sainsbury introduced the Sainsbury's reward card in 1996. A multiparty card program, "Nectar," was launched in the autumn of 2002. Nectar gives the customer a versatile and powerful point-gathering system to be used and redeemed at a variety of stores. In Nectar, Sainsbury's has strong partners such as Barclaycard, British Petroleum, and the department store chain Debenhams. The Nectar card was re-launched in summer 2007 to celebrate its fifth anniversary. The scheme was changed from a reward- to a treats-based program. In its early days, the Nectar scheme was criticized as being among the worst card schemes offered. At the time, it was said that some consumers who spent £5,000 on Barclaycard received as little as £12.50 in points to redeem, while Sainsbury's customers had to spend as much as £1,000 just to get two tickets to the cinema. Today, points on spending in-store are earned at a rate of two points per £1 spent (except 1 point per liter of fuel); 500 points can subsequently be exchanged for a voucher worth £2.50 to spend in Sainsbury's. The card scheme is run by a third-party company, Loyalty Management UK (LMUK), which collects information on behalf of the partner sponsors.

Online Sales Channels

Toward the end of the 1990s, both firms targeted online distribution channels that promised large growth potential. Non-store retailing growth rates were expected to be higher than store-based rates, as online usage gained popularity among British consumers (see Exhibit 3). Following these predictions, the United

Exhibit 3 Retailing: Growth in Value Sales by Broad Sector/ Sector 2001–2006 (percentage of current value growth)

	2005–2006	2001–2006 CAGR	2001–2006 Total
Non-store retailing	13.3	13.8	91.2
Internet retailing	24.8	32.9	313.9
Vending	2.5	5.0	27.7
Home shopping	2.8	3.8	20.6
Direct selling	–1.0	–1.5	–7.4
Store-based retailing	2.4	3.7	19.8
Food retailers	3.0	4.0	21.7
Non-food retailers	1.9	3.4	18.3
Retailing	3.1	4.2	23.1

Source: 2007, Official statistics, trade associations, trade press, company research, trade interviews, Euromonitor International estimates; Euromonitor, U.K. Retail Market: Market overview.

Kingdom has evolved into a leader of Internet retailing in Europe, and growth is continuing.

Tesco[5] has operated on the Internet since 1994 and was the first retailer in the world to offer a robust home-shopping service in 1996. Tesco.com was formally launched in 2000. It also has online operations in the Republic of Ireland and in South Korea. Food sales are available within delivery range of selected stores, goods being hand-picked within each store, in contrast to the warehouse model followed by most competitors (e.g., Ocado[6]), which allows rapid expansion with limited investment. In 2003, Tesco.com's then-CEO, John Browett, received the Wharton Infosys Business Transformation Award for the innovative processes he used to support this online food service. Today, Tesco operates the world's largest food home-shopping service, as well as provides consumer goods, telecommunications, and financial services online. As of November 2006, Tesco was the only food retailer to make online shopping profitable.

Sainsbury's has been involved in e-business and home-shopping development since 2000, when it launched Sainsbury's to You in April of that year. Although some employees transferred from the traditional side of the business, Sainsbury's also hired new staff with Web and marketing skills. Specific training was provided on e-business, as well as cross-functional training. Sainsbury's to You did not completely spin off

but occupied a separate building, thereby combining entrepreneurial flexibility with the strength and security of a strong brand. Sainsbury's Online currently operates from 144 stores and uses two dedicated picking centers that are not open to the public. In addition to food, also available are flowers, wine, gifts, and electronics. In October 2007, Sainsbury's was receiving around 80,000 online orders per week. This represents quite strong growth, but is far less than Tesco, which processes weekly orders of 250,000. Sainsbury's did not release any e-commerce sales figures, but said it was still on track to expand its Web service to 200 stores by March 2010. Tesco.com captured two-thirds of all online food orders in the first seven months of 2007, generating sales of approximately £2.5 million per day. Sainsburystoyou .com took third place with 14 percent, behind ASDA with 16 percent. Customers of Sainsbury's, however, spent the most per order, averaging almost £90, compared to £80 for both Tesco and ASDA. ASDA and Sainsbury's online shoppers also bought more items per order, with both averaging 69 units per order compared to 58 for Tesco. Sainsbury's online customers incurred the lowest average delivery charge during the period, at just over £3. Tesco online customers paid over £4 per delivery, and ASDA online customers paid nearly £5.50.

Diversification into Non-Food

A number of retailers have created such sense of nearness with customers in terms of perception, safety and security that you can refer to them as brands.

—**KAREL VUURSTEEN, CHAIRMAN & CEO, HEINEKEN**

Originally specializing in food, Tesco began to diversify into areas such as discount clothes, consumer electronics, consumer financial services, DVD sales and rentals, compact discs and music downloads, Internet service, consumer telecoms, consumer health insurance, consumer dental plans, and budget software. In these new product segments, Tesco heavily built on its skills in private labels. For example, it introduced brands such as "Cherokee" and "F+F" in clothing, "Technika" and "Digilogic" in consumer electronics, and other labels ranging from DVD players to televisions and computers. Tesco used its food brands "Finest" and "Value" to expand into non-food items. In its Extra stores, Finest health and beauty, home, and clothing lines resulted.

In 1997, Tesco Personal Finance was launched as a fifty-fifty banking joint venture with the Royal Bank of Scotland. Products offered included credit cards, loans, mortgages, savings accounts, and several types of insurance, including car, home, life, pet, and travel. They are promoted by leaflets in Tesco stores and through its

Web site. All of its offers are simple, providing customers few but clear options and choices. Profits were £130 million for the 52 weeks prior to February 24, 2007, of which Tesco's share was £66 million. This move toward the financial sector has diversified the Tesco brand and provides opportunities for growth outside the retailing sector. For example, Tesco offers Clubcard points or free petrol when consumers purchase Tesco car insurance. The company is currently conducting trials at a finance center in the Glasgow Silverburn Extra store, providing free financial advice and quotes for insurance and loans; this service is staffed by trained Royal Bank of Scotland employees. The center also has a Euro cash machine providing commission-free Euros and a Bureau de Change run by Travelex. If successful, this service will be rolled out to more key and flagship stores.

Tesco also entered the telecommunications sector. Though it launched its Internet service provider in 1998, the company was not seriously active in telecommunications until 2003. Rather than purchasing or building its own telecom network, Tesco paired its marketing strength with the expertise of existing telecom operators. In autumn 2003, Tesco Mobile was launched as a joint venture with O2, and Tesco Home Phone was created in partnership with Cable & Wireless. In August 2004, Tesco Broadband, an ADSL-based service delivered via BT phone lines, was launched in partnership with NTL. In January 2006, Tesco Internet Phone, a Voice over Internet Protocol service, was launched in conjunction with Freshtel of Australia. Simple and clear offering logic is also evident in the strategic move into telecommunications. Tesco Mobile offers only four different pay-as-you-go tariffs: Value, Standard, Extra, and Staff (for employees). Tesco announced in December 2004 that it had signed up 500,000 customers to its mobile service in the 12 months since launch. By December 2005, one million customers were using its mobile service, and by April 2006, Tesco claimed over one and, one-half million telecom accounts in total, including mobile, fixed line, and broadband. On December 19, 2006, Tesco Ireland announced that it would enter into a joint venture with O2 Ireland to offer mobile telecommunications services, also under the Tesco Mobile brand.

Recently, Tesco entered the housing market with a self-advertising Web site, Tesco Property Market. Other strategic initiatives into non-food items include, for example, following a successful trial in 2006, "Apple" zones in 12 outlets, where the iPod range is sold alongside Mac computers and other Apple products.

Sainsbury's was much more reluctant to move into non-food retailing. Inspired by the success of its main rivals (ASDA had also moved strongly into the non-food area) and the sheer size of the U.K. non-food retail market (in 2003, it was estimated at over £100 million), it launched 2,500 home and cookware products in September 2003. Copying Tesco, Sainsbury's also used its own food brands and transferred them to non-food items. For example, it extended its clothing range with an organic line. In addition to food and non-food items, Sainsbury's expanded into retail banking and property development. In 1997, Sainsbury's bank was established as a joint venture between J Sainsbury plc and the Bank of Scotland (now HBOS). Sainsbury's bank offers services similar to Tesco's, including travel (insurance and money), savings, and lending; it also offers a Sainsbury's credit card. By 2010, Sainsbury's expects to achieve sales of £3.5 billion, with 33 percent of its total sales coming from non-food businesses.

International Diversification

These results show that our new growth businesses—in international, in non-food and in services—have contributed as much profit as the entire business was making in 1997.

—*CEO TERRY LEAHY, 2005*

Tesco's international expansion[7] began in the late 1970s with the purchase of a small company in the Republic of Ireland. The small-scale nature of this first foray was seen as a weakness, and the company was eventually sold in the mid-1980s. In 1994, Tesco acquired the Scottish supermarket chain William Low. Tesco successfully fought off Sainsbury's for control of the Dundee-based firm, which then operated 57 stores. This paved the way for Tesco to expand its presence in Scotland, where it was weaker than in England. Inverness was recently branded "Tescotown" because well over 50p in every £1 spent on food is believed to be spent in its three Tesco stores. In March 1997, Tesco announced the purchase of the retail arm of Associated British Foods, which consisted of the Quinnsworth, Stewarts, and Crazy Prices chains in the Republic of Ireland and Northern Ireland, as well as associated businesses, for £640 million. This acquisition gave Tesco both a major presence in the Republic of Ireland and a larger presence in Northern Ireland than Sainsbury's, which had begun its move into the province in 1995.

In the 1990s, Tesco strongly expanded overseas by increasing investments in emerging markets such as Hungary, the Czech Republic, Thailand, and South Korea. Tesco was buying into successful companies, a strategy that resulted in strong positions in these markets. In 1997, the new CEO, Terry Leahy, enforced Tesco's international growth strategies beyond Great Britain. However, outside the United Kingdom the supermarket firm's position was far from dominant and remained in the shadow of larger, more high-profile international operators such as Wal-Mart and Carrefour. Tesco then analyzed countries for expansion, putting high emphasis on two dimensions: the market potential for growth and the competitive situation in the market. Only if a market was characterized by relatively high growth potential and relatively low rivalry was it considered a real target market and approached in an orderly fashion.

In 2002, Tesco purchased 13 HIT hypermarkets in Poland. In June 2003, Tesco purchased the C Two-Network in Japan. It also acquired a majority stake in the Turkish supermarket chain Kipa. Another acquisition was the Lotus chain in Thailand. In mid-2006, Tesco purchased an 80 percent stake in Casino's Leader Price supermarkets in Poland, which were subsequently reconfigured as small Tesco stores.

Many British retailers attempting to build international businesses have failed. Tesco has responded to the need to be sensitive to local expectations in foreign countries by entering into joint ventures with local partners, such as Samsung Group in South Korea (Samsung-Tesco Homeplus), and Charoen Pokphand in Thailand (Tesco Lotus), and by appointing a high proportion of local personnel to management positions.

In late 2004, the amount of floor space Tesco operated outside the United Kingdom surpassed its home market space for the first time, although the United Kingdom still accounted for more than 75 percent of group revenue due to lower sales per unit area outside the territory (for an overview of Tesco's international store portfolio, see Exhibit 4). Tesco regularly continues to make small acquisitions to expand its international businesses. For example, in the 2005–06 fiscal year, acquisitions were made in South Korea, Poland, and Japan.

In September 2005, Tesco announced that it was selling its operations in Taiwan to Carrefour and purchasing Carrefour stores in the Czech Republic and Slovakia. Both companies stated that they were concentrating their efforts in countries where they had strong market positions. Tesco entered China by acquiring a 50 percent stake in the Hymall chain from Ting Hsin of

Exhibit 4 Tesco's Store Portfolio "International"

Country	Entered	Stores	Area (m²)	Area (sq ft)	Turnover (£ million)
China	2004	47	392,422	4,224,000	552
Czech Republic	1996	84	381,459	4,106,000	807
France	1992	1	1,400	16,000	Note 3
Hungary	1994	101	448,164	4,824,000	1,180
Republic of Ireland	1997	95	205,780	2,215,000	1,683
Japan	2003	109	29,078	313,000	287
Malaysia	2002	19	174,750	1,881,000	247
Poland	1995	280	606,935	6,533,000	1,135
Slovakia	1996	48	225,475	2,427,000	498
South Korea	1999	81	473,340	5,095,000	2,557
Thailand	1998	370	698,166	7,515,000	1,326
Turkey	2003	30	102,936	1,108,000	256
United States of America	2007	6	Unknown	60,000 (est.)	Unknown

Note 1: The store numbers and floor area figures are as of February 24, 2007, but the turnover figures are for the year 2005, except for the Republic of Ireland data, which are for the year ending February 24, 2007, like the U.K. figures. This information is taken from the 2007 final broker pack.

Note 2: China: Joint venture in February 2006; now a 90 percent–owned subsidiary.

Note 3: France: Tesco owned a French chain called Catteau between 1992 and 1997. Its existing single store in France is a wine warehouse in Calais (opened in 1995 and targeted at British day trippers).

Note 4: Malaysia: Tesco Stores (Malaysia) Sdn Bhd was incepted on November 29, 2001, as a strategic alliance with local conglomerate, Sime Darby Bhd of which the latter holds 30 percent of total shares.

Taiwan in September 2004. In December 2006, it raised its stake to 90 percent in a £180 million deal, which was just after Tesco lost out to Wal-Mart to partner with the Indian group, Bharti, to develop a national retail chain in India.

In February 2006, Tesco announced its intention to move into the United States, opening a chain of convenience stores on the West Coast (Arizona and California), Fresh & Easy Neighborhood Market. The first store was opened in November 2007, with 100 more openings scheduled in the first year. By planning to open a new store in the United States every two-and-one-half days, Tesco intends to mimic the successful expansion of U.S. pharmacy chains such as Walgreens. Tesco's strategy and unorthodox tactics have not been without controversy. In 2005 and 2006, the company covertly sent an advance team consisting of executives in disguise to conduct intelligence on potential competitors. Like a James Bond movie, the company's agents sought to keep their plans secret by posing as Hollywood film producers making a movie about supermarkets, according to *BusinessWeek*. The bold operation collected intelligence on the U.S. market and on competitors such as Wal-Mart, Kroger, Safeway, Albertson's, Whole Foods, and Trader Joe's. The covert operation was so unusual and unsettling that some potential rivals hired security teams to infiltrate Tesco and obtain information about executives involved in the operation. In the end, Tesco did obtain the necessary information to proceed with its store openings. A Tesco senior manager said, "For me, it is remarkable that in five years Tesco has moved from being a U.K.-based supermarket chain to become an international mixed retail and services business. This rapid transformation is based on clarity at the top and a tremendous creativity and energy in making it happen quickly." Sainsbury's international strategy can be described as that of a fast follower, albeit with varying results and to a lesser extent. It expanded its operations into Scotland, opening a store in Darnley in January 1992. In June 1995, Sainsbury's announced its intention to move into the Northern Ireland market, which had until that point been dominated by local companies. Between December 1996 and December 1998, the company opened seven stores. Two others at Sprucefield, Lisburn, and Holywood Exchange, Belfast, would not open until 2003 due to protracted legal challenges. Sainsbury's move into Northern Ireland was undertaken in a very different way than that of Tesco. While Sainsbury's outlets were all new developments, Tesco (apart from one Tesco Metro) instead purchased existing chains from Associated British Foods (see Tesco Ireland). In 1999, Sainsbury's acquired an 80.1 percent share of the Egyptian Distribution Group SAE, a retailer in Egypt with 100 stores and 2,000 employees. However, poor profitability led to the sale of this share in 2001.

Management Teams

At the end of March 2004, Davis was promoted to chairman and was replaced as CEO of Sainsbury's by Justin King. Justin King joined Sainsbury's from Marks and Spencer plc, where he was a director with responsibility for its food division and Kings Super Markets, Inc, a subsidiary in the United States. King was also previously a managing director at ASDA, with responsibility for hypermarkets. In June 2004, Davis was forced to resign as chairman in the face of an impending shareholder revolt over his salary and bonuses. Investors were angered by a bonus share award of over £2 million, despite poor company performance. In July 2004, Philip Hampton was appointed chairman. Hampton had previously worked for British Steel, British Gas, BT, and Lloyds TSB.

King perceived Sainsbury's to be not sufficiently focused on its customers or its main competitors. King ordered a direct mail campaign to one million Sainsbury's customers, asking what they wanted from the company and where the company could improve. Results re-affirmed the commentary of retail analysts; that is, the group was not ensuring that shelves were fully stocked, partly due to the failure of the IT systems introduced by Peter Davis. In October 2004, King unveiled the results of the business review and his plans to revive the company's fortunes. This was generally well received by both the stock market and the media. Immediate plans included terminating 750 headquarters staff and recruiting around 3,000 shop floor staff to improve the quality of service and the firm's problem of stock availability. Another significant announcement was the decision to halve the dividend in order to increase funds available to offer price cuts and to improve quality. The company's fortunes have improved since the launch of this recovery program.

In 2004, King hired Lawrence Christensen, previously an expert in logistics at Safeway, as supply chain director. Immediate supply chain improvements included the reactivation of two distribution centers. In 2006, Christensen commented on the four automated depots introduced by Davis, saying, "[N]ot a single day went by without one, if not all of them, breaking down ... the systems were flawed. They have to stop for four hours every day for maintenance. But because they were constantly breaking down you would be playing catch up. It was a vicious circle." Christensen felt that a fundamental mistake was to build four such depots at once, rather than building one and testing it thoroughly before building the others. In 2007, Sainsbury's announced an additional £12 million investment in its depots to keep pace with sales growth and to remove the failed automated systems from its depots.

The Competitive Landscape Today

The situation today is clear. Tesco has outpaced its closest rival in its local and international markets. Edward Garner, communications director of the TNS Superpanel, said, "TNS supermarket share information shows that the retailer's market share has grown consistently and strongly over the last decade and shows no sign of abating."

These events led to shifts in the competitive landscape. The U.K. retail industry has become highly concentrated. The top four store-based retailers—Tesco, Sainsbury's ASDA, and Morrison's Supermarkets—dominate the market; all are original food retailers. This illustrates the status of food retailers in the market (see Exhibit 5). All are British, except ASDA, which was acquired in 1999 by the U.S. retail giant Wal-Mart.

Discounters adapted to this less-favorable environment by slightly improving their meager U.K. presence by expanding their number of outlets and moving upscale. This was helped by the trend of consumers to increasingly combine bargain shopping with purchases of luxury products or services. This "schizophrenic" shopping behavior blurs previously separate boundaries. The traditional structure of upper, middle, and mass market has been more or less abolished.

Since the launch of King's recovery program, Sainsbury's has reported nine consecutive quarters of sales growth, most recently in March 2007, even outpacing Tesco, making the company's performance the best since its glory days of the 1980s and early 1990s. Sales increases were credited to solving problems with the company's distribution system. More recent sales improvements have been attributed to significant price cuts and the company's focus on fresh and healthy food. On October 4, 2007, Sainsbury's announced plans to relocate their Store Support Centre from Holborn to Kings Cross in 2011. This office, part of a new building complex, will allow both cost savings and energy efficiency.

Despite this positive news, according to the latest Taylor Nelson Sofres rankings published in March 2007, Sainsbury's market share in food retailing remains third in the United Kingdom at 16.37 percent compared to Tesco's 31.35 percent, ASDA's 16.83 percent, and Morrison's 11.08 percent (see Exhibit 6). Tesco remains the clear market leader. In the past, Tesco showed itself

Exhibit 5 Retailing: Company Shares by Value 2004–2006 (in percentage of retail value)

	2004	2005	2006
Tesco plc	10.2	11.0	11.4
J Sainsbury plc	5.4	5.8	5.9
Asda Stores Ltd	4.7	4.9	5.1
Wm Morrison Supermarkets plc	3.7	3.7	3.5
Marks and Spencer plc	2.7	2.7	2.7
Alliance Boots plc	—	—	2.1
Dixons Group plc	1.3	1.4	1.4
Argos plc	1.3	1.4	1.4
B&Q plc	1.5	1.5	1.4
Somerfield Ltd	1.7	1.7	1.3
Waitrose Ltd	1.0	1.0	1.2
Co-operative Group (CWS) Ltd	1.3	1.3	1.2
Next plc	1.0	1.0	1.1
Spar Ltd (UK)	0.8	0.9	0.9
Debenhams Retail plc	0.7	0.8	0.8

Source: 2007, Official statistics, trade associations, trade press, company research, trade interviews, Euromonitor International estimates; Euromonitor, U.K. Retail Market: Market overview.

to be the quickest at seizing expansion opportunities. Furthermore, it has succeeded in building an image of providing good value at low prices.

The recovery in the Sainsbury market share builds on the positive picture already established. This strong performance has been achieved in the face of relentless pressure from Tesco, which continues its recent run of double-digit turnover growth. . . .

Whilst Tesco remains dominant, there are signs that it is experiencing increased competition. It is still growing, but the year-on-year share increase is below the average we were seeing last year. Looking towards the future, Tesco will continue to face challenging competition from its nearest competitor Asda as well as the likes of Sainsbury's, which is showing positive growth trends and Morrisons once the Safeway store conversions are complete. Tesco will need to prove its ability to meet increasingly challenging consumer demands and stay a step ahead of the competition. . . .

Exhibit 6 Food Retailing: Company Shares by Sales 1990–2007 (in percentage of retail value)

	1990	...	1994	1995	...	2002	...	2004	2005	2006	2007
Tesco plc	9.7		11.4	13.4		16.7		27.5	29.8	31.1	31.35
J Sainsbury plc	11.0		12.3	12.2		11.7		15.5	15.9	16.0	16.37
Asda Stores Ltd	6.8		6.7	7.2		10.6		16.6	16.5	16.4	16.83
Wm Morrison Supermarkets plc (Safeway included)						7.5 (only Safeway)		14.4	12.2	11.3	11.08

Source: TNS (Taylor Nelson Sofres) World Panel market-share data released June 2007.

Future Internationalization: It has a long way to go before it overhauls Wal-Mart as the world's biggest grocer—but analysts said the same about overhauling Sainsbury's in the U.K. market 15 years ago and now Tesco is almost double its size.

—**EDWARD GARNER, COMMUNICATIONS DIRECTOR OF TNS SUPERPANEL, 2007**

New Challenges Ahead

After a relatively long period of economic growth during the review period, conditions may well stagnate in the coming years, thus dampening the forecast performance of store-based retailing. Consumer debt levels have reached record highs and, with the United Kingdom's negative saving rate, there is less room for continued growth in consumption. As a result, discounters (both food and non-food) are well placed to gain importance. Euromonitor predicts food retailers to outperform non-food retailers with a value compound annual growth rate of 1 percent. Recent trends, such as health and wellness and ethical concerns, have opened opportunities, even in the saturated food category; however, most food retailers' growth is expected to stem from non-food items.

Consolidation is expected to continue (see the Safeway takeover), with independent shops closing, being taken over, or joining larger chains. This is evident in the decline of the number of total outlets, particularly independent ones.

Sainsbury's might be the target of additional takeover bids, since family investment in the company is only 18 percent. A first private equity bid was considered by CVC Capital Partners, Kohlberg Kravis Roberts (which later left the consortium in order to focus on its bid for Alliance Boots), and Blackstone Group; in February 2007, this also included Goldman Sachs and Texas Pacific Group. The initial offer submitted in April 2007 of 562p a share was rejected after discussions between Sainsbury's top management and the two largest family shareholders. A subsequent offer of 582p a share was also rejected. As a consequence, the CVC-led consortium abandoned its quest, stating "[I]t became clear the consortium would be unable to make a proposal that would result in a successful offer." In April 2007, Delta Two, a Qatari investment company, bought a 14 percent stake in Sainsbury's (causing its share price to rise 7.17 percent); this stake was increased to 25 percent in June 2007. On July 18, 2007, BBC News reported that Delta Two had tabled a conditional bid proposal. On November 5, 2007, it was announced that Delta Two had abandoned its takeover bid due to the "deterioration of credit markets" and concerns about funding the company's pension scheme. Following the withdrawal of the interest of Qatari investment, shares in Sainsbury's dropped about 20 percent (115p) to 440p on the day of this announcement.

Appendix 1 Retail: Number of Employees: 2001–2006 (in thousands)

	2001	2002	2003	2004	2005	2006
Retail employees	3,048	3,077	3,136	3,308	3,329	3,316
% growth	—	1.0	1.9	5.5	0.6	−0.4

Source: 2007, Official statistics, trade associations, trade press, company research, trade interviews, Euromonitor International estimates; Euromonitor, U.K. Retail Market: Market overview.

Appendix 2 Number of Employees of Food Retailers (full-time equivalents)

Employees	2006	2007
Tesco	380,000	318,283
Asda	150,000 90,000 part-time 60,000 full-time	143,125
Sainsbury's	96,200 104,100 part-time 49,200 full-time	95,500 98,100 part-time 48,800 full-time

Appendix 3 Tesco's Financial Figures

52 weeks ended	Turnover (£m)	Profit before Tax (£m)	Profit for Year (£m)	Basic Earnings per Share (p)
2007	46,600	2,653	1,899	22.36
2006	38,300	2,210	1,576	19.70
2005	33,974	1,962	1,366	17.44
2004	30,814	1,600	1,100	15.05
2003	26,337	1,361	946	13.54
2002	23,653	1,201	830	12.05
2001	20,988	1,054	767	11.29
2000	18,796	933	674	10.07
1999	17,158	842	606	9.14
1998	16,452	760	532	8.12

Note: The numbers include non-UK and Ireland results.

Appendix 4 Growth Rates (Tesco vs. Sainsbury) 1990–2007

Growth Rates (%)	Sales	Operating Income	Net Income	Div. Per Share	Equity	Total Assets
Sainsbury's Y2007				21.88		
Tesco Y2007	8.08	5.88	20.51	11.70	12.00	9.86
Sainsbury's Y2006	5.65	7.55	−64.67	2.56	−0.21	9.24
Tesco Y2006	16.50	13.40	16.82	14.15	9.03	11.97
Sainsbury's Y2005	−10.10	−53.04	−84.60	−56.50	−15.48	−7.11
Tesco Y2005	10.26	12.47	24.18	10.53	13.76	10.12
Sainsbury's Y2004	−1.66	−2.03	−12.78	0.70	2.05	4.70
Tesco Y2004	17.00	19.78	16.28	10.32	22.50	12.68

Appendix 4 Growth Rates (Tesco vs. Sainsbury) 1990–2007 (*Continued*)

Growth Rates (%)	Sales	Operating Income	Net Income	Div. Per Share	Equity	Total Assets
Sainsbury's Y2003	1.56	11.46	24.73	4.99	3.30	8.76
Tesco Y2003	11.35	12.49	13.98	10.71	18.24	21.91
Sainsbury's Y2002	7.57	9.95	38.93	3.63	−1.31	6.85
Tesco Y2002	12.70	13.29	8.21	12.45	4.02	16.00
Sainsbury's Y2001	−1.95	−5.78	−24.93	—	3.23	−1.94
Tesco Y2001	11.66	12.55	13.80	11.16	12.05	18.80
Sainsbury's Y2000	−0.99	−25.32	−41.64	—	0.65	4.32
Tesco Y2000	9.55	7.92	11.22	8.74	9.58	13.88
Sainsbury's Y1999	13.33	8.48	22.79	3.02	12.89	10.13
Tesco Y1999	7.81	5.03	20.00	6.54	10.42	15.58
Sainsbury's Y1998	8.25	11.58	20.84	13.01	12.01	25.23
Tesco Y1998	14.60	18.09	−2.88	12.09	−0.36	12.32
Sainsbury's Y1997	6.08	−11.94	−17.42	1.65	3.88	7.88
Tesco Y1997	14.83	6.91	11.59	7.81	8.78	6.74
Sainsbury's Y1996	11.18	−4.09	−8.87	3.43	7.45	15.81
Tesco Y1996	19.73	17.34	22.63	11.61	15.21	5.01
Sainsbury's Y1995	7.31	13.36	278.18	10.38	8.21	6.22
Tesco Y1995	17.45	18.38	27.43	10.99	12.92	18.84
Sainsbury's Y1994	9.27	1.80	−71.84	5.99	0.36	3.95
Tesco Y1994	13.43	−5.53	−28.59	9.13	−0.15	9.82
Sainsbury's Y1993	11.39	17.48	14.74	14.29	14.68	12.26
Tesco Y1993	6.82	15.06	5.56	12.71	12.50	9.03
Sainsbury's Y1992	11.29	14.29	23.37	20.41	57.92	22.22
Tesco Y1992	11.84	20.48	30.69	20.00	13.29	13.01
Sainsbury's Y1991	12.74	23.83	13.23	20.50	18.98	14.75
Tesco Y1991	17.48	25.63	19.27	25.72	72.23	50.90
Sainsbury's Y1990	22.47	17.16	24.88	20.79	20.38	16.97
Tesco Y1990	14.50	20.50	36.23	22.86	21.60	19.75

Source: Thompson Database 2007.

Appendix 5 Financial Leverage and Return on Equity/Assets 1990–2007

Profitability (%)	Financial Leverage Tesco	Financial Leverage Sainsbury's	Return on Equity Tesco	Return on Equity Sainsbury's	Return on Assets Tesco	Return on Assets Sainsbury's
Y2007	42.41	45.42	18.81		8.62	
Y2006	41.59	30.62	17.50	1.67	8.11	1.02
Y2005	44.13	36.50	16.20	−1.10	7.86	1.56
Y2004	42.72	40.12	15.65	8.09	7.31	3.70
Y2003	39.29	41.16	16.17	9.49	7.37	4.59
Y2002	40.51	43.34	15.65	7.71	7.72	4.21
Y2001	45.18	46.92	15.62	5.60	8.30	3.34
Y2000	47.91	44.57	15.26	7.55	8.54	4.12
Y1999	49.78	46.20	14.99	13.71	8.56	6.94
Y1998	52.11	45.07	13.01	12.56	8.08	6.79
Y1997	58.74	50.38	13.98	11.21	8.74	6.63
Y1996	57.64	52.32	14.02	14.29	8.90	8.48
Y1995	52.54	56.39	13.00	16.88	8.08	10.04
Y1994	55.29	55.36	10.84	4.70	6.96	2.77
Y1993	60.81	57.34	16.07	17.74	10.58	10.39
Y1992	58.93	56.13	17.17	19.88	11.18	11.96
Y1991	58.79	43.44	19.36	23.11	11.12	12.05
Y1990	51.51	41.90	21.05	24.40	12.82	12.20

Source: Thompson Database 2007.

Appendix 6 Margins 1990–2007

Profitability (%)	Gross Margin Tesco	Gross Margin Sainsbury's	Op Profit Margin Tesco	Op Profit Margin Sainsbury's	Pretax Prof Margin Tesco	Pretax Prof Margin Sainsbury's
Y2007	7.60	6.83	5.02	3.00	5.91	2.78
Y2006	7.67	6.95	5.13	2.22	5.46	0.65
Y2005	7.77	7.20	5.89	2.21	5.49	0.10
Y2004	7.65	8.89	5.78	4.22	4.92	3.56
Y2003	7.50	8.20	5.64	4.24	4.96	3.83
Y2002	7.51	7.41	5.58	3.86	4.97	3.33

Appendix 6 Margins 1990–2007 (*Continued*)

Profitability (%)	Gross Margin Tesco	Gross Margin Sainsbury's	Op Profit Margin Tesco	Op Profit Margin Sainsbury's	Pretax Prof Margin Tesco	Pretax Prof Margin Sainsbury's
Y2001	7.53	6.69	5.56	3.78	5.01	2.72
Y2000	7.39	6.96	5.51	3.93	4.91	3.12
Y1999	7.77	7.87	5.60	5.22	4.87	5.33
Y1998	7.68	8.05	5.74	5.45	4.67	4.85
Y1997	7.27	7.43	5.57	5.29	5.40	4.40
Y1996	7.65	8.36	5.99	6.37	5.58	5.49
Y1995	7.70	9.29	6.11	7.38	5.45	7.07
Y1994	8.13	9.00	6.06	6.99	5.06	3.48
Y1993	9.33	9.68	7.28	7.50	7.66	7.57
Y1992	8.98	9.44	6.76	7.11	7.69	7.21
Y1991	8.46	9.21	6.27	6.92	6.87	6.63
Y1990	8.39	9.06	5.86	6.30	6.69	6.49

Source: Thompson Database 2007.

Appendix 7 Sales per Share, EPS, and Dividends 1990–2007

Profitability (%)	Sales per Share Data Tesco	Sales per Share Data Sainsbury's	EPS Tesco	EPS Sainsbury's	Dividend Tesco	Dividend Sainsbury's
Y2007	5.37	10.14	0.24	0.19	0.10	0.10
Y2006	5.04	9.57	0.20	0.04	0.09	0.08
Y2005	4.41	8.81	0.18	−0.03	0.08	0.08
Y2004	4.22	10.24	0.15	0.24	0.07	0.18
Y2003	3.77	10.42	0.14	0.27	0.06	0.18
Y2002	3.43	10.28	0.12	0.22	0.06	0.17
Y2001	3.09	9.59	0.11	0.16	0.05	0.16
Y2000	2.81	9.72	0.10	0.21	0.04	0.16
Y1999	2.59	9.84	0.09	0.36	0.04	0.16
Y1998	2.43	8.87	0.08	0.30	0.04	0.16
Y1997	2.14	8.34	0.08	0.25	0.03	0.14
Y1996	1.92	7.94	0.07	0.31	0.03	0.14
Y1995	1.68	7.22	0.06	0.34	0.03	0.13
Y1994	1.46	6.79	0.05	0.09	0.03	0.12
Y1993	1.30	6.27	0.07	0.33	0.02	0.11

(Continued)

Appendix 7 Sales per Share, EPSs and Dividends 1990–2007 (*Continued*)

Profitability (%)	Sales per Share Data Tesco	Sales per Share Data Sainsbury's	EPS Tesco	EPS Sainsbury's	Dividend Tesco	Dividend Sainsbury's
Y1992	1.22	5.83	0.07	0.29	0.02	0.10
Y1991	1.28	5.81	0.06	0.26	0.02	0.08
Y1990	1.13	5.19	0.05	0.24	0.01	0.07

Source: Thompson Database 2007.

Appendix 8 Retailing: Company Shares by Value 2004–2006 (in percentage of retail value)

Company	2004	2005	2006
Tesco plc	10.2	11.0	11.4
J Sainsbury plc	5.4	5.8	5.9
Asda Stores Ltd	4.7	4.9	5.1
Wm Morrison Supermarkets plc	3.7	3.7	3.5
Marks and Spencer plc	2.7	2.7	2.7
Alliance Boots plc	—	—	2.1
Dixons Group plc	1.3	1.4	1.4
Argos plc	1.3	1.4	1.4
B&Q plc	1.5	1.5	1.4
Somerfield Ltd	1.7	1.7	1.3
Waitrose Ltd	1.0	1.0	1.2
Co-operative Group (CWS) Ltd	1.3	1.3	1.2
Next plc	1.0	1.0	1.1
Spar Ltd (UK)	0.8	0.9	0.9
Debenhams Retail plc	0.7	0.8	0.8

Source: 2007, Official statistics, trade associations, trade press, company research, trade interviews, Euromonitor International estimates; Euromonitor, U.K. Retail Market: Market overview.

Appendix 9 Food Retailing: Company Shares by Value 2004–2006 (in percentage of retail value)

Company	2004	2005	2006
Tesco plc	23.0	24.4	25.2
J Sainsbury plc	12.5	13.1	13.3
Asda Stores Ltd	10.9	11.0	11.2
Wm Morrison Supermarkets plc	8.7	8.5	8.1
Somerfield Ltd	4.0	3.8	3.1
Waitrose Ltd	2.3	2.3	2.8

Appendix 9 Food Retailing: Company Shares by Value 2004–2006 (in percentage of retail value) (*Continued*)

Company	2004	2005	2006
Co-operative Group (CWS) Ltd	2.7	2.6	2.5
Spar Ltd (UK)	2.0	2.0	2.0
Musgrave Group plc	1.6	1.8	1.8
Lidl Ltd	1.0	1.1	1.1
Aldi Stores Ltd	0.9	1.0	1.1
Iceland Frozen Foods Ltd.	1.2	1.1	1.0
Others	26.6	24.8	23.6

Source: 2007, Official statistics, trade associations, trade press, company research, trade interviews, Euromonitor International estimates; Euromonitor, U.K. Retail Market: Market overview.

Appendix 10 Food Retailers: Value Sales by Sector 2001–2006 (in millions of pounds, current rsp)

Retailer Type	2001	2002	2003	2004	2005	2006
Supermarkets	40,502.8	42,591.0	43,106.1	44,356.0	45,198.8	46,284.0
Hypermarkets	22,766.5	24,677.2	27,569.9	31,698.9	35,521.1	38,175.9
Convenience stores	10,514.3	11,895.7	13,729.7	14,306.0	14,577.8	14,875.2
Food/drink/tobacco specialists	12,074.0	11,460.6	11,100.0	10,700.0	10,144.0	9,667.0
Independent grocers	8,563.0	8,135.0	7,647.0	7,119.4	6,592.5	6,203.6
Discounters	2,395.0	2,582.6	2,672.2	2,725.4	2,980.2	3,375.5
Other food retailers	2,365.7	2,395.0	2,218.9	2,159.0	2,129.0	2,088.0
Food retailers	99,181.2	102,737.0	108,043.9	113,064.6	117,143.4	120,669.1

Source: 2007, Official statistics, trade associations, trade press, company research, trade interviews, Euromonitor International estimates; Euromonitor, U.K. Retail Market: Market overview.

Appendix 11 Food Retailers: Growth in Value Sales by Sector 2001–2006 (percentage of current value growth)

Retailer Type	2005/2006	2001–2006 CAGR	2001/2006 TOTAL
Hypermarkets	7.5	10.9	67.7
Convenience stores	2.0	7.2	41.5
Discounters	13.3	7.1	40.9
Supermarkets	2.4	2.7	14.3
Other food retailers	−1.9	−2.5	−11.7
Food/drink/tobacco specialists	−4.7	−4.3	−19.9
Independent grocers	−5.9	−6.2	−27.6
Food retailers	3.0	4.0	21.7

Source: 2007, Official statistics, trade associations, trade press, company research, trade interviews, Euromonitor International estimates; Euromonitor, U.K. Retail Market: Market overview.

Appendix 12 Share Price Tesco vs. Sainsbury (1990–2007)

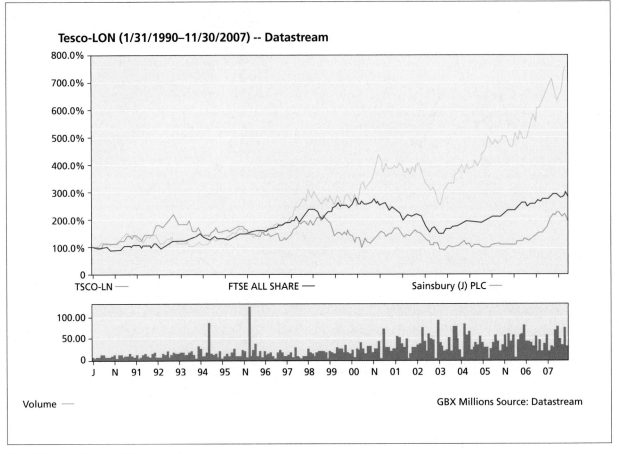

Tesco-LON (1/31/1990–11/30/2007) -- Datastream

TSCO-LN ——   FTSE ALL SHARE ——   Sainsbury (J) PLC ——

Volume ——   GBX Millions Source: Datastream

Source: Thompson Database 2007.

NOTES

1. The largest retailers in the world ranked by sales in 2005, http://www.chainstoreage.com.

2. For more information on ASDA and how the purchase of Asda by Wal-Mart in 1999 changed the competitive scenario of the U.K. retail industry, see, for example, Dhar & Sushma, 2005,: Tesco vs. Asda: UK's retailing battle, ECCH Case: 305-623-1.

3. For more detailed information on Tesco's store formats in 2003, see, for example, Padmini & Himansu, 2003, Tesco in 2003, ECCH Case: 304-173-1.

4. The article "Surpassing Sainsbury" describes Tesco's market-share dominance since the introduction of the Clubcard.

5. For Tesco's online sales strategy, see also Pole, 2007, Tesco's online sales strategy, ECCH Case: 507-024-1; Mukund, 2003, http://www.tesco.com: A rare profitable dotcom, ECCH Case: 903-034-1.

6. Ocado was launched in January 2002, in partnership with Waitrose and is today available to over 13.5 million households in the United Kingdom.

7. For Tesco's global expansion strategies, see also Bhavika & Phani Madhav, 2005, Tesco: The British supermarket chain's global expansion strategies and challenges, ECCH Case: 305-350-1.

Mark Brewer, Brandi Chauvin, Eric Mitchell,
Eric Partington, Mark Rade, Don Riddle,
Yinghong (Sara) Song, Robin Chapman

Arizona State University

Millions of people each year try to come up with a "million dollar" idea. Many believe that it requires an "unfathomable" idea, but sometimes going back to the basics is the key. That's what allowed Kevin Plank, the founder of Under Armour performance apparel, to find success. The task at hand was to simply make a superior T-shirt and nothing more. It all began in 1996 when the former University of Maryland football player wanted to create a shirt that would help control the temperature of an athlete's body, not just soak up the sweat during intense activities. He wanted a shirt that enhanced performance rather than detracted from it. As a result, Plank created a synthetic shirt made of high-tech material that had a snug fit designed to feel like a second skin.

The technology behind Under Armour's diverse product lines for men, women, and youth is complex, but the message is simple: wear HeatGear when it's hot, ColdGear when it's cold, and AllSeasonGear between the extremes. Under Armour's mission is to enhance the experience for all athletes by applying passion, science, and the relentless pursuit of innovation to create clothing with temperature control, comfort, and flexibility.[1]

Under Armour's stated goal is to be "a leading developer, marketer, and distributor of branded performance products." It has been able to successfully penetrate the sports apparel market by using the image and influence of: domestic and international professional teams, collegiate teams, Olympians, and individuals.

Utilizing broad-based, frequently free endorsements and well-received publicity, Under Armour has also reached regular athletes, active outdoor enthusiasts, elite tactical professionals, and active lifestyle consumers.

Under Armour is quickly becoming a leader in the sports apparel industry, and it could be argued that it is an opposing force to Nike in sports apparel, with its widespread popularity amongst top-name athletes and sports programs and teams. This is further evidenced by a 133 percent compound annual growth rate and an equally enormous increase in operating income from $5.7 million to $52.5 million between the years 2003 and 2007. As of 2007, Under Armour had $606 million in sales revenue, far surpassing its first year's revenue in 1996 of $17 thousand (see Exhibits 1 and 2).

Under Armour's products are sold worldwide, with the company's headquarters located in the United States and support offices in Hong Kong and Guangzhou, China. Primary sales are achieved through wholesale distribution and licensing to distributors. Products are offered through the company website and retailers, and company stores in the United States, Europe, Japan, Canada, South Africa, Australia, and New Zealand (see Exhibit 3). Under Armour operates in a highly competitive industry where the dominant competitors have significant breadth of market coverage that it is difficult to find an entry point. The main competitors have been advertising and establishing distribution channels, marketing agreements,

Exhibit 1 Under Armour Net Revenue: 2003–2007

	Year Ended December 31				
(In thousands, except per share amounts)	2007	2006	2005	2004	2003
Statements of Income data:					
Net revenues	$606,561	$430,689	$281,053	$205,181	$115,419

Source: 2008, Under Armour, Inc., Form 10-K 2007 Annual Report, December 31, 26.

Exhibit 2 Under Armour Income Growth from 2005 to 2007

Under Armour, Inc. and Subsidiaries Consolidated Statements of Income (In thousands, except per share amounts)			
	Year Ended December 31		
	2007	**2006**	**2005**
Net revenues	$606,561	$430,689	$281,053
Cost of goods sold	301,517	215,089	145,203
Gross profit	305,044	215,600	135,850
Operating expenses			
Selling, general and administrative expenses	218,779	158,682	100,040
Income from operations	86,265	56,918	35,810
Other income (expense), net	2,778	2,169	(2,836)
Income before income taxes	89,043	59,087	32,974
Provision for income taxes	36,485	20,108	13,255
Net income	52,558	38,979	19,719
Accretion of and cumulative preferred dividends on Series A Preferred Stock	—	—	5,307
Net income available to common stockholders	$52,558	$38,979	$14,412

Source: 2008, Under Armour, Inc., Form 10-K 2007 Annual Report, December 31, 46.

and recognition for many years. Thus the battle for Under Armour was much more uphill than most other new entrants to an established market. However, Under Armour has succeeded in breaking into a mature market and is no longer simply an amateur player in the sports apparel arena. The question is: "How does the company stay on top of its game?"

History of Under Armour

As previously mentioned, when Plank was a football player he grew tired of having to change his damp, heavy t-shirt under his jersey, so he set out to create a unique product that would meet the needs of all athletes. His laboratory was his grandmother's basement in Maryland. After many prototypes, Plank created his first shirt; it was a shiny tight shirt made of high-tech fibers that wicked away moisture, keeping athletes cool, dry, and feeling "light."[2] Plank's shirts truly did regulate athletes' body temperatures, lending to improved performance.[3]

Starting Small

Plank believed that he could make a profitable apparel business with his advanced feature shirts, so he used

Exhibit 3 Net Revenue by Geographic Region

(In thousands)	Year Ended December 31		
	2007	**2006**	**2005**
United States	$562,439	$403,725	$266,048
Canada	23,360	16,485	9,502
Subtotal	585,799	420,210	275,550
Other foreign countries	20,762	10,479	5,503
Total net revenues	$606,561	$430,689	$281,053

Source: 2008, Under Armour, Inc., Form 10-K 2007 Annual Report, December 31, 68.

$20,000 of his savings and ran up $40,000 in credit card debt to launch Under Armour.[4] Success was initially slow in coming, but once Plank made his first big sale to Georgia Tech University,[5] Under Armour grew rapidly. Plank marketed his product by focusing on the value-added concept, and now many high school, college, and professional teams use Under Armour athletic gear.

At the end of its first year of operations, Under Armour had five lines of clothing made for every climate, and the company's operations were moved out of Plank's grandmother's basement into a manufacturing warehouse in Maryland.

Growing into a Recognized Brand

In the late 1990s, Under Armour achieved national recognition. By 1998, it was the official supplier of performance apparel to NFL Europe. In 1999, it signed a contract to feature Under Armour in Warner Brothers' movies. By 2000, Under Armour had become a globally recognized brand and was supplying performance apparel to the National Football League, National Hockey League, and Major League Baseball, USA Baseball, and the U.S. ski team as well as other professional leagues abroad.[6] Currently players from 30 of 32 NFL teams wear Under Armour products.

As of 2005, Under Armour was supplying over 100 NCAA Division 1A football programs and thirty NFL teams, but it was still looking for other areas to branch into within the performance apparel industry.[7] Consequently, Under Armour introduced a loose-fit clothing line and added women's clothing to its product line.[8] Also in 2005, the company went public, seeking to sell as much as $100 million in shares of common stock. Ben Sturner, president of Leverage Sports Agency, a New York–based sports marketing firm, said, "Under Armour is no longer an up-and-coming brand. [It] [has] positioned [itself] as a real player in the industry and in the eyes of consumers in only a few years' time."[9]

During 2007, Under Armour increased its marketing initiatives by opening self-owned retail and outlet stores. Plank recognized that "You can't be a world-class athletic brand without the ability to outfit the athlete head to toe,"[10] so Under Armour developed athletic footwear. As of the first quarter of 2008, Under Armour had 43 percent of the total U.S. performance apparel business sold through sporting goods stores, versus 32 percent for Nike and 5.1 percent for Adidas.[11] A marketing consultant has said, "Under Armour is identified with performance the way Starbucks is identified with better coffee, and that is a huge advantage in entering new categories."[12] Plank attributes the company's success to the fact that "[it] ha[s] grown and reinforced [its] brand name and image through sales to athletes and teams at all levels, from youth to professional, as well as through sales to consumers with active lifestyles around the globe."[13]

Current Product and Sales Profile

Geographic Distribution

Approximately 93 percent of sales in 2007 were in the United States. with the remaining 7 percent split between Canada [4 percent] and all other international markets [3 percent] (see Exhibit 3). Under Armour sells products in 13 countries, including in-house distribution in the United Kingdom, Germany, and France. Sales in other Western European and Asian countries are done through partnerships and third-party distributors. The limited sales outside of the North American market were primarily the result of an emerging international penetration plan that received new emphasis in 2006 with the opening of a European headquarters. In an effort to increase the geographic diversity of sales, these headquarters were opened to manage sales and distribution channels, and additional experienced industry talent was brought on board in 2007 (Exhibit 4 shows where offices and stores are located).

Exhibit 4 Geographic Diversity

Location	Use
Baltimore, MD	Corporate headquarters
Amsterdam, The Netherlands	European headquarters
Glen Bumie, MD	Distribution facilities, 17,000 square foot quick-turn, Special Make-Up Shop manufacturing facility, and 4,500 square foot retail outlet store
Denver, CO	Sales office
Ontario, Canada	Sales office
Guangzhou, China	Quality assurance & sourcing for footwear
Hong Kong	Quality assurance & sourcing for apparel
Various	Retail store space

Source: 2008, Under Armour, Inc., Form 10-K 2007 Annual Report, December 31, 20.

Product Segment Distribution

Under Armour's sales results are broken into apparel, footwear, accessories, and licensed products (see Exhibits 5 and 6). Apparel dominated in 2007 with 84 percent of total sales. Men's apparel made up the "lion's share" of Under Armour's business, representing 68 percent of apparel sales and 57 percent of total sales. The second largest apparel segment was women's with 23 percent of apparel sales and 19 percent of total sales, representing a significant growth and diversification opportunity. Youth products made up the balance of apparel sales.

Under Armour's non-apparel product segments made up the remaining 16 percent of sales: footwear (7 percent), accessories (5 percent), and licensed products (4 percent). Footwear is a new product line that was launched in fourth quarter of 2006. Initially this line only offered baseball, softball, and lacrosse cleats designed for high performance through a highly breathable and lightweight design. The footwear line now includes shoes for golf, football, running, and cross-training. In the near future it will likely introduce basketball shoes and soccer cleats. It captured 20 percent of the U.S. football

Exhibit 5 Net Revenue by Product Category

| (In thousands) | Year Ended December 31 | | |
	2007	2006	2005
Men's	$348,150	$255,681	$189,596
Women's	115,867	85,695	53,500
Youth	48,596	31,845	18,784
Apparel	512,613	373,221	261,880
Footwear	40,878	26,874	—
Accessories	29,054	14,897	9,409
Total net sales	582,545	414,992	271,289
License revenues	24,016	15,697	9,764
Total net revenues	$606,561	$430,689	$281,053

Source: 2008, Under Armour, Inc., Form 10-K 2007 Annual Report, December 31, 68.

Exhibit 6 Net Revenue by Product in 2007

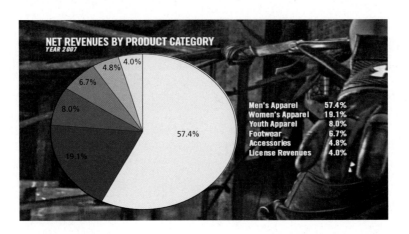

NET REVENUES BY PRODUCT CATEGORY
YEAR 2007

Men's Apparel	57.4%
Women's Apparel	19.1%
Youth Apparel	8.0%
Footwear	6.7%
Accessories	4.8%
License Revenues	4.0%

Source: 2008, Under Armour, Inc., Form 10-K 2007 Annual Report, December 31, Intro.

shoe market in the first year.[14] The company's 2009 first quarter earnings beat analysts' expectations, which the company attributes largely to the new running shoe.[15]

Under Armour's accessories category is developed and managed directly by Under Armour. The primary accessories products are performance gloves for football, baseball, running, and golf aligned to the Heatgear and Coldgear product lines with unique performance features.

Under Armour also licenses its brand name to independent manufacturers for other miscellaneous products such as bags, socks, headwear, eyewear, and watches. The company works with multiple licensees directly throughout the product development process to ensure that the products are aligned with its brand and quality expectations.

Seasonality

There appears to be a trend that sales are higher in the third and fourth quarters of each year, aligning with the football and basketball seasons and the traditional holiday gift-giving season in the United States. Under Armour has contemplated putting more emphasis on its baseball product line to improve the sales balance and reduce the seasonal variability in sales, inventory efforts, and distribution.

Operations and Distributions/ Distributors

Under Armour possesses an efficient operations and distribution network. As with any corporation, this requires a blend of physical-location metrics and strategic qualities.

By leveraging its licensing partners (JR286, Inc. and USG), Under Armour can provide a wider range of branded products to its customers. This broader range of products adds value by reinforcing the brand and generating revenue without having to organically develop capabilities in these adjacent product categories. Through keen selection and effective partner relationships, Under Armour has developed unique products that consumers value.

For the first ten years of its existence, the company was able to sustain operations by using "off the shelf" software programs, but after it went public in 2006, Under Armour invested in a new SAP system. This system is key to the company's ability to add products to its list of offerings, as it allows Under Armour to manage a more diverse inventory and to ship directly to distributors.[16]

Under Armour does not have a patent on any of the materials[17] used in its products. Therefore, it needs to be cautious in its licensing agreements so companies do not steal its know-how and introduce their own versions. Though the materials and technology used to create its products are not exclusive, by implementing an effective corporate strategy Under Armour has been able to fashion itself as a profitable business and remain a key player among competitors.

Major Competitors

There is stiff competition in the athletic apparel industry with companies of various sizes employing different strategies in order to attract consumers to their product and brand. The athletic apparel industry is so diverse that some smaller companies may choose to target a specific area such as yoga; whereas the larger companies try to capture the whole market. The larger companies continuously increase the competition by spending large amounts of money on product innovation, advertising, and sponsorships. Under Armour's three largest competitors in the industry are Nike, Adidas/Reebok, and Columbia Sportswear.[18] There are also smaller competitors such as SportHill that could possibly break through to become larger threats.

Nike[19]

Nike was founded in 1964 by a University of Oregon track star, Phil Knight. Knight saw a need for better running shoes and began selling shoes imported from Asia out of the trunk of his car. By 1972 he severed his relationships with suppliers abroad because they had become strained and developed his first shoe branded as Nike. Nike over time became known as a high-quality, innovative product that consumers and athletes wanted to wear and were willing to pay a premium price to own.

By 1980, Nike had captured 50 percent of the athletic shoe market and in the 1980s began expanding into other areas of the market through acquisitions and product innovation. It produces its three main product segments (footwear, apparel, and equipment) mostly through contract manufacturers rather than operating its own plants. Nike has relationships with some 700 factories in 52 countries, with most in China, Vietnam, and India.[20] Nike is the leader in athletic shoes, apparel, and equipment and grossed $18.6 billion in fiscal year 2007. It sells products for every sport and climate and strives to be the best in every segment. Nike advertises its brand through high-priced endorsement deals, media advertising, event sponsorships, and partnerships and alliances. Nike currently has 30,000 employees spread across six continents and operates in 160 countries. Nike is an industry leader that is continually striving to stay ahead of the competition.

Adidas[21]

Adidas, combined with Reebok (through an acquisition), is the second largest athletic apparel manufacturer in the world. Adidas was founded in 1924 in Germany by Adolf Dassler. Dassler created the first running shoe made by hand without electricity in his mother's kitchen. Dassler's big break came in 1954 when the German soccer team beat Hungary in the World Cup wearing Adidas cleats. From that point forward, Adidas was the industry leader in soccer shoes and apparel.

Changes in leadership during the late 1980s led Adidas to branch out into other markets, but it struggled to find its niche. Through acquisitions and better management it was back on track by the mid-1990s. Adidas acquired three smaller companies: TaylorMade, Salomon Group, and Maxfli. These acquisitions gave it access to the golf and winter sports market segments. In 2006, it merged with athletic apparel and equipment giant Reebok making it the second largest athletic apparel manufacturer in the world. Today the Adidas product line includes shoes and athletic apparel for basketball, soccer, fitness, golf, and outdoor adventure. Adidas operates globally and has 25,000 employees worldwide with 80 subsidiaries and reported $15.6 billion in profits in 2007.

Columbia Sportswear[22]

Columbia Sportswear Company started in the 1930s as a family-owned and operated hat company in Portland, Oregon. Founder Paul Lamfrom grew tired of working with inadequate suppliers and decided to manufacturer his own products. Columbia quickly gained a reputation for its innovative, high-quality products.

Columbia's introduction of waterproof, breathable fabrics triggered the growth it has experienced since the 1980s from a small family-owned business to a billion dollar publicly traded company. Columbia continues to grow thanks to its innovative product development and the acquisitions of Sorel, Mountain Hardware, Pacific Trail, and Montrail. These acquisitions enabled the company to branch out into other market segments.

Columbia Sportswear is now one of the largest manufacturers and sellers of outdoor apparel specializing in skiwear, snowboard gear, and hunting, fishing, hiking, camping, and casual wear. Columbia currently operates in North America, Europe, and Asia, and its products are available in 90 countries. Columbia has 3,000 employees worldwide. In 2007, Columbia posted record net sales of $1.36 billion.

SportHill[23]

SportHill was founded in 1985 by a University of Oregon track runner who saw the need for cold weather track gear. His athletic apparel design concept merged the best American fabrics with European style to make unique athletic apparel. SportHill clothing is designed for use in any climate and for any sport. SportHill utilizes the expertise of elite athletes to perfect its design and innovate new products. It is well known for quality, comfort, and reliability. SportHill's clothing can be found globally in most major retailer stores and can be purchased online. The success of SportHill is apparent in the number of sponsorships it has, including many Olympic athletes and collegiate running teams; however, it is a privately held company so financial information is not available.

Under Armour has been able to remain successful among its competitors in large part due to the strength of character of its founder and other leaders.

Under Armour's Leaders

Under Armour's success may seem unbelievable at first, but it's no accident. Plank's drive to keep trying even during difficult times when it seemed the company might never flourish is what made it possible. In the beginning, when customers would request products that Plank had not created, he would respond, "Of course we make that!" and then immediately go to work with suppliers and contractors to deliver on his promise. Two such examples were when the equipment manager for the Atlanta Falcons wanted long-sleeve Under Armour shirts, and when the equipment manager for Arizona State wanted clothing for cold weather.[24]

"He's one of the hardest workers I've known in my life," says Plank's mother.[25] Plank's humble beginnings give him valuable insight into his business. He knows every aspect of it because at one time he actually did the work himself. Many of his first employees were his college classmates and teammates. Most of them are still with Under Armour and play important roles in management.

He spent five months driving round-trip from Baltimore to Moundsville at least twice a week to help Ella Mae Holmes produce and ship Under Armour products. He left Baltimore at 4 AM, arrived in Moundsville about 8 AM, and worked with Holmes and her boyfriend throughout the day. At 8 PM, Plank would take his shipment to the local FedEx office and drive back to Baltimore.[26]

Plank effectively uses his athletic experience and connections to help Under Armour's marketing and sales teams earn new business. In the athletic world, he is considered by his customers to be "one of them" rather than a CEO of a very profitable business. It frequently takes competitors years to develop a loyal customer, but Under Armour has been able to quickly earn loyalty after a customer has had one or two good experiences with their purchase. Most of the sports teams feel that Plank is truly helping them by providing a better product and not simply trying to sell his brand. Plank embraces and nurtures this connection respectfully and gracefully. He regularly seeks feedback regarding existing products and the need for new products.

Management Style

Having been part of a sports team, Plank manages his company with a unique team-driven style. "Under Armour is one team and my job is to help ensure we operate and execute as one team. Because there's a lot of noise and clutter surrounding our brand, I try to simplify our story and objectives for the team to help keep everyone running on the same wavelength and working towards the same goal: to become the world's number one performance athletic brand."[27]

To remind him of his critical role every day, Plank has written on a whiteboard in his office four things that define his job: (1) make a great product, (2) tell a great story about the product, (3) service the business, and (4) build a great team. Every morning when he arrives at the office and every evening before he leaves, he looks at the board. Plank said, "If I don't work toward those things, I'm not doing my job …. You can overcomplicate your job … It's important that you don't allow the clutter to grow too loud […] and distract you from your mission."[28]

International Leadership

In order to facilitate its international expansion, Under Armour hired several new executives with experience in international business, most notably Peter Mahrer. Mahrer was appointed as president and managing director for Under Armour Europe, B.V. Mahrer, a seasoned industry executive, will oversee Under Armour's European operations headquartered in Amsterdam. Mahrer previously served as head of international sales and general manager for Puma AG.[29]

Under Armour's Business Strategies

Ever since its inception in 1996, Under Armour's leaders have strived to achieve the company's vision of becoming the world's leading performance athletic apparel brand by employing a differentiation strategy through innovation. Under Armour attains physical differentiation through the value chain activities of technological development and procurement. As CEO Kevin Plank puts it, "The key driver is to offer products that are better than what is currently in the market, best in class."[30] Additionally, Under Armour is able to exploit psychological differentiation through its marketing campaign, which has hundreds of professional athletes that not only volunteer to wear Under Armour gear, but actually want to wear it. Most budding stars or wannabe weekend recreational athletes want to wear the gear the pros wear. Plank is fixated on maintaining differentiation from Nike, and uses "authenticity" as his guiding principal to grow or advertise the brand. Under Armour, for example, identifies

itself with team sports, rather than individual sports and fashion. "Everything we do is centered on performance … we aren't ever going to develop products to fill up a sales table," says Plank. Specifically, Under Armour will never use cotton to produce its clothing.[31]

Under Armour's corporate level strategy consists of a low level of diversification. While it does offer more than one product, 84 percent of its revenue comes from athletic apparel and gear. Incorporating a shoe line is helping the company with its diversification efforts, but it is still highly dependent upon premium priced products that are closely related. There is obviously a degree of economic risk associated with the premium pricing and Under Armour is feeling the effects of the current declining retail consumer market that is affecting the broader economy. Additionally, Under Armour is exposed to a degree of risk by offering closely related, nonessential products that are, to a degree, subject to the fashion whims of its customers. Plank said Under Armour is "cautiously optimistic about 2009" and is looking at the year with the "appropriate degree of conservatism."[32]

Under Armour added new domestic sales channels by introducing its first independent retail sales outlet in 2007 in Annapolis, Maryland. However, due to the conservative approach to growth in 2009, no new retail stores will be opened during the year.

Under Armour has placed major emphasis on international expansion. In addition to creating a broader consumer base, "Researchers have found that international diversification can lead to greater operational efficiency, which ultimately leads to higher financial performance."[33] Because its product transcends cultural differences and is appealing to many athletes, regardless of nationality, Under Armour is pursuing a worldwide scope via regionalization. Over the past three years, revenues from foreign sales other than Canada have increased at a rate of 100 percent per year and are expected to increase even more quickly with the international growth emphasis (Exhibit 3). Under Armour is fortunate because performance sports apparel appears to transcend any jingoistic trends and exporting does not require an in-depth knowledge of local customer service. Additionally, Under Armour's products are already manufactured overseas in China; therefore, the new offices in Europe are primarily geared toward marketing and distribution and do not have to contend with the challenges associated with establishing manufacturing plants in foreign countries.

Marketing

Under Armour's marketing strength is twofold. First, its products have proven to be so effective that professional athletes want to use them. Second, Under Armour has become a master of product placement in movies, TV shows, and video games.

Plank believes that word-of-mouth advertising is the most effective method. Plank has said, "We always build a product for the athlete's needs." The customer is willing to pay the price because the Under Armour product has value in it. "Without value, our product is just an expensive t-shirt. But we have the technology in the fabric [and] the design and the features satisfy what the athlete needs."[34] "Our model is getting to the athletes—supplying them with great product that helps them perform better."[35]

Athletes are a valuable marketing resource and the mouthpiece for Under Armour. The company signed a five-year partnership agreement in April 2009 with Cal Ripken, Jr., a retired professional baseball player, to be their official uniform representative. Under Armour feels this is a great opportunity because Ripken previously was partnered with Nike.[36] The company has reached out to capture much of the youth sports industry by sponsoring recreational teams and major youth tournaments, including the Under Armour All-America high school football and lacrosse games (see Exhibit 7).[37]

Under Armour has initiated other sponsorships that help get its name out in public, such as the Baltimore Marathon, which is now named the Under Armour Marathon. In an effort to boost the women's clothing line, Under Armour sponsored the women's U.S. field hockey team and some of the U.S. women's softball and volleyball athletes during the 2008 Olympic Games.[38]

During the first three months of 2008, Under Armour apparel appeared in cable shows nearly 3,000 times, more than any other company, according to Nielsen Media.[39] Ironically, movie studios are asking to use Under Armour's products as opposed to Under Armour having to purchase product placement time. The desire of athletes and movie studios to use Under Armour's products leads to a lower-cost, more effective, grass roots ad campaign. While Under Armour did sponsor its first Super Bowl commercial in 2008, the company will continue to use more guerrilla tactics than traditional expensive ad campaigns.

Strategic Challenges

Like most up-and-coming companies, Under Armour faces several issues and challenges. These challenges include the current economic downturn, competing against major rivals such as Nike and Adidas/Reebok, and maintaining a positive brand image despite setbacks, such as the recent recall of its men's protective athletic gear.[40] In addition, some of the most critical issues involve protection of the differentiation strategy, improvement of production and procurement capabilities, and continued implementation of a sound international expansion strategy.

Under Armour's differentiation strategy has been successful to date; however, the lack of proprietary product rights, intellectual property rights in foreign countries, and a heavy reliance on relatively few third-party suppliers and manufacturers could adversely affect the long-term sustainability of the firm. "The intellectual property rights in the technology, fabrics, and processes used to manufacture our products are generally owned by our suppliers and generally not unique to us."[41] The company's ability to obtain patent protection for its products is limited, and as previously mentioned it does not currently own any fabric or process patents.[42]

Intangible assets such as trademarks are very important to the Under Armour brand, as are licensing arrangements and other legal agreements. The intellectual property rights laws and regulations of countries in the global market vary dramatically. Under Armour relies heavily on suppliers and manufacturers outside of

Exhibit 7 Sponsorship and Other Marketing Commitments

(In thousands)	December 31
	2007
2008	$14,684
2009	14,660
2010	13,110
2011	10,125
2012 and thereafter	1,005
Total future minimum sponsorship and other marketing payments	$53,584

Source: 2008, Under Armour, Inc., Form 10-K 2007 Annual Report, December 31, 60.

the United States. Seventy to 75 percent of the fabric used in its products come from only six suppliers,[43] lending to Under Armour's weak position relative to its suppliers. Additionally, some of its supplies are commodities and thus are subject to price fluctuations; for example, petroleum-based materials are used in Under Armour's products and the petroleum industry has experienced significant swings in price and relative availability in recent months and years.[44]

Under Armour has achieved a level of success in the U.S. domestic market and limited foreign markets, but is relatively small in size and financial strength compared to its major competitors (Nike and Adidas) with similar or competing product offerings. Does Under Armour run the risk of diluting the brand relative to its competitors? Is an acquisition strategy feasible due to the company's current debt situation? Although a cooperative strategy may be beneficial to bridge barriers to entry into desirable markets such as China, how likely is it that Under Armour would pursue this option due to its emphasis on innovation and premium branding? Overall, has Under Armour done a good job in finding key strategic leaders with the experience necessary and does it have the right organization in place to help exe-

cute its international growth strategy? Going forward, how can it maintain the product quality that it has nurtured thus far?

Additional questions that Plank and other managers are pondering are: Can Under Armour maintain strong relationships with its suppliers so that it becomes the customer of choice? Should Under Armour pursue patents or strike agreements to limit the chance of competitors offering identical products? If so, will this effort actually be a defense or will counterfeit merchandise undermine such an investment? Does Under Armour possess appropriate supplier relationships and have an understanding of the inherent economic impacts on raw materials? If not, how will Under Armour acquire or develop these capabilities? What capabilities should Under Armour develop to ensure international success? What barriers to entry exist in additional markets, and is licensing or some other method the best approach based on its current cash position? Will the international strategy be different from Under Armour's overall differentiation and growth strategy? As its founder and CEO has stated, "Under Armour's success in 2010 and beyond will be significantly impacted by the decisions we make in 2009."[45]

NOTES

1. 2008, Investors Relations—About Under Armour, Inc., http://www.underarmour.com.
2. 2008, Five questions with Under Armour CEO, Kevin Plank, *Sports Business Journal*, http://www.sportsbusinessconferences.com/sss-pov/entries/2008/five-questions-with-kevin-plank, August 15.
3. Ibid.
4. Ibid.
5. S. Lyster, 2008, The history of Under Armour—A mastermind for performance apparel, http://www.ezinearticles.com, December 4.
6. 2008, Under Armour performance apparel, *Funding Universe*, http://www.fundinguniverse.com, December 4.
7. Ibid.
8. Ibid.
9. D. Rovell, 2005, Under Armour could offer up to $100 million in stock, http://sports.espn.go.com, August 26.
10. S. N. Mehta, 2009, Under Armour reboots: The sports apparel maker is sprinting into footwear—and trying to take on Nike—with the help of software and science, *Fortune*, http://www.money.cnn.com, March 5.
11. D. Kiley, 2008, Under Armour steps into footwear field: Sports apparel maker set to do battle with Nike and Adidas, *BusinessWeek*, http://www.businessweek.com, January 31.
12. Ibid.
13. 2008, Under Armour 10-K 2007 Annual Report, http://www.underarmour.com/annuals.cfm, February.
14. D. Kiley, 2008, Under Armour steps into footwear field.
15. A. K. Walker, 2009, New shoe helps Under Armour beat expectations, *Baltimore Sun*, http://www.baltimoresun.com, April 29.
16. S. N. Mehta, 2009, Under Armour reboots.
17. D. Kiley, Under Armour steps into footwear field.
18. 2008, Under Armour, *Hoovers*, http://premium.hoovers.com.ezproxy1.lib.asu.edu/subscribe/co/competitors.xhtml?ID=ffffjjjfkrrrhkxsxh.
19. 2008, Nike history, http://www.nikebiz.com/company_overview/history, December 4.
20. 2009, Nike company overview fact sheet, http://www.nikebiz.com; 2009, Nike pulling production from four Asian factories, *Reuters*, http://www.reuters.com, March 24.
21. 2008, Adidas group history, Adidas Group, http://www.adidas-group.com/en/overview/history/default.asp. December 4.
22. 2008, Columbia Sportswear, *Funding Universe*, http://www.fundinguniverse.com/company-histories/Columbia-Sportswear-Company-Company-History1.html, December 4.
23. 2008, http://www.sporthill.com, December 4.
24. M. Hyman, 2003, How I did it: Kevin Plank: For the founder of apparel-maker Under Armour, entrepreneurship is 99% perspiration and 1% polyester, *Inc.*, http://www.inc.com, December.
25. S. Graham, 2004, Kevin Plank's drive makes Under Armour an industry overachiever, *Sports Business Journal*, http://www.sportsbusinessjournal.com/article/36213, January 19.
26. Ibid.
27. 2008, Five questions with Under Armour CEO, Kevin Plank.
28. 2008, How do you define your job? *Business Management Daily*, http://www.businessmanagementdaily.com, November 8.
29. 2007, Under Armour appoints Peter Mahrer as president & managing director, Europe; Experienced sporting goods industry executive to lead sport performance brand's European growth strategy, Baltimore, MD, Under Armour press release, http://www.underarmour.com, July 9.
30. T. Heath, 2008, In pursuit of innovation at Under Armour: Founder Kevin Plank says Super Bowl commercial has generated "buzz," *Washington Post*, February 25, D03.

31. D. Kiley, 2009, Under Armour steps into footwear field.

32. R. Sharrow, 2009, Plank: Under Armour eyeing '09 "with appropriate degree of conservatism," *Baltimore Business Journal*, http://www.baltimore.bizjournals.com, January 29.

33. R. E. Hoskisson, M. Hitt, R. Ireland, & J. Harrison, 2008, *Competing for Advantage*, Thomson Southwestern, 286.

34. 2007, I am, Video interview with Kevin Plank, *CNBC*, http://www.cnbc.com/id/25191722, September 11.

35. M. Hyman, 2003, How I did it: Kevin Plank.

36. R. Sharrow, 2009, Under Armour, Ripken Baseball swing for fences with sportswear pact, *Baltimore Business Journal*, http://www.baltimore.bizjournals.com, April 22.

37. R. Sharrow, 2009, Cal Ripken Jr. nears deal to promote Under Armour, *Baltimore Business Journal*, http://www.baltimore.bizjournals.com, March 20.

38. R. Sharrow, 2008, Under Armour entering an Olympic contest of its own, *Baltimore Business Journal*, http://www.baltimore.bizjournals.com, August 1.

39. A. K. Walker, 2008, Under Armour in public eye, *The Baltimore Sun*, July 24.

40. J. Alper, 2009, Under Armour recalls 200,000 cups: Injuries involve cutting and bruising, *NBC New York Sports*, http://www.nbcnewyork.com/sports, April.

41. 2007, Under Armour, Inc., Form 10-K Annual Report, http://investor.underarmour.com, December 31, 18.

42. Ibid.

43. 2008, Under Armour, Inc., Form 8-K, http://investor.underarmour.com, 6.

44. Ibid.

45. R. Sharrow, 2009, Plank: Under Armour eyeing '09 with appropriate degree of conservatism.

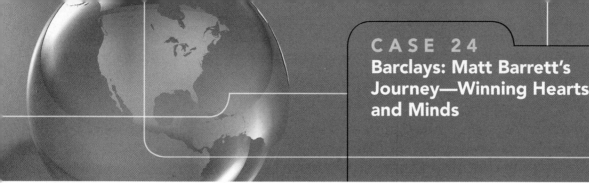

Mtina Buechel

IMD–International Institute for Management Development

Late October, 2001, Matt Barrett, CEO of Barclays, was preparing for a seminal event that was to take place the following week. After 24 months in office, he was comtemplating how best to introduce the Group strategy that he had developed with Marakon Associates to the wider organization.

According to Barrett, his key challenge in transforming Barclays was to move it from a large U.K. bank dabbling overseas to a global bank which happened to have a strong U.K. franchise. Barrett's aim was to improve Barclays's performance rapidly and significantly so it could be a predator and not a victim in the industry consolidation that he felt sure was coming.

From the start, he had worked on changing the mind-set and culture of Barclays. His next step was to try to convince the top 100 company executives that the current model for running the business was inadequate for reaching its goals. He passionately believed that a more fact-based, value-growth orientation to running Barclays was essential. This event was key to ensuring that Barclays's new management model would be widely used within the businesses across the Group.

Barclays History

The history of Barclays dates to 1690 when John Freame and Thomas Gould started trading as Goldsmith bankers on Lombard Street in London. In 1896, the company joined with 19 other private banking businesses to form a new joint-stock bank called Barclay and Company Limited. Almost 30 years later, Barclays began its global expansion. In 1981, it became the first foreign bank to file with the Securities and Exchange Commission in Washington, D.C.

After years of expansion, including the acquisitions of the stockbrokers De Zoete & Bevan in 1986 and Wells Fargo Nikko Investment Advisors in 1995,

Barclays faced a leadership challenge. Between 1995 and 1999, Barclays had five different CEOs. In October 1999, Barclays appointed Matt Barrett, a Canadian/Irish citizen who had been the CEO of the Bank of Montreal for the previous decade. Matt was enjoying his retirement when he received the invitation to run Barclays and saw it as a great opportunity. Having been in the financial services industry from the start of his career, Matt had deep vocational knowledge about how a bank, with its multiple businesses and functions, works.

Business Overview

In 2000, Barclays PLC was one of the four dominant retail and commercial banks in the United Kingdom. It was the ninth-largest bank in Europe by assets, with total assets exceeding £320 billion.

The Group consisted of four divisions, of which Retail Financial Services contributed 61 percent of earnings (see Exhibit 1). Its retail franchise included direct relationships with one in five personal customers in the United Kingdom.

In the corporate banking market, Barclays had a direct relationship with more than 25 percent of U.K. businesses, which it served via a network of more than 1,200 relationship managers.

In 1997, Barclays sold the cash, equities, and corporate finance businesses from its investment banking division—Barclays de Zoete Wedd—to Credit Suisse First Boston. As a result, by 2000, the rebranded Barclays Capital had become a collection of sub-scale businesses united by a focus on debt products.

In 2000, Barclays Global Investors (BGI) offered advanced active and indexed asset management services to about 1,800 institutional clients in 36 countries. It introduced the world's first index fund and was managing £529 billion of assets.

Professor Mtina Buechel wrote this case as a basis for class discussion rather than to illustrate either effective or ineffective handling of a business situation.

Exhibit 1 Barclays PLC Corporate Structure (2000)

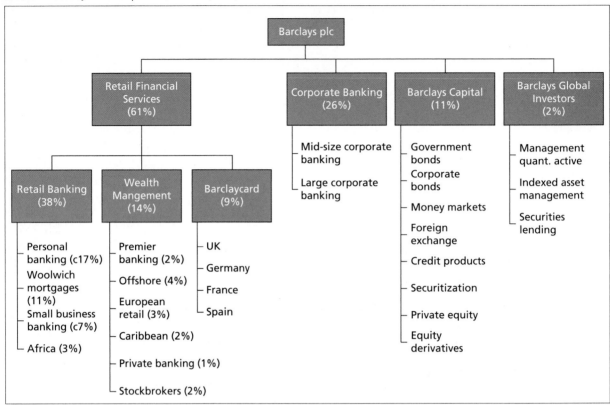

Note: Percentages represent estimated earnings contributions, including pro forma Woolwich.

Source: Company data and Credit Lyonnais Securities Europe estimates.

By 2000, 78 percent of Group revenue and 80 percent of Group profits came from the United Kingdom. Continental Europe generated 10 percent of sales and profits, primarily from high-net-worth retail banking operations in Spain, France, and Portugal. The United States and various African businesses generated the remaining balance.

Situation Assessment

When Barrett joined Barclays, he came across an organization that, according to him, had lost confidence due to years of underperformance and several significant corporate crises. During the 20 years leading up to Matt's arrival, the bank executed 57 divestitures and only two acquisitions. Barclays's global market capitalization rank had fallen from four in 1980 to 22 in 2000 (see Exhibit 2). As a result, predators were circling the company as a potential takeover target and the investor community was increasingly losing patience.

Barclays had lost its way—it had gone from "one of the best" to "one of the rest." Given a prolonged period of underperformance and revolving doors for CEOs, Barclays had become an easy target for the media. Institutional investors were unhappy, employees were demoralized, and the front-line and senior executives had lost confidence. There was at base, however, a great brand and reputation as well as a strong domestic franchise.

Exhibit 2 Barclay's Market Capitalization Rank*

	1980	1985	1990	1995	2000
Rank*	4	13	13	19	22
Mkt Cap (£ bn)	2.0	3.4	7.4	12.4	34.3

*Barclays's rank among the top 100 financial services players globally for any given calendar year.

Source: Marakon Associates.

The Group had no coherent strategic plan, ineffective performance standards and woefully inadequate MIS [management information systems]. We had very little indication where we were losing money and where value was being created. It was like flying a 747 without any controls—exhilarating but life-threatening.

—**MATT BARRETT**

One of Barrett's early discoveries was the excessive cost base. For more than 10 years, Barclays had struggled to make significant inroads into reducing its cost base. By 2000, its cost to income ratio was significantly higher than that of competitors (see Exhibit 3). Part of the reason for the excessive cost base was that divisions set up their own HR, IT, and finance divisions to protect themselves from erratic Group governance. Barrett quickly realized that he had a major task ahead of him—to clean up management incompetence and fix the core infrastructure. Indeed, he soon realized that the bank needed a shift in culture and mind-set, a new strategic direction, a structural overhaul, and an improved communications policy.

Building the Foundation

During his first three months in office, Barrett engaged with employees throughout the Group in what he termed "open forums." These were sessions of two to three hours where he would meet up to 1,000 employees from various functions and hierarchical levels. These sessions would typically start with Barrett summarizing his understanding of the current situation. He would then take questions from the audience. In an effort to prepare the organization for the changes he wanted to make, he would also pose provocative questions to his employees, such as "Do you feel that there are people in your area who do not pull their weight?" and "Is it fair that these people are paid the same as you are?" Barrett met approximately 10,000 employees during this initial three-month period to transmit the message that everyone was in this transformation together. There were no second-class citizens.

At the same time, Barrett developed his own vision for the bank—"earn, invest, and grow." He planned to double Barclays's economic profit in four years.[1] In order to finance growth, he planned to reduce costs by £1 billion (from a cost base of £5.5 billion). He emphasized that the money saved from cost reductions created an opportunity for people to shape their destiny, as they could decide which business areas were worth investing in.

In February 2000, six months after Barrett became CEO, the first top 100 executive event was organized in Brighton. Barrett spoke to the group about his vision for the future and explained the company's new financial and strategic goals. These goals were met with skepticism. As one top executive reflected, "I was initially thinking, if I keep my head down, this too will pass." To those who thought the challenge was too great, Barrett's approach was sympathetic but unyielding. Barrett said, "I recognized that it was a significant challenge, and I

Exhibit 3 Barclays Operating Expense as a Percentage of Income in Comparison with Competition

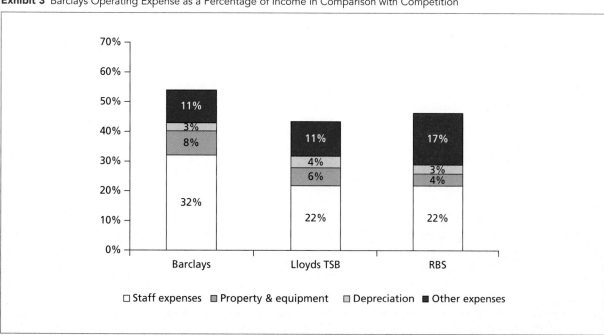

Source: Credit Lyonnais Securities Europe, 2000.

told them that each and every one could count on my support, but that the goal was non-negotiable."

A week later, Barrett publicly committed to these goals to ensure that there would be no scaling back of the commitments. The organization and the top team, while skeptical, were now on the hook to deliver. The goals were to apply equally to him, top management, and everyone in the organization.

Changes at the Top

Barrett started by focusing on his direct reports and spelling out what he believed in—sincerity, encouraging people to take risks, and learning from mistakes. He led as if he had to be reelected the next day. He had to show that he was deeply involved and that he cared.

Barrett quickly turned his sights to realigning the mind-set, and, ultimately, the composition of the top team. He felt that the executive committee (ExCo) was not performing as decision makers but as an administrative body. Each meeting seemed more like a series of bilateral discussions with the CEO than multilateral, high performance dialogues.

At an early ExCo dinner, while the team was having its appetizers, Barrett launched into a direct discussion. He suddenly said he was thinking of disbanding the ExCo meetings if he couldn't make them more productive. There was silence in the room. The team seemed shocked at the prospect of having a FTSE 100 firm that was no longer run by an ExCo (and of each potentially losing his seat at the top table). The team came out vocally against Barrett's proposal and immediately took up his challenge—from then on, their commitment to making the ExCo work became a shared goal. This was reflected in the decision to make co-managing the Barclays Group the primary task of the ExCo and managing their business unit responsibilities the second task. To reflect this change, Barrett realigned ExCo members' rewards, placing more weight on overall company results.

With respect to team composition, Barrett rapidly engineered significant changes on the ExCo. His aim was to undermine opposition to change by bringing in new perspectives and disconnecting existing members from their traditional power bases. Gary Dibb, who had worked for the Bank of Montreal, soon followed Barrett and became the chief administrative officer. John Varley was appointed Group finance director and given ExCo responsibility for delivering cost, productivity, and economic profit goals. This appointment, in particular, was an important step toward building broad organizational confidence in the Group's ability to deliver on its new goals. By spending significant time with the top 100, Barrett was also able to spot and promote young talent to the ExCo, including Gary Hoffman and David Roberts,

who in their late thirties, considerably reduced the average age of the top team.

From an investor's perspective, changes to the senior management team raised concerns about pace and velocity of change. It was, however, positively viewed by equity analysts, such as Credit Lyonnais: "Barclays is undergoing a significant process of change that requires a fresh look and innovative solutions. It can only be assisted by a new senior team."

Gaining Confidence

In October 2000, Barclays acquired Woolwich, a leading mortgage business in the United Kingdom, for £5.4 billion. The acquisition expanded Barclays's product and service portfolio and strengthened an area in which Barclays was weak—residential mortgages. As Barclays had primarily divested in the last 20 years, another purpose of this acquisition was just to show that Barclays could *grow*, not just divest. The Woolwich CEO, John Stewart, moved into Barclays to head Retail.

Value-Based Management Underpins Strategy Development

In the second half of 2000, Barclays Strategic Planning Group, on behalf of the ExCo, reviewed bids from potential advisors to accelerate both the understanding of value and the push for value growth. As Matt Barrett reflected afterwards: "We needed to have tools to make fact-based decisions. There was no cross-organizational discussion of value-adding activities. Barclays was run as four separate pillars and each had its own head office. I used to joke that I was never lonely at the top—there were dozens of 'CEOs.'"

After reviewing the proposals, Barrett and the ExCo decided to work with Marakon Associates, the advisory firm that pioneered "managing for value." Barrett knew Marakon well as he had worked successfully with the company when he was at the Bank of Montreal. Marakon and the ExCo set about looking at all businesses and activities from a value perspective, identifying where value was being created and where it was being destroyed. By assessing all businesses, the supertanker was broken down into a "flotilla of highly maneuverable speedboats," or 20 to 25 smaller value-creating entities, which could be analyzed and managed. The goal was to enable a thorough analysis of each business's potential contribution to the Group.

The value-based approach to developing and delivering strategy was applied within each business. At ExCo meetings, each of the four divisional heads was asked to present two or three alternatives for each business. Each of these strategic options was to be grounded in analysis of industry and company data. Varley characterized the environment as follows: "We are having to up our game, and that is pulling lots of us out of our comfort zones …. All the time we are asking: What makes money and what doesn't? Where are the weaknesses in the business? It had a profound effect— energizing and clarifying …."

As one of the outcomes, it was expected that every investment decision—whether a project, geographic expansion, or new product introduction—presented to the ExCo would have to be assessed using the new value-based management approach. Implicitly, this led to an evaluation of every manager and business unit leader in that sound reasoning had to be used as the foundation for every strategic decision. This method was wildly unpopular at first because it challenged the managers' beliefs. However, as Barnett noted, "We needed to institutionalize the approach. Every meeting we ran had to involve the same questions. Only then would it become part of the DNA."

In the analyst community, the change in management approach did not go unnoticed. As Commerzbank's James Alexander commented: "Value-based management depends on risks and expected profitability, bad debts, and your view of the economy. It's still an art rather than a science. It doesn't entirely help avoid mistakes, but it makes the decision-making process more rigorous."

Developing the Group Strategy

Under Barnett's leadership, and with the help of Marakon's systematic, fact-based approach, the ExCo developed a long-term strategic direction during the first half of 2001. Five full-day ExCo meetings were devoted to debating and agreeing upon a Group strategy. In addition, key opinion formers from across the organization were engaged to provide input and challenge. This resulted in a new strategic direction that called for change along multiple dimensions, including:

- Greater presence outside the United Kingdom, complementing continued strong growth within the U.K. market.

- Greater diversity of sources of economic profit across different product/customer markets, with a greater contribution from asset accumulation and capital markets.
- Growth driven by a more balanced combination of organic and acquisitive moves.
- Selected businesses with full global reach (e.g., Barclays Capital and Barclays Global Investors) leading the way and complementing strong "local" businesses (e.g., UK Retail/Commercial).
- Greater bias of Barclays's personal customer base toward the highly profitable affluent and high-net-worth segments.
- Strongly differentiated customer offers with clearly articulated value for clients, supported by a strong brand and improved distribution, sales, and information.

To drive change, a series of medium-term themes and near-term priorities were developed. As an example, one of the near-term priorities was to develop a "second home market" in continental Europe. This was part of a broader theme to change Barclays's European franchise. Another priority was to expand capital market activities as part of a broader theme to establish world-class global product/customer businesses.

Each of the near-term priorities had a value creation goal attached to it and was led by an ExCo sponsor who had full responsibility for delivering on expectations.

Implementing the Group Strategy

The work with Marakon led to the formal articulation of a Group strategy (see Exhibit 4). In October 2001, this Group strategy was disseminated at the "top 100" meeting in Canary Wharf. Barnett had achieved buy-in from the eight ExCo members, but how would the wider organization receive the Group strategy?

Exhibit 4 Group Strategy Framework

Objective of Our Group Strategy

Our overarching Group Strategy objective is to maximize the economic value of the Group. Accordingly, our Group Strategy has been developed using our value-based strategy development framework and standards.

Components of Our Group Strategy

Our Group Strategic Direction ("Where we are heading")
+Our View of the Future
+Long-Term Direction (5–10 years)
+Medium-Term Strategic Themes (next 2–5 years)
+Near-Term Priorities (next 12 months)

(Continued)

Exhibit 4 Group Strategy Framework (*Continued*)

Our Group Management Model ("How we will run the business")

Group Goals

Our aspiration is to deliver top quartile Total Shareholder Returns vs. our peers over time. However, we do not believe we will be able to continue to deliver against a four-year double-value goal over a 10-year period from our existing business portfolio. As a result, we expect to face a "value gap" in 2010 in the region of £40 billion (£16 billion in today's money) of incremental value creation (as opposed to market capitalization)—broadly equivalent to adding another business of the size of Barclays today over the next 10 years. We expect an economic profit gap of at least £1.5 billion in 2010.

Group Structure

The Group ExCo will have greater involvement in managing cross-Group synergies and "top-down" strategy development; the recent restructuring of the Group into the current model of Clusters, SBUs, and SSUs (Shared Service Units), and the acquisition of Woolwich reflect this evolution.

Group Mission, Beliefs, Practices, and Behaviors

We aspire to be one of the most admired financial services organizations in the world, recognized as an innovative, customer-focused company that delivers superb products and services, ensures excellent careers for our people and contributes positively to the communities in which we live and work. In addition, there are 18 beliefs and practices that outline more specifically the expected operating mode, e.g. Practice 14: We ensure all decisions are fact-based and value-maximizing through our strategy development and agenda management processes. The management team defined an acceptable set of behaviors for the Group. These were—Drive Performance, Build Pride and Passion, Delight Customers, Grow Talent and Capability, Execute at Speed, and Protect and Enhance our Reputation.

Group Decision Rules

Rule 1: Select the strategy/investment alternative which creates the highest economic value (EV).

Rule 2: Select the EV alternative if it meets or exceeds Group/SBU goals for EV, economic profit (EP),[1] and cosW savings.

Rule 3: Select the EV alternative if it is aligned with the Group Strategic Direction.

Rule 4: Select the highest EV if it is aligned with the Group Management Model.

Rule 5: Select the highest EV alternative if it complies with the Group operating policies and standards (e.g., brand, risk, compliance).

Source: Framework developed by Marakon Associates for Barclays.

NOTE

1. Economic profit = net profit after tax less the equity charge, a risk-weighted cost of capital.

*Analia Anderson, Jake Johnson, Pauline Pham,
Adam Schwartz, Richard Till, Craig Vom Lehn,
Elena Wilkening*

Arizona State University

Air transportation powers the U.S. economy—this is an industry that drives economic and social development. Air transportation is a critical part of our nation's infrastructure and should play a vital role in our country's economic recovery ... enabling our cities and smaller communities to connect and compete domestically and globally. It is, therefore, hugely ironic that we enable such economic and business development in the United States—to the tune of more than $1 trillion a year and contribut[ing] some 5 percent of GDP—but have historically and systemically been incapable of earning our cost of capital.

—GLEN TILTON, CHAIRMAN, PRESIDENT, AND CEO OF UNITED AIRLINES[1]

In early 2009, the U.S. economy was mired in its worst recession since the Great Depression. With airline industry business cycles closely mirroring larger economic trends, United Airlines felt the effects of the downturn. United, the fourth-largest U.S. passenger airline, lost more than $5 billion in 2008 and reported further declines in both revenue and traffic in the first quarter of 2009.[2] Even before the economy soured, United managed only minimal profits in 2006 and 2007, which were considered great years for the U.S. airline industry. Prior to that, the company spent three years in Chapter 11 bankruptcy protection as a result of losses early in the decade. In addition, United encountered challenges related to expanding service internationally, introducing subsidiaries in an effort to compete with low-cost carriers (LCCs), and maintaining positive relations with its employees and the unions that represent its employees. Thus, more than just waiting for economic recovery, United is exploring tactics to become profitable again and reclaim the image and success it once experienced.

Early History

United Air Lines, Inc. came into existence in 1931 to provide mail service and passenger transport.[3] United was born uniquely national, with Eastern and Western subsidiaries, and diversified by virtue of its ownership of Boeing Air Transport, an aircraft manufacturer.[4] Early growth in the fledgling industry was funded largely by U.S. government payments for mail service. When accusations of collusion arose from the allocation of routes by the postal service, the government stepped in to regulate both the process and the industry.[5] The resulting Civil Aeronautics Act of 1938 transferred power over route allocation to the newly created Civil Aeronautics Authority,[6] which required United to divest Boeing and several airports it owned, but awarded the company "grandfather certificates on U.S. transcontinental and West Coast routes it was operating when the law took effect."[7]

Like most airlines, United prospered and grew under government regulation. Pricing was regulated, and approval from government regulators was required for an airline to enter or exit a particular route.[8] While the market for passenger travel grew significantly after World War II, artificially high prices limited air travel to wealthier travelers and businessmen. Under regulatory protection, carriers developed hub-and-spoke networks that allowed them to centralize operations and provide convenient connections to passengers. The beginnings of United's network can be seen in Exhibit 1, which shows the airline's route map in 1940. Hubs in Chicago, San Francisco, and Los Angeles were beginning to take shape. Eventually they would be joined by hubs in Denver and Washington D.C.[9] Larger airports often were dominated by one or two carriers, such as United in Denver and Chicago.[10] As a result of regulation

Exhibit 1 United Air Lines Route Map, 1940

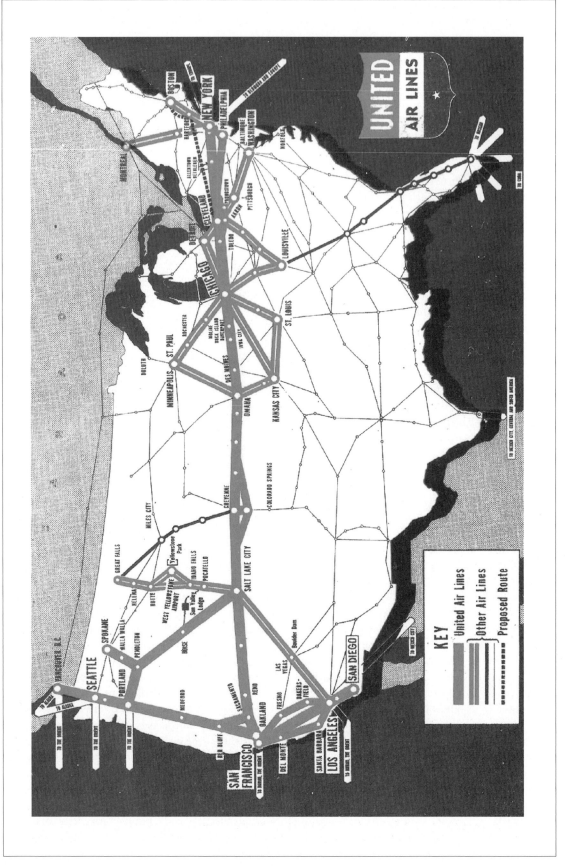

Source: United Air Lines Route 1940, Wikipedia, http://en.wikipedia.org.

and network distribution, competition was restrained, with carriers making small but reliable profits based on the uniqueness of their networks and the convenience of schedules and connections, but deregulation changed all of this.

Deregulation

In 1978, the passage of the Airline Deregulation Act eliminated government oversight of routes and fees, allowing carriers to compete along a much broader range of parameters.[11] Deregulation brought about a glut of new airlines "causing airfares to plummet 40 percent in real terms between 1978 and 1997."[12] For United and its competitors, business cycles have been much more dramatic under deregulation, with profits in years when the economy is strong and heavy losses when it is weak.[13] Along with the challenges came opportunities for expansion. United secured its first Trans-Pacific route in 1983 and subsequently purchased 13 additional Asian routes from the ailing Pan American Airways.[14] In 1990, the company launched service to Europe, and in 1992 it operated flights to South America.[15] By 1995, with the introduction of service to Mumbai, India, United could advertise that it offered "Round the World" service.[16]

Although United was taking advantage of the opportunities that deregulation made possible, the company was struggling with the higher oil prices that resulted from the Persian Gulf War and the emergence of successful low-cost carriers such as Southwest Airlines. By the early 1990s, United was losing money. In 1993, the company attempted to remedy its financial problems by exchanging $5.15 billion of salaries and benefits with its employees for a 53 percent stake in the company.[17] As a result, in 1994, United became the "largest majority employee-owned corporation in the world."[18] Also in 1994, United launched "Shuttle by United" to compete against the low-cost carriers in the western United States; however, in 2001 when air travel diminished and cost savings had not materialized, the Shuttle was assimilated back into the main business.[19] Business took a sharp turn for the worse at the beginning of the new millennium when United declared bankruptcy and confronted other challenges.

Bankruptcy and Beyond

At the end of 2001, United recorded a $2.1 billion loss, the largest in airline history. With losses continuing to mount, United, under newly appointed CEO Glenn Tilton, filed for Chapter 11 bankruptcy protection in December 2002.[20]

Under bankruptcy protection, the company restructured its labor contracts and defaulted on its employee pension plan. United took out a $3 billion loan from investment banks in order to gain approval to exit bankruptcy, which it did on[21] February 1, 2006.[22] The timing was auspicious for the company as the U.S. economy was once again on the rise and airlines, including United, earned profits in 2006 and 2007.[23] The good times came to an end in 2008, however, as the U.S. economy slipped into recession, and United posted its largest-ever loss of $5.2 billion.[24]

In an unusual move for a bankrupt company, United also formed a new business line called Ted, which was a second attempt at creating a low-cost subsidiary.[25] Ted failed to meet expectations and the company announced its closure in 2008.[26]

Company executives have tried to reposition the company since 2006. United bid to merge with Delta in 2007[27] and with both Continental[28] and US Airways in 2008, but none of these negotiations were successful.[29] United was forced to make significant cuts once again, and by June 2008 the company had announced plans to ground 70 planes, eliminate 950 pilot positions, and cut up to 1,600 salaried positions.

While United has suffered many trials since deregulation, it has managed to survive. Many airlines have not been so fortunate, as competition in the airline industry is intense.

Competition

Within the last 30 years the airline industry has undergone significant contraction, as healthier carriers acquired failing competitors or their assets. Exhibit 2 shows the 51 mergers and acquisitions that brought the airline industry to its current state.[30] Six airlines now control 71.4 percent of the U.S. market (see Exhibit 3). The top six carriers consist of five traditional carriers—American, Continental, Delta, United, and US Airways—along with Southwest, the most successful of the LCCs (Exhibit 4 shows relevant financial data).

Competition is becoming more intense among the traditional carriers because the amount of business travel is decreasing.[31] Among the factors contributing to the decline in business travel are the use of videoconferencing, e-mail, and other Internet-based interactive technologies that make it easy to convey information without a face-to-face meeting.[32] Even more significant, perhaps, are cuts in corporate expenditures and increased governance, which lead to fewer approved trips and more price sensitivity among business travelers. The end result of this shift is that "the leisure segment of demand now constitutes the dominant one in air transport today."[33]

The similarities between United and its major competitors (excluding Southwest Airlines) are far greater

Exhibit 2 The Evolution of the U.S. Airline Industry

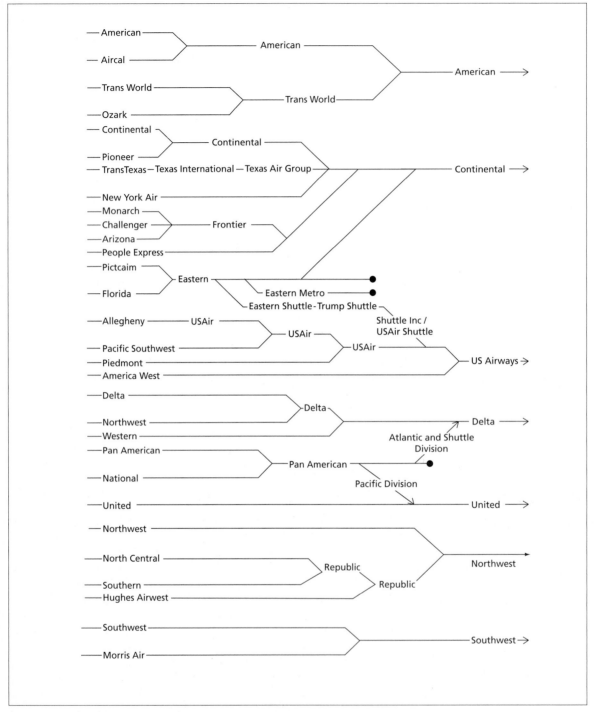

Source: B. Vasigh, K. Fleming, & T. Tacker, 2008, *Introduction to Air Transport Economics*, Ashgate Publishing, 16.

than their differences. All operate a hub-and-spoke route network, seeking to efficiently transfer passengers across the country. They all run a mainline service with large jets and extend their reach through networks of regional affiliates and global alliances. They all focus on the business traveler, offering service upgrades and frequent flyer loyalty programs to appeal to the business segment of the market. These companies differ, however, in their history, size, and hub locations.

American Airlines

Founded in 1934 as the Robertson Aircraft Corporation, American Airlines has grown from a small airmail service to one of the largest passenger airlines with 84,000

Exhibit 3 Airline Domestic Market Share, March 2009

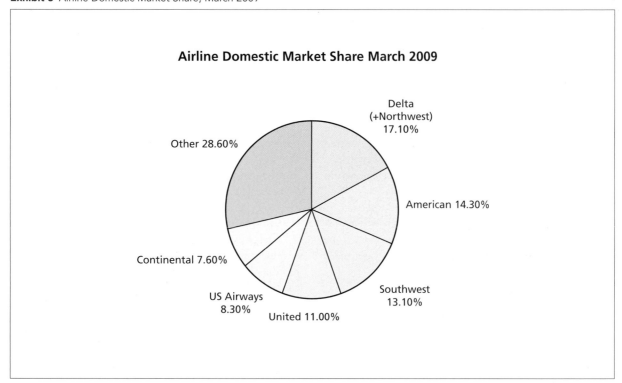

Source: 2009, Chart by authors, data from RITA, http://www.transtats.bts.gov.

Exhibit 4 Comparison of Net Profits between United and Top Competitors

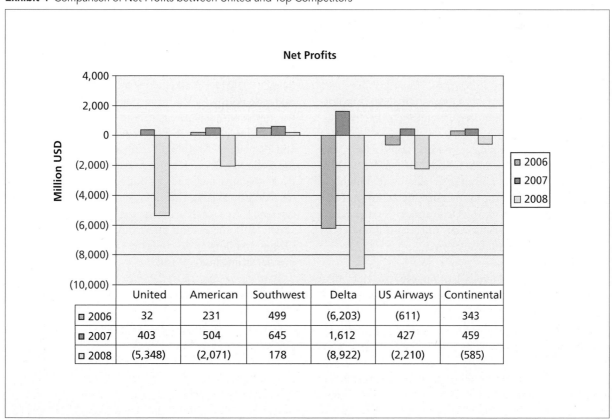

	United	American	Southwest	Delta	US Airways	Continental
2006	32	231	499	(6,203)	(611)	343
2007	403	504	645	1,612	427	459
2008	(5,348)	(2,071)	178	(8,922)	(2,210)	(585)

Source: 2009, Chart by authors using data from the 2008 10-K reports of each company.

employees and a fleet of 900 aircraft.[34] From its corporate headquarters in Dallas and additional major hubs in Chicago, St. Louis, and Miami the company transports 270,000 passengers on 3,300 flights to 250 domestic and international destinations every day.[35] Like most traditional carriers, American operates a mainline business serving larger cities and a regional affiliate network (American Eagle) serving smaller airports. American Eagle accounts for 300 of American's planes, flying 1,800 daily flights to 150 destinations in the United States and the Carribean.[36] American's network is further extended by its participation in the Oneworld global airline alliance.

American is the only large traditional domestic carrier that has not filed for bankruptcy, narrowly avoiding this fate in 2003.[37] In 2008, the company posted the fourth-largest loss among domestic carriers, just under $2.1 billion.[38]

Continental Airlines. Unlike American, Continental Airlines has filed for bankruptcy protection twice—once in 1983 and again in 1990.[39] Since the second bankruptcy, the company's fortunes have improved significantly, leading *Fortune* to name Continental, "The World's Most Admired Airline" for five years running.[40] While several competitors posted multi-billion dollar losses in 2008, Continental's loss was modest by comparison, $585 million.[41]

Continental and its regional affiliates, Continental Express, Continental Micronesia, and Continental Connection, fly more than 2,600 flights per day to 265 domestic and international destinations using a network based on hubs located in Newark, Houston, Cleveland, and Guam.[42] Continental has more than 42,000 employees, 44 percent of whom are covered by collective bargaining agreements.[43]

In 2007, Continental entered into merger talks with United Airlines. The talks subsequently failed to produce a merger, but did result in an alliance that involved Continental terminating its membership in the SkyTeam global alliance (anchored by Delta and Air France KLM) and becoming part of the Star Alliance dominated by United, Lufthansa, and US Airways.[44]

Delta Airlines. Founded in Georgia in 1924 by a cropduster named Huff Daland, Delta's first decades of operation were dominated by agricultural and public service flights, with the majority of its domestic flights dedicated to mail handling, and then for military purposes during World War II.[45]

From the 1940s through the late twentieth century, Delta aggressively pursued a differentiation strategy, known for its innovation and contribution to the art and science of aviation. There were many "firsts" for Delta,

such as being the first airline to offer night service, the first to employ interchange service among flight attendants, the first airline to transport living vegetables and plants, the first airline to use the Douglass DC-8 and DC-9 (which would become standard in the industry for decades), and the first to offer passengers an in-flight telephone system (Airfone). In 1962, Delta had the quickest flight time from coast to coast (Atlanta to Los Angeles); its record time of just less than three hours remains the fastest cross-country passenger flight to date. The hub-and-spoke system was Delta's innovation that improved passenger plane transfers with coordinated flight arrival and departure times.[46]

However, this airline giant has experienced financial trouble in recent years. In September 2005, Delta Airlines filed for Chapter 11 bankruptcy.[47] Goodwill and deferred tax asset write-offs, significant declines in passenger miles, and high fuel costs led management to conclude that "… these results underscore the urgent need to make fundamental changes in the way we do business."[48] A more fundamental shift in industry strategy, however, seemed to underlie the firm's demise. The continued growth of low-cost carriers, intense competitive rivalry within the industry (most notably increased price sensitivity), and increased customer use of the Internet for travel information challenged Delta's differentiation strategy that was framed around exceptional customer service and innovative aviation.

To counter the increasing threats to its firm, Delta finalized its merger with Northwest Airlines in October 2008. Although the combined organization lost $8.9 billion in 2008,[49] Delta hopes to obtain three major benefits from the merger: (1) larger market share by including Northwest's mid- and northwest U.S. routes, along with its Asia routes; (2) improved financial capacity to sustain cyclical downturns in the economy and associated volatility in fuel costs; and (3) synergy of resources created by the combination of the Delta SkyMiles and Northwest WorldPerks frequent flyer programs, facilitated by both airlines membership in the SkyTeam alliance (including over 20 other commercial carriers).[50] As a result of the merger, Delta offers the largest variety of domestic and international commercial routes (378 destinations in 66 countries) and is the largest commercial airline in the world.[51]

US Airways. Headquartered in Tempe, AZ, US Airways is the nation's fifth-largest airline. It employs over 33,000 people and has more than 3,000 departures a day using a fleet of 351 mainline and 299 express aircraft serving 155 domestic and 46 international destinations in 27 different countries from its major hubs in Phoenix, Charlotte, and Philadelphia.[52]

As a result of its acquisition by America West Airlines in September 2005, US Airways avoided filing a second bankruptcy in three years and inevitable liquidation.[53] The new US Airways (under the America West leadership team and CEO Doug Parker) was able to offer "more non-stop flights and better connecting service than either the West-Coast-oriented America West or the old, East-Coast-centric US Airways had before," and even "branded [itself] as 'America's largest low cost carrier.'"[54] The post-merger airline earned $427 million in profit on reported $11.7 billion in revenue in 2007 and $304 million on $11.6 billion in revenue in 2006. The firm reported a net loss of $2.2 billion on increased revenue of $12.1 billion in 2008.[55]

As with many of its competitors, US Airways relies on its regional affiliate, US Airways Express, to provide jet service to passengers traveling in and out of the smaller airports across the country, as well as flying during off-peak hours when it becomes inefficient to operate a larger jet.[56] In addition, US Airways is a member of the Star Alliance, which provides customers with even more access to various destinations across the globe without additional costs for the airline.[57]

US Airways competes on price, flight availability, and level of service provided with both low-cost carriers such as Southwest and AirTran, and full service traditional airlines such as American, Delta, and United.[58] The weakened state of the U.S. economy, a higher operating cost structure than that of true low-cost carriers, and fluctuations in fuel prices make it extremely difficult for the airline to earn profits on an annual basis. In fact, according to the airline officials, "one cent per gallon change in fuel prices will result in a $14 million increase/decrease in annual fuel expense."[59] However, US Airways is determined to be successful by providing the best customer service. But according to the 2008 American Customer Satisfaction survey conducted by the University of Michigan, the airline only scored 59 out 100 and thus has significant room for improvement in this regard.[60]

Southwest Airlines. Founded in 1971, Southwest Airlines introduced a new business model in the U.S. airline industry. It originally flew only intra-state routes in Texas, allowing it to operate outside the price and route regulations inter-state carriers faced.[61] Thus it was able to focus on providing low-cost no-frills travel to price-conscious consumers. When the industry was deregulated in 1978, Southwest began to expand beyond the borders of Texas. By 2007, Southwest had carried nearly 102 million passengers, more than any other airline in the world.[62] At the end of 2008, the company had a fleet of 500 Boeing 737 aircraft that flew 3,300 flights to 65 U.S. cities daily.[63]

Unlike its traditional competitors, Southwest does not rely on a hub-and-spoke network, using instead a point-to-point service between medium and large metropolitan areas.[64] Southwest minimizes costs by standardizing its fleet to reduce training and maintenance expenses, by using secondary airports that charge lower access fees, and by minimizing downtime for both aircraft and employees.[65] While traditional hub-and-spoke networks attempt to coordinate hub arrivals to facilitate shorter layovers for passengers, Southwest makes regular, frequent flights throughout the day. The result is a flatter demand for labor (less peaks and valleys) and higher aircraft utilization because of turnarounds that take half as long as the industry average.[66]

The customer experience on Southwest is described as "no-frills" because the company uses first-come, first-served seating and does not provide complimentary meal service. Southwest was also a pioneer in online bookings, e-ticketing, and self-check kiosks, reducing the cost of the ticketing and check-in process.[67]

Although "no-frills" might indicate a lack of commitment to service, industry statistics and surveys confirm that passengers feel otherwise. In fact, "Southwest Airlines has consistently received the lowest ratio of complaints per passengers boarded of all major U.S. carriers that have been reporting statistics to the Department of Transportation (DOT) since September 1987."[68]

The company earned profits during every year from 1975 to 2008, including recessionary periods in the early 1990s and 2000s when traditional carriers suffered losses.[69] In 2008, while every major traditional U.S. carrier posted a loss, Southwest turned a profit of $178 million.[70] The extent of the threat posed by Southwest and its model is evident in the number of low-cost carriers that have been launched around the world and the extent to which traditional carriers have tried to change their business models in direct response to the growth of low-cost airlines. Primarily, traditional carriers have tried combating low-cost carriers by creating "low-cost" subsidiaries of their own. American Airlines is the only major competitor to avoid this temptation.

Southwest has not posed a threat in regard to international travel because its operations do not yet extend beyond the borders of the United States.

International Transport

Generally speaking, an airline is permitted to carry passengers from a domestic airport to a foreign destination, drop them off, pick up passengers at that airport, and return to its country of origin.[71] Airlines are usually not permitted to carry passengers to other airports in other countries or within any country other than their home nation. Obviously, this situation presents problems for a traveler who wishes to go for example from a small airport in the United States to a small airport in Russia. This traveler would need to purchase separate tickets on a U.S. and a Russian carrier, transfer his or her own baggage, and assume the risks of missed connections between the carriers.

One obvious way around this dilemma is a merger of carriers with domestic rights in both countries. Unfortunately, "U.S. law limits the amount of foreign ownership in its domestic airlines to a maximum of 49 percent, with a maximum of 25 percent control."[72] Because other nations have similar restrictions, international airline mergers are essentially impossible at this time.

To circumvent the limitations related to international routes and restrictions on ownership, airlines have formed global strategic alliances.

Global Alliances

Alliances allow passengers to book end-to-end itineraries to a much larger pool of international destinations through airlines code-sharing on their joint networks.[73] In addition to extending a carrier's network, alliances also allow airlines to expand the value of their Frequent Flyer Programs (FFP) by providing passengers the opportunity to accumulate and redeem awards for other member airlines.[74] These alliances have extended beyond code-sharing and agreements on FFP programs to include food service agreements and maintenance contracts for each other's aircraft. There are three main airline alliances that compete against one another: Oneworld, SkyTeam, and Star. Exhibit 5 shows the airlines participating in each alliance as of June 2009, along with key statistics from 2008 for each alliance.

Star Alliance. The Star Alliance is the largest and the oldest formed by an agreement between United Airlines, Lufthansa, Air Canada, Thai Airways, and SAS (Scandinavian Airlines) in 1997.[75] In its 12-year existence, Star Alliance has grown to 21 member airlines and 3 regional members. The extent to which the alliance has been successful in covering the globe is evident in the combined route map shown in Exhibit 6.

Exhibit 5 Global Alliances

Global Alliances			
Alliance	Oneworld	SkyTeam	Star
Year formed	1999	2000	1997
Countries served	134	169	159
Unique airports	673	905	912
Daily departures	8,419	16,787	16,500
Passengers (thousands)	328,626	462,000	499,900
Lounges	550	447	805
Fleet (operated)	2,226	2,496	3,325
Employees	302,753	356,998	393,559
Full members	American Airlines	Aeroflot	Air Canada
	British Airways	Aeromexico	Air China
	Cathay Pacific Airways	Air France	Air New Zealand
	FinnAir	Alitalia	ANA
	Iberia	China Southern Airlines	Asiana Airlines
	Japan Airlines (JAL)	Continental Airlines*	Austrian
	LAN Airlines	CSA Czech Airlines	bmi
	Malev Hungarian Airlines	Delta Air Lines	EGYPTAIR
	Mexicana	KLM Royal Dutch Airlines	LOT Polish Airlines

Exhibit 5 Global Alliances (*Continued*)

Global Alliances			
Alliance	**Oneworld**	**SkyTeam**	**Star**
	Qantas	Korean Air	Lufthansa
	Royal Jordanian	Northwest Airlines	Scandinavian Airlines
			Shanghai Airlines
			Singapore Airlines
			South African Airways
			Spanair
			SWISS
			TAP Portugal
			THAI
			Turkish Airlines
			United Airlines
			US Airways
Associate/regional members	Air Nostrum	Air Europa	Adria Airways
	American Connection	Copa Airlines	Blue1
	American Eagle	Kenya Airways	Croatia Airlines
	BA Citiflyer		
	Click Mexicana		
	Comair		
	Dragonair		
	J-Air		
	JAL Express		
	JALways		
	Japan Transocean Air		
	Jetconnect		
	LAN Argentina		
	LAN Ecuador		
	LAN Express		
	LAN Peru		
	QantasLink		
	Sun-Air of Scandinavia		

* Continental is transitioning from SkyTeam to Star in 2009.

Source: 2009, Table compiled by authors using data from http://www.oneworld com, http://www.skyteam.com, and http://www.staralliance.com.

Exhibit 6 Star Alliance Route Network

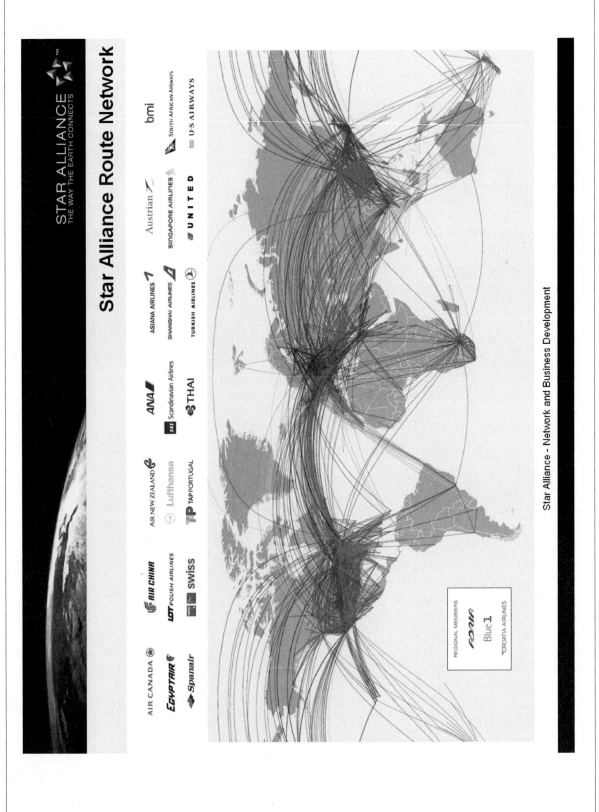

Source: 2008, Network facts & figures, Star Alliance, http://www.staralliance.com, July.

Star Alliance exemplifies both the advantages and disadvantages of global airline alliances. Member airlines have been able to reduce costs and increase convenience for passengers through initiatives such as Star's dedicated terminals in Tokyo, Bangkok, Miami, and elsewhere.[76] Placing Star Alliance member airlines in a single terminal allows passengers to connect faster with shorter walks between gates. It also allows airlines to share lounges as well as personnel and resources used in check-in and ground handling activities.[77]

However, critics of alliances claim that code-sharing arrangements can lead to a reduction in competition, as "all the flights on a route carry the codes of [all] the 'competitors' and are jointly marketed by [all] the airlines."[78] Too many alliance members flying the same routes can also adversely affect the airlines involved, "as new airlines are added to the alliance, the importance of an existing airline may be reduced."[79]

Additionally, airlines face expenses when they join an alliance. Service levels must be standardized, information technology systems must be integrated, and costs are incurred for running the alliance itself.[80] Still, on the whole, there is general agreement that the benefits of alliances outweigh their drawbacks.

Oneworld.
Oneworld is the smallest of the three major alliances. Offering the same basic benefits as Star, Oneworld also consolidated operations in dedicated terminals in Madrid, London Heathrow, Tokyo Narita, and elsewhere.[81] Oneworld seeks to distinguish itself from the Star and SkyTeam alliances by offering innovative fare structures that are designed to appeal to adventurous pleasure travelers as well as frequent business travelers.[82] In the United States, American is the primary Oneworld carrier.

SkyTeam.
Formed in 2000, SkyTeam is the youngest of the major alliances. Like its competitors, SkyTeam is working to reduce member costs and "has opened more than 40 co-locations."[83] Member airlines are currently in the process of repainting some aircraft to emphasize the SkyTeam brand and de-emphasize the individual carrier brands.[84] Exhibit 7 shows a standard Delta branded plane and a new SkyTeam-Delta co-branded model. In 2007, the U.S. market was served by SkyTeam carriers Delta, Northwest, and Continental. Delta acquired Northwest in 2008 and Continental is scheduled to switch to the Star Alliance in 2009, leaving Delta as the sole U.S. airline in SkyTeam. Continental's defection is not surprising given Delta's acquisition of Northwest coupled with "Delta's and Continental's battle on transatlantic routes."[85]

Of the six largest U.S. airlines, Southwest is the only one that is not a member of a global alliance. In fact, no LCC is currently a member of any alliance. LCCs have traditionally avoided global alliances because of the service level requirements that membership places on them, although they do have some domestic code sharing agreements (Southwest had a code sharing agreement with ATA Airlines, for example, until ATA ceased service in 2008). A particularly enlightening case is Aer Lingus, which was in Oneworld, but quit the alliance as part of its attempt to restructure itself as an LCC.[86]

In addition to extending its network globally through the Star Alliance, United extends its network to smaller domestic airports through its regional affiliate, United Express.

United Express.
The goal of this air carrier service is to transport passengers from smaller airports to United hubs for convenient connections to other United and Star Alliance flights.[87] United maintains agreements with regional carriers such as Chautauqua Airlines, Colgan Airlines, Go Jet Airlines, Mesa Airlines, Shuttle America, SkyWest Airlines, and Trans States Airlines, all of which fly planes bearing the United Express insignia; as such, passengers are generally unaware of the relationship and consider these flights to be United Airlines flights.[88] United Express conducts more than 2,000 flights daily and all of the same elements apply, such as acquiring points for the United frequent flier program.

Not only are alliances and networks important considerations for airline companies, but factors of production may be even more crucial.

Factors of Production

Aircraft Manufacturers. The most visible tangible asset of any airline is its fleet of aircraft. For large jet aircraft (more than 100 seats), Boeing and Airbus are currently the only two suppliers in the world.[89] The two companies are relatively evenly matched in terms of capabilities, and "since both manufacturers price their aircraft almost identically, competition occurs in the area of additional services, such as financing agreements or agreed buy-back of older aircraft."[90] Most airlines, including United, tend to maintain a relationship with both manufacturers to avoid becoming overly dependent on either supplier.

Fuel. With recent increases in the cost of oil, fuel has become the largest and most volatile expense for airlines.[91] In 2008 oil prices escalated to a high of $145 per barrel in July, then dropped to $70 a barrel in October, making it difficult for airlines to forecast expenses.[92] To smooth the variance, airlines routinely participate in fuel hedging, but this is not a foolproof practice. United lost $519 million in just the third quarter of 2008 when price decreases lowered the

Exhibit 7 Delta Planes with Traditional Delta Branding and New SkyTeam Branding

Source: 2009, Delta Air Lines N702DN and N844MH, http://www.flickr.com, March 30.

value of its hedges.[93] American, Delta, Continental, and even Southwest also posted losses due to fuel hedges.[94]

Airport Slots. The relationships between airlines and airports are quite complex. While airports generally have significant latitude with regards to the fees they charge airlines to use their facilities, the resulting agreements give airlines significant power over gates, terminals, ticket counters, and slots for takeoffs and landings.[95]

Of particular interest is something called an "airport slot." Essentially, airport slots grant the holder "the right to land or take off from an airport at a given time."[96] Once these slots are granted, they exist in perpetuity as long as the owner uses the slot at least

80 percent of the time.[97] This provides a significant incentive to slot owners to continue flying in every slot they own to keep those slots from becoming available to other carriers.[98]

Labor. Labor relations can be challenging for any company, but for the airline industry, where a large percentage of airline workers are represented by labor unions, it is a very critical component of the business. Unfortunately for United, the firm's history of problems with the labor unions representing its workers continues to plague the company today.

After years of strikes and bitter negotiations, 1994 was something of a watershed moment for United's labor relations. As part of contract negotiations, it became the largest company in the world to be majority owned by its employees. Pilots bought 25 percent of the company, machinists, 20 percent and salaried and management workers, about 10 percent, and several seats on the board of directors were granted to union representatives.[99] It seemed that United and its unions were finally working together; however, that perception ended quickly. While the company's Employee Stock Ownership Plan (ESOP) provided job security for the so-called new "owners," there was little change in employee relations, airline efficiency, or customer satisfaction as workers still had little control over the critical decisions the company made. In retrospect, it seems that there was no intention to create an "ownership culture" by either side. Instead, union leaders "wanted to use ownership to prevent United from breaking up into regional carriers ... and outsourcing work performed by union members," while the company's management saw ESOP "primarily as a way to get wage concessions."[100]

Results of a 2008 employee survey showed that a staggering 70 percent of United's employees remain dissatisfied working for the airline, and only 38 percent were proud of the company, "compared with the average *Fortune* 500 Company, where 84 percent of employees express pride in their employer."[101]

United's pilots, along with the Air Line Pilots Association (ALPA), criticized CEO Glenn Tilton based on the fact that his compensation package remains the highest in the industry by a considerable margin, even while his airline was reporting negative earnings, its employees are being laid off, and customers are being charged extra service fees.[102] Further, United's decision in June 2008 to eliminate 950 pilot jobs, lay off 1,600 salaried positions, and ground 70 aircraft was not received well by the ALPA community.[103] In fact, the union's pilots went on strike; in response, United sued the ALPA claiming it organized an illegal and disruptive "sickout" that caused hundreds of flight cancellations costing the airline millions of dollars in potential revenue and "damaging its reputation with the flying public and disrupting travel plans of about 36,000 passengers."[104] In November 2008, the federal court ruled against United's pilots, stating that their actions were illegal.[105]

Financial Results

During fiscal year 2008, five out of six major domestic carriers sustained losses on their income statements (see Exhibit 8a). Low-cost carrier Southwest Airlines was the only exception to this outcome. Most of these firms, because of liabilities that exceed their total assets, maintain a negative equity position (see Exhibits 8a, 8b, 8c). The extraordinarily high ROE shown simply demonstrates the significant amount of

Exhibit 8a Industry Financial Statistics 2008 (in millions except ratios and per-share figures)

Year Ending 2008	United	American	Southwest	Delta	US Airways	Continental
Income Statement						
Sales	20,194	23,766	11,023	22,697	12,118	15,241
Average daily sales	55	65	30	62	33	42
EBIT	(4,856)	1,348	383	(8,336)	(1,957)	(352)
Total interest	523	723	105	705	253	332
Lease obligations (capital leases)	1	1	25	473	752	195
Net income	(5,348)	(2,071)	178	(8,922)	(2,210)	(585)
Balance Sheet						
Current assets	4,861	5,935	2,893	8,904	2,418	4,347
Accounts receivable	977	811	574	1,844	293	669

(Continued)

Exhibit 8a Industry Financial Statistics 2008 (in millions except ratios and per-share figures) (*Continued*)

Year Ending 2008	United	American	Southwest	Delta	US Airways	Continental
Inventory	237	525	203	388	201	235
Finished goods	NA	NA	NA	NA	NA	NA
Fixed assets	10,312	15,735	11,040	20,627	3,286	7,327
Total assets	19,461	25,175	14,308	45,014	7,214	12,686
Current liabilities	7,281	9,374	2,806	11,022	3,044	4,474
Long-term debt	8,286	9,001	3,498	15,411	3,634	5,371
Total debt	21,926	28,110	9,355	44,140	7,719	12,581
Annual dividend per share	0	0	0	0	0	0
Current market price per share	12	10	9	12	9	19
After-tax earnings per share	(42)	(8)	0	(19)	(22)	(6)
Common shares outstanding	140	285	741	772	114	124
Owner's equity	(2,465)	(2,935)	4,953	874	(505)	(105)
Statement of Cash Flows						
Net change in cash	780	43	(845)	1,607	(914)	37
Profitability						
Profit margin	−26.48%	−8.71%	1.61%	−39.31%	−18.24%	−3.84%
Asset turnover	103.77%	94.40%	77.04%	50.42%	167.98%	120.14%
Return on assets	−27.48%	−8.23%	1.24%	−19.82%	−30.63%	−4.61%
Financial leverage	789.49%	857.75%	288.88%	5,150.34%	1,428.51%	12,081.90%
Return on equity	216.96%	70.56%	3.59%	−1,020.82%	437.62%	557.14%
Liquidity						
Current ratio	0.67	0.63	1.03	0.81	0.79	0.97
Quick ratio	0.64	0.58	0.96	0.77	0.73	0.92
Inventory to net working capital	−0.10	−0.15	2.33	−0.18	−0.32	−1.85
Leverage						
Debt to assets	1.13	1.12	0.65	0.98	1.07	0.99
Debt to equity	−8.89	−9.58	1.89	50.50	−15.29	−119.82
Long-term debt to equity	−3.36	−3.07	0.71	17.63	−7.20	−51.15
Times interest earned	−9.28	1.86	3.65	−11.82	−7.74	−1.06
Fixed-charge coverage	−9.26	1.86	3.14	−6.67	−1.20	−0.30
Activity						
Inventory turnover	NA	NA	NA	NA	NA	NA
Fixed assets turnover	1.96	1.51	1.00	1.10	3.69	2.08

Exhibit 8a Industry Financial Statistics 2008 (in millions except ratios and per-share figures) (*Continued*)

Year Ending 2008	United	American	Southwest	Delta	US Airways	Continental
Total assets turnover	1.04	0.94	0.77	0.50	1.68	1.20
Accounts receivable turnover	20.67	29.30	19.20	12.31	41.36	22.78
Average collecting period	17.66	12.46	19.01	29.65	8.83	16.02
Shareholder's Return						
Dividend yield on common stock	0.00	0.00	0.00	0.00	0.00	0.00
Price-earnings ratio	−0.28	−1.25	37.50	−0.63	−0.41	−3.43
Dividend-payout ratio	0.00	0.00	0.08	0.00	0.00	0.00
Cash flow per share	5.57	0.15	−1.14	2.08	−8.00	0.30

Source: 2009, Table compiled by authors using data from the 2008 10-K reports of each company.

Exhibit 8b Industry Financial Statistics 2007 (in millions except ratios and per-share figures)

Year Ending 2007	United	American	Southwest	Delta	US Airways	Continental
Income Statement						
Sales	20,143	22,935	9,861	19,154	11,700	14,232
Average daily sales	55	63	27	52	32	39
EBIT	1,337	1,398	1,127	2,471	707	922
Total interest	642	894	69	652	273	356
Lease obligations (capital leases)	1,106	846	39	526	765	183
Net income	403	504	645	1,612	427	459
Balance Sheet						
Current assets	6,095	7,229	4,443	5,240	3,347	4,561
Accounts receivable	966	1,027	279	1,208	374	865
Inventory	242	601	259	262	249	271
Finished goods	NA	NA	NA	NA	NA	NA
Fixed assets	11,359	17,153	10,874	11,701	2,488	6,558
Total assets	24,220	28,571	16,772	32,423	8,040	12,105
Current liabilities	7,979	8,483	4,838	6,605	2,434	4,449
Long-term debt	7,521	10,093	2,050	7,986	3,031	4,366
Total debt	21,431	25,914	9,831	22,310	6,601	10,555
Annual dividend per share	0	0	0	0	0	0
Current market price per share	32	13	12	13	13	20
After–tax earnings per share	3	2	1	5	5	4

(*Continued*)

Exhibit 8b Industry Financial Statistics 2007 (in millions except ratios and per-share figures) (*Continued*)

Year Ending 2007	United	American	Southwest	Delta	US Airways	Continental
Common shares outstanding	117	255	808	772	114	124
Owner's equity	2,418	2,657	6,941	10,113	1,439	1,550
Statement of Cash Flows						
Net change in cash	2,573	26	823	614	832	5
Profitability						
Profit margin	2.00%	2.20%	6.54%	8.42%	3.65%	3.23%
Asset turnover	83.17%	80.27%	58.79%	59.08%	145.52%	117.57%
Return on assets	1.66%	1.76%	3.85%	4.97%	5.31%	3.79%
Financial leverage	1,001.65%	1,075.31%	241.64%	320.61%	558.72%	780.97%
Return on equity	16.67%	18.97%	9.29%	15.94%	29.67%	29.61%
Liquidity						
Current ratio	0.76	0.85	0.92	0.79	1.38	1.03
Quick ratio	0.73	0.78	0.86	0.75	1.27	0.96
Inventory to net working capital	–0.13	–0.48	–0.66	–0.19	0.27	2.42
Leverage						
Debt to assets	0.88	0.91	0.59	0.69	0.82	0.87
Debt to equity	8.86	9.75	1.42	2.21	4.59	6.81
Long-term debt to equity	3.11	3.80	0.30	0.79	2.11	2.82
Times interest earned	2.08	1.56	16.33	3.79	2.59	2.59
Fixed-charge coverage	1.40	1.29	10.80	2.54	1.42	2.05
Activity						
Inventory turnover	NA	NA	NA	NA	NA	NA
Fixed-assets turnover	1.77	1.34	0.91	1.64	4.70	2.17
Total-assets turnover	0.83	0.80	0.59	0.59	1.46	1.18
Accounts-receivable turnover	20.85	22.33	35.34	15.86	31.28	16.45
Average collecting period	17.50	16.34	10.33	23.02	11.67	22.18
Shareholder's Return						
Dividend yield on common stock	0.00	0.00	0.00	0.00	0.00	0.00
Price–earnings ratio	9.58	7.30	14.29	2.49	2.79	4.94
Dividend-payout ratio	0.00	0.00	0.02	0.00	0.00	0.00
Cash flow per share	22.01	0.10	1.02	0.80	7.28	0.04

Source: 2009, Table compiled by authors using data from the 2008 10-K reports of each company.

Exhibit 8c Industry Financial Statistics 2006 (in millions except ratios and per-share figures)

Year Ending 2006	United	American	Southwest	Delta	US Airways	Continental
Income Statement						
Sales (millions USD)	17,880	22,563	9,086	17,171	7,117	13,128
Average daily sales	49	62	25	47	19	36
EBIT	511	1,232	867	(6,098)	(379)	752
Total interest	729	1,001	77	870	242	383
Lease obligations (capital leases)	1,350	927	51	387	956	200
Net income	32	231	499	(6,203)	(611)	343
Balance Sheet						
Current assets	6,273	6,902	2,601	5,385	1,413	4,129
Accounts receivable	942	988	241	1,317	252	747
Inventory	218	506	181	181	177	217
Finished goods	NA	NA	NA	NA	NA	NA
Fixed assets	11,463	17,763	10,094	12,973	3,370	6,263
Total assets	25,369	29,145	13,460	19,622	8,422	11,308
Current liabilities	7,945	8,505	2,887	5,769	2,383	3,955
Long-term debt	8,803	12,041	1,567	6,509	2,637	4,859
Total debt	22,860	29,751	7,011	33,215	8,856	10,961
Annual dividend per share	0	0	0	0	0	0
Current market price per share	46	32	15	20	54	45
After-tax earnings per share	197	1	1	(32)	4	3
Common shares outstanding	140	285	808	772	114	124
Owner's equity	2,148	(606)	6,449	(13,593)	(434)	347
Statement of Cash Flows						
Net change in cash	2,183	(17)	(890)	26	(191)	400
Profitability						
Profit margin	0.18%	1.02%	5.49%	−36.12%	−8.59%	2.61%
Asset turnover	70.48%	77.42%	67.50%	87.51%	84.50%	116.09%
Return on assets	0.13%	0.79%	3.71%	−31.61%	−7.25%	3.03%
Financial leverage	1,181.05%	4,809.41%	208.71%	144.35%	1,940.55%	3,258.79%
Return on equity	1.49%	−38.12%	7.74%	45.63%	140.78%	98.85%
Liquidity						
Current ratio	0.79	0.81	0.90	0.93	0.59	1.04

(Continued)

Exhibit 8c Industry Financial Statistics 2006 (in millions except ratios and per-share figures) (*Continued*)

Year Ending 2006	United	American	Southwest	Delta	US Airways	Continental
Quick ratio	0.76	0.75	0.84	0.90	0.52	0.99
Inventory to net working capital	–0.13	–0.32	–0.63	–0.47	–0.18	1.25
Leverage						
Debt to assets	0.90	1.02	0.52	1.69	1.05	0.97
Debt to equity	10.64	–49.09	1.09	–2.44	–20.41	31.59
Long-term debt to equity	4.10	–19.87	0.24	–0.48	–6.08	14.00
Times interest earned	0.70	1.23	11.26	–7.01	–1.57	1.96
Fixed-charge coverage	0.90	1.12	7.17	–4.54	0.48	1.63
Activity						
Inventory turnover	NA	NA	NA	NA	NA	NA
Fixed-assets turnover	1.56	1.27	0.90	1.32	2.11	2.10
Total-assets turnover	0.70	0.77	0.68	0.88	0.85	1.16
Accounts-receivable turnover	18.98	22.84	37.70	13.04	28.24	17.57
Average collecting period	19.23	15.98	9.68	28.00	12.92	20.77
Shareholder's Return						
Dividend yield on common stock	0.00	0.00	0.00	0.00	0.00	0.00
Price–earnings ratio	0.23	32.65	24.59	–0.63	15.38	13.72
Dividend-payout ratio	0.00	0.00	0.03	0.00	0.00	0.00
Cash flow per share	15.59	–0.06	–1.10	0.03	–1.67	3.23

Source: 2009, Table compiled by authors using data from the 2008 10-K reports of each company.

financial leverage that is commonplace in the airline industry.

Competition from low-cost carriers, recent emergence from bankruptcy, and intense competitive rivalry (because of high fixed costs and the need for high turnover) among carriers has forced United to contract its operations. With negative cash flows from operating and financing activities, United was forced to finance its activities by forgoing future investment and liquidating its assets (see Exhibit 9). In 2008, the firm permanently removed 100 aircraft from its fleet, reduced capital spending by $200 million, and cut 6,000 employees from its workforce.[106] In addition, in 2009 the company plans to eliminate 1,400 more workers, limit capital expenditures to $450 million, and reduce premium seats on domestic flights by 20 percent. Net sales of short-term investments accounted for the majority of United's liquidity in 2008 ($2.2 million of $2.7 million on the Statement of Cash Flows).[107]

Volatile fuel costs remain the most significant threat to financial stability for the airline industry as whole, but for United in particular. For the airline industry as a whole, fuel accounts for approximately 30 percent of total operating expenses. In 2008, United witnessed a 59 percent increase in the cost of fuel, leading to a $3.1 billion increase in overall costs related to hedging or direct fuel costs.[108]

United, along with competitors American, Continental, Delta, and Northwest, have implemented fees and reduced service in order to cope with rising fuel costs and decreased traffic. While charging fees for checked baggage seems intuitively counterproductive to increasing passenger traffic for United Airlines, according to CFO Kathryn Mikells, "a la carte pricing is proving to be a very large opportunity," and is expected to provide $700 million in additional income for 2009.[109] However, in many instances, such fees have caused an increase in public ire toward the airline industry. Thus, in an attempt to win back passengers and generate

Exhibit 9 UAL Statement of Cash Flows, 2006 to 2008

Period Ending	12/31/08	12/31/07	12/31/06
Net income	−5,348,000	403,000	22,876,000
Operating Activities, Cash Flows Provided by or Used in			
Depreciation	981,000	925,000	882,000
Adjustments to net income	3,374,000	496,000	636,000
Changes in accounts receivables	195,000	−59,000	43,000
Changes in liabilities	−591,000	638,000	1,447,000
Changes in inventories	—	—	—
Changes in other operating activities	150,000	−269,000	−1,411,000
Total Cash Flows from Operating Activities	−1,239,000	2,134,000	1,539,000
Investing Activities, Cash Flows Provided by or Used in			
Capital expenditures	−415,000	−658,000	−362,000
Investments	2,295,000	−1,951,000	−235,000
Other cash flows from investing activities	841,000	49,000	347,000
Total Cash Flows from Investing Activities	2,721,000	−2,560,000	−250,000
Financing Activities, Cash Flows Provided by or Used in			
Dividends paid	−253,000	—	—
Sale purchase of stock	96,000	24,000	10,000
Net borrowings	−702,000	−2,253,000	770,000
Other cash flows from financing activities	157,000	82,000	2,000
Total Cash Flows from Financing Activities	−702,000	−2,147,000	782,000
Effect of Exchange Rate Changes	—	—	—
Change in Cash and Cash Equivalents	$780,000	−$2,573,000	$2,071,000

Source: 2009, UAL Corporation cash flow, *Yahoo! Finance,* http://finance.yahoo.com.

brand loyalty, United has embraced several marketing strategies.

Marketing Initiatives

In 2008, United began its "Travel Options by United" program in an effort to provide passengers with greater choice and flexibility.[110] The program is comprised of six services that passengers can elect to add to their ticket price: economy plus, Premier Line, door-to-door baggage, travel insurance, award accelerator, and Red Carpet Club.[111] Through the Travel Options program, United is attempting to offer travelers services they will value—even if the service must be purchased by the passenger. The Premier Line, for example, was the result of market research aimed at uncovering customer needs and desires. Dennis Cary, senior vice president and chief marketing and customer officer, described the process as follows: "when we asked our customers what travel services were most important to them they told us the access to priority lines was something they value highly."[112] The Premier Line provides priority access at check-in, security, and boarding for a starting fee of $25.[113]

Another marketing strategy that United is using is its Premium Service, or p.s., flights. According to the company Web site, "in its essence, p.s. is about doing a few things extraordinarily well." The p.s. flights offer the only domestic lie-flat bed in first class, more leg room, laptop power, and a premium menu.[114] Currently, p.s. flights only service three cities: Los Angeles, New York, and San Francisco, providing special accommodations for a select few.[115] For United, p.s. flights are a confirmation of the belief that "to get business travelers to pay more and not simply shift to discount airlines, big airlines may have to find ways to offer premium service travelers will value."[116]

In addition to its marketing efforts to increase passenger transport, United Airlines maintains cargo service to supplement its revenues. United Cargo is the seventh-largest domestic freight company.[117]

Additional Revenue Streams

In 2008, cargo accounted for approximately 4 percent of the United's operating revenue, generating $854 million in freight and mail revenue.[118] While United and most of its competitors derive some revenue from the freight market, "competition in the freight market has grown steadily, and it is becoming less and less likely that airlines treating freight purely as a by-product will be successful."[119] The bulk of the market (which is expected to grow more rapidly than passenger service) is expected to fall to dedicated air freight companies.[120]

Despite all of United's attempts to improve its financial situation and future viability, it faces multiple challenges.

Strategic Challenges

Just three years removed from bankruptcy, United Airlines is suffering financially once again. The company's losses in 2008–2009 combined with its high levels of debt and low liquidity placed the company on shaky ground. The growth of LCCs, especially Southwest, and United's failed attempts at countering their influence are also troubling trends for the firm.

The company must decide how best to face the changing landscape of the passenger airline industry. Can United find a viable merger opportunity? If so, does a merger only postpone resolution of United's problems? Most importantly, can United neutralize the market erosion caused by low-cost carriers, or must it find a way to compete with them directly by lowering its own cost structure? Glenn Tilton and his executive team must find the most viable answers as the pathway for United Airlines to operate in ways that will satisfy all stakeholders, certainly including shareholders.

NOTES

1. 2009, Glenn Tilton remarks to the Phoenix Aviation Symposium, http://www.united.com, March 27.
2. 2009, UAL Corporation reports first quarter 2009 results, United Press Release, http://www.united.com, April 21; 2009, UAL Corporation 2008 Annual Report, http://www.united.com.
3. 2009, Era 2: 1926–1933 Timeline, http://www.united.com.
4. 2009, Era 3: 1934–1940, http://www.united.com.
5. R. Freeman, Walter Folger Brown: The postmaster general who built the U.S. Airline industry, U.S. Centennial of Flight Commission, http://www.centennialofflight.gov/essay/Commercial_Aviation/Brown/Tran3.htm.
6. E. Preston, The Federal Aviation Administration and its predecessor agencies, U.S. Centennial of Flight Commission, http://www.centennialofflight.gov/essay/Government_Role/FAA_History/POL8.htm.
7. Era 3: 1934–1940 Timeline.
8. S. Shaw, 2007, Airline Marketing and Management, 6th ed., Ashgate Publishing, 52.
9. 2008, Star Alliance Facts & Figures, Star Alliance, http://www.staralliance.com, December 11.
10. B. Vasigh, K. Fleming, & T. Tacker, 2008, Introduction to Air Transport Economics: From Theory to Applications, Ashgate Publishing, 227.
11. S. Shaw, Airline Marketing and Management.
12. B. Vasigh, K. Fleming, & T. Tacker, Introduction to Air Transport Economics, 308.
13. Ibid., 2.
14. 2009, Era 7: 1970–1989 Timeline, http://www.united.com.
15. 2009, Era 8: 1990–1993 Timeline, http://www.united.com.
16. 2009, Era 9: 1994–1999 Timeline, http://www.united.com.
17. 2002, United, CBS News, http://www.cbsnews.com, December 9.
18. Era 9: 1994–1999 Timeline.
19. 2009, Era 10: 2000–... Timeline, http://www.united.com.
20. United, CBS News.
21. Ibid.
22. Ibid.
23. 2009, UAL Corporation 2008 Annual Report, http://www.united.com.
24. Ibid.
25. Ibid.
26. M. Maynard, 2008, More cuts as United grounds its low-cost carrier, The New York Times, http://www.nytimes.com, June 5.
27. 2007, Delta, United deny being in merger discussions, MSNBC, http://www.msnbc.msn.com, November 14.
28. M. Maynard, 2008, United and Continental form alliance, The New York Times, http://www.nytimes.com, June 20.
29. United, CBS News; M. Maynard, United and Continental form alliance.
30. B. Vasigh, K. Fleming, & T. Tacker, Introduction to Air Transport Economics: From Theory to Applications, 51.
31. S. Shaw, Airline Marketing and Management, 37.
32. Ibid., 70.
33. Ibid., 37–39.
34. 2009, American Airlines History, http://www.aa.com, March; 2009, AMR Corporation 2008 Annual Report, http://www.aa.com, June.
35. 2008, AMR Corporation – American's Parent Company, http://www.aa.com, August.
36. 2009, American Eagle Airlines: At a glance, http://www.aa.com, May.
37. 2003, American Airlines avoids bankruptcy, BBC News, http://news.bbc.co.uk, April 1.
38. 2009, AMR Corporation 2008 Annual Report, http://www.aa.com.
39. A. Salpukas, 1990, Continental files for bankruptcy, The New York Times, http://www.nytimes.com, December 4.
40. 2008, Continental Airlines ranked No. 1 world's most admired airline by Fortune magazine, Reuters, http://www.reuters.com, March 11.
41. 2009, Continental Airlines 2008 8-K, http://www.continental.com, April, 24.

42. 2009, Continental Airlines facts second quarter 2009, http://www .continental.com; 2009, Continental Airlines 2008 Annual Report, http://www.continental.com, February.

43. Ibid.

44. 2009, Continental to join Star Alliance, Continental Airlines News Release, http://www.continental.com, April 16.

45. 2009, Delta through the decades, http://delta.com, April.

46. Ibid.

47. Ibid.

48. 2009, Delta Air Lines 2005 Annual Report, http://www.delta.com, April.

49. 2009, Delta Air Lines 2008 Annual Report, http://www.delta.com, April.

50. Ibid.

51. Ibid.

52. 2009, US Airways fact sheet, http://www.usairways.com, April; 2009, US Airways 2008 Annual Report, http://www.usairways.com, April.

53. 2009, US Airways chronology, http://www.usairways.com, April.

54. D. Reed, 2008, US Airways highlights drawbacks of consolidation, USA Today, http://www.usatoday.com, May 3; 2009, US Airways & America West Airlines combined route network map, http://www .airlineroutemaps.com, April; 2008, Is US Airways a low-cost carrier?, http://www.associatedcontent.com, February 14.

55. 2009, US Airways 2008 Annual Report, http://www.usairways.com, April.

56. Ibid.

57. Ibid.

58. Ibid.

59. Ibid.

60. S. McCartney, 2009, For the first time in awhile, airline customer satisfaction is up, Wall Street Journal, http://online.wsj.com, May 20.

61. We weren't just airborne yesterday, http://www.southwest.com.

62. 2008, Scheduled passengers carried, World Air Transport Statistics, http://www.iata.org.

63. 2009, Southwest Airlines Fact Sheet, http://www.southwest.com, April 27; 2009, Southwest Airlines Investor Relations, http://www .southwest.com.

64. Ibid.

65. B. Vasigh, K. Fleming, & T. Tacker, Introduction to Air Transport Economics, 309–318.

66. S. Shaw, Airline Marketing and Management, 96.

67. We weren't just airborne yesterday.

68. 2009, Southwest Airlines 2008 Annual Report, http://www .southwest.com, April.

69. S. Shaw, 2007, Airline Marketing and Management, 90.

70. Southwest Airlines 2008 Annual Report.

71. B. Vasigh, K. Fleming, & T. Tacker, Introduction to Air Transport Economics.

72. Ibid., 138.

73. S. Shaw, Airline Marketing and Management, 112.

74. Ibid., 255.

75. 2007, Backgrounder: 10 years Star Alliance from "The airline network for Earth" to "The way the Earth connects"—A chronological history, Star Alliance Press Office, May 14, 2.

76. Ibid., 3.

77. 2009, SkyTeam airline member benefits, http://www.skyteam.com, April.

78. S. Shaw, Airline Marketing and Management, 112.

79. B. Vasigh, K. Fleming, & T. Tacker, Introduction to Air Transport Economics, 173.

80. Ibid.

81. 2007, An introduction to Oneworld: The alliance that revolves around you, http://www.oneworld.com, July 11.

82. Ibid.

83. SkyTeam airline member benefits.

84. 2009, SkyTeam names managing director, introduces aircraft livery, http://www.skyteam.com, April 1.

85. B. Vasigh, K. Fleming, & T. Tacker, Introduction to Air Transport Economics, 173.

86. Ibid.

87. 2009, United Express, http://www.united.com, April.

88. 2009, United Airlines 2008 Annual Report, http://www.united.com, April.

89. B. Vasigh, K. Fleming, & T. Tacker, Introduction to Air Transport Economics, 212.

90. Ibid.

91. J. Lowy, 2008, Pilots: To cut costs, airlines forcing us to fly low on fuel, The Huffington Post, http://www.huffingtonpost.com, August 8.

92. M. Maynard, 2008, United, citing fuel hedging, loses $779 million in quarter, The New York Times http://www.nytimes.com, October, 21.

93. Ibid.

94. Ibid.

95. B. Vasigh, K. Fleming, & T. Tacker, Introduction to Air Transport Economics, 190.

96. Ibid., 191.

97. Ibid.

98. Ibid.

99. Era 9: 1994–1999 Timeline; 2003, United Airlines likely to lose employee ownership, USA Today, http://www.usatoday.com, January 16.

100. C. Rosen, 2002. United Airlines, ESOPs, and employee ownership, The National Center for Employee Ownership, http://www.nceo .org, November.

101. 2008, United Pilots: Leadership void costly for UAL in 2008, UPI, http://www.upi.com, December 29.

102. Ibid.

103. 2008, United Airlines to lay off 950 pilots—cuts in addition to those announced earlier, domain-b.com, http://www.domain-b.com/ aero/unitedairlines/20080624_united_airlines.html, June 24.

104. 2008, United Airlines sues pilots' union, says it caused hundreds of flight cancellations, domain-b.com, http://www.domain-b.com/ aero/unitedairlines/20080731_united_airlines.html, July 31.

105. 2008, Injunction halts United Airline's pilot strike, RoutesOnline, http://www.routesonline.com, November 19.

106. United Airlines 2008 Annual Report.

107. D. Koenig, 2008, Major airlines ready to cut more flights in 2009, Associated Press, http://www.news.yahoo.com, December 2; 2009, United Airways 2008 Annual Report, http://www.united .com; L. Stark, M. Hosford, & K. Barrett, 2008, Layoffs continue for airlines in crisis, ABC News, http://www.abcnews.go.com, June 5.

108. United Airlines 2008 Annual Report.

109. A. Karp, 2008, Downsizing United, Air Transport World, http:// www.atwonline.com, November.

110. 2009, United Airlines, Wikitravel, http://wikitravel.org/en/United_ Airlines, April.

111. 2009, Travel Options by United, https://www.united.com, April.

112. Ibid.

113. 2009, Travel Options by United—Premier Line, https://store.united .com; 2008, Take the fast track through the airport with United's new Premier Line service, http://www.united.com, December 8.

114. S. McCartney, 2008, A posher domestic first class; United sells space and comfy beds on "p.s." flights, Wall Street Journal, http:// online.wsj.com, July 29.

115. 2009, p.s. Experience the comfort of our exclusive coast-to-coast service, http://www.unitedps.com, April.

116. S. McCartney, A posher domestic first class; United sells space and comfy beds on "p.s." flights.

117. Scheduled Freight Tonne—Kilometres, IATA Web site, http://www .iata.org/ps/publications/wats-freight-km.htm.

118. United Airlines 2008 Annual Report.

119. S. Shaw, Airline Marketing and Management, 40.

120. Ibid.

Amy Falter, Scott Thompson

Arizona State University

Netflix is one of the most recognizable online movie rental services in the world. Since the company's launch in 1998, its business model has revolutionized the movie rental business and the way U.S. viewers rent and watch movies. Netflix's service has captured approximately 6.7 million subscribers and offers a video library of more than 90,000 movies, television, and other entertainment videos on DVD.[1] The majority of Netflix subscribers pay about $18 per month and are allowed to keep up to three movies at a time.[2] Although Netflix was the first company to tap this new market of online movie rental, they would not be the last trying to capitalize on its potential.

In August 2004, Blockbuster countered Netflix's entry into the movie rental business with a strategic response by introducing Blockbuster Online, its own online rental service.[3] Blockbuster Online offered the same services as Netflix, putting the two companies in direct competition with each other for the first time. In late 2006, Blockbuster revamped the online rental service and renamed it "Blockbuster Online Total Access."[4] This new Blockbuster service gives the customer the option of either returning the video through the mail or dropping it off at a local Blockbuster store.[5] It does however, encourage customers to return videos rented online to the store by offering a voucher for a new in-store rental.[6] As Blockbuster boasts, "With this kind of access, you'll never have to wait to have a new movie to watch!"[7] The only caveat with the new in-store rental is that normal due dates and late fees typical of brick-and-mortar video rental stores are enforced.[8] Without any physical stores, Netflix executives now face the difficult challenge of finding a legitimate and value-adding way to compete with Blockbuster.

Netflix also faces the development of video streaming and downloads on PCs as well as mobile devices. "Computers, portable MP3 video players, and telephones are now options for watching downloaded TV shows and movies, especially among younger audiences."[9] Companies such as Amazon, Apple, and YouTube have all been looking at ventures in this market.[10] To stay atop the online rental market, Netflix must decide how to adjust its current business model in order to grow and adapt to the market's dynamic environment.

To better understand these salient strategic challenges, the following topics will be touched upon: Netflix's history, current strategic leaders, the competitive environment, supplier relationships, Netflix's current strategies and functional operations, and recent financial outcomes.

Brief History

Reed Hastings founded and incorporated Netflix in August 1997 as a more conventional rental service, with online offerings.[11] It was not until April 1998 that Netflix opened its Internet store for DVD rentals and then offered a subscription service in September 1999.[12] Netflix's rapid growth can be attributed to its early strategic relationships with leading DVD hardware and home theater equipment manufacturers (Sony, Toshiba, RCA /Thomson Consumer Electronics, Pioneer, and Panasonic) and marketing tactics (promotional techniques) to build brand recognition and acceptance among the growing DVD-rental consumer base.[13] In December 1999, Netflix announced the elimination of due dates and late fees, helping it to quickly become a popular rental service, as it also did not charge shipping and handling fees and per-title rental fees.[14] On May 22, 2002, Netflix made an initial public offering (IPO) of 5.5 million shares of common stock at $15 per share.[15]

Due to the overwhelming acceptance of and demand for Netflix services, it became necessary for Netflix to

The authors would like to thank Professor Robert E. Hoskisson for his support under whose direction the case was developed. The authors do not intend to illustrate either effective or ineffective handling of a managerial situation. The case solely provides material for class discussion. This case was developed with contributions from: Garret Lumley, Evan Mallonee, & Terri Phillips.

Exhibit 1 Monthly Plans

Movie Rentals	Cost
1 at-a-time (2 per month)	$ 4.99 per month
1 at-a-time (unlimited)	$ 9.99 per month
2 at-a-time (unlimited)	$14.99 per month
3 at-a-time (unlimited)	$17.99 per month
4 at-a-time (unlimited)	$23.99 per month
5 at-a-time (unlimited)	$29.99 per month
6 at-a-time (unlimited)	$35.99 per month
7 at-a-time (unlimited)	$41.99 per month
8 at-a-time (unlimited)	$47.99 per month

Source: http://www.netflix.com/MediaCenter.

build new distribution and shipping centers every year. In the 2003 fiscal year, Netflix recorded its first profitable year with record revenues of $272.2 million, up 78 percent from the 2002 fiscal year with earnings of $152.8 million.[16] As Netflix grew, it developed tailored service packages based on consumers' desired number of rentals per month (see Exhibit 1). In 2005, the number of subscribers grew to a record high of 4.2 million, 60 percent over the previous year.[17] Both 2005 and 2006 were also solid growth years, leaving CEO Reed Hastings optimistic about future growth and earnings potential: "Our accomplishments during the year [2006]—strong subscriber growth, continued improvement in the customer experience, and increased profitability—together with the recent launch of the first generation of our online video option, leave us better positioned than ever to achieve our long-term objective of being the movie rental leader."[18] In February 2007, Netflix celebrated delivery of its one-billionth DVD by giving the recipient a free lifetime Netflix membership.[19]

Netflix recently offered new features to its subscribers. In January 2007, Netflix launched "Watch Now."[20] This feature allows subscribers not only to rent online and continue to receive DVDs through mail, but also watch more than 1,000 movies and television shows via their PCs.[21] Netflix hopes to eventually bring this type of technology to any device with access to the Internet.[22] Another new endeavor Netflix has launched is Red Envelope Entertainment; this new division "looks to leverage its proprietary technology to offer subscribers unique and original content to which they wouldn't otherwise have access."[23] The unique and original content includes independent films such as those found at the Sundance and Toronto Film festivals.[24]

At year end 2006 Netflix employed 1,300 full-time and 646 temporary employees at the corporate headquarters in Los Gatos, California, and in its shipping centers across the nation.[25] Many of Netflix's senior officers have

been with the company for a majority of the company's lifespan. The current strategic decision makers of Netflix are six key individuals from the C-suite.

Netflix Strategic Leaders

Founder, CEO, and Chairperson. Reed Hastings has served as chairman since the company's inception.[26] Hastings studied mathematics at Bowdoin College in Brunswick, Maine, and was awarded the Smyth Prize in 1981 by the math department and received his BA in 1983.[27] To round out his education, Hastings went to Stanford University and received a master's degree in computer science.[28] A former Netflix director, Bob Pisano, said of Hastings "[he is] an engineer, is analytical and very charismatic . . . that's a rare combination."[29]

Hastings created the vision for Netflix and is in perpetual motion to evolve and sustain his business based on critical factors developed by other members of his management team.

Neil Hunt, Chief Product Officer. Neil Hunt created and manages the Netflix site. He has served in this capacity since 1999.[30] His job and decisions are of critical importance, because his output is the portal customers ultimately interact with via the company. Hunt's focus is "Customization and personalization [ensuring] every Netflix member [receives] a unique experience every time they visit the site. This includes the movies they see on each page, the recommendations they receive on movies, and the critical account management tools they use, such as their dynamic queue to order movies."[31] Mr. Hunt is a noteworthy scientist who has the leadership skills to inspire teams to be innovative, and create powerful software that is user-friendly.

Ted Sarandos, Chief Content Officer. Since 2000, Mr. Sarandos's role is to manage and cultivate relationships with studios, networks, film makers, and producers to gain access to films and distribution channels.[32] His most critical role is making sure customers' needs are satisfied through the current video selection and by staying abreast of new trends within the entertainment industry.

Leslie Kilgore, Chief Marketing Officer. Because Netflix is an online entity, Ms. Kilgore's responsibility is to find the most effective and cost-efficient methods to acquire new subscribers through various marketing approaches.[33] Her success is demonstrated in that "more than 90 percent of trial members convert to paying subscribers and more than 90 percent of those tell family and friends about the service."[34]

Barry McCarthy, Chief Financial Officer. Since 1999 Mr. McCarthy has overseen the financial and legal affairs for Netflix. Barry has vast experience in his field, including work with Credit Suisse First Boston. He has helped Netflix become a billion dollar revenue company within 7 years.[35]

Patty McCord, Chief Talent Officer. Ms. McCord has been with Netflix since 1998 and helps the company attract and retain high-talent employees. Having 16 years of human resources experience with high-tech companies, she plays a large role in establishing a culture in which employees are devoted to superior customer service. "She is adamant about keeping a lean organization in which openness, approachability, and honesty are valued above all else."[36]

The strategic leaders have directed Netflix to target three distinct customer segments: those who like the convenience of free home delivery, the movie buffs who want access to the widest selection of, say, French New Wave or Bollywood films, and the bargain hunters who want to watch 10 or more movies for 18 dollars a month. The challenge is to keep all segments happy at the same time.[37]

Netflix hopes that catering to the needs and desires of its different customer segments will help it remain a key player in this rapidly developing and competitive industry.

Competitive Environment

Until recently, Blockbuster Inc. dominated the movie rental industry, with few threatening competitors and drawing annual revenues of more than $3 billion.[38] Netflix challenged the traditional brick-and-mortar video rental chains. With the continual advent of new technology and widespread Internet adoption and usage, the Netflix business model appealed to many consumers, especially those who were frustrated with Blockbuster's late fees. With Netflix's entire business model focused on providing unique online rental, free delivery to households, no due dates or late fees, and movie recommendations to all its subscribers, Netflix appeared to have found a niche market.[39]

As a result of the short product life cycles in the technological sector, continual improvements in products, and lower costs in technology, it has become more common for consumers around the globe to own their own movie viewing devices and access the Internet from home. Thus, the online movie rental market base is expected to grow continuously. In 2005, the online movie rental industry had more than 6 million subscribers in the United States and Europe, and by the end of 2006 that number rose to more than 8 million subscribers.[40]

Emerging Competitors

Progress in technology is changing the competitive dynamics. The main impetus challenging movie rental companies is video on demand (VOD). Video on demand is gaining more attention and popularity, especially among cable/satellite companies, television networks, and dot-com companies. In contrast to buying or renting a video, VOD allows the user to download the entire movie to a computer or stream the video, where the movie is viewed in realtime.[41]

Downloadable movies are in an embryonic stage, with early adopters experimenting with the service, but are not yet widely utilized among Internet users.[42] A potential current pitfall of this product is that neither downloaded nor streaming videos come in high definition yet, and this could be a deal buster for many consumers who have recently bought into the high definition craze.[43] However, most of the key online rental industry players have sought relationships with video on demand providers to maintain a competitive advantage.

New entrants are crafting technology devices specifically designed to support these new services. One major player will be Apple; movies and television shows can be viewed on Apple TV, iPods, and Macs. Smartphones will also begin to offer the downloadable movie and television show service, acting as portable TVs.[44] The downloadable Amazon Unbox allows consumers to access DVD-quality movies and television shows for rent or purchase.[45] Wal-Mart joined the fight for market share by creating its own downloading movie business in February 2007.[46] Wal-Mart has gained the interest of studios such as 20th Century Fox, Lions Gate, Disney, MGM, MTV Networks, Paramount Pictures, Universal Studios, Sony Pictures Entertainment, and Warner Bros.[47] Wal-Mart currently offers approximately 3,000 titles for download purchase ranging in price from $14.88 to $19.88.[48]

Netflix is in its infancy stage of introducing streaming videos and television shows offered to current subscribers.[49] This new addition of streaming service was built upon the Microsoft infrastructure.[50] Over time, the company hopes to make Netflix's service available on other software combinations, portable devices, and televisions screens.[51] Netflix has also partnered with video recorder maker TiVo to allow TiVo customers access to DVDs on Netflix's Web site.[52] CEO Reed Hastings has stated, "We want to be ready when video on demand happens. That's why the company is [called] Netflix and not DVD-by-mail."[53]

Even though Blockbuster has been Netflix's strongest competitor, other companies are strengthening their competitive position to challenge these two giants and gain market share. These competitors seem to believe they can differentiate their service and product offerings in order to challenge Netflix in an entirely new dimension.

Key Competitors

Blockbuster Inc.

Blockbuster is the world's largest video and video disk retail chain today, with approximately 9,040 company-owned or franchised brick-and-mortar stores located in more than 25 countries (about 60 percent located within the United States).[54] Each year, Blockbuster rents more than a billion videos, DVDs, and video games through its retail outlets.[55] Blockbuster became a video giant through its foresight, acquisition strategy, and prime store locations.

History. In 1982, David P. Cook determined that "most [video] stores were relatively modest family operations that carried a small selection of former big hit movies."[56] Cook wanted to create a nationwide movie rental company chain with a vast selection of videos.[57] The biggest selling point to enter this industry was that he could use his computer skills to create an innovative computing system for inventory control and checkout; therefore, it would decrease manual labor costs and help eliminate high costs associated with theft.[58] Cook used the proceeds from the sale of his computer data services company to open a flashy video rental store that maintained the video catalog via computer bar code systems. He named his new company Blockbuster Entertainment, with the first store opening in Dallas, Texas, in 1985.[59]

Growth Strategy. Initially, Blockbuster's growth strategy included franchising and selling the Blockbuster name and proprietary computer system.[60] After being in existence for only one year, Blockbuster altered its strategy to horizontal acquisitions to spur rapid growth. Blockbuster desired to be the first-mover in the superstore video rental chain.[61] "Blockbuster's management continued to maintain that since the video 'superstore' concept was open for anyone to copy, it needed to grab market share as fast as possible in order to exploit its ground-breaking concept."[62]

Although Blockbuster rapidly expanded nationally and experienced astronomical growth (company earnings in 1988, 1989, and 1990 were 114%, 93%, and 48% respectively), the rental industry was beginning to reach maturity.[63] Blockbuster began to offer video game equipment and games for rental and purchase.[64] In addition, Blockbuster continued to expand globally with market entries in the United Kingdom, Japan, Australia, Europe, and Latin America.[65]

To further diversify its business portfolio, Blockbuster purchased Music Plus and Sound Warehouse, a music retail chain, from Shamrock Holdings in 1992, for $185 million and created Blockbuster Music.[66] Within the past 15 years, Blockbuster has entered into many agreements with movie production companies, communication companies, and other entertainment companies, many of which proved beneficial; but some relationships had to be severed, such as Blockbuster Music (1998), so as to not drain Blockbuster of all its financial resources.

Revenue Sharing Program. The current CEO, John Antioco, took the reins in the summer of 1997 with Blockbuster in a world of mess.[67] Not only was its stock 50 percent below its value from the previous year, but suppliers were not delivering newly released movies on time, and there was not enough qualified staff to allow for effective store operations.[68]

Antioco turned the company on its head. He scaled back on expansion and eliminated the nonrental operations (i.e., selling retail merchandise in Blockbuster stores).[69] He also implemented a revenue sharing program with major Hollywood movie studios. "Now instead of paying $65 for new tapes, Blockbuster paid $4 and turned over 30 to 40 percent of the rental income to the studio."[70] This arrangement allowed Blockbuster to stock more videos on its shelves with a lower cost structure. In 2007 Antioco announced his resignation as chairperson and CEO due to various disagreements with Blockbuster's board about salary.[71] The succeeding CEO James Keyes confronts the challenge of holding market share in a volatile industry.

Challenge to Netflix. As noted previously, in response to the success and popularity of Netflix, Blockbuster launched its Blockbuster Online service in 2004 "where members can rent unlimited DVDs online and have them delivered via mail for a monthly fee."[72] This service has evolved into its current state called Blockbuster Total Access, where DVDs are still ordered online and delivered to households, but now customers can return the DVDs for a free in-store rental.[73] Blockbuster also developed a subscription service called Blockbuster Movie Pass where customers can have 2 or 3 movies out at a time without any late fees.[74]

Most recently, Blockbuster and Weinstein Co. entered into an agreement where Weinstein Co.—an independent American film studio—will sell its titles such as *Sicko, Miss Potter, and Hannibal Rising* exclusively to Blockbuster outlets for a three-year period in exchange for the aforementioned revenue sharing program.[75] This strategic action will prohibit Netflix access to any of the titles produced by this studio. Netflix has pursued its own agreements with independent film producers, so it remains to be seen whether these relationships will prove beneficial for each company.

Also, Blockbuster recently acquired Movielink LLC, an online movie downloading company owned by major Hollywood studios, such as MGM, Paramount Pictures, Sony Pictures Entertainment, Universal Studios, and Warner Brothers.[76] In this agreement, Blockbuster will have long-term deals for content with the major film studios, which will significantly enlarge its current video library used by both the brick-and-mortar stores and online subscribers.[77] Blockbuster has also sought out a video download partner so its customers will have three ways to attain movies—in-store, mail order, or download. "While Blockbuster trailed behind in the online DVD rental business after entering it in 2004—five years after Netflix—it's not taking a wait-and-see attitude toward movie downloads."[78]

Movie Gallery, Inc.

Movie Gallery is the second-largest North American video rental retail chain, with more than 4,700 stores located in all 50 states, Canada, and Mexico.[79] Its growth strategy is internal growth and pursuing selective complementary acquisitions. "By focusing on rural and secondary markets, [Movie Gallery] is able to compete very effectively against the independently owned stores and small regional chains in these areas."[80] Movie Gallery's acquisition of Hollywood Entertainment in 2005 made the company stronger and more competitive with Blockbuster by challenging Blockbuster on its strength—owning stores in prime locations.

By acquiring Hollywood Entertainment, Movie Gallery inherited 74 automated movie vending machine kiosks similar to ATMs, which "provide around the clock availability of movies" for rent.[81] Because of the minimal overhead and fixed costs associated with the kiosks Movie Gallery intends to expand its fleet with a rollout of an additional 200 units through 2007.[82]

Joe Malugen, chairperson, president, and CEO of Movie Gallery, stated "While we firmly believe that our retail brick-and-mortar stores will remain the foundation of our business, over the past three years we have been diligently pursuing alternative delivery platforms to further complement our base business."[83] As such, in March 2007 Movie Gallery purchased MovieBeam, a movies-on-demand service, which was created and funded by Walt Disney Co., Cisco Systems, and Intel Capital.[84] Movies are "beamed" into consumer homes using MovieBeam's patented over-the-air data-casting technology to the set-top box.[85] Currently, this technology is limited to television set use only, but Movie Gallery plans to expand these services to video on demand capability over the Internet.[86]

Hastings Entertainment. Hastings Entertainment operates in approximately 20 midwestern and western states, focusing on small to medium-sized towns with underserved markets (towns with populations of 33,000 to 105,000).[87] This multimedia retailer "combines the sale of new and used CDs, books, videos, and video games, as well as boutique merchandise, with the rental of videos and video games in a superstore format."[88] Sales and rentals of videos and games account for the primary revenue stream (35 percent) with music sales pulling in the second highest amount (25 percent).[89] According to Hoover's Inc., "As is the case throughout most of the rental industry, Hastings video rental sales continue to drop in the face of mail-order rental houses like Netflix and video on demand services from cable companies."[90] Although Blockbuster, Movie Gallery, and Hastings Entertainment are the "Big Three" competitors for Netflix, other movie delivery methods exist and capture some of the market share.

Other Competitors

While movie rentals are the most common method for viewing newly released films or older pictures, other channels are available. These channels include movie retail stores (e.g., Best Buy, Wal-Mart, and Amazon.com); subscription entertainment services (e.g., Showtime and HBO); Internet movie providers (e.g., iTunes, Amazon.com, Movielink, CinemaNow.com, and Vongo); Internet companies (e.g., Yahoo! and Google); and cable and direct broadcast satellite providers.[91]

To remain a key player in the industry it is just as important for Netflix to consider the movie content providers as it is the competitors.

Content Providers

Netflix has exercised great effort in establishing strong relationships with a number of entertainment film providers. They have sought to ensure that the relationships are mutually beneficial. Netflix obtains content from the studios through either revenue sharing agreements or direct purchase. The revenue sharing program provides Netflix with a tremendous cost savings, and in return provides the studios a percentage of Netflix's subscription revenues for a defined period of time. This agreement also allows the studios an additional distribution outlet for new releases, television shows, and so on. Once the defined period for the revenue sharing has ended for a particular movie title, Netflix will destroy the title, purchase the title, or return it to the studio.

Netflix contracts movies offered through its instant-viewing feature with studios and other content providers on a fixed fee or per-view basis. The general arrangement is the same, but the specific terms are often unique to each provider.[92]

Netflix orders movies in two different formats: HD-DVD and Blu-Ray[93] through content providers such as Hollywood Film studios, 20th Century Fox, Walt Disney Studios, Columbia Pictures, Lions Gate Films, New Line Cinema, Paramount Pictures, Universal Pictures, Warner Bros. Pictures, and other independent film studios.[94]

The online rental industry has enjoyed large growth and success up to this point largely due to the distribution rules established by studios. Currently, DVDs are available for movie rental and retail sales three to six months before the movies are available on pay-per-view and VOD, nine months before satellite and cable, and two to three years before basic cable and syndicated networks. The studios have discussed either eliminating the distribution windows or shortening them, which would adversely affect Netflix.[95]

Netflix has been able to establish a relationship with content providers and differentiate itself among competitors through its strategic approach.

Netflix's Strategies and Functional Operations

Netflix is focused on continuous improvement and metrics to add value to the business and the customers' experience.[96] All these goals culminate into one overlying company strategic goal—to maintain a low-cost structure. Dillon states,

The Company's fulfillment costs are about half what Blockbuster's are, which enables profitability at a lower price. Every penny counts in a high-volume business. As we keep lowering our cost, we're able to lower our price. It's a very elastic market; so, the lower the price, the more our market grows.[97]

As mentioned previously, the company developed strategic alliances with sources in the film and television sectors.[98] These arrangements provided a significant cost savings, which freed up funds to use for other projects and investments, such as the continued investment and development of its proprietary software for inventory management, logistics, and shipping.[99]

Netflix has also carefully managed its payroll expenses to keep in line with the low-cost structure. "When the company first started in 1999, Netflix had 75,000 customers and was using 100 employees to package software for customer support."[100] Netflix cut that number roughly in half with just 45 current employees serving more than 6 million subscribers.[101] This dramatic cut in staffing is driven by an essentially self-service Web site and home-grown support software that enables representatives to handle higher volumes.[102] Tom Dillon, COO explains,

We firmly believe in building IT from scratch; this is a custom business. . . . If you want to get it done exactly the way you want, build it yourself. . . . IT is not a strategic weapon in most companies. But in our company, IT is the business. We live and breathe [the idea] that the way you get more competitive, lower your costs, and provide better service is through continuous improvement of the information technology.[103]

Netflix transcended the norms for IT use and will continue to rely on its information technology capabilities and resources. It has built a strong, reliable Web platform that is compatible with all kinds of portals and browsers in order to sustain a large number of users and maintain a positive "brand experience."[104]

Netflix is a company that competes on its strong foundation of mathematical, statistical, and data management expertise and uses these strengths to further distinguish itself from other competitors.[105] It uses analytics in two different ways. Internally created, algorithmically driven software makes movie recommendations for customers through a system called Cinematch.[106] This capability essentially led to the creation of personalized Web sites for each customer who visits Netflix and gives a customized interaction with every individual.[107] Netflix also uses a process called *throttling*. With this process, the company balances the frequent-use and infrequent-use distribution shipping requests of its customers.[108] Infrequent-use customers are given higher priority in shipping than frequent-use customers.[109] Some customers became disgruntled when they learned that Netflix uses the throttling process. Netflix's senior leaders did not seemed concerned about the complaints as shown in a statement by CEO Reed Hastings, "Few customers have complained about this 'fairness algorithm.' We have unbelievably high customer satisfaction ratings." In January, 1995 Netflix changed its "terms of use" to read "In determining priority for shipping and inventory allocation, we give priority to those members who receive the fewest DVDs through our service."[110]

Netflix's services provide value for its large customer base. The value provided has led Netflix to be almost four times larger than Blockbuster's in regard to subscribers for the online service, and to maintain this position, Netflix is continually reinvesting its money into marketing.[111]

Marketing Approaches

Marketing has been a key advantage for Netflix. Early on it established an agreement with Best Buy in that Best Buy set up a cobranded version of the online DVD rental service on its five online Web sites and instituted a joint-marketing program in the 1,800-plus retail stores. In return, Netflix directs its customers interested

Exhibit 2 Advertising Expenditures

As of	Blockbuster	Netflix
December 2006	$154,300,000	$225,524,000
December 2005	252,700,000	144,562,000
December 2004	257,400,000	100,534,000
December 2003	179,400,000	49,949,000

Sources: http://www.marketwatch.com; Netflix SEC10-K 2003, Netflix SEC10-K 2004, Netflix SEC10-K 2005, and Netflix SEC10-K 2006.

Exhibit 3 Historic Stock Price and P/E Ratios

	2006	2005	2004	2003	2002
High Price	33.12	30.25	39.77	30.50	9.10
Low Price	18.12	8.91	9.25	5.93	2.42
Year-End Price	25.86	27.06	12.33	27.35	5.51
High P/E	46.61	47.16	119.18	294.52	−12.25
Low P/E	25.50	13.89	27.72	57.21	−3.26
Year-End P/E	36.39	42.19	36.95	264.05	−7.41

Source: http://stocks.us.reuters.com/stocks/performance.asp?symbol= NFLX.O&WTmodLOC=L2-LeftNav-18-Performace.

in buying DVDs to Best Buy's Web sites.[112] It has a similar agreement with Wal-Mart; both companies have promoted one another since 2005 when Wal-Mart exited the online movie market.[113]

Other marketing efforts include online advertisements such as banner ads, paid search listings, pop-up advertisements, and text on popular Web portals—Yahoo!, MSN, and AOL.[114] Netflix was ranked as being the number two company to spend the most money on online advertisements.[115] Most online retailers face budget restrictions on advertising expenditures, as did Netflix in the beginning, and therefore are selective in the channels of advertising,[116] but as Netflix's subscriber base has grown, so has its advertising budget and expenditures (see Exhibit 2).

Netflix also targets a broad demographic in its advertising plan by running ads on the mainstream networks—ABC, NBC, FOX, and CBS, as well as radio advertisements.[117] Direct mail, print advertising, and promotions in certain consumer package goods are used as well in their marketing strategy.[118]

For online video rental, Netflix pioneered the use of database marketing to develop a personalized relationship with consumers. The database, possible because of Netflix's strengths in IT, allowed Netflix to understand individual customers, aggregate and predict behaviors, and then send customized e-mails informing customers of what new movies are available. Netflix has a strong culture of analytics and a test-and-learn approach to its business.[119] Metrics tracked include Web site users, advertising testing, data mining, subscriber satisfaction, segment research, and marketing material effectiveness.[120] Often, the effectiveness of its marketing endeavors can be assessed by reviewing the company's financials.

Financial Results

Stock Related Issues

Netflix's stock price has been highly volatile since its IPO on May 22, 2002. After adjusting for the eventual 2-for-1 stock split on February 12, 2004, its first year stock was valued anywhere between $2.42 and $9.10.[121] In the following three years, the stock price fluctuated even more until it started showing signs of stabilization in 2006 (see

Exhibit 3). The earnings per share (EPS) for Netflix has been constantly on the rise (see Exhibit 4). Estimates for 2007 and 2008 suggest that this trend will continue at a reasonable rate, which can also be seen in Exhibit 4.

Also important to note is Netflix's P/E ratios. Netflix's 006 P/E ratio of 32.88 (2007) is showing a trend toward becoming more in line with the rest of the industry, which has a current P/E ratio of 29.17.[122] This high P/E ratio indicates that the market views Netflix as having a higher potential for future earning compared to others in the video rental industry. Netflix's P/E ratio has moved from an extremely high number in 2003 to its more stable current P/E ratio. Historic P/E ratios can be found in Exhibit 3.[123]

Company Liquidity

The current ratios for 2002–2006 can be found in Exhibit 6. Netflix has consistently had a high current ratio, always above 1.75.[124] As of December 2006, its current ratio was 2.20, while the rest of the industry had a less favorable ratio of .59.[125] At 2006 year end, the cash ratio was 2.09 and the debt ratio was .319. With all these ratios considered, Netflix seems to be in a favorable position. (See Exhibit 5 for balance sheet information.)

Company Profitability

Netflix has continued to increase revenues since its IPO at a significant rate.[126] The net profit margin has remained in the 4 to 6 range for the past three years and appears to be the most stable profitability ratio. This value is significantly lower than the industry's net profit margin at 14.80.[127] Return on assets, return on stockholders' equity, operating profit margin, and net profit margin have all been computed and listed in Exhibit 7.

Competitor and Industry Financial Ratios

See Exhibit 8 for a list comparing Netflix to its main competitors—Blockbuster, Hastings Entertainment, and Movie Gallery—and to other industry averages.

Exhibit 4 Income Statement

Income Statement
(in US$ thousands, except per share data)

	2002	2003	2004	2005	2006	2007 (est.)	2008E
Revenues	$150,818	$270,410	$500,611	$682,213	$996,660	$1,295,550	$1,595,890
Cost of revenues							
Subscription	77,044	147,736	273,401	393,788	532,621		
Fulfillment expenses	20,421	32,623	58,311	71,987	94,364		
Total cost of revenues	$ 97,465	$180,359	$331,712	$465,775	$626,985		
Gross profit	53,353	90,051	168,899	216,438	369,675	w	
Operating expenses							
Technology and development	$ 17,632	$ 21,863	$ 29,467	$ 35,388	$ 48,379		
Marketing	37,423	51,535	100,534	144,562	225,524		
General and administrative	9,867	13,390	22,104	35,486	36,155		
Gain on disposal of DVDs	(896)	(1,209)	(2,560)	(1,987)	(4,797)		
Total operating expenses	$ 64,026	$ 85,579	$149,545	213,449	$305,261		
Operating income (loss)	$(10,673)	$ 4,472	$ 19,354	$ 2,989	$ 64,414		
Other income (expense)							
Interest and other income	1,697	2,457	2,592	5,753	15,904		
Interest and other expense	(11,972)	(417)	(170)	(407)	–		
Income (loss) before income taxes	$(20,948)	$ 6,512	$ 21,776	$ 8,335	$ 80,318		
Provisions for (benefit from) income taxes	–	–	181	(33,692)	31,236		
Net income (loss)	$(20,948)	$ 6,512	$ 21,595	$ 42,027	$ 49,082		
Net income (loss) per share:							
Basic	$ (0.74)	$ 0.14	$ 0.42	$ 0.79	$ 0.78	$ 0.79	$ 1.04
Diluted	$ (0.74)	$ 0.10	$ 0.33	$ 0.64	$ 0.71		
Weighted average shares outstanding							
Basic	$ 28,204	$ 47,786	$ 51,988	$ 53,528	$ 62,577		
Diluted	$ 28,204	$ 62,884	$ 64,713	$ 65,518	$ 69,075		
Year-end price per share	$ 5.51	$ 27.35	$ 12.33	$ 27.06	$ 25.86		
Price/earnings ratios	(7.45)	273.50	37.36	42.28	36.42	29.83	21.79

Sources: Netflix SEC10-K 2002, Netflix SEC10-K 2003, Netflix SEC10-K 2004, Netflix SEC10-K 2005, and Netflix SEC10-K 2006; http://stocks.us.reuters.com/stocks/estimates.asp?symbol=NFLX.

Exhibit 5 Balance Sheet

Balance Sheet (in US$ thousands, except share and per share data)					
	2002	2003	2004	2005	2006
Assets					
Current assets					
Cash and cash equivalents	$59,814	$89,894	$174,461	$212,256	$400,430
Short-term investments	43,796	45,297	–	7,848	4,742
Prepaid expenses	2,753	2,231	2,741	5,252	9,456
Prepaid revenue sharing expenses	303	905	4,695	13,666	3,155
Other current asses	409	619	5,449	4,669	10,635
Total current assets	107,075	138,946	187,346	243,691	428,418
DVD library, net	9,972	22,238	42,158	57,032	104,908
Intangible assets	6,094	2,948	961	457	969
Property and equipment, net	5,620	9,772	18,728	40,213	55,503
Deposits	1,690	1,272	1,600	1,249	1,316
Deferred tax assets	–	–	–	21,239	15,600
Other assets	79	836	1,000	800	2,065
Total assets	$130,530	$176,012	$251,793	$364,681	$608,779
Liabilities and Stockholders' Equity					
Current liabilities					
Accounts payable	$20,350	$32,654	$ 49,775	$ 63,491	$93,864
Accrued expenses	9,102	11,625	13,131	25,563	29,905
Deferred revenue	9,743	18,324	31,936	48,533	69,678
Current portion of capital lease obligations	1,231	416	68	–	–
Total current liabilities	40,426	63,019	94,910	137,587	193,447
Deferred rent	288	241	600	842	1,121
Capital lease obligations, less current portion	460	44	68	–	–
Total liabilities	$41,174	$63,019	$95,510	$138,429	194,568
Commitments and contingencies					
Stockholders' equity	45	51	53	55	69
Additional paid-in capital	260,044	270,836	292,843	315,868	454,731
Deferred stock-based compensation	(11,702)	(5,482)	(4,693)	–	–
Accumulated other comprehensive income (loss)	774	596	(222)	–	–
Accumulated deficit	(159,805)	(153,293)	(131,698)	(89,671)	(40,589)
Total stockholders' equity	$89,356	$112,708	$156,283	$226,252	$414,211
Total liabilities and stockholders' equity	$130,530	$176,012	$251,793	$364,681	$608,779

Sources: Netflix SEC10-K 2002, Netflix SEC10-K 2003, Netflix SEC10-K 2004, Netflix SEC10-K 2005, and Netflix SEC10-K 2006.

Netflix experienced some financial setbacks in the first quarter of 2007, most of which can be attributed to its key strategic challenges.

Key Strategic Challenges

Netflix faces a rapidly developing competitive environment with new technological innovations affecting product and service offerings among the various movie rental businesses, whether it be a brick-and-mortar store, click-and-mortar store, or online business. However, perhaps the main challenge Netflix will encounter is trying to figure out how to adjust its business model to the new technological pressures while staying true to the company's strengths and providing value to its subscribers.

Churn

Churn is the cancellation of a subscription service. Churn can be triggered by a number of factors: insufficient use of the service does not justify the expense; delivery is

Exhibit 6 Liquidity Ratio

	2002	2003	2004	2005	2006
Current ratio	2.65	2.20	1.97	1.77	2.20

Sources: Netflix SEC10-K 2002, Netflix SEC10-K 2003, Netflix SEC10-K 2004, Netflix SEC10-K 2005, and Netflix SEC10-K 2006.

Exhibit 7 Profitability Ratios

	2002	2003	2004	2005	2006
Return on assets (%)	−19.56	3.70	11.53	11.52	8.06
Return on stockholders' equity	−23.44	5.78	13.93	18.58	11.85
Operating profit	−13.89	2.41	4.35	1.22	8.06
Net profit margin	−13.89	2.41	4.31	6.16	4.92

Sources: Netflix SEC10-K 2002, Netflix SEC10-K 2003, Netflix SEC10-K 2004, Netflix SEC10-K 2005, and Netflix SEC10-K 2006.

Exhibit 8 Comparative Performance of Netflix and Key Competitors

	Blockbuster BBI	Hastings Entertainment HAST	Movie Gallery MOVI.O	Netflix NFLX	Industry Median
Profitability					
Gross profit margin	54.68%	67.62%	60.19%	37.09%	48.94%
Pre-tax profit margin	−0.15%	1.51%	−0.95%	8.06%	16.47%
Net profit margin	1.23%	0.59%	−1.01%	4.93%	14.82%
Return on equity	10.54%	5.22%	–	15.33%	11.84%
Return on assets	2.15%	1.26%	−2.03%	10.08%	6.37%
Valuation					
Price/Sales ratio	0.22	0.12	0.06	1.60	2.82
Price/Earnings ratio	21.43	13.99	–	32.92	18.97
Price/Book ratio	2.06	0.69	–	3.84	3.80
Operations					
Inventory turnover	7.57	3.28	7.30	–	27.08
Asset turnover	1.75	2.13	2.00	2.05	0.52
Financial					
Current ratio	1.12	1.63	0.89	2.22	0.63
Quick ratio	0.88	0.16	0.37	2.22	0.48
Total debt/Equity ratio	1.33	0.42	–	0.00	0.68

Sources: http://stocks.us.reuters.com/stocks/ratios.asp?symbol=NFLX.O&WTmodLOC=L2-LeftNav-16-Ratios; http://stocks.us.reuters.com/stocks/ratios.asp?symbol=BBI.N; http://stocks.us.reuters.com/stocks/ratios.asp?symbol=MOVI.OQ; http://www.investor.reuters.wallst.com/stocks/Ratios.asp?rpc=66&ticker=HAST.O.

too long; poor service; or competitive services provide better added value and/or experience to the consumer. These factors are critical to any online movie rental business, but especially for Netflix because its entire business model is based on attracting and maintaining subscribers (see Exhibits 9 and 10).

Some of the company's key competitors have more brand name recognition, experience, and financial resources to provide value to the customer. This makes it difficult for Netflix to compete at its existing price level or at lower price level structures in the future. Netflix needs to offer services that compete effectively.

Managing Growth

Finally, Netflix must have the ability and foresight to manage extensive growth to maintain its current service

Exhibit 9 Potential Growth for Netflix

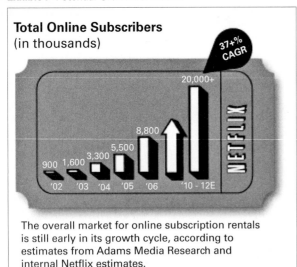

Total Online Subscribers
(in thousands)

37+% CAGR

900 1,600 3,300 5,500 8,800 20,000+
'02   '03   '04   '05   '06   '10 - 12E

The overall market for online subscription rentals is still early in its growth cycle, according to estimates from Adams Media Research and internal Netflix estimates.

Exhibit 11 Subscriber Growth

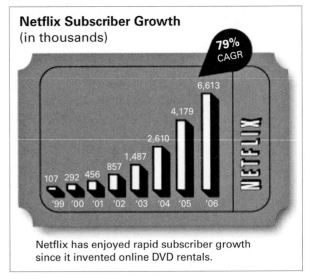

Netflix Subscriber Growth
(in thousands)

79% CAGR

107 292 456 857 1,487 2,610 4,179 6,613
'99 '00 '01 '02 '03   '04   '05   '06

Netflix has enjoyed rapid subscriber growth since it invented online DVD rentals.

Exhibit 10 Subscriber Churn

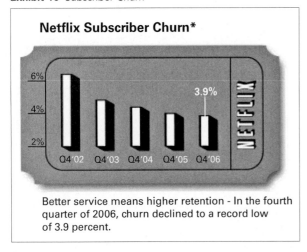

Netflix Subscriber Churn*

6%
4%
2%

3.9%

Q4 '02   Q4 '03   Q4 '04   Q4 '05   Q4 '06

Better service means higher retention - In the fourth quarter of 2006, churn declined to a record low of 3.9 percent.

Exhibit 12 Netflix Distribution Network

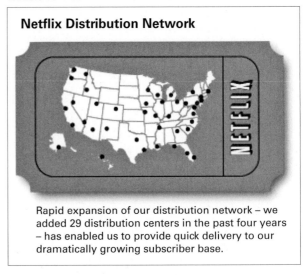

Netflix Distribution Network

Rapid expansion of our distribution network – we added 29 distribution centers in the past four years – has enabled us to provide quick delivery to our dramatically growing subscriber base.

level. Since the company's launch in 1998, Netflix has seen phenomenal growth and profitability (see Exhibit 11). As the company grows, it must add additional distribution centers to its already existing infrastructure (see Exhibit 12). However, if the company does not properly prepare for a continual increase in clientele Netflix's managerial operations and financial resources could be spread too thin, which translates into orders not being met and customer satisfaction levels decreasing.

The Central Question

Reed Hastings started Netflix on the premonition that users would buy into his business concept of online movie rental without the hassle of late fees and due dates while choosing a movie from the confines of their home. With Hastings's vision and charisma, along with his strong supporting cast of IT, marketing, and entertainment industry experts, Netflix set in motion a new wave of how consumers viewed the movie rental business. Netflix was the primary proponent of change in the movie rental business. Now, the key concern is how to cope with industry and technological trends that are evolving. Should Netflix transition from an online movie rental business to solely VOD or streaming services? Or can Netflix maintain its stronghold position with its current business model while making slight improvements to keep current with VOD and other new technologies? Should Netflix's strategic leaders and decision makers consider a merger or a joint venture with another company in order to offer a unique basket of services to consumers? Netflix must weigh its options carefully. It has established brand equity and delivered a distinctive solution during its short history. Now Netflix must realize how it can sustain its business livelihood in a cutthroat, highly competitive industry.

NOTES

1. 2006, Netflix Inc. Annual Report.
2. M. Helft, 2007, Netflix to deliver movies to the PC, *New York Times*, http://www.nytimes.com/2007/01/16/technology/16netflix.html?ex=1326603600&en=71618d2092f5b372&ei=5088&partner=rssnyt&emc=rss, January.
3. 2007, Hoover's Company Reports—Full Overview, Netflix, February 8.
4. 2007, Hoover's Company Reports—Full Overview, Blockbuster Inc., February 10.
5. 2007, Blockbuster Total Access—How It Works, http://www.blockbuster.com.
6. Ibid.
7. Ibid.
8. Ibid.
9. 2007, Netflix, Blockbuster competes for supremacy with new DVD services, *Pittsburgh Post Gazette*, January 30.
10. Hoover's company reports.
11. 2007, About Us, http://www.netflix.com, March.
12. 2007, First online DVD rental stores open, http://www.netflix.com/mediacenter, March.
13. 2007, Netflix's aggressive growth plan, http://www.netflix.com/mediacenter, March.
14. 2007, Netflix.com transforms DVD business eliminating late fees and due dates from movie rentals, http://www.netflix.com/mediacenter, March.
15. 2007, Netflix announces IPO, http://www.netflix.com/mediacenter, March.
16. 2004, Netflix announces Q4 revenue growth of 80% year over year and a 2-for-1 stock split, Netflix financial release, http://www.netflix.com, January 21.
17. 2006, Netflix announces Q4 2005 financial results, Netflix press release, http://www.netflix.com, January 24.
18. 2007, Netflix announces Q4 2006 financial results, Netflix press release, http:// www.netflix.com, January 24.
19. 2007, One billion and counting, http://www.netflix.com/mediacenter, March.
20. 2007, Netflix offers subscribers option of instantly watching movies on their PCs, http://www.netflix.com/mediacenter, March.
21. Ibid.
22. 2007, Netflix press release, http://www.netflix.com/MediaCenter, March 27.
23. 2007, http://www.netflix.com/mediacenter.
24. 2007, Netflix Hoover's Full Overview, http://premium.hoovers.com.
25. 2006 Netflix Inc. Annual Report.
26. 2007, Netflix board of director's committee composition, http://ir.netflix.com/committees.cfm.
27. J. Hopkins, 2006, Charismatic founder keeps Netflix adapting, *USA Today*, http://www.usatoday.com/money/companies/management/2006-04-23-exec-ceo-profile-netflix_x.htm, April 23.
28. Ibid.
29. Ibid.
30. 2007, Management, http://www.netflix.com/mediacenter.
31. Ibid.
32. Ibid.
33. Ibid.
34. Ibid.
35. Ibid.
36. Ibid.
37. P. Sauer, 2005, How I did it: Reed Hastings, Netflix, http://www.inc.com/magazine, December.

38. T. H. Davenport & J. G. Harris, 2007, Competing on analytics: The new science of winning, *The Nature of Analytical Competition*, http://harvardbusinessonline, 3.
39. Ibid., 4.
40. M. Kirdahy, 2007, Blockbuster takes on Netflix, *Forbes*, http://www.forbes.com, January 3.
41. 2007, Video on Demand (VOD): About Broadband Movies, Downloads and More, Broadbandinfo.com, http://www.broadbandinfo.com/got-high-speed/video-on-demand/default.html.
42. 2006, What's next for Netflix? *Financial Times*, http://www.ftpress.com/articles/article.asp?p=671844&rl=1, November 2.
43. 2007, The big picture, Hoovers.com, *Pittsburgh Tribune Review*, January 28.
44. Ibid.
45. 2007, Amazon.com, Amazon Unbox, http://www.amazon.com/gp/video/help/faq.html/ref=atv_dp_faq_dscvr/103-7381394-1357468#discover.
46. P. Gogoi, 2007, Wal-Mart enters the movie download wars, *BusinessWeek*, http://www.businessweek.com, February 6.
47. Ibid.
48. Ibid.
49. Ibid.
50. Ibid.
51. Ibid.
52. T. Krazit, 2004, Netflix, TiVo team up on broadband movie delivery, *PC World*, http://www.pcworld.com, September 30.
53. P. Sauer, How I did it: Reed Hastings, Netflix.
54. 2007, Blockbuster Inc., Netflix Full Overview, http://premium.hoovers.com, February 10.
55. Ibid.
56. Ibid.
57. Ibid.
58. Ibid.
59. Ibid .
60. 2000, Blockbuster Inc., Funding Universe—Company History, *International Directory of Company Histories*, http://www.fundinguniverse.com/company-histories/Blockbuster-Inc-Company-History.html.
61. Ibid.
62. Ibid.
63. Ibid .
64. Ibid.
65. Ibid.
66. Ibid.
67. Ibid.
68. Ibid.
69. Ibid.
70. Ibid.
71. 2007, Blockbuster CEO Antioco to leave company, *Yahoo! Finance*, http://www.finance.yahoo.com, March 23.
72. 2007, Blockbuster, Inc. Full Overview, Hoovers, http://premium.hoovers.com, February 10.
73. Ibid.
74. Ibid.
75. S. Ault, 2006, Blockbuster, Weinsteins sign exclusive deal, http://www.videobusiness.com.
76. M. Halkias, 2007, Blockbuster may buy downloading firm, *The Dallas Morning News*, March 1.
77. Ibid.

78. Ibid.

79. 2007, About Movie Gallery, Moviegallery.com, http://www
.moviegallery.com, March 18.

80. Ibid.

81. 2007, Movie Gallery to introduce online video rental service
and extend automated video vending machine program,
Movie Gallery press release, http://phx.corporate-ir.net/phoenix
.zhtml?c=85959&p=irol-newsArticle&ID=975465&highlight=,
March 25.

82. 2007, Movie Gallery to launch online service, http://www
.businessweek.com, March 19; R.C. Lim, 2007, Movie Gallery
mayhem, *Motley Fool Stock Advisor*, www.fool.com/investing,
July 24.

83. Ibid.

84. P. Sweeting & C. Spielvogel, 2007, Movie Gallery acquires
MovieBeam, www.videobusiness.com, March 7; 2007, Movie
Gallery News Release, http://www.moviegallery.com, March 7.

85. Ibid.

86. Ibid.

87. 2007, Hastings Entertainment, Hoovers.com, http://premium.
hoovers.com/subscribe/co/overview.xhtml?ID=ffffctthjfcxryycrk,
February 10.

88. 2007, About Hastings, Gohastings.com,http://www.gohastings
.com/Investor/AboutHastings.stm, February 10.

89. 2007, Netflix Full Overview, http://premium.hoovers.com, February 10.

90. Ibid.

91. 2006, Netflix Inc. Annual Report.

92. Ibid.

93. Ibid.

94. 2007, Motion Picture access, major film studios in the U.S., http://
ncam.wgbh.org/mopix/studios.html.

95. 2006, Netflix Inc. Annual Report.

96. Ibid.

97. Ibid.

98. Ibid.

99. Ibid.

100. Ibid.

101. Ibid.

102. Ibid.

103. Ibid.

104. M. Levy, 2002, Netflix analyzed via the value framework, http://
www.valueframeworkinstitute.org/May2002/feature.article.htm,
May.

105. T. H. Davenport & J. G. Harris, 2007, Competing on analytics.

106. Ibid.

107. Ibid.

108. Ibid.

109. Ibid.

110. 2006, Frequent Netflix renters sent to the back of the line,
Associated Press, http://www.msnbc.msn.com/id/11262292/,
February 10.

111. P. Sauer, 2005, How I did it: Reed Hastings, Netflix.

112. 2001, Best Buy and Netflix offer co-branded online DVD movie
rental service, *Retailer Merchandiser*, http://www.allbusiness.com/
retail, September 11.

113. P. Sauer, How I did it: Reed Hastings, Netflix.

114. 2006, Netflix Inc. Annual Report.

115. L. Punch, 2007, Advertising to the masses, http://www
.internetretailer.com, January.

116. Ibid.

117. Ibid.

118. 2006 Netflix Inc. Annual Report.

119. Ibid.

120. Ibid.

121. 2007, Historical prices for Netflix Inc., *Yahoo! Finance*, http://
finance
.yahoo.com/q/hp?s=NFLX&a=00&b=5&c=2002&d=03&e=17&f=2
007&g=m.

122. 2007, Summary for Netflix Inc., *Yahoo! Finance*,http://finance.yahoo
.com/q?s=nflx&x=0&y=0.

123. 2007, Netflix Inc. performance, http://stocks.us.reuters.com/stocks/
performance.asp?symbol=NFLX.O&WTmodLOC=L2-LeftNav-18-
Performace.

124. 2006, Netflix Inc. Annual Report.

125. 2007, Netflix Inc. ratios, http://stocks.us.reuters.com/stocks/ratios
.asp?symbol=NFLX.O&WTmodLOC=L2-LeftNav-16-Ratios.

126. 2006, Netflix Inc. Annual Report.

127. Ibid.

CASE 27
Oasis Hong Kong Airlines: The First Long-Haul, Low-Cost Airliner in Asia

Gary Chan, Andrew Lee

The University of Hong Kong, Asia Case Research Centre

It was August 2006, and Stephen Miller, chief executive officer (CEO) of the newly founded Oasis Hong Kong Airlines, was busy rallying his management team for the purpose of launching Asia's first long-haul, low-cost carrier. Oasis intended to pioneer the concept of affordable business class and offer one-way economy-class fares between Hong Kong and London for as little as HK$1,000.[1] Miller was confident that with a unique business model, solid financial backing from a few entrepreneurial investors, and almost 30 years of experience in the aviation industry under his belt, he had what it took to make Oasis a success. Meanwhile, Miller stumbled upon a Singapore Airlines advertisement in the *South China Morning Post* offering a special round-trip fare from Hong Kong to London for HK$2,950 (US$378). As he glanced over the advertisement again, he decided that traditional airlines had thrown down the gauntlet and that the time had come for him to prove that his business model would prosper.

The Airline Industry

The International Airline Industry[2]

The shape of the international airline industry was largely the result of deregulation, privatization, liberal air traffic agreements, and economic downturns. The United States led the world in air traffic deregulation in 1977 when it deregulated its domestic air cargo market, allowing carriers the freedom to choose domestic routes and set fares. This was followed by deregulation in the passenger market, which started in 1978, relaxing restrictions on fares, routes, and mergers. By 1981, all restrictions on routes and services had been eliminated and, by 1983, all rate regulations were ended.

Within approximately 20 years after deregulation, the number of airlines operating in the United States had roughly doubled and passenger traffic had nearly tripled.[3] By one estimate, roughly 85 percent of passengers had a choice of at least two airlines in 2001. Meanwhile, air fares had fallen by 35 percent. Major airlines found themselves settling on a few major hubs as the foundation for connecting passenger and cargo traffic to other destinations. This structure came to be known as the hub-and-spoke.

As deregulation forced U.S. carriers to become more efficient and competitive, the competitive pressure was felt throughout the rest of the world and triggered a series of privatizations of flag carriers in Europe and Japan, many of which had been state-owned. British Airways, for instance, was restructured and floated in 1987. Similarly, in 2000, the Japanese government deregulated its domestic market and privatized Japan Airlines. Nonetheless, many European national carriers that sustained losses were still heavily subsidized by their respective governments, and other carriers outside of Europe and Japan, even if not state-owned, still maintained a very close relationship with their governments. For example, such flag carriers and listed companies as Singapore Airlines, China Airlines, and Air China were all majority-held by entities that could be traced back to their respective national governments.

International air traffic remained regulated by bilateral air services agreements that were negotiated between countries. These agreements were often very elaborate, detailing the granting of different traffic rights and specifying which airlines could fly which routes and at what capacity and frequency. Traffic rights described in these agreements were commonly known as Freedoms of the Air (see Exhibit 1). Since 1992, the United States had

Gary Chan and Andrew Lee prepared this case under the supervision of Dr. Venkat Subramanian for class discussion. This case is not intended to show effective or ineffective handling of decision or business processes.

Exhibit 1 Freedoms of the Air

First Freedom of the Air: The right or privilege, in respect of scheduled international air services, granted by one State to another State or States to fly across its territory without landing. This is also known as a **First Freedom Right.**

Second Freedom of the Air: The right or privilege, in respect of scheduled international air services, granted by one State to another State or States to land in its territory for non-traffic purposes. This is also known as a **Second Freedom Right.**

Third Freedom of the Air: The right or privilege, in respect of scheduled international air services, granted by one State to another State to put down, in the territory of the first State, traffic coming from the home State of the carrier. This is also known as a **Third Freedom Right.**

Fourth Freedom of the Air: The right or privilege, in respect of scheduled international air services, granted by one State to another State to take on, in the territory of the first State, traffic destined for the home State of the carrier. This is also known as a **Fourth Freedom Right.**

Fifth Freedom of the Air: The right or privilege, in respect of scheduled international air services, granted by one State to another State to put down and to take on, in the territory of the first State, traffic coming from or destined for a third State. This is also known as a **Fifth Freedom Right.**

   ICAO characterizes all freedoms beyond the Fifth Freedom as "so-called" because only the first five "freedoms" have been officially recognized as such by international treaty.

Sixth Freedom of the Air: The right or privilege, in respect of scheduled international air services, of transporting, via the home country of the carrier, traffic moving between two other countries. This is also known as a **Sixth Freedom Right.**

Seventh Freedom of the Air: The right or privilege, in respect of scheduled international air services, granted by one State to another State, of transporting traffic between the territory of the granting State and any third State with no requirement to include on such operation any point in the territory of the recipient State (i.e., the service need not connect to or be an extension of any service to or from the home State of the carrier). This is also known as a **Seventh Freedom Right.**

Eighth Freedom of the Air: The right or privilege, in respect of scheduled international air services, of transporting cabotage traffic between two points in the territory of the granting State on a service which originates or terminates in the home country of the foreign carrier or (in connection with the so-called "Seventh Freedom of the Air") outside the territory of the granting State. This is also known as an **Eighth Freedom Right** or **"consecutive cabotage."**

Ninth Freedom of the Air: The right or privilege of transporting cabotage traffic of the granting country on a service performed entirely within the territory of the granting country. This is also known as a **Ninth Freedom Right** or **"stand-alone cabotage."**

Source: ICAO, 2006, Freedoms of the air, http://www.icao.int/icao/en/trivia/freedoms_air.htm (accessed November 19, 2006).

been advocating and signing the so-called Open Skies agreements with foreign governments. These bilateral or multilateral agreements included unrestricted landing rights on each other's soil and unrestricted capacity and frequency; however, these agreements did not allow increased foreign ownership or control of airlines, nor did they grant cabotage freedom in the United States or U.S. domestic traffic rights, to foreign carriers. Meanwhile, the European Union (EU) was increasingly behaving like a single nation. In April 1997, the EU took a major step toward deregulation by allowing an airline from one member state to fly within another member's domestic market.[4] In 2000, the EU established the Common European Aviation Area, comprising all 15 member states and within which airlines of member states would have full traffic rights and ability to set fares.

Types of Carriers

There are three primary types of commercial carriers: scheduled airlines, charter airlines, and feeder airlines.

Scheduled airlines, the most common type and the one with which most passengers are familiar, operate year-round on established schedules. International carriers of this type operate under the framework of the bilateral air services agreements described earlier. Any international carrier that obtains approval to operate under a bilateral agreement is a "designated carrier." Scheduled airlines sell their capacities directly to the public within specified fare levels, which must be filed with and approved by their respective governments.

Charter airlines differ from scheduled airlines in that they do not operate on established schedules, but rather as ad hoc services, either to support the operations of scheduled airlines or to meet the demands of specific groups of customers. Charter airlines do not operate under the normal bilateral agreements, and each flight is separately approved by the respective governments. Some airlines that had started off as charter airlines eventually became scheduled airlines. From time to time, scheduled airlines also operate charter services.

The third type of commercial carrier, feeder airlines, are mostly scheduled airlines operating smaller aircraft for the primary purpose of carrying passengers from smaller cities to larger air traffic hubs for connections with other flights. As the aviation industry evolved, many of these smaller feeder airlines either were bought out by their larger competitors or simply perished under the pressure of fierce competition. Because most feeder airlines operate domestic flights, their operations do not involve any bilateral agreements between nations.

Traditional and Low-Cost Carriers

A commercial scheduled airline could be either a traditional carrier or a low-cost carrier. While most commonly known airlines in 2006 (e.g., United Airlines, British Airways, Cathay Pacific Airways, and Singapore Airlines) were traditional carriers, the late 1990s and early 2000s saw a proliferation of low-cost carriers in almost every part of the world. Inspired by Southwest Airlines' impressive success, as indicated by the fact that Southwest was the only major U.S. airline in 2005 that had remained profitable since the September 11, 2001, terrorist attacks,[5] many attempted to replicate this firm's business model either in the United States or in other parts of the world. By 2006, examples of low-cost carriers could be found in all major regions of the world: Southwest and JetBlue in North America; Ryanair and easyJet in Europe; Kingfisher and Air Deccan in India; Tiger Airways, Jetstar Asia, and Valuair in Singapore; Air Asia in Malaysia; and Jetstar and Virgin Blue in Australia.

Traditional Carriers. Traditional carriers usually provide a full complement of options and services throughout the entire passenger experience, from the point when a booking is made to the end of the return flight. They allow passengers to book tickets through various means, including travel agents (usually via one or more global computer reservation systems) and directly with the airline (which could be by phone, in person, or online), and provide a choice of up to four classes of cabin service. Upon check-in, using the International Air Transport Association (IATA) interline system, a traditional airline can check passengers and their baggage through to connecting flights on other airlines and issue onward boarding passes. For premium-class passengers or members of loyalty clubs, a comfortable waiting lounge is provided with complimentary food and beverages, as well as other services. Once on board, passengers are provided with various in-flight amenities, reading materials, in-flight audio and video programs (on a broadcast or on-demand basis via personal TVs or cabin-based screens), and hot meals and beverages. For some overnight flights, lounges are also available for select passengers to freshen up upon arrival. Service agents are present at arrival gates to assist passengers with connecting flights. Most traditional carriers provide these services at no additional cost to passengers.

Operating on a scheduled basis with a hub-and-spoke model, traditional carriers have multiple origins of sales and multiple destinations. For example, Cathay Pacific Airways, a Hong Kong–based traditional carrier that offered service between Tokyo and Los Angeles via Hong Kong, would sell tickets in Tokyo for both the Tokyo–Hong Kong sector and the Tokyo–Los Angeles sector. At the same time, a portion of seats would be reserved to be sold in Hong Kong for the Hong Kong–Los Angeles sector of the same flight. The proportions of seats assigned to the Tokyo–Los Angeles, Tokyo–Hong Kong, and Hong Kong–Los Angeles sectors would vary from flight to flight, based on the forecasted yield and demand at any particular time of the year, with the overall objective of optimizing profit. There are also many different fare classes within each cabin class that carry different validities and restrictions.

Most traditional carriers serve a variety of long-, medium- and short-haul destinations with a variety of aircraft types. British Airways, for instance, serves destinations from its bases in the United Kingdom, ranging from other points in the United Kingdom that are flights shorter than one hour, to trips to New York, which would take 8 hours, and Hong Kong, which would take 14 hours. To serve such a broad range of destinations, British Airways's fleet at this time consisted of a wide variety of aircraft types: Boeing 737s, 747s, 757s, 767s, and 777s; Airbus A319s, A320s, and A321s; and a few other smaller aircraft types.[6]

Traditional carriers often use expensive primary airports as bases and hubs. The major advantage of this model is that airlines can schedule effectively and capture passengers from more origins to more destinations through the hubs. This additional revenue generation allows carriers to operate flights between cities where point-to-point demand alone does not justify the operation economically. By dominating a hub, airlines may also be able to limit competition on certain routes because the supply of slots at leading airports is limited. Nevertheless, any flight irregularities occurring at the hub can wreak havoc on an airline's entire network.

Traditional carriers usually offer loyalty clubs or frequent-flyer programs, which rewarded frequent travelers with such privileges as lounge access, upgrades, and free tickets. Typically, rewards are based primarily on mileage flown, though mileage could also be earned by purchasing from partnering companies or using airline-branded credit cards. To strengthen and expand their hub-and-spoke networks, traditional airlines have chosen to form alliances. These alliances link the networks of their various member airlines and offer alliance-wide loyalty clubs that provide passengers with privileges throughout an alliance's enlarged network. The world's three largest alliances are Star Alliance, Sky Team, and Oneworld. As of 2005, Star Alliance was the largest, with 18 full members (including Lufthansa Airlines, United Airlines, and Singapore Airlines), and an estimated 23.6 percent share of the international air travel market.[7] Sky Team was the second largest, with 10 full members (including Northwest Airlines, Air France-KLM, and Korean Airlines) and a world market share of 20.7 percent. Oneworld was the smallest among the top three, with eight full members (including American Airlines, British Airways, Cathay Pacific, and Qantas Airways) and a world market share of 13.5 percent.

Low-Cost Carriers. The term "low-cost carriers" commonly refers to airlines that offer low ticket prices and limited services. However, when this term was first used, it referred specifically to carriers with lower operating-cost structures than traditional carriers. As competition and the overall business environment toughened, most airlines, traditional or otherwise, lowered their operating costs significantly, blurring the definition of the term. It was for this reason that low-cost carriers were later distinguished from traditional carriers by ticket prices and services rather than by cost structures.

Unlike traditional carriers, low-cost carriers tend not to use travel agents or computer reservation systems. Instead, they prefer to sell directly and limit their use of travel agents. Low-cost carriers usually provide a single-class cabin and very basic complimentary services such as soft drinks and peanuts. Southwest Airlines, for example, is well known for offering complimentary peanuts. Some also provide limited in-flight entertainment. One such example is JetBlue, which historically provided an in-flight entertainment system that broadcast satellite TV. Low-cost carriers commonly charge for additional services.

Low-cost carriers typically do not adopt the hub-and-spoke network business model. Instead, their networks consist of city pairs that support direct service, or point-to-point traffic. Many low-cost carriers believe that direct service is cheaper than the hub-and-spoke model. One industry observer even suggested that the cost of handling passengers in a hub-and-spoke system was as much as 45 percent higher than in a point-to-point system. With a simpler network, low-cost carriers also tend to have much simpler pricing systems and fewer fare classes than their traditional counterparts. To keep their costs low, low-cost carriers also fly to secondary airports. One example is easyJet, which, instead of flying in and out of London Heathrow, a major air transport hub in Europe, opted to base its London service out of London Gatwick.

Most low-cost carriers focus on short-haul services, flights of less than five hours. Because the type of operations of all the different flights is similar, low-cost carriers usually use just one type of aircraft. Since its inception, Southwest Airlines has flown only Boeing 737s. Although there were different versions of the 737 in the fleet, including the new generation 737, the commonality among the aircraft reduces the cost of both the spares inventory and the training of pilots, flight attendants, and maintenance personnel, and also facilitates quick turnarounds. Likewise, JetBlue adopted a similar model and flew only Airbus A320s, all with the same engine type.

Low-cost airlines were unlikely to be members of the IATA and did not value receiving feeder traffic or feeding traffic to other airlines. As a result, low-cost airlines do not complete interline check-ins or baggage transfers, nor are they members of an alliance. Indeed, Ryanair encourages passengers not to have any checked baggage[8] by reducing ticket prices by £2.5 for these passengers. In contrast, those with checked baggage have to pay £2.5 or £5.

Although typical low-cost carriers keep to themselves and do not collaborate with other airlines in the form of alliances, some are beginning to deviate a bit from this model. Southwest Airlines, which had an unprecedented 33 consecutive years of profit, is an example of a low-cost carrier doing so. In 2005, Southwest Airlines announced a code-sharing agreement[9] with ATA Airlines, allowing customers to book flights on ATA to fly to such destinations as Hawaii.[10] Some low-cost carriers also offer a simpler version of frequent-flyer programs. For example, Southwest Airlines operates a simple frequent-flyer program where points are accumulated based on the number of one-way trips, not mileage flown, and a free round-trip is rewarded for every 18 points accumulated. Similar to frequent flyer programs of traditional carriers, Southwest also allows spending on partner companies and through Southwest-branded credit cards to be converted into frequent flyer points.

Airline Economics

Airlines operate much like many other businesses in that the primary aim is to generate maximum revenue and incur minimum cost to maximize return on invested capital. For these firms, seats and cargo space, which travel at a particular time from one location to another, are the products. As products, passengers and cargo both have a very short shelf life (from the time the schedule is published to the time the gate closes for departure) and are perishable by nature (once an aircraft departs, any unsold products "perish").

To benchmark themselves against each other, airlines often examine their capacities in available seat kilometers (ASKs) for passenger service or available tonne kilometers (ATKs) for total capacity, including passenger and freight[11] (see Exhibit 2 for a glossary of airline terms). Two closely related benchmarks are

Exhibit 2 Glossary of Terms

Terms	Description
Available seat kilometer (ASK)	A measurement of an airline's passenger-carrying capacity, calculated by multiplying the number of seats available by the distance flown in kilometers. If miles are used, available seat mile (ASM) is used instead of ASK.
Available tonne kilometer (ATK)	A measurement of an airline's total capacity (including both passengers and cargo), calculated by multiplying the capacity in tonnes by the distance flown in kilometers. If miles are used, available ton mile (ATM) is used instead of ATK.
Block hours	The distance of a flight leg between two points, from the time when the aircraft is pushed back for takeoff to the time when the aircraft arrives at the gate. Compare with "flying hours."
Break-even load factor	The percentage load factor that represents the point at which an airline breaks even.
Cost per ASK	A unit cost measurement of an airline, calculated by dividing the total operating cost by ASK or ASM. This is regarded as an appropriate measurement for airlines with a predominant focus on passenger service.
Cost per ATK	A unit cost measurement of an airline, calculated by dividing the total operating cost by ATK or ATM. This is regarded as an appropriate measurement for airlines that provide only cargo service, or passenger as well as cargo service.
Cycle	A measurement of utilization, where one cycle equals one takeoff and landing.
Flying hours	The distance of a flight leg between two points, from the time when the aircraft lifts off the ground during takeoff to the time when the aircraft touches the ground during landing. Compare with "block hours."
Load factor	A measurement of capacity utilization in percentage, calculated by dividing RPK by ASK, or RTK by ATK.
Narrow-body aircraft or single-aisle aircraft	An aircraft that has a fuselage diameter of about 3 to 4 meters and has only one aisle in its seat arrangement.
Revenue passenger kilometer (RPK)	A measurement of passenger volume carried by an airline, calculated by multiplying the number of revenue-generating passengers by the distance flow in kilometers. If miles are used, revenue passenger mile (RPM) is used instead of RPK.
Revenue tonne kilometer (RTK)	A measurement of total volume carried by an airline, calculated by multiplying the revenue tonnage by the distance flown in kilometers. If ton and mile are used, revenue ton mile (RTM) is used instead of RTK.
Seat pitch	The distance between two rows of seats, typically in inches, measured from the back of one seat to the back of the seat directly behind it.
Sector	A sector is a direct flight between two cities and is usually represented by the city pair names. For example, Hong Kong–London is one sector and London–Hong Kong is another sector.
Sector length or stage length	The distance of a flight leg measured either in physical distance in kilometers (or miles) or time in hours. When it is measured in time, it can be represented in block hours or flying hours, depending on the purpose.
Wide-body aircraft or twin-aisle aircraft	An aircraft that has a fuselage diameter of about 5 to 6 meters and has only two aisles in its seat arrangement.

Sources: Adapted from http://moneyterms.co.uk, http://en.wikipedia.org, and industry sources.

revenue passenger kilometers (RPKs) and revenue tonne kilometers (RTKs); these benchmarks measure the number of seat kilometers or tonne kilometers that an airline sold during a particular period of time. To measure their financial performance, airlines published their unit costs in cost per ASK or ATK. The fraction of RPK over ASK yields the passenger load factor while the fraction of RTK over ATK shows the overall load factor.

For airlines focusing on passenger service, cost per ASK is used as a primary measure of unit cost. For airlines that also have a sizeable cargo service, a combined measurement, including cost per ATK, is used. Airlines also measure their ability to generate revenue with revenue per ASK and revenue per ATK.

Armed with these numbers and various other figures and forecasting tools, airlines employ sophisticated inventory management and pricing techniques to maximize revenue and profitability and to lower their breakeven load factors (see Exhibits 3 and 4 for the ASKs, ATKs, RPKs, RTKs, and related data of selected airlines).

Exhibit 3 Income Statements and Company Information of Two Low-Cost Carriers

	Southwest Airlines Year Ending December 31, 2005 (in US$ millions)	EasyJet Year Ending September 30, 2005 (in UK£ millions)
Total operating revenue		
Passenger	7,279	1,254
Freight	133	
Other	172	87
	7,584	1,341
Total operating expenses		
Salaries, wages & benefits	2,702[a]	267
Fuel & oil	1,342	260
Maintenance & repairs	430	119
Aircraft rentals	163	124
Landing fees & other rentals	454	339
Depreciation & amortization	469	37[d]
Other operating expenses	1,204	148
	6,764	1,293
Total operating income	820	49
Other expenses (income)		
Interest expense	122	8
Interest income	(47)	(27)
Other (gains) losses, net	(129)	0
	(54)	(19)
Profit before tax	874	68
Taxes	326	25
Net income	548	43

Exhibit 3 Income Statements and Company Information of Two Low-Cost Carriers *(Continued)*

Other information	Southwest Airlines Year Ending December 31, 2005 (in US$ millions)	EasyJet Year Ending September 30, 2005 (in UK£ millions)
Fleet size (averaged)	431[b]	94
Aircraft types	Boeing 737	Boeing 737, Airbus A319
Total trips flown	1,028,639	229,068
Average trips per aircraft per day	6.5[b]	6.7[b]
Average stage length (block hour)	1.84[b]	1.75
Average hours per aircraft per day	12.02[b]	11.70[b]
RPK (thousand)	96,356,960[c]	27,448,000
ASK (thousand)	136,276,472[c]	32,141,000
Passenger load factor	70.7 percent	85.4 percent
Passenger revenue per ASK	5.57 cents	4.17 pence
Operating cost per ASK	4.96 cents	3.97 pence[e]

Notes: Income statement items have been aligned for comparison purposes; [a] included handling charges; [b] estimated by case writer; [c] converted from ASM/RPM; [d] included goodwill amortization of £17.4 m; [e] before goodwill.

Sources: Southwest Airlines, 2005, Annual Report; easyJet, 2005, Annual Report.

Exhibit 4 Income Statements and Selected Information of Two Traditional Airlines

	British Airways Year Ending March 31, 2006 (in UK£ million)	Cathay Pacific Airways Year Ending December 31, 2005 (in HK$ million)
Total operating revenue		
Passenger	6,820	30,274
Freight	498	12,852
Other	1,197[a]	7,783
	8,515	50,909
Total operating expenses		
Salaries, wages & benefits	2,346	9,025
Fuel & oil	1,632	15,588
Maintenance & repairs	473	4,527
Aircraft rentals	112	4,893[e]
Landing fees & other rentals	559	6,947
Depreciation & amortization	717	790[f]
Other operating expenses	1,971[b]	4,996[g]
	7,810	46,766
Total operating income	705	4,143

Exhibit 4 Income Statements and Selected Information of Two Traditional Airlines *(Continued)*

	British Airways Year Ending March 31, 2006 (in UK£ million)	Cathay Pacific Airways Year Ending December 31, 2005 (in HK$ million)
Other expenses (income)		
Interest expense	221	1,605
Interest income	(93)	(1,161)
Other (gains) losses, net	(43)	(269)
	85	175
Profit before tax	620	3,968
Taxes	153	500
Net income	467	3,468
Other information		
Fleet size (averaged)	281[c]	93
Aircraft types	10 major types	4 major types
Total trips flown	368,000	84,000
Average trips per aircraft per day	3.6[c]	2.5[c]
Average stage length (block hour)	2.83[c]	5.06[c]
Average hours per aircraft per day	10.14	12.60
RPK	111,859,000	65,110,000
ASK	147,934,000	82,766,000
Passenger load factor	75.6 percent	78.7 percent
Passenger revenue per ASK	4.61 pence[d]	HK$0.37
ATK	23,106,000	17,751,000
Total revenue per ATK	31.67 pence	HK$2.87
Operating cost per ATK	28.62 pence	HK$2.19

Notes: Income statement items have been aligned for comparison purposes; [a] included fuel surcharge; [b] included selling cost of £449 m; [c] case writer's estimates; [d] before fuel surcharge; [e] for Cathay Pacific this category should be "aircraft depreciation and leases"; [f] for Cathay Pacific this category should be "non-aircraft depreciation and leases"; [g] included commission of HK$555 million.

Sources: British Airways, 2006, Annual Report; Cathay Pacific Airways, 2005, Annual Report.

Airline Cost Structure. Personnel, fuel, capital cost and maintenance cost of assets, selling expenses, and airport and landing fees are the major costs airlines incur. Personnel-related costs are among the largest of the incurred costs for major airlines. Typically, airlines employ large labor forces including pilots, flight attendants, engineers, mechanics, airport service agents, and support staff. Labor in the airline industry is highly unionized, especially in North America and Europe, though strong pilots' and flight attendants' unions were also found in Asia. In 2005, labor costs for a major airline represented 20 to 40 percent of total costs.

The cost of fuel is a major concern for all airlines due to the huge increase in oil prices in the first decade of the 21st century. In 2005 for example, fuel represented approximately 20 to 30 percent of an airline's operating costs in contrast to around 12 to 15 percent during most of the 1990s. A successful fuel hedge program could save an airline a significant amount of money. Southwest Airlines was renowned for its fuel hedging program. In 2005, fuel cost represented about 20 percent of Southwest's operating cost. In 2006, its fuel expenses were approximately 73 percent hedged at about US$36 per barrel, which translated into savings of hundreds of millions of U.S. dollars.

In addition to the costs of offices, fixtures, office equipment, and ticketing equipment, airlines incur substantial capital costs to purchase aircraft and the flight simulators that are used to train pilots. In 2006, the Boeing 737 and the Boeing 777 were the best selling families of the firm's commercial planes. At this time, the list price of a Boeing 737, a single-aisle, narrow-bodied aircraft, ranged between US$47 million and US$80 million. A Boeing 777, a twin-aisle, wide-bodied aircraft, was priced between US$180 million and US$260 million. Although the actual purchase price was usually at least 15 to 20 percent lower than the list price,[12] aircraft capital costs are substantial. Airlines typically finance their purchase of aircraft through a finance/lease[13] arrangement. An operating lease[14] is a viable alternative, but with a typical monthly lease rate of 1 percent of the purchase price for a long-term lease, the rental cost for a brand-new Boeing 737 was still around US$600,000 a year in 2006 while that of a Boeing 777 was US$2.64 million a year.

The cost of maintaining aircraft and engines is another major expense for an airline, accounting for about 6 to 10 percent of operating costs. Managing maintenance costs is interwoven with asset and fuel cost management. For instance, an airline needs to balance the average age of its aircraft (capital costs of older aircraft tended to be cheaper) with maintenance costs, which tend to be more expensive as aircraft age. Also, as aircraft and engines age and enter their heavy maintenance cycles, ground time of up to 45 days for aircraft and 90 days for engines is required, necessitating additional aircraft or engines to uphold schedule integrity. Fuel cost management also plays a part, as older assets are usually less efficient and consume more fuel.

Selling expenses are another category of operational costs for an airline. Traditionally, air tickets were bought through travel agents, who subscribed to global computer reservation systems where airlines made bookings and reservations available. Airlines incurred costs through paying agency commissions and charges for using global computer reservation systems. In the fiscal year ending March 2006, British Airways's selling cost was £449 million (US$829 million), amounting to 5 percent of its total turnover. However, as online bookings and direct sales increased, the cost of agency commissions also came down, especially for low-cost carriers. In 2001, 25 percent of Southwest Airlines's ticket sales were through travel agents, while 24 percent came from reservation centers (where customers could call to make reservations directly) and 39 percent from the Internet. By 2005, Southwest's reliance on travel agents and reservation centers dropped to 11 percent and 15 percent, respectively, while sales generated through the Internet rose to 65 percent.

Operating aircraft incurs airport charges, landing fees, and route costs. For example, British Airways's landing fees and en-route costs amounted to £559 million (US$1.032 billion), or 6.6 percent of total turnover, in the fiscal year ended in March 2006. In stark contrast, easyJet, British Airways's low-cost counterpart, spent £438 million (US$808 million), or 25.2 percent of turnover, on airport charges and navigation expenses.

Airline Profitability. A report published by IATA in 2006,[15] which studied the fiscal performance of 85 of the world's major carriers who together accounted for 85 percent of worldwide passenger numbers and the vast majority of global freight volumes, found that eight of them made operating profits in excess of US$500 million each, among which three made more than US$1 billion. On the other hand, 20 of the carriers surveyed had incurred operating losses, with nine having lost more than US$100 million each. Asian and European carriers were among the highest profit generators, whereas 9 of the 20 who lost money were U.S. carriers. Only 14 carriers had operating margins of greater than 10 percent, many of which were low-cost carriers (see Exhibit 6).

Experience in the United States further suggested that low-cost carriers operating on a point-to-point model displayed higher aircraft utilization rates, lower unit operating costs, and higher staff productivity. For example, in 2004, JetBlue's A320 fleet had an average utilization rate of 13.6 block hours per day, 46 percent higher than Northwest's A320 fleet, and a unit operating cost of US$0.032 per available seat mile (ASM), compared to Northwest's US$0.051.[16]

In Asia, airlines such as Cathay Pacific Airways, Singapore Airlines, Qantas, and Emirates Airlines were among the most profitable commercial carriers in the world, yet they all operated on the traditional hub-and-spoke model. Collectively, these airlines generated over US$6.4 billion in net profits between 2003 and 2005, even after the severe acute respiratory syndrome (SARS) pandemic nearly caused the Asian air travel market to grind to a complete halt in 2003.

Asia also differed from the United States in that the majority of Asian countries did not have large domestic air travel markets, and there were a limited number of secondary airports, which low-cost carriers could use as operating bases. This meant that low-cost carriers were faced with high airport charges, which was contrary to

Exhibit 5 Operating Profits by Airline, Fiscal Year 2005 (* = fiscal 2004)

By Total Operating Profit			By Operating Profit Margin		
Rank	Airline	US$ (mil)	Rank	Airline	%
1	FedEx*	1.414	1	Gol Airlines	23.3
2	British Airways	1,330	2	Ryanair	21.8
3	Air France-KLM	1.200	3	Air Asia	18.9
4	Lufthansa	377	4	COPA	17.3
5	Southwest	820	5	Kenya Airlines	15.6
6	Emirates	786	6	Philippine Airlines	13.7
7	All Nippon	776	7	DHL International*	12.5
8	Qantas*	775	8	Kalitta Air	12.3
9	Singapore Airlines	590	9	Emirates	11.9
10	Cathay Pacific	533	10	Mesa Airlines	11.7
11	Ryanair	459	11	American Eagle	11.3
12	Air China	458	12	SkyWest	11.2
13	Iberia	457	13	Southwest	10.8
14	Air Canada	388	14	Jet Airways	10.3
15	UPS Airlines	293	15	Air China	9.6
16	Thai Airlines	269	16	Virgin Blue	9.6
17	Gol Airlines	266	17	TAM	9.5
18	TAM	232	18	Singapore Airlines	9.1
19	American Eagle	225	19	Royal Jordanian	9.0
20	SkyWest	220	20	Qantas*	8.9
21	Korean Airlines	207	21	Atlantic Southeast	8.5
22	Virgin Blue	184	22	British Airways	8.3
23	China Eastern*	179	23	Aer Lingus	8.2
24	LAN Airlines	142	24	Cathay Pacific	8.1
25	Asiana*	136	25	FedEx*	7.2

Source: IATA, 2006, IATA economic briefing, June 2006.

their basic operating principles. Recently, however, this situation began to change. In 2006, both Singapore's Changi Airport and Malaysia's new airport in Kuala Lumpur opened separate, no-frills terminals that catered to low-cost carriers' needs. However, the airport authority of Hong Kong showed no interest in following suit.

Front-End (Business- and First-Class) Traffic Revenue Contribution. For a typically configured

Boeing 747-400 aircraft flying on a popular transatlantic route between the United States and Europe, the revenue split between first, business, and economy classes would be roughly 20 percent, 60 percent, and 20 percent, respectively. In 2006, typical published fares for such a flight would be around US$14,000, US$7,000, and US$750, with the aircraft equipped with 14, 79, and 265 seats, respectively, for the three classes. Because of the differences between carriers in short-haul and long-haul mixes, primary target markets, load factors, aircraft types, and so on, the resulting revenue mix across the three classes could vary significantly.

In the first half of 2006, front-end traffic accounted for 11 percent of all international traffic and 15 percent of long-haul routes. During this period, the top five route areas accounted for 72 percent of all front-end traffic volume, falling from 82 percent in 2000. Routes within Europe accounted for around one-third of all international front-end traffic, while routes between Europe and East Asia contributed 14 percent (see Exhibit 6). Because of the strong rebounds in trade and investment after the decline triggered by the September 11th terrorist attacks in 2001, front-end traffic between Europe and Asia had grown faster than overall traffic, contributing to strong revenues for airlines in 2005 and 2006.[17]

The International Airline Industry in 2006. In the five years following the September 11, 2001, terrorist attacks, the average financial performance of commercial airlines around the world improved substantially, except for the second and third quarters of 2003, when carriers operating in Asia were badly hit by the SARS pandemic. Between 2000 and 2006, total revenues increased from US$329 billion to a projected US$450 billion while the number of passengers carried increased from 1.672 billion to a projected 2.154 billion, representing an increase of 36.8 percent and 28.8 percent, respectively. Cargo volume grew from 30.4 million tonnes to 39.8 million tonnes, a 30.9 percent increase. Operating profit fluctuated from a high of US$10.7 billion in 2000 to a

loss of US$11.8 billion in 2001 due to the 9–11 terrorist attacks, but rebounded to a projected US$9.8 billion in 2006. However, as fuel expenses skyrocketed from US$46 billion to a projected US$115 billion (a 150 percent increase), airlines' net profit actually decreased from US$3.7 billion to a projected loss of US$1.7 billion. When broken down geographically, North American carriers incurred a US$4.5 billion loss, followed by African carriers at US$0.8 billion. European and Asian carriers earned net profits of US$1.8 billion and US$1.7 billion, respectively.[18]

The Airline Industry in Hong Kong. Located in southern China and historically an important trade port between the East and the West, Hong Kong's catchment area (within five hours of flight time) included most of the urban centers in East Asia, whose cumulative population was about 2 billion in the late 1990s.[19] With flights connecting to over 40 cities in the Chinese Mainland, Hong Kong was also the leading gateway to the rapidly growing Chinese market. In 2005, over 78 scheduled airlines served the Hong Kong International Airport, providing about 5,300 scheduled passenger and all-cargo flights each week between Hong Kong and more than 140 destinations worldwide. In the same year, the airport handled some 40.7 million passengers and 3.4 million tonnes of cargo, making Hong Kong the fifth-busiest international passenger airport and the busiest airport for international cargo in the world. In 2005, the airport also saw more than 19.8 million passenger departures.[20] Among them, South-East

Exhibit 6 Distribution of Front-End Traffic Volume by Route, January–May 2006

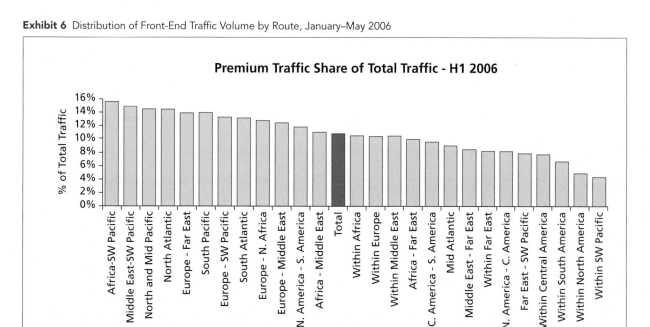

Source: IATA, 2006, IATA economic briefing, August 2006.

Asian destinations contributed 24 percent to the total, followed by mainland China at 21 percent and Taiwan at 19 percent. The remaining traffic was divided among Japan, Europe, North America, Australia, and others.[21]

According to the *Current Market Outlook 2005* published by Boeing,[22] passenger air travel would grow at an annual rate of 4.8 percent from 2005 to 2024, while cargo was forecast to grow at an annual rate of 6.2 percent. In Europe and North America, where the air travel market was mature, a slower growth of 3.4–5.5 percent was expected. The Asia-Pacific region was expected to be a major source of growth. Intra-regional traffic was expected to grow at an annual rate of 5.1 percent, while China was forecast to have an annual growth rate of 8.8 percent in this area. Traffic between Europe and Asia-Pacific was expected to grow 5.4 percent annually, while traffic between North America and Asia-Pacific, 6 percent.

Industry observers believed that Hong Kong, being a major air transport hub between the Far East and the Western world, was uniquely positioned to reap the benefits of this growing trend. However, they cautioned that the growing and rapidly improving mainland Chinese airports might challenge Hong Kong's position as a leading gateway to China. The Guangzhou Baiyun International Airport, Macau International Airport, Shenzhen Baoan International Airport, and Zhuhai Airport are all within 30 minutes by air from Hong Kong and the catchment area of the Pearl River Delta. In addition, direct traffic from Beijing's Capital Airport and Shanghai's Pudong International Airport to Europe and North America was also expected to increase during the 2008 Beijing Olympics and the 2010 Shanghai World Expo.

In response, Hong Kong had been extending its airport's market reach to serve the Pearl River Delta's population of 48 million, as well as the rest of China.[23] Since the early 2000s, Hong Kong International Airport has established multi-modal links that connect Hong Kong with other cities in the Pearl River Delta: the SkyPier provides frequent ferry connections to selected Pearl River Delta cities (including the four airports) and the SkyLimo provides coach services to and from major Pearl River Delta cities. Additionally, there were more than 170 daily coach trips operating between more than 40 Pearl River Delta cities and Hong Kong International Airport. In 2003, the Hong Kong Airport Authority (HKAA) signed a letter of intent with Shanghai Airport Authority to strengthen exchanges and facilitate closer cooperation between the two airports. In 2005, HKAA agreed to buy a major stake in the Hangzhou Xiaoshan International Airport.

Airlines in Hong Kong

In late 2006, seven airlines used Hong Kong as their home base. Among them, six were commercial airlines providing scheduled services to the public: Cathay Pacific Airways, Hong Kong Dragon Airlines, Air Hong Kong, CR Airways, Hong Kong Express Airways, and Oasis Hong Kong Airlines.

Cathay Pacific Airways.   Founded in 1946 by American Roy C. Farrell and Australian Sydney H. de Kantzow, Cathay Pacific Airways was Hong Kong's largest airline and de facto flag carrier. The airline started with passenger service to destinations such as Shanghai, Manila, Singapore, Bangkok, and Guangzhou. In 1948, Butterfield & Swire (which later became the Swire Group) bought 45 percent of the airline and subsequently increased its stake to 5.2 percent. Since the 1960s, the airline has undergone significant expansion, both in fleet size and in the number of destinations served. By 2006, Cathay Pacific served 90 passenger and cargo destinations worldwide and had a fleet of 100 aircraft, including the Boeing 747 and 777 series and the Airbus A330 and A340 series. The average age of its fleet was seven years and the longest non-stop flight on its regular schedule was its Hong Kong–New York flight at 12,968 km and roughly 16 hours of flying time. It operated four daily flights to London's Heathrow airport, two using Airbus A340–300s and two using Boeing B747–400s, with all four offering three classes of service.

Cathay Pacific had a reputation as one of the industry's best airlines, with regular and frequent updates of seats, entertainment systems, meal options, and other in-flight amenities. Its latest first-class seats are equipped with 17-inch personal TVs with Audio-Video on Demand ("AVOD"), massage functions, extendable meal tables, and the largest pitch-flat beds available on a scheduled commercial airline, all enclosed within private areas. Meals could be selected and served at any time. Passengers also received preferential check-in service, access to exclusive lounge facilities, priority luggage handling, and other personalized services. Personal TVs with AVOD were also standard for its business-class service. Menus were created in cooperation with leading local fine-dining establishments and a broad wine selection was also available to passengers in both first and business class. Among its numerous industry awards, Cathay Pacific was named "Airline of the Year" by *Skytrax* in 2003 and 2005 and by *Air Transport World* in 2006.[24]

Cathay Pacific was a founding member of Oneworld. The airline had established a large number of code-share agreements with other carriers, including Air China, American Airlines, British Airways, Japan Airlines, Qantas, and Malaysian Airlines. Cathay Pacific had two loyalty programs: the Marco Polo Club, reserved exclusively for Cathay Pacific customers, and Asia Miles, where membership was available to customers of a number of participating airlines and other merchants, such as restaurants, hotels, and entertainment establishments.

Hong Kong Dragon Airlines.[25] In May 1985, Hong Kong Dragon Airlines ("Dragonair") was established as a wholly owned subsidiary of Hong Kong Macau International Investment Co. on the initiative of a local shipping tycoon, K. P. Chao. The airline, however, struggled under the one-airline-one-route policy of the then British colonial government of Hong Kong. In 1990, CITIC Pacific, the Swire Group, and Cathay Pacific acquired an 89 percent stake in Dragonair. As a result, Dragonair transitioned into a regional carrier with a focus on mainland Chinese destinations. In 1996, at the onset of the sovereignty change of Hong Kong from being a British colony to becoming a Special Administration Region of the People's Republic of China, the China National Aviation Corporation ("CNAC") purchased a 35.86 percent interest in Dragonair, becoming the largest shareholder. CITIC Pacific remained the second-largest shareholder, with a 28.5 percent stake, while the Swire Group and Cathay Pacific together held a 25.5 percent stake.

The new shareholding structure allowed Dragonair to develop outside the shadows of Cathay Pacific. The year 2000 marked a watershed for Dragonair, when it introduced its all-cargo service with a Boeing 747-200 special freighter, competing directly with Air Hong Kong, a wholly owned subsidiary of Cathay Pacific. The following five years saw Dragonair's passenger fleet double in size to 30 aircraft and its freighter fleet grow to four. Meanwhile, Dragonair established its own frequent-flyer program; rolled out a new cabin interior with lie-flat seats and personal TVs in the premium classes; competed with Cathay Pacific head-to-head on passenger services to Taipei, Bangkok, and Tokyo; and won numerous accolades for its outstanding service in the mainland Chinese market.

In June 2006, a joint announcement was made by Air China (the parent company of CNAC and China's flag carrier), CNAC, CITIC Pacific, the Swire Group, and Cathay Pacific about a shareholding realignment that resulted in a cross-shareholding between Air China and Cathay Pacific and made Dragonair a wholly owned subsidiary of Cathay Pacific.[26]

Air Hong Kong.[27] Founded in 1986 and initiating charter services in 1988 with a Boeing 707 freighter, Air Hong Kong was Hong Kong's only all-cargo operator. In 1994, Cathay Pacific bought a 75 percent stake in the company, strengthening Air Hong Kong's market and giving it access to Cathay Pacific's distribution system. In February 2002, Cathay Pacific acquired the remaining 25 percent stake in Air Hong Kong, making it a wholly owned subsidiary. In October 2002, Cathay Pacific and DHL Express announced a joint venture in which DHL Express acquired 30 percent of Air Hong Kong. Under the agreement, an initial investment of about US$300 million was to be committed by 2004 and a further US$100 million by 2010 to purchase a fleet of long-range, wide-body freighters to operate DHL Express's network connecting the major cities in the Asia-Pacific region. In March 2003, DHL Express acquired an additional 10 percent stake in Air Hong Kong from Cathay Pacific. By mid-2006, Air Hong Kong's fleet included eight A300-600GFs and one wet lease[28] Airbus A300-600F, and operated a freighter service network between Hong Kong and Tokyo, Osaka, Seoul, Taipei, Bangkok, Penang, Singapore, and Shanghai.

CR Airways and Hong Kong Express Airways. CR Airways was founded in 2001 and began service with Bombardier CRJ200 and CRJ700 regional jets.[29] In December 2005, it was reported that Hainan Airlines, a mainland Chinese carrier based on the island of Hainan, was interested in acquiring a 60 percent stake in CR Airways. In the same month, CR Airways announced the signing of a Memorandum of Understanding with Boeing to acquire thirty 737-800s and ten 787 Dreamliners. Hainan Airlines later revealed that it would reduce its stake in CR Airways to 45 percent to ensure that CR Airways remained a Hong Kong–based airline. In early 2006, the acquisition was given the green light by the government. CR Airways's service network changed rapidly as new routes were tested for viability and as the airline phased in the 737-800s, the first of which was delivered in early 2006 and coincided with the launch of services to Changsha and Tianjin. More destinations were slated to be added to the network in the second half of 2006, including Chengdu, Xian, Nanjing, and Fuzhou in China, as well as Seoul, Taegu, and Pusan in South Korea. CR Airways was also keen to begin long-haul service and was planning to operate Boeing 777s in the interim before the arrival of its Boeing 787s (which were expected to be delivered from 2010 onwards).

Hong Kong Express Airways Limited (formerly Helicopters Hong Kong Limited) was 51 percent owned by Macau casino tycoon Stanley Ho. Hong Kong Express wanted to take advantage of liberalization of air service between Hong Kong and the Chinese mainland. In September 2005, Hong Kong Express launched its first service to Guangzhou. As the fleet expanded, it added such destinations as Hangzhou, Ningbo, Chongqing, and Chengdu in China, as well as Chiang Mai in Thailand. However, six months after starting service to Guangzhou, they cancelled this route because the load factor fell short of the 30 percent target.[30] In May 2006, Hong Kong Express acknowledged that negotiations were under way regarding a possible capital injection from Hainan Airlines and a merger with CR Airways.[31]

Oasis Hong Kong Airlines

Oasis Hong Kong Airlines was founded by ex-Dragonair CEO Stephen Miller, with principal investment from property developer Raymond Lee and his wife Priscilla. Oasis had a definitive positioning as the only long-haul, low-fare airline operating out of Hong Kong. After developing the idea of a long-haul, low-fare carrier, Miller went to Lee with a proposal. Although initially skeptical, Lee eventually agreed to invest in the proposal Miller brought to him. The Lees provided the majority of the seed funding, which was supplemented by additional investments from Allan Wong, chairman and CEO of VTech Holdings (a multinational corporation), and Richard K. Lee, founder of Trinity Textiles.[32]

The Oasis Model

Oasis marketed itself as a long-haul, low-fare carrier that offered exceptional value with customizable options. It offered two classes of service, targeting both economy- and business-class passengers, whereas other low-cost carriers only offered economy-class service and competed primarily on price. While all other low-cost carriers served short-haul routes, Oasis would only serve long-haul routes. The initial network plan of Oasis included Oakland and Chicago in the United States, Berlin and Cologne in Germany, Milan in Italy, and London Gatwick in the United Kingdom, which would be the airline's launch destination.[33]

While Oasis did not position itself to be a low-cost carrier, competitive pricing was nevertheless one of its competitive advantages. Oasis only sold one-way tickets,

which, on the Hong Kong-London route, would sell for as low as HK$1,000 (US$128) for an economy class seat and HK$6,600 (US$846) for a business class seat, excluding taxes and surcharges. In the long run, at least 10 percent of seats would continue to be sold at these fares.[34] In contrast, for a Hong Kong–London round-trip economy-class ticket departing on October 31, 2006, and returning on November 10, 2006, Cathay Pacific's prices varied from HK$5,880 (US$754) to HK$9,550 (US$1,224), depending on the level of travel restrictions, while British Airways's prices ranged from HK$2,250 (US$288) to HK$4,525 (US$580), and Virgin Atlantic's fell between HK$5,532 (US$709) and HK$17,263 (U$4,525). At these prices, Cathay Pacific was 190 to 380 percent more expensive than Oasis, 112.5 to 130 percent more expensive than British Airways, and 180 to 760 percent more expensive than Virgin Atlantic. For business-class tickets, Cathay Pacific charged HK$44,952 (US$5,763), British Airways HK$21,350 (US$2,737), and Virgin Atlantic between HK$44,897 (US$5,756) and HK$46,813 (US$6,002). In addition to attractive prices, Oasis also had a relatively simple, easily understood fare structure, which the firm expected customers would find appealing (see Exhibit 7).

Operating long-haul flights would also allow the airline to have high average aircraft utilization and efficiency. It was expected that Oasis could achieve average aircraft utilization in excess of 15 hours per day. This would give Oasis a low operating unit cost on a per available seat kilometer basis. Furthermore, by spending a large proportion of time in cruise, an aircraft flying long-haul flights would have fewer takeoffs and landings than one flying short-haul, which would translate into

Exhibit 7 Oasis Hong Kong Airlines Fare Types

Fare Type	Description
Flexi Fare	• Available year-round • Reservation held for 72 hours before payment • Unlimited free changes to flight and date • Changes to passenger name allowed on payment of change penalty plus fare difference • Refundable subject to cancellation penalty
Advance Purchase Fare	• Booked 45, 21, or 14 days in advance • Payment must be made at time of flight confirmation • Changes to flight, date, and passenger name allowed with penalty and fare difference • Refundable subject to cancellation penalty
Value Fare	• Semi-flexible fare available year-round • Payment must be made at time of flight confirmation • Changes to flight, date, and passenger name allowed with penalty and fare difference • Refundable subject to cancellation policy
Hot Deal	• Discount value fare • Payment must be made at the time of flight confirmation • Changes to flight, date, and passenger name not permitted • Non-refundable

Source: Oasis Hong Kong Airlines, 2006, Fare types, http://www.oasishongkong.com/hk/en/services/faredetails.aspx (accessed November 19, 2006).

lower maintenance costs for the airframe and engines, as well as lower fuel consumption.

Another area where Oasis would save on costs was airport landing and parking fees because the airline would use secondary airports such as Gatwick instead of Heathrow in London and Oakland instead of San Francisco in California. Other secondary airports under consideration included Milan in Italy, and Berlin and Cologne in Germany. All these secondary airports were also major hubs of leading low-cost carriers: London Gatwick, Milan, and Berlin were hubs for easyJet; Cologne was the main hub for Germanwings; and Oakland was a hub for Southwest Airlines and a busy port for JetBlue. By flying into the hubs of major low-cost carriers, Oasis hoped to receive feeder traffic from them and feed traffic to these carriers. Doing so would require interline ticket sales, check-ins, and baggage transfers, which were not unusual among low-cost carriers.

Oasis's value proposition was to offer products and services that were not significantly inferior to those of the major competitors at a price that would be considered extremely competitive and of solid value. Oasis's two Boeing 747-400s were configured for 81 business-class seats and 278 economy-class seats.[35] All passengers in economy class would be offered standard complimentary hot meals. For business-class passengers, Oasis would offer standard upgraded meals with complimentary drinks. In-flight entertainment, such as video and audio programs with personal TVs and in-flight magazines, was a part of Oasis's standard offerings. Lounge access, if required, would be available at an additional cost.

On the distribution side, Oasis adopted the traditional carriers' model and relied on brick-and-mortar travel agents to sell tickets. Passengers would also be able to buy tickets directly on the company's Web site or through a call center.

The traditional model for low-cost carriers placed little emphasis on cargo revenue. However, because Hong Kong was a major air cargo hub for the Asia-Pacific region, demand for cargo space was consistently high, and hence the corresponding market prices, especially on routes to Europe and North America, were very high. Thus, Oasis was also looking at tapping into this revenue stream by filling the bellies of its aircraft with freight.

The Plan

Oasis planned to launch its inaugural flight to London Gatwick in late October 2006. It had purchased two Boeing 747-400s from Singapore Airlines. The first was to be delivered in September, just in time for the planned inaugural flight, and the second one was to be delivered in November. With just two aircraft, Oasis could only serve one destination, with over 12 hours of idle time at London Gatwick. As Lee admitted, load factors would have to be extremely high to be profitable.[36] With four

aircraft and the added service to Oakland, the break-even load factor would come down to around 85 percent. With six aircraft, the break-even load factor could come under 80 percent.

The airline's five-year plan called for aggressive growth of fleet size, amounting to 25 aircraft. The challenge was finding the right aircraft at the right price.[37] Oasis wanted the Boeing 747-400, but in 2005–2006, this aircraft was in high demand. With high fuel prices and the availability of more efficient aircraft types, many 747-400s were expected to cease being economical as passenger aircraft. However, with a healthy growth forecast for the air cargo market, many of these aircraft were destined to be converted into freighters. Singapore Airlines, for example, not only had sold or pre-sold 11 of its 747-400s to Cathay Pacific and Dragonair for freighter conversions, but also was planning to convert a few of its own into freighters. Meanwhile, some airlines, including Singapore Airlines, had originally planned to replace their 747-400s with Airbus's A380 super jumbos starting in 2006, but were caught off guard by Airbus's 22-month delay in its A380 program, forcing airlines to hold on to their 747-400s longer than they had planned. In 2005, the market value of a 747-400 manufactured in 1991 ranged from US$33 million to US$52 million (see Exhibit 8).[38]

Exhibit 8 Market Value of a Boeing 747-400 (in US$ millions)

Vintage	Value (market)	Future Value	
	2005	2009	2012
1989	33.9	19.5	13.7
1991	45.5	26.5	18.9
1993	56.9	33.9	24.5
1995	68.4	41.7	30.5
1997	79.9	50.0	37.1
1999	91.4	59.1	44.6
2001	103.0	68.1	52.5
2003	114.5	76.1	60.2

Source: Aircraft Value News, 2005, Semi-annual jet aircraft value listing, September 5.

Rental Cost per Month (in US$ thousands)

Vintage	2005
1989–1995	360–490
1996–2002	470–865

Source: Aircraft Value News, 2005, Widebody lease rates (dry) US$, October 2005.

Other possible aircraft types for Oasis included the Airbus A340-600 and the Boeing 777-300ER. Albeit slightly smaller than the 747-400, the A340-600 could work, but not many were available at this time. Similarly, the 777-300ER, which had been in service for only a few years, was not readily available on the second-hand aircraft market. In 2005, an A340-600 manufactured in 2002 was valued between US$102 million and US$111 million, whereas a 777-300ER manufactured in 2003 was worth between US$117 million and US$132 million. There was always the option of purchasing brand-new aircraft, but because of long production lead times and production slot availability, it would take 36 to 48 months before any new aircraft delivery. Oasis needed to increase capacity and add new services sooner rather than later.

Preparing for Takeoff

Oasis's potential to get off to a successful start depended to a great extent on the global economic situation at the time, as there is a strong positive correlation between gross domestic product growth and the amount of money businesses and individuals are willing to spend on travel and air freight. However, the biggest question was whether Oasis's target customers would readily embrace these services from a newcomer. On its inaugural route from Hong Kong to London, Oasis's service would be judged and compared to such reputable carriers as British Airways, Virgin Atlantic, Cathay Pacific, and Qantas. It was up to Miller and his management team to prove themselves in the marketplace.

NOTES

1. This price excluded surcharges and taxes.
2. This section is adapted from: P. Ferreira, 2001, Systems in transportation: The case of the airline industry, http://web.mit.edu/esd.83/www/notebook/Transportation%20-%20Airline%20Ind.ppt (accessed November 15, 2006); The airline industry and the World Trade Center disaster, Centre for Asian Business Cases, University of Hong Kong.
3. P. Ferreira, 2001, Systems in transportation: The case of the airline industry, http://web.mit.edu/esd.83/www/notebook/Transportation%20-%20Airline%20Ind.ppt (accessed November 15, 2006).
4. The airline industry, http://adg.stanford.edu/aa241/intro/airlineindustry.html (accessed November 15, 2006).
5. M. Schlangenstein, 2005, Southwest Airlines profit jumps: Lower fuel costs let carrier nearly triple its bottom line, Washington Post, April 15.
6. British Airways, 2005–2006 Annual report & accounts.
7. Wikipedia, 2006, Airline alliance, http://en.wikipedia.org/wiki/Airline_alliance (accessed November 20, 2006).
8. 2006, Ryanair turns screw to hold luggage, http://news.cheapflights.co.uk/flights/2006/01/ryanair_turns_s.html (accessed November 21, 2006).
9. A code sharing agreement is a cooperative agreement between two or more airlines whereby a flight operated and marketed by one airline is also marketed by its code share partner(s). In this case, the flight will have more than one flight number—one that is given to it by the operating airline and other one(s) given to it by the code share partner(s)
10. 2005, Southwest Airlines Annual Report.
11. In the parts of the world where the imperial system was prevalent (e.g., the United States), the equivalent terms were Available Seat Mile (ASM) and Available Ton Mile (ATM). Note that "ton" referred to the imperial ton equal to 2,000 pounds, whereas "tonne" in ATK referred to the metric tonne, which was equal to 2,000 kilograms.
12. This was due to the various discounts that aircraft manufacturers would offer to airlines or leasing companies.
13. A finance lease was basically a mortgage arrangement. Typically an airline would set up a special purpose company, which financed the purchase of the aircraft through a syndicate loan and would in turn lease the aircraft back to the airline.
14. As opposed to a finance lease, an operating lease was purely a leasing arrangement between the airline and a leasing company.
15. IATA. 2006, Profitability: Does size matter?, Economics Briefing, June.
16. The airline industry and current challenges, http://web.mit.edu/airlines/www/the-airline-industry/the-airline-industry.htm (accessed November 14, 2006).
17. IATA, 2006, Premium traffic, Economic Briefing, August, 3.
18. IATA Economics, 2006, Industry financial forecast briefing note, September, 4.
19. Trade Development Council, 2006, Air transport, http://logistics.tdctrade.com/ (accessed November 15, 2006).
20. Hong Kong Civil Aviation Department, 2006, Hong Kong International Airport Civil International Air Transport Movements of Aircraft, Passenger and Freight (1998–2006), http://www.cad.gov.hk/english/p-through.html (accessed November 21, 2006).
21. Airport Authority Hong Kong, 2006, Annual report 2006.
22. Boeing Commercial Airplanes, 2005, Current market outlook 2005, 3–5.
23. Airport Authority Hong Kong, 2006, The airport authority, http://www.hongkongairport.com/eng/aboutus/profile.html (accessed October 17, 2006).
24. Cathay Pacific Airways, 2006, Awards and honours, http://www.cathaypacific.com/cpa/en_INTL/aboutus/cxbackground/awardsandhonours (accessed November 29, 2006).
25. This section was adapted from: Hong Kong Dragon Airlines, 2006, History, http://www.dragonair.com/icms/servlet/template?series=98&lang=eng (accessed November 29, 2006).
26. Air China, Cathay Pacific, CNAC, CITIC Pacific, and Swire Pacific 2006, Changes in shareholding structure builds new aviation partnerships in Greater China, Joint Press Release, June 9.
27. This section was adapted from: Air Hong Kong, 2006, History, http://www.airhongkong.com.hk/ahk/en/F300/History/index.jsp (accessed June 21, 2006).
28. A wet lease was an aircraft leasing arrangement between two parties whereby the lessor provided not only the aircraft, but also the crew, maintenance, and insurance to the lessee.
29. Wikipedia, 2006, Hong Kong Airlines, http://en.wikipedia.org/wiki/CR_Airways (accessed November 29, 2006).

30. C. So, 2006, HK Express to drop Guangzhou service, *South China Morning Post*, February 9.

31. R. Barling, 2006, CR Airways and Ho carrier eye merger, *South China Morning Post*, May 9.

32. Asia Travel Tips, 2006, New low cost–long haul Hong Kong-based airline opens for reservations, http://www.asiatraveltips.com/news06/59-OasisHongKongAirlines.shtml (accessed November 23, 2006).

33. Wikipedia, 2006, Oasis Hong Kong Airlines, http://en.wikipedia.org/wiki/Oasis_Hong_Kong_Airlines (accessed November 22, 2006).

34. Wikipedia, 2006, Oasis Hong Kong Airlines, http://en.wikipedia.org/wiki/Oasis_Hong_Kong_Airlines (accessed November 22, 2006).

35. Wikipedia, 2006, Oasis Hong Kong Airlines, http://en.wikipedia.org/wiki/Oasis_Hong_Kong_Airlines (accessed November 22, 2006).

36. R. Barling, 2006, Oasis success still on a wing and a prayer to distant horizon, *South China Morning Post*, October 27.

37. Wikipedia, 2006, Oasis Hong Kong Airlines, http://en.wikipedia.org/wiki/Oasis_Hong_Kong_Airlines (accessed November 22, 2006.

38. Aircraft Value News, 2005, Semi-annual jet aircraft value listing, September 5.

Havovi Joshi, Samuel Tsang

The University of Hong Kong, Asia Case Research Centre

For some time we have believed the game industry is ready for disruption. Not just from Nintendo, but from all game developers. It is what we all need to expand our audience. It is what we all need to expand our imaginations.

— *SATORU IWATA*
  PRESIDENT OF NINTENDO CO. LTD[1]

In the 2008 *BusinessWeek*–Boston Consulting Group ranking of the world's most innovative companies, Nintendo Co. Ltd ("Nintendo") was ranked seventh, up from thirty-ninth the previous year.[2] This improvement was in recognition of Nintendo's transformation into an innovative design powerhouse that challenged the video game industry's prevailing business model.

In 2000, when Sony, Microsoft, and Nintendo (the "big three" of the video game console manufacturers) released their latest products, Sony's PlayStation 2 (PS2) emerged as the clear winner, outselling Microsoft's Xbox, and Nintendo's GameCube. In 2006, these players introduced a new generation of video game consoles, precipitating a new competitive battle in the industry. Microsoft and Sony continued with their previous strategy of increasing the computing power of their newest products and adding a more impressive graphical interface. However, Satoru Iwata, president of Nintendo, believed that the video game industry had been focusing far too much on existing gamers and completely neglecting non-gamers. In light of this belief, the company repositioned itself by developing a radically different console, the Wii (pronounced "we"). The Wii was an interesting machine that used a wand-like remote controller to detect players' hand movements, allowing them to emulate the real-life play of such games as tennis, bowling, and boxing.

The new console proved to be a runaway success. By September 2007, Nintendo had become Japan's most valuable listed company after Toyota, and its market value had tripled since the launch of the Wii. In spite of this initial success, however, it was not clear whether Nintendo had really disrupted the industry and significantly changed the dynamics of competition in it.

History of Nintendo, 1889 to 2002

Nintendo's[3] roots could be traced all the way back to 1889 in Kyoto, Japan, when Fusajiro Yamauchi, the founder of the company, started manufacturing playing cards. In 1907, the company began producing Western playing cards, and by 1951, it had become the Nintendo Playing Card Company. In 1959, it began making theme cards under a licensing agreement with Walt Disney Company; by 1963, the company had gone public and taken its current name. During the period 1970 to 1985, Nintendo began focusing on the manufacture of electronic toys and entered the emerging field of video games (see Exhibit 1).

Interestingly, 1991, the year Nintendo launched the highly popular Super NES in the United States, was also the year Nintendo's vision become Sony's opportunity—and the creation of what could be described as Nintendo's "greatest challenge" for over a decade—the Sony PlayStation (PS). Nintendo had wanted to incorporate CD-ROM into its Super NES, and Sony had agreed to create the PS for this purpose. However, over the next two years there were many conflicts of vision between Nintendo and Sony, and the two finally parted ways. Nintendo went ahead with Philips

Exhibit 1 The History of Nintendo, 1889 to 2002

1889	Fusajiro Yamauchi, the founder of the company, began manufacturing and selling Japanese playing cards.
1907	The company began producing Western playing cards.
1951	Begins using the name "Nintendo Playing Card Company Ltd."
1959	Nintendo began making theme cards under a licensing agreement with Disney.
1962–63	The company went public and took its current name.
1970	Nintendo began focusing on the manufacture of electronic toys and entered the emerging field of video games by licensing Magnavox's Pong technology.
1977	Nintendo developed its first home video game machines, Color TV Game 15 and Color TV Game 6.
1980	Nintendo established its U.S. subsidiary, Nintendo of America. Developed and started selling the first portable LCD video games with a microprocessor.
1981	One of Nintendo's most famous coin-operated games, "Donkey Kong," appeared and was an instant hit in both the United States and Japan.
1983	Nintendo expanded its product range from games and arcade machines to home consoles, and the company released Famicom, a technologically advanced home video game system, in Japan. With its high-quality sound and graphics, Famicom was a huge hit, dominating the Japanese market.
1985	Nintendo successfully launched Famicom in the United States as the Nintendo Entertainment System (NES). The company then marketed a follow-up version of "Super Mario Bros." for the NES, and this classic game helped the NES become a resounding success.
1989	Nintendo released a new console, the Game Boy. The Game Boy was the first major product in the handheld game console industry and became immensely popular because of its portability and accessibility.
1990–92	In 1990, Nintendo launched the Super Family Computer game system in Japan, which also did very well. A year later, the same product was launched as the Super NES in the United States. In 1992, Super NES was released in Europe.
1994	Nintendo formed design alliances with companies such as Silicon Graphics. Released the Super Game Boy, a peripheral for the Super NES, which enabled Game Boy software to be played on the TV screen.
1995	Introduced a 32-bit Virtual Immersion System, known as the "Virtual Boy."
1996	Nintendo launched its 64-bit N64 game system. It launched "Pokémon" on the Game Boy: the game involved trading and training virtual monsters and was the first in a hugely popular video-game series. The company also released another blockbuster video game, "The Legend of Zelda: Ocarina of Time." In just six weeks, 2.5 million units of the game were sold.
1997	It introduces the innovative "Rumble Pak" attachment for the N64 controller, which enabled the game player to feel vibrations while playing the game.
1998	Release of Game Boy Color. "Pokémon" is introduced overseas and becomes a smash hit.
2000	Nintendo acquired a 3 percent stake of convenience store operator Lawson in order to leverage Lawson's online operations and network to sell video games.
2001	Launched the new version of the Game Boy, with a 32-bit CPU. Nintendo GameCube is launched in Japan and the United States.
2002	GameCube is launched in the European and Australian markets.

Source: Nintendo Co. Ltd, 2008, Annual Report, http://www.nintendo.co.jp/ir/pdf/2008/annual0803e.pdf (accessed October 3, 2008).

technology,[4] and Sony was left with the PS, which the company decided to continue developing. Given Sony's clout and resources, when the PS and its wide range of games were finally released in Japan in 1994, the console was an instant success. In 1995, Sony released the PS in the United States, totally uprooting Nintendo's established name in the industry.

For many years, Nintendo was a dominant player in the video game industry. It had sold more than two billion games since 1985. Its top-selling series included nonviolent and easy-to-play games such as "Super Mario Bros." and "The Legend of Zelda." Its games were so successful largely because they appealed to all age groups across different cultures. The title of a book published in 1993 summed up Nintendo's supremacy: *Game Over: How Nintendo Zapped an American Industry, Captured Your Dollars, and Enslaved Your Children.* Suddenly, after the debut of the Sony PS, it was no longer the leader of the video game industry.

Nintendo tried various strategies to counter Sony. However, competition continued to intensify, and the PS2 also captured a significant portion of the video game market, maintaining a dominant position in the industry. In May 2001, Microsoft too entered the video game market by introducing the Xbox console, leaving Nintendo with an even smaller piece of the market.

In 2002, Nintendo appointed Satoru Iwata[5] as president of the company. It was hoped that, with his experience and deep insights into how the market evolved, Iwata would help the company develop a brand-new vision and approach.[6]

The Video Game Industry

History

The video game industry was born in the 1970s. In the early days, notable players such as Atari from the United States and Namco from Japan brought video games to teenagers in the form of arcade games found in malls and video game arcades. With the introduction of home consoles, video games began to make their way into households around the globe.

In the 1980s and early 1990s, many new players came to the market. With the increasing popularity of personal computers (PCs), gamers were no longer limited to playing their favorite video game titles on proprietary consoles. Although the market was affected by the introduction of PCs, video game makers achieved steady growth.

Nevertheless, the target customer group of video game consoles was narrowly confined to teenagers. Armed with insightful targeting and positioning, image-conscious branding, and superb graphics technologies, Sony introduced the PS in the mid-1990s. The Japanese electronics giant revolutionized the perception of video game consoles and successfully captured new players, thereby helping the industry grow substantially. Video gaming suddenly became the new popular entertainment. It was especially well received by young adults, mostly males in their late 20s or early 30s, and often with substantial disposable incomes. By the time Sony launched the PS2 in 2000, technology giant Microsoft realized that it could no longer ignore the runaway success of this product or the effect the booming video

game market was having on its traditional PC and software domains. Thus Microsoft's video game console, the Xbox, was launched in 2001.

Since the early 2000s, the convergence of information technology, telecommunications, media, and entertainment has brought dramatic social and technological changes. With the new socio-technological movement and a wider audience base, the big video game console markers such as Sony and Microsoft began to realize that there were new opportunities for their video gaming and console product offerings, which would play a far greater role in people's lives than mere entertainment.

Trends in the Industry

With the broad availability of broadband Internet, increasing sophistication of high-definition (HD) video technologies, and decreasing cost of hard-drive storage, video game console manufacturers realized that their products no longer had to be for gaming only. In fact, many players such as Sony and Microsoft envisioned their game consoles as all-encompassing home entertainment centers. Further, given the increasing speed achieved by broadband connections, Internet users were increasingly able to access large quantities of data files, especially those containing HD audio and video. Consequently, these console producers developed and offered online libraries as a new service enabling users to download and stream a variety of movies, music, and television shows through their consoles.

As top-quality video materials became more readily available through HD broadcasting and Internet downloads, a new recording medium with increased storage capacity was required. Two formats, the Blu-ray format[7] developed by a consortium led by Sony, and the HD-DVD format developed by a consortium led by Toshiba, competed to become the standard in this area.

By offering online games based on new and existing titles, console makers could provide similar social-networking or virtual-world services to get online gamers to play, connect, and form loyal communities. Such communities were expected to help create a perpetual demand for services and products created by the video game makers and their alliance partners. In fact, in-game advertising had already started and offered a new revenue stream to video game developers.

Nintendo: Innovation and the Launch of the Wii

Traditionally, Sony, Microsoft, and Nintendo would enter a new cycle or a new competitive battle every five to six years, and in 2000, Sony's PS2 emerged as the clear winner.[8] Since then, the industry's focus turned even more to the technological advancement of the console hardware, particularly in terms of faster processing speed, higher definition of video quality, and increasing complexity of the games. The relentless pursuit of superior technologies became the driver of the industry's dynamics.

However, the former leader in the video game industry, Nintendo, adopted a vastly different viewpoint about the industry's future development. Some years before the battle that began in 2006, Iwata saw the potential threats facing the industry. He observed that the video game market in Japan was shrinking. Based on various market trends and data, the key factor causing this reduction appeared to be the increasing complexity of video games, which required players to invest a significant amount of their time to learn and play them using increasingly complicated controllers with combinations of buttons and joysticks. Consequently, occasional gamers with busy lives had stopped playing. Further, for novices and non-gamers, the time required to learn and play these games was a major deterrent for potential newcomers to join the camp. Iwata also saw that the video game industry had largely ignored non-gamers and was focused on the existing players. Armed with these insights, Iwata decided to devise a radically new strategy as the foundation for leading Nintendo down an unorthodox path.

The new strategy's objective was to reach out to non-gamers in order to create a bigger market. Iwata's mandate was for simpler games to be developed, targeting all customers, irrespective of age, gender, or gaming experience. These new games were to take no more than a few minutes to set up and play. In addition, they would require an easy-to-use controller. He also wanted the game scenarios to be largely based on real-life situations rather than fantasies.

In order to pilot Iwata's idea, Nintendo first developed a new handheld gaming device called the DS, which stood for "double screen." It was launched in 2004. The DS was positioned as "the machine that enriches the owner's daily life."[9] One of the key features of this device was a touch-screen that gamers could tap or write on with a stylus. This innovative design enabled gamers to play without using complicated sets of buttons or a mini-joystick. The company then launched the Nintendo Wi-Fi Connection, an innovative service that allowed DS system players to play with other users through a wireless network. The DS was a huge success, and by April 2008, more than 70 million units had been sold worldwide.[10]

Among the many DS game titles, the most popular was "Nintendogs," particularly among female gamers. Players of "Nintendogs" could interact with their virtual pets through the DS's built-in microphone and "touch" them via the touch-screen. They could take these dogs for walks, teach them tricks, and enter them into competitions. Another popular game was "Brainage," which featured brain-training games that were basically puzzles.

Following the success of the DS, Nintendo rolled out the DS Lite in 2006. With its mature Game Boy and innovative DS systems, Nintendo remained the leader in the handheld console segment and continued to retain well over 90 percent of the handheld device market that it had captured since 1989.

However, the deciding factor in Nintendo's success was the video game console segment. Since 2000, Nintendo had lost control of the fixed console market to Sony's PS. With its new strategy to capture non-gamers and expand the market, coupled with the lessons learned from the DS handheld device, Nintendo developed its new console, the Wii, which arrived about the same time as the rollout of Microsoft's Xbox 360 and Sony's PS3, and just in time for the 2006 holiday shopping season (see Exhibit 2 for a timeline).

Our goal was to come up with a machine that moms would want—easy to use, quick to start up, not a huge energy drain, and quiet while it was running. Rather than just picking new technology, we thought seriously about what a game console should be. Iwata wanted a console that would play every Nintendo game ever made.

—Shigeru Miyamoto,
Member of the Wii Development Team[11]

The Wii was an impressive, well-designed, tiny machine that was controlled with a wand-like controller that resembled a TV remote control. Without an elaborate joystick and wire, gamers could navigate the system simply by moving the controller. Motion detectors would then translate the movement of the wand into on-screen action, enabling simulation of real-life games such as tennis, bowling, and boxing. The games were sold on optical discs similar to DVDs. The Wii could also be connected to the Internet for online news and weather updates and to access Nintendo's classic game catalogue, which could be downloaded from the Web. To do this, players could access the Virtual Console service, whereby games originally released for the SNES and N64 could be downloaded from the Wii Shop Channel and accessed from the Wii.

Nintendo positioned the Wii as "a machine that puts smiles on surrounding people's faces," encouraging communication among family members as each of them found something personally relevant and were motivated to turn on the console every day in order to enjoy "the new life with Wii."[12] To promote the Wii, Nintendo adopted the same word-of-mouth strategy that had proven successful in promoting the DS. The company "recruited a handful of carefully chosen

Exhibit 2 Significant Milestones in the Video Game Console Industry

1967	German engineer Baer and co-workers designed the first video game console and developed the first set of games, the Brown Box.
1972	Magnavox approved of the Brown Box and developed Magnavox Odyssey, the first commercial video game console.
1975	Atari, a company founded by Bushnell in 1972, had its first major hit with the arcade game "Pong." "Pong" introduced at-home video games to the masses and Atari became hugely popular.
1977	With Warner Bros. having bought Atari in 1976, the Atari VCS, a cartridge-based system that played multiple games, was developed and released, and became a resounding success.
1980	Mattel entered the market and released Intellivision, a console featuring synthesized voices.
1983–84	Unlicensed games flooded the market and, with many new home systems such as the Atari 5200, the video game industry crashed. Nintendo launched Famicom in Japan.
1985	Nintendo released the NES in the United States.
1989	Nintendo released its second smash hit, the Game Boy.
1991	Nintendo released the Super NES in the United States, a year after its launch in Japan.
1995	Sony launched the PS.
1996	The N64, the last mass-market system to use cartridges, was released by Nintendo.
2000	Sony released the PS2.
2001	Microsoft released the Xbox.
2002	Nintendo released the Game Boy Advance.
2004	Nintendo launched the DS.
2005	In early 2005, Sony released the PSP. In November, Microsoft released the Xbox 360.
2006	Nintendo launched the Wii. Sony launched the PS3.

Source: *Time*, 2005, Video game console timeline—video game history—Xbox 360, http://www.time.com/covers/1101050523/console_timeline/ (accessed August 13, 2008).

suburban housewives to spread the word among their friends that the Wii was a gaming console the whole family could enjoy together."[13] The Wii was also featured in the gamers' self-made video, which was then shared through YouTube and social networking sites. This once-experimental approach was more effective than the traditional advertising or mass-media campaigns used by Sony and Microsoft.

In addition to becoming the home gaming system for the family, Wii also helped expand "exergaming," which was the combination of on-screen action with physical exercise. The origins of exergaming can be traced to 1989, when Nintendo released the Power Pad and Power Glove, two accessories for its gaming console. The Power Pad was a "large plastic platform that plugged into the console and contained pressure sensors on which gamers could step or jump to play sports games."[14] The Power Glove was a "glove-like controller that translated various gestures into on-screen movements."[15] However, these two accessories had not sold well. Now, with the introduction of the Wii into millions of households, boxing, tennis, bowling, golf, and baseball games would require players to act out the physical movements involved in these sports. Consequently, it was predicted that the Wii would spawn a whole new generation of exergaming that would go far beyond the existing games that used dance mats or video cameras to detect players' actions, as the Wii's controller could detect more subtle movements and could be used to record and analyze these movements through intelligent software to determine the players' physical fitness levels.[16]

The Wii proved to be a runaway success and by September 2007, Nintendo became Japan's most valuable listed company after Toyota, at US$72 billion in market value—nearly tripling in value since the launch of the Wii (see Exhibits 3 and 4).[17]

Exhibit 3 Nintendo's Income Statements, 2006 to 2008 (US$ Millions)

	March 31, 2006, Restated	March 31, 2007, Restated	March 31, 2008
Revenues	4,736.0	8,988.8	15,553.5
Cost of Goods Sold	2,735.4	5,289.1	9,043.0
Gross Profit	2,000.6	3,699.7	6,510.6
Selling, General and Administrative Expenses	850.4	1,219.0	1,602.0
R&D Expenses	284.5	350.7	344.1
Depreciation	16.4	24.8	31.7
Other Operating Expenses	1,151.3	1,594.4	1,977.8
OPERATING INCOME	849.3	2,105.2	4,532.8
Interest Expense	0.0	—	—
Interest and Investment Income	209.2	316.1	410.7
Currency Exchange Gains	423.3	239.4	−858.8
Other Non-Operating Income	22.3	28.7	16.5
Earnings before Tax (excluding unusual items)	1,504.1	2,689.3	4,101.1
Gain on Sale of Investments	32.8	5.2	−101.2
Gain on Sale of Assets	−0.2	−1.2	34.1
Other Unusual Items, Total	11.5	—	—
Earnings before Tax (including unusual items)	1,548.2	2,693.3	4,034.1
Income Tax Expense	633.7	1,072.7	1,641.7
Earnings from Continuing Operations	914.9	1,620.9	2,393.3
NET INCOME	914.9	1,620.9	2,393.3

Source: Adapted from *BusinessWeek*, 2008, Financial results for Nintendo Co. Ltd, www.investing.businessweek.com/research/stocks/financials (accessed August 4, 2008).

Key Players in the Video Game Industry

Video Game Hardware

Other than Nintendo, the video game hardware industry (essentially comprising the manufacture of consoles and devices) was dominated by Sony with its PS family, and Microsoft with the Xbox 360.

Sony.[18] For decades, Sony defined the leading edge in gadgetry, producing transistor radios in the 1950s, Trinitron TVs in the 1960s, and the revolutionary Walkman in the 1970s.[19] Similarly, when the company introduced the PS in Japan in March 1994 and in the United States in 1995, it brought the technology of video gaming to a whole new level (see Exhibit 5). With Sony's strategy of attracting older teenagers and young adults (who had significantly more disposable income)

by offering more sophisticated and often more violent games, the PS dominated the market.

In 2000, the PS2 was released and completely won over the video game market. The PS2 was not only backward-compatible with the PS, but could also be used to play CDs and DVDs. For most people who bought the PS2, it was their first DVD player. In July 2008, Sony announced that worldwide PS2 console sales exceeded 140 million,[20] making the PS2 the best-selling console in history.

In order to compete against Nintendo, the ruler of the handheld video game market, Sony introduced the PlayStation Portable ("PSP") in 2004. In the meantime, Sony continued to release other electronics, such as Sony Connect, an online music service; Vaio Pocket, a portable music player designed to compete with Apple's iPod; and Network Walkman, which was the first Walkman with a hard drive.

Exhibit 4 Nintendo's Consolidated Sales Information for the Six Months Ending September 30, 2007 (US$ Millions)

		Year Ending March 31, 2007	Six Months Ending September 30, 2006	Six Months Ending September 30, 2007
Hardware	Handheld	3,241	1,349	1,827
	Console	1,356	33	1,741
	Others	470	79	355
	Total	5,068	1,461	3,923
Software	Handheld	2,530	1,019	1,322
	Console	714	93	719
	Others	46	10	44
	Total	3,289	1,121	2,085
Total Electronic Entertainment Products Division		8,357	2,582	6,008
Others (playing cards, etc.)		19	7	13
TOTAL		8,376	2,589	6,021

(US$1 = ¥115.4 on March 31, 2008)

Source: Nintendo Co. Ltd, 2007, Consolidated financial statements for the six months ending September 30, 2007, http://www.nintendo.com/corp/report/FY07FinanciaiP£SiiltsYdf, October 25 (accessed August 1, 2008).

Although the PS product line dominated the market, the sales of Sony's other electronics (e.g., DVD recorders, TVs, and computers) and music products dropped significantly. Consumer demand remained weak as there was a battle over prices, with Apple's iPod undermining the sales of Sony's CD and MiniDisc Walkmans, as well as their TV products. These challenges, in addition to the costs incurred in streamlining operations, significantly decreased Sony's market value, and in 2004 the company reported a loss. Sony, once acknowledged globally for its cutting-edge technological innovations, was coming to be perceived as a bureaucratic conglomerate.

In order to rectify the situation, in 2005 Sony brought in Sir Howard Stringer to replace Nobuyuki Idei as chairman and chief executive. Stringer was the first non-Japanese chief of the company and, prior to this post, had been the head of the company's U.S. and electronics divisions. After taking over, Stringer announced Project Nippon, a corporate restructuring plan designed to revamp Sony's electronics business and foster better collaboration between the company's divisions. His plan called for eliminating 10,000 jobs (the company had 150,000 employees) and closing 11 of Sony's 65 factories. Stringer also revealed plans for improved research-and-development (R&D) with a stronger focus on consumer demand, aiming to reestablish Sony's presence in Japan. Sony's emphasis became HD products for consumers and broadcasters, and semiconductors designed to improve performance in the company's products.

As one of the major weapons in Sir Stringer's grand plan, Sony planned to introduce and leverage the PS3 to regain its position in the electronics industry. The PS3 was designed to be a multimedia entertainment hub. Thus, people would buy the PS3 to watch movies in addition to playing games. Its computing power would also allow users to chat online, listen to music, and view high-quality animations. The machine would also be backward-compatible with games designed for previous PS consoles. Sony hoped that it would be able to utilize the Cell computer chip, jointly developed with IBM and Toshiba, in other products too, such as selling home servers broadband and high-definition television (HDTV) systems. This powerful chip would power the new PS3, whose games would also be the first mass utilization of the Blu-ray format.[21]

In November 2006, after several delays, Sony's PS3 was released nearly a year after Microsoft's Xbox 360 and within a week of the debut of Nintendo's Wii. However, the results were largely disappointing. Supply problems and the high price tag of the PS3 resulted in Sony losing its dominant position in the console market to Nintendo. To boost sales, the company slashed the price of the PS3 in mid-2007. Around the same time, because of continuous setbacks in terms of delays and inability to ramp up production, Sony fired Ken Kutaragi, who was the chief architect of the PS product line.

Exhibit 5 Evolution of Technology in the Video Game Console Industry's War for Supremacy

First Generation 1972–1977	Simple gameplay and basic visuals, such as Atari's "Pong."
Second Generation 1977–1984	Consoles such as the Atari 2600 were launched. The 8-bit cartridge appeared. This era ended with the video game market crashing.
Third Generation 1983–1987	The 8-bit cartridge continued. The first console war took place between Nintendo's NES and Sega's Master System, with Nintendo emerging as the leader. Games such as "Super Mario Bros." and "Metal Gear" were launched and became huge successes. The handheld market, allowing mobility while playing games, was introduced with Nintendo's Game Boy and Sega's Game Gear.
Fourth Generation 1987–1996	The 16-bit cartridge arrived. Graphics became increasingly well defined. Nintendo again won the war against Sega, with its SNES sales exceeding those of the Sega Mega Drive.
Fifth Generation 1995–2002	32-bit, 64-bit, and 3D graphics were introduced. In this era, Sony launched the PS and the CD format arrived—two events that completely revolutionized the industry. In the format war of CD versus cartridge, the cartridge just did not have the capacity of the CD to store games, which were increasingly complex and featured high-quality graphics. Further, while there was a possibility the CD could be pirated, it had the advantage of being cheaper than the cartridge. Nintendo's N64 was the last cartridge-based console to be produced.
Sixth Generation 1998–2004	The 128-bit era began. Sony launched the PS2, which used the DVD format and got exclusive licenses for games such as "Grand Theft Auto" and "Metal Gear Solid 2," making it the winner of this round of competition. Microsoft launched the Xbox and took second place. Nintendo's Game Cube trailed in third. Sega's Dreamcast lagged at fourth place.
Seventh Generation 2004–2008	The Xbox 360 and the PS3 introduced HD gaming and graphics. The PS3 had now moved ahead from the DVD to the Blu-ray format, and this combination of HD and Blu-ray implied far superior storage capacity and graphics. Nintendo's Wii had motion sensors.

Source: Adapted from D. Lero, 2007, A history of gaming, http://www.gamespot.com/pages/unions/home.php?union_id=Contributions, November 14 (accessed August 13, 2008).

In July 2008, 20 months after the release of the PS3, the console had barely achieved 10 percent of its sales target. At the end of Sony's fiscal year in March 2008, sales were 12.85 million, and the company expected to sell just about 10 million in the fiscal year ending March 2009.[22] Sony's more pressing need was to steer the PS3 to profitability, which was estimated to finally happen by 2009 (see Exhibits 6 and 7). Given the shaky situation, Sony had no plans to cease development of games for the older PS2 system and planned to continue rolling out titles specifically for it.[23]

Microsoft. Entering the video game business in 2001 was one of Microsoft's diversification moves when the company recognized the remarkable success of Sony's PS2 and the potential threat the video game market posed to its stronghold in the PC market. The Xbox was the company's first foray into the industry and was launched to compete directly with Sony's PS2 and Nintendo's GameCube. In November 2002, the company launched Xbox Live, allowing subscribers to play online Xbox games with other subscribers around the world. By mid-2005, the service had attracted about two million subscribers worldwide.

However, by May 2005, the software giant had sold only 21.3 million Xbox units, which put the company in a distant second place behind Sony's PS2 (which had sold 83.5 million units) and slightly ahead of Nintendo's GameCube (with sales of 18.3 million units).[24] By August 2005, Microsoft's Xbox division had cost the company US$4 billion.[25] Soon after, production of the Xbox was ended in favor of the Xbox 360.

Microsoft was determined to capture the top spot in the market with the launch of the Xbox 360 in November 2005, several months ahead of its rivals (Sony's PS3 appeared in the market in late 2006, about a week after Nintendo's Wii). Some believed that the previous success of Sony's PS2 was partly due to its advantage in reaching the market earlier than its rivals; thus, Microsoft imitated this marketing strategy and became the first game console in the new business cycle. Further, having learned a hard lesson from the flop of the original Xbox in Japan, Microsoft worked closely with the producers of Japanese games in an attempt to neutralize the traditional advantages of its two main rivals. The company also abandoned its previous approach of using off-the-shelf parts provided by Intel and NVIDIA to build its consoles because while such an approach was efficient, it lacked the flexibility that Microsoft's rivals enjoyed in reducing costs and increasing profit margins during a console's lifetime.[26] (For instance, Sony had gradually reduced the number of chips required by its

Exhibit 6 Sony's Income Statement, 2006–2008 (US$ Millions)

	March 31, 2006	March 31, 2007	March 31, 2008
Revenue	63,541.2	70,513.4	89,601.3
Cost of Goods Sold	43,786.9	54,652.4	68,885.3
Gross Profit	19,754.3	15,861.0	20,716.0
Gross Profit Margin	31.1%	22.5%	23.1%
Selling, General and Administrative Expenses	12,446.4	8,719.8	9,525.6
Depreciation	5,682.2	6,531.3	7,408.1
Operating Income	1,625.7	609.9	3,782.3
Operating Margin	2.6%	0.9%	4.2%
Non-Operating Income	1,054.6	489.3	1,159.1
Non-Operating Expenses	246.5	231.9	231.6
Income before Taxes	2,433.8	867.3	4,709.8
Income Taxes	1,500.4	458.0	2,055.1
Net Income after Taxes	933.4	409.3	2,654.7
Continuing Operations	1,050.7	1,073.8	3,731.3
Total Net Income	1,050.7	1,073.8	3,731.3
Net Profit Margin	1.7%	1.5%	4.2%

Source: Adapted from C. Colbert, 2008, Sony Corporation, Hoover's Company Information.

PS2 without sacrificing its performance.) Subsequently, Microsoft adopted a new design for its Xbox 360 in the hope that this would achieve a new degree of manufacturing flexibility that could help integrate various components and increase profitability in the future (see Exhibit 8).[27]

Video Game Software

The computer game industry, one of the biggest money-spinners in the global entertainment industry, routinely spent amounts ranging from US$12 million to US$20 million to develop each game. As the consoles became more expensive, the cost of developing games for them also increased. However, Nintendo turned its lower-cost hardware into another competitive advantage. By focusing on characters rather than special effects, developing Wii games cost the company about half what its competition was spending on Xbox and PS games, and thus the expense could be recouped at a much lower sales volume. Nintendo had also thrown in

Exhibit 7 Analysis of Sony's Income Statement for the Year Ending March 31, 2008

> Sony's increase in revenues was largely due to the group's electronics segment, comprising televisions and digital cameras, which saw an 8.9 percent increase in sales. The video game segment increased sales by 26.3 percent to US$12.2 billion, largely due to an increase in sales of the PS3. In all, 9.24 million PS3 units were sold during the year, an increase of 5.63 million units over the previous year. With Sony increasing software sales to 57.9 million units (from 44.6 million) and reducing hardware costs, the losses in the PS3 segment declined to US$1.18 billion from US$ 2.21 billion in the previous year.
>
> PSP sales increased by 4.36 million units to 13.89 million, and PSP software sales rose by 0.8 million to 55.5 million units. PS2 sales declined by 0.98 million units to 13.73 million, with PSP software sales decreasing by 39.5 million units to 154 million.
>
> For the year ending March 31, 2009, Sony expected game segment sales to decline and the PS2 business to shrink. However, the company was optimistic that profitability would increase with more titles available for the PS3 and reductions in hardware costs. There would be an estimated 22 percent reduction in profits, taking into account the one-off increase in the March 2008 financials due to property sales and the floating of the group's financial services segment.

Source: Adapted from D. Jenkins, 2008, "Sony's game division sees 26% sales jump, http://www.gamasutra.com/php-bin/news-index.php?story=8638, May 14 (accessed August 11, 2008).

Exhibit 8 Microsoft's Income Statement, 2005–2007 (US$ Millions)

	June 30, 2005	June 30, 2006	June 30, 2007
Revenue	39,788	44,282	51,122
Cost of Goods Sold	6,200	7,650	10,693
Gross Profit	33,588	36,632	40,429
Gross Profit Margin	84.4%	82.7%	79.1%
Selling, General, and Administrative Expenses	18,172	19,257	20,465
Depreciation	855	903	1,440
Operating Income	14,561	16,472	18,524
Operating Margin	36.6%	37.2%	36.2%
Non-Operating Income	2,067	1,572	1,577
Income before Taxes	16,628	18,262	20,101
Income Taxes	4,374	5,663	6,036
Net Income after Taxes	12,254	12,599	14,065
Net Profit Margin	30.8%	28.5%	27.5%

Source: Adapted from S. Shafer, 2008, Microsoft Corporation, Hoover's Company Information.

five simple but highly addictive games, Wii Sports, with each console so that the buyer was getting a "complete" product at a great price. Sony and Microsoft, on the other hand, incurred losses on the consoles they sold, despite their high price. To compensate for these losses, they sold their games with high licensing royalties. As of July 2008, 6 of the 10 most popular games worldwide were for Nintendo consoles (see Exhibit 9).

Nintendo also focused on developing first-party titles. Nintendo had placed its top software designers at the helm of hardware design. Thus, while Sony and Microsoft relied heavily on third parties to develop titles,

Exhibit 9 Top 10 Games Worldwide, July 2008 (approximate number of units in thousands)

Rank	Console	Game	Publisher	Number of Weeks Since Launch	Sales for the Week Ending July 25, 2008	Sales Since Launch by July 25, 2008
1	Wii	Wii Sports	Nintendo	88	333	26,826
2	Wii	Wii Fit	Nintendo	35	206	6,010
3	DS	Dragon Quest V	Square Enix	2	181	861
4	Wii	Mario Kart Wii	Nintendo	16	167	6,604
5	Wii	Wii Play	Nintendo	87	144	13,840
6	DS	Pokemon Mysterious Dungeon 2	Nintendo	46	117	2,919
7	DS	Guitar Hero: On Tour	Activision	3	116	740
8	Wii	Super Smash Bros. Brawl	Nintendo	26	95	6,430
9	PS2	Powerful Pro Baseball 15	Konami	1	88	88
10	Xbox 360	NCCA Football 09	Electronic Arts	2	84	374

Source: Adapted from VGChartz, 2008, "Worldwide chart for week ending July 25, 2008, http://www.vgchartz.com (accessed August 4, 2008).

Nintendo's consoles were designed to suit the concepts of the games that would run on them, allowing the creation of early first-party titles that really showcased the hardware, including low-profit and offbeat games like Brainage. Such games would have been impossible on another company's hardware.[28]

The sales of hardware consoles such as the Wii, Xbox, and PS were highly correlated to the launch and sale of the video games that could be played on them. For instance, in March 2008, Nintendo launched its exclusive hit game "Super Smash Bros. Brawl" for the Wii and, in that month, along with selling 2.7 million copies of the game, the company sold more video game consoles in the United States than Sony and Microsoft combined.[29]

The Battle Begins

Until the launch of the Wii at the end of 2006, competition in the video game market was straightforward. The leader was the company that introduced a wider array of games with high-quality graphics and increasingly complex gameplay. Then Microsoft introduced the Xbox 360 in November 2005, and Nintendo and Sony followed about a year later with the Wii and PS3. It was apparent that the rules of competition had changed.

Sony continued to claim success in selling the aging PS2 console. Given its long history in the market, the PS2 had outsold both the Xbox 360 and the Wii. Microsoft also remained confident about its Xbox 360. As of May 2008, Microsoft announced its Xbox 360 game machine had beaten the Wii and PS3 to reach 10 million units in U.S. sales.[30] The head start of several months in selling the Xbox 360 gave Microsoft an edge over Sony's PS3 and Nintendo's Wii. The lead time also helped Microsoft and its partners build a vast library of games, which was a major factor for consideration when gamers chose a particular console.

However, within a month of Microsoft's announcement that it was the leader in the U.S. console war, the June 2008 figures were released and it was evident that the Wii had usurped the Xbox 360 as the leader. A total of 10.9 million Wiis were sold in the United States since its launch in November 2006, whereas a total of 10.4 million Xbox 360s were sold since its launch a year earlier.[31] The PS3 came in a distant third with 4.8 million units sold. In the United States, which was Nintendo's largest market,[32] the Wii had taken off the fastest by selling 600,000 units in the first eight days, generating US$190 million in sales.[33] In fact, because of its high demand and market buzz, many consumers found it difficult to get their hands on the machine even months after the launch (see Exhibit 10). The same story about demand existed

Exhibit 10 Sales Figures of Wii, PS3, and Xbox 360 in the United States (approximate number of units in thousands)

	Xbox 360	Nintendo Wii	Sony PS2	Sony PS3
September 2006	259	0	300	0
October 2006	217	0	235	0
November 2006	511	476	664	197
December 2006	1,132	604	1,400	491
January 2007	294	436	299	244
February 2007	228	335	295	127
March 2007	199	259	280	130
April 2007	174	360	194	82
May 2007	155	338	188	82
June 2007	198	382	270	95
July 2007	170	425	222	159
August 2007	277	404	202	131
September 2007	528	501	215	119
October 2007	366	519	184	121

Exhibit 10 Sales Figures of Wii, PS3, and Xbox 360 in the United States (approximate number of units in thousands) (*Continued*)

	Xbox 360	Nintendo Wii	Sony PS2	Sony PS3
November 2007	770	981	496	466
December 2007	1,260	1,350	1,100	798
January 2008	230	274	264	269
February 2008	254	432	352	281
March 2008	262	721	216	257
April 2008	188	714	124	187
May 2008	187	675	133	209
June 2008	220	667	189	406
TOTAL	8,079*	10,853	7,822	4,851

*Cumulative sales of the Xbox 360 from the launch date in November 2005 to September 2006 equaled 2,414 units, bringing the total from launch to June 2008 to 10.5 million units.

Source: Adapted from PVC Forum, 2008, "Games sales chart—monthly console hardware sales in America, www.forum.pcvsconsole.com, July 17 (accessed August 11, 2008).

in other parts of the world, and Nintendo emerged as the clear month-on-month leader with the outstanding success of its new console (see Exhibit 11).

In terms of profitability, Nintendo was in an enviable position of making a profit on each Wii console sold from the first day (see Exhibit 12). Sony, on the other hand, had already slashed the price of the PS3 by US$100 to US$499 to help boost sales of the console. This was still US$20 more than Microsoft's most expensive version of the Xbox 360 and about twice the price of Nintendo's Wii.[34]

Exhibit 11 Worldwide Sales Figures of Wii, PS3, and Xbox Units (approximate number of units in thousands)

	Xbox 360	Nintendo Wii	Sony PS2	Sony PS3
September 2006	446	0	859	0
October 2006	431	0	793	0
November 2006	1,263	1,068	2,016	516
December 2006	2,028	2,418	3,282	843
January 2007	692	1,308	981	546
February 2007	648	1,315	954	389
March 2007	438	900	708	954
April 2007	395	1,060	648	530
May 2007	482	1,522	746	418
June 2007	392	1,245	647	298
July 2007	350	1,371	735	419

	Xbox 360	Nintendo Wii	Sony PS2	Sony PS3
August 2007	636	1,612	882	609
September 2007	837	1,149	754	428
October 2007	1,007	1,234	699	632
November 2007	1,516	2,698	1,334	1,525
December 2007	2,215	4,267	2,456	2,389
January 2008	1,064	2,961	1,271	1,480
February 2008	648	1,606	830	948
March 2008	710	1,730	765	929
April 2008	886	2,545	668	1,189
May 2008	796	2,331	488	939
June 2008	618	1,921	499	995
TOTAL	18,498	35,596	23,015	15,981

Source: Estimated data adapted from VGChartz, July 2008, World hardware sales—weekly comparison, http://www.vgchartz.com/aweekly.php (accessed August 16, 2008).

Exhibit 12 The Economics of the Game: Wii, PS3, and the Xbox 360

Microsoft and Sony were prepared for initial losses in producing their Xbox 360 and PS3 in the hopes that there would be a long-term profit from software sales. However, by integrating hardware and software development, Nintendo made profits on both from the very start. In the United States and Europe, where the Wii's retail price was higher than in Japan and it came bundled with Wii Sports, it was estimated that it made a healthy gross profit margin per console of US$49 in the United States and US$74 in Europe, factoring in currency conversions.[37]

Nintendo also outsourced nearly all production of the Wii and the DS. Its strategy of having more than one supplier for the same part meant that it got the parts cheaper and increasing production was not difficult. Sony, on the other hand, produced an estimated 40 percent of its components in-house.[38] The massive costs of investing in the game console, which was equipped with a Blu-ray player and the powerful Cell chip, meant that Sony continued to incur a loss on each PS3 sold.[39] Electronics supply chain researcher iSuppli's analysis in November 2006 showed that Sony's selling price of US$499 per 20GB PS3 resulted in a unit loss of about US$306.85, not including packaging, controller, and cables.[40]

As for Microsoft, at launch the Xbox 360 was estimated to be losing about US$125 per console.[41] By November 2006, the company streamlined processes and reduced manufacturing costs by almost 40 percent, thereby making an estimated profit of US$75.70 on the retail price of US$399.[42] However, the year ending 2007 remained difficult for the company's Xbox 360 division, which managed both hardware and software sales. The division posted a net loss of US$2 billion. This was primarily due to Microsoft incurring costs exceeding US$1.1 billion by extending the warranty on the product from one year to three years, mainly due to "red ring o' death" issues (a problem that arose due to a defective graphic chip and which caused the console to die while in use). It was only for the year ending June 30, 2008, that a yearly operating profit—amounting to US$426 million—was reported.

Finally, unlike Sony's and Microsoft's reliance on third-party development of games, Nintendo's focus on in-house titles had a pronounced impact on revenues. These were far more profitable than third-party titles, for which the console manufacturer might get only 10 to 15 percent of the price of the game.[43]

It was becoming clear that, in this latest battle between the Xbox 360, PS3, and Wii, the Wii was the clear winner of the game.

Nintendo's Disruptive Strategy

It was not just the video game industry that had felt the impact of the innovative Wii. With the December 2007 release of Wii Fit (an extension of the Wii for exercise activities utilizing the Wii Balances Board peripheral), the potential for capturing yet another class of non-gamers was significantly increased. Wii Fit aimed to integrate health and entertainment and featured approximately 40 different activities, including yoga, pushups, and other exercises. It was described as a way to help get families to exercise together. Within six months of being released, the product had sold two million copies in Japan and had long queues waiting for its delivery in many parts of the world. Its effect on the health industry was already evident, with doctors and therapists recommending it for various purposes, such as body balance, strength training, keeping patients interested in performing repetitive and tedious exercises, and for the elderly to enjoy expanding their range of motion.

Nintendo's business model was also exciting for small, independent software producers. In May 2008, Nintendo made the strategic move of loosening its traditionally tight control over content by launching WiiWare in the United States and Europe. WiiWare, an online channel for distributing downloadable games, enabled users to download new games by independent developers. Reggis Fils-Aime, president of Nintendo of America,[35] said, "Independent developers armed with small budgets and big ideas will be able to get their original games into the marketplace to see if we can find the next smash hit. WiiWare brings new levels of creativity and value to the ever-growing population of Wii owners."

While it was still too early to predict the final results, Nintendo's Wii has revolutionized and changed the nature of competition, and not just in the video-game industry. Would this disruptive transformation of the video game industry leave the competitors in the cold? What course of action was available to them?

Appendix
Disruptive Technology

The term "disruptive technology" was coined by Clayton M. Christensen, a professor at the Harvard Business School. Christensen believed that leading companies, despite having followed all the right practices (i.e., keeping a close watch on competition, listening to their customers, and investing aggressively in new technologies), still lost their top positions when confronted with disruptive changes in technology and market structure. He suggested that, while keeping close to customers was critical for current success, it was paradoxically also the cause for companies' failure to meet the technological demands of customers in the future.

To remain at the top of their industries, managers must first be able to spot disruptive technologies. To pursue these technologies, managers must protect them from the processes and incentives that are geared to serving mainstream customers. And the only way to do that is to create organizations that are completely independent of the mainstream business.[36]

Disruptive technology is an innovation that uses a "disruptive strategy"' rather than a "sustaining" strategy (one which improved the performance of an established product) or a "revolutionary" strategy (one which introduced products with dramatically improved features). Christensen argued that following good business practices could ultimately weaken a great company because truly important breakthrough technologies were often rejected by mainstream customers because they could not immediately use them. Companies with a strong customer focus would thus reject those strategically important innovations. As a result, it was left to the more nimble, entrepreneurial companies to pursue those disruptive opportunities, which might result in worse product performance in the short term, but in the long run were of strategic importance in creating new markets and finding new customers for future products.

NOTES

1. S. Iwata, 2006, GDC keynote address, *Nintendo World Report*, http://www.nintendoworldreport.com/newsArt.cfm, March 23 (accessed July 31, 2008).
2. J. McGregor, 2008, The world's most innovative companies, *BusinessWeek*, http://www.businessweek.com/magazine/content/08, April 17 (accessed July 10, 2008).
3. "Nintendo," loosely translated from Japanese, means "leave luck to heaven."
4. Under this deal, Philips, one of Sony's principal rivals, would produce an add-on device for Nintendo game players allowing them to use optical compact discs with greater storage capacities than game cartridges.

5. Iwata joined HAL Laboratories in 1982 and shortly after became the company's coordinator for software production, where he helped create video games such as "Kirby." In 1993, he became president of HAL, a post he held until 2000, when he joined Nintendo as head of the corporate planning division. When Yamauchi retired in 2002, Iwata became president of Nintendo.

6. C. Colbert, 2007, Nintendo Co. Ltd, Hoover's Company Information; M. Sanchanta, 2007, Nintendo market cap rockets, *Financial Times*, September 26; 2006, Playing a Different Game, *The Economist*, October 26.

7. Blu-ray was a new DVD format derived from the blue laser, which had a short wavelength of 405 nm. Blu-ray discs could store substantially more data than the DVD format, which was derived from red-laser (650 nm) technology.

8. The PS2 had been updated since introduction and was available in a much smaller format than the original.

9. Nintendo, 2007, Consolidated financial statements for the six months ending September 30, 2007, http://www.nintendo.com/corp/report/FY07FinancialResults.pdf, October 25 (accessed August 1, 2008).

10. Data sourced from VGChartz.com (week ending April 5, 2008), Hardware table, http://www.vgchartz.com (accessed August 1, 2008).

11. K. Hall, 2006, The big ideas behind Nintendo's Wii, *BusinessWeek*, http://www.businessweek.com/technolgy/content/nov2006, November 16 (accessed June 25, 2008).

12. Nintendo, 2007, Consolidated financial statements for the six months ending September 30, 2007, http://www.nintendo.com/corp/report/FY07FinancialResults.pdf (accessed August 1, 2008).

13. 2007, "Building buzz: Marketing, 2007, *The Economist*, 383(8525): 64.

14. http://www.wordspy.com/words/exergaming.asp?r=16.9423217396108&svr=9&lang=en_us& (accessed August 1, 2008).

15. Ibid.

16. C. Colbert, 2007, Nintendo Co. Ltd, Hoover's Company Information; 2007, Let's get physical, *The Economist*, March 8.

17. K. Takenaka, 2007, Nintendo becomes Japan's second most valuable company, *Reuters*, http://www.reuters.com/article/technology-media-telco, September 25 (accessed August 1, 2008).

18. This chapter contains excerpts from A. Farhoomand & S. Tsang, 2006, Microsoft's diversification strategy, Asia Case Research Centre, The University of Hong Kong.

19. L. Stahl, 2006, Sir Howard Stringer: Sony's savior? *CBS News 60 Minutes*, http://www.cbsnews.com/stories/2006/01/06/60minutes/main1183023_page3.shtml, January 8 (accessed June 25, 2008).

20. C. Nutall, 2008, Sony sets 150m sales target for PS3, *Financial Times*, http://www.ft.com/cms/s/0/1c46ad2e-5678. July 20 (accessed August 14, 2008).

21. Sony joined Matsushita and Samsung, plus a few other companies, to jointly develop the Blu-ray format. The alliance, formed in 2004, aimed to establish the new DVD format for optical storage media. In late 2004, Disney agreed to use the Blu-ray format.

22. C. Nutall, 2008, Sony sets 150m sales target for PS3, *Financial Times*, http://www.ft.com/cms/s/0/1c46ad2e-5678, July 20 (accessed August 14, 2008).

23. C. Colbert, 2007, Nintendo Co. Ltd, Hoover's Company Information.

24. Data sourced from http://vgchartz.com, 2005, Hardware table, May 28 (accessed July 30, 2008).

25. V. Murphy, 2005, Microsoft's midlife crisis, *Forbes*, http://www.forbes.com/2005/09/12, September 13 (accessed August 1, 2008).

26. Lifetime refers to the complete stages of the product's life cycle: from conception, through design and production, to its service and, finally, disposal.

27. This chapter contains excerpts from A. Farhoomand & S. Tsang, 2006, Microsoft's diversification strategy, Asia Case Research Centre, The University of Hong Kong.

28. R. Ehrenberg, 2007, Game console wars II: Nintendo shaves off profits, leaving competition scruffy, *Seeking Alpha*, http://seekingalpha.com/article/34357-game-console-wars-ii-nintendo-shaves-off-profits-leaving-competition-scruffy, May 3 (accessed August 14, 2008).

29. P. McDougall, 2008, Nintendo Wii sales trounce Xbox 360, Playstation 3, *Information Week*, http://www.informationweek.com/news/hardware/, April 18 (accessed July 15, 2008).

30. D. Wakabayashi, 2008, Xbox 360 sales surpass Wii, PS3, *Reuters*, http://www.reuters.com/article/technologyNews, May 15 (accessed June 25, 2008).

31. T. Ricker, 2008, NPD: Wii usurps Xbox as best selling U.S. game console, pulling away, *Engadget*, http://www.engadget.com/2008/07/18/npd-wii-usurps-xbox-360-as-best-selling-us-game-console, July 18 (accessed August 11, 2008).

32. The United States comprised 36 percent of Nintendo's total sales for the year ending March 2007, followed by Japan with 34 percent.

33. C. Colbert, 2007, Nintendo Co. Ltd, Hoover's Company Information.

34. CNN, 2007, Sony slashes PS3 price tag by about $100, http://www.cnn.com/2007/TECH/fun.games/07/09/sony.prie.reut/index, July 9 (accessed August 11, 2008).

35. J. L. Bower & C. Christensen, 1995, Disruptive technologies: Catching the wave, *Harvard Business Review*, http://www.hbsp.harvard.edu/b01/en/common/item_detail.jhtml, January 1 (accessed August 11, 2008).

36. M. Sanchanta, 2007, Nintendo Wii success helps component makers score, *Financial Times*, http://ft.com/cms/s/0/4f9a9108-6467-11dc-90ea-00009fd2ac.html, September 16 (accessed August 14. 2008).

37. Ibid.

38. C. Nutall, 2008, Sony sets 150m sales target for PS3, *Financial Times*, http://www.ft.com/cms/s/0/1c46ad2e-5678. July 20 (accessed August 14, 2008).

39. Edge Online, 2006, iSuppli: 60GB PS3 costs US$840 to produce, http://www.edge-online.com/news/isuppli-60gb-ps3-costs-840-produce, November 16 (accessed August 14, 2008).

40. Ibid.

41. J. Mann, 2006, Microsoft makes tiny profit on Xbox 360 hardware, *TechSpot News*, http://www.techspot.com/news/23612-microsoft-makes-a-tiny-profit-on-xbox-360-hardware.html, November 20 (accessed August 14, 2008).

42. R. Ehrenberg, 2007, Game console wars II: Nintendo shaves off profits, leaving competition scruffy, *Seeking Alpha*, http://seekingalpha.com/article/34357-game-console-wars-ii-nintendo-shaves-off-profits-leaving-competition-scruffy, May 3 (accessed August 14, 2008).

43. R. Ehrenberg, 2007, Game console wars II: Nintendo shaves off profits, leaving competition scruffy, Seeking Alpha, http://seekingalpha.com/article/34357-game-console-wars-ii-nintendo-shaves-off-profits-leaving-competition-scruffy, May 3 (accessed August 14, 2008).

Jim Kayalar

Ivey Management Services

Richard Ivey School of Business
The University of Western Ontario

"I am working harder and longer hours than ever before and making less money," thought Kevin Wilson as he drove his van to work one morning in Knoxville, Tennessee. Wilson was the sole owner and manager of Pro Clean LLC, a carpet cleaning business. He was still the first one to arrive at work and the last one to leave. As a result, he felt he was neglecting his family, leading to tension in his marriage.

The issue was fast becoming not one of working harder and longer for less money but simply surviving. Looking back at his decision to expand his business, he was close to admitting that he had made a mistake. Was there still a chance to rectify his mistake, or would his business spiral ever faster into bankruptcy?

Knoxville

Knoxville was the third-largest city in Tennessee. It is located in a broad valley between the Cumberland Mountains to the northwest and the Great Smoky Mountains to the southeast.[1]

Knoxville had a population of 183,546 in 2007, and the population had grown by 4.6 percent since 2000. The estimated median household income in 2005 was $30,473 (it was $27,492 in 2000), and the estimated median house/condo value in 2005 was $100,400 (it was $78,000 in 2000). Knoxville had a land area of 92.7 square miles.[2]

Knoxville had a highly diversified economy that did not rely heavily on any single industry. The local economy had recently seen substantial growth in the areas of trade, transportation, utilities, and financial activities.

The Market

The residential house cleaning market in Knoxville was serviced predominately by independent companies. There were also a few large franchises competing for market share. Residential house cleaning services were divided into different categories: maid or house cleaners, carpet cleaners, window cleaners, and a variety of other service providers. The carpet cleaning market consisted of approximately 60 cleaners. The figure was close to 80 if one took into account the cleaners in the distant Knoxville counties. Roughly 90 percent were owner/operators that had one van. There was one large national franchise, which had seven vans and 18 to 20 employees. The remaining companies operated with two or three vans. The market grew approximately 5 percent per year, which was what Wilson's business averaged as well. Over time, Pro Clean had built up a respectable 5 percent market share in Knoxville.

The commercial cleaning market was serviced by janitorial service providers that offered a one-stop service to commercial businesses with diverse services such as general office cleaning, carpet cleaning, and window cleaning.

Regardless of the saturated marketplace, a number of national janitorial cleaning and carpet cleaning chains were advertising aggressively to establish new franchises in the city.

Pro Clean

Wilson was an old-timer in the carpet cleaning business. He had run his own carpet cleaning business as an owner/operator in Chicago for seven years and had moved to

Exhibit 1 Cleaning Methodology

There were two methods of carpet cleaning available in the market:

- Steam cleaning
- Low moisture/chemical cleaning

Steam Cleaning

- Eighty-five percent of the professional carpet cleaning business in the United States was steam cleaning
- Steam cleaning done with the right equipment and trained technicians dried within 3 to 4 hours of application and dried in full within 12 to 16 hours
- Steam cleaning flushed the carpet with hot water piped in from the van with a long retractable hose at 180 to 220 degrees ("steam" was the term used to help buyers visualize the service better)
- Carpet manufacturers required steam cleaning every 12 to 16 months to keep maintenance warranties valid

Steam cleaning advantages:

- Preferred by clients as cleaning method of choice
- Required by carpet manufacturers
- Best deep-down cleaning (fibers were flushed and extracted to remove all contaminants)
- Better overall results

Steam cleaning disadvantages:

- Average truck-mounted cleaning system started at $17,000 and could cost as much as $40,000 (not including van)
- Longer setup time
- Longer cleaning time
- Longer drying time
- Longer training time for new technicians
- More equipment maintenance and downtime
- More fuel costs to operate equipment

Dry Cleaning/Chemical Cleaning

The cleaning process consisted of using a chemical compound to treat the carpet and then using a cotton bonnet spinning on a rotary machine, with the bonnet absorbing the dirt into the cotton pad.

Low moisture/chemical cleaning advantages:

- Faster dry times—30 to 60 minutes after initial application
- Faster setup and cleaning time
- Faster learning curve
- No fuel costs to run machines
- Low equipment cost ($700 to $1,000)

Low moisture/chemical cleaning disadvantages:

- Limited to surface cleaning of fibers
- Did not rinse carpet of contaminants
- No extraction
- Most consumers did not prefer it for fear of chemicals

Source: Kevin Wilson, Ivey School of Business.

Knoxville eight years ago after his wife received an offer to run a medical clinic there. He had worked hard to establish himself in Knoxville and was able to do so. He was now making $75,000 a year as an owner/operator. The Wilsons settled comfortably in Tennessee and had two young children in elementary school.

Wilson offered both steam cleaning and dry cleaning options to his customers, but the method of choice was steam cleaning (see Exhibit 1).

As an owner/operator, Wilson managed the following daily functions:

- Scheduling
- Estimates
- Cleaning
- Inventory management
- Training
- Ordering
- Payroll
- Marketing
- Customer care management
- Van and equipment maintenance
- Accounting

Exhibit 2 Pro Clean HR Data

1. Kevin Wilson, Owner

   - Age: 48
   - Education: Some community college
   - Past Experience: Fifteen years of experience in the carpet cleaning industry

2. Andrew Scott, Sales/Office Manager

   - Age: 47
   - Education: High school diploma
   - Past Experience: Owned and operated a limousine rental service for eight years in Kansas before moving to Knoxville (company went out of business); worked in Knoxville as a call center operator, handling customer service complaints for a large national appliance manufacturer
   - Worked as a cleaning technician before making the switch to sales/office manager
   - Hired him for his business experience and ability to deal with people

3. Alexander Martinez, Technician

   - Age: 51
   - Education: High school diploma
   - Past Experience: Twenty years of experience in air conditioning installation (company went out of business)
   - Hired because he was eager to take the job (due in part to the good health benefits) and was mechanically inclined

4. Jeremy Turner, Technician

   - Age: 27
   - Education: High school diploma
   - Past Experience: Five years of experience working in different janitorial cleaning service companies in the Knoxville area
   - Hired because he had good references, was a hard and reliable worker, and knew the Knoxville area well

Source: Kevin Wilson, Ivey School of Business.

Wilson used QuickBooks software to do his accounting because he was not good with numbers. He also was not good at selling and avoided public speaking at all costs. After 15 years of hard work, long hours, and incessant back pains, he finally decided that it was time for him to hang up his overalls and leave the cleaning to others.

Business Expansion

Wilson had long envied the high prices that one of his competitors, King Rug, charged and had tried to emulate the business model of that company. Two years ago he had hired three workers to do the cleaning, (see Exhibit 2), moved the business out of his home to a newly rented commercial facility, and purchased two new vans on lease. Upon the suggestion of a fellow member of the Knoxville Chamber of Commerce, he had also invested in a basic Web site. He thought that with four employees, three vans, and a Web site, Pro Clean was ready to take on even the best in Knoxville. Wilson wanted to become the new King Rug of Knoxville.

Expansion Pains

The expansion process was exhilarating at first. He trained the new employees and outfitted them in Pro Clean–branded overalls. A new Pro Clean logo was designed and painted on the side of all company vans. At the onset of the expansion, the business had started to churn cash as a result of the increased payroll expenses and the lease payments for the new vans. Wilson's return on investment was dismal. Increasing capacity threefold had not increased business to the same degree, and the company's cleaning technicians were spending at least two thirds of the day sitting idly at the new office. Cash flow quickly became a problem, and Wilson resorted to using his business and personal credit cards to finance his business.

Looking for ways out of his predicament, he had tried to get help from peers at the Chamber of Commerce, but to no avail. As a last resort, he sought help online and found a carpet cleaning guru in Memphis, Tennessee, who went by the title of "King of Klean." The King of Klean promised guaranteed results and Wilson enrolled in the program, paying for the $20,000 workshop and tutorials with his already overextended credit card.

He had tried to the best of his knowledge to enact the standardized marketing templates that had brought fame and glory to the King of Klean. What had worked for the King of Klean and turned him into a millionaire had unfortunately not worked for Wilson, as he was not able to replicate the great man's success.

Exhibit 3 Map of Knoxville, Tennessee

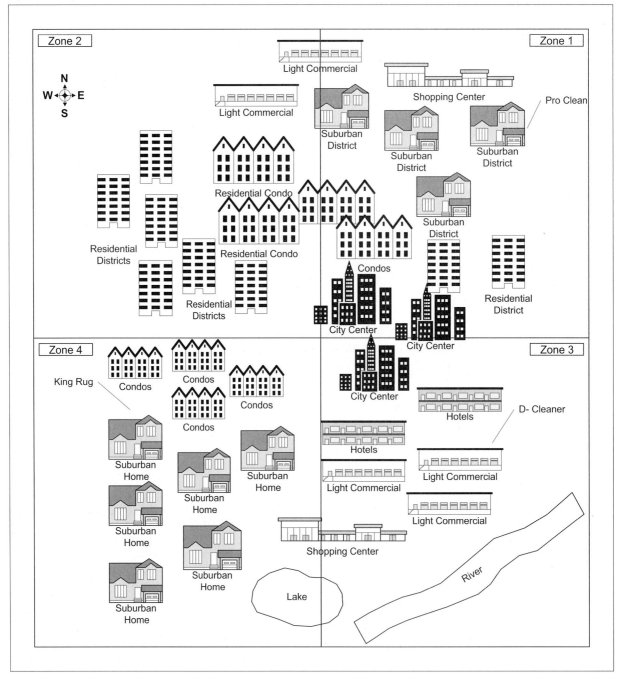

Source: Author.

Restructuring

Accepting that his expansion plans had run into trouble, Wilson had to lay off one of his cleaning technicians. Desperately in need of new business and in response to one of the remaining cleaning technicians, who had problems adapting to the rigor of cleaning, he had temporarily transformed the cleaning technician position to that of sales and office administration. The change in

position was made permanent shortly thereafter, along with a pay raise and the new title of sales and office manager.

The Restructured Pro Clean Organization

Initially, the new sales/office manager spent a lot of time stuffing envelopes with direct mail material, answering phones, giving estimates, and so on. After six months of spending most of his time in the office and with little additional business to show for it, he had started to visit real estate agents and business owners to garner referrals and do in-home estimates for residential prospects that called in. He had also started to visit current business clients to build stronger relationships.

The sales/office manager now routinely visited real estate agents and other referral sources for half of the day and spent the remainder of the day in the office, usually when Wilson was out. He had also seemingly been doing a lot of work from his home, with full online access to the Pro Clean computer network, and claimed that he clocked-in at least 60 hours a week. The two men had established a good rapport and Wilson regularly conferred with him before making business decisions.

The other cleaning technician had not been available to clean after hours or on weekends, and Wilson himself was back to cleaning on one of the vans for after-hours and weekend cleaning jobs. The rest of Wilson's time was spent trying to develop the business as well as dealing with administrative and clerical tasks.

Marketing Strategy

Pro Clean's strategy was to target all potential residential customers in Knoxville without bothering to focus on demographics—a paying customer was a paying customer. In the past, it had done some commercial cleaning and hoped that it could build on that, targeting small businesses with carpets no larger than 10,000 square feet. The commercial business was not a cash business and required receivables follow-up and payments were usually late. Pro Clean tried to stay in touch with all its customers by sending out quarterly newsletters.

Pro Clean Customer Profile

- Income greater than $250,000 per year
- Mostly single-income families
- Most homes had pets/young children
- Stay-at-home spouse made the purchasing decision
- Mostly paid in cash
- Want a safe, healthy, quality service
- Want to protect their investments with regular maintenance

Purchasing Patterns

- The average Pro Clean customer had their carpets cleaned every 12 months
- Frequent-use customers had their carpets cleaned every six months

- Frequent-use customers made up approximately 20 percent of the business
- Most carpet owners cared for their carpets themselves regularly on a weekly or bi-monthly basis using standard household vacuum cleaners

Source of Business

Pro Clean had a loyal and satisfied customer base which provided most of the business. Sixty percent of Pro Clean's business was repeat business, with marketing accounting for 10 percent, referrals 8.5 percent, other sources such as walk-ups and calls from people that saw the van accounting for 19.5 percent, and Internet-based sales for 3 percent. The Pro Clean Web site had not lived up to expectations and Wilson had tried to upgrade it himself with the help of a high school student.

Source of Revenue

Carpet cleaning accounted for 77 percent of Pro Clean's revenue. Upholstery cleaning accounted for 9 percent, area rug cleaning 5 percent, tile and grout cleaning 5 percent, carpet and fabric protection 3 percent, and drapery cleaning a mere 1 percent.

Wilson suspected that his competitors generated considerable revenue by up-selling customers extra services in addition to carpet cleaning. It was a wellknown fact in the carpet cleaning industry of Knoxville that King Rug derived a substantive portion of its revenue from rug cleaning at its place of business and did well with cross selling and up-selling. Pro Clean, however, did not (or, admittedly, could not) successfully up-sell.

Sales Incentives

Pro Clean had a commission system in place for its technicians that paid 10 percent of each new job. After each job, technicians were encouraged to distribute flyers to two or three houses across the street and one on each side of the house they were cleaning. The technicians, however, rarely bothered to distribute flyers, as their previous efforts had yielded no results.

Scheduling

Pro Clean divided Knoxville into zones and tried to schedule cleaning jobs on a one-zone-a-day basis to save fuel. More often than not, trucks would have to service two or more zones a day (see Exhibit 3).

Customers were given time options to accommodate their own schedules. The size of the cleaning job was not prioritized unless it affected Pro Clean's punctuality.

While the new vans were 40 percent more fuel efficient, they did complicate scheduling because of their faster setup and cleaning times versus the older van.

New Service Offering

Wilson was thinking of offering a new service to his clients. He had carefully studied the competitive landscape and seen that only one company offered hardwood floor cleaning. He planned to introduce the new service as soon as he had been trained for it.

Sales and Cleaning Process

New Customers: Residential and Commercial

Potential customers would call to get information and prices as a result of interest sparked by Pro Clean's marketing effort. The sales/office manager would prequalify the sales leads, visit the prospective customer, and prepare an on-site estimate after measuring the areas to be cleaned. Potential customers would usually take a couple days to come to a decision. Most of them would contact other carpet cleaners and ask for estimates. Once the job was given to Pro Clean, a cleaning technician would be dispatched to clean at the agreed-upon day and time. The technician would also collect the cash payment upon completing the job (see Exhibits 4 and 5).

Existing Customers

Existing customers' details were stored on the Pro Clean computer. The price estimate would be given over the phone unless the customer required additional spaces to be cleaned or asked for new services. A technician would then be dispatched at the agreed-upon day and time to clean (see Exhibits 6).

Exhibit 4 New Residential Customer Sales, Cleaning, and Collection Process

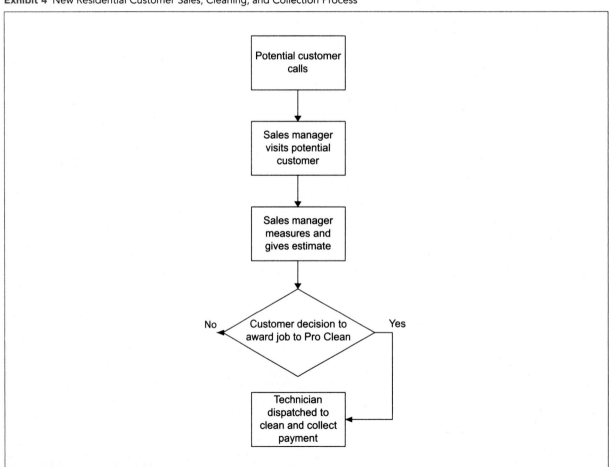

Source: Kevin Wilson, Ivey School of Business.

Exhibit 5 New Commercial Customer Sales, Cleaning and Collection Process

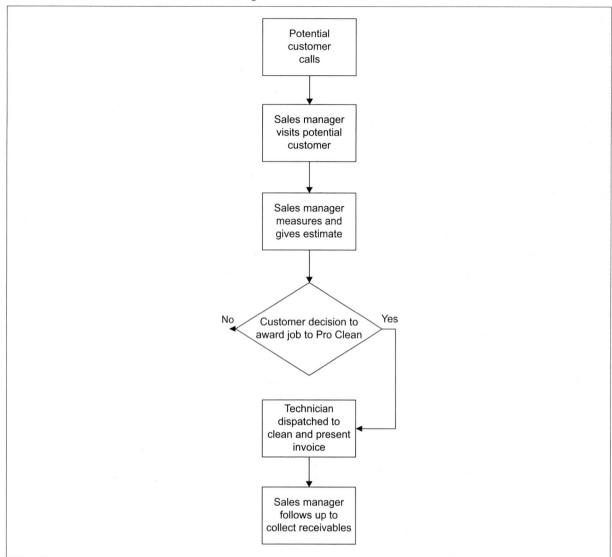

Source: Kevin Wilson, Ivey School of Business.

On-Site Estimates versus Phone Estimates

Only King Rug and Pro Clean made on-site estimate visits. Wilson thought that doing on-site estimate calculations was one way to impress customers and emulate King Rug. At times, he had watched the young, professional King Rug technicians' interactions with customers and admired the way they managed the customer interaction process in a standardized way. The only other cleaner that had a similar level of standardized proficiency was D-Cleaner, a large national chain.

All other cleaners gave approximate estimates over the phone and followed up with a detailed price once they were on-site to clean. This was when the inevitable up-selling began and greatly increased the low estimate given over the phone.

Wilson was not very good at selling, so Andrew Scott made most of the visits for Pro Clean. Alexander Martinez preferred just to clean as his closing ratio on the few times he had made on-site estimate visits was dismal. Scott had a higher closing ratio with elderly customers, with whom he claimed he was able to "connect" better. His approach did not work as well with other age groups or with commercial buyers.

The Pro Clean estimate kit consisted of a tape measure, calculator, and pre-printed estimate form, of which a copy was given to the customer. Wilson taught Scott and Martinez how to do the calculations and fill out the

Exhibit 6 Existing Residential Customer Sales, Cleaning, and Collection Process

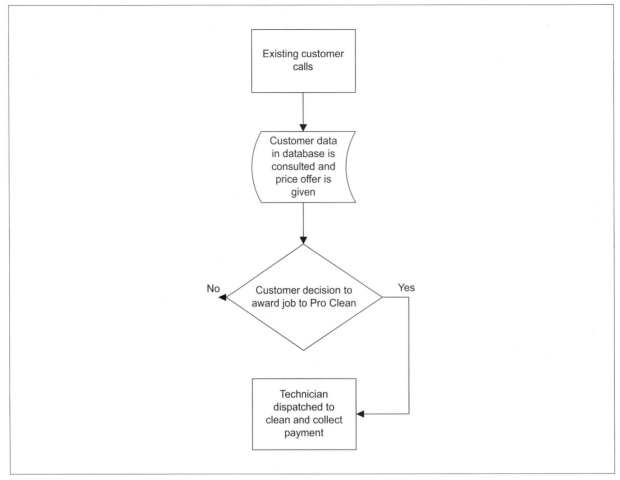

Source: Kevin Wilson, Ivey School of Business.

estimate form in their first week at work after showing them how to clean.

Competitive Challenges Facing Pro Clean

Pro Clean had more than 80 direct competitors in Knoxville providing carpet cleaning services. The market was very price-competitive and there was a large national chain, D-Cleaner, with high brand recognition that advertised aggressively at the national and local levels. D-Cleaner had successfully acquired a good portion of the market with a low price for standard cleaning services. D-Cleaner advertised prices by area rather than by square feet and a favorite ploy was to advertise a $199 all-inclusive price for five areas of a standard home, which was usually upsold by at least 50 percent by aggressive point-of-sale bait-and-switch tactics.

The exception to price-based competition was King Rug, which was able to attract a wealthier clientele. King Rug had 20-plus years of business presence in the Knoxville area, operated four top-of-the-line vans and equipment, and worked out of a nice building with a warehouse where oriental rugs were treated. King Rug charged on average 50 to 100 percent higher for its services than its competitors.

At the bottom of the price spectrum was Kleen Clean, run by Kim Lee, a Korean-American, which offered low-cost dry/chemical cleaning services (see Exhibit 7).

Wilson had tried a number of approaches to meet the competitive challenges in the market, but to date none of them had helped Pro Clean to achieve the progress in the market desired. He had sought to increase the business scale, but had not achieved a positive result. He had sought to replicate the strategy of the upscale competitor (King Rug), but had been unable as yet to realize this objective as well. He had even tried to learn better principals of success and leadership. What else could he do to achieve his desires for his business and improve his competitive success?

Exhibit 7 Competitive Analysis

Competitive Analysis	Pro Clean	D-Cleaner	King Rug	Green Clean	Right Clean	Kleen Clean
BUSINESS BASICS						
Number of vans	3	7	4	2	2	1
Number of employees	3	18–20	5	3	5	1
Number of years in business	15	50	20	8	18	5
MARKET FOCUS						
Residential	Y	Y	Y	Y	Y	Y
Commercial	N	N	N	N	N	N
CLEANING METHOD						
Steam	Y	Y	Y	Y	Y	N
Chemical	Optional	N	N	N	N	Y
CLEANING SERVICES						
Carpets	Y	Y	Y	Y	Y	Y
Upholstery	Y	Y	Y	Y	Y	Y
Rugs	Y	N	Y	N	N	N
Tiles	Y	Y	Y	Y	Y	N
Drapery	Y	Y	N	Y	Y	N
Air ducts	N	Y	N	Y	Y	N
Odor treatment	Y	Y	Y	Y	Y	Y
Natural stone car	Y	N	Y	N	N	N
House exteriors	N	N	N	N	N	N
RVs, trailers	Y	Y	Y	Y	Y	Y
Hardwood floor restoration	N	Y	N	N	N	N
Hardwood floor cleaning	Y	Y	N	N	N	N
MARKETING						
Carpet cleaning packages	N	Y	N	Y	Y	Y
Referral program	Y	N	Y	N	N	N
Coupons	N	Y	N	Y	Y	Y
Newsletter	Y	N	Y	Y	N	N
Advertising	N	Y	N	Y	Y	N
Loyalty program	N	N	Y	N	N	N
Unconditional guarantee	Y	N	Y	Y	Y	N
Good web page	N	Y	Y	N	N	N

Exhibit 7 Competitive Analysis (*Continued*)

Competitive Analysis	Pro Clean	D-Cleaner	King Rug	Green Clean	Right Clean	Kleen Clean
PRODUCT SALES						
Flooring goods	N	Y	N	N	N	N
GEOGRAPHICAL FOCUS						
Focus on metro Knoxville	Y	Y	Y	Y	Y	Y
Focus on other counties	N	N	N	N	N	N
Close to customer base	Y	Y	Y	Y	Y	Y
PRICING						
Carpet	$0.27 per sq. ft.	$36 per room	$0.60 per sq. ft.	$36 per room	$30 per room	$33 per room
Sofa upholstery cleaning (per piece)	$85	$80	N	$75	$60	N
Love seat cleaning (per piece)	$60	$60	N	$55	$50	N
Chair cleaning (per piece)	$55	$50	N	$35	$30	N
Rug cleaning (sq. ft.)	$2.00	$1.50	$3.00	$1.75	$1.50	$1.50
Tile cleaning (sq. ft.)	$0.90	$0.65	$1.25	$0.75	$0.75	N
Drapery cleaning (per pleat)	$1.75	N	N	N	N	N
Upholstery cleaning (by linear ft.)	N	N	$15	N	N	N

Source: Kevin Wilson, Ivey School of Business.

NOTES

1. http://www.cityofknoxville.org/about/history.asp.
2. http://www.city-data.com/us-cities/The-South/Knoxville-Population-Profile.html.

Case Title	Manu-facturing	Service	Consumer Goods	Food/Retail	High Tech-nology	Internet	Transportation/Communication	International Perspective	Social/Ethical Issues	Industry Perspective
Biovail			•		•			•	•	
Wal-Mart Stores				•				•	•	
Room and Board				•					•	
Alibaba		•				•		•		
eBay, Inc.		•			•	•		•		•
Boeing	•							•		•
Motorola, Inc.	•		•					•		•
Southwest Airlines		•					•			•
Apple Computer, Inc.	•	•			•	•	•			•
Blockbuster			•	•		•				•
South Beauty Group		•		•				•		
Cinemaplex		•		•						•
JetBlue		•					•	•		•
Dell	•		•		•	•				•
Home Depot		•		•				•		
Henkel	•		•					•		
Citibank		•			•	•		•		
Nucor	•						•	•		•
Baidu		•				•		•		
TNK-BP	•							•		
The New York Times Company		•				•	•			•
Tesco versus Sainsbury's			•	•				•		
Under Armour			•					•		•
Barclays		•						•		
United Airlines		•					•	•		•
Netflix		•		•						
Oasis Hong Kong Airlines		•					•	•		
Nintendo			•		•	•		•		•
Pro Clean		•		•						

Case Title	Chapter												
	1	2	3	4	5	6	7	8	9	10	11	12	13
Biovail								●		●	●	●	
Wal-Mart Stores	●	●	●	●									
Room and Board			●	●					●			●	●
Alibaba				●		●		●			●		
eBay, Inc.	●				●	●			●				●
Boeing				●	●			●	●				
Motorola, Inc.		●		●		●	●					●	●
Southwest Airlines		●	●	●	●							●	●
Apple Computer, Inc.			●	●	●				●				●
Blockbuster			●		●	●	●						
South Beauty Group	●	●		●								●	●
Cinemaplex		●	●	●	●				●				
JetBlue		●		●	●								
Dell		●		●	●						●	●	
Home Depot				●	●							●	
Henkel			●	●			●	●			●		
Citibank		●	●	●				●	●		●		
Nucor		●	●	●	●						●	●	
Baidu			●		●			●					
TNK-BP		●				●	●	●		●			
The New York Times Company	●	●		●					●			●	
Tesco versus Sainsbury's					●	●	●	●					
Under Armour	●		●	●				●				●	●
Barclays	●	●	●			●						●	
United Airlines		●		●				●	●				
Netflix		●	●		●							●	
Oasis Hong Kong Airlines		●	●	●				●					
Nintendo		●	●	●				●			●		
Pro Clean		●	●	●								●	●